GOOD DATA

Edited by Angela Daly,

S. Kate Devitt

and Monique Mann

Theory on Demand #29
Good Data

Editors: Angela Daly, S. Kate Devitt and Monique Mann

Copy editor: Harley Williams
Editorial assistant: Kayleigh Murphy

Funding: Queensland University of Technology Faculty of Law

Cover design: Katja van Stiphout
Design and EPUB development: Barbara Dubbeldam

Published by the Institute of Network Cultures, Amsterdam, 2019

ISBN 978-94-92302-27-4

Contact
Institute of Network Cultures
Phone: +3120 5951865
Email: info@networkcultures.org
Web: http://www.networkcultures.org

This publication is available through various print on demand services and freely downloadable from http://networkcultures.org/publications

This publication is licensed under the Creative Commons Attribution-NonCommercial-NoDerivatives 4.0 International (CC BY-NC-SA 4.0).

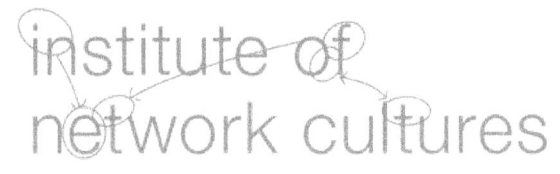

institute of
network cultures

CONTENTS

1: Introduction: What is (in) Good Data?   8

Monique Mann, Kate Devitt and Angela Daly

THEME 1: GOOD DATA MANIFESTOS AND PRACTICES

2: Good Data Practices for Indigenous Data Sovereignty and Governance   26

Raymond Lovett, Vanessa Lee, Tahu Kukutai, Donna Cormack, Stephanie Carroll Rainie and Jennifer Walker

3: The Good Data Manifesto   37

Claire Trenham and Adam Steer

4: The Good, the Bad and the Beauty of 'Good Enough Data'   54

Miren Gutiérrez

5: An Energy Data Manifesto   77

Declan Kuch, Naomi Stringer, Luke Marshall, Sharon Young, Mike Roberts, Iain MacGill, Anna Bruce and Rob Passey

THEME 2: GOOD DATA AND JUSTICE

6: Trade-offs in Algorithmic Risk Assessment: An Australian Domestic Violence Case Study   96

Daniel McNamara, Timothy Graham, Ellen Broad and Cheng Soon Ong

7: Unlawful Data Access and Abuse of Metadata for Mass Persecution of Dissidents in Turkey: the ByLock Case   117

A. Sefa Ozalp

8: Not as Good as Gold? Genomics, Data and Dignity   135

Bruce Baer Arnold and Wendy Elizabeth Bonython

9: Data Localization: Policymaking or Gambling?   156

Nikita Melashchenko

THEME 3: GOOD DATA AS OPEN AND SHARED DATA

10: Making Data Public? The Open Data Index as Participatory Device   174

Jonathan Gray and Danny Lämmerhirt

11: Data Journalism and the Ethics of Open Source   189

Colin Porlezza

12: Governance of Communal Data Sharing   202

Chih-Hsing Ho and Tyng-Ruey Chuang

THEME 4: GOOD DATA ACTIVISM AND RESEARCH

13: Provocations for Social Media Research: Toward Good Data Ethics   216

Andrea Zeffiro

14: Data for the Social Good: Toward a Data-Activist Research Agenda 244

Becky Kazansky, Guillén Torres, Lonneke van der Velden, Kersti Wissenbach and Stefania Milan

15: Good Data is Critical Data: An Appeal for Critical Digital Studies   260

Chiara Poletti and Daniel Gray

16: The Fieldnotes Plugin: Making Network Visualisation in Gephi Accountable   277

Maranke Wieringa, Daniela van Geenen, Karin van Es and Jelmer van Nuss

THEME 5: GOOD DATA AND SMART CITIES AND HOMES

17: Algorithmic Mapmaking in 'Smart Cities': Data Protection Impact Assessments as a means of Protection for Groups — 298

Gerard Jan Ritsema van Eck

18: Truly Smart Cities. Buen Conocer, Digital Activism and Urban Agroecology in Colombia — 317

Juan-Carlos Valencia and Paula Restrepo

19: Intelligent Warning Systems: 'Technological Nudges' to Enhance User Control of IoT Data Collection, Storage and Use — 330

Rachelle Bosua, Karin Clark, Megan Richardson and Jeb Webb

20: Domesticating Data: Socio-Legal Perspectives on Smart Homes and Good Data Design — 344

Martin Flintham, Murray Goulden, Dominic Price and Lachlan Urquhart

Bibliographies — 361

1. WHAT IS (IN) GOOD DATA?

MONIQUE MANN, S. KATE DEVITT AND ANGELA DALY

1. Introduction: Why Good Data?

In recent years, there has been an exponential increase in the collection, aggregation and automated analysis of information by government and private actors. In response to this there has been significant critique regarding what could be termed 'bad' data practices in the globalised digital economy. These include the mass gathering of data about individuals, in opaque, unethical and at times illegal ways, and the increased use of that data in unaccountable and discriminatory forms of algorithmic decision-making.

This edited collection has emerged from our frustration and depression over the previous years of our academic and activist careers critiquing these dystopian 'Bad Data' practices. Rather, in this text on 'Good Data' we seek to move our work from critique to imagining and articulating a more optimistic vision of the datafied future. We see many previous considerations of Bad Data practices, including our own, as only providing critiques rather than engaging constructively with a new vision of how digital technologies and data can be used productively and justly to further social, economic, cultural and political goals. The objective of the Good Data project is to start a multi-disciplinary and multi-stakeholder conversation around promoting good and ethical data practices and initiatives, towards a fair and just digital economy and society. In doing so, we combine expertise from various disciplines and sectors, including law, criminology, justice, public health, data science, digital media, and philosophy. The contributors to this text also have expertise in areas such as renewable energy, sociology, social media, digital humanities, and political science. There are many fields of knowledge that need to come together to build the Good Data future. This project has also brought together academic, government and industry experts along with rights advocates and activists to examine and propose initiatives that seeks to promote and embed social justice, due process rights, autonomy, freedom from discrimination and environmental sustainability principles.

We acknowledge that we are not the first people to start thinking about ethical data and data justice.[1] But we view 'Good Data' as being a broader, and more open-ended, idea than data ethics or data justice, which may confine the conversation, for instance, to philosophical questions or a consideration of 'inserting' ethics in technical aspects, and not engage with wider political, historical, social, cultural, technological and economic issues.

We also wanted to take a more global approach to Good Data given much of the discussion and critique on data practices emanates from the Global North/West, in the spirit of creating and supporting Southern scholarship about data issues.[2] In this edited text there are contri-

---

1   See Data Justice Lab, https://datajusticelab.org/.
2   See: Stefania Milan and Emiliano Treré, 'Big Data from the South: The beginning of a conversation we must have', *DATACTIVE Blog*, 16 October 2017, https://data-activism.net/2017/10/bigdatasur/;

butions from five continents which we view as a step towards broadening the good and ethical data discussions out from the Global North/West, although we acknowledge our position of privilege as academics based in the 'Global North-in-South'.[3] Furthermore, we acknowledge limitations of the book in this regard that we do not have a contribution from the African continent, and also our choice of language in the form of English. We hope that in the future Good Data discussions will be broadened to include more contributions from authors based in more geographical locations and in more languages than we have managed with this book.

The Good Data project was developed and initiated by us when we were all based together at Queensland University of Technology (QUT) in Brisbane/Meanjin - located on traditional Turbal land in what is now known as Australia - in late 2017. Each of us had been working on research engaging with social science aspects of data and digital technologies, and Angela and Monique had also been very active in digital rights activism in Australia. The situation in Australia was then, and still is, far from 'best practice' in data and digital issues - the lack of an enforceable constitutional right to privacy, the Australian government's ongoing digital colonialism perpetuated against Indigenous peoples, refugees and other marginalised people and a myriad of other ways in which unethical data practices were being implemented.[4] We had spent a lot of time and energy criticising these practices from both academic and activist perspectives, but we realised that we had not presented a positive alternative: how could data and digital technologies be designed and used in 'good ways', for 'good' purposes? If digitisation and data are inevitabilities, then we have to (re)imagine the kind of digitised world and data we want to see rather than only offering a naysaying critique of the status quo.

The Good Data project formally commenced with a multi-stakeholder workshop hosted by us and funded by the QUT Faculty of Law in late 2017. We designed the workshop to gather representatives of different academic disciplines and people who had in some way created, used or implemented 'Good Data' practices. The workshop was invite-only, and we organised an outreach public event in the evening featuring well-known digital rights activist Asher Wolf (@Asher_Wolf) in conversation. We would like to thank Thoughtworks Brisbane for hosting our public event and providing catering for the audience.

We wanted the workshop and public event to be just the beginning of our enquiry into Good Data. Given the interest and engagement in our project, we thought that the next step was a book project on Good Data with an open call for contributions. From the beginning we knew that the book would have to encompass and showcase Good Data practices itself. Firstly, we are delighted to be working with the Institute of Network Cultures (INC) given their commitment to quick open access publishing on innovative topics related to digital network cultures. So many texts related to Good Data reside behind paywalls and as a result are not widely accessible, particularly to those outside of the academy. Furthermore, with the increasing

---

Kerry Carrington, Russell Hogg, John Scott and Maximo Sozzo, *The Palgrave Handbook of Criminology and the Global South*, Cham: Palgrave Macmillan, 2018; Raewyn Connell, *Southern Theory: The Global Dynamics of Knowledge in Social Science*, New South Wales: Allen & Unwin, 2007.

3   Monique Mann and Angela Daly, '(Big) Data and the North-*in*-South: Australia's Informational Imperialism and Digital Colonialism', *Television and New Media*, (in press, 2019).

4   Ibid.

and all-encompassing datafication of society and the economy, we were keen to issue this collection on Good Data in a rapid and timely manner (whose publication is taking place a little over a year after our initial Good Data workshop). We have extensive experience ourselves in waiting for our (academic) writing to see the light of day (often behind a paywall) and so we also appreciated the speed with which the INC could facilitate this collection getting out into the world. We also asked contributors for short chapters which would be accessible to non-specialists in order to widen the book's appeal.

Perhaps the first question that should be asked when writing a book about Good Data is what is the nature of 'good'. What is 'goodness'? In our call for papers we were deliberately agnostic with regards to a conceptual analysis of 'good' because it intentionally sought transdisciplinary, culturally diverse and inclusive contributions. Foundational questions on 'goodness' for society and individuals from a western philosophical perspective - a perspective in which we ourselves are situated - might consider 'goodness' as increasing wellbeing (including hedonic, desire-theories and objective list-based theories), sustainability, fairness, justice, virtue and so on. For example, how would a utilitarian or Rawlsian design a smart city? How should app developers incorporate feminist ethics of care - that prioritises relationships and responsibilities over the individual - into their choice architecture? Yet, data discourses from underrepresented, disenfranchised and disempowered voices need to be prioritised rather than hegemonic conceptual structures. For example, (how) can autonomous vehicle data regulation incorporate intersectional feminist or Marxist political agendas? When and who should participate in radical data resistance and erasure? We believe this book is just one step into a long term project of interrogating diverse ethical, cultural and political theoretical frameworks into data practices.

Since we view 'Good Data' as a discussion which transcends atomised academic fields, we are pleased to see contributors and contributions to this book coming from cross/multi/transdisciplinary perspectives. Another of our aims was to move the discussion on Good Data beyond one disciplinary or professional sphere, and we are also pleased to see academics, activists, civil society representatives and technical experts contribute chapters to this book. Finally, we gave authors the option to have their chapter peer-reviewed or editor-reviewed. We thought that the option of editor review would ensure that people from other fields beyond academia could contribute to the collection.

In the next section we offer an overview of the authors' contributions to this collection under each theme. We acknowledge that many of the contributions are relevant to more than one theme, but we have grouped them as best we can under some headings which give a flavour of the chapters:

1. Good Data Manifestos and Practices;
2. Good Data and Justice;
3. Good Data as Open and Shared Data;
4. Good Data Activism and Research; and
5. Good and Smart Data.

Finally, we would like to offer our sincere thanks to our research and editorial assistants who have helped us bring this book to fruition. Our particular thanks go to Dr Kayleigh Murphy and Ms Harley Williamson without whose hard work and dedication we would not have been able to complete the book project within such a speedy timeframe. We would also like to thank Anna Carlson who assisted us at the beginning of the project and organised a wonderful outdoor public event in November 2017 on 'Data Activism and Digital Rights'[5] (at which Angela spoke) for the Brisbane Free University, 'an autonomous space in which the empowering processes of teaching and learning belong to everybody'.[6] Anna also wrote a series of Good Data blogposts for the DATACTIVE Big Data Sur blog.[7] Last, but far from least, we would like to thank all of the peer reviewers who contributed their time and expert insights to commenting on the peer-reviewed chapters, thereby strengthening the final versions of the chapters, and this book overall.

2. What's in the Good Data book?

Theme 1: Good Data Manifestos and Practices

We kick off the book with a selection of manifestos and guidance on what 'Good Data' is, or should be, and how it should be used, or not.

First, in **Chapter 2**, we are delighted to have a multi-authored contribution on Good Data Practices for Indigenous Data Sovereignty and Governance from a group of prominent international Indigenous scholars, namely Raymond Lovett, Vanessa Lee, Tahu Kukutai, Donna Cormack, Stephanie Carroll Rainie and Jennifer Walker. Indigenous Data Sovereignty (IDS) and Indigenous Data Governance are Indigenous-led movements and practices through which Indigenous peoples are setting their own visions for good data regarding data generated and collected by and about them. IDS movements and practices can be seen as a manifestation of Indigenous peoples' sovereignty more generally and as an alternative vision of data, centreing Indigenous peoples' rights to self-determination and autonomy.[8] IDS also challenges conventional, western colonial data practices, which have been utilised against Indigenous peoples since colonisation and continue to be used against them in the digital environment. The authors set out the context for, and emergence of, IDS movements and provide an overview of IDS developments including the IDS networks such as Te Mana Raraunga, the Maori Data Sovereignty Network in Aotearoa/New Zealand.

In **Chapter 3**, we then move to Claire Trenham and Adam Steer's Good Data Manifesto, which draws on their practical experience as data scientists working with geospatial data. Their man-

---

5   BFU presents: "Don't be Evil" - Data Activism and Digital Rights. Public Panel Discussion by Brisbane Free University, West End, Brisbane, 8 November 2017.
    https://brisbanefreeuniversity.org/2017/11/06/bfu-presents-dont-be-evil-data-activism-and-digital-rights/.
6   Brisbane Free University, About, https://brisbanefreeuniversity.org/about/.
7   Starting with: Anna Carlson, 'Imagining 'Good' Data: Northern Utopias, Southern Lessons', *Big Data from the South blog*, 25 May 2018, https://data-activism.net/2018/05/bigdatasur-blog-13-imagining-good-data-northern-utopias-southern-lessons/.
8   See also: Tahu Kukutai and John Taylor (eds), *Indigenous Data Sovereignty: Towards an Agenda*, Canberra: ANU Press, 2016.

ifesto sets out a series of 'Good Data' questions that data producers and consumers should ask, constituting a set of principles which can be used to guide data collection, storage, and re-use. According to the authors, good data should be: usable and fit for purpose; collected with respect to humans and their rights, and the natural world; published; revisable; and form useful social capital. They draw on various examples to illustrate these questions and principles, with a focus on geospatial data which is often voluminous, ubiquitous and also - significant from a data protection perspective - personal.

Chapter 4 by Miren Gutiérrez, considers the question of 'good enough data', particularly for social activism. 'Good enough' is contrasted with institutional, government or corporate data collection that may be systematic, but also imbued with control mechanisms to protect data stakeholders. Good enough data is thus a way to promote the use of data by grass roots activists and citizens to impose political pressure for social ends. The author thus defends 'good enough data' as data created, valued and interpreted by ordinary people, such as environmental data and citizen sensing. Good enough to sustain ongoing legal investigations. She offers the example of the Berkeley Human Rights Investigation Lab (HRC Lab) that used the Syrian archive to categorise chemical attacks on a Syrian city as evidence for violations of international humanitarian law as well as violations other regulations and treaties.

Finally, we turn to our next manifesto in **Chapter 5**, this time for good energy data, authored by Declan Kuch, Naomi Stringer, Luke Marshall, Sharon Young, Mike Roberts, Iain MacGill, Anna Bruce and Rob Passey. The authors are Australia-based energy researchers who view a close link between access to energy data and the country's transition to a sustainable and just community-based energy future, which they argue is currently hampered by some major incumbent energy sector businesses and politicians. Rooftop solar (PV) panels are popular additions to Australian homes but individuals do not have access to the data about the energy they produce and consume. Access to this data would empower individuals and collectives such as community energy groups, and accordingly could hasten Australia's take-up and implementation of sustainable energy in a sustainable, communal way. The authors provide a series of recommended actions in their manifesto which would lead to this goal.

Theme 2: Good Data and Justice

Data justice is a term which has become very prominent in recent times. We acknowledge in particular the work of the Data Justice Lab based at Cardiff University,[9] and their conceptualisation of 'data justice' as 'a conceptual foundation for exploring how data-driven surveillance implicates different understandings of social justice as well as a potential action-building tool for addressing such implications'.[10] We also acknowledge Taylor's work on elucidating a concept of international data justice based on three 'pillars' of '(in)visibility, (dis)engagement with technology and antidiscrimination'.[11]

---

9   Data Justice Lab, https://datajusticelab.org/.
10 Lina Dencik, Arne Hintz and Jonathan Cable, 'Towards data justice? The ambiguity of anti-surveillance resistance in political activism', *Big Data & Society* 3.2 (2016): 9.
11 Linnet Taylor, 'What is data justice? The case for connecting digital rights and freedoms globally', *Big Data & Society* 4.2 (2017): 8.

The chapters in this theme contribute to, and extend, the idea of data justice, through case studies on data justice topics in different areas such as criminal justice, genomics and cross-border data flows. We see these chapters as also contributing to discussions on digital criminology,[12] by widening the discipline's traditional focus beyond 'The Cyber' and cyber-crime to look at wider socio-political contexts of digital citizenship.

What is meant by 'fairness' is a central consideration in 'Good Data.' This question is addressed by McNamara, Graham, Broad, and Ong on (racial) bias[13] in **Chapter 6** that examines actuarial models of criminal justice. McNamara and colleagues examine assumptions that underpin recidivism prediction methods in Australia, with the objective of identifying and rectifying bias, specifically in relation to domestic violence cases. Significantly, the authors draw attention to the politics of data collection and statistical inference. For example, they question Indigenous status being selected as a predictor variable, and argue that the social context of algorithmic decision-making is an important determinant of outcomes in criminal justice. Their examination of the predictive validity of risk assessment tools demonstrates that there are serious consequences for 'trade-offs' in adopting various definitions of 'fairness'. Accordingly, the authors re-design the predictive model in order to reduce the discriminatory impact of the model towards Indigenous persons, yet this comes at the 'trade-off' of reduced predictive accuracy. With these findings identified, the authors outline various approaches to algorithmic fairness in all stages of data collection and processing. Their analysis demonstrates the importance of incorporating explicit fairness criterion into predictive models - and making trade-offs in fairness explicit - as Good Data practice.

Ozalp's chapter - **Chapter 7** - presents a detailed case study of the ByLock case concerning unlawful data access leading to mass persecution of dissidents in Turkey. Through the lens of moral panic analysis Ozalp recounts a case study of what can go bad without good information security, providing a concrete real world example of the oppressive potential of bad data practices, and while questioning what we can learn for Good Data. In doing so, Ozalp outlines how digital communication technologies and strong information security are essential to support what he terms a 'good democracy' - including protection for the rights such as freedom of expression, political thought, religion, association and privacy. Accordingly, it is argued that counter-surveillance practices, online anonymity and encryption tools are integral to a good democracy.

Next under the data justice theme is **Chapter 8:** Arnold and Bonython's examination of genomic data. They argue that recent technological developments in this area, a 'perfect storm' may be brewing where governments want to implement population-wide genomic

---

12   Anastasia Powell, Gregory Stratton and Robin Cameron, *Digital Criminology: Crime Justice in Digital Society*, New York: Routledge, 2018.
13   See also: Simone Browne, *Dark Matters: On the Surveillance of Blackness*, Durham: Duke University Press, 2015; Andrew Ferguson, *The Rise of Big Data Policing: Surveillance, Race, and the Future of Law Enforcement*, New York: NYU Press, 2017; Safiya Umoja Noble, *Algorithms of oppression: How search engines reinforce racism*, New York: NYU Press, 2018; Christian Sandvig, Kevin Hamilton, Karrie Karahalios and Cedric Langbort, 'When the algorithm itself is a racist: Diagnosing ethical harm in the basic components of software' *International Journal of Communication*, 10 (2016): 4972-4990.

databases, private corporations attempt to commodify genomic data through the intellectual property system, and direct-to-consumer genomic testing opens a Pandora's Box of legal, political and ethical issues. Their chapter is a timely and crucial contribution to conceptualising 'Good Data' in this area. Underpinning 'goodness' regarding genomic data is, according to the authors, a fundamental respect for human dignity which ought to manifest, for instance, in truly consensual, fair and transparent data collection and use. The authors also emphasise an 'ethic of responsibility' regarding genomic data which ought to be implemented in various ways, including through regulation and government intervention, professional codes, public education, and decision-making by public bodies funding research and development in this area.

The final contribution to this section is **Chapter 9**, where Melashchenko tackles the contentious issue of data localisation,[14] or stipulations that data be physically held on machines within the territory of a particular country or jurisdiction. Data localisation policies in some countries evidence the materiality of data. Data does not have an ethereal existence but exists in a physical location. This is significant as principles of territoriality underpin the state's legitimacy to police and govern. The issue of data localisation goes to the heart of (digital) geopolitics and legal geographies of digital technologies, since it may or may not be desirable from different perspective for data to be held in a particular country, or for it to be held 'offshore' in order to evade certain laws and policies. Melashchenko considers data localisation in the context of trade, data justice and privacy. He identifies that data localisation policies are far from a monolith and may differ in their intensity and detail, and accordingly maps out some 'variables' and 'types' of these policies. This is followed by the introduction of some normative criteria against which data localisation policies can be assessed as being 'smart data regulation' which facilitates data justice, and ultimately a vision of Good Data.

Theme 3: Good Data as Open and Shared Data

Our next theme centres ideas of open data and shared data as forms of Good Data. Discussions of open data have preceded much of the contemporary focus on privacy as being a main 'Good Data' issue, although concerns about the unintended consequences of (some) open data for privacy and other rights are now prominent. Reconciling tensions between open data and data protection (and other interests) is a key challenge for this area.

In the first chapter in this theme - **Chapter 10** - Gray and Lämmerhirt consider the social life of the Open Data Index, a civil society project that aims to measure and influence how

---

14 See also: Jack Goldsmith and Tim Wu, *Who Controls the Internet: Illusions of a Borderless World*, New York: Oxford University Press, 2006; Mireille Hilderbrandt, 'Extraterritorial jurisdiction to enforce in cyberspace: Bodin, Schmitt, Grotius in cyberspace', *University of Toronto Law Journal* 63 (2013), 196-224; Murray Lee, 'Crime and the Cyber Periphery: Criminological Theory Beyond Time and Space', in Kerry Carrington, Russell Hogg, John Scott and Maximo Sozzo (eds), *The Palgrave Handbook of Criminology and the Global South*, Cham: Palgrave Macmillan, 2018, pp. 223-244; Monique Mann, and Ian Warren, 'The digital and legal divide: Silk Road, transnational online policing and Southern criminology', in Kerry Carrington, Russell Hogg, John Scott and Maximo Sozzo (eds), *The Palgrave Handbook of Criminology and the Global South*, Cham, Switzerland: Palgrave Macmillan, 2018, pp. 245-260; Monique Mann, Ian Warren and Sally Kennedy, 'The legal geographies of transnational cyber-prosecutions: Extradition, human rights and forum shifting', *Global Crime* 9.2 (2018): 107-124.

much government data is made available. In particular they attend to how the index organises participation and data politics, comparing indexes to the political mobilisation afforded by rallies, petitions and hashtags. Indexes represent social facts but also reshape the social world - quantifying and thus enabling normative claims about data practices of different countries, and encouraging participation to resolve them. The Open Data Index aims to intervene around what is considered 'Good Data' by assessing the extent to which the publication of government data conforms with specific legal and technical norms and conventions. As a database about data, it can measure accountability and intervene on official regimes of quantification and datification. This is relevant to other chapters considered in the volume including smart cities and good enough data that consider the role of government versus citizen data and the role of data activism. The discussion of the role of indexes (ratings and rankings) is also relevant to the data visualization chapter that acknowledges the impact of visualisations on the epistemology of users. Visualizations are heavily employed by indexes to attempt political and social change (e.g. Corruption Perceptions Index). The Open Data index chapter is thus able to contribute to a larger conversation around the importance of empowering citizens with good data.

We then turn to **Chapter 11**, where Porlezza addresses open source ethics in data journalism, broadly speaking the use of computer science and statistical analytic methods in journalism practice, including programming, data analysis and visualisations to inform reporting. The author identifies four open source normative concepts to guide activity in this area, namely transparency, participation, tinkering, and iteration, which he argues can facilitate Good Data journalism. Drawing on empirical research conducted with data journalists in Italy and Switzerland, actual data journalism practices are assessed against these four concepts to evaluate the extent to which these activities fulfil and align with open source ethics. Various differences are identified in how data journalists in both countries approach, adhere to and implement these ethical principles in their work, which Porlezza mainly attributes to structural differences between the journalism environment in the two countries rather than individual journalists' own moral codes.

In the final chapter in this theme, **Chapter 12**, Ho and Chuang critique neoliberal data protection models which emphasise individual autonomy and choice through concepts such as consent and anonymisation. Instead, the authors propose an alternative model for data use and sharing based on community participation in decision-making and self-governance, drawing from commoning scholarship and practice, and computational methods. They look to examples including data cooperatives to analyse how community participation can occur regarding data governance, in ways which can facilitate use and sharing of that data but are also trusted by the collective. In this way, communal data sharing models present a Good Data alternative to the current widespread proprietary and extractive models.

Theme 4: Good Data Activism and Research

Ethical research and activism is a key component of 'Good Data'. In an age of fighting back against Bad Data, government surveillance and corporate capture of civil society and academia (see for instance Funding Matters' recent resistance to Palantir's sponsorship of the Amsterdam Privacy Conference),[15] it is crucially important for the Good Data agenda to outline approaches to ethical activism and research. Chapters within this theme advance and consider what 'Good' activism and research looks like and outline principled approaches to conducting Good Data activism and research. Chapters within this theme also consider the interaction between activists and academics research agendas and outline models for ethical data-activist collaborations.

The theme's first chapter - **Chapter 13** - by Zeffiro investigates research ethics boards at funding bodies and universities in Canada and found that they share a piecemeal approach to research ethics in the face of changing technologies. She proposes a united effort to create ethical guidance for using social media data for whole of life-cycle research that acknowledges the diversity of needs of different interdisciplinary researchers. At its core researchers must be transparent about their methodologies for generating, collecting, processing analysing and storing social media data. Social media data is likely to be harvested without informed consent, without concern for the welfare of participants and potentially without sensitivity to vulnerable or at risk participants. Zeffiro notes that third party disclaimers on social platforms are not sufficient for ethical and informed consent by research participants. Participant data accrued from social media participants must be kept anonymous, yet researchers must acknowledge that confidentiality cannot be guaranteed for data sent via the internet by any third parties. Researchers must recognise that their social media dataset has been generated by human participants who are likely unaware of how their inputs have been quantified and that they are complicit with the platforms themselves if they rely on them for research data. Zeffiro argues that the term 'c/overt research' should be used by researchers to acknowledge the ethical challenges with collecting and using social media data and the limitations of research ethics boards. Zeffiro proposes researchers question who they feel accountable towards, are self-reflective with regards to their own situated perspective and identify their duties to participants; maintaining a flexible and adaptable approach, rather than seeking a 'one-size-fits-all' solution to research.

Writing reflectively from the experiences of the DATACTIVE team at the University of Amsterdam, in **Chapter 14** Kazansky, Torres, van der Velden, Wissenbach and Milan consider what data activism research for the social good could look like aligned with the Good Data agenda. They question what forms of active and productive roles academics can play in advancing data activism, and also research agendas. In doing so, they examine the co-production of knowledge and the specific work of the DATACTIVE team and their direct involvement as activists with the communities that they study. Their main contribution is the proposal of an 'engaged' approach and epistemology to research that aims to contribute to activist causes - that is, doing research 'with' rather than 'about'. They outline an approach to ethical data activist research as a process rather than a checklist and as inspired by Association of Internet Researchers (AoIR) ethical codes and feminist ethics of care.

Similarly, in **Chapter 15** Poletti and Gray outline what is 'Good' when it comes to critical digital studies, and advance an emancipatory method inspired by Marxist and critical eth-

---

15   Funding Matters, https://fundingmatters.tech/.

ical approaches. They argue that 'Good Data' is that which can be used to critique power dynamics associated with the use of data, and with a focus on economic and technological environments and contexts in which they are generated. They commence their examination by drawing attention to global informational capitalism and the asymmetric and extractive exploitation of data by companies such as Google, Facebook, Amazon etc, while advocating for reflection on the production system where data are created and collected and sold - and the tensions between ethical research and capitalist research (such as, for example, as revealed by the Facebook-Cambridge Analytica scandal). Poletti and Gray highlight the challenges to critical researchers in producing valid and ethical research in a data ecosystem of capitalist production and also that is formed and exists in cross/multi jurisdictional contexts. Drawing from the work of Antonio Casilli, Christian Fuchs and Karen Gregory they propose an approach to critical ethical data research that considers the economic and political order, and ground data ethics in a critique of neoliberal economic systems and digital labor and capitalist relations. They conclude that Good Data are data that can be used to bring about change in modern informational capitalism, but for this to occur there is a need to challenge the dominant rhetoric and further reflexivity in critical digital studies.

In **Chapter 16** Wieringa, van Geenen, van Es and van Nuss focus on a particular kind of research data communication format: network visualisations. Network visualisations are used to represent the geometric interconnectedness and interrelatedness of data, providing a more nuanced way of experiencing complex data than normal charts, graphs or tables. However, network visualisations can bias readers into believing the data presented is objective and complete; rather than interpretive and limited. The authors argue that the assumptions, methodologies and justifications behind the visualisation need to be more transparent and have created a plug-in for common data visualisation tool 'Gephi' to make them more accountable. Specifically their fieldnotes plugin allows users to export the details of the ethnographic, working process, including iterations of the graph file over time. The authors argue that the plugin is of relevance to critical data scholars more widely.

Theme 5: Good and Smart Data

The book's final theme focuses on the changes ubiquitous interconnectedness brings to our cities, homes, personal and interpersonal information ecosystems. Governments, research institutions and corporations are invested in an innovation agenda that relies on extensive access to citizen data via smart phones; urban and domestic surveillance and the Internet of Things (IoT) to create 'smart' algorithms for 'smart cities' and 'smart homes'. Families, groups and communities share personal data in homes and online and have collective interests beyond those of the individual. Technologies are usually touted as bringing convenience, efficiency, ease and wellbeing improvements to consumers, often in overtly technological determinist terms. However, ethical, regulatory and legal frameworks often lag behind consumer trust in these devices and networks. This theme brings together authors who consider data activism and citizen protection under the onslaught of data in private and public spheres. The authors consider citizen use of public, private and interpersonal data, offering insights and good data practices to protect individuals and groups.

In the first chapter in this theme, **Chapter 17**, Ritsema van Eck argues that mapmaking has changed as 'smart cities' gather data via video, audio, and other kinds of Internet of Things (IoT) sensing devices. The data-streams they generate can be combined with volunteered data to create a vast multitude of interactive maps on which individuals are constantly (re) grouped on the basis of abnormality, deviation, and desirability. Instead of extending personal data protection rights to groups - that is awkward within the current European Union data protection framework, which is the chapter's focus - the author suggests protection can be achieved via Data Protection Impact Assessments (DPIAs), which are mandatory to carry out when the 'systematic monitoring of a publicly accessible area on a large scale' necessary for mapmaking takes place. DPIAs can identify risks such as discrimination at an early stage. Furthermore, by including representatives of local (disadvantaged) groups, the strong performative qualities of maps can offer occasions for groups of citizens in smart cities to proactively shape the environments in which they live. However the author acknowledges that substantial legislative change would be required to the DPIA process to ensure affected data subjects and their representatives were included in the consultative process.

Smart cities are promoted as creating more economically thriving, social and environmentally sustainable cities. However, in **Chapter 18** Valencia and Restrepo argue that they are usually driven by governments and corporations that promote a neoliberal, colonialist agenda to retain power and influence over citizens through increased surveillance and data secrecy. Citizens' data is collected, analysed and used to drive political agendas, often without citizen consent or access. The authors investigate the possibility of citizen led smart cities that could lead to data empowered citizens. Rather than rejecting datatification, the authors discuss citizen organisations and resistance communities that demand open data and the production of citizen-led data and software to produce bottom-up smart cities instead of top-down. They argue that true smart cities can only emerge from inclusive and citizen-led social data practices. They focus particularly on an instance of urban agriculture in Colombia, where a citizen-led environmental resistance movement endorses open data and software, citizen-data gathering, digital activism, community connection and communication. The chapter explores how data activism can progress an agroecological political agenda and social movements.

This is followed by **Chapter 19**, in which Bosua, Clark, Richardson and Webb investigate user control of personal data in a connected digital world. They argue that the Internet of Things has the paradoxical result of introducing a new era of 'smart computing' while reducing the intelligent control that individuals can exercise over their personal data. Users should be able to exert greater control over the collection, storage and use of their personal data. In this chapter the authors provide early design concepts of systems that could improve personal control of data including privacy, data protection and cybersecurity. They argue that personal data empowerment can be achieved through better design that make data flows more transparent to users. In particular they focus on IoT data that is particularly vulnerable because it is frequently unencrypted and uncontrolled. They propose creating an Intelligent Warning App DataMind, using 'privacy-by-design' principles to incorporate 'nudges' to alert individuals about data issues of potential interest to them, thereby empowering them to take control of their personal data.

In **Chapter 20**, the last chapter of the book, Flintham, Goulden, Price and Urquhart warn of a future in which the Internet of Things creates group data that overwhelm the efforts of individual group members to manage personal information that other members have access to - what they call 'interpersonal data', because it is drawn from, and carries consequences for, the relationships between intimate groups. The authors examine European Union law (as the most proactive regulatory regime in this space) using design fiction methodologies to consider what good interpersonal data might look like and how to avoid it becoming 'bad data' through inappropriate design, or legal consequence. Data in homes is often co-constructed, yet legal protection is constrained to individualised notions of one user, one device. Homes are shared spaces between diverse individuals who participate in wide range of social practices including access to and control of data. These homes comprise not just nuclear units and are not necessarily safe for all parties to have agency. The authors point to divorce, break ups and domestic violence as particular challenges, but also discuss the risks to the agency of teenagers and children. Thus the specific danger within homes it is not a distant bad actor who constitutes the greatest threat but those most intimately connected to individuals. Smart devices digitise domestic interpersonal relations demonstrating how IoT technologies carry novel implications for interpersonal relations, and the data generated around them. Designing smart devices with the law in mind goes some way towards good data practices, however users have latitude to change settings that open up new challenges within their context of use. Data driven technologies must respect interpersonal relationships, and the distribution of agency amongst them, both socially and legally. They must also, in doing so, recognise the moral choices they are making in involving themselves in these spaces, and redefining their possibilities. The next generation of smart devices should, potentially, actively and disruptively, deliver data protection norms into the home including informed and visible transactions around data and designing personalised privacy interventions. However, given limited legal protections and fast-paced technological innovation, it is possible that the best data at home is not smart at all.

3. What (else) is Good Data?

We are very pleased to include 20 Chapters of Good Data discussions with differing perspectives on the question of what Good Data is. But, like data itself, it is impossible for us to cover everything encompassed by 'Good Data' and accordingly we cannot offer a 'complete', 'comprehensive' or 'perfect' account of good data at this stage (if indeed ever). This book is but a partial reflection of the 'Good Data' reality or possibility. But that is exciting because we are just the beginning of a process of establishing Good Data frameworks, processes and guidelines.

As we mentioned earlier in this introduction, we acknowledge that this book still has a bias to the Global North in the contributions we received and included in this book, and we also acknowledge that our choice of language also may have excluded contributions. For Good Data going forward, a more global approach needs to be taken to the issue, rather than just (re)centering perspectives from the Global North, as already noted - and critiqued - by Arora.[16]

---

16   Payal Arora, 'The Bottom of the Data Pyramid: Big Data and the Global South', *International Journal of Communication*, 10 (2016): 1681-1699.

In order to see more Global South perspectives on Good Data, and many other topics, Global North(-in-South) scholars such as ourselves need to take more steps to be inclusive and facilitate such perspectives, for instance by providing resources such as translation, access to academic databases and other assistance to our colleagues and comrades in the Global South. This is a increasingly crucial as we see a more multi-polar digital world, with the rise of China as an Internet giant and the large online - and increasingly datafied - populations of countries such as India (with its highly controversial Aadhar whole-of-population biometric database), Indonesia and Nigeria - to name but a few.

In addition to more Global Southern perspectives on Good Data, we also think that more account should be taken of how Bad Data practices impact specifically and more acutely on marginalised people and communities, and that Good Data thinking and practices must taken an intersectional approach to acknowledging the different and intersecting oppressions faced by People of Colour, Indigenous people, queer people, and disabled people. We are very pleased and honoured to have the chapter from Lovett and others in this book on Indigenous Data Sovereignty. Going forward, Good Data conversations, including our own, must take more account of intersectional perspectives.

We would also like to see more scholarship and thinking at various levels on Good Data in the form of theories, methodologies and practices for Good Data, in order to gain power for individuals and communities. While we are critical of technological determinist views of data, digital technologies and datafication, we do not include much on technical aspects of data in this book. We do not think that 'only' 'hard-coding' rights, interests, values etc into technology is enough to ensure Good Data practices; but we also do not think that it is unimportant either. We would like to see more ideas, discussion and scholarship, from an interdisciplinary perspective, about how this might happen. Finally, we have included some domain or sector-specific contributions in this book on the question and idea of Good Data; but given that 'Good Data' might look somewhat different in different contexts, we would also like to see more analysis and recommendations for specific domains and sectors such as science, agriculture, health and education.

For us, Good Data also goes beyond the digital, including when studying the digital as researchers. Social media and other digital data are tempting for researchers as they offer rich, complex and extensive insights into human behaviours, attitudes, beliefs and desires. However, researchers utilising digital data sources such as social media must be self-reflective regarding their methodologies and acknowledge their complicity with platform ethical commitments (or lack thereof) when they benefit from harvested platform data. Researchers also need to appreciate the limits of data scraped from public sources that may not reveal a full picture of participant views but instead present a carefully filtered representation. So the fight is deeper than the methodologies themselves and indeed extends to challenging various aspects of the contemporary neoliberal culture of research as a whole. A call for Good Data for holistically ethical research encourages researchers to strive towards higher order ethical norms, beyond the minimum required of 'do not harm' and instead a cry to do more, to 'do good'.

4. Next steps: How do we start building Good Data initiatives?

An important question following from this book is how do we start to build, develop and reward Good Data initiatives? This is the logical next step in the Good Data project: moving from theory and academic inquiry (as we present in this collection) to progressing initiatives in practice. Good Data is but the first step in a long journey towards a just or ethical digital economy and society. With the utmost humility, we admit that we do not have all the answers to this question, but we have some ideas as where to place the next steps, and we present them as open questions in this final section.

There is first and foremost a need to take stock and question what tools - conceptual, theoretical, practical, legal and technical - that we need to build the Good Data future. Despite being socio-legal researchers working within Law Faculties, we do not think that law and regulation is the solution,[17] and there are limits to looking to the law (and data protection law).[18] With that said, we do see some potentially promising provisions such as Article 25 of the EU's General Data Protection Regulation on 'data protection by design and default.' But, we have questions about how this translates (if indeed if it is possible to do so) into the design or hardcoding of systems.[19] We also recognise this also needs to be about more than privacy,[20] and it may be more fruitful if we shift the focus away from privacy, and towards data ethics, human rights more generally and social justice as we have attempted to do here in this Good Data book.

There is also a critical question about how do we engage and empower technologists, designers and end-users in building Good Data initiatives and communities of change? How do we educate and encourage them to be more ethical in their work, and indeed protest Bad Data practices, as we have recently witnessed.[21] How can we work better with technologists, designers and end-users to co-design and co-educate each other about Good Data ethics, ideas and practices?

---

17 See: Roger Brownsword, Eloise Scotford, and Karen Yeung (eds), *The Oxford Handbook of Law Regulation and Technology*, Oxford: Oxford University Press, 2017.
18 See: Bert-Jaap Koops, 'The trouble with European data protection law', *International Data Privacy Law*, 4.4 (2014): 250-261.
19 See: Bert-Jaap Koops and Ronald Leenes, 'Privacy regulation cannot be hardcoded. A critical comment on the 'privacy by design' provisions in data-protection law', *International Review of Law, Computers and Technology*, 28.2 (2014): 159-171.
20 See: Tobias Matzner, 'Why privacy is not enough privacy in the context of "ubiquitous computing" and "big data"', *Journal of Information, Communication and Ethics in Society* 12.2 (2014): 93-106.
21 See: Mike Montiero, 'Ethics can't be a Side Hustle', *Dear Design Student*, 19 March 2017, https://deardesignstudent.com/ethics-cant-be-a-side-hustle-b9e78c090aee ; Hamza Shaban, 'Amazon Employees Demand Company Cut Ties with ICE', *Washington Post*, 22 June 2018, https://www.washingtonpost.com/news/the-switch/wp/2018/06/22/amazon-employees-demand-company-cut-ties-with-ice/?utm_term=.713db9c3092a; Sara Salinas and Jillian D'Onfro, 'Google Employees: We no Longer believe the company places values over profit', *CNBC*, 27 November 2018, https://www.cnbc.com/2018/11/27/read-google-employees-open-letter-protesting-project-dragonfly.html.

It is here we see our future work heading. With *Good Data* we have moved our work from critique to imagining and articulating a more optimistic vision of the datafied future, with our enormous gratitude to this book's contributors for assisting us in doing so. The next steps for us all are to build the Good Data future we want to see rather than letting governments and companies build a Bad Data future for us.

References

Arora, Payal. 'The Bottom of the Data Pyramid: Big Data and the Global South', *International Journal of Communication* 10 (2016): 1681-1699.

BFU presents: "Don't be Evil" - Data Activism and Digital Rights. Public Panel Discussion by Brisbane Free University, West End, Brisbane, 8 November 2017, https://brisbanefreeuniversity.org/2017/11/06/bfu-presents-dont-be-evil-data-activism-and-digital-rights/.

Brisbane Free University. About, https://brisbanefreeuniversity.org/about/.

Browne, Simone. *Dark Matters: On the Surveillance of Blackness*, Durham: Duke University Press, 2015.

Brownsword, Roger, Eloise Scotford, and Karen Yeung (eds). *The Oxford Handbook of Law Regulation and Technology*, Oxford: Oxford University Press, 2017.

Carlson, Anna. 'Imagining 'Good' Data: Northern Utopias, Southern Lessons', *Big Data from the South blog*, 25 May 2018 https://data-activism.net/2018/05/bigdatasur-blog-13-imagining-good-data-northern-utopias-southern-lessons/.

Carrington, Kerry, Russell Hogg, John Scott and Maximo Sozzo. *The Palgrave Handbook of Criminology and the Global South*, Cham, Switzerland: Palgrave Macmillan, 2018.

Connell, Raewyn. *Southern Theory: The Global Dynamics of Knowledge in Social Science*, New South Wales: Allen & Unwin, 2007.

Data Justice Lab. https://datajusticelab.org/.

Dencik, Lina, Arne Hintz and Jonathan Cable. 'Towards data justice? The ambiguity of anti- surveillance resistance in political activism', *Big Data & Society* 3.2 (2016): 1-12.

Ferguson, Andrew. *The Rise of Big Data Policing: Surveillance, Race, and the Future of Law Enforcement*, New York: NYU Press, 2017.

Funding Matters, https://fundingmatters.tech/.

Goldsmith, Jack and Tim Wu, *Who Controls the Internet: Illusions of a Borderless World*, New York: Oxford University Press, 2006.

Hilderbrandt, Mireille. 'Extraterritorial jurisdiction to enforce in cyberspace: Bodin, Schmitt, Grotius in cyberspace', *University of Toronto Law Journal* 63 (2013), 196-224.

Koops, Bert-Jaap. 'The trouble with European data protection law', *International Data Privacy Law*, 4.4 (2014): 250-261.

Koops, Bert-Jaap and Ronald Leenes. 'Privacy regulation cannot be hardcoded. A critical comment on the 'privacy by design' provisions in data-protection law', *International Review of Law, Computers and Technology*, 28.2 (2014): 159-171.

Kukutai, Tahu and John Taylor (eds). *Indigenous Data Sovereignty: Towards an Agenda*. Canberra: ANU Press, 2016.

Lee, Murray. 'Crime and the Cyber Periphery: Criminological Theory Beyond Time and Space.' in Kerry Carrington, Russell Hogg, John Scott and Maximo Sozzo (eds), *The Palgrave Handbook of Criminology and the Global South*, Cham: Palgrave Macmillan, 2018, pp. 223-244.

Mann, Monique and Angela Daly. '(Big) Data and the North-*in*-South: Australia's Informational Imperialism and Digital Colonialism', *Television and New Media* (in press, 2019).

Mann, Monique and Ian Warren. 'The digital and legal divide: Silk Road, transnational online policing and Southern criminology', in Kerry Carrington, Russell Hogg, John Scott and Maximo Sozzo (eds.), *The Palgrave Handbook of Criminology and the Global South*, Cham: Palgrave Macmillan, 2018, pp. 245-260.

Mann, Monique, Ian Warren and Sally Kennedy. 'The legal geographies of transnational cyber-prosecutions: Extradition, human rights and forum shifting', *Global Crime* 9.2 (2018): 107-124.

Matzner, Tobias. 'Why privacy is not enough privacy in the context of "ubiquitous computing" and "big data"', *Journal of Information, Communication and Ethics in Society*, 12.2 (2014): 93-106.

Milan, Stefania and Emiliano Treré. 'Big Data from the South: The beginning of a conversation we must have', *DATACTVE Blog*, 16 October 2017, https://data-activism.net/2017/10/bigdatasur/.

Montiero, Mike. 'Ethics can't be a Side Hustle', *Dear Design Student,* 19 March 2017, https://deardesignstudent.com/ethics-cant-be-a-side-hustle-b9e78c090aee.

Noble, Safiya Umoja. *Algorithms of oppression: How search engines reinforce racism*, New York: NYU Press, 2018.

Powell, Anastasia, Gregory Stratton & Robin Cameron. *Digital Criminology: Crime Justice in Digital Society*, New York: Routledge, 2018.

Salinas, Sara and Jillian D'Onfro, 'Google Employees: We no Longer believe the company places values over profit', *CNBC*, 27 November 2018, https://www.cnbc.com/2018/11/27/read-google-employees-open-letter-protesting-project-dragonfly.html.

Sandvig, Christian, Kevin Hamilton, Karrie Karahalios and Cedric Langbort. 'When the algorithm itself is a racist: Diagnosing ethical harm in the basic components of software', *International Journal of Communication* 10 (2016): 4972-4990.

Shaban, Hamza. 'Amazon Employees Demand Company Cut Ties with ICE', *Washington Post*, 22 June 2018, https://www.washingtonpost.com/news/the-switch/wp/2018/06/22/amazon-employees-demand-company-cut-ties-with-ice/?utm_term=.713db9c3092a.

Taylor, Linnet. 'What is data justice? The case for connecting digital rights and freedoms globally', *Big Data & Society* 4.2 (2017): 1-14.

THEME 1:
GOOD DATA MANIFESTOS AND PRACTICES

2: GOOD DATA PRACTICES FOR INDIGENOUS DATA SOVEREIGNTY AND GOVERNANCE

RAYMOND LOVETT, VANESSA LEE, TAHU KUKUTAI, DONNA CORMACK, STEPHANIE CARROLL RAINIE AND JENNIFER WALKER

Introduction

Indigenous Data Sovereignty (IDS) and Indigenous Data Governance (IDG) are terms increasingly being used across community, research, policy and in practice. The IDS movement has emerged in response to poor data practices, from the conceptualisation of data items through to reporting of data about Indigenous peoples. This chapter aims to provide clarity concerning the definitions of IDS and IDG; provide an overview of the historical context in which IDS has emerged; and provide examples of IDS and IDG across the spectrum of community, policy and practice.

For Indigenous peoples, historical encounters with statistics have been fraught, and none more so than when involving official data produced as part of colonial attempts at statecraft. Governments in the settler states of Australasia and North America have amassed large amounts of data on their Indigenous populations to generate statistics as 'evidence' for population monitoring and policy interventions.[1] Set against this, Indigenous nations, communities and data activists have responded with their own agendas for 'good data'; Indigenous Data Sovereignty (IDS) and Indigenous Data Governance (IDG) movements are contemporary articulations of 'good data' and are the central focus of this chapter.

At the heart of IDS and IDG is the right of Indigenous peoples and nations to decide what data development occurs and the controls over the collection, governance, ownership, and application of data about their peoples, territories, lifeways and natural resources.[2] IDS is grounded in Indigenous understandings of sovereignty that challenge dominant 'data sovereignty' discourse and current practice, and is supported by global human rights instruments such as the United Nations Declaration on the Rights of Indigenous Peoples (UNDRIP). This chapter provides perspectives from Indigenous scholars across Australia, Aotearoa, and North America to explain the genesis and development of the IDS movement, acknowledging the nascent IDS movements outside these areas.[3] We begin with a brief discussion of the historical context of Indigenous statistics. We then discuss the defining elements of IDS and IDG, and

---

1   Tahu Kukutai and Maggie Walter, 'Recognition and Indigenizing Official Statistics: Reflections from Aotearoa New Zealand and Australia', *Statistical Journal of the IAOS* 31.2 (2015).
2   Tahu Kukutai and John Taylor, 'Data Sovereignty for Indigenous Peoples: Current Practice and Future Needs', in Tahu Kukutai and John Taylor (eds), *Indigenous Data Sovereignty: Towards an Agenda*, Canberra: ANU Press, 2016, pp. 1-25.
3   S. Carroll Rainie, M. Walter, P. Axelsson, M. Hudson, J. Walker and O. Figueroa-Rodríguez, 'Indigenous Data Sovereignty: Global Progression Roundtable', *North American and Indigenous Studies (NAISA) Tenth Annual Meeting*, Los Angeles 18 May 2018.

the development of country-specific IDS processes. We conclude with three examples of IDS and IDG in practice. The intent of this chapter is to inform others on how the application of IDS and IDG can lead to good data and good decision-making.

Defining Data

The idea of data is a broad concept, but in the context of this chapter, we define data as information that may be recorded in various forms. In the contemporary context, this mostly includes digital data. The Indigenous data ecosystem is extensive and includes data generated or held by Indigenous communities and organisations, governments, the public sector, international governmental organisations (IGOs), NGOs, research institutions and commercial entities. Therefore, the application of IDS and IDG crosses many boundaries.[4]

Defining Indigenous Data Sovereignty

'Data sovereignty' is the management of information in a way that aligns with the laws, practices and customs of a nation-state in which it is located.[5] In the Indigenous context this may manifest at the group (iwi(tribe)/mob/Maori) levels.

Defining Indigenous Data Governance

Data governance is the power and authority over the design, ownership, access to and use of data. The governance of data has emerged as a highly contested area of debate between Indigenous peoples and the states within which they reside. For Indigenous peoples, whose traditional modes of governance were disrupted by western modes of democratic governance, re-asserting themselves through self-determined governance structures is critical. Ownership of governance structures commences at the development stage, and continues through the ethics application stage and through the collection, analysis and reporting of data, and through policy translation. Indigenous peoples' ownership is integral to autonomy.

Historical context of Data Sovereignty

Indigenous peoples have always been data collectors and protectors. Data gathering and preservation existed in most, if not all, Indigenous cultures in the form of art and pictorial calendars (e.g. Lakota winter counts), chants, songs, the recitation of genealogies and other cultural practices that have been passed on across generations. With colonisation these practices were disrupted (and often heavily censured), but not extinguished. In many contexts, the census was an indispensable tool of colonisation; indeed, the census has long been tied to the exercise of power and statecraft.[6] The word 'census' comes from the Latin word 'censere',

---

4 Ibid.
5 C Matthew Snipp, 'What Does Data Sovereignty Imply: What Does It Look Like?', in Tahu Kukutai and John Taylor (eds), *Indigenous Data Sovereignty: Towards an Agenda*, Canberra: ANU Press, 2016, pp. 39-55.
6 David I Kertzer and Dominique Arel, 'Censuses, Identity Formation, and the Struggle for Political Power', *Census and identity: The politics of race, ethnicity, and language in national censuses* 1 (2002).

which means to tax or assess, and the origins of the census coincide with the rise of early Chinese, Egyptian and Roman states and their extraction of resources from the population, either through taxation, labour or military conscription.[7] With the expansion of colonial powers into new lands, the census facilitated the surveillance and control of Indigenous peoples and their lands, and political projects of segregation and/or assimilation. In Aotearoa NZ, for example, the counting of 'half-castes' in 19th and early 20th century censuses was clearly linked to colonial policies of racial amalgamation.[8] Across what is currently Canada, representatives of the British Crown and the Canadian government have undertaken counts and established lists of Indigenous people since before Canadian Confederation in 1867. Colonial legislation, in the form of the Indian Act (1876 to present), has resulted in registration lists of First Nations and Inuit peoples, termed the 'Indian Register'.[9]

In Australia, a long-standing committee advised on government held data pertaining to Aboriginal and Torres Strait Islander people. The Australian Institute of Health and Welfare (AIHW) in conjunction with the Australian Bureau of Statistics (ABS) convened the National Advisory Group on Aboriginal and Torres Strait Islander Health Information and Data (NAGATSIHID). The main role of NAGATSIHID was to provide strategic advice to the Australian Health Ministers Advisory Council (AHMAC) on Indigenous health data issues as part of a national strategy towards closing the data gap in life expectancy between Indigenous and non-Indigenous people.[10] However, in 2017 this group was disbanded in a review of committees, and the gap remains. There is now no national level mechanism to advise on the use of Indigenous health information. As a result, Aboriginal and Torres Strait Islander voices in the process are minimal, at a time of policy change surrounding government administrative data, including increasing the availability and improving the use of data in Australia.[11]

One of the more egregious contemporary examples of the misuse of Indigenous data is the well-known Havasupai case.[12] In 2004, concerns escalated in Arizona and nationwide in the United States related to biological samples collected from the Havasupai Tribe, with human subject violations cited.[13] In the 1990s, an Arizona State University researcher conducted

---

7   Kukutai and Taylor, 'Data Sovereignty for Indigenous Peoples: Current Practice and Future Needs'.
8   Kukutai and Walter, 'Recognition and Indigenizing Official Statistics: Reflections from Aotearoa New Zealand and Australia'.
9   'Indian Act (R.S.C. C. I-5),' (1985).
10 AIHW, 'National Advisory Group on Aboriginal and Torres Strait Islander Health Information and Data: Strategic Plan 2010-2015', Canberra, 2011; C. Coleman, B. Elias, V. Lee, J. Smylie, J. Waldon, F.S. Hodge, and I. Ring, 'International Group for Indigenous Health Measurement: Recommendations for best practice for estimation of Indigenous mortality'. *Statistical Journal of the IAOS* 32 (2016): 729-738, 729, DOI: 10.3233/SJI-161023.
11 Productivity Commission, 'Data Availability and Use: Overview & Recommendations', Canberra, 2017.
12 Katherine Drabiak-Syed, 'Lessons from Havasupai Tribe V. Arizona State University Board of Regents: Recognizing Group, Cultural, and Dignity Harms as Legitimate Risks Warranting Integration into Research Practice', *J. Health & Biomedical L.* 6 (2010).
13 Christina M Pacheco et al, 'Moving Forward: Breaking the Cycle of Mistrust between American Indians and Researchers' *American journal of public health* 103.12 (2013): Rebecca Tsosie, *Cultural Challenges to Biotechnology: Native American Genetic Resources and the Concept of Cultural Harm*, Los Angeles: SAGE Publications, 2007.

a genetics of diabetes study with the Havasupai Tribe, taking DNA samples from over 400 tribal members with consent for primary use of the biological materials. The study failed to find a genetic link to diabetes. Later, the researcher directed secondary analyses of the DNA samples with respect to schizophrenia. When this secondary use of specimens came to light, the tribe filed a lawsuit alleging lack of informed consent and misuse of genetic materials. The lawsuit settled out of court, but lasting damage to research relationships as well as a ban on genetics research at Havasupai and other tribes remain.

Contemporary IDS was pioneered by the work of Canadian First Nations communities. In 1995, tired of non-Indigenous data users assuming the mantle of unbiased experts and speaking with authority about First Nations realities, data sovereignty was demanded as a prerequisite for a government health survey in First Nations communities. A new model was developed by First Nations that established First Nations' collective and broad-based control of their own data. This model became known as OCAP® with the acronym trademarked to prevent its use except by First Nations[14]. In this acronym the O is Ownership; C is the Control First Nations hold on how the data are collected, used and disclosed; A is Access, whereby First Nations have access to any data about them; and P is Possession whereby all First Nations data fall within First Nations' jurisdiction. Since the establishment of OCAP® principles by First Nations, similar and adapted sets of principles have emerged in other Indigenous groups within Canada. For example, the recent National Inuit Strategy on Research establishes Inuit ownership, control and access with respect to Inuit data and information. To some degree, these principles are now acknowledged by federal departments and agencies, such as Statistics Canada. These principles are primarily used in the area of data collection, but not in the analysis of existing data collected through the census or other government surveys.

Emergence of IDS movements

Indigenous groups across the world have increasingly become engaged in the data space in response to historical practice and to guide good practice going forward. This has included the establishment of country specific networks including the US Indigenous Data Sovereignty Network (USIDSN) to support IDS through data-driven research, policy advocacy, and education. The Aotearoa New Zealand-based Te Mana Raraunga - Maori Data Sovereignty Network, was formed in 2015,[15] and argues that data that are collected about Indigenous people should be subjected to the laws of the nation from which it is collected, including tribal nations. The First Nations Information Governance Centre advocates for and coordinates Indigenous data governance efforts for First Nations in Canada; the Maiam nayri Wingara Aboriginal and Torres Strait Islander Data Sovereignty Collective in Australia was formed in early 2017[16] to develop Aboriginal and Torres Strait Islander data sovereignty principles and to identify Aboriginal and Torres Strait Islander strategic data assets.

---

14 The First Nations Information Governance Centre, 'Ownership, Control, Access and Possession (Ocap™): The Path to First Nations Information Governance', Ottawa: The First Nations Information Governance Centre, 2014.
15 Te Mana Raraunga, 'Te Mana Raraunga - Maori Data Sovereignty Network Charter', https://www.temanararaunga.maori.nz/tutohinga/.
16 AIATSIS, *National Indigenous Research Conference* 2017.

The intent of these groups is to advocate for rights (informed by UNDRIP) using data to inform development.

United Nations Declaration on the Rights of Indigenous Peoples (UNDRIP)

UNDRIP was the result of a quarter of a century work to develop minimum standards to protect Indigenous peoples' rights. After a series of changes to the draft (initially submitted in 1994), the United Nations Declaration on the Rights of Indigenous Peoples (UNDRIP) was adopted by the General Assembly on 13 September 2007.[17] A majority of 144 states voted in favour, four voted against (notably Australia, New Zealand, Canada and the United States), and 11 abstained.[18] Australia did not adopt the declaration until 2009, even though it played a key role in the development of the United Nations' Declaration of Human Rights.[19] Aotearoa and the United States adopted the Declaration the following year in 2010.[20] Canada issued a Statement of Support in November 2010, but the Minister of Indigenous and Northern Affairs did not announce Canada's full commitment until May 2016.[21]

Article 18 of the UNDRIP specifies that 'Indigenous peoples have the right to participate in decision-making in matters which affect their rights, through representatives chosen by themselves in accordance with their own procedures, as well as to maintain and develop their own Indigenous decision-making institutions'.[22] Article 19 stipulates that states are required to 'consult and cooperate in good faith with Indigenous peoples through their own representative institutions in order to obtain their free, prior and informed consent before adopting and implementing legislative or administrative measures that may affect them'.[23] As Tauli-Corpuz suggests,[24] measures are needed to gauge Indigenous peoples access and ownership of land, how they participate in decision-making and control on their development and application processes, and control over the data and knowledge. In the same foundational publication, Kukutai and Taylor highlight that to give 'practical effect' to UNDRIP, Indigenous peoples should assert (and are asserting) control of data from nation states.[25] Both UNDRIP articles require data to appropriately inform legislative and administrative decisions.

---

17 Kukutai and Taylor, 'Data Sovereignty for Indigenous Peoples: Current Practice and Future Needs'.
18 United Nations, 'The United Nations Declaration on the Rights of Indigenous Peoples', 2008 https://www.un.org/development/desa/indigenouspeoples/declaration-on-the-rights-of-indigenous-peoples.html.
19 Australian Human Rights Commission, 'Australia and the Universal Declaration on Human Rights', https://www.humanrights.gov.au/publications/australia-and-niversaldeclaration-human-rights.
20 N.B In 2010, the State Department released, 'Announcement of U.S. Support for the United Nations Declaration on the Rights of Indigenous Peoples'. To read the full statement, go to http://www.achp.gov/docs/US%20Support%20for%20Declaration%2012-10.pdf.
21 Indigenous and Northern Affairs, 'United Nations Declaration on the Rights of Indigenous Peoples', Government of Canada, https://www.aadnc-aandc.gc.ca/eng/1309374407406/1309374458958.
22 Nations, 'The United Nations Declaration on the Rights of Indigenous Peoples'.
23 Ibid.
24 Kukutai and Taylor, 'Data Sovereignty for Indigenous Peoples: Current Practice and Future Needs'.
25 Ibid.

Based on the groundwork from First Nations in Canada and with additional impetus provided through UNDRIP, Indigenous groups have, over time, developed principles specific to their IDS context.

IDS principles in the Asia Pacific and North American States

Research Data Alliance (RDA) International Indigenous Data Sovereignty Interest Group

Generate recommendations for principles and best practices in IDS (currently in the principles development phase).

Aotearoa/NZ. Te Mana Raraunga, the Maori Data Sovereignty Network

Whakapapa and whanaungatanga: Recognising the connectedness between the material, natural and spiritual worlds

Rangatiratanga: Iwi(tribal)/Maori rights to own, access, control and possess data from them or about them and their environs

Kotahitanga: Collective vision and unity of purpose

Manaakitanga: Ethical data use to progress iwi/Maori aspirations for wellbeing

Kaitiakitanga: Sustainable data stewardship

United States - US Indigenous Data Sovereignty Network (USIDSN)

The USIDSN is in the principles development phase. Draft principles include recognition of inherent sovereignty; protection of Indigenous data; a commitment to aligning with Indigenous values for intergenerational collective wellbeing; a focus on relationships between Indigenous nations and other stakeholders; for IDG; and the honouring of Indigenous knowledge.

Canada (First Nations) - OCAP®

Ownership of data
Control - First Nations hold on how the data are collected, used and disclosed,
Access - whereby First Nations have access to any data about them
Possession - whereby all First Nations data fall within First Nations jurisdiction

Australia - Maiam nayri Wingara
Maiam nayri Wingara is the most recent of the IDS groups and has recently developed their principles.[26]

Table 1 - IDS principles in the Asia Pacific and North American States.

Indigenous Data Sovereignty and Governance in practice

Here we present examples of IDS and IDG in practice. The first example from Australia concerns both IDS and IDG.

Australia

The Mayi Kuwayu: The National Study of Aboriginal and Torres Strait Islander Wellbeing (meaning 'to follow Aboriginal people' in Ngiyampaa language) is a national Aboriginal and Torres Strait Islander longitudinal study. The aim of the study is to develop national-level cultural indicators and examine how culture interacts with health and wellbeing. It is publicly funded research and is housed at the Australian National University (ANU) in Australia.[27] The study development processes are designed to adhere to IDS and IDG. The data development considerations in the Mayi Kuwayu Study include:

- Development of new data items that represent cultural expression and practice (data of importance to Aboriginal and Torres Strait Islander peoples).

- The Australian Code for the Responsible Conduct of Research (the Code), that requires research data ownership and storage to be described.

- Research ethics[28] and intellectual property,[29] to acknowledge the sources of information and those who have contributed to the research. If Indigenous knowledge contributes to intellectual property, recognising the contribution, where appropriate, by transferring or sharing intellectual property and any benefits that result from the research'.[30]

- An Indigenous Data Governance group that develops data access and release protocols based on IDS principles.

---

26 Maiam nayri Wingara and the Australian Indigenous Governance Institute, *Indigenous Data Sovereignty Summit and Indigenous Data Sovereignty Communique,* Canberra, 2018, www.maiamnayriwingara.org.
27 KA Thurber, R Jones, J Chapman et al, 'Our Cultures Count: Mayi Kuwayu - the National Longitudinal Study of Aboriginal and Torres Strait Islander Wellbeing', *BMJ Open* (in press, 2018).
28 AIATSIS, 'Gerais Guidelines for Ethical Research in Australian Indigenous Studies' Canberra: Australian Institute of Aboriginal and Torres Strait Islander Studies, 2012.
29 Australian National University, 'Intellectual Property Policy', https://policies.anu.edu.au/ppl/document/ANUP_003603.
30 AIATSIS, 'Gerais Guidelines for Ethical Research in Australian Indigenous Studies'.

The Mayi Kuwayu Study has developed a number of mechanisms to address many of the existing data processes identified above. This includes ensuring Aboriginal and Torres Strait Islander leadership and management of the study from the outset, through leadership of the study by majority Aboriginal Chief Investigators and research staff. Further, in the development of cultural data items, the research team undertook 24 focus groups with a diverse range of Aboriginal and Torres Strait islander groups across Australia, embedding their feedback into priorities for measurement while also seeking suggestions on cultural appropriateness of questions and methods.

In the MK Study, ongoing data collection and ownership of the data set is shared between the research institute and participants under institutional policy (and its use is currently governed by the Study's Governance group that includes investigators and representatives from Aboriginal institutional project partners and community). Further, the research team and study governance group are developing protocols for data storage, access, analysis, and dissemination.

Aotearoa (New Zealand)

Aotearoa NZ is one of the world's most advanced digital nations.[31] Data is seen as a key national strategic asset,[32] and several key policy and legislative initiatives are underway to facilitate easier data sharing and linkage. A flagship project is the Integrated Data Infrastructure (IDI), a world-leading research database under the stewardship of Statistics New Zealand that contains de-identified data (including Maori data) from more than 50 surveys and administrative datasets across the state, research and NGO sectors. With a greater focus on data-driven policy-making has come an increased interest in how 'social license'[33] can enable more flexible data sharing without explicit individual consent. Missing from these innovations, however, are robust models of data governance and ethics, value creation and benefit-sharing to enhance 'good data' and 'good outcomes'.

Maori have often been at the sharp end of intrusive data surveillance and misuse but have well-tested 'tikanga' (ethics, processes, principles) around the protection and sharing of knowledge for collective benefit that can be readily adapted to digital data environments. Maori Data Sovereignty (MDS) advocates are developing a number of tikanga-based solutions including: models of Maori/iwi (tribal) data governance for the IDI and wider government ecosystem; 'cultural license' as the 'social license' alternative for community acceptability of data use; and a Maori Data Audit Tool to assess organisational readiness to incorporate MDS principles. Many of the assumptions underpinning old and emerging data ecosystems rest on Anglo-European

---

31 N.B Aotearoa is part of the D7 network of the world's most advanced digital nations. The others are: Estonia, Israel, South Korea, United Kingdom, Canada and Uruguay.

32 N.B. The strategic importance of data ecosystems in Aotearoa NZ is reflected in government strategies such as the Data Futures Partnership, the Government ICT Strategy, Open Government Data Programme and the establishment of a Social Investment Unit; research initiatives such as the New Zealand Law Foundation Information Law & Policy Project and the Virtual Health Information Network (VHIN); and the recent appointments of a Government Chief Digital Officer and Chief Data Steward.

33 See, for example: http://datafutures.co.nz/our-work-2/talking-to-new-zealanders/.

legal concepts, such as individual privacy and ownership, which translate poorly into the big and open data environments. What is needed is a radically different way of conceptualising rights that relate to massive quantities of data and the value that can be extracted from. The direct beneficiaries of the 'data revolution' have largely been data producers and controllers, not the individuals and collectives from which data are drawn. IDS and MDS demands clear lines of accountability and benefit sharing; at the heart of these demands is a call for power sharing. Seen this way, the potential benefits of embedding MDS principles across government data ecosystems extend beyond Maori to include the wider public.

As a result of the rapidity of changes in data capabilities and technology, there can be a tension between responding to technological imperatives and to changes being driven by other actors (e.g. Government and corporations) and focusing on Maori aspirations and priorities. The MDS space is also a creative space where there is potential for Maori to (re-)imagine relationships and practices that realise Maori aspirations for data sovereignty, including those that may operate outside currently existing structures.

North America

One of the landmark results of the establishment of OCAP® principles in Canada has been the multiphase First Nations Regional Health Survey, which is designed, implemented and analyzed by First Nations organizations in Canada.[34] A coordinating national organization, the First Nations Information Governance Centre was established to lead the efforts to expand this First Nations-driven survey approach to education, labour and employment and other key areas.

Across Canada, each of the three distinct Indigenous Peoples in Canada (First Nations, Métis and Inuit) have also asserted sovereignty over the data that are held about their encounters with the provincial health system.[35] This has resulted in a mosaic of relationships, Data Sharing Agreements, and Data Governance Agreements in each Canadian province to ensure that decisions about the use and sharing of First Nations, Inuit, and Métis data are made by the respective governance organizations.

Conclusions

While the IDS movement has emerged in response to poor data practices and exclusion, IDS and IDG provide opportunities to reconfigure current approaches to data, including embedding good governance of Indigenous data that supports self-determination and wellbeing for Indigenous communities. Good data, including good data governance, are necessary to ensure Indigenous peoples benefit from current and future data practices and to mitigate the potential for continued harm. IDS movements also support broader transformative aims of developing Indigenous-owned and controlled data infrastructures, protocols and community capabilities that lie beyond the reach of nation states and corporations.

---

34 See: http://fnigc.ca/our-work/regional-health-survey/about-rhs.html.
35 Evelyn Pyper et al, 'Walking the Path Together: Indigenous Health Data at Ices', *Healthcare Quarterly* 20.4 (2018).

References

AIATSIS. 'Gerais Guidelines for Ethical Research in Australian Indigenous Studies'. Canberra: Australian Institute of Aboriginal and Torres Strait Islander Studies, 2012.

AIATSIS. *National Indigenous Research Conference,* 2017.

AIHW. 'National Advisory Group on Aboriginal and Torres Strait Islander Health Information and Data: Strategic Plan 2010-2015', Canberra, 2011.

Australian Human Rights Commission. 'Australia and the Universal Declaration on Human Rights'.

Australian National University. 'Intellectual Property Policy', https://policies.anu.edu.au/ppl/document/ANUP_003603.

Coleman, C., B. Elias, V. Lee, J. Smylie, J. Waldon, F.S. Hodge, and I. Ring. 'International Group for Indigenous Health Measurement: Recommendations for best practice for estimation of Indigenous mortality'. *Statistical Journal of the IAOS* 32 (2016) 729-73, DOI: 10.3233/SJI-161023.

Drabiak-Syed, Katherine. 'Lessons from Havasupai Tribe V. Arizona State University Board of Regents: Recognizing Group, Cultural, and Dignity Harms as Legitimate Risks Warranting Integration into Research Practice', *J. Health & Biomedical L.* 6 (2010): 175.

Indian Act R.S.C. C. I-5 (1985). http://laws-lois.justice.gc.ca/eng/acts/I-5/page-2.html.

Indigenous and Northern Affairs. 'United Nations Declaration on the Rights of Indigenous Peoples', Government of Canada, https://www.aadnc-aandc.gc.ca/eng/1309374407406/1309374458958.

Jones R, KA Thurber, J Chapman et al. 'Our Cultures Count: Mayi Kuwayu - the National Longitudinal Study of Aboriginal and Torres Strait Islander Wellbeing'. *BMJ Open* (in press 2018).

Kertzer, David I, and Dominique Arel. 'Censuses, Identity Formation, and the Struggle for Political Power', *Census and identity: The politics of race, ethnicity, and language in national censuses* 1 (2002): 1.

Kukutai, Tahu, and John Taylor. 'Data Sovereignty for Indigenous Peoples: Current Practice and Future Needs', in Tahu Kukutai and John Taylor (eds), *Indigenous Data Sovereignty: Towards an Agenda*, Canberra: ANU Press, 2016, pp. 1-25.

Kukutai, Tahu, and Maggie Walter. 'Recognition and Indigenizing Official Statistics: Reflections from Aotearoa New Zealand and Australia', *Statistical Journal of the IAOS* 31.2 (2015): 317-26.

Maiam nayri Wingara and the Australian Indigenous Governance Institute, Indigenous Data Sovereignty Summit and Indigenous Data Sovereignty Communique, Canberra, 2018, http://www.maiamnayriwingara.org.

Pacheco, Christina M, Sean M Daley, Travis Brown, Melissa Filippi, K Allen Greiner and Christine M Daley. 'Moving Forward: Breaking the Cycle of Mistrust between American Indians and Researchers', *American journal of public health* 103.12 (2013): 2152-59.

Productivity Commission. 'Data Availability and Use: Overview & Recommendations', Canberra, 2017.

Pyper, Evelyn et al. 'Walking the Path Together: Indigenous Health Data at Ices.' *Healthcare Quarterly* 20.4 (2018): 6-9.

Snipp, C Matthew. 'What Does Data Sovereignty Imply: What Does It Look Like?' in Tahu Kukutai and John Taylor (eds) *Indigenous Data Sovereignty: Towards an Agenda*, Canberra: ANU Press, 2016, pp. 39-56.

Te Mana Raraunga. 'Te Mana Raraunga - Maori Data Sovereignty Network Charter', https://www.temanararaunga.maori.nz/tutohinga/.

The First Nations Information Governance Centre. 'Ownership, Control, Access and Possession (OCAP™): The Path to First Nations Information Governance', Ottawa: The First Nations Information Governance Centre, 2014.

Tsosie, Rebecca. *Cultural Challenges to Biotechnology: Native American Genetic Resources and the Concept of Cultural Harm*, Los Angeles: SAGE Publications, 2007.

United Nations. 'The United Nations Declaration on the Rights of Indigenous Peoples', 2008.

3: THE GOOD DATA MANIFESTO

CLAIRE TRENHAM AND ADAM STEER

Introduction

The Good Data Manifesto sketches out a set of principles which can be used to guide data collection, storage, and re-use. In an increasingly data-rich world, we have long failed to fully consider many implications of how data might be used, once collected and stored. On the technical front - how do we manage, move, and pay for the storage of data? How long can we assume that infrastructure-scale computing is a sustainable solution? And on the human side, how can we adequately protect our rights to privacy and individuality, or even to be forgotten? While some research fields consider ethics deeply in their data management, others have not traditionally done so, thus our aim is to develop principles that might broadly apply across disciplines, to address the question '*what makes data good?*'. We draw on examples from a number of fields, but with a general focus on geospatial data which is often large in volume, ubiquitous, and personal. We aim to help data collectors and managers consider more fully how they go about their task, and to help data users critically consider the applicability of datasets to their need.

Data exist everywhere. In a growing technological society, humans are increasingly recording, cataloguing and exploiting observations of the world and ourselves. We are also getting better at producing data - inferences, models and predictions of the world and our behaviour - driven by a growing ability to collect and collate observations, together with increasing computational power to integrate this data with complex theoretical models. Invariably, this leads to new problems: what do we do with all these data? How do we catalogue them? How should we use them?

Less often we consider the questions: *should* we collect, aggregate, catalogue and exploit these data? If so, how? What would be ethical means for doing so? These questions have been deeply considered in health and human-related sciences (e.g. psychology, sociology). Driven by Europe's implementation of General Data Protection Regulation (GPDR),[1] these questions are also under active consideration in high-resolution earth observation,[2] and wherever ubiquitous, commercialised personal data collection takes place (e.g. ride sharing apps).[3]

---

1   European Commission, '2018 reform of EU data protection rules', 2018, https://ec.europa.eu/commission/priorities/justice-and-fundamental-rights/data-protection/2018-reform-eu-data-protection-rules_en.
2   DroneRules.eu, '8 Data Protection Guiding Principles under the GDPR for Drone Pilots', 2018 http://dronerules.eu/en/professional/news/8-data-protection-principles-under-the-gdpr-for-drone-pilots; 'Accurate Privacy Blurring at Scale', *The Mapillary* Blog, 2018, https://blog.mapillary.com/update/2018/04/19/accurate-privacy-blurring-at-scale.html.
3   'Uber Privacy Policy', https://privacy.uber.com/policy.

Historically, these questions are rarely asked before amassing collections of data containing explicit and/or implicit (e.g. location tracks) personal information, until something goes wrong: for example, the 2018 revelation of a major social media company's collection and third party exploitation of user data.[4]

The preparation of this book is timely, with a number of groups around the world considering what "good data" and data ethics mean.[5] [6] The authors of this chapter are not ethicists, nor data privacy experts. We are Australian data practitioners with experience managing and working with petabyte-scale data collections; advisors on and contributors to continent-scale data infrastructures. We love high quality data but want to make sure the data we produce and consume considers more than fidelity, precision, accuracy, and reproducibility. This chapter is written with a focus on Australian concerns. We focus often on geospatial data or data with a geospatial component, however our goal in this chapter is to touch on considerations across a broad range of data fields.

Boundaries between geospatial data and personal data are increasingly blurry. Data warehouses and practitioners must consider multiple data types and myriad layers of licensing, ethical and access concerns. In this chapter we present a generalised manifesto for 'good data', with the aim of creating a set of principles which can guide operations whilst avoiding harm.[7] We ask, '*what attributes make data good?*'

The Good Data Manifesto

There are international efforts devoted to various kinds of data collection 'goodness', for example the Research Data Alliance, the Open Geospatial Consortium, the ISO, and the IEEE. These organisations are typically concerned with (meta)data standards and focus on technical aspects with little attention to ethical aspects. We ask, '*should* the data be collected?' If so, how and why? How long should it persist? What makes it useful/good? Aspects we consider that contribute to 'good data' are described in this chapter.

4　Cambridge Analytica series, *The Guardian*, 2018, https://www.theguardian.com/uk-news/cambridge-analytica.
5　'IEEE Ethically Aligned Design', *IEEE Global Initiative*, v2, 2017, https://ethicsinaction.ieee.org/.
6　D. E. O'Leary, 'Ethics for Big Data and Analytics', *IEEE Intelligent Systems*, 31.4 (2016): 81-84, DOI: 10.1109/MIS.2016.70.
7　S. Dixon and L. Quirke, 'What's the harm?...', *Teaching Sociology*, 46.1 (2018): 12-24, DOI: 10.1177/0092055X17711230.

Good data are...	Considerations	Questions we may ask
Usable: fit for purpose	3.1.1 Well described 3.1.2 Include uncertainties/limitations 3.1.3 Readable 3.1.4 FAIR (Findable, Accessible, Interoperable, Reusable) 3.1.5 Reproducible 3.1.6 Timely 3.1.7 Appropriately licenced	- Is the purpose of the dataset well defined? - Are these the best data for the task? - Are the data well described, including limitations and uncertainties? - Is the dataset discoverable, accessible, and readable? - Are the data reproducible? - Is the method by which open data was produced also open?
Collected with respect to...	3.2.1 humans and their rights 3.2.2 the natural world	- Was the data collected/produced for this purpose, not incidentally?
Published	3.3.1 with respect to openness 3.3.2 maintaining privacy 3.3.3 carrying owner licensing	- Is the dataset published with a DOI and version? - Does the data carry an appropriate licence?
Revisable	3.4.1 Personal: opt-in/out alternatives 3.4.2 Long term accuracy: data may change over time 3.4.3 Older versions of data may be decommissioned	- For human-related data, could participants realistically opt-out? - Are the data time dependent?
Form useful social capital	3.5 Valuable to society 'FAIR', persistent, open Available for ethical use	- Have we considered ethics around the data?

Table 1: Guidelines for 'good data'.

The above questions might assist data producers and consumers to consider the impacts on their research outcomes.

3.1 Good Data are fit for Purpose

For data to be 'good' they must meet the consumer's needs (and indeed, the data producer's needs). This may include measuring the right things, measuring appropriately, and with an understanding of uncertainties in the data (that is, data is accurate, and data has an appropriate level of precision). Data should be internally consistent within the dataset (e.g. angles should consistently be measured in degrees *or* radians), or in the case of non-numeric data, language uncertainties should be minimised (e.g. is a survey conducted in the native tongue of the respondents? Could there be translation uncertainties between respondents and analysts?). When possible, Controlled Vocabularies - which provide taxonomies for cataloguing information in particular fields - should be used.

Data that is created to answer a specific question may be more useful than 'incidental' data. Use of data should be 'defensible', i.e. it is demonstrable that the data can be validly used for its primary, or secondary, purposes. For example, population biases exist in social media analytics that could be deliberately avoided in constructing random populations for surveying, but the data may be much harder to collect. Similarly, in marine science when using tracers of a measurable quantity to infer values of another quantity, how strongly correlated is the effect? Is measuring the desired variable possible? What is the uncertainty associated with use of a notionally equivalent metric?

3.1.1 Good Data are Well Described

Good data need to have a plan, and be curated according to that plan, which may change over time.[8] Datasets contain, or are accompanied by, *metadata* describing the dataset. This metadata must contain a description of how the dataset was created - measurement techniques, associated uncertainties, and dataset provenance. It should also provide transparency: who funded and collected the data, what was the purpose, any post-processing steps that have occurred, when the original data was collected, and when the data product was created, as well as versioning information if the dataset has been updated or re-produced. Metadata must be accessible in a machine-readable format, but good metadata are also human-readable. Google have recently released a Dataset Search tool which relies on the use of open metadata standards in contributing datasets.[9]

3.1.2 Good Data Include Uncertainty Estimates or Description of Limitations

Good data are self-deferential, datasets are open about limitations. Every observation has some uncertainty. Good data describe uncertainties, and are not asserted as canonical truth. Data collectors must consider all sources of error and uncertainty in their data, and ensure this information is available to downstream consumers of the data.

3.1.3 Good Data are Readable

Good Data are written in common Open formats with standards-governed specifications. If proprietary formats must be used to meet community standards, thought is given to how the data should be accessed in 10 years' time when standard software may well have

---

8   J. Wang et al, 'The A, B, C, D, E, F of Multipurpose Active Data Management Plans...', *eResearch Australasia, Brisbane*, 2015, www.researchgate.net/publication/309704990_The_A_B_C_D_E_F_of_Multipurpose_Active_Data_Management_Plans_to_Facilitate_Multiscale_Interdisciplinary_Science.
9   N. Noy, 'Making it easier to discover datasets', *Google Blog*, 2018, https://www.blog.google/products/search/making-it-easier-discover-datasets/.

changed. Open formats include .txt, .csv, .html, .mp3, .gzip, .png, .geoTIFF, .nc, .hdf, and more. Because open formats adhere to published standards, maintaining support for these formats in the future is easier than when formats are proprietary.

Examples of closed or proprietary data formats that may also be appropriate to use due to their ubiquitous community uptake include .pdf, .doc, .xls, .gif. The vast number of files written in these formats means that backward compatibility for these file types is likely to persist for some time.

3.1.4 Good Data do better than FAIR

Data should be *findable*. Digital Object Identifiers (DOIs) should be minted for datasets.

Data should be *accessible*. Not hidden behind paywalls or obscure metadata redirection servers.

Data should be *interoperable*. Data can be meaningfully read by multiple, ideally non-proprietary software products.

Data should *reusable*. Data are available for use.

Data should be *ethical*. No entity will be harmed in the collection or use of the data.

Data should be *revisable*. Errata can be filed, corrections made, and updated versions released with older versions archived.

The FAIR data principles have been widely adopted among public data providers including data.gov.au, and online assessment tools have been developed to rate compliance with FAIR principles.[10] However, FAIR data may not be 'good'. Adding the terms 'ethical' and 'revisable' to make FAIRER data is a good step - but may still be applied to data which miss metadata; are not appropriately licensed; which do not describe uncertainties or whose definition of 'ethical' may differ from a common usage concept.

3.1.5 Good Data are Reproducible

If a dataset cannot be reproduced (other than time-dependent observations of a dynamic system), its value is severely limited. Reliability of data depends on its reproducibility.

- For medical and social research, have the populations tested been constructed such that the same results would be produced if the study was repeated using appropriately sampled individuals?

---

10   ARDC, 'FAIR data assessment tool', https://www.ands-nectar-rds.org.au/fair-tool; 'Accurate Privacy Blurring at Scale', *The Mapillary Blog*, 2018, https://blog.mapillary.com/update/2018/04/19/accurate-privacy-blurring-at-scale.html.

- For survey data, will the same people give the same answers if surveyed again (barring interventions designed to change responses)? Were populations appropriately randomly selected? Could language barriers contribute issues around reproducibility?

- For observed data, will instruments produce consistent results (i.e. are they well calibrated)?

- For modelled data, is the code that produced it open source and available to be run on other systems by other people; and can the code be associated with the data it produced?[11]

- For data collected by 'apps', is the software used by the app open, versioned, and adhering to relevant standards? Are algorithms published?

Reliability outside of a laboratory context with controlled conditions takes different meanings for different fields. For example, a satellite image captured at position *(x,y)* at time *t=0* will never be repeated at a later time. But if a static object can be reliably identified, measurements of that object should return consistent results.

The question of reproducibility is difficult in non-controlled, time-dependent data collection - a feature of many social media or personal geolocation platforms. In these scenarios, reliability may be cast as capacity to understand the conditions and algorithms which led to the data being collected/created.

Additionally, data which cannot be reproduced for ethical reasons (for example, experiments on humans in war time),[12] could be open and published and may contribute important understandings of e.g. human physiology, but the data are limited by the fact that they must not be reproduced. In other words, data could be FAIR but that does not make it 'good'.

"Good data" can be recreated when conditions of their original formation can be controlled.

3.1.6 Good Data are Timely

Data should be released to primary consumers as soon as possible after collection. They should still be relevant when they are released to the wider community. It may be reasonable to issue a metadata record rapidly after data collection with the accompanying data to be published later. The risks of early release (e.g. needing to correct errors in the data) are important, and quality checking and control is crucial, as is anonymising human data.

---

11 D. Irving, 'A minimum standard for publishing computational results in the weather and climate sciences', *BAMS*, 2015, DOI: 10.1175/BAMS-D-15-00010.1; M. Katerbow & G. Feulner, 'Recommendations on the development, use and provision of Research Software', *Zenodo*, 16 March 2018, DOI: 10.5281/zenodo.1172988.

12 H. Brody et al, 'United States Responses to Japanese Wartime Inhuman Experimentation after World War II: National Security and Wartime Exigency', *Cambridge Quarterly of Healthcare Ethics*, 23.2 (2014): 220-230, DOI: 10.1017/S0963180113000753.

Sometimes the funding associated with data acquisition necessitates an embargo period for the funder to maximise return on investment in the early period, however there is likely to be broader benefits to releasing data to the community that will indirectly benefit the funder. Delaying release means the data may no longer be fit for use.

3.1.7 Good Data are Appropriately Licensed

Ambiguity about how data may be used (assuming ethical and anonymity criteria are met) is resolved by application of an appropriate license. In Australia, without a license, data are considered 'all rights reserved'[13] which may not be the intention of the data publisher. A license may not meet the desires of all parties wishing to re-use data - but it must, at least, resolve ambiguity about whether data can be used for a particular purpose.

A range of creative commons (CC-BY) licenses are available for canonical data (data which are generally immutable, e.g. observations of temperature). Where data may be edited, or version-controlled, software licenses may be more appropriate (e.g. https://choosealicense.com). The terms of software licenses are better designed for the case where the licensed collection may evolve over time - and may be more permissive of contributions. Licensing is the collective decision of the data producers, owners, and custodians, who should become familiar with the various licenses available.

3.2 Good Data Respects Rights

Good data are collected with respect to various rights, including human rights, property rights, and privacy rights.[14] Here we take 'rights' to mean human rights in a broad sense (privacy, freedom to live without harassment) and the rights of the natural world, in the sociocultural context at the time of collection. Other principles that may be considered are 'responsibilities' of the data collector - sustainability (environmental and financial cost of maintaining the data), fairness/equitability, and path to impact; as well as 'value', which may have a range of meanings.

3.2.1 Human Privacy

The Australian Government recently tightened requirements around reporting of data breaches which could impact on privacy (via the *Privacy Amendment (Notifiable Data Breaches) Act 2017*).[15] Organisations storing personal data are required to strengthen security and establish/review data breach reporting processes. While not protecting privacy directly, it enables citizens to know when their personal data may have been breached. Significant numbers of

---

13 ANDS, 'Licensing and copyright for data reuse', https://www.ands.org.au/working-with-data/publishing-and-reusing-data/licensing-for-reuse.
14 UN, 'Universal Declaration of Human Rights', 1948, http://www.un.org/en/universal-declaration-human-rights/.
15 OAIC, 'Notifiable Data Breaches scheme', *Australian Government Office of the Australian Information Commissioner*, https://www.oaic.gov.au/privacy-law/privacy-act/notifiable-data-breaches-scheme.

breaches have been reported to date across government and industry.[16]

The European Union have legislated for greater control of personal data for their citizens via the General Data Protection Regulation (GDPR).[17] The GDPR sets a high standard for data privacy. The changes have had wide-reaching impacts on mobile apps and websites that collect data.

3.2.2 The Natural World

Data collection may have implications for the natural world. Consider the possible impacts of increasingly high resolution remote-sensed imagery. There are implications of sensor data being used in detection and monitoring of threatened species: there are conservation benefits, but potential black-market risks. If it were deemed that fossil fuel extraction harms the planet, this affects models and observational datasets used to detect such deposits. This is of particular interest in heretofore unspoilt wilderness areas such as Antarctica.[18]

The physical cost of holding, cataloguing, accessing and processing data is important. Infrastructure scale computing, data storage and data retention is expensive; as is large scale data transmission and energy infrastructure. Costs of unnecessary data collection and retention are ethical and environmental, as well as financial.[19] We should aim to minimise the impact of data collection and retention on the natural world.

3.3 Good Data are Published

If data remain solely accessible by an individual, group, or corporation, then utility and defensibility of process and products is limited. Good data are 'as open as possible'; ranging from CCBY-4 licensing to pay-per-access. The utility (or 'goodness') of any data is always restricted if nobody knows they exist, so publication of metadata, even without the accompanying data, is very important. There can be no means of assessing data quality and veracity if the data are not published and comparable with other datasets.

---

16 OAIC, 'Annual Report 2016-2017', *Australian Government Office of the Australian Information Commissioner, 2017,* https://www.oaic.gov.au/annualreport2016-17, p.80; P. Farrell, 'Darknet sale of Medicare data "traditional criminal activity", minister says', *The Guardian*, 2017, https://www.theguardian.com/australia-news/2017/jul/04/federal-police-asked-to-investigate-darkweb-sale-of-medicare-data; OAIC, 'Notifiable Data Breaches Quarterly Statistics Report: 1 April - 30 June 2018', 2018, https://www.oaic.gov.au/resources/privacy-law/privacy-act/notifiable-data-breaches-scheme/quarterly-statistics/notifiable-data-breaches-quarterly-statistics-report-1-april-30-june-2018.pdf.
17 European Commission, '2018 reform of EU data protection rules', 2018, https://ec.europa.eu/commission/priorities/justice-and-fundamental-rights/data-protection/2018-reform-eu-data-protection-rules_en.
18 Secretariat of the Antarctic Treaty, 'The Protocol on Environmental Protection to the Antarctic Treaty', 1991, https://www.ats.aq/e/ep.htm.
19 NCI, 'NCI Annual Report 2016-2017', 2017, https://nci.org.au/wp-content/uploads/2014/12/NCI-Report-2017-web-sm-updated.pdf, p.65.

There must be exceptions where privacy or ethics are concerned to maintain the rights of the data subject(s), but aggregated and de-identified data (which cannot be re-identified) should be published where possible.

Publishing data is not simply making it accessible via a web server. If datasets are formally published, DOIs can be minted, increasing the value of the data as a citable resource. In turn this provides incentive for academic data collectors to release valuable data collections, as it helps researchers to accrue credit in the academic system. DOIs also provide a permanent metadata record for the dataset.

3.3.1 Open Data should be Published Openly

Data should be openly available in compliance with FAIR data principles. Licence restrictions may be required, but the barrier to access should be low, to encourage reuse. Data access should not have a monetary cost, as exemplified by the Australian Government's Research Data Storage Infrastructure scheme (2010-2015), which provided infrastructure and support for nationally significant data collections. Cost recovery models are understandable, but the data should be accessible by all people.[20] Publicly funded research should be published openly, both data and journal articles.[21] Ideally, 'for profit' or 'commercial' data should also be available for discovery in an open fashion.

3.3.2 Published Data must Maintain Privacy

It is important that no individual (person, government, corporation, or the Earth itself) should have their privacy damaged as a result of data publication. Significant thought has been given to data privacy in medical contexts.[22] However, emerging fields in ubiquitous data are only now facing these issues, prompted in part by the EU's GDPR, and by the public response to data breaches and unexpected information sharing revealed in the media. Data released in Strava's Heatmap demonstrated an unexpected privacy violation;[23] similarly the Earth and humanity may be better served if the location of critically endangered species (e.g., the Wollemi Pine)[24] is kept secret.

---

20 European Commission, 'Creating value through open data', *EU Publications*, 2015, DOI: 10.2759/328101.
21 Science Europe, 'cOAlition S', 2018, https://www.scienceeurope.org/coalition-s/.
22 OAIC, 'Health Information and medical research', *Australian Government Office of the Australian Information Commissioner*, https://www.oaic.gov.au/privacy-law/privacy-act/health-and-medical-research.
23 R. Pérez-Peña & M. Rosenberg, 'Strava Fitness App Can Reveal Military Sites, Analysts Say', *NYTimes*, 29 January 2018, https://www.nytimes.com/2018/01/29/world/middleeast/strava-heat-map.html; Violet Blue, 'Strava's fitness heatmaps are a "potential catastrophe"', *Engadget*, 2 February 2018, https://www.engadget.com/2018/02/02/strava-s-fitness-heatmaps-are-a-potential-catastrophe.
24 J. Kidd, 'Wollemi Pines: Secret plantation in Blue Mountains to ensure species' survival', *ABC News*, 21 September 2014, http://www.abc.net.au/news/2014-09-21/secret-bid-to-save-prehistoric-wollemi-pines/5758542.

3.3.3 Published Data should Carry Owner Licensing

The data owner should be able to decide what license terms they apply to their data and may wish to control limitations about what users can do with the data, and whether they can profit from modifications to it. Attribution should not be lost when data is used for downstream applications, and derived data products should contain acknowledgement of or reference to the parent dataset(s). In Australia, CC-BY licensing does not compromise moral rights under copyright law.[25]

3.4 Good Data are Revisable

Data may have a lifespan. It is important that datasets are maintained, reviewed periodically and retired to an archive if need be. In the built environment, Ingress (www.ingress.com) is an Augmented Reality mobile game built around user-identified 'portals' attached to real world objects, in which users are able to submit edits and corrections, and flag portals for removal if the object in the real world no longer exists.

Humans have successfully asserted that their personal data be 'forgotten',[26] arguing that the right to privacy over-rides historical record. In these cases, electronic records of history are revised - not necessarily removed - with aggregate or non-personal data and information potentially retained for historical purposes.

3.4.1 Personal Data should be Opt-in

Keßler and McKenzie construct a *Geoprivacy Manifesto* designed to address an internet-age trend of personal data collection *and storage* being the default for many web-based services.[27] This leads to potential exposure of individuals through various inadvertent means - their location, which services they used, how they communicated. In a good data scenario, these data would be retained just long enough: exploited *at the time of usage*, then forgotten, unless the individual expressly opted for their data to be retained.

In the context of ubiquitous data collection about individuals, 'good data' respects the right to be forgotten.[28] Should records of a person attending a specific place be retained? What if the person may be unaware that their location is being recorded, or if cultural sensitivity requires consideration of deceased persons? There may be ethical advantages to data retention which appropriately considers privacy, e.g. notification of people who may have been exposed to a toxin because they visited an infected location in a given timeframe.

---

25 Thinh, 'CC, Open Access, and moral rights', *Science Commons Blog,* 2007, http://sciencecommons.org/weblog/archives/2007/11/07/cc-oa-moral-rights/.
26 L. Floridi et al. *'The Advisory Council to Google on the Right to be Forgotten', 2015,* https://static.googleusercontent.com/media/archive.google.com/en//advisorycouncil/advisement/advisory-report.pdf.
27 C. Keßler and G. McKenzie, 'A geoprivacy manifesto', *Transactions in GIS* 22:3-19 (2018), DOI: 10.1111/tgis.12305.
28 (The right to be forgotten), https://en.wikipedia.org/wiki/Right_to_be_forgotten.

3.4.2 Good Data may Change over Time

The world is not static. Considering geospatial datasets for example, population distributions change over time which may diminish accuracy and trustworthiness of an ecological dataset. Projects like the Atlas of Living Australia help researchers track these changes.[29] The built environment changes at an even higher rate. In response, Australian state mapping authorities release regularly updated maps to ensure data is effectively versioned, and consumers can access the most accurate data available. Conversely, the use of an older map collection implies a level of uncertainty with respect to present day locations. In other words, the 'goodness' of geospatial data may decay over time.

Data formats and conventions can also change specification over time, and good datasets may need to be updated to meet new standards or be converted to new formats to maintain interoperability.

3.4.3 Older Versions of Data may be Decommissioned

Good data are versioned and timestamped, so that when data become un-useful they can be decommissioned. This does not mean erased - historical data contributing social capital may be retained - simply removed from active usage.

This highlights the need for versioned datasets. Real-world applications may be interested in the present state of geospatially referenced objects, or they may be interested in changes over time, for example land use, coastlines, or urban development (e.g. an historical New York cartography project and mapping of historical photos).[30]

Dataset production should consider the valid lifetime of its data, and if it can change over time, how data should be marked as out-of-date. For example some states of Australia have a fuel price monitoring body, but due to rapid fluctuations in fuel prices, these products may flag some locations as being inaccurate due to age. Data should not be thrown away without good cause. Older versions of datasets should be kept for research purposes at a later date to study trends, for example.

3.5 Good Data form Useful Social Capital

'Social capital' aims to describe a collection of resources and networks that enable social interaction and understanding[31]. A concise definition might specify '*the shared values and understandings that enable people to trust each other*.'[32]

---

29 Atlas of Living Australia, https://www.ala.org.au/.
30 NYC Space/Time Directory, *New York Public Library*, http://spacetime.nypl.org/; OldNYC: Mapping historical photos from the NYPL, https://www.oldnyc.org/.
31 T. Claridge, *Social Capital and Natural Resource Management: An important role for social capital?*, Unpublished Thesis, University of Queensland, Brisbane, Australia, 2004, https://www.socialcapitalresearch.com/literature/definition/.
32 OECD Insights: Human Capital, *Organisation for Economic Cooperation & Development*, 2007,

Good data are a social asset, a platform upon which trust and cooperation can be built, enabling a 'social license to operate'. This may occur between scientists - for example field scientists collecting measurements and providing them to systems modellers; or anyone - for example, trusting a restaurant address is correct, or a weather forecast is mostly accurate.

Even private or sensitive data form a useful social asset - while they may not be openly accessible, 'good data' are reliable and their veracity can be examined by whoever has the appropriate permission to use it.

Examples of Good Data and Conclusion

To the authors, a dataset is 'good' if it can reasonably address the questions suggested in Table 1. We do not expect a 'good' dataset to be able to 'tick every box', indeed that may be logically impossible for some data, our thesis here is aimed at helping data producers and consumers think qualitatively about the goodness of their data. Quantitative measures of FAIR data principles exist, but we hope to encourage data practitioners to step beyond these metrics.

The following four examples represent, by these guidelines, 'good data'.

a.	Data can have power in numbers. Not only in the literal sense, rather, just as repeatability is important, so aggregation and meta-analysis of repeated and comparable studies acts to reduce the uncertainty of individual studies. Cochrane reviews in medical research carry a good deal of weight for this reason and are considered 'gold standard'.[33] These reviews reduce the influence of individual companies or vested interests, and lead to more informed health policy.

b.	A spatial dataset which meets all relevant criteria is the National Public Toilet Map,[34] available through data.gov.au. This dataset contains historical versions allowing changes to be monitored over time. It meets 'good data' requirements around publication, licensing, availability, versioning, formats (both human- and computer readable), and it also forms useful social capital. This data enables apps to be built,[35] which are of high impact to families with infants, people with medical continence issues for whom knowing where these facilities are can be vital, and accessibility information benefits those with reduced mobility. The dataset contains not only the location of public toilet facilities, but metadata about the facilities.

c.	OpenStreetMap (www.openstreetmap.org) is a geospatial dataset forming a social asset. It is built by volunteers and geospatial professionals alike, maintained by an active community, editable by anyone, and governed by a code of conduct.

---

	https://www.oecd.org/insights/37966934.pdf.
33	Cochrane Collaboration, http://www.cochrane.org.
34	data.gov.au, 'National Public Toilet Map', *Australian Government data.gov.au*, 2018, https://data.gov.au/dataset/553b3049-2b8b-46a2-95e6-640d7986a8c1.
35	Web: https://toiletmap.gov.au/, also available on iTunes.

d.   The Australian Electoral Commission (AEC),[36] and state-based electoral commissions, provide polling data that is open and accessible down to polling place level (without compromising privacy, though a voter can choose to vote below the line in a Hare Clark election such that their vote may be uniquely identifiable, due to the possible permutations of preferences combined with small numbers of persons voting at each booth). Transparency in democracy is a powerful thing.

Collected Thoughts on 'Good Data'

Posing a question[37] about what make 'good data' resulted in the themes 'consistency' - agreement about what to call things between data providers, 'accessibility' with regard to cost and licensing, and 'provenance' - knowing where data come from. In a largely geospatial cohort, ethical aspects were not widely discussed. One person we spoke to likened 'good data' to edge pieces of a jigsaw puzzle. Every piece of data is like part of the puzzle that is how the world works (and some are poorly formed!), but good data are the pieces that allow you to constrain the others.

In the context of developing countries,[38] another contributor noted considerations including faith in the data collectors - data not hearsay; how money sponsoring data collection is spent - bias that might result in donor organisations being seen to do good things; is government intimidation a concern? Consistency within data records can be problematic, and survey responses can vary as those interviewed may say what they think the interviewer wants to hear.

Conclusion

As well as the EU's GDPR, we are aware of a Manifesto for Data Practises,[39] a Code of Ethics for Data Science,[40] a Geoprivacy Manifesto,[41] and an Open Geospatial Consortium and World Wide Web Consortium note on 'Spatial Data on the Web Best Practices'. [42] The proliferation of these considerations suggests that in the near future, these ideas may crystallize into formal guidelines just as medical ethics did during the 20th Century.[43]

---

36 Australian Electoral Commission, www.aec.gov.au.
37 @adamdsteer, Twitter post, 18 January 2018, 11:54AM, https://twitter.com/adamdsteer/status/953792786607742977.
38 D. Serwadda et al, 'Open data sharing and the Global South - Who benefits?', *Science* 359.6376 (2018): 642-643, DOI: 10.1126/science.aap8395.
39 Manifesto for Data Practices, https://datapractices.org/manifesto/.
40 DJ Patil, 'A code of Ethics for Data Science', *Medium*, 1 February 2018, https://medium.com/@dpatil/a-code-of-ethics-for-data-science-cda27d1fac1.
41 Keßler and McKenzie, 'A geoprivacy manifesto'.
42 J. Tandy, L. van den Brink, and P. Barnaghi (eds), 'Spatial Data on the Web Best Practices', *W3C Working Group Note*, 2017, https://www.w3.org/TR/sdw-bp/.
43 UMKC, 'History of Research Ethics', *UMKC Office of the Vice Chancellor*, date unknown, http://ors.umkc.edu/research-compliance-(iacuc-ibc-irb-rsc)/institutional-review-board-(irb)/history-of-research-ethics.

The size and variety of data created and available continues to grow, and we are moving from 'the 3 V's of Big Data' to 10 V's[44] (or even 17![45]). In the context of 'good data' we need to consider validity, veracity, volatility, vulnerability, and value. This manifesto outlines the concepts that we believe act toward making data good.

Why are all data not inherently good data? And what are the risks of creating data which are not designed with 'good data' principles in mind? These questions are critical, but the possible answers too numerous to be included in this introduction of what we think 'good data' could be. As you consider this book, we invite you to reflect on those questions in your own data environment.

As data producers and consumers, we challenge ourselves to consider the principles presented in Table 1 in our work and encourage others to do the same. We only see part of the complete 'data picture' ourselves; and the picture changes more rapidly than we can keep pace with. It is our hope that this chapter inspires discussion and reflection on what 'good data' means to you.

Acknowledgements

We thank our employers for flexibility to contribute to this project, and the organisers for promoting the discussion. Thanks to those who provided valuable insights in writing this chapter, including Dr Rowan Martin-Hughes, Lanes Koeu, and Twitter users @SimoneMantovan3, @bestqualitycrab, and @ellenbroad. Thanks to John Morrissey, Gareth Williams, Tristan Kenderdine, and the chapter reviewers for critical feedback. Claire Trenham is supported by the CSIRO Climate Science Centre. We are thankful for experience in Open Data resulting from work with the National Computational Infrastructure (NCI) through the Research Data Services (RDS) project; both supported by the Australian Government.

References

@adamdsteer, Twitter post, 18 January 2018, https://twitter.com/adamdsteer/status/953792786607742977.

Arockia, P. S., S.S. Varnekha and K.A. Veneshia. 'The 17 V's of Big Data'. *International Research Journal of Engineering and Technology (IRJET)*, 4.9 (2017): 329-333, https://irjet.net/archives/V4/i9/IRJET-V4I957.pdf.

Atlas of Living Australia, https://www.ala.org.au/.

Australian Electoral Commission, https://www.aec.gov.au.

Australian National Data Service [ANDS], 'Licensing and copyright for data reuse', https://www.ands.org.au/working-with-data/publishing-and-reusing-data/licensing-for-reuse.

---

44 G. Firican, 'The 10 V's of Big Data', *Transforming Data with Intelligence*, February 2017, https://tdwi.org/articles/2017/02/08/10-vs-of-big-data.aspx.
45 P.S. Arockia et al, 'The 17 V's Of Big Data', *IRJET* 4.9 (2017), https://www.irjet.net/archives/V4/i9/IRJET-V4I957.pdf.

Australian Research Data Commons [ARDC], 'FAIR data assessment tool', https://www.ands-nectar-rds.org.au/fair-tool.

Brody, H., S.E. Leonard, J-B. Nie and P. Weindling. 'United States Responses to Japanese Wartime Inhuman Experimentation after World War II: National Security and Wartime Exigency', *Cambridge Quarterly of Healthcare Ethics* 23.2 (2014): 220-230, DOI: 10.1017/S0963180113000753.

(Cambridge Analytica series), *The Guardian*, 2018, https://www.theguardian.com/uk-news/cambridge-analytica.

Claridge, T. *Social Capital and Natural Resource Management: An important role for social capital?*, Unpublished Thesis, University of Queensland, Brisbane, Australia, 2004, https://www.socialcapitalresearch.com/literature/definition/.

Cochrane Collaboration, http://www.cochrane.org.

data.gov.au, 'National Public Toilet Map', *Australian Government data.gov.au*, 2018, https://data.gov.au/dataset/553b3049-2b8b-46a2-95e6-640d7986a8c1.

Dixon, S. and L. Quirke. 'What's the harm? ...', *Teaching Sociology* 46.1 (2018):12-24, DOI: 10.1177/0092055X17711230.

DroneRules.eu, '8 Data Protection Guiding Principles under the GDPR for Drone Pilots', 23 May 2018, http://dronerules.eu/en/professional/news/8-data-protection-principles-under-the-gdpr-for-drone-pilots.

European Commission, 'Creating value through open data', *EU Publications*, 2015, DOI: 10.2759/328101.

European Commission, '2018 reform of EU data protection rules', 2018, https://ec.europa.eu/commission/priorities/justice-and-fundamental-rights/data-protection/2018-reform-eu-data-protection-rules_en.

Farrell, P. 'Darknet sale of Medicare data 'traditional criminal activity', minister says', *The Guardian*, 4 July 2017, https://www.theguardian.com/australia-news/2017/jul/04/federal-police-asked-to-investigate-darkweb-sale-of-medicare-data.

Firican, G. 'The 10 V's of Big Data', *Transforming Data with Intelligence*, 8 February 2017, https://tdwi.org/articles/2017/02/08/10-vs-of-big-data.aspx.

Floridi, L., S. Kauggman, L. Kolucka-Zuk, F. La Rue, S. Leutheusser-Schnarrenberger, J-L Piñar and J. Wales. '*The Advisory Council to Google on the Right to be Forgotten'*, 6 February 2015, https://static.googleusercontent.com/media/archive.google.com/en//advisorycouncil/advisement/advisory-report.pdf.

IEEE, 'Ethically Aligned Design', IEEE Global Initiative, v2, December 2017, https://ethicsinaction.ieee.org/.

Irving, D. 'A minimum standard for publishing computational results in the weather and climate sciences', *BAMS*, 2015, DOI: 10.1175/BAMS-D-15-00010.1.

Katerbow, M. and G. Feulner. 'Recommendations on the development, use and provision of Research Software', *Zenodo*, 16 March 2018, DOI: 10.5281/zenodo.1172988.

Keßler, C. and G. McKenzie. 'A geoprivacy manifesto', *Transactions in GIS*, 22 (2018) :3-19, DOI: 10.1111/tgis.12305.

Kidd, J. 'Wollemi Pines: Secret plantation in Blue Mountains to ensure species' survival', *ABC News*, 21 September 2014, http://www.abc.net.au/news/2014-09-21/secret-bid-to-save-prehistoric-wollemi-pines/5758542.

Manifesto for Data Practices. 2018, https://datapractices.org/manifesto/.

Mapillary. 'Accurate Privacy Blurring at Scale', *The Mapillary* Blog, 19 April 2018, https://blog.mapillary.com/update/2018/04/19/accurate-privacy-blurring-at-scale.html.

National Computational Infrastructure Australia [NCI]. 'NCI Annual Report 2016-2017', 2017, https://nci.org.au/wp-content/uploads/2014/12/NCI-Report-2017-web-sm-updated.pdf, p.65.

Noy, N. 'Making it easier to discover datasets', *Google Blog*, 5 September 2018, https://www.blog.google/products/search/making-it-easier-discover-datasets/.

New York Public Library [NYPL]. 'NYC Space/Time Directory', *New York Public Library*, http://spacetime.nypl.org/.

_____. 'OldNYC: Mapping historical photos from the NYPL', *New York Public Library*, https://www.oldnyc.org/.

OAIC. 'Notifiable Data Breaches scheme', *Australian Government Office of the Australian Information Commissioner*, https://www.oaic.gov.au/privacy-law/privacy-act/notifiable-data-breaches-scheme.

_____. 'Annual Report 2016-2017', *Australian Government Office of the Australian Information Commissioner, 2017,* https://www.oaic.gov.au/annualreport2016-17, p.80.

_____. 'Notifiable Data Breaches Quarterly Statistics Report: 1 April - 30 June 2018', *Australian Government Office of the Australian Information Commissioner,* 2018, https://www.oaic.gov.au/resources/privacy-law/privacy-act/notifiable-data-breaches-scheme/quarterly-statistics/notifiable-data-breaches-quarterly-statistics-report-1-april-30-june-2018.pdf.

_____. 'Health Information and medical research', *Australian Government Office of the Australian Information Commissioner*, https://www.oaic.gov.au/privacy-law/privacy-act/health-and-medical-research.

OECD, 'OECD Insights: Human Capital', *Organisation for Economic Cooperation & Development*, 2007, https://www.oecd.org/insights/37966934.pdf.

O'Leary, D.E. 'Ethics for Big Data and Analytics', *IEEE Intelligent Systems*, 31.4 (2016): 81-84, DOI: 10.1109/MIS.2016.70.

Patil, DJ. 'A code of Ethics for Data Science', *Medium*, 1 February 2018, https://medium.com/@dpatil/a-code-of-ethics-for-data-science-cda27d1fac1.

Pérez-Peña, R. and M. Rosenberg. 'Strava Fitness App Can Reveal Military Sites, Analysts Say', *NYTimes*, 29 January 2018, https://www.nytimes.com/2018/01/29/world/middleeast/strava-heat-map.html.

Science Europe. 'cOAlition S', September 2018, https://www.scienceeurope.org/coalition-s/.

Secretariat of the Antarctic Treaty. 'The Protocol on Environmental Protection to the Antarctic Treaty', 1991, https://www.ats.aq/e/ep.htm.

Serwadda, D., P. Ndebele, M.K. Grabowski, F. Bajunirwe and R.K. Wanyenze. 'Open data sharing and the Global South - Who benefits?', *Science*. 359.6376 (2018): 642-643, DOI: 10.1126/science.aap8395.

Tandy, J., L. van den Brink, and P. Barnaghi (eds). 'Spatial Data on the Web Best Practices', *W3C Working Group Note*, 2017, https://www.w3.org/TR/sdw-bp/.

Thinh. 'CC, Open Access, and moral rights', *Science Commons Blog,* 7 November 2007, http://sciencecommons.org/weblog/archives/2007/11/07/cc-oa-moral-rights/.

Uber. 'Privacy Policy', https://privacy.uber.com/policy.

UMKC. 'History of Research Ethics', *UMKC Office of the Vice Chancellor*, date unknown, http://ors.umkc.edu/research-compliance-(iacuc-ibc-irb-rsc)/institutional-review-board-(irb)/history-of-research-ethics.

United Nations [UN]. 'Universal Declaration of Human Rights', *United Nations General Assembly*, 1948, http://www.un.org/en/universal-declaration-human-rights/.

Violet Blue. 'Strava's fitness heatmaps are a "potential catastrophe"', *Engadget,* 2 February 2018, https://www.engadget.com/2018/02/02/strava-s-fitness-heatmaps-are-a-potential-catastrophe.

Wang, J., B. Evans, L.A.I. Wyborn, K. Gohar, I. Bastrakova, C. Trenham and K. Druken. 'The A, B, C, D, E, F of Multipurpose Active Data Management Plans to Facilitate Multiscale Interdisciplinary Science'. *eResearch Australasia 2015, Brisbane, Australia*, 2015, https://www.researchgate.net/publication/309704990_The_A_B_C_D_E_F_of_Multipurpose_Active_Data_Management_Plans_to_Facilitate_Multiscale_Interdisciplinary_Science.

Wikipedia contributors. 'The right to be forgotten', https://en.wikipedia.org/wiki/Right_to_be_forgotten, accessed 13 March 2018.

Yu, J. and S. Cox.'5-Star Data Rating Tool', v3, *CSIRO Software Collection*, 2017, DOI: 10.4225/08/5a12348f8567b.

4: THE GOOD, THE BAD AND THE BEAUTY OF 'GOOD ENOUGH DATA'

MIREN GUTIÉRREZ

Introduction

Drawing on the concept of 'good enough data'[1], which apply to citizen data collected via sensors this chapter looks critically at data in 'proactive data activism,' understood as a social practice that uses the data infrastructure politically and proactively to foster social change.[2] This chapter examines how data are generated and employed in proactive data activism, expanding and applying the term 'good enough data' beyond citizen sensing and the environment. This analysis derives from a taxonomy of activists based on how they go about obtaining data.[3] It offers too an unsentimental view on the failures and contradictions of data activism regarding the collection, analysis and communication of data.[4] The chapter employs the Syrian Archive - an organization that curates and documents data related to the Syrian conflict for activism - as a pivotal case to look at the new standards applied to data gathering and verification in data activism from the South, as well as their challenges, so data become 'good enough' to produce reliable evidence for social change. Data were obtained too thorough in-depth interviews, fieldwork and empirical observation.

On 25 and 30 March 2017, the town of al-Lataminah, in northern Syria, suffered two chemical attacks possibly committed by Syrian government aircraft.[5] Since 2011, Syria has been engulfed by a multi-sided armed conflict between forces led by President Bashar al-Assad, together with its international allies, and other forces opposing both the government and each other in varying groupings.[6] International organizations have blamed the Syrian government,

---

1   Jennifer Gabrys, Helen Pritchard, and Benjamin Barratt. 'This Is the Other Aspect of "just" Good Enough Data -that Citizen Data Could Provide Ways of Realising Environmental and Social Justice', *Big Data & Society* 1.14 (2016): 14.
2   Stefania Milan and Miren Gutierrez, 'Citizens' Media Meets Big Data: The Emergence of Data Activism', *Mediaciones* 14 (June, 2015): 120-133.
3   Miren Gutierrez, *Data Activism and Social Change*, London: Palgrave Macmillan, 2018.
4   See: Mel Hogan and Sarah T. Roberts, 'Data Flows and Water Woes: An Interview With Media Scholar Mél Hogan', *Big Data & Society,* 12 August 2015, http://bigdatasoc.blogspot.com.es/2015/08/data-flows-and-water-woes-interview.html; Lindsay Palmer, 'Ushahidi at the Google Interface: Critiquing the "geospatial Visualization of Testimony"', *Continuum* 28.3 (2014): 342-56; Wayan Vota, 'Dead Ushahidi: A Stark Reminder for Sustainability Planning in ICT4D', *ICT Works*, 9 July 2012, http://www.ictworks.org/2012/07/09/dead-ushahidi-stark-reminder-sustainability-planning-ict4d/.
5   See: Colum Lynch, 'Soviet-Era Bomb Used in Syria Chemical Weapon Attack, Claims Rights Group'. *Foreign Policy*, 5 January 2017, http://foreignpolicy.com/2017/05/01/soviet-era-bomb-used-in-syria-chemical-weapon-attack-claims-rights-group/; Ole Solvang, 'Key Finding on Use of Chemical Weapons in Syria', *Human Rights Watch,* 5 October 2017, https://www.hrw.org/news/2017/10/05/key-finding-use-chemical-weapons-syria.
6   Al Jazeera News, 'Syria's Civil War Explained from the Beginning'. *Al Jazeera*, 14 April 2018, https://www.aljazeera.com/news/2016/05/syria-civil-war-explained-160505084119966.html.

and its ally, Russia, opponent rebel groups and the coalition led by the United States of human rights violations,[7] including attacks with chemical weapons against civilians. The main forces implicated in the Syrian conflict - that is, Iran, Russia, Syria and the United States - are parties to the Weapons Convention, which entered into force in 1997, prohibiting the production, possession and use of chemical weapons, and should comply with its obligations.[8] However, since 2013, there have been some forty recorded instances of alleged chemical weapons use in Syria,[9] and no mechanism to attribute responsibility exists.[10]

As with other assaults, the source for the attacks against al-Lataminah remained unclear until a team of students at the Berkeley Human Rights Investigation Lab (HRC Lab) went through nine videos uploaded by people identified as journalists and ordinary citizens on Twitter, YouTube and Facebook. This analysis suggested that the attacks had indeed involved chemical weapons and that, at least in the case of the 25 March strike, the target was a medical facility.[11] Their report concludes that the perpetrators were in potential violation of international humanitarian law, as well as other regulations and treaties.[12]

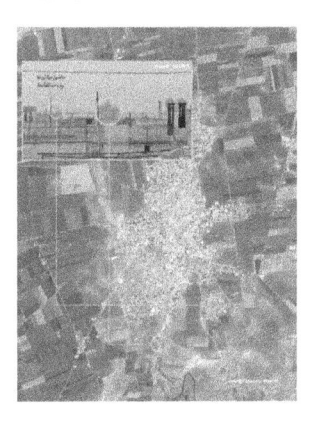

Figure 1: Chemical Strikes on Al-Lataminah. Source: (Syrian Archive, 2018).

Syrian Archive was the supplier of the videos. This organization gathers visual accounts about human rights violations committed by all sides of the Syrian conflict.[13] It was founded in 2014

---

7   Amnesty International, 'Exposed: Child Labour behind Smart Phone and Electric Car Batteries'. 19 July 2016, https://www.amnesty.org/en/latest/news/2016/01/child-labour-behind-smart-phone-and-electric-car-batteries/
8   Organisation for the Prohibition of Chemical Weapons, 'Chemical Weapons Convention', 2015 https://www.opcw.org/sites/default/files/documents/CWC/CWC_en.pdf.
9   Marc Weller, 'Syria Air Strikes: Were They Legal?' *BBC News*, 14 April 2018, https://www.bbc.com/news/world-middle-east-43766556.
10 Izumi Nakamitsu, 'The Situation in the Middle East'. Briefing S/PV.8344, New York: Security Council, 6 September 2018, https://www.securitycouncilreport.org/atf/cf/%7b65BFCF9B-6D27-4E9C-8CD3-CF6E4FF96FF9%7d/s_pv_8344.pdf.
11 Anna Banchik et al, 'Chemical Strikes on Al-Lataminah', *Berkeley Human Rights Investigation Lab*, 25, 30 March 2017, https://syrianarchive.org/assets/hama/Syrian_Archive_Hama_Report_Final.pdf.
12 Ibid.
13 Syrian Archive, About, https://syrianarchive.org/en/about.

by human rights activists with the aim of investigating and preserving digital content as a form of 'a digital memory' of human rights infringements and building a corpus of substantiation that could be used for advocacy, reporting and law cases.[14] Syrian Archive is sustained by donations but accepts no money from governments directly involved in the conflict.[15]

Syrian Archive could be regarded as a proactive data activist organization, or activism that employs the data infrastructure politically and proactively to provide diagnoses and evidence for social change.[16] The massive collection and automated analysis of private data by governments and corporations have generated the emergence of reactive data activists, who use the data infrastructure to shelter their interactions from data surveillance.[17] The chapter is focused on the data practices employed by the former type of activism, which embodies a reversal to what Poell, Kennedy and van Dijck call *dataveillance*.[18] In the face of discriminatory, opaque or unethical private data gathered for obscure purposes without people's knowledge or consent, proactive data activists engage in a variety of methods to obtain and analyze data, sidestepping conventional data actors and systems, enhancing their data agency, and correcting the asymmetries embedded in top-down datafication processes.[19]

Activists have demonstrated ingenuity in creating data, and can be classified from the ways they go about obtaining them: from the easiest way to the most difficult, they can rely on whistleblowers who hand over datasets anonymously (first type) or resort to public datasets (second); and when data are not available, create platforms to crowdsource citizen data (third); appropriate data, becoming whistleblowers themselves (fourth), and generate data on their own terms, for example, via data-gathering devices (fifth).[20]

Syrian Archive combines mainly the second and third kinds of data extraction methods: it counts on data uploaded by ordinary citizens, journalists and activists on sharing and social media platforms. That is, it relies on data that has been made public by people (i.e. a form of public data). These data have been harvested through platforms which were not set up by the activists themselves but by social media service providers (i.e. a form of crowdsourced data). Other data activists specialize in using just one of these methods.[21] For example, the deployers of 'Ayuda Ecuador' - an application of the Ushahidi platform launched to gather data on the crisis unleashed by the earthquake in 2016 in Ecuador - established the means to collect data submitted via mobile technology, emails and websites, using the third type of data extraction method. Although crowdsourcing citizen data is its main data mining method, Ushahidi also resorts to data scraping from websites and social media for verification pur-

---

14 Ibid.
15 Ibid.
16 Stefania Milan and Miren Gutierrez, 'Citizens´ Media Meets Big Data: The Emergence of Data Activism', *Mediaciones* 14 (June, 2015): 120-133.
17 Ibid.
18 Thomas Poell, Helen Kennedy, and Jose van Dijck, 'Special Theme: Data & Agency', *Big Data & Society*, 2 (July, 2015): 1-7.
19 Gutierrez, *Data Activism and Social Change*.
20 Ibid.
21 Ibid.

poses (i.e. a form of data appropriation). Meanwhile, the citizen data on air quality Gabrys, Pritchard and Barratt talk about were gathered via sensors,[22] namely, the fifth technique. Data activists are resourceful and often combine repertoires of action and strategies seeking the best solutions for each case.

Proactive data activism often relies on good enough data, a concept coined by Gabrys, Pritchard and Barratt to indicate data created, valued and interpreted by ordinary people, which these authors apply to environmental data and citizen sensing.[23] The good enough data practices in these authors' study meet the criteria of being a) based on datasets gathered by ordinary people, b) aimed at creating new types of data and data stories, and c) useful to generate evidence that can be employed in decision-making.[24] This concept pertains to other types of data activism too, as seen later.

However, data activism is neither pure nor neutral; it embeds some contradictions and unbalances. For example, like in other deployments of the Ushahidi platform, 'Ayuda Ecuador' places digital humanitarians (i.e. the deployers of the application) in the role of gatekeepers of good enough data as they are the ones enforcing the data authentication systems and controlling the crisis map. These data asymmetries are reviewed later too.

To look at good enough data in activism, I rely on fieldwork, empirical observation of significant cases, a case study, and in-depth interviews with relevant actors involved in data curation processes from several organizations. The case study methodology aims at showing how data practices look like based not on the actors' opinions, but on evaluations, scientific literature and website content.[25] Syrian Archive is a data activist initiative that embodies the highest standards of data curation in activism. Because of the delicate tasks they have been set to confront, its managers have developed a meticulous data protocol, based on international standards, to conserve data so they are *good enough* to sustain further legal investigations. This is a single-focused, descriptive study that employs an instance to offer a common framework for future studies.[26] Syrian Archive provides a case of a class of phenomena; that is, activism that utilizes the data infrastructure for knowledge and action. The case study methodology is helpful when the boundaries between a phenomenon and its context are not apparent.[27] This organization has been chosen based on the fact that background conditions are relevant to the inspection of data practices in activism.

Five interviewees - chosen for their in-depth knowledge data practices and protocols in activism and beyond - were questioned about their data mining and curation methodologies. Although the questions vary in line with their expertise, the questionnaires sent to these prac-

---

22 Gabrys, Pritchard, and Barratt, 'This Is the Other Aspect of "just" Good Enough Data'.
23 Ibid, 1.
24 Ibid, 11.
25 Arch Woodside, *Case Study Research: Theory, Methods and Practice*, United Kingdom: Emerald, 2010, p. 322.
26 Ibid.
27 Robert K Yin, *Case Study Research: Design and Methods,* Applied Social Research Methods Series. Thousand Oaks: SAGE,* 2002, p. 13.

titioners include open questions such as: 'How can you aspire to data robustness taking into account that your data sources may have their own agendas?' The idea behind the interviews is to capture what these interviewees think they do.[28] The questions were designed to last for one hour, and sent by email or formulated in phone discussions. Interviewee 1 works for a crowdsourcing platform that visualizes citizen data for digital humanitarianism. Interviewee 2 has designed smart grids that channel data for real-time decision-making in water management. Interviewees 3 and 4 have an exhaustive knowledge of Syrian Archive. In charge of an index that ranks countries by their frailty, Interviewee 5 - not a data activist - has been included here for contrast, as in the case of Interviewee 2. Although their data methods and approaches vary, their tenets do not differ so much.

The next sections offer an exploration of data in activism from the perspective of data, followed by an inspection of Syrian Archive and a comparison with other initiatives, concluding with a proposed definition for *good enough data in activism* that can be used as a heuristic tool in other analyses.

Perfect Data, Big Data and Small Data

Most researchers, journalists and activists who handle data employ 'small data', namely, data that appears in a volume and format that makes them usable and analyzable.[29] In contrast, 'big data' are so vast and complex that they cannot be managed with traditional data processing methods.[30] The big data infrastructure allows the collection of data and metadata continually, surreptitiously and comprehensively: every click and every 'like' is stored and analyzed in real-time.[31] Big data are understood as 'datasets whose volume, velocity or variety' is extremely high and show a high degree of 'veracity' and a potential for 'value'.[32]

The employment of big data techniques can give rise to thought-provoking insights. For example, Stephens-Davidowitz's *Everybody Lies* explores how people lie in polls and pretend on social media while removing their masks when they search for information online.[33] Based on

---

28 Philip Balsiger, and Alexandre Lambelet, 'Participant Observation', in Donatella della Porta (ed.), M*ethodological Practices in Social Movement Research*, Oxford: Oxford University Press, 2014, pp. 144-72; Russell H. Bernard, *Research Methods in Anthropology: Qualitative and Quantitative Approaches*, fourth edition, Maryland: AltaMira Press, 2006; D. Cohen and B. Crabtree, 'Qualitative Research Guidelines Project', The Robert Wood Johnson Foundation: Semi-Structured Interviews, July 2006, http://www.qualres.org/HomeSemi-3629.html.
29 Rob Kitchin and Tracey P. Lauriault, 'Small Data, Data Infrastructures and Big Data', *GeoJournal*, The Programmable City Working Paper 1, 80.4 (2014): 463.
30 Viktor Mayer-Schönberger and Kenneth Cukier, *Big Data: A Revolution That Will Transform How We Live, Work, and Think*, Boston: Houghton Mifflin Harcourt, 2013.
31 Jose van Dijck, 'Datafication, Dataism and Dataveillance: Big Data between Scientific Paradigm and Ideology', *Surveillance & Society* 12.2 (2014): 197-208.
32 International Telecommunication Union, 'Measuring the Information Society Report', *Geneva: International Telecommunication Union (ITU)*, http://www.itu.int/en/ITU-D/Statistics/Documents/publications/misr2015/MISR2015-w5.pdf, 2014.
33 Seth Stephens-Davidowitz, *Everybody Lies: Big Data, New Data, and What the Internet Can Tell Us About Who We Really Are*, London: Bloomsbury Publishing, 2017.

the massive analysis of Google searches, other search engines and websites, he discovers that people are much more racist, sexist and ignoble than they think or admit.[34] Big data-based research is revolutionizing not only surveillance and marketing, but scientific disciplines as well, from sociology to historiography. For instance, only a few years ago it was only possible to examine fragments of big *corpora* and science focussed on getting information from limited fragments.[35] The study of the 13th century Korean Buddhist canon, which contains 52 million characters distributed across 166,000 pages, is an example; with data analytics, the whole text can now be interrogated in its totality in every search.[36] Are big data, then, better data, as Cukier argues?[37] The simple answer is: not necessarily. Data *goodness* depends on the quality of both the data and processes involved to analyze them, as well as on the purpose of the analysis. Namely, it is not a question only of quantity, but also of quality and intent.

No matter how big, data can never be perfect because they cannot be raw.[38] Borges's tale of frustrated mapmakers could be read as a warning about the impossibility of perfect science, or data.[39] In 'On Exactitude in Science,' Borges speaks about an empire where pursuing scientific authenticity, cartographers made maps as big as the land they portrayed, whereupon these charts failed to be useful and were forgotten.[40] The same way that 'the map is not the territory',[41] data cannot be considered 'straightforward representations of given phenomena'.[42] Data are not free of ideology, as they do not emerge free of the views, methods and technologies of the people that conceive, generate, process, curate, analyze and store them.[43] Data are not natural but *cultural resources* 'cooked' in processes of collection and use, which are also 'cooked',[44] thus, they can embed biases, gaps and asymmetries. As Interviewee 5 notes, 'every qualitative data source is arguably open to bias.' Paraphrasing Gitelman,[45] *perfect data* is another oxymoron.

---

34 Ibid.
35 Harvey J. Miller, 'The Data Avalanche is Here: Shouldn't we be Digging?' Wiley Periodicals, Inc., 22 August 2009, 2.
36 Lewis Lancaster, 'From Text to Image to Analysis: Visualization of Chinese Buddhist Canon', *Digital Humanities*, 2010, pp. 1-3.
37 Kenneth Cukier, 'Big Data Is Better Data', presented at the Berlin TEDSalon, Berlin, June 2014, http://www.ted.com/talks/kenneth_cukier_big_data_is_better_data?language=en.
38 Lisa Gitelman (ed.), *Raw Data Is an Oxymoron*, Cambridge MA/London: MIT Press, 2013.
39 Jorge Luis Borges, 'Del Rigor En La Ciencia', *Palabra Virtual*, 12 February 2007, http://www.palabravirtual.com/index.php?ir=ver_voz1.php&wid=726&p=Jorge%20Luis%20Borges&t=Del%20rigor%20en%20la%20ciencia&o=Jorge%20Luis%20Borges.
40 Ibid.
41 Alfred Korzybski, *Science and Sanity: An Introduction to Non-Aristotelian Systems and General Semantics*, fifth edition, New York: Institute of General Semantics, 1994, p. 58.
42 Sabina Leonelli, 'What Counts as Scientific Data? A Relational Framework', *Philosophy of Science* 82.5 (2015): 810.
43 Tracey P. Lauriault, 'Data, Infrastructures and Geographical Imaginations', Ottawa: Carleton University, 2012, https://curve.carleton.ca/system/files/etd/7eb756c8-3ceb-4929-8220-3b20cf3242cb/etd_pdf/79f3425e913cc42aba9aa2b9094a9a53/lauriault-datainfrastructuresandgeographicalimaginations.pdf.
44 Tom Boellstorff, 'Making Big Data, in Theory', *First Monday* 18.10 (2013), http://firstmonday.org/article/view/4869/3750.
45 Gitelman (ed.), *Raw Data Is an Oxymoron*.

Errors and biases can be introduced accidentally in data processes. An artificial intelligence (AI) algorithm learned to associate women with kitchen images because more women appear photographed in kitchens on the web.[46] In the process of *learning*, the algorithm then multiplied the bias present in the initial dataset, amplifying - not simply replicating - the biased association between kitchens and women.[47] This study by the University of Virginia is among several others that recently show that artificial intelligence systems can incorporate, and even multiply, biases if their design or the data on which they are based are not revised carefully.

Besides, data can also be manipulated. Edward Snowden's 2013 revelations include examples of big data-based manipulation; they showed that the intelligence services of the US government, with the collaboration of companies and other governments, had established a dense layer of surveillance and data interception on the communications of millions of people globally without their knowledge.[48] More recently, it was revealed that Cambridge Analytica, a data analytics firm, had collaborated with Donald Trump's election team in 2016 to harvest millions of Facebook profiles of US voters to design personalized campaign messages for them.[49] Critical scholars, including Braman,[50] Tufekci,[51] and Gangadharan,[52] describe how big data techniques are employed to profile people, discriminate against vulnerable groups and promote relentless, omnipresent and preventive monitoring. In *Weapons of Math Destruction*, O'Neil presents too that data-based programs increase the efficiency of 'predatory advertising' that undermines democracy.[53]

This paper's aim is not to determine the difference between *good* and *good enough* because to do that, and it would have to establish first the philosophical question of the meaning *good*, over which there is no consensus. Gabrys, Pritchard and Barrat do not fathom what *good* means related to data either.[54] Thus, good enough is to be initially understood as robust enough - devoid of significant unfair or impairing manipulation - to sustain research for socially

---

46   Jieyu Zhao, Tianlu Wang, Mark Yatskar, Vicente Ordonez, and Vicente Chang, 'Men Also Like Shopping: Reducing Gender Bias Amplification Using Corpus-Level Constraints', *Association for Computational Linguistics* (2017): 2979-2989, DOI: https://doi.org/10.18653/v1/D17-1323.
47   Ibid.
48   See: David Lyon, 'Surveillance, Snowden, and Big Data: Capacities, Consequences', *Big Data & Society* (July, 2014): 1-13; Andy Greenberg, 'These Are the Emails Snowden Sent to First Introduce His Epic NSA Leaks', *The Wired*, 13 October 2014, https://www.wired.com/2014/10/snowdens-first-emails-to-poitras/; Bettina Berendt, Marco Büchler and Geoffrey Rockwell, 'Is It Research or Is It Spying? Thinking-Through Ethics in Big Data AI and Other Knowledge Science', *Künstliche Intelligenz* 29.223 (2015), DOI: https://doi.org/10.1007/s13218-015-0355-2.
49   Carole Cadwalladr and Emma Graham-Harrison, 'Revealed: 50 Million Facebook Profiles Harvested for Cambridge Analytica in Major Data Breach', *The Guardian*, 17 March 2018, https://www.theguardian.com/news/2018/mar/17/cambridge-analytica-facebook-influence-us-election.
50   Sandra Braman, *Change of State: Information, Policy, and Power*, Cambridge MA: MIT Press, 2009.
51   Zeynep Tufekci, 'Engineering the Public: Internet, Surveillance and Computational Politics.' *First Monday* 19.7 (2014), https://firstmonday.org/ojs/index.php/fm/article/view/4901/4097.
52   Seeta Peña Gangadharan, 'Digital Inclusion and Data Profiling', *First Monday,* 17.5 (2012), http://firstmonday.org/article/view/3821/3199.
53   Cathy O'Neil, *Weapons of Math Destruction: How Big Data Increases Inequality and Threatens Democracy*, New York: Crown Publishers, 2016.
54   Gabrys, Pritchard, and Barratt, 'This Is the Other Aspect of "just" Good Enough Data'.

beneficial purposes. Coming back to Cukier's assertion,[55] it seems that instead of asking how big our datasets are to determine whether they are good, we should start by asking first 'for what', as Robert Staughton Lynd suggested about science,[56] and then look for data and processes that are strong enough to support such research.

Good Enough Data

Data analysis is not for everyone. In a show of enthusiasm, Rogers compared data analysis with punk music in 2012 because 'anyone can do it'.[57] Unfortunately, this is not the case. Not only are data not available to anyone, but, as Innerarity points out,[58] the tools to make them useful are not available to anyone either. However, the barriers to access both data and their infrastructure - understood as the software, hardware and processes necessary to render them useful - have been falling in recent years.[59] Activists of all stripes are using data, in combination with the geoweb, satellite technology, sensing devices and information and communication technologies (ICTs), to create datasets and generate diagnoses and social change, as I have considered elsewhere.[60] Examples abound. Forensic Architecture, supported by Amnesty International, has created an interactive model of Syria's most notorious prison, Saydnaya, using the memories of sounds narrated by survivors who had been kept captive in the dark. The project aims to show the conditions inside the prison.[61] WeRobotics employs 'community drones' to collect data on the conditions of glaciers in Nepal to analyze the data and launch alarms when there is the danger of flash floods.[62] InfoAmazonia, among other things, has published a calendar that superimposes the time counted by the Indigenous peoples of the Tiquié River, Brazil, and the time measured in the Gregorian calendar, in a dialogue between the local and the global that never existed before.[63] Meanwhile, the Ushahidi platform is deployed to generate crisis maps that can visualize citizen data in quasi-real-time to assist humanitarian operations. Namely, when data are not available, people and organizations create them.

Gabrys, Pritchard and Barratt refer to 'just good enough' data generated by non-experts to gauge pollution.[64] Citizen data are often good enough to produce 'patterns of evidence' that can mobilize community responses to connect with regulators, request follow-up monitoring,

---

55 Cukier, 'Big Data Is Better Data'.
56 Robert Staughton Lynd, *Knowledge for What: The Place of Social Science in American Culture*, Princeton: Princeton University Press, 1967.
57 Simon Rogers, 'John Snow's Data Journalism: The Cholera Map That Changed the World', *The Guardian*, 15 March 2012, http://www.theguardian.com/news/datablog/2013/mar/15/john-snow-cholera-map.
58 Daniel Innerarity, 'Ricos Y Pobres En Datos', *Globernance.org*, 22 February 2016, http://www.danielinnerarity.es/opinion-preblog/ricos-y-pobres-en-datos/.
59 Milan and Gutierrez, 'Citizens' Media Meets Big Data'.
60 See: Gutierrez, *Data Activism and Social Change*.
61 Forensic Architecture, 'About Saydnaya', http://www.forensic-architecture.org/case/saydnaya/.
62 WeRobotics, 'About', http://werobotics.org/.
63 InfoAmazonia, 'The Annual Cycles of the Indigenous Peoples of the Rio Tiquié, 2005-2006', 2016. https://ciclostiquie.socioambiental.org/en/index.html.
64 Gabrys, Pritchard, and Barratt, 'This Is the Other Aspect of "just" Good Enough Data'.

make a case for improved regulation and accountability, and keep track of exposures both on an individual and collective level.[65] Although these authors imply citizen sensing and environmental data gathering, the concept of good enough data can be applied to other areas where citizens and organizations are creating their own datasets, robust enough to generate new types of data and data practices, and impactful bottom-up narratives. The same way that alternative journalism argues that different forms of knowledge may be generated, representing 'multiple versions of reality from those of the mass media',[66] good enough data - as an alternative to conventional big data - can produce trustworthy analysis and visualizations which shed light on complex issues and are the basis for action. The examples of Syrian Archive, Forensic Architecture, WeRobotics, InfoAmazonia and Ushahidi show that, beyond citizen sensing, activists can produce reliable results based on good enough data in the areas of human rights evidence, crisis mapping and alert systems, and advocacy. The selection of these cases - based on the complexity in their data processes - draws from my previous work on data activism.[67]

That is not to say that data in activism is devoid of inconsistencies. Some Ushahidi deployments, for instance, have been set up and then abandoned,[68] creating a cyber-graveyard of 'dead Ushahidi' maps for lack of communities reporting data.[69] Also, Ushahidi's verification system has not forestalled some glitches, with on-the-ground consequences.[70] Besides, data activist projects often resort to proprietary, corporate inventions, with entrenched imbalances and harmful practices (i.e. semi-slave labor in the extraction of the cobalt needed in smartphones),[71] which are then embedded in the initiative.[72] Data processes in activism can also include asymmetries in the relationships established within their networks, integrating their own 'power inequalities, unbalances and mediations'.[73] The interviewees in this study admit that faulty datasets must be corrected. However, constant verification allows imperfect datasets to improve and lead to alternative and useful insights.

---

65 Ibid, p. 8.
66 John D. H. Downing (ed.), *Encyclopedia of Social Movement Media*. Thousand Oaks: SAGE, 2011, p. 18.
67 Gutierrez, *Data Activism and Social Change*; Miren Gutierrez, 'Maputopias: Cartographies of Knowledge, Communication and Action in the Big Data Society - The Cases of Ushahidi and InfoAmazonia'. *GeoJournal*, (2018): 1-20, DOI: https://doi.org/https://doi.org/10.1007/s10708-018-9853-8; Miren Gutierrez, 'The Public Sphere in Light of Data Activism', *Krisis* (2018).
68 Dirk Slater, 'What I've Learned about Mapping Violence', *Fab Riders*, 3 April 2016, http://www.fabriders.net/mapping-violence/.
69 Wayan Voya, 'Dead Ushahidi: A Stark Reminder for Sustainability Planning in ICT4D', *ICT Works*, 9 July 2012. http://www.ictworks.org/2012/07/09/dead-ushahidi-stark-reminder-sustainability-planning-ict4d/.
70 Heather Ford, 'Can Ushahidi Rely on Crowdsourced Verifications?' *H Blog*, 3 September 2012, https://hblog.org/2012/03/09/can-ushahidi-rely-on-crowdsourced-verifications/.
71 Amnesty International, 'Exposed: Child Labour behind Smart Phone and Electric Car Batteries'.
72 See: Gutierrez, *Data Activism and Social Change*; Hogan and Roberts, 'Data Flows and Water Woes'; Lindsay Palmer, 'Ushahidi at the Google Interface: Critiquing the "geospatial Visualization of Testimony"', *Continuum* 28.3 (2014): 342-56, DOI: https://doi.org/10.1080/10304312.2014.893989.
73 Gutierrez, *Data Activism and Social Change*.

Summarizing, good enough data in activism could be explained as data, however flawed, which are obtained, gathered, curated and analyzed by citizens and activists through procedures aimed at generating action-oriented analysis for beneficial social change and humanitarianism. This definition is reviewed later.

Syrian Archive

In 2016, Syrian Archive team verified 1748 videos and published a report pointing to an 'overwhelming' Russian participation in the bombardment and airstrikes against civilians in the city of Aleppo, Syria.[74] Although all parties have perpetrated violations, the visual evidence demonstrated that the Russian forces were accountable for the largest amount of violations in Aleppo.[75] Meanwhile, the Office of the UN High Commissioner for Human Rights (OHCHR) issued a carefully phrased statement in which it blamed 'all parties to the Syrian conflict' of perpetrating violations resulting in civilian casualties, although it also admitted that 'government and pro-government forces' (i.e. Russian) were attacking hospitals, schools and water stations.[76] The difference in language could be attributed to the attitude of a non-governmental organization compared with that of a UN agency, which has to collaborate with governments to be able to function. However, the contrast in data methodologies may also be at the bottom of what each said about the bombings. While the OHCHR report was based on interviews with people after the events, Syrian Archive relied on video evidence mostly uploaded by people on social media without the intervention of the non-profit (although some video evidence was sent directly to Syrian Archive).[77]

The traditional practices of evidence gathering in human rights law 'is grounded in witness interviews often conducted well after the fact'.[78] Even if surveys and interviews offer crucial information about armed conflicts, the violence can shape responses 'in ways that limit their value'.[79] Namely, the distortions that violence can elicit in the witnesses' testimonies and the time-lapse between the facts and the interviews can affect the reliability of an inquest. The medialization of conflicts makes the new activist's data gathering techniques relevant. Syrian Archive does not only resort to what victims and witnesses say they remember, but they also rely on what witnesses *recorded as events unfolded* in real-time. Most of the evidence included in Syrian Archive report on Aleppo was mentioned in the OHCHR report, but the non-profit also found new evidence that had not been cited before.[80]

---

74   Syrian Archive, 'Research Methodology', 6 January 2017, https://syrianarchive.org/p/page/methodology_digital_evidence_workflow/.
75   Ibid.
76   Office of the UN High Commissioner for Human Rights, 'Warring Parties Continued to Target Civilians for Abuses over Last Seven Months - UN Commission', *United Nations*, 14 March 2017, http://www.ohchr.org/EN/NewsEvents/Pages/DisplayNews.aspx?NewsID=21370&LangID=E.
77   Ibid.
78   Forensic Architecture 'Project', http://www.forensic-architecture.org/project/.
79   William G. Axinn, Dirgha Ghimire and Nathalie E. Williams, 'Collecting Survey Data during Armed Conflict', *J Off Stat* 28.2 (2012): 153.
80   Ben Knight, 'Syrian Archive Finds "Overwhelming" Russian Atrocities in Aleppo'. *DW*, 28 March 2017, http://www.dw.com/en/syrian-archive-finds-overwhelming-russian-atrocities-in-aleppo/a-38169808.

Syrian Archive's methodology used in carrying out the Aleppo bombings research include the identification, collection and preservation of data, followed by two layers of confirmation with increasing depth.[81] Syrian Archive has identified three hundred sources in Syria - including media organizations and citizen journalists - and checked their reliability by tracking them and examining their social media accounts over time.[82] The organization is aware of the fact that these sources are 'partisan' and require 'caution', and that is why it also relies on other groups of sources, which offer additional information.[83]

When Syrian Archive obtains a video, the first thing is to save it; next, the identity of the source of the video is verified with the on-the-ground network. Then, the source's track record is examined looking at whether the source has posted other videos from the same location or different locations.[84] As investigative reporters counting on deep throats, Syrian Archive does not scrutinize the sources' motivations, as Interviewee 4 notes:

> We don't care about their agendas. What we are trying to do here is to look at the content itself, and cross-reference the content with hundreds of thousands of other contents to conclude whether it is true or not. We are aware of the types of problems that our sources endure (for example blockages by the Syrian government), but we do not look at that. As much as we can understand limitations for sources, our job is to verify the contents.

Subsequently, the recording is examined to establish its location using methods that can include the identification of a natural feature of the landscape (e.g. a line of trees) and buildings and landmarks (e.g. a mosque's minaret).[85] Syrian Archive compares the footage with satellite images from Google Earth, Microsoft Bing, OpenStreetMap, Panoramio or DigitalGlobe, and looks at the metadata from the video, which also can provide information about its whereabouts. The video is then compared with the testimonies of witnesses interviewed by trustworthy media outlets and human rights organizations. Videos in Arabic are also scrutinized to determine the dialect and location to which they might be linked. When possible, Syrian Archive contacts the source directly to confirm the location and teams up with organizations specialized in verifying images, such as Bellingcat.[86] The materials are categorized using the classification of human rights abuses issued by the UN, which includes, among others, 'massacres and other unlawful killings', 'arbitrary arrest and unlawful detention' and 'hostage-taking'.[87] On Syrian Archive website, information is classified by the kind of weapon utilized, the location or the kind of violation or abuse. Figure 2 summarizes the process.

---

81 'Research Methodology'. 6 January 2017, p. 3, https://syrianarchive.org/p/page/methodology_digital_evidence_workflow/.
82 Ibid.
83 Ibid.
84 Ibid.
85 Ibid.
86 Ibid.
87 Human Rights Council, 'Report of the Independent International Commission of Inquiry on the Syrian Arab Republic', UN General Assembly, 5 Februrary 2013, http://www.ohchr.org/Documents/HRBodies/HRCouncil/ColSyria/A.HRC.22.59_en.pdf.

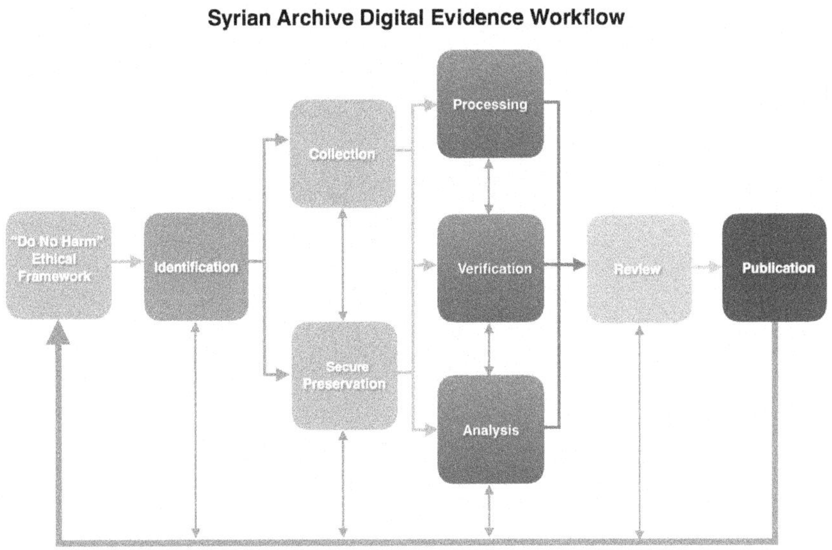

Syrian Archive Digital Evidence Workflow

Figure 2: Syrian Archive digital evidence workflow.[88]

Based on the examination of footage, the research of the Aleppo bombings from July to December 2016 includes overwhelming evidence of 'unlawful attacks,' illegal weapons, attacks against civilians, humanitarian workers, journalists and civilian facilities such as hospitals, schools or markets, and the use of incendiary and cluster munitions.[89] Given that rebel groups and terrorist militias like the Islamic State do not have air forces, Syrian Archive concludes that most of the airstrikes are carried out by Russian aircraft.[90] Figure 3 shows a static snapshot of the location of verified attacks; the interactive chart available online allows users to access the videos that sustain it.

---

88 Source: Syrian Archive, 'About', https://syrianarchive.org/en/about.
89 Syrian Archive, 'Research Methodology', 19-20. https://syrianarchive.org/p/page/methodology_digital_evidence_workflow/; 'Violations Database', https://syrianarchive.org/en/database?location=%D8%AD%D9%84%D8%A8%20:%20%D8%AD%D9%84%D8%A8&after=2016-07-01&before=2016-12-31.
90 Ibid.

Map of Visual Evidence about Attacks in Aleppo City [July - Dec 2016]

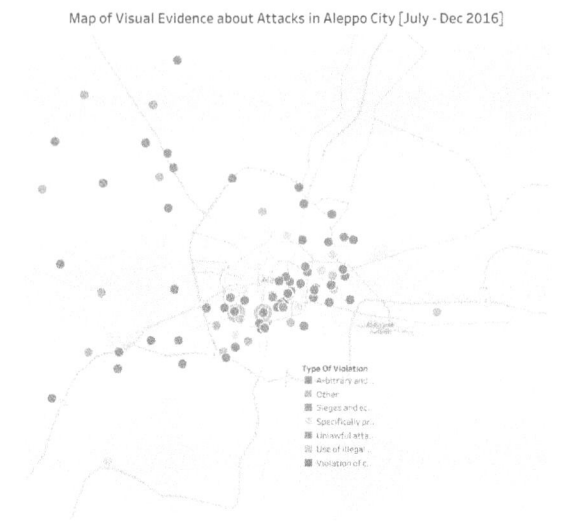

Figure 3: Map of visual evidence about attacks in Aleppo City (July - December 2016).[91]

Syrian Archive exhibits the ingenuity that characterizes data activists; however, not all data activist initiatives employ the same data methods. Next, the commonalities in good enough data gathering practices are examined. First, Syrian Archive's data are inspected through the lens of the criteria for 'just good enough data' (see Table 1).[92] Second, based on the taxonomy of data gathering methods offered earlier,[93] several data activist initiatives are compared with Syrian Archive looking at the variety of data mining approaches they employ (see Table 2). And third, how the interviewees themselves definite 'good enough' is explored to extract more insights.

Comparison and discussion

Meeting the criteria for 'good enough'

First, Gabrys, Pritchard and Barratt refer to datasets generated by citizens, that is, ordinary people understood as non-experts.[94] Meanwhile, although based on citizen data, the team at Syrian Archive includes 'researchers, journalists, technologists and digital security experts who have been working in the field of human rights, verification, open source technologies and investigation methodologies for the past ten years'.[95] According to the Syrian Archive's protocols, experts determine the data rules, and ordinary people (citizen journalists and

---

91 Source: Syrian Archive, 'Research Methodology', https://syrianarchive.org/p/page/methodology_digital_evidence_workflow/.
92 Gabrys, Pritchard, and Barratt, 'This Is the Other Aspect of "just" Good Enough Data'.
93 Gutierrez, *Data Activism and Social Change*.
94 See Gabrys, Pritchard, and Barratt, 'This Is the Other Aspect of "just" Good Enough Data'.
95 Syrian Archive, 'About', https://syrianarchive.org/en/about.

contributors) and other experts (conventional journalists) provide the data from the ground. At face value, this constitutes a difference. However, Gabrys, Pritchard and Barratt also acknowledge that expert mediation was required in citizen data sensing 'given the disjuncture between the expertise needed to analyze the data and the researchers' and residents' skills in undertaking data analysis'.[96] Namely, good enough data analysis involved citizens but requires a degree of expertise. However, the 'good enough' condition does not depend on distinctions between ordinary people and experts: data are either good enough or not. Gabrys, Pritchard and Barratt note 'regulators, scientists and polluters' have attempted 'to discredit citizen data' due to concerns about their know-how.[97] Nevertheless, as they also say, 'questions about validity do not pertain to citizen data alone'.[98] Thus, the level of expertise of either data gatherers or data interpreters does not seem to be relevant as long as the data are robust.

Second, Syrian Archive provides new types of data and data stories, since no other actor, official or not, is producing them. Likewise, Gabrys, Pritchard and Barratt suggest that the citizens involved in the data sensing exercises are compelled to act by the absence of information and institutional support;[99] that is, they are filling a gap. This is the case of Syrian Archive too; for instance, the official UN report on Aleppo shows only part of the story. This characteristic has to do with the ability of data activists of crafting alternative maps, stories and solutions.[100] The purpose of filling gaps suggests that there is a particular amount of information needed to tell a human rights story accurately, and that activism can help secure this information. That is why good enough data implies to the right amount of data - not necessarily big - that activists needs to produce.

Third, as the Aleppo investigation suggests, the result of the analysis of the video footage was useful to generate new 'forms of evidence', paraphrasing Gabrys, Pritchard and Barratt,[101] which were good enough to reveal a Russian or Syrian intervention in the bombing of the city. Thus, good enough data can be evidential data, since they can satisfy the need to provide sufficient support for ongoing legal investigations.

This paper proposes a new criterion. To be deemed good enough, data should also be suitable for the goals of the initiative in which the data are being employed, as Interviewee 3 suggests:

> What is good enough data depends on the purpose of what you are doing (...) (For Syrian Archive) the dataset in question has to be the result of an investigation, it has to be cross-referenced, the product of a collaboration, it has to be in a standardized form if it comes from different platforms and media types, and it has to be preserved to be handed over for legal accountability and the end user, for example, a UN report.

---

96 Gabrys, Pritchard, and Barratt, 'This Is the Other Aspect of "just" Good Enough Data', p. 6.
97 Ibid, p. 2.
98 Ibid.
99 Ibid.
100 Gutierrez, 'Maputopias: Cartographies of Knowledge, Communication and Action in the Big Data Society'.
101 Gabrys, Pritchard, and Barratt, 'This Is the Other Aspect of "just" Good Enough Data', p. 6.

It might be said that Syrian Archive's long-term mission is to promote social change in Syria, but there are various means by which change might be promoted. Syrian Archive goes about fulfilling its mission in its own way: producing evidence of abuses that can withstand examination in court. The nature of what counts as 'good enough' data is *unavoidably* contextual. The data in the Syrian Archive are good enough to show that there are human rights violations in the military conflict. It appears we cannot ask whether a pertinent dataset is good enough without further formulating the specific use to which the data will be put; that is, without stipulating a) the specific role the data play in how change is to be fostered, and b) what change is to be advanced. The question of whether data are 'good enough' must be framed by the context in which the data are being used; it should respond to the question 'what for'. And Syrian Archive's data are good enough for the purposes of the organization, while they are new and are generating alternative data stories and evidence that can be the basis for court cases.

How Syrian Archive fares in comparison with other cases

Data activists can resort to different data methods. Table 1 shows how Syrian Archive compares with the other cases mentioned before. The purpose of this table is to spell out the different origins, type of data activism and means to understand good enough data more broadly and provide a taxonomy that can be used as a tool to enhance the comparability of case studies.

	Origins of data	Type of data activism	Means
Syrian Archive	Videos on social media (posted by citizens and others)	2nd (public data) and 3rd (crowdsourced data)	Videos uploaded by citizens, journalists and activists on sharing platforms and social media, news media; public satellite imagery; news media; testimonies from a network of sources
Forensic Architecture	Satellite imagery and data, ballistic analysis, news, citizen data	2nd (public data) and 5th (own data)	Public satellite imagery and data (i.e. AIS signals); news media; sensors; a variety of means
WeRobotics	Drone-based imagery (gathered by citizens)	5th (own data)	Drones; people as data/images analyzers
InfoAmazonia	Satellite imagery, crowdsourced citizen data, citizen sensing	2nd (public data), 3rd (crowdsourced data) and 5th (own data)	Public satellite imagery; crowdsourcing platform; sensors (i.e. water quality)

Ushahidi	Crowdsourced citizen data; websites and social media	2nd (public data) and 3rd (crowdsourced data)	Crowdsourcing platform and scraping methods (i.e. for verification); scraping
Citizen sensing in Gabrys, Pritchard and Barratt (2016)	Citizen sensing	5th (own data)	Sensors

Table 1: Comparison of Data Initiatives by Their Origins[102]

Forensic Architecture employs advanced architectural and media research on behalf of international prosecutors, human rights organizations and campaigning groups to produce evidence of human rights abuses.[103] WeRobotics launches 'flying labs' and swimming robots to capture data and images for social uses.[104] Focused on promoting conservation via data transparency, InfoAmazonia visualizes journalistic stories and advocacy content on maps, sets up sensor networks to capture water data, creates alarm systems and crowdsources data from indigenous communities.[105] Meanwhile, Ushahidi has created a crowdsourcing platform that gathers, verifies and visualizes citizen data to support humanitarian operations.[106] One difference can be identified looking at their data sources is that, while the people who submit documents on social media may not know they are going to be used by Syrian Archive, the reporters of the Ushahidi platform and the citizens gathering data via sensors are creating data deliberately as part of the effort from its inception. The act of documenting a case of abuse and sharing the video may reveal an intention to denounce it and an acceptance that the information can be used by third parties, but it is not a given. Interviewees 3 and 4 say that some reporters send the footage directly to the organization; however, part of the Syrian Archive reporters' involvement in the project is indirect.

In any case, these initiatives rely wholly or partially on citizens, and the interviews illustrate the importance of citizen data for their projects. Talking about Syrian Archive Interviewee 3 puts it like this:

> (Syrian) footage gathered by ordinary citizens and journalists and posted online has started to appear as evidence in courtrooms. In August 2017, the International Criminal Court used a video posted on YouTube to get an international arrest warrant on an officer of the Libyan army accused of war crimes. Open information obtained from social media is increasingly recognized in court as potential evidence, which is really encouraging.

---

102 Elaboration by the author based on Gutierrez, *Data Activism and Social Change*.
103 Forensic Architecture 'Project', 2028, http://www.forensic-architecture.org/project/.
104 WeRobotics, 'About', http://werobotics.org/.
105 InfoAmazonia, 'About', https://infoamazonia.org/en/about/.
106 Ushahidi, 'About', https://www.ushahidi.com/about.

Interviewee 1 notes that the high value of citizen data in crisis mapping employed in digital humanitarianism:

> Especially in times of disaster, the best people to give direction on what is needed on the ground are the people directly affected by the crisis, the otherwise assumed to be "passive recipients" of information.

Even the two non-activist interviewees integrate some forms of citizen data in their projects. Although the fragile states index does not incorporate them 'because it is too difficult to verify at that high level', social media or citizen data are part of 'more ground-level, localized community assessments', says Interviewee 5. The water grids designed to distribute water in cities and communities by Interviewee 2 employ user data to identify loss and malfunction within the grids.

However, there is a distinction to be made when the lens of volume and data roles are taken into account. In the case of Syrian Archive and Forensic Architecture, citizen data are incorporated on a case by case basis; WeRobotics, Ushahidi, InfoAmazonia and citizen sensing integrate citizens not only as data gatherers but also as analyzers and users.

Another trend that can be spotted is the alternative use practitioners make of data-harvesting technologies. For example, while drones - crewless aerial vehicles - were created originally for military purposes, they have been appropriated by WeRobotics and other data activists for social and humanitarian uses. Likewise, maps have been traditionally the monopoly of the state; these organizations and projects have seized them to generate alternative narratives and oppose top-down approaches.[107] The same observations can be made about the data infrastructure being employed in activism, not its primary purpose. That is, these data practices not only generate new datasets and data stories; they also reverse top-down approaches to the data infrastructure.

The interviewees: Verification and usefulness

What else can be said about good enough data? Next, the interviewees provide more clues as to what is good enough. For example, Interviewee 1 notes something that appears obvious: data have to be accurate to be valuable. To make sure this is the case, data practitioners resort to verification processes with a variety of techniques, which are, again, context related.

> Verification mechanisms (...) vary from one deployment to another, depending on the context and intensity of the situation. Children mapping out the cost of chicken across the world will have a less rigorous verification process as compared to election monitors in Kenya. In most cases, verification will involve corroboration with trusted sources online, and on the ground, and mainstream media sources (...) I think the definition of good enough data is something that can only be determined from one deployment to another. Is it relevant to the topic of interest/goal of your deployment?

---

107 Gutierrez, 'Maputopias: Cartographies of Knowledge, Communication and Action in the Big Data Society'.

> Do the submissions give you enough information to act?

Interviewee 2 also highlights the fact that, while good enough data is a relative concept, all data have to be standardized and validated to be usable:

> Good enough data is really a moving target. Each data submission (...) can lead to new, unsupported data that needs to be analyzed and added to our *raw* input data validation and normalization stage. We also need to have a data QA stage that extracts statistics that let us inspect incoming data and adjust accordingly. Our definition of good data could be: It passes our initial raw input data validation filters; it's normalized to our system's internal requirements; it doesn't produce abnormalities in data QA (quality assurance) statistics, and it fits into each of the system's internal data structures.

Interviewees 1, 2 and 4 suggest that what is good enough today, can become *not so good* tomorrow, and that this is a work in progress. The interviewees imply too that achieving good enough data is a collective effort that requires meticulous team-work. Interviewee 4 adds the concepts of comparability and accessibility, as well as the requirement to integrate feedback to correct errors and avoid misinformation:

> Good enough data are data that have been verified and offered in an accessible and standardized, easy manner, which can collaborate with other types of data. It is also important that they are accessible, so potential problems are fixed through feedback. We see people working regarding collecting data (on human rights) based on published data but without any criteria of verification. The risk there is to spread propaganda.

Syrian Archive devotes significant resources to verify not only the data but also the data sources. Likewise, Interviewee 5 points out the need to rely on credible sources to apply verification tests.

> It is basically a reasonability test. In assessing 178 countries on such a broad breadth of indicators every year, it is impossible to directly verify every one of the 50 million or so data points that we analyze. To that degree, a certain amount of trust is necessary for the credibility of the sources included in the sample by the content aggregation process. The data may never be perfect; however, our process of triangulation with different types of data is a way of 'balancing' it and ensuring it is providing reasonable outputs.

The interviewees stress the demand for data to be enough in quantity and accurate, which requires verification processes that integrate corrections back into the system. Some of them use similar methods. For example, the triangulation in the vulnerable countries index resembles Syrian Archive's process in that the latter includes three layers of data identification and confirmation as well. These interviews add new perspectives on the concept of good enough data: data should be standardized and comparable so they can endure verification processes, they should employ trustworthy sources and embed the capacity for absorbing corrections.

Towards a definition of good enough data in activism

Building blocks that emerge from the comparisons, interviews and definitions above include: good enough data in activism can/should: 1) be robust enough in quantity and quality; 2) refer to forms of citizens' involvement as data gatherers and other roles; 3) generate impact/action-oriented new data and data stories; 4) involve alternative uses of the data infrastructure and other technologies, and a variety of mining methods; 5) resort to credible data sources; 6) include standardization, comparability, accessibility, usability and accuracy, as well as verification, testing and feedback integration processes; 7) involve collaboration; 8) be relevant for the context and aims of the research questions; and 9) be preserved for further use, including as evidence in court cases.

The comparison between the reports on Aleppo issued by Syrian Archive and by OHCHR, and between activist and non-activist data gathering exercises show that data activism has potential to produce good enough data to generate dependable information, filling gaps, complementing and supporting other actors' efforts and, paraphrasing Gabrys, Pritchard and Barratt,[108] creating patterns of actionable evidence that can mobilize policy changes, community responses, follow-up monitoring, and improved accountability.

Compliance with Ethics Requirements

The author declares that she has no conflict of interest. The author has permission to use the images included in the article. Informed consent was obtained from all interviewees for being included in the study.

References

Al Jazeera News. 'Syria's Civil War Explained from the Beginning', *Al Jazeera*, 14 April 2018, https://www.aljazeera.com/news/2016/05/syria-civil-war-explained-160505084119966.html.

Amnesty International. 'Exposed: Child Labour behind Smart Phone and Electric Car Batteries', 19 July 2016, https://www.amnesty.org/en/latest/news/2016/01/child-labour-behind-smart-phone-and-electric-car-batteries/.

_____.'Syria: "War Of Annihilation": Devastating Toll On Civilians, Raqqa Syria', 2018, https://www.amnesty.org/en/documents/mde24/8367/2018/en/.

Axinn, William G., Dirgha Ghimire and Nathalie E. Williams. 'Collecting Survey Data during Armed Conflict', *J Off Stat* 28.2 (2012): 153-171.

Balsiger, Philip, and Alexandre Lambelet. 'Participant Observation', in Donatella della Porta (ed.), M*ethodological Practices in Social Movement Research*, Oxford: Oxford University Press, 2014, pp. 144-72.

Banchik, Anna, et al. 'Chemical Strikes on Al-Lataminah'. *Berkeley Human Rights Investigation Lab*, 25, 30 March 2017, https://syrianarchive.org/assets/hama/Syrian_Archive_Hama_Report_Final.pdf.

---

108 Gabrys, Pritchard, and Barratt, 'This Is the Other Aspect of "just" Good Enough Data'.

Berendt, Bettina, Marco Büchler, and Geoffrey Rockwell. 'Is It Research or Is It Spying? Thinking-Through Ethics in Big Data AI and Other Knowledge Science', *Künstliche Intelligenz* 29.223 (2015), https://doi.org/10.1007/s13218-015-0355-2.

Bernard, H. Russell. *Research Methods in Anthropology: Qualitative and Quantitative Approaches*, Fourth Edition, Maryland: AltaMira Press, 2006.

Boellstorff, Tom. 'Making Big Data, in Theory', *First Monday* 18.10 (2013), http://firstmonday.org/article/view/4869/3750.

Borges, Jorge Luis. 'Del Rigor En La Ciencia', *Palabra Virtual*, 12 February 2007, http://www.palabra-virtual.com/index.php?ir=ver_voz1.php&wid=726&p=Jorge%20Luis%20Borges&t=Del%20rigor%20en%20la%20ciencia&o=Jorge%20Luis%20Borges.

Braman, Sandra. 2009. *Change of State: Information, Policy, and Power*. Cambridge: MIT Press.

Cadwalladr, Carole, and Emma Graham-Harrison. 'Revealed: 50 Million Facebook Profiles Harvested for Cambridge Analytica in Major Data Breach'. *The Guardian*, 17 March 2018, https://www.theguardian.com/news/2018/mar/17/cambridge-analytica-facebook-influence-us-election.

Cohen, D., and B. Crabtree. 'Qualitative Research Guidelines Project'. The Robert Wood Johnson Foundation: Semi-Structured Interviews. July 2006, http://www.qualres.org/HomeSemi-3629.html.

Cukier, Kenneth. 'Big Data Is Better Data'. presented at the Berlin TEDSalon, Berlin, June 2014, http://www.ted.com/talks/kenneth_cukier_big_data_is_better_data?language=en.

Dijck, Jose van. 'Datafication, Dataism and Dataveillance: Big Data between Scientific Paradigm and Ideology'. *Surveillance & Society* 12.2 (2014): 197-208.

Downing, John D. H. (ed.). *Encyclopedia of Social Movement Media*, Thousand Oaks: SAGE, 2011.

Ford, Heather. 'Can Ushahidi Rely on Crowdsourced Verifications?', *H Blog*, 3 September 2012, https://hblog.org/2012/03/09/can-ushahidi-rely-on-crowdsourced-verifications/.

Forensic Architecture. 'About Saydnaya', 2017, http://www.forensic-architecture.org/case/saydnaya/.

_____.'Project', 2028, http://www.forensic-architecture.org/project/.

Gabrys, Jennifer, and Helen Pritchard. 2015. 'Next-Generation Environmental Sensing: Moving beyond Regulatory Benchmarks for Citizen-Gathered Data', in AJ Berre, S Schade, and J Piera (eds), *Proceedings of the Workshop 'Environmental Infrastructures and Platforms 2015*, Barcelona, pp. 57-65, http://ecsa.citizen-science.net/sites/default/ files/envip-2015-draft-binder.pdf.

Gabrys, Jennifer, Helen Pritchard, and Benjamin Barratt. 'This Is the Other Aspect of "just" Good Enough Data that Citizen Data Could Provide Ways of Realising Environmental and Social Justice', *Big Data & Society* 1.14 (2016): 14.

Gangadharan, Seeta Peña. 'Digital Inclusion and Data Profiling'. *First Monday* 17.5 (2012), http://firstmonday.org/article/view/3821/3199.

Gitelman, Lisa (ed.). *Raw Data Is an Oxymoron*, Cambridge MA/London: MIT Press, 2013.

Greenberg, Andy. 'These Are the Emails Snowden Sent to First Introduce His Epic NSA Leaks', *The Wired*, 13 October 2014, https://www.wired.com/2014/10/snowdens-first-emails-to-poitras/.

Gutierrez, Miren. *Data Activism and Social Change*, London: Palgrave Macmillan, 2018.'Maputopias: Cartographies of Knowledge, Communication and Action in the Big Data Society - The Cases of Ushahidi and InfoAmazonia'. *GeoJournal* (2018): 1-20, https://doi.org/https://doi.org/10.1007/s10708-018-9853-8.

_____.'The Public Sphere in Light of Data Activism'. *Krisis* (2018).

Hogan, Mel, and Sarah T. Roberts. 'Data Flows and Water Woes: An Interview With Media Scholar Mél Hogan'. 2015, http://bigdatasoc.blogspot.com.es/2015/08/data-flows-and-water-woes-interview.html.

Human Rights Council, 'Report of the Independent International Commission of Inquiry on the Syrian Arab Republic', UN General Assembly, 5 Februrary, 2013, http://www.ohchr.org/Documents/HRBodies/HRCouncil/ColSyria/A.HRC.22.59_en.pdf.

InfoAmazonia. 'THE ANNUAL CYCLES of the Indigenous Peoples of the Rio Tiquié 2005-2006'. 2016, https://ciclostiquie.socioambiental.org/en/index.html.

_____. 2017.'About'. 2017, https://infoamazonia.org/en/about/.

Innerarity, Daniel.'Ricos Y Pobres En Datos', *Globernance.org*, 22 February 2016, http://www.danielinnerarity.es/opinion-preblog/ricos-y-pobres-en-datos/.

International Telecommunication Union. 'Measuring the Information Society Report' 2014. Geneva: International Telecommunication Union (ITU), http://www.itu.int/en/ITU-D/Statistics/Documents/publications/misr2015/MISR2015-w5.pdf.

Kitchin, Rob, and Tracey P. Lauriault. 'Small Data, Data Infrastructures and Big Data', *GeoJournal*, The Programmable City Working Paper 1, 80.4 (2014): 463-75.

Knight, Ben. 'Syrian Archive Finds "Overwhelming" Russian Atrocities in Aleppo'. *DW*, 28 March 2017, http://www.dw.com/en/syrian-archive-finds-overwhelming-russian-atrocities-in-aleppo/a-38169808.

Korzybski, Alfred. *Science and Sanity: An Introduction to Non-Aristotelian Systems and General Semantics*, fifth edition, New York: Institute of General Semantics, 1994.

Lancaster, Lewis. 'From Text to Image to Analysis: Visualization of Chinese Buddhist Canon', *Digital Humanities, 2010*, http://dh2010.cch.kcl.ac.uk/academic-programme/abstracts/papers/pdf/ab-670.pdf.

Lauriault, Tracey P.'Data, Infrastructures and Geographical Imaginations', 2012, Ottawa: Carleton University, https://curve.carleton.ca/system/files/etd/7eb756c8-3ceb-4929-8220-3b20cf3242cb/etd_pdf/79f3425e913cc42aba9aa2b9094a9a53/lauriault-datainfrastructuresandgeographicalimaginations.pdf.

Leonelli, Sabina. 'What Counts as Scientific Data? A Relational Framework', *Philosophy of Science* 82.5 (2015): 810-21.

Lynch, Colum. 'Soviet-Era Bomb Used in Syria Chemical Weapon Attack, Claims Rights Group'. *Foreign Policy*, 5 January 2017, http://foreignpolicy.com/2017/05/01/soviet-era-bomb-used-in-syria-chemical-weapon-attack-claims-rights-group/.

Lynd,Robert Staughton. *Knowledge for What: The Place of Social Science in American Culture*, Princeton: Princeton University Press, 1967.

Lyon, David. 'Surveillance, Snowden, and Big Data: Capacities, Consequences', *Big Data & Society* (July, 2014): 1-13.

Mayer-Schönberger, Viktor, and Kenneth Cukier. *Big Data: A Revolution That Will Transform How We Live, Work, and Think*, Boston: Houghton Mifflin Harcourt, 2013.

Milan, Stefania and Miren Gutierrez. 'Citizens´ Media Meets Big Data: The Emergence of Data Activism'. *Mediaciones* 14 (June, 2015), http://biblioteca.uniminuto.edu/ojs/index.php/med/article/view/1086/1027.

Miller, Harvey J. 'The Data Avalanche Is Here: Shouldn't We Be Digging?' *Wiley Periodicals*, 22 August 2009.Nakamitsu, Izumi. 'The Situation in the Middle East', Briefing S/PV.8344, New York: Security Council, 6 September 2018, https://www.securitycouncilreport.org/atf/cf/%7b65BFCF9B-6D27-4E9C-8CD3-CF6E4FF96FF9%7d/s_pv_8344.pdf.

Office of the UN High Commissioner for Human Rights. 'Warring Parties Continued to Target Civilians for Abuses over Last Seven Months - UN Commission', *United Nations,* 14 March, 2017, http://www.ohchr.org/EN/NewsEvents/Pages/DisplayNews.aspx?NewsID=21370&LangID=E.

O'Neil, Cathy. *Weapons of Math Destruction: How Big Data Increases Inequality and Threatens Democracy*, New York: Crown Publishers, 2016.

Organisation for the Prohibition of Chemical Weapons. 'Chemical Weapons Convention', 2005, https://www.opcw.org/sites/default/files/documents/CWC/CWC_en.pdf.

Palmer, Lindsay. 'Ushahidi at the Google Interface: Critiquing the "geospatial Visualization of Testimony"', *Continuum* 28.3 (2014): 342-56, DOI: https://doi.org/10.1080/10304312.2014.893989.

Poell, Thomas, Helen Kennedy, and Jose van Dijck. 'Special Theme: Data & Agency', *Big Data & Society*, 2 (July, 2015): 1-7, http://bigdatasoc.blogspot.com.es/2015/12/special-theme-data-agency.html.

Rogers, Simon. 'John Snow's Data Journalism: The Cholera Map That Changed the World', *The Guardian*, 15 March 2012, http://www.theguardian.com/news/datablog/2013/mar/15/john-snow-cholera-map.

Slater, Dirk. 'What I've Learned about Mapping Violence', *Fab Riders*, 3 April 2016, http://www.fabriders.net/mapping-violence/.

Solvang, Ole. 'Key Finding on Use of Chemical Weapons in Syria'. Human Rights Watch, 2017, https://www.hrw.org/news/2017/10/05/key-finding-use-chemical-weapons-syria.

Stephens-Davidowitz, Seth. *Everybody Lies: Big Data, New Data, and What the Internet Can Tell Us About Who We Really Are*, New York: Dey Street Books, 2017.

Syrian Archive. 'About', 2017, https://syrianarchive.org/en/about.

_____. 'Research Methodology'. 6 January 2017, https://syrianarchive.org/p/page/methodology_digital_evidence_workflow/.

_____. 'Violations Database', Database. 2016, https://syrianarchive.org/en/database?location=%D8%AD%D9%84%D8%A8%20:%20D8%AD%D9%84%D8%A8&after=2016-07-01&before=2016-12-31.

_____.'Eyes on Aleppo: Visual Evidence Analysis of Human Rights Violations Committed in Aleppo - July - Dec 2016', 2017, https://media.syrianarchive.org/blog/5th_blog/Eyes%20on%20Aleppo.pdf.

Tufekci, Zeynep. 'Engineering the Public: Internet, Surveillance and Computational Politics', *First Monday* 19.7 (2014).

Ushahidi, 'About', 2017, https://www.ushahidi.com/about.

Vota, Wayan. 'Dead Ushahidi: A Stark Reminder for Sustainability Planning in ICT4D'. *ICT Works,* 9 July 2012, http://www.ictworks.org/2012/07/09/dead-ushahidi-stark-reminder-sustainability-planning-ict4d/.

Weller, Marc. 'Syria Air Strikes: Were They Legal?' *BBC News*, 14 April 2018, https://www.bbc.com/news/world-middle-east-43766556.

WeRobotics, 'About', 2017, http://werobotics.org/.

Woodside, Arch. *Case Study Research: Theory, Methods and Practice*, United Kingdom: Emerald, 2010.

Yin, Robert K. *Case Study Research: Design and Methods,* Applied Social Research Methods Series. Thousand Oaks: SAGE,* 2002.

Zhao, Jieyu, Tianlu Wang, Mark Yatskar, Vicente Ordonez and Vicente Chang. 'Men Also Like Shopping: Reducing Gender Bias Amplification Using Corpus-Level Constraints', *Proceedings of the 2017 Conference on Empirical Methods in Natural Language Processing,* Copenhagen, Denmark, 7-11 September 2017, pp. 2979-2989.

5: AN ENERGY DATA MANIFESTO

DECLAN KUCH, NAOMI STRINGER, LUKE MARSHALL, SHARON YOUNG, MIKE ROBERTS, IAIN MACGILL, ANNA BRUCE AND ROB PASSEY

Introduction

This collaborative manifesto, co-written by a social scientist and engineers, situates the demands for data about energy use and planning by regulators, consumers and policy-makers in an historical and regulatory context, most notably the shift from state ownership of large coal power plants to competition policy. We outline paths forward in three overlapping areas: firstly, data for the empowerment of consumers should see easier access to usage data provided by retailers, whilst new collectives to produce energy should be encouraged and enabled. Secondly under the umbrella of 'data for accountability', we situate practical work we have undertake in open source modelling in a wider set of concerns about how retailers and electricity supply (poles and wires) businesses are run. Finally, building on these two areas, we speculate how moving past the binary between individual versus corporate interest may enable a more democratic and accountable research capacity into energy planning. We conclude noting the scale and scope of challenges facing energy policy makers in Australia and underscore the importance of a strategic 'technopolitics' – the technical details of market design – to both effective action on climate change and robust, sustainable energy systems.

A spectre is haunting Australia – the spectre of an energy transition. All the powers of the old energy sector have entered an unholy alliance to exorcise this spectre.[1] Enabled by rapid technological changes, including developments in distributed solar, storage, metering and control, the prospect of an environmentally sustainable, equitable and reliable energy system driven by community knowledge and engagement has emerged. The control of the resultant explosion of energy data lies at the heart of the battle for our energy future. Although enthusiasm for much broader access to energy data to monitor and facilitate this transition is growing, some key incumbent energy sector businesses, politicians and others are pushing to maintain present asymmetries in energy data collection and access. Two things result from the struggle to remedy these asymmetries:

1. A revolution in how we collect and disseminate energy data - especially that of end-users - is sorely needed. This is widely acknowledged by Australian policy-makers.

2. Appropriate frameworks are urgently needed for collecting and sharing suitably anonymised energy data to enable a rapid transition to a democratic and sustainable energy future.

---

[1] Of course, we understand this is not entirely true, and that toxic politics is a major barrier, but we adapt this quote from another famous manifesto to illustrate the difficulties being faced by proponents of sustainable energy in Australia.

As energy researchers, we use energy data to inform our work, build our models and provide insights on possible energy transition futures. By collectively and openly publishing our views about what good energy data access and oversight might look like, and the prospects for an energy data revolution, we hope to facilitate public debate to help bring about a just transition in the energy sector in ways that empower and enable communities to determine their own futures.

We focus on the electricity sector that is the primary subject of our work, and where the quantity and complexity of energy data is increasing rapidly, with only limited guidance from policy-makers regarding who should have access and under what terms. This work is both technical and political – it redraws the boundaries of which actors have access to relevant data, and, therefore, who can make decisions. Political structures are important in shaping regulation, but equally, politics and regulations are shaped by technical details and flows of data.

A History of the Current Paradigm Through Data

The history of the Australian electricity system is a history of paradigms: small, local generation and governance at the municipal level has given way to large, state-owned, and generally vertically integrated electricity commissions. These became responsible for planning, building and operating large centralised generation assets and networks to serve energy consumers under a social contract of affordable and reliable electricity provision. Unlike some jurisdictions, such as those States in the US that established Utility Commissions to oversee monopoly electricity utilities, there was remarkably little transparency about the operation of these Australian state electricity commissions. To this day, Utilities themselves have had very limited information on nearly all energy consumers because data infrastructure has typically comprised simple accumulation meters that provided only quarterly consumption data.

Events in the 1980s, such as attempts to build power stations for an aluminium smelting boom that never materialised, increased pressure to establish greater government and public oversight of the Utilities in some key states. However, these initiatives were overtaken by a micro-economic reform agenda in the early 1990s that established a very different direction for the electricity sector.

The reform agenda for electricity focussed on the vertical separation of generation and retail from the natural monopoly networks, the introduction of competition and the sale of publicly-owned electricity generation, transmission and distribution assets to the private sector.[2] The key role of publicly available data (see Box 1) to facilitate an effective market in electricity provision was appreciated at an early stage of this restructuring.[3]

---

2   George Wilkenfeld, 'Cutting greenhouse emissions-what would we do if we really meant it?', *Australian Review of Public Affairs*, (2007) http://www.australianreview.net/digest/2007/08/wilkenfeld.html; George Wilkenfeld & Peter Spearritt, 'Electrifying Sydney', Sydney: EnergyAustralia, 2004.
3   The Australian National Electricity Market uses detailed data regarding large-scale generation, namely five-minute market offers of all scheduled generators, their dispatch and market prices.

A key objective of micro-economic reform was to provide energy consumers with greater choice, which according to economic rationalist theory would put them at the heart of decision-making in the industry.[4] There was far less focus on the role of public energy data (Box 1) to facilitate effective engagement at the distribution network and retail market level.

> **Box 1: What is 'Public Energy Data'?**
>
> Energy data typically refers to information over time regarding the level of energy consumption, generation, quality,[5] and price. When coupled with metadata (such as consumer location or demographics), this data can yield valuable insights for researchers, and policymakers in domains such as urban planning, demography, and sociology. We use the prefix '*public*' to refer to energy data which is freely and publicly available. This can be contrasted to proprietary data held by privately owned retailers or within government departments. Public refers to both the state of accessibility and the process of making otherwise enclosed data freely available.

Market design decisions in the 1990s mean that key parameters of the energy markets are published online. The Federal regulator AEMO publishes energy consumption and wholesale price across regions (such as New South Wales) and updates this information every five minutes. energy data demonstrate the importance of aggregation.[5] When household data includes thousands or even millions of households, it yields insights relevant to decision-making about the supply and distribution system (poles and wires), retail and wholesale markets. Because Retailer and Network Business access to consumer data is generally far superior to that of consumers, regulators or researchers, there are substantial information asymmetries with implications for competition, regulation and broader decision-making.

Data for Empowerment of Consumers and New Collectives

Decarbonising an electricity sector governed through the competition policy paradigm has proven incredibly problematic.[6] A new paradigm of governing carbon emissions through a nationally regulated cap and trade scheme spluttered into life briefly in 2012 before being snuffed out by the Coalition Government of Tony Abbott in 2014.

In this contentious policy context, private action by households to reduce emissions by deploying household PV has been one of the few environmental success stories for effective transition to a sustainable energy system in Australia. Collectives have also sprung up in the ashes of the carbon emissions trading regime seeking to make the transition to sustainable electricity industry infrastructure. The competition policy paradigm preserves universal indi-

---

4 This is of course not true as consumers would still only be responding to the products offered to them.
5 Available on the Australian Energy Market Operator's website: https://www.aemo.com.au/.
6 Iain MacGill and Stephen Healy, 'Is electricity industry reform the right answer to the wrong question? Lessons from Australian restructuring and climate policy.', in Fereidoon P. Sioshansi (ed.), *Evolution of Global Electricity Markets*, Cambridge MA: Academic Press, 2013, pp. 615-644.

vidual household access to competitive retail markets. However, these markets have generally served retailers better than their customers. Moreover, the competition policy paradigm has constrained collectives at the community scale seeking to building mini or microgrids or develop shared energy resources like solar and batteries. Crucially, groups organising around contracts that would effectively remove choice of provider have been scuppered by competition justifications. Furthermore, competition policies have further constrained access to data by locking these groups into market arrangements where legacy retail businesses have advantages of scale and incumbency.

At present, households can be both consumers and producers of energy (prosumers) yet do not have real-time access to their energy consumption data. This data is collected by the metering service providers and then passed to the electricity retailers and network companies for billing, sales and planning needs. While consumers are able to obtain their past consumption data, it is usually not a straightforward process and there is no consistent format of delivery. As decentralised energy becomes increasingly prevalent, secure energy data sharing is needed to facilitate new markets and options.

Community groups such as Pingala and ClearSky Solar have been asking the question, 'who should have energy usage data and under what circumstances?' with quite different perspectives to those of network operators, the large retailers and Federal regulators that are a legacy of the old paradigm. These community groups seek to democratise ownership of the energy system through facilitating communities' investment in solar PV assets and sale of the electricity generated.[7] However, without visibility over relevant data to investment decision-making and electricity loads, participation in the electricity market is more difficult. Managing a decentralised, variable renewable energy supply requires an accurate and time-sensitive set of monitoring tools.

While millions of rooftop distributed solar generators have been installed across Australia, the required data acquisition tools have not been deployed in parallel at a similar scale. Distributed resources to monitor and forecast their own operation are much better able to integrate with and respond to price signals, especially when aggregated into Virtual Power Plants – where a host of smaller controllable loads such as battery systems, electric cars, air conditioners and/or pool pumps act together like a physical power station.

In this political and regulatory context, data empowerment for the grassroots provides hope. For individual consumers, this can simply mean being able to compare their retail offer with others. This has been made somewhat possible, to the extent possible just by using bill data, via the Australian Government's 'Energy Made Easy' website, while the Australian Consumer Association, Choice, is also developing a tool to inform consumers in the marketplace, particularly around purchases of solar or batteries. For communities, empowerment can mean accessing the electricity usage data of one or more sites like breweries or community halls, to size an appropriate suite of distributed energy technologies to reduce dependence on

---

7   See Declan Kuch and Bronwen Morgan, 'Dissonant Justifications: an organisational perspective of support for Australian community energy', *People Place and Policy* 9 (2015): 177-218.

what are often unfair contracts with retailers. Or it can be as complex as using high temporal resolution load and generation data to facilitate real-time peer-to-peer local energy trading in a microgrid or across the network as exemplified by Power Ledger or LO3. However, even timeseries usage data from a single site is currently typically not available or easily accessible. Rather than being "allowed" retrospective access to their data, there are collective benefits in households having real-time access to their energy use data, with the ability to control access to that data and to share it with trusted organisations.

A proposed trial in the sunny Byron Bay region of Northern NSW provides an apt example for a new paradigm of data flows. In this case, community owned retailer Enova is seeking to enable local sharing of generated solar power between consumers in an arts and industrial estate and is considering battery energy storage to increase the volume of solar power consumer locally.[8] In this instance, the data is essential to allowing peer-to-peer energy trading, which otherwise would not be possible and critically, understanding of the collective energy needs for the estate would not be known. Furthermore, the ability for a battery to provide network benefits requires understanding of network conditions, typically known only by the local distribution network service provider.[9] Open Utility in the UK is a similar example, enabling consumers to trade peer-to-peer through a retailer, and looking to offer networks flexibility services.[10]

These examples demonstrate that appropriate data access can foster creativity with legal structures and contracts which enables communities to work around the intransigence of incumbent organisations and rules, and for new collectives to form. These new collectives are based on the sharing of data on energy loads in ways that can catalyse a transition to distributed, sustainable energy economy.

Recommendations

- Opt-in data access to energy use data beyond just networks and retailers.

- Residential consumers be granted straightforward access to their own energy use data and be given consent to give or withdraw data for specific purposes; and so are able to easily come together to produce and consume energy as community energy groups.

- Further experimentation with the legal form of electricity businesses that will enable investments in renewable energy.

---

8   See https://enovaenergy.com.au/about-us/#structure for Enova's corporate structure, which includes a holding company divided into a retailer which channels 50% of profits into its non-profit arm. Enova's constitution specifies that most shareholders must reside locally to the Northern Rivers region of NSW.
9   We note that there are ongoing efforts to make network information more widely available, for instance through the Australian Renewable Energy Mapping Infrastructure project.
10 Scottish and Southern Electricity Networks (SSEN), 'SSEN and Open Utility partner to trial revolutionary smart grid platform', 2018, http://news.ssen.co.uk/news/all-articles/2018/april/ssen-open-utility-smart-grid-platform/.

Data for Accountability

The corporatisation of large centralised generation and transmission brings with it requirements of accountability. The displacement of a public service provision model with market and corporate logics has resulted in incentives to seek rents on what was public infrastructure, as electricity systems globally are becoming more decentralised and decarbonised.

Decentralisation presents is both an opportunity to empower new collectives, and brings with it risks of high costs and new power imbalances. The Australian Energy Market Operator have recently identified a potential cost reduction of nearly $4 billion if distributed energy resources (namely rooftop solar PV and battery energy storage) are effectively integrated,[11] whilst also flagging the substantial risks associated with the lack of visibility and control that distributed energy resources afford.[12] In this context of technological change and associated market and regulatory reform, we see public energy data as a critical tool in a) ensuring efficient outcomes, particularly as they can remedy historical incentives and incumbent player advantages, and; b) supporting fair outcomes by increasing visibility of the distribution of costs and benefits associated with the transition.

Network Service Providers (NSPs) own and operate the 'poles and wires' across Australia and present a particular challenge for regulators and rule makers. As regulated monopolies, they need to be effectively supervised without stifling innovation. They are subject to five yearly reviews in which their revenue for the upcoming 'regulatory period' is set by the Australian Energy Regulator (AER), based on information provided by the NSPs. Their regulated task of ensuring energy supply is technically complex and they are increasingly challenged as distributed energy resources such as rooftop photovoltaic solar (the most common form of flat, black panels on roofs) grow in number. Technologies such as solar can reduce consumer bills and therefore utility profitability. Therefore, without transparency about network investment there is a risk that technical challenges can be used to justify limiting access to networks, or the use of tariff structures that disadvantage consumers that install these technologies. Improved independent oversight of technical conditions in the depths of the network (e.g. Box 2) may lead to more efficient and fair investment and operational outcomes.

---

11   AEMO, 'Integrated System Plan', 2018.
12   AEMO, 'Visibility of Distributed Energy Resources', 2017.

> **Box 2: The importance of voltage data for integrating distributed renewables**
>
> Understanding how networks are functioning at both the high voltage transmission and low voltage distribution ends is crucial to integrating renewable energy resources effectively and at a fair cost to society. For instance, as PV uptake continues, a technical upper voltage limit is reached at local transformers, at which point it is difficult for additional PV to connect to the network. The responsibility of Network Service Providers to maintain a stable electricity network can lead them to a cautious approach to integration of distributed renewables, and in some jurisdictions, this has resulted in NSPs drastically restricting deployment of residential PV.[14] However, recent data analysis – which used information captured from independent monitoring of household PV systems – shows that network voltages are generally high due to historic network decision making (distribution transformer set points were generally set at a high voltage, leaving minimal 'headroom' for PV).[15] This has implications for exporting rooftop PV electricity to the national grid. The visibility afforded by voltage data readings across the network may enable scrutiny of network expenditure to ensure money is spent in a judicious manner;[16] there may be cost-effective solutions to maintain grid stability without placing unnecessary restrictions on deployment of distributed PV. Access to such data is key to overcoming integration barriers and market asymmetries, and as such is an important companion to wider policies on a just energy transition that have received more widespread attention such as the Renewable Energy Target and carbon pricing schemes.

We believe the existing regulatory hierarchy of access rights to electricity usage data requires restructuring. As things stand, incumbent retailers automatically have full access to their customers' data which they can use for commercial purposes beyond just ensuring accurate billing, such as targeted marketing. While recent regulatory changes give customers the right to access their electricity consumption data from retailers or NSPs, [13] householders must apply retrospectively for the data, while both the application process and the format of data supplied lack consistency and clarity. Although the regulation allows a customer to authorise a third party to access their data, as yet there is no consistent mechanism for obtaining multiple consents, nor for making bulk data requests, while these bulk requests are exempted from the time limits imposed on retailers and NSPs to provide data. This leaves researchers, along with community groups and other players needing data from multiple users, at the bottom of the pile. The creation of Consumer Data Rights will likely entrench this hierarchy, further entrenching a regulatory mindset of 'individual household vs. corporations', hobbling collectively forms of action from these other forms of actors.

---

13   AEMC, 'Final Rule Determination: National Electricity Amendment (Customer access to information about their energy consumption)', 2014.
14   G. Simpson, 'Network operators and the transition to decentralised electricity: An Australian socio-technical case study', *Energy Policy* 110 (2017): 422-433.
15   Naomi Stringer, Anna Bruce and Iain MacGill, 'Data driven exploration of voltage conditions in the Low Voltage network for sites with distributed solar PV', paper presented at the *Asia Pacific Solar Research Conference*, Melbourne, Australia, 2017.
16   See also the 'network opportunities map' project by UTS ISF: https://www.uts.edu.au/research-and-teaching/our-research/institute-sustainable-futures/our-research/energy-and-climate-2.

A hierarchy based on the purpose of data usage could be designed to require customer opt-in to allow their retailer (or other parties) to access their data for targeted sales. Conversely, use of anonymised data for public-interest research or for non-profit, community-based engagement in the energy market could be opt-out for initiatives like Enova, contingent on strict standards of data-protection and governance schemes that include ongoing re-evaluation of the data usage. Customers should be empowered to easily give or withdraw consent to access their data for specific purposes, which may involve a role for a delegated authority (similar to the community representative committees in Nepal)[17] to respond to specific access requests on their behalf.

A good energy data regime cannot continue to play by the incumbent rules. Good policy-making and robust regulation depend on access to data and the development of appropriate models and methods for analysis that allow efficiency, competition and equity to be assessed. Outdated rules must be reformed so that data can be harnessed by individual consumers and those that act on their behalf, community energy groups and consumer-advocates.[18]

It has been especially challenging for consumer advocacy groups, NGOs, and general public to effectively participate and engage in regulatory decision-making processes. Network operators' submissions to regulatory process could be made available to consumer groups and researchers for greater scrutiny. To effectively engage with these groups, they should also provide access to appropriate analysis and modelling platforms. CEEM's tariff analysis tool (Box 3) provides an example of a transparent and open-source modelling platform that can improve stakeholder engagement around electricity prices.

Box 3: Opening the black boxes: CEEM's Tariff Analysis Tool

CEEM's tariff analysis tool is an example of an open source model which is accessible by stakeholders like think tanks, community energy organisations, local councils and policy-makers.[20]

Consumers' ability to reduce their consumption using energy efficiency and solar is altering the distribution of revenue collection from consumers via tariffs, and has drawn attention to apparent cross-subsidies from traditional electricity-consuming customers to solar 'prosumers', while users of air-conditioning have also been identified as placing an unfair cost burden on other customers. Along with emerging costs of transforming the electricity network to a more distributed model, this has driven regulatory changes that now require network utilities to develop more cost-reflective tariffs.

---

17 See https://medium.com/@accountability/leadership-by-local-communities-in-nepal-paves-the-path-for-development-that-respects-rights-bdb906f43209.
18 Michel Callon and Fabian Muniesa, 'Peripheral vision: Economic markets as calculative collective devices.' *Organization studies*, 26.8 (2005): 1229-1250.
19 Rob Passey, Navid Haghdadi, Anna Bruce & Iain MacGill, 'Designing more cost reflective electricity network tariffs with demand charges', *Energy Policy* 109 (2017): 642-649.

> However, the proprietary energy models used by network providers and their private consultants are often complex, opaque and based on assumed variables, making it possible for the energy modellers to exploit uncertainties within a regulatory context biased towards recovering capital expenditure on electricity infrastructure.
>
> To overcome this information asymmetry, CEEM's tariff tool allows stakeholders to test different electricity network tariffs on different sets of customers and investigate the impact on users' electricity bills, their cost-reflectivity, and distributional impacts using anonymised load data. Because it is open-source, the tool and results can be easily verified and can therefore facilitate transparency and more robust regulatory decisions.
>
> Unlike black-box and expensive proprietary energy models which are usually only available to powerful incumbent stakeholders, open source modelling platforms can be used, expanded, scrutinised, and verified by any interested stakeholders. This democratisation of tariff analysis is an example of how open source tools can empower more stakeholders, improve the operation of markets, regulation and policymaking.

Regulators of energy retail licenses (AER), energy reliability (AEMO) and market competition and power (ACCC) have particularly important roles in maintaining the accountability of energy market players. and existing so-called markets in energy services have some fundamental problems at the retailer level: incumbent retailers have some unfair advantages selling energy devices and services to their customers because they have energy use data that is unavailable, or at least challenging to obtain, for other potential energy service providers.

Recommendations

- Retailers be required to obtain opt-in permission for targeted sales.

- The expansion of tools to enhance market participation of individual consumers and community groups, created in the public interest.

- Some communities of modellers be granted delegated authority to access fine-grain energy data: good energy data requires an appropriate interface between energy users, regulators and power providers.

- Increased expert resources for regulators to enable them to access to usage and tariff data.

- Support for open-source modelling and data transparency in regulatory decision-making to reduce reliance on opaque analysis from private consultants.

Data for the People: The Potential of Standards

Ethical protocols of informed consent for research serve to formalise relationships through a bureaucratic agency and assist universities in managing risks to research participants and to their own reputation. Rights to privacy, to withdraw from research and so forth, can act as valuable bulwarks against the abuse of the powers and privileges to access sensitive data.

But singular moments of 'consent' are not ideal for the dynamics of energy data research, nor are they suitable for the digital platforms upon which much of today's interactions take place. Blurred boundaries between public-interest research and commercially-driven consultancy (exacerbated by privatisation of public institutions and increased corporatisation of universities) sharpen the need for consent conditional on the *purpose* of proposed data usage. Data activist Paul-Olivier Dehaye has recently quipped that a lot of 'data protection issues come from a narrow-minded business view of personal data as commodity. Much better is to embrace the European view, with a notion of personhood covering flows of personal data as well'.[20] This move from liberal privacy to communal personhood, he suggests is analogous to the shift from property rights to granting rights to rivers.

Ongoing public dialogue over the trade-off between privacy concerns and the granularity and reliability of data for analysis is required in such a shift – especially where the appropriation of data for private gain has often occurred at the behest of government agencies. Privacy, granularity and reliability of data for analysis and decision-making are intimately related for the purposes of infrastructure planning. Usage data at varying temporal and spatial resolutions is valuable to researchers, consumers and networks. For example, electricity consumption data at specific points in the electricity network is essential to network operators and useful to new energy business models based on sharing or aggregating consumer load and generation, and also potentially to other market participants and researchers. Since individual household data cannot typically be extracted from such data, there is little privacy or commercial risk involved in releasing it. However, the same data identified by street address, while potentially even more useful for certain purposes, requires more careful handling.

Public debate over energy data privacy often focuses on an individual's place of residence. This is often a result of imagining an individual household as a final fortress in an increasingly invasively connected world. As a result, energy researchers are hamstrung by highly anonymised data sets, for instance limiting geographical specificity to a postcode area. There are two primary challenges arising from this abstraction of data:

1. The first arises because the fabric of everyday life sustained through energy networks is vastly complicated. Electricity networks do not fit neatly into postcode-shaped areas. Aggregation of data points and the capacity to assess the impacts of decisions on the wider network is severely limited by the lack of granularity. For instance, the contribution of a certain customer demographics to peak demand on their local network infrastructure requires researchers to make clear connections between household and distribution

---

20 See https://twitter.com/podehaye/status/1030773658975981569.

network usage data. This connection is important because it forms the basis of significant supply, demand and network investment decisions.

2. The second arises because of the extremely rapid growth of distributed generation such as rooftop PV and batteries. These systems can have significant impacts on the security of the electricity system (i.e. the ability for the system to keep working without significant risk of power quality issues),[21] however their behaviours need to be understood in the context of their local network. Postcode level anonymisation makes this near impossible, whereas street location or even location on a specific section of the 'poles and wires' would be ideal.

Just as a more communal notion of personhood can foster better data practice outcomes, social scientists have argued that shifting the focus away from individual choice towards collective responsibility is key to effective climate action.[22] During our research, we have observed that individual consumers do not act as rational agents without help from material devices that enable calculation: they need apps, meters, interfaces and other market tools to act as 'rational actors' in the context of competitive retail markets. Moreover, it is often only through co-ordinated activity – selling aggregated generation from multiple small PV systems, co-ordinating temporal shifting of their electricity use to periods of low demand or applying the output of a collectively owned generator to their aggregated load – that they can engage effectively with the market.

Accessing data requires careful consideration about the purpose and access rights granted in research. Household-level electricity usage data can yield rich and diverse insights for effective energy research for public good and bad. Consider the identification of illicit facilities and improved network planning, yet also opportunities for well-resourced burglars to identify unattended dwellings, or for targeted advertising campaigns based on identification of existing appliances through their usage footprints. Highlighted in the rollout of 'smart meters' or Advanced Metering Infrastructure across Victoria,[23] similar challenges are also flagged by the CSIRO in its ongoing Energy Use Data Model project,[24] which seeks to collect an array of data across Australia for research and consultancy purposes.[25]

Data misuse, targeted marketing or malicious attacks on the energy market participants

---

21   Debra Lew, Mark Asano, Jens Boemer, Colton Ching, Ulrich Focken, Richard Hydzik, Mathias Lange and Amber Motley, 'The Power of Small - The Effects of Distributed Energy Resources on System Reliability', *IEEE Power & Energy Magazine,* 15 (2017): 50-60.
22   Elizabeth Shove, 'Beyond the ABC: climate change policy and theories of social change.' *Environment and planning A*, 42.6 (2010): 1273-1285.
23   Lockstep Consulting, 'Privacy Impact Assessment Report Advanced Metering Infrastructure (AMI)', Dept of Primary Industries, 2011.
24   CSIRO, 'Energy Use Data Model (EUDM)', 2015, https://research.csiro.au/distributed-systems-security/projects/energy-data-use-model/.
25   CSIRO 'partners with small and large companies, government and industry in Australia and around the world' https://www.csiro.au/en/Research/EF/Areas/Electricity-grids-and-systems/Economic-modelling/Energy-Use-Data-Model.

requires vigilance and effectively resourced regulators.[26] As researchers, we are mindful of the trust we solicit when we ask for data at a time when purposeful exploitation of personal data is a commonplace business model. If we cannot engender trust, we rightly risk losing access to appropriate data.

The rights and responsibilities of all energy data stakeholders need to be rebalanced to harness the power of energy data in the interests of energy users and society. Privacy is vital but should be considered in this wider context. Policies mandating social and ethical responsibilities integrated with public research and innovation,[27] such as those in the EU Horizon 2020, offer one platform to address the challenge of maintaining trust. Researchers have a responsibility to maintain security and confidentiality, through de-identification of individual data in the context of ongoing dialogue and its potential commercial uses. A suitable consent-for-purpose mechanism would support sharing of anonymised data with other public-interest researchers and groups and undermine commercial exploitation of publicly-funded or personally-sourced data.

Box 4: Making a Data Commons from Household Photovoltaic Solar Output
http://pvoutput.org

PVOutput is a free online service for sharing and comparing distributed photovoltaic solar generation unit output data across time. It provides both manual and automatic data uploading facilities for households to contribute the outputs from their photovoltaic system. PVOutput began in 2010 as an open-access commons in response to the interest and enthusiasm of many households deploying PV to let others know of their system performance. It then, unintentionally but certainly fortuitously, came to fill the growing need for an aggregate measurement of the contribution of photovoltaic solar to the grid. The site has become a public resource that is used by a wide range of market participants, including those seeking to facilitate rule changes that recognise the value of distributed PV systems, and others seeking to improve network planning. Today there are over 1.7m households in Australia with photovoltaic solar and PVoutput.org has played a key role in helping researchers and other stakeholders understand the challenges and opportunities this presents.

Standards are sorely needed

Research currently requires a pragmatic approach to making sense of data. Metadata is often incomplete or incorrect. Strings of numbers with no indication of the units of measurement (e.g. kWh, kW or kVA) have little value. Time stamps are particularly vexatious, as inconsistent treatment of daylight-saving periods, time zones and even time period 'ending' or 'starting' can all lead to misleading analysis outcomes. The detail on exactly what a data set contains

---

26 S.N. Islam, M. A. Mahmud and A.M.T. Oo, 'Impact of optimal false data injection attacks on local energy trading in a residential microgrid.' *ICT Express*, 4.1 (2018): 30-34, DOI: http://doi:10.1016/j.icte.2018.01.015.
27 Richard Owen, Phil Macnaghten and Jack Stilgoe, 'Responsible research and innovation: From science in society to science for society, with society', *Science and public policy*, 39.6 (2012): 751-760.

must be documented (and kept current) and have a clear standard across the industry.

The Australian Energy Market Operator has recently gone to great lengths to establish a data communication standard at the utility scale,[28] whilst requirements for a new register of distributed energy resource metadata is in the final stages of consultation.[29]

> **Box 5: The Green Button Initiative has empowered electricity consumers**
>
> 'The Green Button initiative is an industry-led effort that responds to a 2012 White House call-to-action to provide utility customers with easy and secure access to their energy usage information in a consumer-friendly and computer-friendly format for electricity, natural gas, and water usage.' [31] Inspired by the success of the Blue Button in providing access to health records, Green Button was an initiative of the US Chief Technology Officer that was taken up by utilities, network operators, technology suppliers and integrators, policy makers and regulators. Green Button is a standardised API web service and a common data format for transmission of energy data.

Standardised reporting criteria and formats enable collective knowledge-sharing.[31] By standardising energy data, consumers, researchers and industry will be able to build tools and perform analysis upon a stable platform, eliminating a wide range of common errors and miscalculations. As such, we recommend that, through collaboration between research groups, a standardised energy time-series data format be developed, with the following criteria as an initial basis for discussion:

- Human-readability (e.g. standardised labelling, sensible time series)
- Cross-compatibility between common processing platforms (Excel, Matlab, Python, R)
- Standard use of Unicode file formats for internationalisation
- Development of open-source tools for standard conversions (e.g., JSON -> CSV) and translations (e.g. labels English -> Chinese)
- Standard labelling & protocols for handling missing data
- Clear labelling of data types (e.g. Power, Energy, Real vs. Reactive)
- Mandatory fields (e.g. period length, time)
- Standardised time format (suggest addition of Unix and/or GMT timestamp for elimination of general ambiguity)
- Standardisation of time-ending data (vs. time-starting data)
- Standardisation of metadata, with common fields (e.g. Location and range, Country of origin, Postcode etc.)
- Standardised procedure for de-identification and anonymisation of datasets
- Standard approach for data quality assessment

---

28 AEMO, 'Visibility of Distributed Energy Resources', 2017.
29 AEMC, 'National Electricity Amendment (Register of distributed energy resources) Rule', 2018.
30 Green Button Alliance. 'Green Button Data', 2015, http://www.greenbuttondata.org/.
31 Matthias Björnmalm, Matthew Faria and Frank Caruso. 'Increasing the Impact of Materials in and beyond Bio-Nano Science', *Journal of the American Chemical Society* 138.41 (2016): 13449-13456, DOI:10.1021/jacs.6b08673.

- Standard platform to validate the meta-data
- Standardised data compression protocols for storage

It is also important to consider the current impact of inadequate data standards on the emerging market for distributed energy resources. A lack of clear data formats may represent a significant barrier to entry for some markets. In the Australian National Electricity Market, for example, metering data for billing is required to be collected and distributed in a standardised format (NEM12), as specified in detail by the Australian Energy Market Operator. This format is however effectively non-human-readable and could be classified as a type of low-level machine code. Interpretation of NEM12 data requires conversion to a different format before it can be interpreted in any meaningful way, yet there are no tools provided by the market operator to help the public interpret these files. This means that energy data in the NEM12 format is inherently opaque for the consumer; further, it means that developers of new energy systems (which may not have the expansive IT infrastructure of their retail competitors) must invest heavily in custom data processing software simply to be able to bill their customers. Anecdotal evidence has suggested that these overheads can cost solar developers significant sums in setup and metering costs, as well as lost revenues from inaccurate file conversion (and hence miscalculated bills).

From a market design perspective, if distributed energy resources are to be integrated into operational decision-making in restructured electricity markets, a stable, trusted and interrogable data format is required so more organisations can observe or participate in the market. Additionally, the emergence of real-time energy metering may require a rethink of how energy is sent and received between participants. In computing terms, these protocols are generally referred to as APIs (application programming interfaces) - broadly, languages and protocols that are used to send messages between smart meters, cloud infrastructure, market participants and consumers.

Data retrieval services have historically been designed by a mixture of hardware and software developers, as well as regulators and operators (such as AEMO in the Australian context), using diverse languages and designs, which may have different security, frequency and formatting characteristics. This means that enforcement of security, reliability and data quality is incredibly difficult across existing meters and platforms. All is not lost however, as the rollout of smart metering infrastructure is still in its infancy in many parts of Australia and the rest of the world. We believe that a regulator-enforced, set of clear standards for the transmission of energy data from energy meters to cloud infrastructure would enable adequate security and clarity as the proportion of internet-connected meters grows.

The impetus for such standards becomes clearer when we examine the coming wave of controllable, dispatchable energy resources such as batteries. Without a standardised language with which these devices can communicate, control of a large proportion of the electricity network may fall to a cloistered, privately controlled and relatively small subset of stakeholders, namely the manufacturers of popular distributed energy resource devices. It appears reasonable to ask that devices connected to a national electricity network be required to allow regulators or operators access to ensure stability of supply; such access would require the development of a set of standardised formats for these different stakeholders to share worthwhile data to enable new community enterprises to flourish and wrest power from the incumbents.

Recommendations

- Maintain appropriate privacy in the context of existing information and power asymmetries with a view to opening up a more communal notion of personhood upon which trustworthy data sharing may occur.

- Learn from other successful delegated authorities in other countries: make consumers aware of benefits of good governance. For example, in Nepal there are representative committees at community level that can make decisions on behalf of others.

- Some communities of modellers be granted delegated authority to access fine-grain energy data. Good energy data requires an appropriate interface between energy users, regulators and power providers.

We underscore

- The importance of creating a process for communities to access data and enable studies based on energy use data.

- That good data is embedded in good governance. Community energy projects need to build their authority to make decisions.

- The need for ongoing dialogue about how and where data is used. Analysis can discover new valuable insights that may require consent to be re-evaluated - one form isn't enough!

- Researchers have responsibility to act in the public interest when using public funds or public data and be mindful of data security and anonymity, and the importance of allowing broad access to their algorithms, data, assumptions and findings.

Conclusions

The operators and regulators of an increasingly complex energy system have a duty to the public interest, which requires them to be transparent about their decision-making process. This means clearly stating their assumptions, allowing access to their data, and opening up their models for testing and scrutiny. Similarly, researchers and academics, often working with public money, must champion open modelling, share their data generously and communicate their findings broadly to break open the struggle between neoliberal rationality on one hand and individual privacy on the other.

Our recommendations may not seem radical. However, energy debates have been shaped by a range of political constraints: the opacity of market design decisions, slow speed of rule changes, an increasing political disconnect between voter opinion and administrative decision-making in electricity market design, and especially the polarised nature of policy debates about the suitable role for Australian institutions in addressing climate change mitigation obligations.

Political advocacy aimed at challenging these various constraints remains a profound challenge. Traditional political advocacy focused on building coalitions, writing letters, protesting and so forth remains vital to reforming energy politics, but it has also proved entirely insufficient. Political advocacy can be complemented with what Donald MacKenzie has termed 'technopolitics': an attention to details of policy designs that may be highly consequential to the efficacy or otherwise of political interventions such as climate change policies.[32]

Climate change debates demonstrate that simply sharing evidence is insufficient to swaying political opinion. A growing body of Science and Technology Studies literature shows, instead, that evidence-making is situated in peculiar contexts according to the issues considered and audience. Evidence is contextual,[33] and this is consequential to how distinctions between technology and politics are drawn, how and why coalitions around energy policies succeed or fail to affect political power structures. Our energy data manifesto should be read in this context – a call for a new energy society.

References

AEMC. 'Final Rule Determination: National Electricity Amendment (Customer access to information about their energy consumption)', 2014.

AEMC. 'National Electricity Amendment (Register of distributed energy resources) Rule', 2018.

AEMO. Power System Data Communication Standard, 2018.

AEMO. 'Integrated System Plan', 2018.

AEMO. 'Visibility of Distributed Energy Resources', 2017.

Björnmalm, Mattias, Matthew Faria and Frank Caruso. 'Increasing the Impact of Materials in and beyond Bio-Nano Science' *Journal of the American Chemical Society* 138.41 (2016): 13449-13456. DOI:10.1021/jacs.6b08673.

Callon, Michel and Fabian Muniesa. 'Peripheral vision: Economic markets as calculative collective devices', *Organization studies* 26.8 (2005):1229-1250.

CSIRO. 'Energy Use Data Model (EUDM)', 2015, https://research.csiro.au/distributed-systems-security/projects/energy-data-use-model/.

Green Button Alliance. 'Green Button Data', 2015, http://www.greenbuttondata.org/.

---

32   Donald MacKenzie, 'Constructing Carbon Markets: Learning from Experiments in the Technopolitics of Emissions Trading Schemes', in A. Lakoff (ed.), *Disaster and the Politics of Intervention*, New York: Columbia University Press, 2010, pp. 130-149.
33   Catherine Trundle, 'Biopolitical endpoints: Diagnosing a deserving British nuclear test veteran.' *Social Science & Medicine* 73.6 (2011): 882-888.

International Energy Agency. 'Digitization and Energy', 2017 http://www.iea.org/publications/freepublications/publication/DigitalizationandEnergy3.pdf.

Islam, S. N., M. A. Mahmud and A.M.T. Oo. 'Impact of optimal false data injection attacks on local energy trading in a residential microgrid.' *ICT Express*, 4.1 (2018): 30-34, DOI: http://doi:10.1016/j.icte.2018.01.015.

Kuch, Declan and Bronwen Morgan. 'Dissonant Justifications: an organisational perspective of support for Australian community energy', *People Place and Policy* 9 (2015): 177-218.

Lew, Debra, Mark Asano, Jens Boemer, Colton Ching, Ulrich Focken, Richard Hydzik, Mathias Lange and Amber Motley. 'The Power of Small - The Effects of Distributed Energy Resources on System Reliability', *IEEE Power & Energy Magazine*. 15 (2017): 50-60.

Lockstep Consulting. 'Privacy Impact Assessment Report Advanced Metering Infrastructure (AMI)', Dept of Primary Industries, 2011.

MacGill, Iain, and Stephen Healy. 'Is electricity industry reform the right answer to the wrong question? Lessons from Australian restructuring and climate policy.', in Fereidoon P. Sioshansi (ed.), *Evolution of Global Electricity Markets*, Cambridge MA: Academic Press, 2013, pp. 615-644.

MacGill, Iain, and Robert Smith. 'Consumers or prosumers, customers or competitors?-Some Australian perspectives on possible energy users of the future.' *Economics of Energy & Environmental Policy* 6.1 (2017).

MacKenzie, Donald. 'Constructing Carbon Markets: Learning from Experiments in the Technopolitics of Emissions Trading Schemes', in A. Lakoff (ed.), *Disaster and the Politics of Intervention*, New York: Columbia University Press, 2010, pp. 130-149.

Owen, Richard, Phil Macnaghten and Jack Stilgoe. 'Responsible research and innovation: From science in society to science for society, with society'. *Science and public policy*, 39.6 (2012): 751-760.

Passey, Rob, Navid Haghdadi, Anna Bruce and Iain MacGill. 'Designing more cost reflective electricity network tariffs with demand charges', *Energy Policy*, 109 (2017): 642-649.

Rhodes, T., K. Lancaster, M. Harris, M and C. Treloar. 'Evidence-making controversies: the case of hepatitis C treatment and the promise of viral elimination.' *Critical Public Health* (2018): 1-14.

Scottish and Southern Electricity Networks (SSEN). 'SSEN and Open Utility partner to trial revolutionary smart grid platform', 2018,http://news.ssen.co.uk/news/all-articles/2018/april/ssen-open-utility-smart-grid-platform/.

Shove, Elizabeth. 'Beyond the ABC: climate change policy and theories of social change' *Environment and planning A*, 42.6 (2010): 1273-1285.

Simpson, G. 'Network operators and the transition to decentralised electricity: An Australian socio-technical case study.' *Energy Policy*, 110 (2017): 422-433.

Stringer, Naomi, Anna Bruce and Iain MacGill. 'Data driven exploration of voltage conditions in the Low Voltage network for sites with distributed solar PV', paper presented at the *Asia Pacific Solar Research Conference*, Melbourne, Australia, 2017.

Trundle, Catherine. 'Biopolitical endpoints: Diagnosing a deserving British nuclear test veteran.' *Social Science & Medicine* 73.6 (2011): 882-888.

Wilkenfeld, George. 'Cutting greenhouse emissions-what would we do if we really meant it?', *Australian Review of Public Affairs*, 2007, http://www.australianreview.net/digest/2007/08/wilkenfeld.html.

Wilkenfeld, George and Peter Spearritt. 'Electrifying Sydney', Sydney: EnergyAustralia, 2004.

THEME 2:
GOOD DATA AND JUSTICE

6: TRADE-OFFS IN ALGORITHMIC RISK ASSESSMENT: AN AUSTRALIAN DOMESTIC VIOLENCE CASE STUDY

DANIEL MCNAMARA, TIMOTHY GRAHAM, ELLEN BROAD AND CHENG SOON ONG

Introduction

Actuarial methods have been part of criminal law and its enforcement in jurisdictions around the world for nearly a century.[1] These methods employ probability theory to shape risk management tools designed to help humans make decisions about who to search, what geographical areas to police, eligibility for bail, eligibility for parole, the length of a criminal sentence and the kind of prison a convicted offender should be incarcerated in.[2] The criminal justice system can be said to have been employing algorithms and crunching 'big' data for decision-making long before these words became part of the popular lexicon surrounding automated decisions.

These days, a range of commercial and government providers are developing software that embed actuarial methods in code, using machine learning methods on large bodies of data and marketed under the umbrella of 'artificial intelligence' (AI).[3] While the effects of using these kinds of probabilistic methods in criminal justice contexts - such as higher incarceration rates among certain racial groups and distorted future predictions - have been critiqued by legal and social science scholars for several years,[4] they have only recently become issues for the computer scientists and engineers developing these software solutions.

In-depth investigations of commercial criminal recidivism algorithms, like the COMPAS software developed by US-based company Equivant (formerly known as Northpointe), have become flash points in discussions of bias and prejudice in AI.[5] Within the computer science community, developing quantitative methods to potentially reduce bias and build fairer, more transparent decision-making systems is an increasingly important research area.[6] This chapter trials one quantitative approach to 'fairness', designed to reduce bias in the outputs of a pre-existing case study predicting domestic violence recidivism in the Australian context.

---

1   Bernard Harcourt, *Against Prediction: Profiling, Policing and Punishing in an Actuarial Age*, Chicago: University of Chicago Press, 2006.
2   Ibid.
3   Richard Berk, *Criminal Justice Forecasts of Risk: A Machine Learning Approach*, Cham: Springer, 2012.
4   Marnie Rice and Grant Harris, 'Violent Recidivism: Assessing Predictive Validity', *Journal of Consulting and Clinical Psychology* 63 (1995).
5   Julia Angwin et al, 'Machine Bias', *ProPublica* (2016), https://www.propublica.org/article/machine-bias-risk-assessments-in-criminal-sentencing.
6   Arvind Nayaranan, 'Tutorial: 21 Fairness Definitions and their Politics', *Conference on Fairness, Accountability and Transparency* 2018, https://www.youtube.com/watch?v=jIXIuYdnyyk.

There is no one authoritative definition of fairness,[7] in computer science or in any other discipline. 'Fairness' as a word carries significant cultural heritage.[8] John Rawls' famed 'veil of ignorance' proposes an approach to fairness akin to an impartial observer, who does not know what status they will have in society and how the definition of fairness is agreed on.[9] Other scholars have noted this abstract approach of fairness, when put into practice, does not reduce perceptions of unfair outcomes.[10] Previous explorations of varied definitions of fairness in disciplines as diverse as philosophy, law, neuroscience and information theory have concluded there is no single foundation on which to rest for the purposes of fair algorithms.[11]

To paraphrase the science fiction author Margaret Atwood: 'Fair never means fairer for everyone. It always means worse, for some'.[12] This chapter does not assert its approach to fairness as the 'right' one. What is 'fair' is not a technical consideration, but a moral one.[13] We are interested in the insights that quantitative methods for fairness give human decision makers, allowing us to make explicit certain implicit trade-offs that have long been part of how humans make decisions. Efforts to quantify what is 'fair' allow us to measure the impact of these trade-offs.

Used effectively in a criminal justice context, these methods could help human decision makers make more transparent, informed decisions about a person's likelihood of recidivism. But they also speak to enduring challenges unpicking and rectifying bias in actuarial methods (and the AI systems that absorb these methods). Whatever definition of 'fairness' is employed, there are real world consequences. The impact of varying trade-offs in 'fair' decision-making on victims and offenders should be handled with great caution in a domestic violence context.

6.1 Algorithmic Risk Assessment in an Australian Domestic Violence Context

In a 2016 paper, Australian researchers Robin Fitzgerald and Timothy Graham evaluated the potential of using existing administrative data drawn from the NSW Bureau of Crime Statistics and Research (BOCSAR) Re-offending Database (ROD) to predict domestic violence-related recidivism.[14] Being able to reliably and accurately assess which offenders, in which contexts, are likely to recommit domestic violence is a priority for law enforcement, victim support services and, of course, for victims themselves.

---

7   Shira Mitchell and Jackie Shadlen, 'Mirror Mirror: Reflections on Quantitative Fairness' (2018), https://speak-statistics-to-power.github.io/fairness/.
8   Anna Wierzbicka, *English: Meaning and Culture*, Oxford: Oxford University Press, 2006.
9   John Rawls, *A Theory of Justice*, Cambridge MA: Harvard University Press, 1971.
10 Stefan Trautmann and Gijs van de Kuilen, 'Process Fairness, Outcome Fairness, and Dynamic Consistency: Experimental Evidence for Risk and Ambiguity', *Journal of Risk and Uncertainty* 53 (2016).
11 Aditya Menon and Robert Williamson, 'The Cost of Fairness in Binary Classification', *Conference on Fairness, Accountability and Transparency* 2018.
12 Margaret Atwood, *The Handmaid's Tale*, Toronto: McClelland and Stewart, 1985.
13 Nayaranan, 'Tutorial: 21 Fairness Definitions and their Politics'.
14 Robin Fitzgerald and Timothy Graham, 'Assessing the Risk of Domestic Violence Recidivism', *Crime and Justice Bulletin* 189 (2016); NSW Bureau of Crime Statistics and Research, *Re-offending Statistics for NSW*, 2018.

Domestic violence (DV), also referred to as family violence or domestic abuse, is defined as a pattern of violence, intimidation or abuse between individuals in a current or former intimate relationship. A World Health Organization study found that within each of dozens of studies conducted around the world, between 10% and 69% of women reported having experienced physical abuse by an intimate partner, and between 5% and 52% reported having experienced sexual violence by an intimate partner.[15]

In Australia, one in six women and one in twenty men have experienced at least one instance of domestic violence since the age of 15.[16] On average, police in Australia respond to a domestic violence matter every two minutes.[17] These statistics emphasize the scale and the gendered nature of this issue. Indeed, aggregate prevalence rates further highlight the negative impact of DV and family violence more broadly. DV is one of the top ten risk factors contributing to disease burden among adult women,[18] and the economic costs of violence against women and children in Australia (including both domestic and non-domestic violence) are estimated at around $13.6 billion per year.[19] Existing statistics and surveys suggest that Indigenous communities face domestic violence issues at much greater rates than the rest of the population.[20]

6.1.1 The Evolution of Algorithmic Risk Assessments

Actuarial methods and probability theory have been employed to help humans make decisions in a criminal justice context for many years.[21] It is only recently that they have been embedded in software.[22] While these longstanding methods could be said to be 'algorithmic' in nature,[23] taking a rule-based approach to predictions - for the purposes of this chapter we use the term 'algorithmic risk assessment' to refer to the more recent automated, software-driven systems.

---

15 Etienne Krug et al, 'The World Report on Violence and Health', World Health Organization (2002).
16 Australian Bureau of Statistics, *Personal Safety Survey 2016* (2017); Peta Cox, 'Violence Against Women in Australia: Additional Analysis of the Australian Bureau of Statistics' Personal Safety Survey', Horizons Research Report, Australia's National Research Organisation for Women's Safety (2012).
17 Clare Bulmer. 'Australian Police Deal with a Domestic Violence Matter Every Two Minutes', *ABC News*, 5 June 2015, http://www.abc.net.au/news/2015-05-29/domestic-violence-data/6503734.
18 Australian Institute of Health and Welfare and Australia's National Research Organisation for Women's Safety, 'Examination of the Health Outcomes of Intimate Partner Violence against Women: State of Knowledge Paper' (2016); Australian Institute of Health and Welfare, 'Family, Domestic and Sexual Violence in Australia', (2018).
19 Department of Social Services. 'The Cost of Violence against Women and their Children', Report of the National Council to Reduce Violence against Women and their Children (2009).
20 In NSW in 2016, 2.9% of the population were Indigenous (Australian Bureau of Statistics, *Census 2016*, 2017) while 65% of victims of family and domestic violence overall were Indigenous (Australian Bureau of Statistics, *Recorded Crime - Victims, Australia 2016*, 2017).
21 Harcourt, *Against Prediction: Profiling, Policing and Punishing in an Actuarial Age*.
22 Sarah Desmarais and Jay Singh, 'Risk Assessment Instruments Validated and Implemented in Correctional Settings in the United States' (2013).
23 Informally, an algorithm is simply a series of steps or operations undertaken to solve a problem or produce a particular outcome/output. For instance, in a rudimentary way a cake recipe can be thought of as an algorithm that, if the steps are followed precisely, produces a cake.

An example is the Public Safety Assessment,[24] which is used in the US states of Kentucky, Arizona and New Jersey and several other US counties.[25]

Algorithmic risk assessment systems have several potential advantages. They offer a mechanism to improve the accuracy of decisions made in the criminal justice system.[26] They are readily scalable, offering greater consistency than human judgment.[27] They offer increased transparency of decisions, if the system's code, methodology and input data are accessible.[28] And they often have adjustable parameters (as in this work), which render trade-offs explicit in decision-making and allow them to be managed.

However, investigations of existing algorithmic risk assessment systems have demonstrated that these systems can - by choice - also be shrouded in secrecy, unnecessarily complex and reinforce existing bias.[29] It has been shown that COMPAS - which used over a hundred variables for predictions - performs no better than a logistic regression classifier using age and total number of previous convictions.[30] A controversial recent example of a risk assessment system in the Australian context is the Suspect Targeting Management Plan (STMP).[31] In the cases of both COMPAS and STMP, concerns have been raised that the systems are unfair, in the former case towards African-Americans and in the latter case towards Indigenous Australians.[32]

6.1.2 Predicting Domestic Violence Recidivism using Administrative Data

A primary aim of any recidivism prediction is accuracy. That is, to accurately identify which offenders are most likely to recommit a crime and subsequently: (1) adjust their access to bail or parole, or period of incarceration accordingly; and (2) understand the risk factors associated with recidivism in order to better target resources and programs aimed at crime prevention. But what is considered an 'accurate' prediction is complicated by risk-based, profiling approaches to policing that inevitably see certain populations overrepresented in data about past offenders, which is then used for making future predictions. Is a prediction

---

24 Laura and John Arnold Foundation, 'Public Safety Assessment: Risk Factors and Formula', 2017, https://www.arnoldfoundation.org/wp-content/uploads/PSA-Risk-Factors-and-Formula.pdf.
25 Laura and John Arnold Foundation, 'Public Safety Assessment Frequently Asked Questions', https://www.psapretrial.org/about/faqs.
26 For example, a recent study using data from more than 750,000 pre-trial release decisions made by New York City judges found that, at the same jailing rate as human judges, an algorithm could reduce crime by 14.4-24.7%. Alternatively, without any increase in crime, an algorithm could reduce jail rates by 18.5-41.9%. Jon Kleinberg et al, 'Human Decisions and Machine Predictions', *The Quarterly Journal of Economics* 133.1 (2017).
27 Ibid.
28 Jiaming Zeng, Berk Ustun and Cynthia Rudin, 'Interpretable Classification Models for Recidivism Prediction', *Journal of the Royal Statistical Society: Series A (Statistics in Society)* 180.3 (2017).
29 Angwin et al, 'Machine Bias'.
30 Julia Dressel and Hany Farid. 'The Accuracy, Fairness, and Limits of Predicting Recidivism', *Science Advances* 4.1 (2018).
31 NSW Police Force, 'NSW Police Force Corporate Plan 2016-18' (2016).
32 Angwin et al, 'Machine Bias'; Vicki Sentas and Camilla Pandolfini, 'Policing Young People in NSW: A Study of the Suspect Targeting Management Plan', Youth Justice Coalition (2017).

based on this past data 'fair'? Answering this question depends on identifying and managing the trade-offs involved in the design of recidivism assessments.

Although domestic violence (DV) is a serious problem in Australia, to date there has been relatively little research on the risks associated with family violence and DV recidivism in the Australian context.[33] Recidivism in this paper refers to reoffending following conviction for an offence. Broadly speaking, a 'recidivist' or 'reoffender' is an individual who is a repeat or chronic offender. In the context of DV recidivism, national and state-based agencies have begun to develop and implement computerized decision support systems (DSS) and risk assessment tools that draw on standardized data (within and/or across agencies) to help understand the risk of DV recidivism for sub-groups within the population. There is increasing interest in evidence-based crime and social welfare governance that draw on data science and big data, perhaps due to a perception that these kinds of DSS and risk assessment tools are more efficient, objective and less costly than existing approaches.[34]

To be sure, the point of these DSS and risk assessment tools is to enhance, refine and better target programs and resources to prevent DV, rather than simply punishment and control. While computer-based DSS have been criticized in, for example, child welfare and protection,[35] recent studies suggest that DV-related risk assessment tools can be effective, particularly to assist under-resourced front-line agencies to make informed and speedy decisions about detention, bail and victim assistance.[36] A standard practice is to measure the accuracy of risk assessment tools using Receiver Operating Characteristic (ROC) curve analysis,[37] known as Area Under the Curve (AUC), and predictive risk assessment tools for DV recidivism have been shown to provide reasonably high levels of predictive performance, with AUC scores in the high 0.6 to low 0.7 range.[38]

---

33 Hayley Boxall, Lisa Rosevear, and Jason Payne, 'Identifying First Time Family Violence Perpetrators: The Usefulness and Utility of Categorisations Based on Police Offence Records', *Trends and Issues in Crime and Criminal Justice* 487 (2015); Fitzgerald and Graham, 'Assessing the Risk of Domestic Violence Recidivism'.
34 Philip Gillingham and Timothy Graham, 'Big Data in Social Welfare: The Development of a Critical Perspective on Social Work's Latest Electronic Turn', *Australian Social Work* 70.2 (2017).
35 Philip Gillingham, 'Risk Assessment in Child Protection: Problem Rather than Solution?', *Australian Social Work* 59.1 (2006).
36 Ron Mason and Roberta Julian, 'Analysis of the Tasmania Police Risk Assessment Screening Tool (RAST), Final Report', Tasmanian Institute of Law Enforcement Studies, University of Tasmania (2009); Jill Theresa Messing et al, 'The Lethality Screen: the Predictive Validity of an Intimate Partner Violence Risk Assessment for Use by First Responders', *Journal of Interpersonal Violence* 32.2 (2017).
37 Tom Fawcett, 'ROC Graphs: Notes and Practical Considerations for Researchers', HP Laboratories (2004).
38 Marnie Rice, Grant Harris and Zoe Hilton, 'The Violence Risk Appraisal Guide and Sex Offender Risk Appraisal Guide for Violence Risk Assessment', in Randy K Otto and Kevin S Douglas (eds), *Handbook of Violence Risk Assessment,* London: Routledge, 2010. AUC can be interpreted as the probability that a randomly selected reoffender will receive a higher risk score than a randomly selected non-reoffender. A random guess has expected AUC of 0.5 while the perfect prediction has AUC of 1.

6.1.3 Findings from Previous Studies

Fitzgerald and Graham applied statistical methods to existing administrative data on NSW offenders who had committed domestic violence, to examine the kinds of factors - for example, socioeconomic status, history of past offences, Indigenous or non-Indigenous status - which were predictive of future domestic violence offences.[39] They used logistic regression to examine the future risk of violent DV offending among a cohort of individuals convicted of any DV offence (regardless of whether it is violent or not) over a specific time period. They found that applying their models to unseen data achieved AUC of 0:69, indicating a reasonable level of predictive accuracy, on par with other risk assessment tools in other countries and contexts. A follow-up study explored using a decision tree induction approach on the same dataset.[40] Although these results show the potential for such models to be deployed to enhance targeted programs and resources for DV prevention, Fitzgerald and Graham also highlighted a significant problem that has yet to be addressed: in short, the authors found that their model was racially biased.

Fitzgerald and Graham argued that whilst DSS that incorporate logistic regression might offer a satisfactory tool for predicting the risk of domestic violence recidivism in the overall population, the efficacy is reduced for making predictions for particular sub-groups, particularly for individuals who identify as Indigenous. Indigenous status showed relatively large discrepancies in the test sample between the averages of the observed and predicted rates of violent DV reconviction. Indeed, Indigenous individuals were more than twice as likely to be predicted as reoffenders (29.4%) by the model compared to the observed rate (13.7%), whereas non-Indigenous individuals were less than half as likely to be predicted as reoffenders (2.3%) compared to the observed rate (6.1%).[41]

In other words, when it came to predicting DV recidivism for the Indigenous sub-group, Fitzgerald and Graham found that the model was biased on two fronts: over-predicting Indigenous reoffenders and under-predicting non-Indigenous reoffenders. If deployed as a risk assessment tool, this model could have serious negative consequences that may reinforce existing inequalities that have resulted from historical and contemporary injustices and oppression of Indigenous Australians.

The output of the model not only reflects but also potentially amplifies and reinforces these inequalities. Indeed, the fact that Indigenous status (as an independent variable) appears at all in the dataset brings to light the politics of data collection and statistical forms of reasoning. The data provided through the BOCSAR ROD, and subsequently used in the study by Fitzgerald and Graham, reflects a 'practical politics' that involves negotiating and deciding what to

---

39 Fitzgerald and Graham, 'Assessing the Risk of Domestic Violence Recidivism'.
40 Senuri Wijenayake, Timothy Graham and Peter Christen. 'A Decision Tree Approach to Predicting Recidivism in Domestic Violence', *arXiv* (2018).
41 Looking at the entire population the predicted (7.4%) and observed (7.6%) recidivism rates are relatively well-aligned. The large differences between predicted and observed recidivism rates only become visible looking separately at the Indigenous and non-Indigenous cohorts.

render visible (and invisible) in an information system context.[42] This example shows that the issue of fairness in algorithmic decision-making is of utmost importance as we move towards computerized risk assessment tools in criminal justice and social welfare. At the same time, caution needs to be taken in how such fairness is defined and achieved.

6.2 Designing Fair Algorithmic Risk Assessments

The impact of an algorithmic risk assessment is determined by both its design and the context in which it is used. This context - which includes human judgment, policy settings and broader social trends - will remain an important determinant of outcomes in the justice system and elsewhere. No algorithm can rectify all of the past and present structural disadvantage faced by a particular social group. However, algorithmic risk assessments influence human decisions, which in turn determine the extent to which structural disadvantage is entrenched. Hence, algorithm design can play a part in making an overall system fairer - or indeed in reinforcing the unfairness of a system. Considerable research is underway to incorporate fairness into the design of algorithmic systems. This approach requires clear definitions of fairness, and modifications to algorithm design to accommodate these definitions.

6.2.1 Quantitative Definitions of Fairness

While defining fairness is a topic as old as human society, the advent of algorithmic predictions has necessitated the quantification of these definitions. We must be precise about what we mean if we are to embed fairness in computer code - a definition that seems simplistic or reductionist is still preferable to none at all. Therefore we necessarily consider a narrow subset of the possible meanings of 'fairness'. Quantitative definitions often describe fairness as avoiding discrimination on the basis of a particular kind of group membership, such as race or gender. Three types of definition have emerged, which we state informally:[43]

- **Parity**: Predictions should be similar for different groups

- **Independence**: Predictions should be independent of group membership

- **Causality**: Predictions should not be caused by group membership.

While each of these approaches has its advantages, our analysis focuses on definitions based on parity. A predictive model that achieves parity between groups is mathematically equivalent to one that is independent of group membership. However, (dis)parity may be measured on a continuous scale, unlike an all-or-nothing statement about independence. Unlike causality-based definitions,[44] parity measures can be computed using only an algo-

---

42 Geoffrey Bowker and Susan Star, 'How Things (Actor-Net)Work: Classification, Magic and the Ubiquity of Standards', *Philosophia* 25.3 (1996).
43 For further details, see Mitchell and Shadlen, 'Mirror Mirror: Reflections on Quantitative Fairness'.
44 Matt Kusner et al, 'Counterfactual Fairness', *Advances in Neural Information Processing Systems* (2017).

rithm's outputs without the knowledge of its functional form, so that external auditing can be carried out without the co-operation of the algorithm's owner. Parity measures also do not require the selection of variables that are permitted to cause decisions (known as resolving variables),[45] which potentially could include proxies for group membership (e.g. 'redlining' where neighborhood is used a proxy for race). Finally, parity-based measures are arguably the simplest to understand for a lay audience, which is significant given the risk of excluding participants from non-quantitative backgrounds in debates about fairness.[46]

An important design choice is selecting a subset of the population to which these definitions are applied. We then ask for fair predictions - according to whichever definition we choose - only within this subset, and permit differences in predictions between subsets. For example, in the recidivism context we might consider all individuals, or only those who reoffended, or only those who did not reoffend. If the subset consists of individuals who are similar according to some metric, we have a definition known in the quantitative fairness literature as individual fairness.[47]

Several mathematical results have shown that, for a particular set of fairness definitions, it is impossible for a predictive model to simultaneously satisfy all definitions in the set.[48] The COMPAS controversy showed this in practice: while ProPublica's critique identified unfairness according to particular definitions,[49] COMPAS owner Equivant/Northpointe used different definitions to argue that the algorithm was not unfair.[50] Within a particular context, different definitions are aligned to the interests of particular stakeholders.[51] Furthermore, when predictions are also measured on their accuracy, the definitions of accuracy and fairness are in general not aligned.[52]

---

45 Niki Kilbertus et al. 'Avoiding Discrimination through Causal Reasoning', *Advances in Neural Information Processing Systems* (2017).
46 Mitchell and Shadlen, 'Mirror Mirror: Reflections on Quantitative Fairness'.
47 Cynthia Dwork et al, 'Fairness Through Awareness', *Innovations in Theoretical Computer Science Conference* 2012; Mitchell and Shadlen, 'Mirror Mirror: Reflections on Quantitative Fairness'.
48 Alexandra Chouldechova, 'Fair Prediction with Disparate Impact: A Study of Bias in Recidivism Prediction Instruments', *Big Data* 5.2 (2017); Jon Kleinberg, Sendhil Mullainathan and Manish Raghavan, 'Inherent Trade-offs in the Fair Determination of Risk Scores', *arXiv* (2016); Zachary Lipton, Alexandra Chouldechova and Julian McAuley, 'Does Mitigating ML's Impact Disparity Require Treatment Disparity?', *arXiv* (2017); Geoff Pleiss et al, 'On Fairness and Calibration', *Advances in Neural Information Processing Systems* (2017).
49 Angwin et al, 'Machine Bias'.
50 William Dieterich, Christina Mendoza and Tim Brennan, 'COMPAS Risk Scales: Demonstrating Accuracy Equity and Predictive Parity', Northpointe Inc. (2016); Anthony Flores, Kristin Bechtel and Christopher Lowenkamp. 'False Positives, False Negatives, and False Analyses: A Rejoinder to Machine Bias', *Federal Probation* 80 (2016).
51 Nayaranan, 'Tutorial: 21 Fairness Definitions and their Politics'.
52 Sam Corbett-Davies et al, 'Algorithmic Decision Making and the Cost of Fairness', *International Conference on Knowledge Discovery and Data Mining* 2017; Menon and Williamson, 'The Cost of Fairness in Binary Classification'; Sam Corbett-Davies and Sharad Goel, 'The Measure and Mismeasure of Fairness: A Critical Review of Fair Machine Learning', *arXiv* (2018).

6.2.2 Defining Fairness in the Australian DV Recidivism Context

Parity-based definitions may be used to assess the fairness of a recidivism risk assessment model which generates a probability that an individual will reoffend. Given the issues associated with the context of DV in Australia, parity between Indigenous and non-Indigenous populations in the criminal justice system is of special interest. Consider the difference between Indigenous and non-Indigenous populations for each of the following:

- **Predicted reoffence rate:** the average probability of reoffence predicted by the model.

- **Predicted reoffence rate for non-reoffenders**: the average probability of reoffence predicted by the model, for those individuals who were not observed to reoffend.

- **Predicted reoffence rate for reoffenders:** the average probability of reoffence predicted by the model, for those individuals who were observed to reoffend.

Parity between groups of predicted reoffence rates among non-reoffenders is referred to as equality of opportunity in the quantitative fairness literature.[53] If we also have parity of predicted reoffence rates among reoffenders, this is referred to as equalized odds (also known as avoiding disparate mistreatment).[54] Enforcing these parity measures between Indigenous and non-Indigenous populations has some intuitive appeal, since it ensures that disagreements between the algorithm's predictions and the subsequently observed data do not disproportionately impact one racial group. However, these measures are sensitive to the way in which the reoffence data was collected. Profiling of particular populations, based on pre-existing risk assessments, can distort trends in reoffending. A feedback loop may be created, where this reoffence data in turn influences future risk assessments.[55]

Overall parity between groups of predicted reoffence rate is referred to in the quantitative fair-ness literature as statistical parity or avoiding disparate impact.[56] We may not want overall parity of predicted reoffence rate if the observed rates of reoffence for Indigenous and non-Indigenous populations are different. However, overall parity has the advantage that it does not depend on the way that reoffence data was collected, which may systematically disadvantage one group.[57] Furthermore, an actual difference in reoffence rates between groups may be the result of a complex historical process. In the case of Indigenous Australians this includes founding violence, structural violence, cultural breakdown, intergenerational trauma,

---

53 Moritz Hardt, Eric Price and Nati Srebro, 'Equality of Opportunity in Supervised Learning', *Advances in Neural Information Processing Systems* (2016).
54 Ibid; Muhammad Bilal Zafar et al, 'Fairness Beyond Disparate Treatment & Disparate Impact: Learning Classification Without Disparate Mistreatment', *International Conference on World Wide Web* 2017.
55 Cathy O'Neil, *Weapons of Math Destruction: How Big Data Increases Inequality and Threatens Democracy*, New York: Broadway Books, 2017.
56 Dwork et al, 'Fairness Through Awareness'; Zafar et al, 'Fairness Beyond Disparate Treatment & Disparate Impact: Learning Classification Without Disparate Mistreatment'.
57 Solon Barocas and Andrew Selbst, 'Big Data's Disparate Impact', *California Law Review* 104 (2016).

disempowerment, and alcohol and drugs.[58] Legal decision-makers may wish to intervene in this process by reducing the discrepancy between incarceration rates for Indigenous and non-Indigenous populations.[59] To support this intervention, it may be appropriate for the design of a risk assessment system to incorporate greater parity in predicted reoffence rates. By contrast, other fairness definitions may be used to justify and perpetuate current rates of Indigenous incarceration.

A risk assessment model should also be accurate, subject to the previous caveat that reoffence data is likely to be imperfect and is possibly biased. While the AUC accuracy measure does not consider fairness with respect to group membership, it is related to fairness insofar as it measures the extent to which reoffenders are assessed as higher risk than non-reoffenders.

6.2.3 Techniques for Algorithmic Fairness

Recent work on quantitative fairness has, in addition to proposing fairness definitions, developed techniques to incorporate fairness into algorithm design.[60] One framework for organizing these fairness techniques divides them into three categories:

- **Pre-processing:** modify the data that the algorithm learns from;[61]

- **In-processing:** modify the algorithm itself;[62]

- **Post-processing:** modify the predictions produced by the algorithm.[63]

Pre-processing, the approach which we use in our analysis, has the advantage that it creates a *separation of concerns* between the data producer who controls the pre-processing and the data user who controls the algorithm. This means that fairness is guaranteed for any use of the pre-processed data, even if the data user is an *adversary* (i.e. they are deliberately unfair).[64] This has the potential to make regulation more practical to enforce.

Several pre-processing approaches have been proposed. To describe these, it is useful viewing a dataset as a sample from a probability distribution. The distribution jointly depends on a sensitive variable S, encoding an individual's group membership (e.g. their race), an input variable X, encoding other characteristics of the individual (e.g. their past criminal record), and

---

58 The Healing Foundation and White Ribbon Australia, 'Towards an Aboriginal and Torres Strait Islander Violence Prevention Framework for Men and Boys' (2017).
59 As of 2017, the incarceration rate of Australia's Aboriginal and Torres Strait Islander population stood at 2434 per 100,000 people, versus 160 per 100,000 people for the non-Indigenous population. Australian Bureau of Statistics, *Prisoners in Australia 2017*, 2017.
60 For a review of this work in the context of recidivism prediction, see Richard Berk et al, 'Fairness in Criminal Justice Risk Assessments: the State of the Art', *arXiv* (2017).
61
62 See e.g. Menon and Williamson, 'The Cost of Fairness in Binary Classification'.
63 See e.g. Hardt, Price and Srebro, 'Equality of Opportunity in Supervised Learning'.
64 Daniel McNamara, Cheng Soon Ong and Bob Williamson, 'Provably Fair Representations', *arXiv* (2017).

a target variable Y, encoding something we wish to predict (e.g. whether or not the individual reoffended). The ultimate objective is to predict the target variable Y using the input variable X.

The result of the pre-processing is to produce a sample of a cleaned variable Z, which is a modification of X that no longer contains information that can be used to infer S. This cleaned data can be used as an input to any subsequent algorithm instead of the original input data. In the following section we will use the concrete example of race as the sensitive variable S, past criminal record as the input variable X, reoffence as the target variable Y, and a cleaned version of past criminal record as Z. However, it is worth remembering that the approach works in general for other sets of variables.

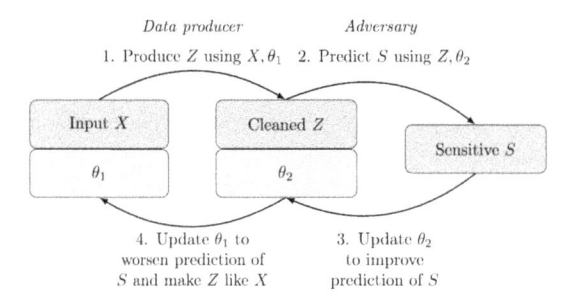

Figure 1: Learning fair representations with an adversary. In the text we use the example of X=criminal record, Z=the cleaned version of the criminal record, S=race, Y=whether the person reoffended. 1 and 2 are parameters of the learning algorithm.

One approach to pre-processing is to design the cleaned variable (Z) such that the distributions of Z conditioned on different values of race (S) are similar.[65] In addition to this requirement, the pre-processing procedure may optimize the independence of the cleaned variable (Z) and race (S).[66] Another pre-processing approach is to design the cleaned variable (Z) such that it is maximally informative about reoffence (Y), subject to a constraint that it is uninformative about race (S).[67]

6.2.4 *Learning Fair Representations* with an Adversary

We adopt a pre-processing approach,[68] which involves learning a cleaned variable (Z) such

---

65   Michael Feldman et al, 'Certifying and Removing Disparate Impact', *International Conference on Knowledge Discovery and Data Mining* 2015; James Johndrow and Kristian Lum, 'An Algorithm for Removing Sensitive Information: Application to Race-Independent Recidivism Prediction', *arXiv* (2017).
66   Christos Louizos et al, 'The Variational Fair Autoencoder', *International Conference on Learning Representations* 2016.
67   AmirEmad Ghassami, Sajad Khodadadian, and Negar Kiyavash, 'Fairness in Supervised Learning: An Information Theoretic Approach', *arXiv* (2018).
68   This approach was proposed in Harrison Edwards and Amos Storkey, 'Censoring Representations with an Adversary', *International Conference on Learning Representations* 2016.

that an adversary is unable to predict race (S) from it, while also trying to make the cleaned variable similar to the original input (X). In our case we assume that the data producer does not have access to whether the person has reoffended (Y),[69] which simplifies the learning algorithm and means that it is not affected by any bias in the way that reoffence data is collected. We refer to this approach as *learning fair representations with an adversary*, since the pre-processing step can be seen as a modification to the representation of the data provided to the algorithm.

We introduce a parameter λ (lambda), a non-negative constant (once set, its value stays the same), to control the trade-off between the two objectives involved in the construction of the cleaned variable (Z). When λ is large, the algorithm focuses more on making the adversary unable to predict race (S). When λ approaches zero, the algorithm focuses more on making the original records and cleaned records similar. The algorithm does not provide any guidance as to how to select λ. Rather, this depends on a decision about the relative importance assigned to fairness and accuracy in the design of the algorithmic risk assessment. Such a decision is a social, political and regulatory one - the algorithm simply provides an implementation for whatever decision is made.

The learning steps of the algorithm are summarized in Figure 1.[70] The data producer learns a neural network parameterized by weights θ_1, which produces cleaned records from input records. The adversary learns a neural network parameterized by weights θ_2, which predicts race from the cleaned records. Four steps are repeated for each batch of examples from the training data:

Feature	Description
Offender demographic characteristics	
Gender	Whether the offender was recorded in ROD as male or female.
Age	The age category of the offender at the court appearance, derived from the date of birth of the offender and the date of finalization for the court appearance.
Indigenous status	Recorded in ROD as 'Indigenous' if the offender had ever identified as being of Aboriginal or Torres Strait Islander descent, otherwise 'non-Indigenous'.

---

69 As in McNamara, Ong, and Williamson, 'Provably Fair Representations'.
70 See McNamara, Ong and Williamson for further details. We also considered a variant of the adversary training objective proposed in David Madras et al, 'Learning Adversarially Fair and Transferable Representations', *arXiv* (2018), but found it did not substantively change the results.

Disadvantaged areas index Quartile	Measures disadvantage of an offender's residential postcode at the time of the offence. Based on the Socio-Economic Index for Areas (SEIFA) score produced by the Australian Bureau of Statistics.
Conviction characteristics	
Concurrent offences	Number of concurrent proven offences, including the principal offence, at the offender's court appearance.
AVO breaches	Number of proven breaches of Apprehended Violence Order (AVO) at the court appearance.
Criminal history characteristics	
Prior juvenile or adult convictions	Number of Youth Justice Conferences or finalized court appearances with any proven offences as a juvenile or adult prior to the court appearance.
Prior serious violent offence conviction past 5 years	Number of Youth Justice Conferences or finalized court appearances in the 5 years prior with any proven homicide or serious assault.
Prior DV-related property damage offence conviction past 2 years	Number of Youth Justice Conferences or finalized court appearances in the 2 years prior with any proven DV-related property damage offence.
Prior bonds past 5 years	Number of finalized court appearances in the 5 years prior at which given a bond.
Prior prison or custodial order	Number of previous finalized court appearances at which given a full-time prison sentence or custodial order.

Table 1: Independent features in the BOCSAR dataset.

1. On receiving examples of X, the data producer passes them through a neural network with weights θ_1 to produce examples of Z

2. On receiving examples of Z, the adversary passes them through a neural network with weights θ_2 to predict the values of S

3. By comparing the true values of S to its predictions for these examples, the adversary updates θ_2 to improve its prediction of S in the future

4. By comparing the true values of S to the adversary's predictions for these examples, the data producer updates θ_1 to worsen the adversary's prediction of S in the future while

also trying make *Z* similar to *X*. The trade-off between these two objectives is governed by the parameter λ.

Once learning is complete, for each individual the data producer passes their input record through a neural network with weights θ_1. This cleaned record is then provided to the data user, who uses it to make a prediction about whether the individual will reoffend.

6.3 Predicting DV Recidivism with the BOCSAR Dataset

We apply learning fair representations with an adversary to the prediction of DV recidivism in Australia with the BOCSAR ROD used in the study by Fitzgerald and Graham.[71] As a result, we achieve improved fairness compared to Fitzgerald and Graham's study on several measures. However, this case study also highlights the inevitable trade-offs involved. Our proposed approach allows us to reduce the disadvantage faced by Indigenous defendants incurred by using the original input data, but at the cost of predictive accuracy.

6.3.1 BOCSAR Dataset Experiments

The BOCSAR ROD contains 14776 examples and 11 categorical and ordinal input features for each example, as shown in Table 1. The input features are grouped to represent the offender, offence, and criminal history related characteristics of the offenders.

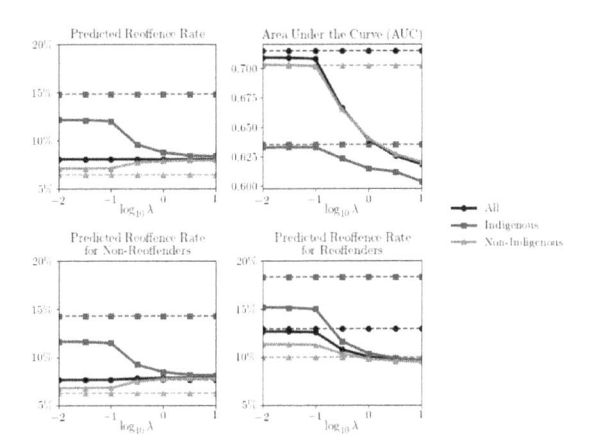

Figure 2: Results of applying pre-processing to the BOCSAR dataset, followed by logistic regression, to predict DV reoffences. Baselines using logistic regression without pre-processing are shown as dashed lines. The y-axes show several fairness and accuracy measures of interest on the test data. The x-axes show the parameter λ used in pre-processing on a logarithmic scale.

The target variable is whether or not an individual re-committed a DV related offence within a

---

71 Fitzgerald and Graham, 'Assessing the Risk of Domestic Violence Recidivism'.

duration of 24 months since the first court appearance finalization date. DV related offences include any physical, verbal, emotional, and/or psychological violence or intimidation between domestic partners. We use a random 50% sample for training and the remaining 50% for testing, as in some experiments in Fitzgerald and Graham.

Our baseline experiments use the original data, including the Indigenous status variable. We also tested the pre-processing method described in Section 6.2.4 for several values of the parameter λ. We predicted recidivism from the data - the original data in the baseline experiments and the pre-processed data in the other experiments - using logistic regression as in Fitzgerald and Graham's study, which predicts the probability of reoffence for each individual. We applied the definitions of fairness and accuracy presented in Section 6.2.2, as shown in Figure 2. We computed each of these metrics for all individuals, for Indigenous individuals and for non-Indigenous individuals.

6.3.2 Discussion of the BOCSAR Dataset Results

We discuss our results by comparing the performance of the baseline method with our proposed pre-processing method. Using the original data, there are significant differences in the average predicted reoffence rates for Indigenous and non-Indigenous individuals. These predicted rates are closely related to the observed rates in the test set: for Indigenous 14.9% predicted vs 14.6% observed, and for non-Indigenous 6.4% predicted vs 6.5% observed. Our baseline does not display the severe overestimation of Indigenous reoffence observed in the Fitzgerald and Graham's model. Furthermore, the baseline test set AUC is 0.71 (slightly superior to the 0.69 previously reported by Fitzgerald and Graham), indicating that the model has some predictive accuracy.

However, there are still several potential issues with the baseline:

- variations in the way that reoffence data is collected among Indigenous and non-Indigenous populations may influence and be reinforced by predictions made by the model;

- among observed non-reoffenders the average predicted reoffence rate is 14.3% for Indigenous vs 6.2% for non-Indigenous populations, indicating that non-reoffending Indigenous individuals are rated more than twice as risky as a non-reoffending non-Indigenous individuals;

- among observed reoffenders, the average predicted reoffence rate is 18.3% for Indigenous vs 10.0% for non-Indigenous populations, indicating that reoffending non-Indigenous individuals are rated only just over half as risky as a reoffending Indigenous individuals;[72]

---

72 It can be shown mathematically that if predicted reoffence rates are equal to observed reoffence rates for both Indigenous and non-Indigenous populations, and that the observed Indigenous and non-Indigenous reoffence rates are different from each other, and that the model is not perfectly accurate, then the predicted reoffence rate for non-reoffenders is different between Indigenous and

- from a process perspective, it may be viewed as unfair that a person's Indigenous status is considered by the model.

Removing the Indigenous status column in the data is a possible step towards remediating these issues. It would address the final concern around fair process. However, our results show that the first three concerns stand even without the presence of this column. The solid lines on the left-hand side of the plots, where λ approaches zero and the data is effectively left untouched except for the exclusion of the Indigenous status column, indicate that while the discrepancies between the Indigenous and non-Indigenous populations are not as acute as in the baseline case, they are still very much present. Information contained in the other columns still results in different outcomes for Indigenous and non-Indigenous populations, a phenomenon known as *redundant encoding*.[73]

Applying pre-processing with increasing values of λ, the above issues are addressed:

- the predicted reoffence rate for non-reoffenders is more similar for Indigenous and non-Indigenous populations (for $\lambda = 10$, 8.1% for Indigenous vs 7.8% for non-Indigenous);

- the predicted reoffence rate for reoffenders is more similar for Indigenous and non-Indigenous populations (for $\lambda = 10$, 9.7% for Indigenous vs 9.5% for non-Indigenous);

- the predicted reoffence rate overall is more similar for Indigenous and non-Indigenous populations (for $\lambda = 10$, 8.3% for Indigenous vs 7.9% for non-Indigenous).

There is a cost to pre-processing in terms of accurately predicting reoffence. The AUC drops to 0.62, so that the predictions are less accurate than the baseline (AUC 0.71), while still significantly more accurate than a random prediction (AUC 0.5).[74] Overall predicted reoffence rates for non-reoffenders are higher compared to the baseline: 7.9% for $\lambda = 10$ vs 7.6% for the baseline, a 10.2% increase. Overall predicted reoffence rates for reoffenders are lower compared to the baseline: 9.6% for $\lambda = 10$ vs 12.9% for the baseline, a 26.0% decrease. This reduced accuracy is not surprising as the pre-processing removes information from the dataset. The decrease in predicted reoffence rates for reoffenders caused by the pre-processing is undesirable from the perspective of potential victims of domestic violence. Furthermore, this decrease is greater for Indigenous individuals, whose potential victims are more likely to also be Indigenous.

---

non-Indigenous populations and/or the predicted reoffence rate for reoffenders is different between Indigenous and non-Indigenous populations.

73   Dwork et al, 'Fairness Through Awareness'.
74   It can be shown mathematically that given equal Indigenous and non-Indigenous predicted reoffence rates among reoffenders, among non-reoffenders and overall, the predicted reoffence rates for reoffenders and non-reoffenders must be equal (assuming that the observed Indigenous and non-Indigenous reoffence rates are unequal).

In summary, our approach improved on several measures of fairness compared to Fitzgerald and Graham's study. The naive approach of learning from the original input data results in a prediction that indicates that the average risk associated with Indigenous individuals is more than twice that of their non-Indigenous counterparts, even among non-reoffenders - while for a value of $\lambda = 10$ these risks are comparable. As discussed previously, this could not have been achieved simply by removing the Indigenous status column from the data. However, achieving comparable risks comes at the cost of overall predictive accuracy (AUC 0.71 to AUC 0.62). It is worth repeating that our approach does not prescribe a particular value of the trade-off parameter λ, but rather provides a quantitative tool to estimate the effect of this trade-off. We discuss further implications of fairness trade-offs in our conclusion.

6.4 Conclusion: Trade-offs in Algorithmic Risk Assessment

The Australian DV case study shows that without incorporating an explicit fairness criterion into algorithm design, individuals from one racial group may be marked higher risk than another, even when considering only reoffenders or only non-reoffenders. This is still true when race is simply dropped from the input data: blindness is not enough. Incorporating a fairness criterion - such as via data pre-processing - yields more equal predicted reoffence rates for different racial groups: among reoffenders, among non-reoffenders and overall.

The case study also reveals an important trade-off involved in the design of algorithmic risk assessments. From the perspective of Indigenous defendants who in the baseline scenario were considered higher risk than non-Indigenous defendants, both among reoffenders and among non-reoffenders, this pre-processing makes the system fairer. The flipside is that non-Indigenous non-reoffenders are judged to be more risky. And all reoffenders - particularly Indigenous reoffenders - are judged to be less risky, which is not in the interests of potential victims.

The trade-off between the interests of different stakeholders is equally a part of human decision-making in the criminal justice system. The advantage of our approach is making this trade-off explicit and precisely controllable through a model parameter, which may be set according to whatever weighting is deemed appropriate by society. The approach we propose - involving an explicit trade-off between certain quantitative definitions of accuracy and fairness - also applies to other contexts where prediction algorithms are used to support decisions about individuals such as the provision of credit or insurance, and to other demographic groups besides racial groups.

There is a second trade-off involved here: between explicit and implicit explanations for decisions. Transparency allows individuals to better understand the social systems - including the criminal justice system - that make decisions about their lives. However, when the rationale for these decisions is laid bare, they may be less palatable than when they are opaque. Algorithms - with their stark rules implemented in code - have the effect of illuminating the myriad forms of inclusion and exclusion that invisibly form our social fabric. Perhaps the more profound trade-off is determining to what extent we are willing to shine that light.

References

Angwin, Julia, Jeff Larson, Surya Mattu and Lauren Kirchner, 'Machine Bias', *ProPublica* (2016), https://www.propublica.org/article/machine-bias-risk-assessments-in-criminal-sentencing.

Atwood, Margaret. *The Handmaid's Tale*, Toronto: McClelland and Stewart, 1985.

Australian Bureau of Statistics. *Census 2016*, 2017.

_____. *Personal Safety Survey 2016*, 2017.

_____. *Prisoners in Australia 2017*, 2017.

_____. *Recorded Crime - Victims, Australia 2016*, 2017.

Australian Institute of Health and Welfare. 'Family, Domestic and Sexual Violence in Australia', 2018.

Australian Institute of Health and Welfare and Australia's National Research Organisation for Women's Safety. 'Examination of the Health Outcomes of Intimate Partner Violence against Women: State of Knowledge Paper', 2016.

Barocas, Solon and Andrew Selbst. 'Big Data's Disparate Impact', *California Law Review* 104 (2016).

Berk, Richard. *Criminal Justice Forecasts of Risk: A Machine Learning Approach*, Cham: Springer, 2012.

Berk, Richard, Hoda Heidari, Shahin Jabbari, Michael Kearns and Aaron Roth. 'Fairness in Criminal Justice Risk Assessments: the State of the Art', *arXiv* (2017).

Bowker, Geoffrey and Susan Star. 'How Things (Actor-Net)Work: Classification, Magic and the Ubiquity of Standards', *Philosophia* 25.3 (1996).

Boxall, Hayley, Lisa Rosevear and Jason Payne. 'Identifying First Time Family Violence Perpetrators: The Usefulness and Utility of Categorisations Based on Police Offence Records'. *Trends and Issues in Crime and Criminal Justice* 487 (2015).

Bulmer, Clare. 'Australian Police Deal with a Domestic Violence Matter Every Two Minutes', *ABC News*, 5 June 2015, http://www.abc.net.au/news/2015-05-29/domestic-violence-data/6503734.

Chouldechova, Alexandra. 'Fair Prediction with Disparate Impact: A Study of Bias in Recidivism Prediction Instruments', *Big Data* 5.2 (2017).

Corbett-Davies, Sam and Sharad Goel. 'The Measure and Mismeasure of Fairness: A Critical Review of Fair Machine Learning', arXiv (2018).

Corbett-Davies, Sam, Emma Pierson, Avi Feller, Sharad Goel and Aziz Huq. 'Algorithmic Decision Making and the Cost of Fairness', *International Conference on Knowledge Discovery and Data Mining*, 2017.

Cox, Peta. 'Violence Against Women in Australia: Additional Analysis of the Australian Bureau of Statistics' Personal Safety Survey', Horizons Research Report, Australia's National Research Organisation for Women's Safety (2012).

Department of Social Services. 'The Cost of Violence against Women and their Children', Report of the National Council to Reduce Violence against Women and their Children (2009).

Desmarais, Sarah and Jay Singh. 'Risk Assessment Instruments Validated and Implemented in Correctional Settings in the United States' (2013).

Dieterich, William, Christina Mendoza, and Tim Brennan. 'COMPAS Risk Scales: Demonstrating Accuracy Equity and Predictive Parity', Northpointe Inc. (2016).

Dressel, Julia and Hany Farid. 'The Accuracy, Fairness, and Limits of Predicting Recidivism', *Science Advances* 4.1 (2018).

Dwork, Cynthia, Moritz Hardt, Toniann Pitassi, Omer Reingold and Richard Zemel. 'Fairness Through Awareness', *Innovations in Theoretical Computer Science Conference* 2012.

Edwards, Harrison and Amos Storkey. 'Censoring Representations with an Adversary', *International Conference on Learning Representations* 2016.

Fawcett Tom. 'ROC Graphs: Notes and Practical Considerations for Researchers', HP Laboratories (2004).

Feldman, Michael, Sorelle Friedler, John Moeller, Carlos Scheidegger and Suresh Venkatasubramanian. 'Certifying and Removing Disparate Impact', *International Conference on Knowledge Discovery and Data Mining* (2015).

Fitzgerald, Robin and Timothy Graham. 'Assessing the Risk of Domestic Violence Recidivism', *Crime and Justice Bulletin* 189 (2016).

Flores, Anthony, Kristin Bechtel, and Christopher Lowenkamp. 'False Positives, False Negatives, and False Analyses: A Rejoinder to Machine Bias', *Federal Probation* 80 (2016).

Ghassami, AmirEmad, Sajad Khodadadian, and Negar Kiyavash. 'Fairness in Supervised Learning: An Information Theoretic Approach', *arXiv* (2018).

Gillingham, Philip. 'Risk Assessment in Child Protection: Problem Rather than Solution?', *Australian Social Work* 59.1 (2006).

Gillingham, Philip and Timothy Graham. 'Big Data in Social Welfare: The Development of a Critical Perspective on Social Work's Latest Electronic Turn', *Australian Social Work* 70.2 (2017).

Harcourt, Bernard. *Against Prediction: Profiling, Policing and Punishing in an Actuarial Age*, Chicago: University of Chicago Press, 2006.

Hardt, Moritz, Eric Price, and Nati Srebro. 'Equality of Opportunity in Supervised Learning', *Advances in Neural Information Processing* Systems (2016).

Johndrow, James and Kristian Lum. 'An Algorithm for Removing Sensitive Information: Application to Race-Independent Recidivism Prediction', *arXiv* (2017).

Kilbertus, Niki, Mateo Rojas Carulla, Giambattista Parascandolo, Moritz Hardt, Dominik Janzing and Bernhard Schölkopf. 'Avoiding Discrimination through Causal Reasoning', *Advances in Neural Information Processing* Systems (2017).

Kleinberg, Jon, Sendhil Mullainathan, and Manish Raghavan. 'Inherent Trade-offs in the Fair Determination of Risk Scores', *arXiv* (2016).

Kleinberg, Jon, Himabindu Lakkaraju, Jure Leskovec, Jens Ludwig and Sendhil Mullainathan. 'Human Decisions and Machine Predictions', *The Quarterly Journal of Economics* 133.1 (2017).

Krug, Etienne, Linda Dahlberg, James Mercy, Anthony Zwi, and Rafael Lozano. 'The World Report on Violence and Health', World Health Organization (2002).

Kusner, Matt, Joshua Loftus, Chris Russell and Ricardo Silva. 'Counterfactual Fairness', *Advances in Neural Information Processing Systems* (2017).

Laura and John Arnold Foundation. 'Public Safety Assessment Frequently Asked Questions', https://www.psapretrial.org/about/faqs.

_____. 'Public Safety Assessment: Risk Factors and Formula', 2017, https://www.arnoldfoundation.org/wp-content/uploads/PSA-Risk-Factors-and-Formula.pdf.

Lipton, Zachary, Alexandra Chouldechova, and Julian McAuley. 'Does Mitigating ML's Impact Disparity Require Treatment Disparity?', *arXiv* (2017).

Louizos, Christos, Kevin Swersky, Yujia Li, Richard Zemel and Max Welling. 'The Variational Fair Autoencoder', *International Conference on Learning Representations* 2016.

Madras, David, Elliot Creager, Toniann Pitassi and Richard Zemel. 'Learning Adversarially Fair and Transferable Representations', *arXiv* (2018).

Mason, Ron and Roberta Julian. 'Analysis of the Tasmania Police Risk Assessment Screening Tool (RAST), Final Report', Tasmanian Institute of Law Enforcement Studies, University of Tasmania (2009).

McNamara, Daniel, Cheng Soon Ong and Bob Williamson. 'Provably Fair Representations', *arXiv* (2017).

Menon, Aditya and Robert Williamson. 'The Cost of Fairness in Binary Classification', *Conference on Fairness, Accountability and Transparency* (2018).

Messing, Jill Theresa, Jacquelyn Campbell, Janet Sullivan Wilson, Sheryll Brown and Beverly Patchell. 'The Lethality Screen: the Predictive Validity of an Intimate Partner Violence Risk Assessment for Use by First Responders', *Journal of Interpersonal Violence* 32.2 (2017).

Mitchell, Shira and Jackie Shadlen. 'Mirror: Reflections on Quantitative Fairness' (2018). https://speak-statistics-to-power.github.io/fairness/.

Nayaranan, Arvind. 'Tutorial: 21 Fairness Definitions and their Politics', *Conference on Fairness, Accountability and Transparency*, 2018, https://www.youtube.com/watch?v=jIXluYdnyyk.

NSW Bureau of Crime Statistics and Research, *Re-offending Statistics for NSW*, 2018.

NSW Police Force. 'NSW Police Force Corporate Plan 2016-18' (2016).

O'Neil, Cathy. *Weapons of Math Destruction: How Big Data Increases Inequality and Threatens Democracy*. New York: Broadway Books, 2017.

Pleiss, Geoff, Manish Raghavan, Felix Wu, Jon Kleinberg and Kilian Weinberger. 'On Fairness and Calibration', *Advances in Neural Information Processing Systems* (2017).

Rawls, John. *A Theory of Justice*, Cambridge MA: Harvard University Press, 1971.

Rice, Marnie, Grant Harris and Zoe Hilton. 'The Violence Risk Appraisal Guide and Sex Offender Risk Appraisal Guide for Violence Risk Assessment', in Randy K Otto and Kevin S Douglas (eds), *Handbook of Violence Risk Assessment*, London: Routledge, 2010.

Rice, Marnie and Harris, Grant. 'Violent Recidivism: Assessing Predictive Validity', *Journal of Consulting and Clinical Psychology* 63 (1995).

Sentas, Vicki and Camilla Pandolfini. 'Policing Young People in NSW: A Study of the Suspect Targeting Management Plan', Youth Justice Coalition (2017).

The Healing Foundation and White Ribbon Australia. 'Towards an Aboriginal and Torres Strait Islander Violence Prevention Framework for Men and Boys' (2017).

Trautmann, Stefan and Gijs van de Kuilen. 'Process Fairness, Outcome Fairness, and Dynamic Consistency: Experimental Evidence for Risk and Ambiguity', *Journal of Risk and Uncertainty* 53 (2016).

Wierzbicka, Anna. *English: Meaning and Culture*, Oxford: Oxford University Press, 2006.

Wijenayake, Senuri, Timothy Graham, and Peter Christen. 'A Decision Tree Approach to Predicting Recidivism in Domestic Violence', *arXiv* (2018).

Zafar, Muhammad Bilal, Isabel Valera, Manuel Gomez Rodriguez and Krishna Gummadi. 'Fairness Beyond Disparate Treatment & Disparate Impact: Learning Classification Without Disparate Mistreatment', *International Conference on World Wide Web* 2017.

Zemel, Rich, Yu Wu, Kevin Swersky, Toni Pitassi and Cynthia Dwork. 'Learning Fair Representations', *International Conference on Machine Learning* (2013).

Zeng, Jiaming, Berk Ustun and Cynthia Rudin. 'Interpretable Classification Models for Recidivism Prediction', *Journal of the Royal Statistical Society: Series A (Statistics in Society)* 180.3 (2017).

7: UNLAWFUL DATA ACCESS AND ABUSE OF METADATA FOR MASS PERSECUTION OF DISSIDENTS IN TURKEY: THE BYLOCK CASE

A. SEFA OZALP

Introduction

This chapter presents a critical case study of unlawful metadata access and retroactive criminalization of encryption to persecute perceived dissidents by focusing on ByLock prosecutions in Turkey. Although ByLock was a public and free encrypted mobile chat application, the Turkish government argues that ByLock was exclusively used by the members of the Gulen Movement (GM), which the Turkish government accuses of organizing the failed coup attempt against President Erdogan in 2016. Under post-coup measures, tens of thousands of alleged ByLock users have been arrested under GM probe and handed down heavy prison sentences on terrorism charges. This chapter aims to highlight the threat of 'bad data' practices, such as criminalization of encryption, unlawful data access and abuse of communications metadata to persecute perceived dissidents, by unpicking the Turkish state's claims and the evidence presented to courts by the Turkish state during the ByLock trials. By doing so, this chapter contributes to current metadata retention and lawful access debate by detailing material effects of metadata exploitation for political purposes by government authorities. This chapter contends that lessons learned from the ByLock case illustrate how critical 'Good Data' principles and the integrity of encrypted and secure communication channels are for democracies.

Digital communication technologies (DCTs) have altered the way we generate, share and receive information. For the most part, DCTs have made public and private communications faster, cheaper, and easier. Although these advancements have been beneficial for people in general, DCTs have introduced new threats to privacy and information security. As the Snowden leaks revealed, DCT infrastructures have enabled state actors to access 'bulk' digital communications data and increased the surveillance capabilities of state actors exponentially.[1] Dissidents, minority populations and activists have been disproportionally affected by the increased digital surveillance efforts of state actors.[2]

In the age of DCTs, many fundamental rights essential for a 'Good Democracy' - such as the freedom of expression, the freedom of political thought, the freedom of religion, the freedom of association, and the right to privacy - are dependent on having strong information security. Freedom of expression is defined as the 'freedom to hold opinions and to receive and impart

---

1 Lina Dencik, Arne Hintz, and Jonathan Cable, 'Towards Data Justice? The Ambiguity of Anti-Surveillance Resistance in Political Activism,' *Big Data & Society* 3.2 (2016), DOI: https://doi.org/10.1177/f2053951716679678.
2 G Greenwald and R Gallagher, 'Snowden Documents Reveal Covert Surveillance and Pressure Tactics Aimed at WikiLeaks and Its Supporters' *The Intercept,* 2014, https://theintercept.com/2014/02/18/snowden-docs-reveal-covert-surveillance-and-pressure-tactics-aimed-at-wikileaks-and-its-supporters/.

information and ideas without interference by public authority and regardless of frontiers' in the Charter of Fundamental Rights of the European Union (CFR).[3] In order to have a 'Good Democracy', activists, dissidents, or people in general need to be able to communicate securely to enjoy the freedom 'to receive and impart information without interference by public authority'.[4] Therefore, 'Good Data' and counter-surveillance practices such as online anonymity and encryption tools are integral to having a 'Good Democracy'. Since encryption is an essential tool to secure DCTs from state surveillance, encrypted and secure communication platforms frequently come under the attack by states, citing national security concerns.[5] These attacks constitute 'bad data' practices because they involve attempts to pass backdoor legislation, unlawfully spying on dissidents, activists and NGOs such as Privacy International,[6] and the use of unlawfully acquired or manipulated (meta)data to prosecute and/or persecute government critics.

To illustrate the oppressive potentials of 'bad data' practices, I introduce a case study of mass persecution of perceived government critics over their alleged usage of an encrypted communication application called ByLock in Turkey. ByLock was a free and public chat application which was downloaded more than 500,000 times from the App Store and Google Play Store between April 2014 and March 2016,[7] when it was deactivated when its developers stopped paying for the servers hosting the app.[8] Turkish Intelligence Agency (in Turkish Millî İstihbarat Teşkilatı, henceforth MIT) claimed that ByLock was a secret communication tool for Gulen Movement (henceforth GM) members - a social movement that the Turkish government holds responsible for the failed coup against Erdogan in 2016. In the aftermath of the coup attempt, the Turkish government accused any individual with perceived links to GM of being 'terrorists' and started an unprecedented purge. Shortly after the coup attempt, Turkish media reported that the MIT had hacked ByLock's servers in Lithuania, in an attempt to uncover ByLock users, perceived to be Gulenists.[9] MIT further claimed that they had identified thousands of ByLock users via metadata provided by Internet Service Providers (ISPs) and Mobile Network Operators (MNOs). Although the number of individuals ensnared under the ByLock investigation has not been officially released, Freedom House reported that 'Tens of thousands of Turkish citizens have been arbitrarily detained for their alleged use of the encrypted communications app ByLock'.[10] Mass arrests based on alleged ByLock usage have attracted severe criticism outside Turkey. The UN Human Rights Council called ByLock prosecutions a 'criminalization

---

3   European Union, 'Charter of Fundamental Rights of the European Union,' 2012, 391-407, https://doi.org/10.1108/03090550310770974.
4   Ibid.
5   David Lyon, *Surveillance After Snowden*, Cambridge: Polity Press, 2015.
6   Privacy International, 'Press Release: UK Intelligence Agency Admits Unlawfully Spying on Privacy International | Privacy International,' 2018, https://privacyinternational.org/press-release/2283/press-release-uk-intelligence-agency-admits-unlawfully-spying-privacy.
7   Fox-IT, 'Expert Witness Report on ByLock Investigation', Delft, 2017, https://foxitsecurity.files.wordpress.com/2017/09/bylock-fox-it-expert-witness-report-english.pdf.
8   Yasir Gokce, 'The Bylock Fallacy: An In-Depth Analysis of the Bylock Investigations in Turkey,' *Digital Investigation* (March, 2018): 2, https://doi.org/10.1016/j.diin.2018.06.002.
9   Freedom House, 'Freedom on the Net 2017 Report,' 2017, 15, https://freedomhouse.org/sites/default/files/FOTN 2017_Turkey.pdf.
10 Ibid, 14.

of encryption', noting that the 'evidence presented [by Turkish authorities] is often ambiguous'.[11] Amnesty International (AI) criticized ByLock prosecutions by stating that 'possession of internationally available and widely downloaded application does not represent a criminal offence' and the 'Turkish Government's methods for identifying users are seriously flawed in general'.[12] Similarly, Privacy International condemned the ByLock prosecutions and called for the immediate release of those arrested solely for using ByLock.[13]

Drawing on Cohen's moral panic theory,[14] I conduct a critical analysis of the post-coup measures taken by the Turkish regime, especially focusing on evidence cited in ByLock prosecutions. I conclude that the abuse of metadata to punish political enemies is not necessarily limited to authoritarian governments such as Turkey, as metadata are retained globally. By doing so, I present a cautionary case study from Turkey, detailing material effects of metadata exploitation for political purposes by government authorities, which digital activists and scholars around the world can draw on in the metadata retention and lawful access debates.[15] I argue that the abuse of metadata and unscrupulous law-enforcement powers can be easily justified in 'moral panics' when 'a condition, episode, person or group of persons emerges to become defined as a threat to societal values and interests'.[16] I further argue that, supranational human rights legislation may be ineffective to prevent state surveillance, privacy breaches and metadata abuse. Finally, I contend that lessons learned from the ByLock case illustrate the importance of the 'Good Data' practices and the integrity of DCTs for 'good democracy'.

Digital Communication Technologies, Metadata and State Access

Before the emergence of DCTs, mass communication and public information campaigns were conducted through pre-digital information sharing mechanisms (ISMs) such as print media, radio, and television. Because of the nation-state-led developments in the technological infrastructure they relied on, pre-digital ISMs were relatively easier to influence for states and the powerful.[17] With the emergence of the internet and the DCTs, some scholars and

---

11 UN Human Rights Council, 'Report of the Special Rapporteur on the Promotion and Protection of the Right to Freedom of Opinion and Expression on His Mission to Turkey' (A/HRC/35/22/Add.3, 2017), 14, http://www.refworld.org/docid/59394c904.html.
12 Amnesty International, 'BRIEFING: Prosecution Of 11 Human Rights Defenders,' 2017, 7, https://www.amnesty.org/download/Documents/EUR4473292017ENGLISH.pdf.
13 Privacy International, 'Encryption At The Centre Of Mass Arrests : One Year On From Turkey's Failed Coup,' Privacy International, 2017, https://medium.com/@privacyint/encryption-at-the-centre-of-mass-arrests-one-year-on-from-turkeys-failed-coup-e6ecd0ef77c9.
14 Stanley Cohen, *Folk Devils and Moral Panics: The Creation of the Mods and Rockers*, third edition, London/New York: Routledge, 2002.
15 Amory Starr et al, 'The Impacts of State Surveillance on Political Assembly and Association: A Socio-Legal Analysis', *Qualitative Sociology* 31.3 (2008): 251-70, DOI: https://doi.org/10.1007/s11133-008-9107-z. ; Lisa M. Austin, 'Lawful Illegality: What Snowden Has Taught Us About the Legal Infrastructure of the Surveillance State,' *SSRN* (2014), DOI: https://doi.org/10.2139/ssrn.2524653.
16 Cohen, *Folk Devils and Moral Panics: The Creation of the Mods and Rockers*, 282:1.
17 Hannu Nieminen, 'Digital Divide and beyond: What Do We Know of Information and Communications Technology's Long-Term Social Effects? Some Uncomfortable Questions', *European Journal of Communication* 31.1 (2016): 19-32, DOI: https://doi.org/10.1177/0267323115614198.

activists argued that these new media provided an opportunity to overcome some of the above challenges. One of the primary arguments brought forward was that the internet provided a decentralized infrastructure that allowed active participation of individuals online, which, in turn had the potential to disturb the pre-digital ISMs.[18] When equipped with 'Good Data' principles, DCTs provided a window of opportunity for activists and dissidents to revolutionize public and private communications. For instance, during the Arab Spring protests, online social media networks served as 'a common medium for professional journalism and citizen journalism, and as a site of global information flow' which, allowed activists to overcome state blackout and 'facilitating the revolutions'.[19] The revolutionary aspect of DCTs led some to believe - perhaps naively - that DCTs could provide users with an opportunity to become anonymous and protected from intrusive state surveillance. Current political, legal, and academic debates, however, illustrates that this is not the case.

One of the primary debates around DCTs concerns the retention of metadata and risks to user privacy.[20] In the context of DCTs, metadata are information about communications that users leave behind while using DCTs. For instance, while contents of the visited webpages are data, IP access logs and timestamps stored by ISPs are metadata. All user activities on DCTs, such as phone conversations, search queries, emails, website visits, ad-clicks, social media activities, and peer-to-peer messages, generate metadata which can be logged and stored automatically. Riley called this perennial form of large scale (meta)data collection 'dataveillance'.[21] Metadata can be aggregated, analyzed and sold to third parties. Using metadata, users can be profiled based on their political leanings, ethnic background, and sexual orientation. Inferences drawn from (meta)data analyses can be used for anti-democratic purposes, such as election meddling, as observed in the Cambridge Analytica case.[22] Metadata expand the surveillance capacities of state actors by revealing personal information such as 'who', 'when', 'what (type of communication)', 'how', 'where' which, in turn, 'can provide very detailed information regarding an individual's beliefs, preferences and behaviour'.[23] In fact, in the *Big Brother Watch vs UK* ruling, the European Court of Human Rights (ECtHR) ruled that 'metadata can be just as intrusive as the interception of content'.[24] Considering nation states are actively trying to exploit DCTs using both legal and illegal means,[25] the ease of access to

---

18 Peter Ferdinand, 'The Internet, Democracy and Democratization', *Democratization* 7.1 (2000): 1-17, DOI: https://doi.org/10.1080/13510340008403642.
19 Gilad Lotan et al, 'The Arab Spring| The Revolutions Were Tweeted: Information Flows during the 2011 Tunisian and Egyptian Revolutions,' *International Journal of Communication* 5 (2011): 1377.
20 Monique Mann et al., 'The Limits of (Digital) Constitutionalism: Exploring the Privacy-Security (Im) Balance in Australia,' *International Communication Gazette* (in press, 2018), DOI: https://doi.org/10.1177/1748048518757141.
21 Rita Raley, 'Dataveilance and Countervailance' in in L Gitelman, *Raw Data' Is an Oxymoron*, Cambridge MA: MIT Press, 2013.
22 CNBC, 'Facebook-Cambridge Analytica: A Timeline of the Data Hijacking Scandal,' 2018, https://www.cnbc.com/2018/04/10/facebook-cambridge-analytica-a-timeline-of-the-data-hijacking-scandal.html.
23 Nora Ni Loideain, 'EU Law and Mass Internet Metadata Surveillance in the Post-Snowden Era,' *Media and Communication* 3.2 (2015): 54, DOI: https://doi.org/10.17645/mac.v3i2.297.
24 M Milanovic, 'ECtHR Judgment in Big Brother Watch v. UK,' EJIL:Talk!, 2018, https://www.ejiltalk.org/ecthr-judgment-in-big-brother-watch-v-uk/.
25 Amnesty International, 'Encryption. A Matter of Human Rights,' 2016, http://www.amnestyusa.org/sites/

metadata can be especially dangerous for political activists, dissident groups and perceived political opponents, who are subject to disproportionate and intrusive state surveillance.[26]

To date, national and supranational legal mechanisms have failed to provide comprehensive privacy protection for individuals. Governments around the world increasingly pass new laws that require metadata retention based on the argument of public security, pre-empting crime and terrorism.[27] Even in the EU context, where mechanisms such as CFR, ECtHR and the Court of Justice of the European Union (CJEU) provide a supranational level of legal protection against human rights breaches,[28] it is hard to talk about sufficient legal protection against government efforts to breach user privacy. For instance, the UK Government passed the Data Retention and Investigatory Powers Act 2014 (DRIPA) which required DCT providers to retain indiscriminate metadata on the grounds of national security and crime prevention. Both the Divisional Court and the Court of Justice of the European Union (CJEU) held that DRIPA was incompatible with EU law.[29] In a subsequent joint case ruling, CJEU found that the mass collection and analysis of metadata would lead to the violation of Article 7 [Respect to private and family life] and Article 8 [Protection of personal data] of the CFR, 'which could be justified only by the objective of fighting serious crime'.[30] Even though privacy organizations and activists welcomed this ruling, the CJEU left it to Member States to define what constitutes serious crime, hence the ability to adjust the balance of privacy versus national security. Indeed, in December 2016, the UK government replaced DRIPA with the Investigatory Powers Act which replicated the problematic elements of the DRIPA i.e. requirement for metadata retention and broad access by government agencies, even on non-crime related grounds.

Moral Panics and the Abuse of Metadata

To understand the true risks of metadata retention, it is beneficial to look at cases where authoritarian regimes exploit communications metadata to target political enemies and to facilitate oppression of dissidents - this is the focus of my analysis. In most cases, oppression faced by dissidents is a perennial process. Historical oppression of Kurds by the Turkish state and successive governments from different political backgrounds is a prime example of the continual oppression observed by dissidents.[31] However, in some cases, new political opponents can become targets. The latter is better observed within moral panics emerging

---

default/files/encryption_-_a_matter_of_human_rights_-_pol_40-3682-2016.pdf.
26 Marcus Michaelsen, 'Exit and Voice in a Digital Age: Iran's Exiled Activists and the Authoritarian State', *Globalizations* 15.2 (2018): 248-64, DOI: https://doi.org/10.1080/14747731.2016.1263078.
27 UN Human Rights Council, 'Report of the Special Rapporteur on the Promotion and Protection of the Right to Freedom of Opinion and Expression, David Kaye,' *Human Rights Council* (A/HRC/29/32: UN Human Rights Council, 2015).
28 The EU General Data Protection Regulation (GDPR) is not included here - despite being the most recent and comprehensive legislation which aims to protect user privacy - since its effectiveness in practice remains to be seen.
29 Isabella Buono and Aaron Taylor, 'Mass Surveillance in the CJEU: Forging a European Consensus', *The Cambridge Law Journal* 76.2 (2017): 250-53, DOI: https://doi.org/doi:10.1017/S0008197317000526.
30 Ibid, 251.
31 William Gourlay, 'Oppression, Solidarity, Resistance: The Forging of Kurdish Identity in Turkey', *Ethnopolitics* 17.2 (2018): 130-46, DOI: https://doi.org/10.1080/17449057.2017.1339425.

in the aftermath of political upheavals.

Goode and Ben-Yehuda's attributional model provides a useful theoretical perspective for understanding moral panics.[32] They propose five defining 'elements of criteria' i.e. *concern, hostility, consensus, disproportion* and *volatility* for moral panics. Authoritarian regimes are adept at constructing and propagating a 'folk devil' narrative to rationalize the persecution of political enemies and dissidents. These oppressive efforts increase when moral panics emege. Folk-devil narratives, constructed by authoritarian regimes, take advantage of widespread public *concerns* 'over the behaviour of a certain group or category'.[33] *Concerns* may be latent in society or be *volatile* i.e. surfacing suddenly following political upheavals. An example of the latter would be socially disruptive incidents, such as terror attacks, which act as 'trigger events',[34] and result in a 'heightened level of concern over the behaviour of a certain group or category.[35] In the aftermath of trigger events, the public becomes susceptible to be influenced by constructed folk devil narratives and 'an increased level of *hostility* towards targeted groups may be observed.[36] Actively propagating 'folk devil' narratives may result in partial or complete *consensus* that 'the threat is real, serious and caused by the wrongdoing group members and their behaviour' across society.[37] Once there is a *consensus* of *hostility* towards the folk devils, *disproportionate* social and official reactions may be observed. Furthermore, disproportionate reactions may become '*routinized* or *institutionalized*', [38] and lead to impulsive and reactionary changes in 'legislation, enforcement practices, informal interpersonal norms or practices for punishing transgressors'.[39] As a result, overreactions can even be more damaging than the original threat for the public.

Correspondingly, abuse of communications metadata to confer criminality upon political enemies and dissidents can be easily justified following trigger events. As UNHRC Special Rapporteur David Kaye warned, 'efforts to restrict encryption and anonymity also tend to be quick reactions to terrorism, even when the attackers themselves are not alleged to have used encryption or anonymity to plan or carry out an attack'.[40] Extra-judicial mass surveillance programs of intelligence agencies, which would have been scrutinized and criticized by the public in normal times,[41] can be introduced in order to identify so-called 'terrorists'. Regimes can abandon established legal procedures and human rights protections such as 'the burden

---

32 Erich Goode and Nachman Ben-Yehuda, *Moral Panics The Social Construction of Deviance*, second edition, Chichester: Wiley-Blackwell, 2009.
33 Ibid, 37.
34 R D King and G M Sutton, 'High Times for Hate Crime: Explaining the Temporal Clustering of Hate Motivated Offending,' *Criminology* 51 (2013), DOI: https://doi.org/10.1111/1745-9125.12022.
35 Goode and Ben-Yehuda, *Moral Panics The Social Construction of Deviance*, 37.
36 Ibid, 38.
37 Ibid.
38 Ibid, 41. Emphasis in original.
39 Ibid.
40 UN Human Rights Council, 'Report of the Special Rapporteur on the Promotion and Protection of the Right to Freedom of Opinion and Expression, David Kaye,' 13.
41 The UNHRC Special Rapporteur highlights that it is critical to have a 'transparent public debate' over privacy restrictions and intrusions. See para 35 of the 'Report of the Special Rapporteur on the Promotion and Protection of the Right to Freedom of Opinion and Expression, David Kaye.'

of proof' or 'right to a fair trial' in pursuit of punishing political enemies. The oppression of dissidents can be facilitated by metadata abuse for political purposes i.e. citing unlawfully accessed or unreliable communications metadata to confer guilt on dissidents. To illustrate the oppressive potentials of such metadata abuse, I will look at the reactions to the coup attempt in Turkey, and the mass ByLock prosecutions in the aftermath.

The Turkish Coup Attempt and the Subsequent Purge

On 15 July 2016, a rogue group in the Turkish military took to the streets to topple President Erdogan. The coup had little chance of success: only a marginally small fraction of the Turkish military was involved,[42] and there was very little public support. While over two hundred soldiers and civilians were killed during the clashes, no government official was apprehended. By the morning, those involved in the coup were arrested and the coup attempt was suppressed. President Erdogan and the ruling Justice and Development Party (henceforth AKP) ministers publicly announced that the coup was organized by the GM, a social and religious movement who were at odds with the AKP at the time.[43] Erdogan personally called the attempt a 'gift from the God (sic)' which would 'allow him to cleanse the army and the state of terrorists [i.e. perceived GM supporters]'.[44] On the other hand, Gulen publicly denied any connection to the coup attempt, and called for an international commission to investigate the attempt; further

---

42 The International Institute for Strategic Studies, 'Turkey: The Attempted Coup and Its Troubling Aftermath,' *Strategic Comments* 22.5 (2016): v-vii, DOI: https://doi.org/10.1080/13567888.2016.1217082.
43 Space precludes a lengthier explanation of the fallout between the GM and AKP, but a short summary is needed to provide context for the reader. Even before the coup attempt, the GM was under heavy state pressure in Turkey. Both AKP and GM are Islam-inspired organisations, but they have categorical differences in interpretation. While the AKP is a political party founded by Erdogan and his allies in 2001 which adheres to nationalism and political Islam, the GM is a civil society organisation founded in Turkey in the late 1960s by the now-US-based Islamic cleric Fethullah Gulen, which prefers a civil interpretation of Islam with an emphasis on education. In terms of supporters, AKP is the largest party in Turkey with half of the popular vote (roughly 23 out of 46 million), the official number of GM sympathisers is unknown but estimates put it around 200,000-300,000. The GM used to run more than 2000 education facilities such as primary schools, high schools, and universities in Turkey, all of which have been confiscated by the AKP government. The GM runs more than a thousand education facilities outside Turkey in more than 100 countries. Despite being on good terms for nearly a decade since the AKP first won plurality in the 2002 legislative elections, the GM and AKP started diverging after 2012 over political disagreements. AKP accused GM of infiltrating state organs and forming a 'parallel state' i.e. having too many influential followers in state positions. The GM dismissed this criticism by arguing this was natural given that it provided good education to pupils in its institutions. When prosecutors in Istanbul opened Turkey's largest corruption investigations to date in late 2013, incriminating an Iranian-Turkish gold trader Reza Zarrab and Erdogan's son along with four cabinet ministers and their sons with credible evidence, Erdogan called the corruption investigation a 'judicial coup' and publicly declared GM as 'public enemy number one'. Media organisations affiliated with the GM ran stories defending the corruption probes and individuals representing GM started criticising AKP government vocally. From this point on, GM started facing a crackdown in Turkey. Just months before July 2016, the GM was declared a terrorist organisation by authorities and individuals allegedly linked to the movement started being arrested on terrorism charges.
44 Marc Pierini, 'Turkey's Gift From God' *Carnegie Europe*, 2017, http://carnegieeurope.eu/strategiceurope/?fa=67826.

stating that if any of his sympathizers were involved, they would have violated his values.[45] The extent of GM-linked individuals' possible involvement in the coup attempt is beyond the scope of this chapter. However, it is clear that following the coup attempt, GM faced extreme stigmatization from Turkish society both inside and outside Turkey,[46] leading GM members to leave Turkey for other countries and seek safety abroad.[47]

In the immediate aftermath of the coup attempt, the AKP government launched an unprecedented purge against perceived Gulenists. One day after the coup attempt, more than 2700 judges were dismissed,[48] and many were later arrested.[49] Even though the coup attempt was suppressed within hours, AKP government declared a state of emergency (henceforth SoE) and derogated from European Convention on Human Rights (ECHR) and the International Covenant on Civil and Political Rights (ICCPR). The derogation notice listed derogations from 13 articles such as the right to liberty, security, fair trial, privacy, the humane treatment of detainees, and the right to remedy, the latter two of which cannot be subject to derogation under any circumstances, according to the UN Human Rights Committee.[50] Additionally, the SoE allowed the AKP government to pass decrees without parliamentary scrutiny. For instance, SoE decrees provided full financial, administrative and criminal impunity to state officials for their actions during the SoE, which resulted in frequent torture and ill-treatment of detainees,[51] mass arbitrary arrests, arbitrary dismissal of state employees, and the removal of due process.[52] Consequently, dismissals have extended to perceived critics from other political backgrounds such as leftists, human rights defenders and Kurdish politicians. According to the latest figures,[53] more than 170,000 civil servants, including academics, teachers, police and military officers have been dismissed from their jobs without due process,[54] with 142,874

---

45   Emre Celik, 'Fethullah Gülen: 'I Call For An International Investigation Into The Failed Putsch In Turkey' *Huffington Post,* 2016, https://www.huffingtonpost.com/emre-celik/fethullah-guelen-i-call-f_b_11480974.html.
46   David Tittensor, 'The Gülen Movement and Surviving in Exile: The Case of Australia', *Politics, Religion & Ideology* 19.1 (2018): 123-38, DOI: https://doi.org/10.1080/21567689.2018.1453272.
47   Liza Dumovich, 'Pious Creativity: Negotiating Hizmet in South America after July 2016', *Politics, Religion and Ideology* 19.1 (2018): 81-94, DOI: https://doi.org/10.1080/21567689.2018.1453267.
48   This number later climbed over 4200 which amounts to one third of the total judges and prosecutors in Turkey.
49   Harry Cockburn, 'Turkey Coup: 2,700 Judges Removed from Duty Following Failed Overthrow Attempt' *The Independent,* 2016, https://www.independent.co.uk/news/world/europe/turkey-coup-latest-news-erdogan-istanbul-judges-removed-from-duty-failed-government-overthrow-a7140661.html.
50   United Nations Human Rights Committee, 'International Covenant on Civil and Political Rights - General Comment No. 29', *Annual Review of Population Law* 44470.29 (2001): 8, DOI: https://doi.org/10.1007/978-1-4020-9160-5_533.
51   Human Rights Watch, 'A BLANK CHECK: Turkey's Post-Coup Suspension of Safeguards Against Torture', 2016, https://www.hrw.org/sites/default/files/report_pdf/turkey1016_web.pdf.
52   Erol Önderoglu, 'Turkey: State of Emergency State of Arbitrary', *Reporters Without Borders,* (September, 2016): 15, https://rsf.org/sites/default/files/turquie.etatdurgence.eng_.def_.pdf.
53   When I submitted the first draft of this chapter, the figures were 150,000 dismissed, 133,257 detained, 64,998 arrested. By the time I submitted the second draft, the figures increased to over 170,000 dismissed, 142,874 detained, 81,417 arrested. These figures alone should be enough to illustrate the severity and arbitrary nature of the purge.
54   Amnesty International, 'NO END IN SIGHT: Purged Public Sector Workers Denied a Future in Turkey,' 2017, https://www.amnesty.org/download/Documents/EUR4462722017ENGLISH.PDF.

people detained and 81,417 people arrested.[55] These negative legislative and judicial developments have been demonstrated to be disproportionate, in breach of Article 4(1) of ICCPR,[56] and have had an extremely negative impact on the rule of law and individual liberties in Turkey.

In parallel with the regressive judicial and legislative developments, exploiting public concern and social tensions in the aftermath of the failed coup attempt, pro-AKP media and influential AKP figures constructed a 'Gulenist' narrative: covert terrorists and plotters infiltrated into society and the state, trying to demolish the state from within. Anyone suspected of being a GM member, supporter or sympathizer is a traitor and a terrorist. In this context, any activities performed by GM-affiliated individuals, such as charity work, donations, working in GM-linked institutions, organizing religious meetings or even simply *communicating with each other* have been ostracized and criminalized. This was exacerbated by Erdogan's presidential pleas for spying on family members and friends who are suspected to be Gulenists and reporting them to authorities.[57] Drawing on moral panic theory, we can see that the coup attempt has acted as a trigger event and the GM have been effectively declared the folk devils -'a category of people who, presumably, engage in evil practices and are blamed for menacing a society's culture, way of life, and central values' in the aftermath.[58] AKP government took advantage of public *concern* in the aftermath of the coup attempt aimed to construct a narrative to achieve *consensus* of *hostility* against GM. This was followed by disproportionate social, legislative, and judicial reactions. In this *volatile* social and political environment, it was relatively easy for the AKP government to weaken the established legal norms and individual safeguards their political enemies. It is fair to argue that, rather than the coup attempt, it was the AKP government's exorbitant and vindictive reactions to the coup attempt which resulted in mass human rights breaches, the eradication of the rule of law and individual liberties in Turkey.

ByLock Prosecutions: Mass Arrest of Perceived Opponents on Terrorism Charges over Encrypted App Usage

ByLock prosecutions were built on inaccurate claims and proceeded with disrespect to established legal standards and individual protections. Shortly after the coup attempt, AKP-linked media outlets published stories that coup plotters and their supporters communicated over ByLock during the coup attempt.[59] However, this claim is false, as Fox-IT clearly illustrated that the Bylock.net domain was deactivated in March 2016, hence ByLock 'could not have been used in the period from April 2016 leading up to 15 July 2016'.[60] The Turkish gov-

---

55 Turkey Purge, 'Turkey Purge I Monitoring Human Rights Abuses in Turkey's Post-Coup Crackdown,' 2018, https://turkeypurge.com/.
56 Ignatius Yordan Nugraha, 'Human Rights Derogation during Coup Situations', *International Journal of Human Rights* 22.2 (2018): 194-206, DOI: https://doi.org/10.1080/13642987.2017.1359551.
57 Laura Pitel, 'Erdogan's Informers: Turkey's Descent into Fear and Betrayal,' *The Financial Times*, 2017, https://www.ft.com/content/6af8aaea-0906-11e7-97d1-5e720a26771b.
58 Goode and Ben-Yehuda, *Moral Panics The Social Construction of Deviance*, 2.
59 Haber7.com, 'Darbeciler ByLock'tan Bu Mesajı Gönderdi! [English: Putchists Sent This Message on Bylock],' 2016, http://www.haber7.com/guncel/haber/2144267-darbeciler-bylocktan-bu-mesaji-gonderdi.
60 Fox-IT, 'Expert Witness Report on ByLock Investigation,' 9.

ernment also claimed that MIT identified ByLock user lists using 'special cyber methods' i.e. hacking Baltic/Cherry Servers in Lithuania which were hosting the ByLock app.[61] This means that MIT's access to ByLock server data was unlawful and such unlawfully acquired data 'shall not be presented before a court' and 'shall not constitute a factual ground for a possible conviction' under Turkish criminal law.[62] Both Lithuanian authorities[63] and Baltic/Cherry Servers[64] declared that they neither received a legal request from nor shared data with Turkish authorities, confirming Gokce's unlawful access observation. This is especially egregious because the ByLock prosecutions, which led to the arrest of tens of thousands of perceived GM members, were built on communication (meta)data accessed unlawfully.

Once the ByLock prosecutions started, MIT submitted a 'ByLock technical report' to trial courts, and this report constituted the technical basis of ByLock prosecutions.[65] The MIT report claimed that ByLock: (1) offered strong cryptography; (2) was disguised as a global application (i.e. presenting itself deceptively as a global application while the aim was to provide GM with an intra-organizational communication app); (3) was aimed at security and anonymity; (4) used a self-signed certificate; (5) offered communication only suitable for a cell-structure (as ByLock did not ask for a phone number to register, MIT argued that ByLock users could only exchange ByLock contact details after initially meeting face-to-face); (6) was designed to prevent access in case of legal confiscation; (7) offered identity hiding features (such as an automatic self-destruct, using long passwords features); and thus, concluded that 'ByLock has been offered to the exclusive use of the 'FTÖ/PDY' members [Gulenists]'.[66] Citing this report amongst evidence, first instance courts sentenced thousands of alleged ByLock users on terrorism charges (over alleged links to GM), ranging from 6 to 15 years.[67] The court of cassation, which acts as the unifying court of appeals in criminal prosecutions in Turkey, approved the evidential status of the alleged ByLock usage,[68] permitting the collective punishment of alleged ByLock users based on dubious lists created by MIT.

Despite the grave consequences for alleged ByLock users, the MIT report was found to be biased, insubstantial and unreliable when scrutinized by the Dutch cyber security firm Fox-IT.[69]

---

61 Gokce, 'The Bylock Fallacy: An In-Depth Analysis of the Bylock Investigations in Turkey,' 2.
62 Gokce, 3.
63 EN.DELFI, 'Lithuania Didn't Provide Turkey with ByLock User Data - Lithuania - m.En.Delfi.Lt,' 2017, http://m.en.delfi.lt/lithuania/article.php?id=76099973.
64 Gokce, 'The Bylock Fallacy: An In-Depth Analysis of the Bylock Investigations in Turkey.'
65 Although this report was not released to the public, it was distributed widely on social media. Fox-IT released the MIT report along with their own condemning report unpicking the inconsistencies and even deliberate manipulations in the former. Readers can find the Turkish version of the MIT report here: https://foxitsecurity.files.wordpress.com/2017/09/bylock-mit-technical-report-turkish.pdf.
66 Fox-IT, 'Expert Witness Report on ByLock Investigation,' 20.
67 The relevant article is Turkish Penal Code 314/2. See https://www.legislationline.org/download/action/download/id/6453/file/Turkey_CC_2004_am2016_en.pdf, p. 104.
68 Reporters Without Borders, 'Journalists in New Wave of Arrests in Turkey,' 2017, https://rsf.org/en/news/journalists-new-wave-arrests-turkey.
69 Fox-IT illustrates tens of factual errors, irregularities, questionable and incorrect claims, and biased statements in MIT's technical report but space precludes the inclusion of all points illustrated. Fox-IT's report is so damning that it calls MIT's credibility in general into question.

By reverse engineering ByLock app's source code and online fact-checking, Fox-IT addressed claims put forward in the MIT report and found that: (1) 'security measures implemented in ByLock are not exceptional and actually on par with widely used chat applications';[70](2) the disguise of global application argument is 'not backed by evidence, questionable or incorrect';[71](3) ByLock developer's aim for security and anonymity 'does not imply an intent for use in illegal activities',[72] and 'in no way an indication that ByLock is aimed at a specific user group';[73](4) the incentive behind using a self-signed certificate is not necessarily to prevent authorities accessing the ByLock data, as self-signed certificates 'are easier to implement and are free of cost'; (5) rather than meeting face-to-face, users could have exchanged ByLock details using another communication method (e.g. WhatsApp, Facebook, phone call), casting a shadow over MIT's 'ByLock was designed for communications in a cell structure argument'; (6) MIT is 'jumping to conclusions on the intent of the developer' when concluding ByLock was designed to 'prevent access in case of legal confusion';[74] and (7) measures such as self-destruct and using long passwords is a common feature also found in other communication applications such as Snapchat and Signal. As a result, Fox-IT concluded that MIT report is 'biased towards a predefined outcome', 'does not adhere to forensic principles', and is 'fundamentally flawed due to the contradicted and unfounded findings, lack of objectivity and lack of transparency'.[75]

MIT report also raised serious doubts about the integrity of data cited as evidence in ByLock prosecutions. Fox-IT noted that it is impossible to verify whether MIT tempered with ByLock server data or not because MIT did not calculate 'cryptographic hashes' of server data and did not 'generate an audit trail'.[76] Given that MIT is reported to have hacked ByLock servers, this is a crucial point that casts a great doubt over the evidential status of ByLock server data cited in prosecutions. In fact, screenshots used in the MIT report detailing the so-called investigation of the server data contain multiple inconsistencies 'that indicate manipulation of results and/or screenshots by MIT'.[77] In Figure 1, Gokce illustrates that the SQL query result screenshots presented in the MIT report (allegedly from data acquired from ByLock servers) are deliberately manipulated by MIT which 'points out the great likelihood that MIT and other Turkish authorities manipulated the Bylock database and fabricated false Bylock records'.[78]

---

70 Fox-IT, 'Expert Witness Report on ByLock Investigation,' 25.
71 Fox-IT, 20.
72 Fox-IT, 20.
73 Fox-IT, 25.
74 Fox-IT, 21.
75 Fox-IT, 28.
76 Fox-IT, 8.
77 Fox-IT, 29.
78 Gokce, 'The Bylock Fallacy: An In-Depth Analysis of the Bylock Investigations in Turkey,' 10.

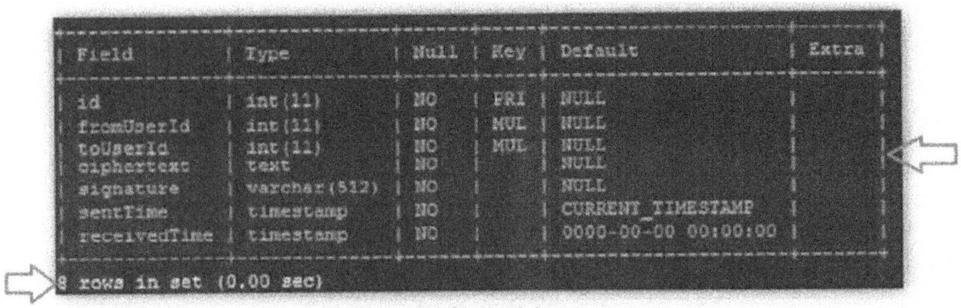

Field	Type	Null	Key	Default	Extra
id	int(11)	NO	PRI	NULL	
fromUserId	int(11)	NO	MUL	NULL	
toUserId	int(11)	NO	MUL	NULL	
ciphertext	text	NO		NULL	
signature	varchar(512)	NO		NULL	
sentTime	timestamp	NO		CURRENT_TIMESTAMP	
receivedTime	timestamp	NO		0000-00-00 00:00:00	

8 rows in set (0.00 sec)

Figure 5 at page 31 of the MIT Bylock Report

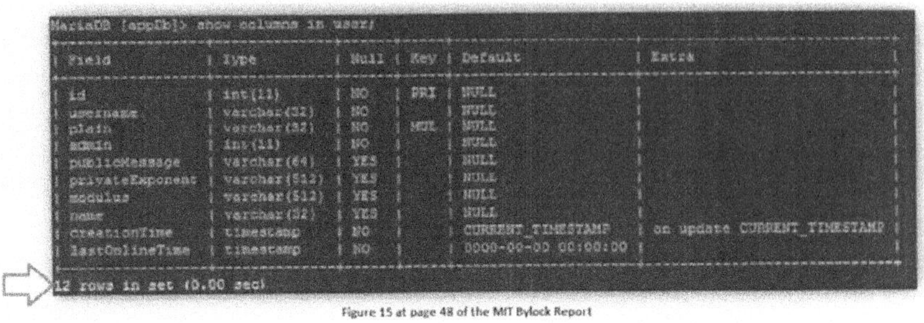

MariaDB [appDb]> show columns in user;

Field	Type	Null	Key	Default	Extra
id	int(11)	NO	PRI	NULL	
username	varchar(32)	NO		NULL	
plain	varchar(32)	NO	MUL	NULL	
admin	int(11)	NO		NULL	
publicMessage	varchar(64)	YES		NULL	
privateExponent	varchar(512)	YES		NULL	
modulus	varchar(512)	YES		NULL	
name	varchar(32)	YES		NULL	
creationTime	timestamp	NO		CURRENT_TIMESTAMP	on update CURRENT_TIMESTAMP
lastOnlineTime	timestamp	NO		0000-00-00 00:00:00	

12 rows in set (0.00 sec)

Figure 15 at page 48 of the MIT Bylock Report

Figure 1: Screenshots from MIT report, allegedly from ByLock database. Total numbers of rows returned by the SQL queries (7 and 10 respectively) do not match total numbers of rows shown at the bottom of the query results (8 and 12 respectively). Figure taken from Gokce (2018).

Although manipulation of evidence is a serious claim, Gokce makes a compelling argument that other not only MIT but also other Turkish authorities may also have 'fabricated' communications metadata (internet traffic records) to facilitate the sentencing of alleged ByLock users.[79] MIT report claimed ByLock users were identified by acquiring IP address logs from the ByLock server database, but it omits methods used to attribute these IP addresses to individuals. During criminal proceedings, it was revealed that the state relied on internet traffic metadata - namely IAL which contain information about date/time, public and private IP address of the user, target IP of the server connected amongst others - as evidence to identify individuals who communicated with ByLock's servers.[80] In Turkey, IAL are retained by the Information and Communication Technologies Authority (Bilgi Teknolojileri Kurumu in Turkish, henceforth BTK) which is the government institution authorized to collect and store metadata provided from ISPs and MNOs, which are private companies. In one scathing example of metadata fabrication, Gokce presents an alleged ByLock user's mobile IAL, which was exhibited to a criminal court during proceedings.[81] While the IAL produced by the MNO contains no data in the 'target IP' column for the specified time frame, the IAL produced by the BTK lists ByLock server's IP address in the 'target IP' column for the specified time

79 Gokce, 7.

80 The Arrested Lawyers Initiative, 'Ever-Changing Evidence ByLock: Turkish Government's Favourite Tool to Arrest Its Critics,' 2017, 14, https://arrestedlawyers.files.wordpress.com/2018/01/bylock_report_by_the_arrested_lawyers.pdf.

81 Gokce, 'The Bylock Fallacy: An In-Depth Analysis of the Bylock Investigations in Turkey,' 9.

frame. As BTK can only store metadata provided by MNOs and ISPs, one would expect no variation between IAL from BTK and MNO over the same time frame. Given this, the fact that only the IAL provided by BTK had 'target IP' information (i.e. IP addresses of servers hosting the ByLock app) indicates metadata manipulation and/or injection on BTK's side. This is a crucial point that lends support for Gokce's 'BTK doctored internet traffic records it received from telecommunication companies' argument.[82] These, coupled with the fact that Turkish authorities reduced the reported total number of ByLock users arbitrarily,[83] led critics to suggest that Turkish authorities have altered ByLock user lists arbitrarily to target perceived GM supporters. [84]

Even if we were to set aside claims of metadata manipulation, citing communications metadata as evidence in criminal prosecutions is unreliable because of IP-based attribution challenges. Without corroborating offline evidence, using IP addresses alone to identify individuals that are suspected for a crime is unreliable.[85] This issue is more frequently observed for mobile device IPs which connect to internet over a network provided by MNOs. Around the world, 92% of MNOs use Carrier Grade Network Address Translation (CGNAT),[86] which are network designs that distribute a small number of global IP addresses to many private users. This means, same public IP address can be shared by hundreds of users at a particular time, making it almost impossible to identify individual users via communications metadata. Indeed, EUROPOL reported that '90% of European cybercrime investigators regularly encounter attribution problems related to CGN technologies'.[87] Similarly, Turkish MNOs use CGNAT, which makes attempts to identify alleged ByLock users using communications metadata exceptionally error prone. In addition, individuals might have relied on 'Good Data' practices - such as using a VPN, a proxy server or Tor - to hide their IP addresses.[88] This makes attribution of ByLock usage based on communications metadata significantly unreliable. Furthermore, handing down lengthy prison sentences to individuals based on such unreliable metadata as evidence is likely to amount to a miscarriage of justice.

---

82 Gokce, 10.
83 The Arrested Lawyers Initiative, 'Ever-Changing Evidence ByLock: Turkish Government's Favourite Tool to Arrest Its Critics.'
84 Turkish Minister of Science and Technology first argued to have identified 215,000 ByLock users in September 2016. Then, in April 2017, AKP-linked media reported that the number of ByLock users had decreased to 102,000. In December 2017, Ankara Chief Prosecutor's Office announced over 11,000 misidentifications in ByLock lists, decreasing the final number to just over 90,000. Furthermore, the prosecution did not share digital data/evidence with defendants and their counsel. This led critics to suspect 'fabrication, alteration or corruption of the data' used in ByLock trials. See: The Arrested Lawyers Initiative report for an extensive summary.
85 Aaron Mackey, Seth Schoen, and Cindy Cohn, 'Unreliable Informants: IP Addresses, Digital Tips and Police Raids. How Police and Courts Are Misusing Unreliable IP Address Information and What They Can Do to Better Verify Electronic Tips', *Electronic Frontier Foundation*, 2016, https://www.eff.org/files/2016/09/22/2016.09.20_final_formatted_ip_address_white_paper.pdf.
86 Philipp Richter et al, 'A Multi-Perspective Analysis of Carrier-Grade NAT Deployment,' *IMC '16 Proceedings of the 2016 Internet Measurement Conference*, 2016: 223, DOI: https://doi.org/10.1145/2987443.2987474.
87 Europol, 'IOCTA 2016: Internet Organised Crime Threat Assessment' (The Hague, 2016), 58, DOI: https://doi.org/10.2813/275589.
88 Mackey, Schoen, and Cohn, 'Unreliable Informants: IP Addresses, Digital Tips and Police Raids'.

In their report scrutinizing the Bylock prosecutions and the legality of actions of the Turkish state following the coup attempt, British criminal lawyers Clegg and Baker illustrated four significant breaches of the ECHR. First, alleged ByLock use does not satisfy the requirement of the ECHR Article 5:1(c)[reasonable suspicion of having committed and offence] and therefore, 'detention of persons on the basis that they had downloaded the Bylock App use is arbitrary and in breach of Article 5 of the convention [right to liberty and security]'.[89] Second, the MIT report is a clear breach of Article 6(3)(d) [right to examine or have examined witnesses against him and to obtain the attendance and examination of witnesses on his behalf under the same conditions as witnesses against him], because 'authors of [the MIT] report are not identified' and 'no questions can be asked to the authors of the report'.[90] Third, mass dismissal and arrest of members of judiciary 'strikes at the heart of judicial independence and appears to be a further clear breach of Article 6 [the right to a fair trial]'.[91] Lastly, since both membership of GM and use of the ByLock app was legal before the coup attempt, to convict persons of membership of a terrorist organization on alleged ByLock use is 'clearly retrospective criminality and a clear breach of Article 7'.[92] The Turkish regime's breaches of the ECHR in the aftermath of the coup attempt - despite being a signatory of the ECHR - demonstrates that supranational human rights legislation may be ineffective to prevent metadata abuses by states. In the context of unlawful access and metadata retention debates, this means that 'broad mandatory [meta]data retention policies'[93] and 'A priori [meta] data retention or collection'[94] capabilities of states leave dissidents and political enemies of the states extremely vulnerable.

Lessons from the ByLock Case: Good Data Practices

In this chapter, by critically engaging with the ByLock prosecutions I detailed the material effects of metadata exploitation for political purposes outside of doctrinal analyses. This case study contributes to the metadata retention and lawful access debates, demonstrating both how existing capabilities of DCTs can be abused, and how extrajudicial - even illegal - investigative techniques can be introduced to oppress dissidents. Authoritarian governments like Turkey can and/or will take advantage of moral panics following political upheavals. 'Bad data' practices such as unlawful access and large-scale (meta)data retention and (meta)data manipulation can be instrumental to confer criminality on dissidents and political enemies, as observed in the ByLock case. Although regimes frequently spy on and surveil dissidents and

---

[89] William Clegg and Simon Baker, 'Opinion on the Legality of the Actions of the Turkish State in the Aftermath of the Failed Coup Attempt in 2016 and the Reliance on Use of the Bylock App as Evidence of Membership of a Terrorist Organisation', London, 2017, 24, http://2oq5cg28288838bmfu32g94v-wpengine.netdna-ssl.com/wp-content/uploads/2017/09/Redacted-Opinion.pdf.
[90] Clegg and Baker, 25.
[91] Clegg and Baker, 26.
[92] Clegg and Baker, 28.
[93] UN Human Rights Council, 'Report of the Special Rapporteur on the Promotion and Protection of the Right to Freedom of Opinion and Expression, David Kaye,' 19.
[94] Amie Stepanovich and Drew Mitnick, 'Universal Implementation Guide for the International Principles on the Application of Human Rights to Communications Surveillance,' *Access Now*, 2015, 41, https://www.accessnow.org/cms/assets/uploads/archive/docs/Implementation_guide_-_July_10_print.pdf.

activists in normal times, moral panics certainly help regimes to justify unlawful, extrajudicial even illegal measures - such as criminalizing encryption usage - that would have been harder to implement in normal times.

Even though the scale and scope of mass arbitrary arrest of dissidents in the ByLock prosecutions are unprecedented, the threat of (meta)data abuse is not unique to dissidents in authoritarian regimes like Turkey. As metadata are being collected in 'bulk' globally, the very availability of metadata can be tempting for states to surveil dissidents, minority populations, activists, whistleblowers and government critics. On the other hand, although supranational human rights legislation and supranational judicial mechanisms have provided a degree of protection for human rights, their effectiveness in the face of oppression is questionable. Despite being a signatory of ECHR and a member of ECtHR, the Turkish regime has significantly breached the ECHR without facing any significant repercussions since the failed coup attempt. The mass human rights breaches observed in Turkey in the aftermath of the coup attempt call the credibility of supranational judicial mechanisms into question. Regimes can simply ignore or suspend the supranational judicial legislation citing perceived or even imagined national security concerns, as observed in the ByLock case. Given the possibility of the further rise of more authoritarian regimes in previously liberal countries, this case may be a grim precedent for things to come.

The ByLock case illustrates how critical 'Good Data' principles and the integrity of encrypted and secure communication channels are for 'Good Democracy'. In the age of DCTs, in order to exercise fundamental human rights - such as the freedom of speech, the freedom of political thought, the freedom of religion, and the freedom of association - strong and secure encrypted communications are essential. If we are not mindful and do not uphold, promote and defend 'Good Data' principles - whether they be more comprehensive and practical human rights legislation or technological solutions such as encrypted communications and anonymization tools - globally, regimes can and will compromise DCTs for 'bad' purposes, and the consequences for dissidents and governments critics are severe, as observed in the ByLock case. Therefore, we should remember that the ultimate promise of the 'Good Data' principles are not staying outside states' surveillance nets or communicating secretly; it is democracy itself.

References

Amnesty International. 'BRIEFING: Prosecution Of 11 Human Rights Defenders', 2017, https://www.amnesty.org/download/Documents/EUR4473292017ENGLISH.pdf.

_____. 'Encryption. A Matter of Human Rights', 2016, http://www.amnestyusa.org/sites/default/files/encryption_-_a_matter_of_human_rights_-_pol_40-3682-2016.pdf.

_____. 'NO END IN SIGHT: Purged Public Sector Workers Denied a Future in Turkey', 2017, https://www.amnesty.org/download/Documents/EUR4462722017ENGLISH.PDF.

Austin, Lisa M. 'Lawful Illegality: What Snowden Has Taught Us About the Legal Infrastructure of the Surveillance State.' *SSRN* (2014): 1-25, DOI: https://doi.org/10.2139/ssrn.2524653.

Buono, Isabella, and Aaron Taylor. 'Mass Surveillance in the CJEU: Forming a European Consensus', *The Cambridge Law Journal* 76.2 (2017): 250-53, DOI: https://doi.org/doi:10.1017/S0008197317000526.

Clegg, William, and Simon Baker. 'Opinion on the Legality of the Actions of the Turkish State in the Aftermath of the Failed Coup Attempt in 2016 and the Reliance on Use of the Bylock App as Evidence of Membership of a Terrorist Organisation.' London, 2017. http://2oq5cg28288838bm-fu32g94v-wpengine.netdna-ssl.com/wp-content/uploads/2017/09/Redacted-Opinion.pdf.

CNBC. 'Facebook-Cambridge Analytica: A Timeline of the Data Hijacking Scandal,' 2018, https://www.cnbc.com/2018/04/10/facebook-cambridge-analytica-a-timeline-of-the-data-hijacking-scandal.html.

Cockburn, Harry. 'Turkey Coup: 2,700 Judges Removed from Duty Following Failed Overthrow Attempt' *The Independent*, 2016. https://www.independent.co.uk/news/world/europe/turkey-coup-latest-news-erdogan-istanbul-judges-removed-from-duty-failed-government-overthrow-a7140661.html.

Cohen, Stanley. *Folk Devils and Moral Panics: The Creation of the Mods and Rockers*, third edition, London/New York: Routledge, 2002.

Dencik, Lina, Arne Hintz, and Jonathan Cable. 'Towards Data Justice? The Ambiguity of Anti-Surveillance Resistance in Political Activism', *Big Data & Society* 3.2 (2016), DOI: https://doi.org/10.1177/2053951716679678.

Dumovich, Liza. 'Pious Creativity: Negotiating Hizmet in South America after July 2016', *Politics, Religion and Ideology* 19.1 (2018): 81-94, DOI: https://doi.org/10.1080/21567689.2018.1453267.

Emre Celik. 'Fethullah Gülen: 'I Call For An International Investigation Into The Failed Putsch In Turkey', *Huffington Post*, 2016. https://www.huffingtonpost.com/emre-celik/fethullah-guelen-i-call-f_b_11480974.html.

EN.DELFI. 'Lithuania Didn't Provide Turkey with ByLock User Data - Lithuania - m.En.Delfi.Lt,' 2017, http://m.en.delfi.lt/lithuania/article.php?id=76099973.

European Union. 'Charter of Fundamental Rights of the European Union,' 2012, 391-407, DOI: https://doi.org/10.1108/03090550310770974.

Europol. 'IOCTA 2016: Internet Organised Crime Threat Assessment', The Hague, 2016, DOI: https://doi.org/10.2813/275589.

Ferdinand, Peter. 'The Internet, Democracy and Democratization', *Democratization* 7.1 (2000): 1-17, DOI: https://doi.org/10.1080/13510340008403642.

Fox-IT. 'Expert Witness Report on ByLock Investigation.' Delft, 2017, https://foxitsecurity.files.wordpress.com/2017/09/bylock-fox-it-expert-witness-report-english.pdf.

Freedom House. 'Freedom on the Net 2017 Report,' 2017, https://freedomhouse.org/sites/default/files/FOTN 2017_Turkey.pdf.

Gokce, Yasir. 'The Bylock Fallacy: An In-Depth Analysis of the Bylock Investigations in Turkey', *Digital Investigation* (March, 2018): 1-11, DOI: https://doi.org/10.1016/j.diin.2018.06.002.

Goode, Erich, and Nachman Ben-Yehuda. *Moral Panics The Social Construction of Deviance*, second edition, Chichester: Wiley-Blackwell, 2009.

Gourlay, William. 'Oppression, Solidarity, Resistance: The Forging of Kurdish Identity in Turkey', *Ethnopolitics* 17.2 (2018): 130-46, DOI: https://doi.org/10.1080/17449057.2017.1339425.

Greenwald, G, and R Gallagher. 'Snowden Documents Reveal Covert Surveillance and Pressure Tactics Aimed at WikiLeaks and Its Supporters', *The Intercept*, 2014, https://theintercept.com/2014/02/18/snowden-docs-reveal-covert-surveillance-and-pressure-tactics-aimed-at-wikileaks-and-its-supporters/.

Haber7.com. 'Darbeciler ByLock'tan Bu Mesajı Gönderdi! [English: Putchists Sent This Message on Bylock]', 2016, http://www.haber7.com/guncel/haber/2144267-darbeciler-bylocktan-bu-mesaji-gonderdi.

Human Rights Watch. 'A BLANK CHECK: Turkey's Post-Coup Suspension of Safeguards Against Torture,' 2016, https://www.hrw.org/sites/default/files/report_pdf/turkey1016_web.pdf.

King, R D, and G M Sutton. 'High Times for Hate Crime: Explaining the Temporal Clustering of Hate Motivated Offending', *Criminology* 51 (2013), DOI: https://doi.org/10.1111/1745-9125.12022.

Laura Pitel. 'Erdogan's Informers: Turkey's Descent into Fear and Betrayal.' *The Financial Times*, 2017, https://www.ft.com/content/6af8aaea-0906-11e7-97d1-5e720a26771b.

Lotan, Gilad, Erhardt Graeff, Mike Ananny, Devin Gaffney, Ian Pearce and danah boyd. 'The Arab Spring I The Revolutions Were Tweeted: Information Flows during the 2011 Tunisian and Egyptian Revolutions', *International Journal of Communication* 5 (2011): 31.

Lyon, D. *Surveillance After Snowden*, Cambridge: Polity Press, 2015.

Mackey, Aaron, Seth Schoen and Cindy Cohn. 'Unreliable Informants: IP Addresses, Digital Tips and Police Raids. How Police and Courts Are Misusing Unreliable IP Address Information and What They Can Do to Better Verify Electronic Tips', *Electronic Frontier Foundation*, 2016, https://www.eff.org/files/2016/09/22/2016.09.20_final_formatted_ip_address_white_paper.pdf.

Mann, Monique, Angela Daly, Michael Wilson and Nicolas Suzor. 'The Limits of (Digital) Constitutionalism: Exploring the Privacy-Security (Im)Balance in Australia', *International Communication Gazette* (in press, 2018): DOI: https://doi.org/10.1177/1748048518757141.

Marc Pierini. 'Turkey's Gift From God' *Carnegie Europe*, 2017, http://carnegieeurope.eu/strategiceurope/?fa=67826.

Michaelsen, Marcus.'Exit and Voice in a Digital Age: Iran's Exiled Activists and the Authoritarian State', *Globalizations* 15.2 (2018): 248-64, DOI: https://doi.org/10.1080/14747731.2016.1263078.

Milanovic, M. 'ECtHR Judgment in Big Brother Watch v. UK.' EJIL:Talk!, 2018, https://www.ejiltalk.org/ecthr-judgment-in-big-brother-watch-v-uk/.

Ni Loideain, Nora. 'EU Law and Mass Internet Metadata Surveillance in the Post-Snowden Era', *Media and Communication* 3.2 (2015): 53, DOI: https://doi.org/10.17645/mac.v3i2.297.

Nieminen, Hannu. 'Digital Divide and beyond: What Do We Know of Information and Communications Technology's Long-Term Social Effects? Some Uncomfortable Questions', *European Journal of Communication* 31.1 (2016): 19-32, DOI: https://doi.org/10.1177/0267323115614198.

Nugraha, Ignatius Yordan. 'Human Rights Derogation during Coup Situations', *International Journal of Human Rights* 22.2 (2018): 194-206, DOI: https://doi.org/10.1080/13642987.2017.1359551.

Önderoglu, Erol. 'Turkey: State of Emergency State of Arbitrary', *Reporters Without Borders* (September, 2016): 15, https://rsf.org/sites/default/files/turquie.etatdurgence.eng_.def_.pdf.

Privacy International. 'Encryption At The Centre Of Mass Arrests : One Year On From Turkey's Failed Coup.' *Privacy International*, 2017, https://medium.com/@privacyint/encryption-at-the-centre-of-mass-arrests-one-year-on-from-turkeys-failed-coup-e6ecd0ef77c9.

_____. 'Press Release: UK Intelligence Agency Admits Unlawfully Spying on Privacy International I Privacy International,' 2018, https://privacyinternational.org/press-release/2283/press-release-uk-intelligence-agency-admits-unlawfully-spying-privacy.

Raley, R. 'Dataveillance and Countervailance' in L Gitelman, *Raw Data' Is an Oxymoron*, Cambridge, MA: MIT Press, 2013.

Reporters Without Borders.'Journalists in New Wave of Arrests in Turkey', 2017. https://rsf.org/en/news/journalists-new-wave-arrests-turkey.

Richter, Philipp, Florian Wohlfart, Narseo Vallina-Rodriguez, Mark Allman, Randy Bush, Anja Feldmann, Christian Kreibich, Nicholas Weaver and Vern Paxson. 'A Multi-Perspective Analysis of

Carrier-Grade NAT Deployment', *IMC '16 Proceedings of the 2016 Internet Measurement Conference*, 2016, 215-29, DOI: https://doi.org/10.1145/2987443.2987474.

Starr, Amory, Luis A. Fernandez, Randall Amster, Lesley J. Wood,and Manuel J. Caro. 'The Impacts of State Surveillance on Political Assembly and Association: A Socio-Legal Analysis', *Qualitative Sociology* 31.3 (2008): 251-70, DOI: https://doi.org/10.1007/s11133-008-9107-z.

Stepanovich, Amie, and Drew Mitnick. 'Universal Implementation Guide for the International Principles on the Application of Human Rights to Communications Surveillance' *Access Now*, 2015, https://www.accessnow.org/cms/assets/uploads/archive/docs/Implementation_guide_-_July_10_print.pdf.

The Arrested Lawyers Initiative. 'Ever-Changing Evidence ByLock: Turkish Government's Favourite Tool to Arrest Its Critics', 2017, https://arrestedlawyers.files.wordpress.com/2018/01/bylock_report_by_the_arrested_lawyers.pdf.

The International Institute for Strategic Studies. 'Turkey: The Attempted Coup and Its Troubling Aftermath', *Strategic Comments* 22.5 (2016): v-vii, DOI: https://doi.org/10.1080/13567888.2016.1217082.

Tittensor, David. 'The Gülen Movement and Surviving in Exile: The Case of Australia', *Politics, Religion & Ideology* 19.1 (2018): 123-38, DOI: https://doi.org/10.1080/21567689.2018.1453272.

Turkey Purge. 'Turkey Purge | Monitoring Human Rights Abuses in Turkey's Post-Coup Crackdown', 2018, https://turkeypurge.com/.

UN Human Rights Council. 'Report of the Special Rapporteur on the Promotion and Protection of the Right to Freedom of Opinion and Expression, David Kaye.' *Human Rights Council*. A/HRC/29/32: UN Human Rights Council, 2015.

_____. 'Report of the Special Rapporteur on the Promotion and Protection of the Right to Freedom of Opinion and Expression on His Mission to Turkey.' A/HRC/35/22/Add.3, 2017. http://www.refworld.org/docid/59394c904.html.

United Nations Human Rights Committee. 'International Covenant on Civil and Political Rights - General Comment No. 29.' *Annual Review of Population Law* 44470.29 (2001): 8, DOI: https://doi.org/10.1007/978-1-4020-9160-5_533.

8: NOT AS GOOD AS GOLD? GENOMICS, DATA AND DIGNITY

BRUCE BAER ARNOLD AND WENDY ELIZABETH BONYTHON

Introduction

Genomics enables us to read individuals and populations as abstractions - repositories of genetic data rather than persons. Through that lens it is tempting to regard 'good data' as a matter of what is big (comprehensive) and better (more accurate), rather than considering whether it is beneficial to or respectful of its human contributors. As nations move swiftly to whole-of-population data collection, analysis and sharing, this chapter suggests that construing bigger and better data as necessarily beneficial to people is contrary to the dignity that is central to personhood. From both a bioethics and legal perspective we are often asking the wrong questions about 'good data'. The chapter critiques contemporary genomic initiatives such as the Genographic Project, Ancestry.com, deCODE and 23andMe in arguing it is imperative to consider meaningful consent regarding data collection and use, alongside establishment of a genomic commons that addresses problems inherent in propertization of the genome through patent law. Public and private goods can be fostered through regulation that ensures data quality and an information framework centred on public education about genomic data, encouraging responsible use of data within and across national borders. If the genome is 'the book of life' we must ensure that 'good' data is available to all and is understood rather than monopolized, mishandled or misread.

The genomics revolution - opening, understanding and manipulating 'the book of life' - results in fruitful questions about 'good data', dignity, ethics and law.[1]

They are fruitful because they require engagement with issues that extend beyond diagnostics, therapeutic practice and the interaction of life-sciences research with business.[2] They are also fruitful because they can be addressed through reference to past philosophical inquiries by figures such as Kant and Locke and to instances such the exploitation of vulnerable people in Nazi Germany and Jim Crow America where scientific ends were deemed to justify outrageous means.

We live in a world where there is excitement about genomic tools such as CRISPR,[3] where governments are endorsing the establishment of population-scale health databases to facilitate advances in public health while strengthening national champions in an emerging global

---

1   Elizabeth Pennisi, 'Finally, the book of life and instructions for navigating it', *Science* 288.5475 (2000): 2304.
2   Wendy Bonython and Bruce Baer Arnold, 'Privacy, Personhood, and Property in the Age of Genomics', *Laws* 4.3 (2015): 377.
3   Jennifer A. Doudna and Samuel H. Sternberg, *A Crack in Creation: Gene editing and the unthinkable power to control evolution*, New York: Houghton Mifflin Harcourt, 2017.

bioeconomy,[4] where corporations such as Myriad are exploiting genomic patents,[5] and where consumers are unwarily gifting familial data to private sector initiatives such as 23andMe[6] or Ancestry.com.[7]

In that world it is pertinent to examine assumptions about the nature, derivation and use of genomic data. Such an examination offers an opportunity for thinking about ways in which potential harms can be minimized, so that data functions as a social good rather than as a commodity subject to data strip-mining.[8] It also offers an opportunity to think about personhood. Most saliently, in an age of Big Data and algorithmic governance are individuals: people who must be respected, or commodities that can be mined by the artificial persons that we characterize as corporations and governments, creations that exist to foster our flourishing?[9]

This chapter accordingly considers 'good data' - and good data practice - through a lens of genomics. The chapter initially discusses genomics as a way of seeing that enables us to read individuals and populations as abstractions: repositories of genetic data (and hence potential susceptibilities, disorders and even behavioural traits) rather than persons. Through that lens it is tempting for the researcher to regard 'good data' as a matter of what is big (comprehensive) and better (more accurate) and commodifiable through law that provides patent holders with exclusive rights. As nations move swiftly to whole-of-population data collection, analysis and sharing, the chapter suggests that construing bigger and better as necessarily beneficial to people is contrary to the dignity that is central to personhood.[10] From both a bioethics and legal perspective, typically centred on property rights, we are often asking the wrong questions about 'good data'. 'Bigger' and 'better' may be beneficial from a data perspective; without

---

4   Kean Birch, Les Levidow and Theo Papaioannou, 'Self-fulfilling prophecies of the European knowledge-based bio-economy: The discursive shaping of institutional and policy frameworks in the bio-pharmaceuticals sector', *Journal of the Knowledge Economy* 5.1 (2014): 1; Ruha Benjamin, 'A lab of their own: Genomic sovereignty as postcolonial science policy' *Policy and Society* 28 (2009): 341; and Kean Birch, 'The neoliberal underpinnings of the bioeconomy: the ideological discourses and practices of economic competitiveness', *Genomics, Society and Policy* 2.3 (2006): 1.
5   Matthew Rimmer, 'An Exorbitant Monopoly: The High Court of Australia, Myriad Genetics, and Gene Patents', in Duncan Matthews and Herbert Zech (eds), *Research Handbook on Intellectual Property and the Life Sciences*, Cheltenham: Edward Elgar, 2017, p. 56; Lori Andrews and Jordan Paradise, 'Gene patents: The need for bioethics scrutiny and legal change' *Yale Journal of Health Policy Law & Ethics* 5 (2005): 403; and Brad Sherman, 'Before The High Court: D'Arcy v Myriad Genetics Inc.: Patenting Genes in Australia' *Sydney Law Review* 37.1 (2015): 135.
6   http://www.23andme.com.
7   https://www.ancestry.com/dna/.
8   Bruce Baer Arnold and Wendy Bonython, 'Should we stripmine your eHealth data', *Health Voices* 15 (2014): 18.
9   Kazimierz Krzysztofek, 'The algorithmic society: digitarians of the world unite', in Paul Kidd (ed.), *European Visions for the Knowledge Age. A Quest for New Horizons in the Information Society*, Henbury: Cheshire Henbury, 2007: p. 89; and Angela Daly, 'The ethics of big data', *Ethics Quarterly* 97 (2014): 22.
10 George Kateb, *Human Dignity*, Cambridge MA: Harvard University Press, 2011; Martha Nussbaum, *Frontiers of Justice: Disability, Nationality, Species Membership*, Cambridge MA: Harvard University Press, 2006, p. 44; and Susan Shell, 'Kant on Human Dignity', in Robert Kraynak and Glenn Tinder (eds), *In Defense of Human Dignity: Essays for Our Times*, Notre Dame: University of Notre Dame Press, 2003, p. 53.

an adequate ethical and legal framework, however, those benefits will not necessarily be extended to its human contributors.

The chapter accordingly critiques contemporary genomic initiatives such as Ancestry.com, National Geographic's Genographic Project,[11] deCODE[12] and 23andMe in arguing it is imperative to consider meaningful consent regarding data collection and use, alongside establishment of a genomic commons that addresses problems inherent in propertization of the genome through patent law. Public and private goods can be fostered through regulation that ensures data quality and an information framework centred on public education about genomic data, encouraging responsible use of data within and across national borders.

The chapter concludes by arguing that if the genome is 'the book of life' we must ensure that 'good' data is available to all and is understood rather than monopolized, mishandled or misread. Goodness may be fostered by respectful clinical protocols, best practice on the part of research funders/regulators and enhanced awareness on the part of consumers rather than merely by exclusions under intellectual property law or an international agreement regarding genetic privacy and genomic rights.[13]

You are Data

Valorization of humans as entities deserving respect, a status often characterized as dignity and differentiated from other life forms, is a feature of Western philosophy and debate about political economy.[14] Kant saliently articulated a categorical imperative that condemned treatment of people as means to a political or other end.[15] After World War Two and the Nuremberg trials, the value of the personhood has been formally recognized through development of binding codes of ethical research and practice entrenching respect for the dignity and autonomy of people as patients and research participants, for example.[16]

---

11 Spencer Wells, *Deep Ancestry: Inside the Genographic Project, Washington:* National Geographic Books, 2006.
12 Michael Fortun, *Promising Genomics: Iceland and deCODE Genetics in a World of Speculation*, Berkeley: University of California Press, 2008; David Winickoff, 'A Bold Experiment: Iceland's Genomic Venture' in Deborah Mascalzoni (ed.), *Ethics, Law and Governance of Biobanking*, Dordrecht: Springer Netherlands, 2015, p. 187; and Gísli Pálsson. 'Decode Me!' *Current Anthropology* 53 (2012): S185.
13 Shawn Harmon. 'The significance of UNESCO's universal declaration on the human genome and human rights' *SCRIPT-ed* 2 (2005): 18; and 'Ethical rhetoric: Genomics and the moral content of UNESCO's 'universal' declarations' *Journal of Medical Ethics* 34 (2008): e24.
14 Kateb, *Human Dignity*; and Jürgen Habermas, 'The Concept of Human Dignity and the Realistic Utopia of Human Rights' *Metaphilosophy* 44.4 (2010): 444.
15 Immanuel Kant. *Groundwork of the Metaphysics of Morals,* trans. Mary Gregor, Cambridge: Cambridge University Press, 1997, first published 1785: pp. 14, 31.
16 Debra Mathews and Leila Jamal, 'Revisiting respect for persons in genomic research' *Genes* 5 (2014): 1; Deryck Beyleveld and Roger Brownsword, 'Human dignity, human rights, and human genetics', *Modern Law Review* 61 (1998): 661; and National Commission for the Protection of Human Subjects of Biomedical and Behavioral Research, *Belmont Report: Ethical Principles and Guidelines for the Protection of Human Subjects of Research*, Washington: United States Government Printing Office, 1978.

Movements in psychosocial medicine, for example, reflect the ideal of treating patients as a whole, rather than as an embodiment of discrete conditions that happen to be stored in a common vessel.[17]

Conversely, nation states have long read individuals and communities in terms of gender, social status, military capability, religious affiliation, age, ethnicity, lineage, tax liability, criminality and nationality.[18] Some of those attributes are innate. Some are mutable. Many can be subverted or evaded. Information tools such as the population census, initially often crude head counts mapped to specific locations, have been supplemented through technologies that collect biometric data in forms such as fingerprints and mugshots.[19]

The aggregation, rapid sorting and interpretation of such data will be increasingly pervasive as public and private sector entities across the globe deploy sophisticated algorithms for biometric data analysis (for example at international airports and other transport nodes),[20] and leverage communication networks that foster the sharing of data between diverse government agencies and private sector proxies.[21]

A rich scholarly literature over the past forty years has identified privacy and other dignitarian concerns regarding the identification of citizens and non-citizens - the latter being potentially especially vulnerable as people situated outside the law that protects their citizen peers - as data subjects. Those subjects are entities that are administered as and because they are manifestations of specific attributes rather than as individuals who are more than a social security number, a tax file number, an affirmative action tag or an entry on a national security watch list. In essence they are depersonalized, made subordinate to their embodiment of a particular type of data.

Such abstraction is inherent in 'seeing like a state',[22] a practice that embodies inescapable tensions about data and data subjects. Abstraction fosters the bureaucratic rationality, discussed below, that is a salient feature of the modern state and more broadly of modernity.[23]

---

17 See for example Pekka Martikainen, Mel Bartley and Eero Lahelma, 'Psychosocial determinants of health in social epidemiology' *International Journal of Epidemiology* 31.6 (2002): 1091; and Sheldon Cohen, 'Psychosocial models of the role of social support in the etiology of physical disease', *Health Psychology* 7.3 (1988): 269.
18 For example see Edward Higgs, *The Information State in England: The Central Collection of Information on Citizens since 1500*, Basingstoke: Palgrave Macmillan, 2004; and *Identifying the English: a History of Personal Identification 1500 to the Present*, London: Continuum, 2011.
19 Richard Hopkins. 'An introduction to biometrics and large scale civilian identification', *International Review of Law, Computers & Technology* 13.3 (1999): 337.
20 Benjamin Muller, *Security, Risk and the Biometric State: Governing Borders and Bodies*, London: Routledge, 2010.
21 Joel R Reidenberg, 'The data surveillance state in the United States and Europe', *Wake Forest Law Review* 49.2 (2014): 583.
22 James Scott, *Seeing Like a State: How Certain Schemes to Improve the Human Condition have Failed*, New Haven: Yale University Press, 1998.
23 Anthony Giddens, *Modernity and Self-Identity: Self and Society in the Late Modern Age,* Cambridge: Polity Press, 1991; and Marshall Berman, *All That Is Solid Melts Into Air: The Experience of Modernity*,

Like is treated alike. Decisions are made on the basis of facts (that is, what are deemed to be value-free data). Entitlements and disabilities are addressed on the basis of shared identity with other members of a cohort, rather than on the basis of an administrator's whim or personal values. Increasingly, decisions may be made by algorithms without any direct human intervention.[24]

An inflection point in our identification and potential understanding of human animals and other life forms came in the 1950s with discoveries regarding DNA, notably publication by Watson and Crick regarding the 'double helix', the code found in all people and characterized by some scholars as the 'book of life'.[25] It is a book that contrary to tabloid enthusiasm about genetics still contains many secrets: we can see the letters but still struggle to read the syntax and the meaning.[26]

An implication of genomics is that we can abstractly construe people as genetic files. Using a genomic lens you are, for example, a set of genomic data. You are a file that came into being at conception and that will be relatively stable throughout your life, reflected in comments that although you can change your name, nationality and gender you cannot change your genes.[27] Your genomic data represents genes that may determine your life-span, susceptibility to specific medical disorders and potential as a champion athlete rather than merely your hair color, gender and skin pigmentation.[28]

As a file your data can be primarily be isolated from a blood or other biological sample. It can be expressed in a way that enable analysis and facilitate the transmission of data across jurisdictions and between discrete databases or users. It also facilitates comparison with data relating to other people. That identification is something that is increasingly automated. It is a practice that is routinized in applications such as paternity testing or forensic analysis regarding homicides and sexual assaults, with DNA testing for example replacing fingerprint testing as a trope in popular culture.[29] Such identification seeks to differentiate one person from another or to confirm a questioned identity through reference to data embodied in a crime scene sample or a law enforcement register of offenders/suspects.[30]

London: Verso, 2001.
24 Frank Pasquale. *The Black Box Society: The secret algorithms that control money and information*, Cambridge MA: Harvard University Press, 2015.
25 Elizabeth Pennisi, 'Finally, the book of life and instructions for navigating it'; and Bruce Baer Arnold and Wendy Bonython, 'Sharing the Book of Life: Privacy, the new genomics and health sector managers' *Privacy Law Bulletin* 12 (2015): 9.
26 International Human Genome Sequencing Consortium, 'Initial sequencing and analysis of the human genome' *Nature* 409 (2001): 860; and Kevin Davies. *The $1,000 Genome: The Revolution in DNA Sequencing and the New Era of Personalized Medicine*, New York: Simon and Schuster, 2010.
27 Wendy Elizabeth Bonython and Bruce Baer Arnold, 'Direct to consumer genetic testing and the libertarian right to test' *Journal of Medical Ethics* (August 2017): 14.
28 Wendy Elizabeth Bonython and Bruce Baer Arnold, 'Privacy, Personhood and Property'.
29 Barbara L Ley, Natalie Jankowski, and Paul R Brewer, 'Investigating CSI: Portrayals of DNA testing on a forensic crime show and their potential effects' *Public Understanding of Science* 21.1 (2012): 51.
30 Sheldon Krimsky and Tania Simoncelli, *Genetic Justice: DNA Data Banks, Criminal Investigations, and Civil Liberties*, New York: Columbia University Press, 2013.

Genomic good data, for some law enforcement personnel, is accordingly a comprehensive digital biobank that is parsed in order to point to a suspected offender, providing a basis for specific investigation and potentially offering what courts regard as conclusive evidence. It is good because it enables law enforcement and facilitates justice.[31]

Genomics is not, however, restricted to authoritative differentiation between yourself, your neighbor and any other reader of this chapter. If we think of you as a living file of genetic data, a physical embodiment or expression of instructions, potentials and disabilities in your genetic code, we should be unsurprised that insurers, developers of diagnostic tools and pharmaceuticals, public policymakers, behavioral scientists, epidemiologists and other medical researchers are interested in what the genome can tell us about health and what opportunities it provides for medicine, personalized or otherwise. Governments are endorsing population-scale genomic initiatives alongside private ventures such as 23andMe that are marketed as recreational genomics.[32] Such activity is complemented by public and private sector plans, notably in the United Kingdom and Israel, to share population-scale health records - for example data about everyone who has attended a hospital or general practitioner in England under the National Health Service. Recent studies have also identified health data and health institutions as key targets for cyberattack.[33]

Using the files of individuals, communities and national populations offers potentials for breakthroughs in medical research. It also offers investors potential rewards that dwarf those reaped by figures such as Bill Gates, George Soros, Mark Zuckerberg and Larry Ellison.

We are thus seeing disputes about claims to own genes, most prominently in litigation about molecular diagnostic patents gained by Myriad Genetics Inc. regarding breast cancer diagnosis. Those disputes follow litigation regarding the highly lucrative exploitation of body samples from people such as Henrietta Lacks.[34] They pose questions about privacy,[35] ethics,[36] trade

---

31 David Lazer (ed), *DNA and the Criminal Justice System: The Technology of Justice*, Cambridge: The MIT Press, 2004.
32 Pascal Su, 'Direct to consumer Genetic Testing: A Comprehensive View' *Yale Journal of Biology & Medicine* 86 (2013): 359; Amy McGuire and Wylie Burke, 'An unwelcome side effect of direct to consumer personal genome testing: Raiding the medical commons' *Journal of the American Medical Association* 300 (2008): 2669.
33 Clemens Scott Kruse, Benjamin Frederick, Taylor Jacobson, and D. Kyle Monticone, 'Cybersecurity in healthcare: A systematic review of modern threats and trends' *Technology and Health Care* 25.1 (2017): 1.
34 Rebecca Skloot, *The Immortal Life of Henrietta Lacks*, New York: Crown, 2010; Maureen Dorney, 'Moore v. The Regents of the University of California: Balancing the need for biotechnology innovation against the right of informed consent', *High Technology Law Journal* 5 (1989): 333; and Jasper Bovenberg, 'Inalienably yours? The new case for an inalienable property right in human biological material: Empowerment of sample donors or a recipe for a tragic anti-commons', *SCRIPT-ed* 1 (2004): 545.
35 Sheri Alpert, 'Protecting medical privacy: Challenges in the age of genetic information', *Journal of Social Issues* 59 (2003): 301; and Jessica Litman, 'Information Privacy/Information Property', *Stanford Law Review* 152 (2000): 1283.
36 Bernice Elger, *Ethical Issues of Human Genetic Databases: A Challenge to Classical Health Research Ethics?* Aldershot: Ashgate, 2013.

secrets,[37] treating data as property,[38] and about the appropriateness of exclusive ownership of genomic data that is not unique to a particular individual but is instead common to that person's siblings.[39] They involve conundrums about the balance between public benefit and the private interests of people who have knowingly or otherwise shared their genomic data, not necessarily addressed through promises regarding de-identification to make data good.[40] The effectiveness of de-identification mechanisms remains contentious,[41] given the scope for associating individual/familial genomic data with other identifiers in the public and private realms - a manifestation of the 'big data' explored elsewhere in this book. The disputes require thought about incentives for innovation and about regulatory incapacity in a global economy where data may be readily harvested in one jurisdiction, analyzed in another jurisdiction and used or misused in other jurisdictions. They require thought about the balance between public and private goods, with an absolute de-identification for example vitiating much research.

As such they encourage thought about the nature of 'good data', explored in the following part of this chapter, and what might be done to minimize harms without forgoing the advancement of research in the life-sciences or disregarding perceptions that data gathered through the public health system is one of the few major assets that might be privatized by neoliberal governments in an era of budget stringency.

Goodness

The goodness of data is a founding value of modernity.[42] Data legitimizes public policy in the contemporary liberal democratic state. Data is perceived as freeing us from superstition and alleviating fear of what is unknown or misunderstood. Data is a matter of disenchantment, truth rather than fantasy. It enables bureaucratic rationality that is a marker of efficient public administration and commerce. Data allows a coherent evaluation of the past, management of the present and prediction of the future. Data is a prerequisite of fact-based medicine

---

37 Christi J. Guerrini, Amy L. McGuire and Mary A. Majumder, 'Myriad take two: Can genomic databases remain secret?', *Science* 356.6338 (2017): 586; and Craig R. Smith, 'A Biotechnology Dilemma: Patent Your Inventions (if you can) or Keep Them Secret', *Journal of Commercial Biotechnology* 23.2 (2017): 74.
38 Richard Spinello. 'Property rights in genetic information', *Ethics and Information Technology* 6 (2004): 29; and Alexandra George, 'The Difficulty of Defining 'Property', *Oxford Journal of Legal Studies* 25 (2005): 793.
39 Wendy Bonython, and Bruce Baer Arnold. 'Privacy, Personhood, and Property in the Age of Genomics', *Laws* 4.3 (2015): 377; Muireann Quigley. 'Propertisation and Commercialisation: On Controlling the Uses of Human Biomaterials', *Modern Law Review* 77 (2014): 677; and Catherine Heeney, Naomi Hawkins, Jantina de Vries, Paula Boddington, and Jane Kaye, 'Assessing the privacy risks of data sharing in genomics' *Public Health Genomics* 14.1 (2011): 17.
40 See for example Khaled El Emam, Elizabeth Jonker, Luk Arbuckle, and Bradley Malin, 'A systematic review of re-identification attacks on health data', *PloS one* 6.12 (2011): e28071 1; and Khaled El Emam, *Guide to the De-Identification of Personal Health Information*, Boca Raton: CRC Press, 2013.
41 See for example Melissa Gymrek, Amy L McGuire, David Golan, Eran Halperin and Yaniv Erlich, 'Identifying Personal Genomes by Surname Inference' *Science* 339.6117 (2013): 321.
42 Theodore Porter, *Trust in Numbers: The Pursuit of Objectivity in Science and Human Life*, Princeton: Princeton University Press, 1996.

and public health initiatives, evident in for example disquiet about homeopathy and much 'new age' therapy. Data's perceived innate goodness is implicit in catchphrases such as 'the facts speak for themselves', 'statistics show', 'facts are power', 'the facts, just the facts' and 'the evidence proves'. It is implicit in the primacy of national statistical agencies (and the mandatory status of much census activity), the culture of risk-management on the basis of population-scale data resources that influence the provision of financial services,[43] and the valorization of epidemiological studies since at least the time of John Snow's mapping of cholera in Georgian London.[44]

Reality is, of course, somewhat more complicated. Rob Kitchin, in referring to a 'knowledge pyramid', contextualized 'data' by commenting that 'data precedes information, which precedes knowledge, which precedes understanding and wisdom'.[45] In considering what genomic 'good data' is through a lens of community benefit and individual dignity, we might accordingly conceptualize data as a tool, rather than an outcome. On that basis goodness might be assessed through reference to how the tool is devised and used rather than merely whether the products of its use - the understanding, diagnostics, therapies and revenue - are beneficent.

If we look beyond the 'data is good' rhetoric noted above we might for example recognize that some data collection is egregiously wrong, fundamentally tainting knowledge that results from the tool. Provenance matters. We might also recognize that although the tool was devised with care for human dignity and used without any intention to harm some outcomes of its use may be subjectively or objectively bad. Recognition acknowledges differentials in who gets to collect data, who defines data, who analyses data, who acts upon it and who disseminates (or chooses not to disseminate) data.

Good data is thus more than a matter of accuracy, an accuracy that is often reflective of care to identify and thence reduce error in data collection and analysis. Accuracy may be a function of the scale of data collection, with a survey of a large number of people for example producing data that is 'good' because it is representative rather than being skewed to a specific cohort. That emphasis on comprehensiveness has driven the large-scale genomic initiatives discussed later in this chapter, with researchers and investors aspiring to population-scale mapping of the human genome and health.

'Goodness' might also be construed in terms of efficiency, with data collection being assessed in terms of the cost of data collection/analysis and more broadly in terms of the knowledge that results from the collection, knowledge that is valuable for investors or public administrators. In the age of the neoliberal enterprise university, where funders are wary of disinterested research, it is axiomatic that institutions deal with data to generate financially tangible out-

---

43 Frank Pasquale, *The Black Box Society*.
44 Donald Cameron and Ian G. Jones, 'John Snow, the Broad Street pump and modern epidemiology', *International Journal of Epidemiology* 12.4 (1983): 393.
45 Rob Kitchin, *The Data Revolution: Big Data, Open Data, Data Infrastructures and Their Consequences* Thousand Oaks: SAGE, 2014, p. 9.

comes: there is no collection for data's sake.[46]

In the life sciences several data collection projects over the past seventy years provide a framework for conceptualizing data goodness in considering genomic initiatives.

One project, in Nazi Germany, involved the collection by medical researchers of data about the resilience of the human body under extreme stress, with the expectation that the resultant knowledge would enable life-saving practices. The collection involved researchers placing concentration camp inmates in freezing water, in high pressure chambers, or depriving them of air. Those data objects - people - were not provided with painkillers. They were not in a position to consent, and were denied dignity.[47] Many died during the data collection. The data collected during what we now characterize in law as a crime against humanity might have been accurate and useful but is fundamentally tainted.[48]

The same can be said for the Pernkopf anatomical atlas, a masterly depiction of the human body and accordingly acclaimed over several editions for its accuracy and usefulness for medical students.[49] From that perspective it is an artefact of good data. It is however a work that draws on the bodies of concentration camp inmates, some of whom may have been 'killed to order' for the anatomists. It prompts disquieting questions about goodness.

We can see other egregious denials of dignity in data collection and use closer to our own time. Recall for example, the Tuskagee Syphilis Study in the United States, where researchers tracked the health of communities containing residents infected with syphilis. Similar studies involved prisoners and people in Guatemala.[50] Saliently, the people were not offered therapies, were not alerted to the nature of any symptoms (meaning that they did not gain treatment from other clinicians) and were in a subordinate position. National security was invoked to justify research for the US Central Intelligence Agency into the effects of LSD.[51] Staff at the Alder Hey hospital, and other institutions in the UK, harvested organs for research purposes

---

46   Simon Marginson and Mark Considine, *The Enterprise University: Power, Governance and Reinvention in Australia*, Cambridge: Cambridge University Press, 2000; and Hans Radder (ed.), *The Commodification of Academic Research: Science and the Modern University*, Pittsburgh: University of Pittsburgh Press, 2010.
47   Benno Muller-Hill, *Murderous Science*, Oxford: Oxford University Press, 1988; and Robert Lifton, *The Nazi Doctors: Medical Killing and the Psychology of Genocide*, New York: Basic Books, 1986.
48   George Annas and Michael Grodin (eds), *The Nazi Doctors and the Nuremberg Code: Human Rights in Human Experimentation,* Oxford: Oxford University Press, 1992.
49   Chris Hubbard, 'Eduard Pernkopf's atlas of topographical and applied human anatomy: The continuing ethical controversy', *The Anatomical Record 265*.5 (2001): 207; and Michel C Atlas, 'Ethics and Access to Teaching Materials in the Medical Library: The Case of the Pernkopf Atlas' *Bulletin of the Medical Library Association* 89.1 (2001): 51.
50   Giselle Corbie-Smith. 'The continuing legacy of the Tuskegee Syphilis Study: considerations for clinical investigation', *American Journal of the Medical Sciences* 317.1 (1999): 5; and Susan M Reverby, 'Ethical failures and history lessons: the US Public Health Service research studies in Tuskegee and Guatemala', *Public Health Reviews* 34.1 (2012): 13.
51   Alfred W McCoy, 'Science in Dachau's shadow: Hebb, Beecher, and the development of CIA psychological torture and modern medical ethics', *Journal of the History of the Behavioral Sciences* 43.4 (2007): 401.

without family consent.[52] Those organs are embodiments of genomic data and potentially beneficial for teaching; the practice means however that the data was not 'good'. US surgeons famously commodified Henrietta Lacks; no consent was obtained from Ms Lacks or her family for culturing and marketing of a cell line cultured from her cancer biopsy (now used in laboratories across the globe), there was no acknowledgement and no compensation was provided for appropriation of her genetic material.[53]

In construing the goodness of data we might accordingly be alert to questions about whether the tool is ethical rather than merely accurate and efficient. Does it for example respect dignity? Is the knowledge that results from the data fair?

'Good' Data, Bad Practice?

Those questions underpin a consideration of contemporary genomic initiatives, particularly those that are marketed as 'recreational genomics', and gene patents such as those held by Myriad Inc. More broadly they underpin thought about population-scale health data initiatives such as the UK care.data program that, as discussed below, encountered fundamental difficulties because bureaucratic indifference to consent eroded its perceived legitimacy.[54] Data in public and private collections, for research or other purposes, may be good because accurate but was its generation respectful and is its use fair? In essence, 'goodness' as a matter of legitimacy may be a function of provenance rather than accuracy.

Excitement over the wonders of genomics, evident in characterisations such as reading 'the book of life', and fundamental reductions in the cost of genomic data processing have resulted in the emergence of recreational genomics. Put simply, consumers provide a genomic service such as 23andMe and Ancestry.com with a body sample, typically in the form of a painless swab from the mouth. That provision might be as a gift, with the consumer neither paying a fee nor receiving a payment. It might instead be on a consumer pays fee for service basis. In return, consumers receive reports that relate them to contemporary/historic cohorts (for example under the Genographic Project indicate that x percent of your ancestors were Vikings or came from Africa) or point to specific genetic traits, such as a dislike of certain vegetables, or phenotypic (physical) phenomena.[55] The data that appears in those reports is the property of the service provider.

---

52 Veronica English and Ann Sommerville, 'Presumed consent for transplantation: a dead issue after Alder Hey?', *Journal of Medical Ethics* 29.3 (2003): 147; and Sarah Ramsay, '105 000 body parts retained in the UK, census says', *The Lancet* 357.9253 (2001): 365.
53 Rebecca Skloot, *The Immortal Life of Henrietta Lacks,* New York: Crown, 2010.
54 Pam Carter, Graeme Laurie, and Mary Dixon-Woods, 'The social licence for research: Why care.data ran into trouble', *Journal of Medical Ethics* 41 (2015): 404.
55 Jennifer Wagner, Jill D. Cooper, Rene Sterling and Charmaine D. Royal, 'Tilting at windmills no longer: A data-driven discussion of DTC DNA ancestry tests', *Genetics in Medicine* 14 (2012): 586; and Ugo Perego, Ann Turner, Jayne E. Ekins, and Scott R. Woodward, 'The science of molecular genealogy', *National Genealogical Society Quarterly* 93 (2005): 245.

The marketing of those services has emphasized recreation, for example as part of a genealogical hobby, rather than therapy. They appeal to novelty and a popular desire for social connectedness. Although they use the language of science and rely on popular faith in the liberating effects of medical data they are typically situated outside health regulation frameworks. They do not require prescription or guidance by a clinician. They might be dourly viewed as akin to genomic fortune telling: an entertainment service that is correspondingly weakly regulated because outside the health realm.[56]

Recreational genomics poses several issues. Consumers and some regulators may not appreciate the implications of the data that can emerge from the sequencing. From the perspective of privacy scholars the initiatives are problematic because individuals are not genetically unique. Some of our genes are common to biological relatives, especially siblings. Inferences of varying accuracy can be drawn about the genomic characteristics of close and distant relatives. If we conceptualize a person as a genomic file, an embodiment of genomic data, we can see that participants in recreational genomics are unilaterally offering service providers data about other people rather than just about themselves. Some people with concerns about potential genetic discrimination - the genomic redlining by insurers, employers and others that has featured in legal literature over the past twenty years - may choose not to participate in recreational genomics and be disquieted that others are tacitly co-opting them through undisclosed provision of swabs.[57] The authors of this chapter have highlighted concerns about a 'right not to know' (freedom from an unwanted disclosure within a family circle of a health condition identified in a genomic report gained by a relative),[58] and about the accuracy of reports from service providers and their potential misinterpretation by consumers.[59]

Those concerns co-exist with weakness of national and international regulation of the services, which typically operate globally and are inadequately constrained by national privacy law that is often based on the principle that protections are waived if consumers consent to data collection, processing and sharing. Genomic data collection for aggregation and sale is likely to be the unstated or even express business model of recreational genomic services, given the value of large-scale genomic and other health repositories. That value was a driver of the contentious UK care.data initiative, with the British government proposing to sell several decades

---

56 Gert van Ommen and Martina Cornel, 'Recreational genomics? Dreams and fears of genetic susceptibility screening', *European Journal of Human Genetics* 16 (2008): 403.
57 Janneke Gerards, Aalt Willem Heringa and Heleen Janssen, *Genetic Discrimination and Genetic Privacy in a Comparative Perspective,* Antwerp: Intersentia, 2005; and Larry Gostin, 'Genetic discrimination: The use of genetically based diagnostic and prognostic tests by employers and insurers', *American Journal of Law & Medicine* 17 (1991): 109.
58 Bruce Baer Arnold and Wendy Elizabeth Bonython, 'Australian reforms enabling disclosure of genetic information to genetic relatives by health practitioners', *Journal of Law and Medicine* 21.4 (2014): 810.
59 Gregory Kutz, 'Direct to consumer Genetic Tests: Misleading Test Results Are Further Complicated by Deceptive Marketing and Other Questionable Practices-Testimony. Before the Subcommittee on Oversight and Investigations, Committee on Energy and Commerce, House of Representatives', United States Government Accountability Office, 2010; Rachel Kalf, Rachel Bakker, and Cecile Janssens, 'Predictive ability of direct to consumer pharmacogenetic testing: When is lack of evidence really lack of evidence?' *Pharmacogenomics* 14 (2013): 341; and Michael Murray, 'Why We Should Care About What You Get for 'Only $99' from a Personal Genomic Service', *Annals of Internal Medicine* 160 (2014): 507.

of National Health Service records (i.e. from hospitals and general practitioners) about all English patients, without patient consent on the basis that the data would be de-identified.[60]

It is arguable that there is insufficiently informed consent on the part of many recreational genomics consumers, who are unaware of (or indifferent to) whether the data they provide is being sold to or otherwise shared with third parties such as pharmaceutical companies.[61] Some presumably trust that the services will rigorously protect what in time will amount to global genomic databases that, like financial databases, are susceptible to unauthorized disclosure by insiders and hacking by outsiders. Few consumers will have much sense of the scope for law enforcement and national security agencies to override the often vague undertakings made by the services and access the data without disclosure to the affected individuals.

Services conceptualize genomic data as property, an asset that can be bounded by confidentiality and employment law and that can be assigned a value for sale or security. Entities outside the recreational genomics sector have also conceptualized genomic data in terms of exclusive rights that enable a substantial return on investment. A salient example is Myriad Inc., a United States corporation that has aggressively sought and asserted patent rights regarding the BRCA 1 gene, associated with breast cancer.[62] The prevalence of breast cancer, the morbidity of its occurrence and perceptions that life-threatening illness can be predicted for pre-emptive surgery or other therapy means that Myriad's patents are commercially very valuable. Unsurprisingly, Myriad has sought to exploit what is often misreported as 'ownership' of genes or more accurately as a tool with some diagnostic value, resulting in criticism across the globe that its pricing and asserted monopoly exclude the disadvantaged. Analysts have questioned whether gene patents as such should be recognized in law, either on grounds of public policy or because they involve discovery rather than invention. Others argue that much of the data at the heart of gene patents was gained through publicly-funded research, so any patent revenue should be shared with the state.

---

60   Justin Keen, Radu Calinescu, Richard Paige and John Rooksby, 'Big data + politics = open data: The case of health care data in England', *Policy and Internet* 5.2 (2013): 228; Pam Carter, Graeme Laurie, and Mary Dixon-Woods, 'The social licence for research: Why care.data ran into trouble' *Journal of Medical Ethics* 41 (2015): 404; Jon Hoeksma. 'The NHS's care.data scheme: What are the risks to privacy?' *British Medical Journal* 348 (2014): g1547; and Paraskevas Vezyridis and Stephen Timmons, 'Understanding the care.data conundrum: New information flows for economic growth' *Big Data & Society* 4.1 (2017): 1.
61   Ma'n H. Zawati, Pascal Borry, and Heidi Carmen Howard, 'Closure of population biobanks and direct-to-consumer genetic testing companies', *Human Genetics* 130.3 (2011): 425; Ole Andreas Brekke and Thorvald Sirnes, 'Population biobanks: the ethical gravity of informed consent' *BioSocieties* 1.4 (2006): 385; and Laura Donnelly, 'NHS hospital records used by private marketing firms' *The Telegraph*, 3 March 2014.
62   Matthew Rimmer, 'An Exorbitant Monopoly: The High Court of Australia, Myriad Genetics, and Gene Patents', in Duncan Matthews and Herbert Zech (eds), *Research Handbook on Intellectual Property and the Life Sciences*, Cheltenham: Edward Elgar, 2017: p. 56; and Gregory D. Graff, Devon Phillips, Zhen Lei, Sooyoung Oh, Carol Nottenburg and Philip G. Pardey, 'Not quite a myriad of gene patents', *Nature biotechnology* 31.5 (2013): 404.

A Genomic Commons?

One response to propertization of genomic data (i.e. characterising it as something over which a discoverer, collector or aggregator has exclusive rights that are legally enforceable and that can be commodified through sale, licence or gift) is to treat the human genome as a commons, something that is properly considered as requiring a public understanding that extends beyond debates about potential commodification of resources on the basis of exclusive rights.[63]

Recognition of the genome as something that is a global resource that must be both socially understood and curated rather than strip-mined on an opportunistic basis will strike some readers as legally or politically naive. It would require change to national law and interpretation of international intellectual property agreements. It would not chill discovery, consistent with a history of research that was funded by government and philanthropic institutions that valorised the common good through an emphasis on what would now be characterized as 'open data', i.e. publication in readily accessible journals. (Such publication would prevent much patent activity, given that the 'invention' to be protected would not be novel.)

A commons would not resolve conundrums regarding genomic privacy. A solution to those conundrums lies outside patent law.

Genomics and Data in a Good Society

Infolibertarian John Perry Barlow envisaged that in the imminent age of data - bits and bytes - the state would wither because neither relevant nor effective, with what he construed as the individualistic values underlying the US Constitution becoming universal. [64] Regulation, seen as innately restrictive of creativity and thus of individual goods, would cease to be viable in a digital world without borders, a market integrated by the internet rather than by state agreements such as the Agreement on Trade-Related Aspects of Intellectual Property (TRIPS). Nicholas Negroponte more vividly pictured the irrelevant state evaporating like a mothball.[65] A succinct response was provided by Bart Kosko: 'we'll have governments as long as we have atoms to protect'.[66] The past two decades have shown that the lions are reluctant to lie

---

63 Elinor Ostrom. 'Beyond markets and states: polycentric governance of complex economic systems', *American Economic Review* 100.3 (2010): 641; Brett Frischmann, Michael Madison and Katherine Strandburg (eds), *Governing Knowledge Commons*, Oxford: Oxford University Press, 2014; and Lee Anne Fennell, 'Ostrom's Law: Property rights in the commons', *International Journal of the Commons* 5.1 (2011): 9.

64 John Perry Barlow, 'A Declaration of the Independence of Cyberspace' in Peter Ludlow (ed), *Crypto Anarchy, Cyberstates, and Pirate Utopias*, Cambridge MA: MIT Press, 2001, pp. 27-28; and John Perry Barlow, 'The Economy of Ideas: A Framework for Patents and Copyrights in the Digital Age (Everything You Know about Intellectual Property is Wrong)' *Wired* 2.3 (March 1994): 1.

65 Nicholas Negroponte, *Being Digital*. New York: Vintage, 1995, p. 238.

66 Bart Kosko, *Heaven in a Chip: Fuzzy Visions of Science and Society in the Digital Age*, New York: Three Rivers Press, 2000: p. 43. See also Michael Birnhack and Niva Elkin-Koren, 'The Invisible Handshake: The Reemergence of the State in the Digital Environment' *Virginia Journal of Law and Technology* 8.2 (2003): 1, 6.

down with the lambs. National borders (and national interests) remain powerful. The law of man - as distinct from Barlow and Lessig's law of code - continues to shape both investment and consumption.[67] In thinking about good data we need to think about the good society, one that John Rawls would consider to be fair,[68] and that Martha Nussbaum would endorse as fostering the capabilities of all members of the state.[69] Good data from that perspective is data and practice that underpins the good society. It is not solely or primarily a matter of property and of law regarding property.

It is unlikely that we will see an international reworking of international intellectual property law to specifically exclude the genome from patent protection. An inability to achieve such a reworking reflects the difficulties evident in global trade negotiations over the past five decades, with the slowing of economic growth and the mercantilism evident in statements by US President Trump, for example, exacerbating the recalcitrance of key actors about surrendering what they see as national advantages. Leading corporations appear unlikely to relinquish what they perceive as key competitive advantages in terms of exploiting genomic information, with public policymakers being influenced by a genomic data version of the axiom that what's good for General Motors is good for the US.

There is perhaps more hope at the national level, especially in response to egregious rent-seeking of the type highlighted by Martin Shkreli.[70] In the age of big data states remain relevant because they permit private actors to exercise power (something that is not inherently bad) and have scope to intervene through a range of policy levers when those actors fail to exhibit adequate internal restraints. Liberal democratic states have tended to acknowledge private property rights and offset market inefficiencies by respecting patents but subsidising the price of key pharmaceuticals for consumers. In essence, the taxpayer fills the gap so that disadvantaged consumers can flourish, and trade sanctions will not be instituted. We might act more boldly.

Such action would recognise genomic patents, such as those gained by Myriad, but cap the prices charged for products embodying those patents and attributable to genomic data. That restriction can be deemed as legitimate both in terms of rationales for intellectual property protection - patents are not an end in themselves - and because much genomic research is founded on discovery in the public domain by public institutions or funded by public agencies.

Lawyers and legal academics typically conceptualize problems and solutions in terms of law, with data, for example, being addressed in terms of jurisprudence regarding copyright, evidence, employment, computer and confidentiality law. Conceptualising good data in relation

---

67 Lawrence Lessig, *Code and Other Laws of Cyberspace,* New York: Basic Books, 1999.
68 John Rawls, 'The Sense of Justice', in Samuel Freeman (ed), *John Rawls: Collected Papers,* Cambridge: Harvard University Press, 1999: p. 115; and *Justice as Fairness: A Restatement*, Cambridge: Harvard University Press, 2001.
69 Martha Nussbaum, *Creating Capabilities: The Human Development Approach,* Cambridge: Harvard University Press, 2011: p. 33.
70 Robin Feldman, Evan Frondorf, Andrew K. Cordova, and Connie Wang, 'Empirical Evidence of Drug Pricing Games - A Citizen's Pathway Gone Astray' *Stanford Technology Law Review* 20.1 (2017): 39.

to a good society requires an acknowledgement that there is scope for regulation outside international agreements, national statutes and judgments. The preceding paragraphs imply that we might look to the behaviour of clinicians and researchers, bounded at an individual and institutional level by ethical codes regarding the exploitation of human subjects, the oversight of research (which often has an institutional or cross-institutional basis) and the allocation of funding. Can researchers refuse to partner with corporations deemed to be unduly exploitative, a refusal that is likely to be career limiting? Can research institutions more easily refuse to licence to those corporations or, despite government pressure to be self-sustaining through an aggressive patent-building strategy, emphasise placing genomic research in the public domain. Is 'Good Data' that which is available to all, across borders and without the tyranny of the quarterly return?

A contention in this chapter is that dignity is inextricably associated with agency, at its simplest the ability to make decisions, enjoy benefits (individual or social) and take responsibility. The genomic initiatives critiqued above typically deny agency.

That denial is a matter of obfuscation where providers of genetic material, for example participants in recreational genomics projects such as 23andMe, are not equipped with the information they need to make informed choices about the consequences for themselves and relatives of that participation. Respect for the capacity of consumers to make decisions, including what we might construe as foolish decisions, should be reflected in both fuller disclosure as part of the initiatives and more broadly by a public education program that informs people about public policy issues rather than merely about the wonders of gene sequencing and the likelihood of achieving fundamental medical breakthroughs from large-scale data capture. Education might reduce some privacy harms by alerting people of the potential consequences of unilaterally providing data about close/distant relatives, particularly if law changed to inhibit genomic discrimination.[71]

Measures to foster that public understanding of what is 'good' data and good data practice would importantly serve to inform community debate about initiatives where people have been denied agency by having no choice about whether their data is mandatorily conscripted for national health databases such as Care. Data or by having little real choice because use of 'opt out' mechanisms is designed to be unduly onerous.

Conclusion

This chapter began by referring to pre-genomic conceptions of what is good, with Kant for example addressing Aristotle's questions about 'the good' by exhorting us not to treat people as a means to an end, abstractions without dignity that can be sacrificed for personal, institutional or political needs. In an era where investors, governments and researchers are awed by 'big data' - the bigger the better - it is useful to recall statements such as Stalin's 'the death of one person is a tragedy, the death of a million is a mere statistic' and the fetishization of

---

71 Alison Harvey, 'Genetic risks and healthy choices: Creating citizen-consumers of genetic services through empowerment and facilitation', *Sociology of Health & Illness* 32 (2010): 365.

bigness in Mao's China where the demise of millions was an acceptable price to pay for an industrial leap forward.[72]

The collection, study and exploitation of genomic data does not have to be dystopian. Bigness is not inherently bad; nor is profit. A contention running through this chapter is that the 'goodness' of genomic data is a function of respect for human dignity, something that requires thinking beyond specific data collection mechanisms and applications.

Good genomic data is not a matter of bulk and breadth: the number of data subjects and their representativeness of a national or global population. It is not a matter of good title: recognized property rights under patent or other law. It is instead more usefully conceived in terms of a mindset, a response to questions that are best addressed through an ethic of responsibility rather than ownership.[73] As we increasingly make sense of the book of life we might accordingly choose to exercise our own agency, and the agency of the governments that are accountable to us, and conceptualize good data as a matter of curation for the common good rather than property in which a fortunate few have exclusive rights. The potential agency of government has been disregarded or dismissed by proponents of neoliberalism, i.e. an ideology in which the invisible hand of the market solves all policy questions. In considering genomic data we suggest that agency may be construed in terms of intellectual property and other legal frameworks at both global and national levels, alongside state-sanctioned professional codes and decision-making by government funders of genomic research. Agency may also be construed in terms of action by public sector entities, a matter of formal authority to intervene in markets, of expertise to both understand and articulate questions about genomic data, and a culture in which regulators are willing to intervene. That intervention - what might be characterized as a reintroduction of state - should provide legitimacy for the state (a social good) and foster understanding by individuals about how we collectively and individually manage the genome. An ultimate function of the state is enabling discourse about what is good.

References

Alpert, Sheri. 'Protecting medical privacy: Challenges in the age of genetic information', *Journal of Social Issues* 59 (2003): 301-322.

Andrews, Lori and Jordan Paradise. 'Gene patents: The need for bioethics scrutiny and legal change', *Yale Journal of Health Policy Law & Ethics* 5 (2005): 403-412.

Annas, George and Michael Grodin (eds). *The Nazi Doctors and the Nuremberg Code: Human Rights in Human Experimentation,* Oxford: Oxford University Press, 1992.

Arnold, Bruce Baer and Wendy Elizabeth Bonython. 'Australian reforms enabling disclosure of genetic information to genetic relatives by health practitioners', *Journal of Law and Medicine* 21.4 (2014): 810-812.

Arnold, Bruce Baer and Wendy Bonython. 'Should we stripmine your eHealth data', *Health Voices* 15 (2014): 18-19.

---

72 Kimberley Manning and Felix Wemheuer (eds), *Eating Bitterness: New Perspectives on China's Great Leap Forward and Famine*, Vancouver: UBC Press, 2011.
73 David Winickoff and Larissa B. Neumann, 'Towards a social contract for genomics: Property and the public in the 'biotrust' model', *Life Sciences Society and Policy* 1 (2005): 8.

Arnold, Bruce Baer and Wendy Bonython. 'Sharing the Book of Life: Privacy, the new genomics and health sector managers', *Privacy Law Bulletin* 12 (2015): 9-14.

Atlas, Michel C. 'Ethics and Access to Teaching Materials in the Medical Library: The Case of the Pernkopf Atlas', *Bulletin of the Medical Library Association* 89.1 (2001): 51-58.

Barlow, John Perry. 'The Economy of Ideas: A Framework for Patents and Copyrights in the Digital Age (Everything You Know about Intellectual Property is Wrong)', *Wired* 2.3 (March 1994): 1-13.

Barlow, John Perry. 'A Declaration of the Independence of Cyberspace', in Peter Ludlow (ed.), *Crypto Anarchy, Cyberstates, and Pirate Utopias,* Cambridge MA: MIT Press, 2001: 27-30.

Benjamin, Ruha. 'A lab of their own: Genomic sovereignty as postcolonial science policy', *Policy and Society* 28 (2009): 341-355.

Berman, Marshall. *All That Is Solid Melts Into Air: The Experience of Modernity,* London: Verso, 2001.

Beyleveld, Deryck and Roger Brownsword. 'Human dignity, human rights, and human genetics', *Modern Law Review* 61 (1998): 661-680.

Birch, Kean. 'The neoliberal underpinnings of the bioeconomy: the ideological discourses and practices of economic competitiveness', *Genomics, Society and Policy* 2.3 (2006): 1-15.

Birch, Kean, Les Levidow and Theo Papaioannou. 'Self-fulfilling prophecies of the European knowledge-based bio-economy: The discursive shaping of institutional and policy frameworks in the bio-pharmaceuticals sector', *Journal of the Knowledge Economy* 5.1 (2014): 1-18.

Birnhack, Michael and Niva Elkin-Koren. 'The Invisible Handshake: The Reemergence of the State in the Digital Environment', *Virginia Journal of Law and Technology* 8.2 (2003): 1-57.

Bonython, Wendy and Bruce Baer Arnold. 'Privacy, Personhood, and Property in the Age of Genomics', *Laws* 4.3 (2015): 377-412.

Bonython, Wendy Elizabeth and Bruce Baer Arnold. 'Direct to consumer genetic testing and the libertarian right to test', *Journal of Medical Ethics* (August 2017).

Bovenberg, Jasper. 'Inalienably yours? The new case for an inalienable property right in human biological material: Empowerment of sample donors or a recipe for a tragic anti-commons' *SCRIPT-ed* 1 (2004): 545-585.

Brekke, Ole Andreas, and Thorvald Sirnes. 'Population biobanks: the ethical gravity of informed consent', *BioSocieties* 1.4 (2006): 385-398.

Cameron, Donald, and Ian G. Jones. 'John Snow, the Broad Street pump and modern epidemiology', *International journal of epidemiology* 12.4 (1983): 393-396.

Carter, Pam, Graeme Laurie, and Mary Dixon-Woods. 'The social licence for research: Why care.data ran into trouble', *Journal of Medical Ethics* 41 (2015): 404-409.

Cohen, Sheldon. 'Psychosocial models of the role of social support in the etiology of physical disease', *Health Psychology* 7.3 (1988): 269-297.

Corbie-Smith, Giselle. 'The continuing legacy of the Tuskegee Syphilis Study: considerations for clinical investigation', *American Journal of the Medical Sciences* 317.1 (1999): 5-8.

Daly, Angela. 'The ethics of big data', *Ethics Quarterly* 97 (Spring 2014): 22-23.

Davies, Kevin. *The $1,000 Genome: The Revolution in DNA Sequencing and the New Era of Personalized Medicine*, New York: Simon and Schuster, 2010.

Dorney, Maureen. 'Moore v. The Regents of the University of California: Balancing the need for biotechnology innovation against the right of informed consent', *High Technology Law Journal* 5 (1989): 333-369.

Doudna, Jennifer and Samuel Sternberg. *A crack in creation: Gene editing and the unthinkable power to control evolution*, New York: Houghton Mifflin Harcourt, 2017.

El Emam, Khaled, Elizabeth Jonker, Luk Arbuckle and Bradley Malin. 'A systematic review of re-identification attacks on health data', *PloS one* 6.12 (2011): e28071 1-12.

El Emam, Khaled. *Guide to the De-Identification of Personal Health Information*, Boca Raton: CRC Press, 2013.

Elger, Bernice. *Ethical Issues of Human Genetic Databases: A Challenge to Classical Health Research Ethics?*, Aldershot: Ashgate, 2013.

English, Veronica and Ann Sommerville. 'Presumed consent for transplantation: a dead issue after Alder Hey?', *Journal of Medical Ethics* 29.3 (2003): 147-152.

Feldman, Robin, Evan Frondorf, Andrew K. Cordova and Connie Wang. 'Empirical Evidence of Drug Pricing Games - A Citizen's Pathway Gone Astray', *Stanford Technology Law Review* 20.1 (2017): 39-92.

Fennell, Lee Anne. 'Ostrom's Law: Property rights in the commons', *International Journal of the Commons* 5.1 (2011) 9-27.

Fortun, Michael. *Promising Genomics: Iceland and deCODE Genetics in a World of Speculation*. Berkeley: University of California Press, 2008.

Frischmann, Brett, Michael Madison, and Katherine Strandburg (eds). *Governing Knowledge Commons*, Oxford: Oxford University Press, 2014.

George, Alexandra. 'The Difficulty of Defining 'Property'', *Oxford Journal of Legal Studies* 25 (2005): 793-813.

Gerards, Janneke, Aalt Willem Heringa and Heleen Janssen. *Genetic Discrimination and Genetic Privacy in a Comparative Perspective*, Antwerp: Intersentia, 2005.

Giddens, Anthony. *Modernity and Self-Identity: Self and Society in the Late Modern Age,* Cambridge: Polity Press, 1991.

Gostin, Larry. 'Genetic discrimination: The use of genetically based diagnostic and prognostic tests by employers and insurers', *American Journal of Law & Medicine* 17 (1991): 109-144.

Graff, Gregory D., Devon Phillips, Zhen Lei, Sooyoung Oh, Carol Nottenburg and Philip G. Pardey. 'Not quite a myriad of gene patents' *Nature biotechnology* 31.5 (2013): 404-410.

Guerrini, Christi J., Amy L. McGuire, and Mary A. Majumder. 'Myriad take two: Can genomic databases remain secret?', *Science* 356.6338 (2017): 586-587.

Gymrek, Melissa, Amy L McGuire, David Golan, Eran Halperin and Yaniv Erlich. 'Identifying Personal Genomes by Surname Inference', *Science* 339.6117 (2013): 321-324.

Habermas, Jürgen. 'The Concept of Human Dignity and the Realistic Utopia of Human Rights' *Metaphilosophy,* 44.4 (2010): 444-480.

Harmon, Shawn. 'The significance of UNESCO's universal declaration on the human genome and human rights', *SCRIPT-ed* 2 (2005): 18-38.

_____. 'Ethical rhetoric: Genomics and the moral content of UNESCO's 'universal' declarations', *Journal of Medical Ethics* 34 (2008): e24.

Harvey, Alison. 'Genetic risks and healthy choices: Creating citizen-consumers of genetic services through empowerment and facilitation', *Sociology of Health & Illness* 32 (2010): 365-381.

Heeney, Catherine, Naomi Hawkins, Jantina de Vries, Paula Boddington and Jane Kaye. 'Assessing the privacy risks of data sharing in genomics', *Public Health Genomics* 14.1 (2011): 17-25.

Higgs, Edward. *The Information State in England: The Central Collection of Information on Citizens since 1500*, Basingstoke: Palgrave Macmillan, 2004.

____. *Identifying the English: a History of Personal Identification 1500 to the Present*, London: Continuum, 2011.

Hoeksma, Jon. 'The NHS's care.data scheme: What are the risks to privacy?', *British Medical Journal* 348 (2014): g1547.

Hopkins, Richard. 'An introduction to biometrics and large scale civilian identification', *International Review of Law, Computers & Technology* 13.3 (1999): 337-363.

Hubbard, Chris. 'Eduard Pernkopf's atlas of topographical and applied human anatomy: The continuing ethical controversy' *The Anatomical Record 265*.5 (2001): 207-211.

International Human Genome Sequencing Consortium. 'Initial sequencing and analysis of the human genome', *Nature* 409 (2001): 860-921.

Kalf, Rachel, Rachel Bakker and Cecile Janssens. 'Predictive ability of direct to consumer pharmacogenetic testing: When is lack of evidence really lack of evidence?', *Pharmacogenomics* 14 (2013): 341-344.

Kant, Immanuel. *Groundwork of the Metaphysics of Morals*, trans Mary Gregor, Cambridge: Cambridge University Press, 1997, first published 1785.

Kateb, George. *Human Dignity*, Cambridge: Harvard University Press, 2011.

Keen, Justin, Radu Calinescu, Richard Paige and John Rooksby. 'Big data + politics = open data: The case of health care data in England', *Policy and Internet* 5.2 (2013): 228-243.

Kosko, Bart. *Heaven in A Chip: Fuzzy Visions of Science and Society in the Digital Age,* New York: Three Rivers Press, 2000.

Krimsky, Sheldon and Tania Simoncelli. *Genetic Justice: DNA Data Banks, Criminal Investigations, and Civil Liberties.* New York: Columbia University Press, 2013.

Kruse, Clemens Scott, Benjamin Frederick, Taylor Jacobson, and D. Kyle Monticone. 'Cybersecurity in healthcare: A systematic review of modern threats and trends', *Technology and Health Care* 25.1 (2017): 1-10.

Krzysztofek, Kazimierz. The algorithmic society: digitarians of the world unite', in Paul Kidd (ed.), *European Visions for the Knowledge Age. A Quest for New Horizons in the Information Society,* Henbury: Cheshire Henbury, 2007: 89-103.

Kutz, Gregory. 'Direct to consumer Genetic Tests: Misleading Test Results Are Further Complicated by Deceptive Marketing and Other Questionable Practices-Testimony. Before the Subcommittee on Oversight and Investigations, Committee on Energy and Commerce, House of Representatives', United States Government Accountability Office, 2010.

Lazer, David (ed.). *DNA and the Criminal Justice System: The Technology of Justice.* Cambridge: MIT Press, 2004.

Lessig, Lawrence. *Code and Other Laws of Cyberspace,* New York: Basic Books, 1999.

Ley, Barbara L, Natalie Jankowski, and Paul R. Brewer. 'Investigating CSI: Portrayals of DNA testing on a forensic crime show and their potential effects', *Public Understanding of Science* 21.1 (2012): 51-67.

Lifton, Robert. *The Nazi Doctors: Medical Killing and the Psychology of Genocide*, New York: Basic Books, 1986.

Litman, Jessica. 'Information Privacy/Information Property', *Stanford Law Review* 152 (2000): 1283-1313.

Manning, Kimberley and Felix Wemheuer (eds). *Eating Bitterness: New Perspectives on China's Great Leap Forward and Famine*, Vancouver: UBC Press, 2011.

Marginson, Simon and Mark Considine. *The Enterprise University: Power, Governance and Reinvention in Australia,* Cambridge: Cambridge University Press, 2000.

Martikainen, Pekka, Mel Bartley and Eero Lahelma. 'Psychosocial determinants of health in social epidemiology', *International Journal of Epidemiology* 31.6 (2002): 1091-1093.

Mathews, Debra and Leila Jamal. 'Revisiting respect for persons in genomic research' *Genes* 5 (2014): 1-12.

McCoy, Alfred W. 'Science in Dachau's shadow: Hebb, Beecher, and the development of CIA psychological torture and modern medical ethics', *Journal of the History of the Behavioral Sciences* 43.4 (2007): 401-417.

McGuire, Amy and Wylie Burke, 'An unwelcome side effect of direct to consumer personal genome testing: Raiding the medical commons' *Journal of the American Medical Association* 300 (2008): 2669-2671.

Muller, Benjamin. *Security, Risk and the Biometric State: Governing Borders and Bodies,* London: Routledge, 2010.

Muller-Hill, Benno. *Murderous Science*, Oxford: Oxford University Press, 1988.

Murray, Michael. 'Why We Should Care About What You Get for 'Only $99' from a Personal Genomic Service', *Annals of Internal Medicine* 160 (2014): 507-508.

National Commission for the Protection of Human Subjects of Biomedical and Behavioral Research, *Belmont Report: Ethical Principles and Guidelines for the Protection of Human Subjects of Research*, Washington: United States Government Printing Office, 1978.

Negroponte, Nicholas. *Being Digital,* New York: Vintage, 1995.

Nussbaum, Martha. *Frontiers of Justice: Disability, Nationality, Species Membership,* Cambridge: Harvard University Press, 2006.

Nussbaum, Martha. *Creating Capabilities: The Human Development Approach*, Cambridge: Harvard University Press, 2011.

Ostrom, Elinor. 'Beyond markets and states: polycentric governance of complex economic systems', *American Economic Review* 100.3 (2010): 641-672.

Pálsson, Gísli. 'Decode Me!', *Current Anthropology* 53 (2012): S185-195.

Pasquale, Frank. *The Black Box Society: The Secret Algorithms that Control Money and Information*, Cambridge: Harvard University Press, 2015.

Pennisi, Elizabeth. 'Finally, the book of life and instructions for navigating it', *Science* 288.5475 (2000): 2304-2307.

Perego, Ugo, Ann Turner, Jayne E. Ekins and Scott R. Woodward. 'The science of molecular genealogy', *National Genealogical Society Quarterly* 93 (2005): 245-259.

Porter, Theodore. *Trust in Numbers: The Pursuit of Objectivity in Science and Human Life*, Princeton: Princeton University Press, 1996.

Quigley, Muireann. 'Propertisation and Commercialisation: On Controlling the Uses of Human Biomaterials', *Modern Law Review* 77 (2014): 677-702.

Radder, Hans (ed.). *The Commodification of Academic Research: Science and the Modern University*, Pittsburgh: University of Pittsburgh Press, 2010.

Ramsay, Sarah. '105 000 body parts retained in the UK, census says', *The Lancet* 357.9253 (2001): 365.

Rawls, John. 'The Sense of Justice', in Samuel Freeman (ed), *John Rawls: Collected Papers,* Cambridge: Harvard University Press, 1999: 96-116.

_____. *Justice as Fairness: A Restatement*, Cambridge: Harvard University Press, 2001.

Reidenberg, Joel R. 'The data surveillance state in the United States and Europe', *Wake Forest Law Review* 49.2 (2014): 583-605.

Reverby, Susan M. 'Ethical failures and history lessons: the US Public Health Service research studies in Tuskegee and Guatemala', *Public Health Reviews* 34.1 (2012): 13-18.

Rimmer, Matthew. 'An Exorbitant Monopoly: The High Court of Australia, Myriad Genetics, and Gene Patents', in Duncan Matthews and Herbert Zech (eds), *Research Handbook on Intellectual Property and the Life Sciences*, Cheltenham: Edward Elgar, 2017: 56-103.

Scott, James. *Seeing Like A State: How Certain Schemes to Improve the Human Condition have Failed*, New Haven: Yale University Press, 1998.

Shell, Susan. 'Kant on Human Dignity', in Robert Kraynak and Glenn Tinder (eds), *In Defense of Human Dignity: Essays for Our Times,* Notre Dame: University of Notre Dame Press, 2003: 53-75.

Sherman, Brad. 'Before The High Court: D'Arcy v Myriad Genetics Inc.: Patenting Genes in Australia', *Sydney Law Review* 37.1 (2015): 135-147.

Skloot, Rebecca. *The Immortal Life of Henrietta Lacks*, New York: Crown, 2010.

Smith, Craig R. 'A Biotechnology Dilemma: Patent Your Inventions (if you can) or Keep Them Secret', *Journal of Commercial Biotechnology* 23.2 (2017): 74-81.

Spinello, Richard. 'Property rights in genetic information', *Ethics and Information Technology* 6 (2004): 29-42.

Su, Pascal. 'Direct to consumer Genetic Testing: A Comprehensive View', *Yale Journal of Biology & Medicine* 86 (2013): 359-365.

Van Ommen, Gert and Martina Cornel. 'Recreational genomics? Dreams and fears of genetic susceptibility screening', *European Journal of Human Genetics* 16 (2008): 403-404.

Vezyridis, Paraskevas and Stephen Timmons. 'Understanding the care.data conundrum: New information flows for economic growth', *Big Data & Society* 4.1 (2017): 1-12.

Wagner, Jennifer, Jill D. Cooper, Rene Sterling and Charmaine D. Royal. 'Tilting at windmills no longer: A data-driven discussion of DTC DNA ancestry tests', *Genetics in Medicine* 14 (2012): 586-593.

Wells, Spencer. *Deep ancestry: Inside the Genographic Project, Washington:* National Geographic Books, 2006.

Winickoff, David. 'A Bold Experiment: Iceland's Genomic Venture', in Deborah Mascalzoni (ed.), *Ethics, Law and Governance of Biobanking*, Dordrecht: Springer Netherlands, 2015: 187-209.

Winickoff, David and Larissa B. Neumann. 'Towards a social contract for genomics: Property and the public in the 'biotrust' model', *Life Sciences Society and Policy* 1 (2005): 8-21.

Zawati, Ma'n H., Pascal Borry and Heidi Carmen Howard. 'Closure of population biobanks and direct-to-consumer genetic testing companies', *Human Genetics* 130.3 (2011): 425-432.

9: DATA LOCALIZATION: POLICYMAKING OR GAMBLING?

NIKITA MELASHCHENKO[1]

>'Sir, the possibility of successfully navigating an asteroid field is approximately 3,720 to 1.' C-3PO, Star Wars: The Empire Strikes Back

Introduction

The benefits of the information society come at the price of increasing data dependency. This creates tensions between economic, privacy, and public security interests. While data fuels the digital economy and production of cross-border value, it also affects power relations between states and other actors. In response, data localization policies have emerged addressing data flows in the context of information sovereignty. This chapter unfolds the basic concept of data localization and outlines how the underlying policy objectives correspond within the WTO framework. It further examines the principles of data regulation drawing on the nature of information and its lifecycles. The chapter concludes with a mapping tool for data localization policies and moves towards the analytical framework for data regulation.

Data has a location and its regulation matters. Whether data constitutes paper records collecting dust on a shelf, or electronic records embedded in a database, it is physically stored somewhere. In a data dependent society, the governance of data and specifically its physical infrastructure is critically important as they are the basis of all activities, particularly which take place in virtual reality. No services provided in cyberspace (e.g. messengers, online video games or cloud storage) can work without servers maintained in the real world.

However, the whole architecture of storing data while providing services is invisible to users and is therefore seen as a technical matter.[2] Nonetheless, depending on the regulatory model, physical infrastructure might affect social welfare in one way or another. This is evident in the emerging fight for allocation and redistribution of data among storage facilities in various jurisdictions. One of the tools states use in this struggle is data localization (DL) - the reason why LinkedIn stopped operating in Russia, Apple is opening data centers in China and moving encryption keys onshore, and Microsoft wallowed in disputes with the US Government.[3]

---

1   ^*^ PhD Candidate, Victoria University of Wellington. I wish to thank Professor Susy Frankel and Dr Mark Bennett for suggesting improvements to this chapter.
2   World Wide Web and email services based on a client-server model and peer-to-peer applications imply among other things the work of physical components (e.g. processors, storage devices). See David D. Clark, 'Designs for an Internet' (2017): pp. 9-11, https://groups.csail.mit.edu/ana/People/DDC/lbook-arch.pdf.
3   See 'LinkedIn to be Blocked in Russia', *RAPSI*, 10 November 2016, http://www.rapsinews.com/judicial/_news/20161110/277106589.html; Cicilia Kang and Katie Benner, 'Russia Requires Apple and Google to Remove LinkedIn From Local App Stores', *The New York Times*, 6 January 2017, https://

States have been utilizing the localization of technology and information as a policy tool for years.[4] When states adopted privacy and data protection regulations in the 1970s, scholars began analyzing the possibility of data privacy and international laws colliding.[5] The discussion eventually recognized important international trade issues: data is foundational to most business interactions, meaning that limiting data flows directly affects trade.[6] However, little attention has been paid to the variety of DL regulations and how such variety affects the end results of regulatory policies.

To keep up with the social and business expectations and practices the DL discussion has to transform.[7] Designing smart data regulations and calibrating DL is necessary given the dependency of the global community on data. However, this is impossible unless we consider the diverse kinds of information and the different regulatory goals that states seek to achieve through controlling information. Thus, DL is not a single, uniform policy measure that always has the same positive or negative consequences; it all depends on what DL measure is adopted. If regulators fail to make DL measures that are fair and just, they risk causing conflict, whether at domestic or international levels.

This chapter explains the essence of DL policies, including the basic goals they seek to achieve. It reviews DL policy taxonomies and explains their limitations. Then, it outlines the

---

www.nytimes.com/2017/01/06/technology/linkedin-blocked-in-russia.html; Paul Mozur, Daisuke Wakabayashi, and Nick Wingfield, 'Apple Opening Data Center in China to Comply With Cybersecurity Law', *The New York Times*, 12 July 2017, https://www.nytimes.com/2017/07/12/business/apple-china-data-center-cybersecurity.html; Robert McMillan and Tripp Mickle, 'Apple to Start Putting Sensitive Encryption Keys in China', *Wall Street Journal*, 24 February 2018, https://www.wsj.com/articles/apple-to-start-putting-sensitive-encryption-keys-in-china-1519497574; Richard Waters, 'Microsoft setback in cloud era test case', *Financial Times*, 1 August 2014, https://www.ft.com/content/0649c042-18e6-11e4-933e-00144feabdc0; 'Microsoft wins battle with US over data privacy', *Financial Times*, 15 July 2016, https://www.ft.com/content/6a3d84ca-49f5-11e6-8d68-72e9211e86ab; Hannah Kuchler, 'Microsoft faces key ruling in data privacy case', *Financial Times*, 17 October 2017, https://www.ft.com/content/7d22f1ae-b28d-11e7-a398-73d59db9e399; 'United States v. Microsoft Corp.', *SCOTUSblog*, 2017, http://www.scotusblog.com/case-files/cases/united-states-v-microsoft-corp/.

4   Consider regulatory institutes such as restrictions on technology export and state secrets.
5   For instance, Sweden adopted the Swedish Data Bank Statute as early as 1973. This was a response to the overseas storage of data connected to Swedish citizens. See John M. Eger, 'Emerging Restrictions on Transnational Data Flows: Privacy Protection or Non-Tariff Trade Barriers', *Law & Policy in International Business* 10.4 (1978): 1065-81; Christopher Kuner, 'Data Nationalism and its Discontents', *Emory Law Journal* 64 (2015): 2091-93; Anupam Chander and Uyên P. Lê, 'Data Nationalism', *Emory Law Journal* 64.3 (2015): 713-39.
6   At large DL analysis presents taxonomy and being surrounded by countless dichotomies (e.g. data/information, privacy/public security, etc.) was trapped within the binary constraints of traditional regulatory approaches. Justice of the US Supreme Court Anthony M. Kennedy has provided a great example of binary regulatory choices during the oral argument in the *United States v. Microsoft Corporation*. In the course of extraterritoriality discussion Justice Kennedy has raised a question of why should SCOTUS be focused on data location storage v. data location disclosure and whether SCOTUS is forced to make such a choice. See 'United States v. Microsoft Corporation (Oral Argument Transcription)', Official Website, (2018), https://www.supremecourt.gov/oral_arguments/argument_transcripts/2017/17-2_j4ek.pdf.
7   Valerie Braithwaite, 'Closing the Gap Between Regulation and the Community', in Peter Drahos (ed.), *Regulatory Theory: Foundations and Applications* Canberra: ANU Press, 2017, pp. 30-33.

tensions between privacy, information sovereignty and international trade in the context of the World Trade Organization (WTO). Against this background, it examines the role of information management cycles (IMCs) and regulatory principles in data regulation. This allows the final analysis that maps DL policies and provides insights into how DL features such as storage location and technological implementation could affect the output of DL policy - providing the key analytical framework for crafting data regulations that avoid negative consequences. While mapping is not a new theory, it is the analytical framework that should initiate the transition from DL taxonomical description to data policy evaluation, modelling and projection.

What is Data Localization?

The term *data localization* refers to compulsory legal requirements to store data in a specific territory. This broad concept is implemented in a myriad of laws and regulations.[8]

DL policy aims to achieve multiple social goals and potentially may disrupt the informational environment, where agents interact and contribute to improvement of social welfare.[9] This is due to conceptual labyrinth where states are forced to regulate the use of technologies that facilitate universal human rights, promote economic activities and enhance national security, despite the way that these values can come into conflict. Encrypted apps such as Telegram and Zello are the examples of technological progress reaching twofold results. On one hand, they protect privacy and globally improve welfare; on the other they raise national security issues by limiting opportunities to enforce domestic legislation regarding users and their own activities.[10]

DL practices continuously evolve and have drawn wide attention of scholars in the last few years. There have been several taxonomies of DL practices that are substantively different, but similar in descriptive approach.[11] Broad measures embrace as much data as possible, while narrow DL measures can specify particular sets of data or particular businesses that are obliged to localize data.[12] On a broad approach DL measures could be defined as any measures that affect cross-border data transfer. Further, they could be grouped by the forms of implementation: (i) rules prohibiting overseas data transfers; (ii) rules restricting overseas data transfers by authorization; (iii) rules requiring *per se* localization of data; (iv) taxes on

---

8   'Data Localization Snapshot (Current as of January 19, 2017)', Information Technology Industry Council, (2017), https://www.itic.org/public-policy/SnapshotofDataLocalizationMeasures1-19-2017.pdf.
9   On the concept of *infosphere* see Luciano Floridi, *The Ethics of Information*, Oxford: Oxford University Press, 2013, p. 6.
10 Issie Lapowsky, 'Voice Chat App Zello Turned a Blind Eye to Jihadis for Years', *WIRED*, 16 March 2018, https://www.wired.com/story/zello-app-turned-blind-eye-to-jihadis-for-years/.
11 Chander and Lê, 'Data Nationalism': 708-13.
12 DL measures introduced in Australia (health related data) and Canada (data in possession of public institutions) are examples of a narrow approach. On the contrary, measures adopted by Russia (personal data (PII), communications metadata and content), China (PII and important data collected by 'network operators') and Vietnam (data important for national security) fall under a broad approach. See Scott Livingston and Graham Greenleaf, 'Data Localisation in China and Other APEC Jurisdictions', *Privacy Laws & Business International Report* 143 (2016): 2-5.

data export.[13] Such classification is not exhaustive. It could be supplemented at least with two additional types of DL: (v) disclosure of cryptographic keys; and (vi) obligatory disclosure of the requested information by entities subject to a particular jurisdiction regardless of the storage location.[14] Relying on the broad approach scholars also distinguish two more categories of DL measures by distinguishing between different technological means of implementation. Thus, states invoke policies of localized data hosting (e.g. sole or local copy) and localized data routing (e.g. data packets routing through the designated routes).[15] Such state interventions in data traffic are usually ensured by cooperation with internet service providers such as content filtering (censorship), access control (website blocking) and regulation of privacy enhancing technologies such as virtual private networks.[16] On the narrow approach to DL, there are three types of DL measures: (i) requirements to store *all* data in facilities located inside of the state; (ii) requirements to store *specific* sets of data in facilities located inside of the state; and (iii) requirements to transfer data only to states with adequate legislative and security measures in place with particular purposes and for a limited time.[17]

Whatever particular DL measures are taken, they may be seen as information barriers,[18] as they can limit information flows in various ways within the infosphere or specifically within a particular political agent like a state or economic union.[19] DL makes access to localized data harder for some agents and increases the informational gap between them, while strengthening privacy and information sovereignty protection. However, DL is not only about building informational walls to exclude access of external agents, because the data also becomes more accessible for agents in the jurisdiction to which it is localized. Hence, DL can be a tool for preventing or facilitating access to information, depending on how it is used.

---

13 Chander and Lê, 'Data Nationalism': 680.
14 See Clarifying Lawful Overseas Use of Data Act, 18 U.S.C. § 2713 (2018); Federal'nyi Zakon RF ob Informacii, informacionnyh tehnologijah i o zashite informacii [Federal law of the Russian Federation on Information, Information technologies and Protection of Information], Rossiiskaia Gazeta, July 31, 2006, item 10.1(4.1).
15 Localized data hosting - a requirement to store certain data on servers physically based within the state's territory. Localized data routing - the requirement to send data packets through servers physically based within the state's territory. John Selby, 'Data Localization Laws: Trade Barriers or Legitimate Responses to Cybersecurity Risks, or Both?', *International Journal of Law and Information Technology*, 25.3 (2017): 214.
16 Content filtering - censorship of data packets based on subject matter or technological requirements. 'Work Programme on Electronic Commerce. Removing Cyberspace Trade Barriers: Towards a Digital Trade Environment with Reciprocally Equal Access. Non-Paper from the Separate Customs Territory of Taiwan, Penghu, Kinmen and Matsu', Council for Trade in Goods General Council, Council for Trade in Services, Council for Trade-Related Aspects of Intellectual Property Rights, Committee on Trade and Development, JOB/GC/170, JOB/CTG/12 JOB/SERV/277, JOB/IP/29 JOB/DEV/53, 16 February 2018 1, para. 1.3, https://docs.wto.org/dol2fe/Pages/SS/directdoc.aspx?filename=q:/JOBs/GC/170.pdf.
17 Shin-yi Peng and Han-wei Liu, 'The Legality of Data Residency Requirements: How Can the Trans-Pacific Partnership Help?', *Journal of World Trade* 51.2 (2017): 193-94.
18 In addition, consider the following examples: data leak prevention systems, rules regarding state secrets, commercial secrets, confidential information, and intellectual property.
19 Floridi, *The Ethics of Information*, 232.

Before proceeding to examine and evaluate possible DL outcomes, it will be necessary to understand the legal and policy problems that arise from the tension between the three concepts that provided grounds for DL in the first place.

Localization Tensions: Privacy - Data Sovereignty - International Trade

DL raises theoretical and practical issues on many levels. First, there is the issue of individual privacy, in particular the desire to protect personal (identifiable) information (PII) from others. Privacy over PII is the ability 'to determine [...] when, how, and to what extent information about [...] [*individuals, groups, institutions*] is communicated to others'.[20] Second, states as independent agents interact with individuals as well as other states. They also have an interest in protecting and accessing information that has value to them. Thus, a notion of data sovereignty arises, which in fact is very similar to individuals' privacy in terms of guarding data of a critical importance by an independent agent. Finally, DL policy affects the free use of information in markets including cross-border trade, where an agenda to liberalize trade by reducing restrictions on imports and exports prevails.

These layers are inter-dependent. Privacy determines not only personal security, but also state security (e.g. consider a Twitter bot that is tracking movements of top public officials,[21] a fitness app exposing military bases,[22] a security breach exposing records of active military).[23] In turn, data sovereignty provides both individual and institutional data protection (e.g. in 2007 the government of Estonia had to cut off the country from the outside internet in order to stop a cyber-attack and prevent possible data loss).[24] International trade therefore has an interface with domestic and international regulation of privacy as well as rules regarding the use of state information (e.g. requirements established for activities related to critical information infrastructure).[25]

---

20 Alan F. Westin, *Privacy and Freedom*, New York: Atheneum, 1967, p. 7.
21 Amar Toor, 'This Twitter Bot is Tracking Dictators' Flights In and Out of Geneva', *The Verge*, 16 October 2016, https://www.theverge.com/2016/10/13/13243072/twitter-bot-tracks-dictator-planes-geneva-gva-tracker.
22 Richard Perez-Pena and Matthew Rosenberg, 'Strava Fitness App Can Reveal Military Sites, Analysts Say', *The New York Times*, 29 January 2018, https://www.nytimes.com/2018/01/29/world/middleeast/strava-heat-map.html.
23 Jason Murdock, 'U.S. Marines Email Leak Exposes Secrets of 21,000 Soldiers, Civilians', *Newsweek*, 1 March 2018, http://www.newsweek.com/us-marines-data-breach-leak-soldier-secrets-hits-21000-soldiers-civilians-825382.
24 Mark Landler and John Markoff, 'Digital Fears Emerge After Data Siege in Estonia', *The New York Times*, 29 May 2007, http://www.nytimes.com/2007/05/29/technology/29estonia.html.
25 See Daniel Gervais, 'Regulation of Inchoate Technologies', *Houston Law Review* 47.3 (2010): 679-80. Also see 'New Legislation Regulating Cyber Security and the Internet in Russia', *Clifford Chance Resources*, 3 March, 2017, https://www.cliffordchance.com/briefings/2017/10/new_legislation_regulatingcybersecurityandth.html; 'China Cybersecurity Law Update: Finally, Draft Regulations on 'Critical Information Infrastructure' *Bird & Bird News Centre*, 3 March, 2017, https://www.twobirds.com/en/news/articles/2017/china/draft-regulations-on-critical-information-infrastructure.

Consequently, problems arise where information restrictions provided by the first two layers start to compete between each other and conflict with international obligations established by the third. In particular, the WTO covered agreements[26] establish the most inclusive liberalized trade regime in the world by requiring non-discrimination and predictable market access.[27] Nonetheless, WTO members frequently restrict non-discrimination obligations and market access for foreign goods and services and this includes restrictions on data flows.[28] Under trade rules, DL measures might constitute a type of non-tariff barrier in digital trade, which might affect trade in services, goods and intellectual property (IP) or constitute a technical barrier to trade. However, none of the legal issues raised by DL implementation have been tested before the WTO dispute resolution body, and therefore the application of the WTO rules (about which there are different interpretations in existing disputes) remains a matter of debate.[29]

In theory the WTO regime should provide certainty and predictability of international trade, but currently it does not do so in relation to data flows. Data usage falls under numerous legal categories and the WTO Agreement provides various exceptions for legitimate non-compliance to achieve goals such as the protection of individuals' privacy.[30] Such protection has to be related to PII processing and dissemination. Another exception is focused on states' safety, which in turn can mean many things. There is also a general exception concerning public order, which applies in the event of a 'genuine and sufficiently serious threat to important societal values'.[31] Finally, states could purport to rely on a security exception which permits to impose any measures that they consider necessary in time of emergency in international relations. States with DL regulation may claim any of these broad exceptions as justification for protecting data sovereignty. Although these matters (particularly, the DL measure's necessity to achieve the goal) arise under the WTO regime and therefore they should be resolved accordingly by means of treaties interpretation and their application to particular facts, one inevitably will face a dilemma of weighing importance of societal values.

In assessing various state DL measures' compliance with WTO obligations, one will ask the following long-standing questions. Is privacy more important than national security? Is it vice versa? Should cross-border data flows be enforced to ensure international trade in any event at the expense of these values? How does one determine the balance between several societal values? How should regulatory practices look to reach and preserve such a balance? In the end of the day, do DL measures serve data justice within a complex multi-agent system? Do

---

26   WTO Agreement: Marrakesh Agreement Establishing the World Trade Organization, Apr. 15, 1994, 1867 U.N.T.S. 154, 33 I.L.M. 1144 (1994).
27   Peter van den Bossche and Denise Prevost, *Essentials of WTO Law*, Cambridge: Cambridge University Press, 2016, pp. 13, 49.
28   Ibid, 49.
29   E-Commerce WP - Taiwan (2018), 3, para. 3.1.
30   GATT 1994: General Agreement on Tariffs and Trade 1994, arts. XX(a), XX(b), XX(d), XXI(b)(iii), Apr. 15, 1994, Marrakesh Agreement Establishing the World Trade Organization, Annex 1A, 1867 U.N.T.S. 187, 33 I.L.M. 1153 (1994); GATS: General Agreement on Trade in Services, arts. XIV(a), XIV(c)(ii), XIV(c)(iii), XIVbis(1)(b)(iii), Apr. 15, 1994, Marrakesh Agreement Establishing the World Trade Organization, Annex 1B, 1869 U.N.T.S. 183, 33 I.L.M. 1167 (1994).
31   GATS, art XIV(a), fn 5.

they amount to smart and fair data regulation? These kinds of questions cannot and should not be answered solely in context of the existing law.[32] Consequently, we should look beyond that to other approaches that may provide guidance.

Regulating Information Management Cycles

Rapid datafication consisting of data computerization and reevaluation has sparked the discussion of data power and its connection to social justice.[33] This gave rise to the idea of data justice - an ethical guide for information society and the basis of data regulation. Data justice being a fairly new phenomenon is the subject of research within various fields of study.[34] The notion of data justice reflects on data governance and its effects on social and economic justice. Data justice in the context of DL policing highlights the role of data within the tripartite power relations between individuals, states and international institutions explained above. In other words, data justice is the pursuit of fair data use by agents aimed at corporate and state surveillance, privacy protection and free data flows for the purpose of economic and technological development. This chapter posits that data justice and hence smart data regulation analysis should take into account the variety of regulatory institutions concerning data such as PII and IP in all their numerous forms, and efficient information lifecycle management consisting of generation, collection, storage, processing, distribution, usage, and erasure as a coherent system because the regulatory system is the foundation of any kind of justice and contemporary society is not only driven by information but also depends on it to function properly.[35]

Current research has been limited by the binary constraints of traditional regulatory approaches that currently characterize the discussion of the balance between private and public interests regarding the treatment of IMCs (i.e. ensuring data justice). This prevents the elaboration of satisfactory solutions that can maintain complex multi-level systems such as DL. Hence, it is necessary to overcome such limitations.

Conceptually it is reasonable to assume that, depending on the particular structure of a DL policy, a measure could serve one or more policy goals by countless means. At the same time, such means should be analyzed as whole since one small detail could determine the output of the system. For instance, would a measure fully depriving individuals of their autonomy to guard data serve the purpose of privacy protection? How does a DL system technically incapable of enforcing a law - or prone to over-enforcement - contribute to serving data justice and account for necessity? Mapping DL practices should help answer these questions.

---

32   Christopher Kuner, 'Data Nationalism and its Discontents', 2096.
33   Lina Dencik, Arne Hintz, and Jonathan Cable, 'Towards Data Justice? The Ambiguity of Anti-Surveillance Resistance in Political Activism', *Big Data & Society*, 3.2 (2016): 8-9.
34   Linnet Taylor, 'What is Data Justice? The Case for Connecting Digital Rights and Freedoms Globally', *Big Data & Society*, 4.2 (2017): 1-4.
35   Braithwaite, 'Closing the Gap', 30-33.

Any data regulatory practice should be evaluated on the basis of how it affects the well-being of agents and the informational environment. Any decrease in size or corrosion of quality of information will cause the infosphere to shrink in terms of content, forms and patterns.[36] This leads to fewer opportunities for agents to beneficially interact and thus to contribute to welfare. Hence, the more restrictive DL policy, the higher the deficit of information and the less space for agents to communicate. However, it does not mean that information processes should not be regulated at all. Clearly, such values as privacy, national security and trade are all important. There have always been certain types of data and information processes that states rigorously restricted on domestic and international levels for the benefit of all agents. But what matters is how states give effect to restrictive information policies and what the overall output of such regulatory system is.[37]

General regulatory principles such as consistency, certainty, effective implementation, stability, minimization of costs and market distortions, compatibility with trade facilitation and others are meant to provide regulators with the framework under which states are more likely to come up with a better output for the society.[38] Thus, no society needs a regulatory mechanism (e.g. regarding theft) that is inconsistent and impossible to implement because the effect of such regulation tends to zero, resulting in more risks for the society.

In the context of data, that would mean an unjustified and unnecessary fracture of the IMCs. Consider the following example. IP is information identified as a specific category of information, the control of which is treated by the society in a special way. The Berne Convention provides regulation for literary works and covers the whole IMC.[39] For instance, creation and record are governed by the norms regarding the form of literary works, publication and formalities (Articles 2, 3, 5); processing and collection are resembled in provisions regarding derivative works (Article 2); distribution is covered by rules on reproduction (Article 9); provi-

---

36   Floridi, *The Ethics of Information*, 65-67.
37   As an alternative to DL policies scholars sometimes refer to the Mutual Legal Assistance Treaties (MLATs). While under MLATs states may agree on information exchange and establish an effective regime of cross-border data interception, this mechanism is extremely time consuming and of a highly political nature. In most cases the request for the information exchange under MLATs may be easily denied. Thus, under the MLAT between Russia and the United States 'the execution of the request [may be denied if it] would prejudice the security or other essential interests of the Requested Party'. Apparently, the category of essential interests is broad and would have different meanings for both Russia and the United States especially considering the current state of international relations between both actors. Hence, while recognizing the role, although somewhat limited, of MLATs in controlling cross-border data flows, this chapter leaves the question of their potential to constitute a substitute to DL polices open and subject to the future research. See Chander and Lê, 'Data Nationalism', 730-735; Peng and Liu, 'The Legality of Data Residency Requirements', 201-202; 'Rethinking Data, Geography, and Jurisdiction: Towards a Common Framework for Harmonizing Global Data Flow Controls', New America, (2018), 5-8, https://newamerica.org/documents/2084/Rethinking_Data_Geography_Jurisdiction_2.21.pdf.
38   'Principles for Good Governance of Regulators (Public Consultation Draft)', Organisation for Economic Co-operation and Development, (2013), http://www.oecd.org/gov/regulatory-policy/Governance%20of%20Regulators%20FN%202.docx.
39   Berne Convention for the Protection of Literary and Artistic Works, Sep. 9, 1886, revised at Paris July 24, 1979, 828 U.N.T.S. 221, S. Treaty Doc. No. 99-27, 99th Cong. (1986).

sions concerning use without charge regulate information consumption (Article 10); erasure is envisaged by prescribed moral rights (Article 6*bis*). By over- or non-regulation of a particular section of the literary work management cycle, the regulator could break it, eventually resulting in the underproduction of literary works. This negative effect on generation, dissemination and consumption of information consequently would affect the state of welfare.[40]

This system also demonstrates tensions between private and public monopoly over information and international obligations. Rephrasing our previously introduced traditional definition of privacy, we might say that the 'right to exclude others' in IP is the right to determine when, how, and to what extent information *created* by individuals, groups or institutions is communicated to others. States have their own interests regarding information flows of the category *literary works* and the Berne Convention provides them with a possibility of legitimate non-compliance by the right of censorship (Article 17). However, as the Berne Convention is a unification act and therefore relies on states' regulatory autonomy and modus of creativity, states independently decide on how they are going to construct their censorship policy, what constitutes necessity, to what extent they are willing to sacrifice regulatory principles in order to reach their objectives. Inevitably, some regulatory practices will appear better than others.

The same structure applies to DL measures dealing with storage location and processing of information (which in fact in many cases includes not only PII, but other categories of information such as IP) that might result in data injustices and disrupt information lifecycles, thus making them inefficient. General regulatory principles aimed at maximizing win-win regulatory end results could therefore provide a threshold against which it would be possible to compare DL models. The following section is dedicated to informational construction of DL and evaluation of regulatory practices.

Mapping Data Localization Regulatory Practices

DL could be dynamically modelled depending on the chosen regulatory tools (variables) and their subject matter (types), which in turn constitute each of the policy goals (observables) (Figure 1). Each sequence of typed variables uniquely determines the subject matter of observables and therefore the output of the DL policy.[41] Such output in terms of welfare consequences then could be measured against regulatory principles.

---

40   Peter Drahos, *A Philosophy of Intellectual Property*, Aldershot: Ashgate Publishing Company, 1996, p. 180.
41   See Luciano Floridi, 'The Method of Levels of Abstraction', *Minds & Machines,* 18.3 (2008): 305-306.

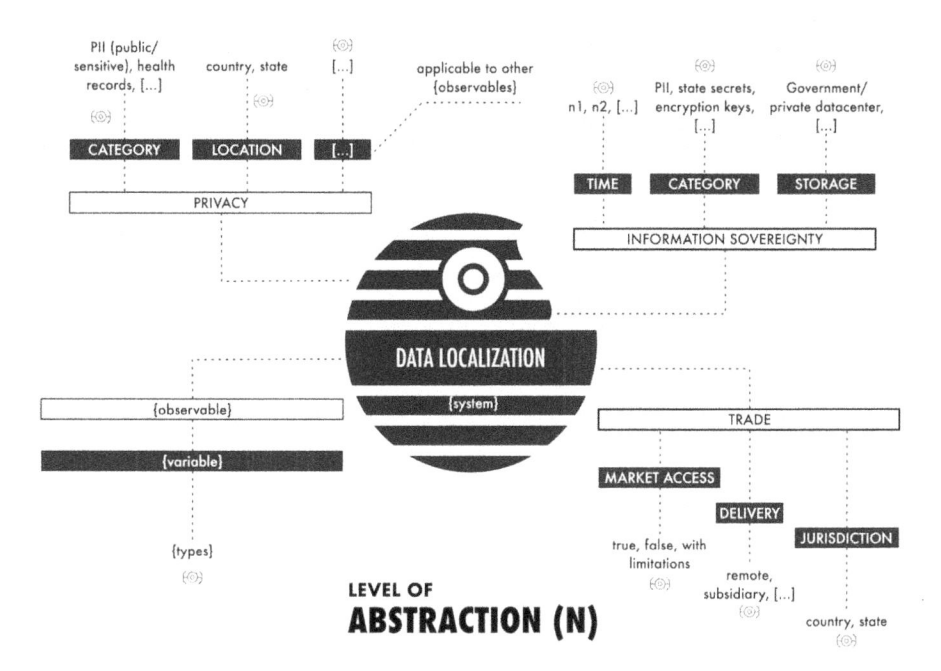

Figure 1.

Depending on collection of variables, their types and interpretation it is possible to construct many variants of DL systems. For instance, *category* variable determines the scope and thus differently characterizes observables. Thus, localization of governmental data should affect the correlation of privacy, sovereignty and trade differently compared to localization of undefined categories of PII. The broader the scope, the more it attributes to the protection of privacy and data sovereignty because data subjects and states acquire more effective control over data as it is physically available to them. However, it becomes more burdensome for international trade and domestic market actors as their economic costs rise as well as more restrictive on individual liberties because the autonomy to decide the fate of data shrinks.

Moreover, this relationship depends on the legal form and meaning of the *types*. For instance, in terms of categories Russia requires the localization of (i) PII and (ii) communications, while Australia requires the localization of (iii) personally controlled electronic health records (PCEHR).[42] The reason why researchers classify (i) and (ii) as broad and (iii) as narrow is that they differ in scope and hence the amount of data required to localize. In Russia PII means any information that can identify a person. Communications in turn include metadata and content data or any information transmitted/received by user over the internet/other means of telecommunications.[43] On the other hand, PCEHR constitutes information about

---

42 'Data Localization Snapshot', www.itic.org.
43 Content data - information aimed at the public (e.g. text messages, audio- and video-files). Metadata - data about information aimed at the public (e.g. IP-address and device the content was sent from, time of the content exchange, format of the content).

and connected to the customer, which is related to health and recorded in a special system or register. Obviously, the scope differs considerably depending on the attributes *any, transmitted,* and *related to health.* The broader the meaning of a category the more policy space a state acquires in the course of sovereignty protection. However, it creates uncertainty for individuals and international market participants that might result in an overall disadvantage.

Although, this system is not static and the output changes if other variables are introduced. Thus, for (i) regulated agents include any persons that are involved in PII management cycle at any stage and specific entities that ensure communications regarding measure (ii). For measure (iii), regulated agents are envisaged in the closed list of entities that are authorized to work with PCEHR. Again, these attributes make the scope narrower or broader. Further, all measures contain a non-finite amount of information formats and mediums (e.g. personal and public records, health records, audio, video, etc.). This attribute broadens the definition of data for all compared measures.

Such variables as location and method of storage also greatly affect the output. In case DL mechanism prescribes storage of data in a particular region or even in a particular datacenter, it creates and worsens to a degree the so-called jackpot and protected local provider (PLP) problems.[44] It is one thing to prescribe storage within a particular territory thus limiting the market by territory, technical capabilities and competition, and another if a regulator specifies authorized market players thus limiting the environment even more. In this regard even forms of ownership (e.g. public or private) should play a crucial role, since owners of datacenters and their numbers determine the market.

The enforcement framework matters as well. DL measures are usually enforced by common regimes of legal sanctions or technical enforcement such as blocking schemes that preclude service providers from operating on a particular territory. Just as the wording of a statute makes a difference in the course of its application, technical characteristics of the blocking scheme determine the output of a DL measure. For example, in many instances DL in Russia is based on blocking IP addresses, while DL in New Zealand is based on blocking of a combination of IP and URL addresses. Both methods provide different outputs. While the former is easier and cheaper (this is relevant for those who pay for such enforcement, e.g. state or internet providers) to implement, it blocks every resource that is assigned to a blocked IP address, hence resulting in over-enforcement. The latter on the other hand allows the conducting of additional filtering by URL and provides for a precision-guided enforcement mechanism.[45]

---

44 Chander and Lê, 'Data Nationalism', 716-17. Jackpot problem - a centralized data storage that simplifies access for the intruder (e.g. designating a state-owned data center for an obligatory data storage). Protected local provider problem - a deterioration of local data processing services as a result of a limited competition established by the DL policy (i.e. data processing market shrinks by excluding international businesses).

45 'Analiz Sushestvujushih Metodov Upravlenija Dostupom k Internet-Resursam i Rekomendatsii po ih Primeneniju', (*Analysis of Existing Methods Regarding Administration of the Access to Internet-Resources and Recommendations on Their Application*), [in Russian], Official Website of Federal Service for Supervision of Communications, Information Technology and Mass Media, (2013), https://

It is important to note that the legal bases for invoking such technical enforcement are also of a great significance. For example, it is reasonable to assume that judicial review might reduce possible negative effects of technical enforcement, particularly regarding IP-based mass blocking, more effectively if compared to administrative review. On top of that, the efficiency of these features depends on the meta framework - the rule of law. Regardless of how legal and technological enforcement is formally constructed, in the absence of the rule of law no mechanism would work properly. This applies to the construction of any regulation.

The same rationale applies to a feature of localization of encryption keys, which could be achieved by various means such as compulsory assistance, lawful hacking and prior design of backdoors.[46] Each method has its own advantages and disadvantages but once again it is crucial to emphasize the importance of legal and technical implementation frameworks. For instance, compulsory assistance that implies sending encryption keys over unsecured means of communication is not better than lawful hacking against an undefined set of persons without any form of legal review.[47]

Hence, there is a plethora of elements that at the end of the day may invoke the law of unintended consequences and turn a DL mechanism intended to regain control over data for the sake of privacy and security into something quite the opposite.[48] It is considerably difficult to argue that a DL scheme consisting of an obligatory centralized governmental data storage regarding broad categories of data and compulsory assistance scheme contributes to privacy protection as this mechanism clearly erodes individuals' autonomy to determine the fate of their data. Neither does it amount to reasonable standards of security protection as such a model elevates jackpot and PLP problems to a critical level. However, it is only when DL is considered as a complex system should the output be considered because otherwise policymaking turns into gambling.[49]

Based on this could it be reasonably assumed that the Australian measure is *smarter* because it requires the storage of less data? Or could it be concluded that all DL measures are bad regulatory practices just because they establish more burdens? Indeed, either scenario results

---

rkn.gov.ru/docs/Analysys_and_recommendations_comments_fin.pdf; 'Digital Child Exploitation Filtering System', The New Zealand Department of Internal Affairs, (2009), http://www.dia.govt.nz/pubforms.nsf/URL/DCESF-PublicInformationPack.pdf/$file/DCESF-PublicInformationPack.pdf.

46 'Encryption Policy in Democratic Regimes: Finding Convergent Paths and Balanced Solutions', EastWest Institute, (2018), 32-38, https://www.eastwest.ngo/sites/default/files/ewi-encryption.pdf.

47 'Telegram Loses Bid to Block Russia From Encryption Keys', *Bloomberg*, 21 March 2018, https://www.bloomberg.com/news/articles/2018-03-20/telegram-loses-bid-to-stop-russia-from-getting-encryption-keys. One of the arguments within discussion of this case was that the Russian Federal Security Service does not provide for a secure means of encryption keys disclosure and allows them to be sent over unsecured mail or email.

48 Gervais, 'Regulation of Inchoate Technologies', 684-88.

49 Consider the following. Russian measures require storing data onshore, but do not prohibit data being transferred abroad in full. Australian measures require storing data onshore by prohibiting any transfer of PCEHR overseas unless redacted, anonymized and conducted by an authorized public agency. Obviously, without taking into consideration other features of the systems it is impossible to conclude whether any of them amount to smart regulatory practice.

in the distortion of IMCs. Consequently, DL measures should be constructed as to prevent and remove such distortion by adherence to regulatory principles.

This discussion cannot canvass every link between DL features and regulatory principles. However, the Australian measure, for instance, provides more certainty as it raises less questions about what actually regulated persons ought to store. In contrast, Russian DL measures are very similar to Russian famous 'yes, no, maybe', which means a negative reaction of a high uncertainty and possibility to be changed into 'yes' and 'no' in the future. In other words, it contains a general but not detailed enough meaning, which is contrary to the principle of legal certainty. This is the exact reason why experts cannot even agree on economic consequences because no one knows how much data shall be stored.[50]

Overall, such an approach correlates with the precautionary principle that is familiar to international law including the WTO framework and many legal systems.[51] The precautionary principle has emerged as a response to human activities resulting in environmental degradation and serves as the basis for safeguarding humans' safety.[52] However, this principle may be applied to regulation of inchoate technologies and therefore IMCs that are constituent to them.[53]

Generally, the precautionary principle aims at preserving conditions critical for humans by eliminating potential negative activities that may alter such conditions even in the absence of a clear and unambiguous causation.[54] Indeed, DL policies look like precautionary measures called to protect states' data sovereignty and individuals' privacy. However, under this veil data flows are seen as a potential source of harm and their value (e.g. social, economic, etc.) is often disregarded. Moreover, such one-sided regulatory interventionism allows for trade protectionism only worsening localization tensions explained above. Accordingly, the focus of precautionary protection should also incorporate IMCs which create the operational environment for states, individuals and trade actors.

Finally, uncertainty is the trigger for the precautionary principle.[55] Data flows as well as inchoate technology generate unpredictable events for all the actors of informational environment and therefore sovereignty, privacy and trade. Hence, there is a genuine interest to eliminate uncertainty by introducing precautionary measures. However, the only way to reduce uncertainty is by introducing legal certainty aligned with social expectations which means adherence to the regulatory principles.

---

50   By various estimates only the costs of communications data localisation will be anywhere from $50 million to $154 billion. See 'Russia's "Big Brother Law" to Cost Telecoms $154Bln - Report', *The Moscow Times*, 26 August 2016, https://themoscowtimes.com/news/anti-terror-big-brother-law-to-cost-russian-companies-154bln-says-expert-55125.
51   See A. Wallace Hayes, 'The Precautionary Principle', *Archives Indus. Hygiene & Toxicology* 56 (2005): 161-62.
52   Ibid.
53   Gervais, 'Regulation of Inchoate Technologies', 693-704.
54   However, there is a plethora of formulas for the precautionary principle depending on the applicable sector and wording. See Hayes, 'The Precautionary Principle', 162.
55   Gervais, 'Regulation of Inchoate Technologies', 697.

By all means, the determination of a threshold of legal certainty regarding IMCs is a nontrivial task. Adopting an approach oriented at IMCs, it is proposed to subject DL policies to the following criteria placed in a hierarchical order:[56]

1. under no circumstances shall a DL policy generate legal uncertainty;
2. a DL policy shall prevent legal uncertainty;
3. a DL policy shall reduce legal uncertainty;
4. a DL policy shall benefit data flows.

The first criterion is of a critical importance and therefore failure to adhere to it would result in over-enforcement. In turn, legal uncertainty exists where a DL policy is inconsistent, disproportionate, technologically and economically unreasonable. For instance, a DL policy introducing a broad localization scheme for undefined data categories, establishing a censorship mechanism at the tremendous cost of private parties that amounts to *carpet website blockings* and on top of that which is arbitrary enforced, would not be justified under the proposed framework in any event. This is due to the fact that it generates legal uncertainty instead of preventing or reducing it. While such a scheme could be highly beneficial for protecting information sovereignty, the generated legal uncertainty would inadequately affect privacy and trade. On the other hand, a DL policy of a high-accuracy that requires law enforcement agencies' access to communications metadata, regardless of the storage location, with a legally provided possibility to copy such data for security precautions and a blocking scheme, would have higher chances to be justified under the proposed framework. Accordingly, such a DL policy arguably reduces legal uncertainty for all the actors while also benefiting the development of IMCs by eliminating harmful activities. Ultimately, a DL policy requiring the disclosure of software code in the event that such software is exploited for governmental purposes or there is a good reason to believe that a product contains backdoors, which could be used for concealed data collection or result in data breach, also has a better chance to be justified. Respectively, this would be possible because such DL policy would prevent legal uncertainty caused by software products and benefit IMCs by securing confidential data before the event.

As previously described and demonstrated in Figure 1 some features of a DL system might reduce the overall effect of DL, while others worsen its notorious effect. Taking into account the regulatory principles, the more definitive and precise a DL measure is, the more adequate the link between the measure and the policy objective is, the better a possibility to construct a smarter data regulatory regime. Approaching data regulation as a complex system should result in a highly scrutinized regulatory scheme. This might be more effective compared to binary choices.

Conclusion

Data justice or balance within the framework of power relations over data is obviously necessary in today's world, but it is impossible to approach without smart data regulation. Far from

---

56   The proposed framework reflects on the four ethical principles of Information Ethics. See Floridi, *The Ethics of* Information, 70-74.

being a fully designed concept, it is plausible to infer that smart data regulation regarding DL should constitute a small-scaled policy based on an adequate number of regulatory tools (variables) with well-defined subject matter (types) rather than extensive and broad regulation. This is more likely to sustain and enrich IMCs, while ensuring the competing interests of all information agents by means of preserving the balance between legally certain regulatory interventions and private autonomy.

Each detail in a data regulatory mechanism matters. From the overall purpose and wording, to technical nature and implementation. By abstracting elements the regulator risks creating expensive, ineffective and damaging regulations resulting in unintended consequences. The regulator has to be sensitive to every action against information flows and provide safety nets as negligence might result in data injustices and affect societal welfare.

References

'Analiz Sushestvujushih Metodov Upravlenija Dostupom K Internet-Resursam I Rekomendatsii Po Ih Primeneniju', (*Analysis of Existing Methods Regarding Administration of the Access to Internet-Resources and Recommendations on Their Application*). [In Russian]. Official Website of Federal Service for Supervision of Communications, Information Technology and Mass Media, 2013.

Berne Convention for the Protection of Literary and Artistic Works, Sep. 9, 1886, revised at Paris July 24, 1979, 828 U.N.T.S. 221, S. Treaty Doc. No. 99-27, 99th Cong, (1986).

Bossche, Peter van den, and Denise Prevost. *Essentials of WTO Law*, Cambridge: Cambridge University Press, 2016.

Braithwaite, Valerie. 'Closing the Gap between Regulation and the Community', in Peter Drahos (ed.), *Regulatory Theory: Foundations and Applications*, Canberra: ANU Press, 2017.

Chander, Anupam, and Uyên P. Lê. 'Data Nationalism', *Emory Law Journal* 64.3 (2015).

'China Cybersecurity Law Update: Finally, Draft Regulations on "Critical Information Infrastructure"'. *Bird & Bird News Centre*, 2017.

Clarifying Lawful Overseas Use of Data Act, 18 U.S.C. § 2713 (2018).

Clark, David D. *Designs for an Internet*. 2017.

'Data Localization Snapshot'. Information Technology Industry Council. 2017.

Dencik, Lina, Arne Hintz and Jonathan Cable. 'Towards Data Justice? The Ambiguity of Anti-Surveillance Resistance in Political Activism', *Big Data & Society* 3.2 (2016): 1-12.

'Digital Child Exploitation Filtering System'. The New Zealand Department of Internal Affairs, 2009.

Drahos, Peter. *A Philosophy of Intellectual Property*, Aldershot: Ashgate Publishing Company, 1996.

Eger, John M. 'Emerging Restrictions on Transnational Data Flows: Privacy Protection or Non-Tariff Trade Barriers', *Law & Policy in International Business* 10.4 (1978): 1055-103.

'Encryption Policy in Democratic Regimes: Finding Convergent Paths and Balanced Solutions'. East-West Institute, 2018.

Federal'nyi Zakon RF ob Informacii, informacionnyh tehnologijah i o zashite informacii [Federal law of the Russian Federation on Information, Information technologies and Protection of Information], Rossiiskaia Gazeta, July 31, 2006.

Floridi, Luciano. *The Ethics of Information*, Oxford: Oxford University Press, 2013.

_____. 'The Method of Levels of Abstraction', *Minds & Machines* 18.3 (2008): 303-29.

GATS: General Agreement on Trade in Services, Apr. 15, 1994, Marrakesh Agreement Establishing the World Trade Organization, Annex 1B, 1869 U.N.T.S. 183, 33 I.L.M. 1167 (1994).

GATT 1994: General Agreement on Tariffs and Trade 1994, Apr. 15, 1994, Marrakesh Agreement Establishing the World Trade Organization, Annex 1A, 1867 U.N.T.S. 187, 33 I.L.M. 1153 (1994).

Gervais, Daniel. 'Regulation of Inchoate Technologies', *Houston Law Review* 47.3 (2010): 665-705.

Hayes, A. Wallace. 'The Precautionary Principle', *Archives Indus. Hygiene & Toxicology* 56 (2005): 161-166.

Kang, Cicilia, and Katie Benner. 'Russia Requires Apple and Google to Remove Linkedin from Local App Stores.' *The New York Times*, 6 January 2017.

Kuchler, Hannah. 'Microsoft Faces Key Ruling in Data Privacy Case.' *Financial Times*, 17 October 2017.

Kuner, Christopher. 'Data Nationalism and Its Discontents', *Emory Law Journal* 64 (2015): 2089-98.

Landler, Mark, and John Markoff. 'Digital Fears Emerge after Data Siege in Estonia.' *The New York Times*, 29 May 2007.

Lapowsky, Issie. 'Voice Chat App Zello Turned a Blind Eye to Jihadis for Years.' *WIRED*, 16 March 2018.

'Linkedin to Be Blocked in Russia'. *RAPSI*, 10 November 2016.

Livingston, Scott, and Graham Greenleaf. 'Data Localisation in China and Other APEC Jurisdictions', *Privacy Laws & Business International Report* 143 (2016): 22-26.

McMillan, Robert, and Tripp Mickle. 'Apple to Start Putting Sensitive Encryption Keys in China.' *Wall Street Journal*, 24 February 2018.

Mozur, Paul, Daisuke Wakabayashi, and Nick Wingfield. 'Apple Opening Data Center in China to Comply with Cybersecurity Law.' *The New York Times*, 12 July 2017.

Murdock, Jason. 'U.S. Marines Email Leak Exposes Secrets of 21,000 Soldiers, Civilians.' *Newsweek*, 1 March 2018.

'New Legislation Regulating Cyber Security and the Internet in Russia'. *Clifford Chance Resources*. 2017.

Peng, Shin-yi, and Han-wei Liu. 'The Legality of Data Residency Requirements: How Can the Trans-Pacific Partnership Help?', *Journal of World Trade* 51.2 (2017): 183-204.

Perez-Pena, Richard and Matthew Rosenberg. 'Strava Fitness App Can Reveal Military Sites, Analysts Say'. *The New York Times*, 29 January 2018.

'Principles for Good Governance of Regulators (Public Consultation Draft)'. Organisation for Economic Co-operation and Development, 2013.

'Rethinking Data, Geography, and Jurisdiction: Towards a Common Framework for Harmonizing Global Data Flow Controls'. New America, 2018.

'Russia's "Big Brother Law" to Cost Telecoms $154bln - Report'. *The Moscow Times*. 26 August 2016.

Selby, John. 'Data Localization Laws: Trade Barriers or Legitimate Responses to Cybersecurity Risks, or Both?', *International Journal of Law and Information Technology* 25.3 (2017): 213-32.

Taylor, Linnet. 'What Is Data Justice? The Case for Connecting Digital Rights and Freedoms Globally', *Big Data & Society* 4.2 (2017): 1-14.

'Telegram Loses Bid to Block Russia from Encryption Keys'. *Bloomberg.* 21 March 2018.

Toor, Amar. 'This Twitter Bot Is Tracking Dictators' Flights in and out of Geneva'. *The Verge.* 16 October 2016.

'United States v. Microsoft Corp.'. *SCOTUSblog.* 2017.

'United States v. Microsoft Corporation (Oral Argument Transcription)'. Supreme Court of the United States. *Official Website.* 2018.

Waters, Richard. 'Microsoft Setback in Cloud Era Test Case.' *Financial Times*, 1 August 2014.

_____. 'Microsoft Wins Battle with Us over Data Privacy.' *Financial Times*, 15 July 2016.

Westin, Alan F. *Privacy and Freedom*, New York: Atheneum, 1967.

'Work Programme on Electronic Commerce. Removing Cyberspace Trade Barriers: Towards a Digital Trade Environment with Reciprocally Equal Access. Non-Paper from the Separate Customs Territory of Taiwan, Penghu, Kinmen and Matsu'. General Council, Council for Trade in Goods, Council for Trade in Services, Council for Trade-Related Aspects of Intellectual Property Rights, Committee on Trade and Development. '2018.

WTO Agreement: Marrakesh Agreement Establishing the World Trade Organization, Apr. 15, 1994, 1867 U.N.T.S. 154, 33 I.L.M. 1144 (1994).

THEME 3:
GOOD DATA AS OPEN AND SHARED DATA

10: MAKING DATA PUBLIC? THE OPEN DATA INDEX AS PARTICIPATORY DEVICE

JONATHAN GRAY AND DANNY LÄMMERHIRT

Introduction

The Open Data Index is a 'civil society audit' which strives to shape the availability and openness of public sector data from around the world. In this chapter we examine the social life of this project, including how it evolved, the changing visions and practices associated with it, and how it serves to assemble and involve different publics in the assessment of institutional practices and forms of datafication. Drawing on recent work on statactivism, data activism and the performative effects of numbers, rankings and indices, we look at how the index organises participation and data politics in specific ways, raising questions about not only making data public but also the making of public data. It plays two roles which are sometimes in tension: (i) conventionalising assessment to facilitate comparability, and (ii) reflecting the diversity of different interests, issues and settings involved in opening up public sector data. It also facilitates the creation of 'enumerated entities' as objects of concern in open data advocacy and policy. The Open Data Index may thus be viewed as a site where participation is both configured and contested, and where practices of valuation and enumeration are both conventionalised and brought into question.

How can various publics participate in shaping what data is created, collected and distributed by states? How might public participation around the availability and openness of public data lead to 'good data' (or at least 'better data')? In this chapter we reflect on the social life of the Open Data Index, a civil society project which aims to measure and influence how government data is made available. In particular we attend to how the index organises participation and data politics in specific ways, raising questions about not only making data public but also the making of public data.

There are many ways that one might appraise such an initiative. From the perspective of what Bruno Latour calls an 'anthropology of modernity',[1] there is a lot to be unpacked in these three little words: 'open', 'data' and 'index'. For example, one might consider imaginaries and practices of the 'index' in light of research on cultures of auditing and accountability.[2] One might tell a tale of the rise of the index as a style of political mobilisation alongside the rally, the petition or the hashtag. As well as public sector indices such as the United Nations 'Human Development Index' and 'Human Poverty Index', there are now a wide variety of

---

1   Bruno Latour, *An Inquiry into Modes of Existence: An Anthropology of the Moderns*, trans C. Porter, Cambridge MA: Harvard University Press, 2013.
2   Michael Power, *The Audit Society: Rituals of Verification*, Oxford: Oxford University Press, 1999; Marilyn Strathern, *Audit Cultures: Anthropological Studies in Accountability, Ethics and the Academy*, London: Routledge, 2000.

non-governmental and civil society indices, such as the 'Corruption Perceptions Index', the 'Press Freedom Index', the 'Happy Planet Index', the 'Financial Secrecy Index', the 'Global Slavery Index' and the 'Global Food Index'.[3]

The rise of the index can also be understood in relation to recent research exploring the social life and performative effects of rankings, indices and indicators.[4] Indices not only *represent* aspects of the world, they can also participate in *shaping* the world, including through reactive effects. They enable scores, rankings and comparisons of different issues across countries through processes of commensuration and quantification. Indices can thus be envisaged as devices for the production of social facts, which in turn enable different dynamics of competition and concern. The following passage from the press release accompanying a recent edition of the 'Corruption Perceptions Index', presented alongside coloured maps and rankings, provides an example of how indices can give rise to 'enumerated entities'[5] as objects of attention and concern:

> This year, New Zealand and Denmark rank highest with scores of 89 and 88 respectively. Syria, South Sudan and Somalia rank lowest with scores of 14, 12 and 9 respectively. The best performing region is Western Europe with an average score of 66. The worst performing regions are Sub-Saharan Africa (average score 32) and Eastern Europe and Central Asia (average score 34).[6]

Here the function of the index is render corruption across different countries commensurable, comparable and quantifiable. The scores enable normative claims about which countries are doing better and worse, and aspirations for future action.[7]

The Open Data Index may be considered a *database about data*, as it is concerned with the availability of governmental data across borders. Along with other similar initiatives such as the Open Data Barometer, the index raises questions about which data is to be made available and how it is to be made available. In doing so it also surfaces issues around the governance and politics of public data, such as who gets to decide what is measured and what kinds of reactive effects are imagined and observed. While previous literature discusses this index in

---

3   The corresponding organisation in order of the indices named: Transparency International, Reporters Without Border, New Economics Foundation, Tax Justice Network, Walk Free, Oxfam.
4   Wendy N. Espeland and Michael Sauder, 'Rankings and Reactivity: How Public Measures Recreate Social Worlds', *American Journal of Sociology*, 113 (2007): 1-40. Richard Rottenburg, Sally E. Merry, Sung-Joon Park, and Johanna Mugler (eds.), *The World of Indicators: The Making of Governmental Knowledge through Quantification*, Cambridge: Cambridge University Press, 2015.
5   Helen Verran, 'Number as an inventive frontier in knowing and working Australia's water resources', *Anthropological Theory*, 10 (2010): 171-178; Helen Verran, 'Enumerated Entities in Public Policy and Governance', in Ernest Davis and Philip J. Davis (eds), *Mathematics, Substance and Surmise,* New York: Springer, 2015, pp. 365-379.
6   Transparency International, 'Corruption Perceptions Index', *Transparency International blog*, 21 February 2018, https://www.transparency.org/news/feature/corruption_perceptions_index_2017.
7   Jane Guyer, 'Percentages and perchance: archaic forms in the twenty-first century', *Distinktion, Journal of Social Theory* 15 (2014): 155-173.

the context of information policy and the practices of public institutions,[8] it can also be considered in terms of recent work on data politics, including 'stactivism'[9] and 'data activism'.[10] The Open Data Index can be envisaged not only as a way to measure accessibility but also as a particular kind of intervention around official regimes of quantification and datafication - including around the horizons of intelligibility, the formation of collectives and the varieties of transnational coordination that they give rise to.[11]

Year	Number of submissions	Number of countries	% of "open" datasets
2012	177	34	Not given
2013	597	77	16%
2014	970	97	12%
2015	1586	122	9%
2016/17	1410	94	11%

Table 1: Numbers of submissions, numbers of countries and % of open datasets from Open Data Index and Open Data Census 2012-2017. Numbers obtained from archived websites and materials.

In what follows we examine what the Open Data Index is, what it does and how it has developed from 2012 to 2017 (Table 1) with reference to its various websites (current and archived), blog posts, reports, events, videos, software repositories, mailing lists and other materials. We also draw on our own involvement with the project in various capacities. We are particularly interested in how it organises participation around both *making public data* (i.e. what counts, what is counted, the forms of quantification and datafication which are held to matter) and *making data public* (i.e. the specific social and technical arrangements for making information available). We consider the index as an online 'device',[12] which both

---

8   Sharon S. Dawes, Lyudmila Vidiasova and Olga Parkhimovich, 'Planning and designing open government data programs: An ecosystem approach', *Government Information Quarterly* 33 (2016): 15-27; Jeffrey Thorsby, Genie N.L. Stowers, Kristen Wolslegel, and Ellie Tumbuan, 'Understanding the content and features of open data portals in American cities', *Government Information Quarterly* 34 (2017): 53-61.
9   Isabelle Bruno, Emmanuel Didier and Tommaso Vitale 'Statactivism: Forms of Action Between Disclosure and Affirmation', *Partecipazione e Conflitto*, 7 (2014).
10 Stefania Milan and Lonneke van der Velden, 'The Alternative Epistemologies of Data Activism', *Digital Culture & Society* 2 (2016): 57-74.
11 Jonathan Gray, 'Three Aspects of Data Worlds', *Krisis: Journal for Contemporary Philosophy* (2018).
12 John Law and Evelyn Ruppert, 'The Social Life of Methods: Devices', *Journal of Cultural Economy* 6 (2013): 229-240.

shapes and is shaped by the assembly of publics around the openness and availability of data as a 'matter of concern'.[13]

As a participatory device, the index plays two roles which may sometimes be in tension: (i) to *conventionalise* the assessment of the openness of data (thus facilitating comparability, objectivity and coordination across settings); and (ii) to facilitate public involvement in a way which is *receptive and flexible* enough to align with diverse interests, issues and activities around opening up governmental data. With the Open Data Index it is notable that this tension between conventionalisation and receptivity plays out through an open-ended invitation from a non-profit organisation to involve various publics through open source software and replicable components which enable the adaptation and multiplication of projects, including through forking.[14]

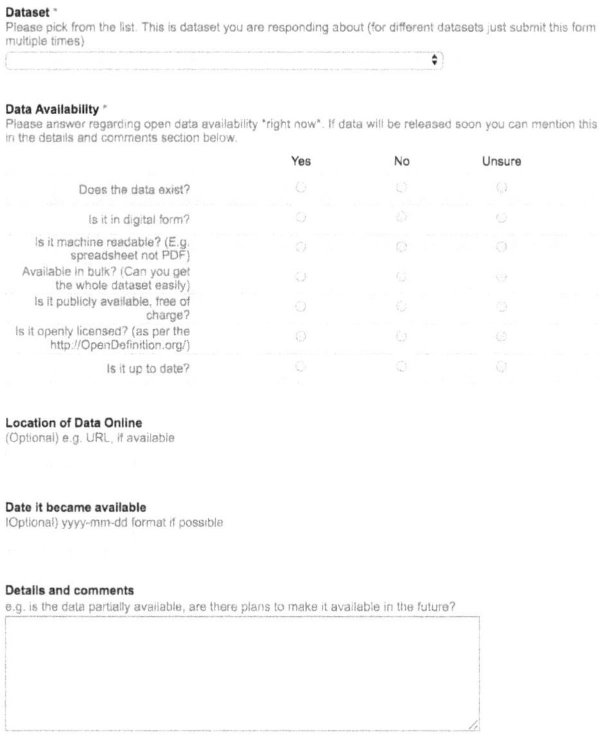

Dataset *
Please pick from the list. This is dataset you are responding about (for different datasets just submit this form multiple times)

Data Availability *
Please answer regarding open data availability *right now*. If data will be released soon you can mention this in the details and comments section below.

	Yes	No	Unsure
Does the data exist?			
Is it in digital form?			
Is it machine readable? (E.g. spreadsheet not PDF)			
Available in bulk? (Can you get the whole dataset easily)			
Is it publicly available, free of charge?			
Is it openly licensed? (as per the http://OpenDefinition.org/)			
Is it up to date?			

Location of Data Online
(Optional) e.g. URL, if available

Date it became available
(Optional) yyyy-mm-dd format if possible

Details and comments
e.g. is the data partially available, are there plans to make it available in the future?

Figure 1: Detail of Open Data Census submission form showing types of data availability.

13 Bruno Latour, 'Why Has Critique Run out of Steam? From Matters of Fact to Matters of Concern', *Critical Inquiry* 30 (2004): 225-248.

14 Nathaniel Tkacz, *Wikipedia and the Politics of Openness*, Chicago: University Of Chicago Press, 2014.

In July 2011 the idea of an index on 'Open Knowledge' or 'Open Data' arose on the mailing list of a working group on 'open economics', advocating for open access to economic data, publications, code and other materials. As one group member put it:

> There are many indices out there - for tracking democracy, corruption, innovation and human development - so why not a measure to track progress in opening government?

The immediate predecessor to the project was the 'Open Data Census', conceived in 2011 and described as 'an attempt to monitor the current status of open data across the globe'. Information about these government datasets was initially gathered with a Google Form embedded on a dedicated website, which recognised and recorded four types of availability: 'a) available in a digital form; b) machine-readable; c) publicly available, free of charge; d) openly licensed'. This later developed into seven questions about data availability (Figure 1), which were used to evaluate the openness of ten areas of data 'which most governments could reasonably be expected to collect':

1. Election Results (national)
2. Company Register
3. National Map (Low resolution: 1:250,000 or better)
4. Government Budget (high level - spending by sector)
5. Government Budget (detailed - transactional level data)
6. Legislation (laws and statutes)
7. National Statistical Office Data (economic and demographic information)
8. National Postcode/ZIP database
9. Public Transport Timetables
10. Environmental Data on major sources of pollutants (e.g. location, emissions)

The census was promoted via email lists, events, blog posts and social media platforms, including through two URLs: one for submissions (with the embedded Google Form) and one with visualisations and numbers summarising the results (Figure 2).

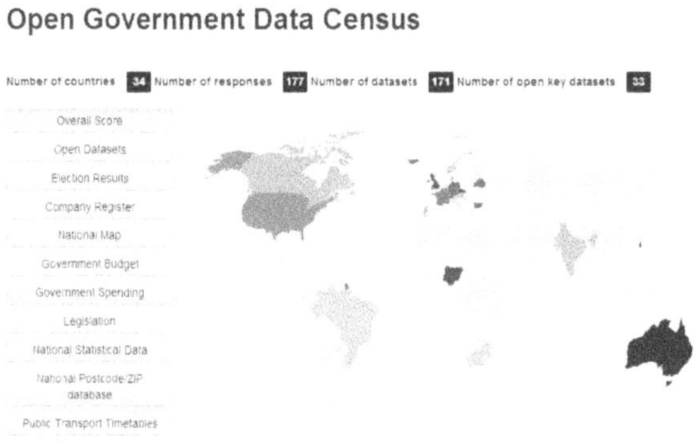

Open Government Data Census

Figure 2: Map showing preliminary results of the 2012 Open Government Data Census.

The Open Data Census was originally envisaged as a means to 'gather responses from every country in the world' around the openness of different types of government data through pre-structured options ('yes', 'no', 'unsure') to questions through which this could be evaluated. This basic format served as the basis for the Open Data Index and associated projects. As the project served to assemble publics to monitor the openness of government data, we can consider it not only as in terms of its *analytical* capacities, but also in terms of its *interactivity* as a form of 'infrastructuring' around public sector data.[15] In the case of the 2012 census, the input was structured through the form, and feedback was invited through an email alias and a public mailing list.

What kind of participation does the index facilitate? One approach would be to consider the dynamics between the 'formal social enterprise' of Open Knowledge International, the non-governmental organisation which coordinates the project;[16] and its 'organised publics', i.e. the various contributors to the census.[17] The politics of the project play out between the views of contributors, how project coordinators manage input and resolve issues, and how the project was situated in relation to the strategic and organisational prerogatives of its host NGO, its collaborators, funders, states, IGOs, and other actors. Some of these issues were raised in a blog post by open data advocate David Eaves highlighting the potential risk that 'British biases - with its highly centralized national government - have strongly shaped the census':

> Thus, while the census evaluates countries some of the data sets being counted are not controlled by national governments. For example - will national governments Canada or the United States get counted for public transport data if any of their cities release transit data? Indeed, transit data - while demonstrably useful - strikes me as an odd duck choice since it is almost always not managed by national governments. The same can be said for company/corporate registers, in which the most important data sets are managed by sub-national entities.[18]

Inquiring about the 'details about the selection process' regarding the datasets included in the 2012 census, he further suggested others that he wished to see added to the list, including:

- Access to Information (ATIP or FOIA) made, completed, rejected and average response time, broken down by government entity
- Government procurements and contracts, broken down by government entity
- Electoral Boundary Data
- Voting Booth Locations

---

15   Christopher A Le Dantec, and Carl DiSalvo, 'Infrastructuring and the formation of publics in participatory design', *Social Studies of Science* 43 (2013).
16   The NGO underwent several name changes over the course of the project. It started as Open Knowledge Foundation (OKF), then became Open Knowledge (OK) and finally Open Knowledge International (OKI). For clarity we use the current name throughout.
17   Adam Fish, Christopher M. Kelty, Luis F.R. Murillo, Lilly Nguyen, and Aaron Panofsky, 'Birds of the Internet', *Journal of Cultural Economy* 4 (2011): 157-187.
18   David Eaves, 'How To Evaluate The State Of Open Data', *Techpresident*, 8 May 2012, http://techpresident.com/news/wegov/22161/how-evaluate-state-open-data.

- Land Registry Data
- Payments to Government for Extractive Industry Resources
- Foreign Aid Data
- Campaign Finance Data
- Registered Lobbyists List

In 2013 saw the release of the Open Data Index as a 'community-based effort' which is 'compiled using contributions from civil society members and open data practitioners around the world' and 'peer-reviewed and checked by expert open data editors'.[19] Described as 'a Scoreboard for Open Government Data', it was explicitly positioned in relation to other civil society index projects:

> Inspired by work such as Open Budget Index from the International Budget Partnership, the Aid Transparency Index from Publish What You Fund, the Corruption Perception Index from Transparency International and many more, we felt a key aspect is to distill the results into a single overall ranking and present this clearly.[20]

The transition from 'census' to 'index' brought a number of changes. The census remained the mechanism for collecting data about the openness of government data, and the index became the mechanism for displaying rankings. A numerical score was introduced for each country by weighting different aspects of data availability (Figure 3). These weightings rewarded specific legal and technical conventions associated with open data.[21] For example, while 5 points (out of a total of 100) would be added if the dataset was available in digital form, 15 points would be accrued if it was 'machine readable' and 30 points if a dataset was 'openly licensed'. These dataset scores would then be used as the basis for an overall country score. Any number of submissions could come in for a given country through the website. These would be reviewed by a 'country editor' (which could be one person or a shared role), who would check and approve incoming submissions (Figure 4). A community manager at OKI worked to coordinate the project and communicate with contributors and editors.

---

19 Open Knowledge International, 'Government data still not open enough - new survey on eve of London summit', *Open Knowledge International blog*, 28 October 2013, https://blog.okfn.org/2013/10/28/government-data-still-not-open-enough/.
20 Rufus Pollock, 'The Open Data Census - Tracking the State of Open Data Around the World', *Open Knowledge International blog*, 20 February 2013, https://blog.okfn.org/2013/02/20/open-data-census-tracking-the-state-of-open-data-around-the-world/.
21 Jonathan Gray, 'Three Aspects of Data Worlds', *Krisis: Journal for Contemporary Philosophy* (2018).

Question	Details	Weighting
Does the data exist?	Does the data exist at all? The data can be in any form (paper or digital, offline or online etc). If the answer is "no", then please submit the form (below); there is no need to answer any further questions.	5
Is data in digital form?	Is it in digital form (stored on computers or digital storage) or is it only in e.g. paper form.	5
Publicly available?	Is the data 'public' - this does NOT require freely available but does require that "someone" outside of the government can access in some form (e.g. if the data is available for purchase it is public, if the timetables exist as PDFs on a website that you can access it is public, if you can get it in paper form it is public). If a freedom of information request or similar is needed to access the data, answer "no".	5
Is the data available for free?	Is the data available for free or is there a charge? If there is a charge please note this in the further information below.	15
Is the data available online?	Is the data available online from an official source. If yes please put the URL in the Source field below.	5
Is the data machine readable?	Data is machine readable if it is in a format that can be easily processed by a computer. Data can be digital but not machine readable. For example, consider a PDF document containing tables of data. These are definitely digital but are not machine-readable because a computer would struggle to access the tabular information (even though they are very human readable!). The equivalent tables in a format such as a spreadsheet would be machine readable. Note: The appropriate machine readable format may vary by type of data – so, for example, machine readable formats for geographic data may be different than for tabular data. In general, HTML and PDF are "not" machine-readable.	15
Available in bulk?	Data is available in bulk if you download or access the "'whole'" dataset easily. Conversely it is non-bulk if you are limited to just getting parts of the dataset (for example, are you restricted to querying a web form and retrieving a few results at a time from a very large database).	10
Openly licensed?	As per http://opendefinition.org/ - does the terms or use or license allow anyone to freely use, reuse or redistribute the data (subject at most to attribution or sharealike requirements). It is vital that a licence is available (if there is no licence, the data is not openly licensed). Open Licences which meet the requirements of the Open Definition are listed at http://opendefinition.org/licenses/	30
Is the data provided on a timely and up to date basis?	Is the data up to date and timely or long delayed. For example, for election data is it made available immediately or soon after the election or is it only available many years later. Please add comments below if you have uncertainty here.	10

Figure 3: Table showing weightings for Open Data Index 2013.

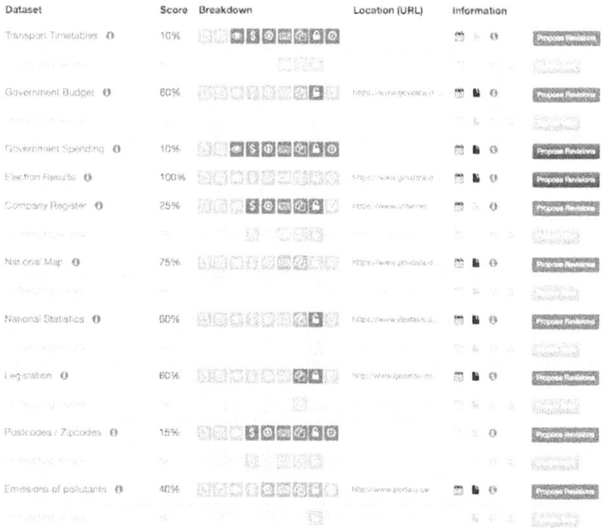

Figure 4: Review process for contributors and editors, Open Data Index 2013.

In terms of its material organisation, the index was a *bricolage* of different elements. It continued to use a Google Form embedded on a website to gather submissions accompanied by a review process conducted with Google Spreadsheets. Submissions were gathered through the census, then normalised, reviewed and published as part of the index. Results were displayed on a NodeJS application, deployed on Heroku, and the code was made available on GitHub. A dedicated '[open-data-census]' public mailing list was set up for contributors to discuss and support the review process. On Twitter the hashtags #OpenDataCensus and #OpenDataIndex were used to promote activity and discussion around the project.

Activity around the census was organised to align with relevant international events. An 'Open Data Census Challenge' was hosted on International Open Data Day in February 2013 to encourage public involvement in the assessment of not only country-level data, but also city-level datasets. Events and activities took place in Amsterdam, Berlin, Prague, London, Shanghai, Montevideo and other cities, organised in association with local groups and partners such as the newspaper Zeit Online in Germany and the Fond Otakara Motejla in the Czech Republic, resulting in a dedicated city-focused section of the census (census.okfn.org/city).[22] Another push of activity took place in the run up to the 39th G8 Summit in Lough Erne, UK, which included a focus on 'tax and transparency' and the release of a G8 'Open Data Charter'.[23] Another mini-site focusing on G8 members was released ahead of the summit.[24] This was editorialised with a press release contending that 'G8 countries must work harder to open up essential data' and that 'progress is lagging behind promise', which was translated into several languages by volunteers.[25] These two examples suggest how the index was adapted and aligned with subnational and transnational events and advocacy opportunities, in order to intervene at different scales in accordance with different event-based and policy-oriented rhythms.

The mailing lists and communications activities around the index also surfaced frictions in the process of creating a single score and ranking for the openness of data in countries and cities around the world. Submissions included comments and queries about pricing, licensing and the availability of data - such as concerns that the norms of the index were in tension with administrative and governance arrangements of countries being scored. A researcher contributing to the Canadian assessment suggested 'the methodology does not work well for federations with divisions of powers and thus different data responsibilities at different levels of jurisdiction'.[26] In a similar vein, a submission for Germany stated:

---

22 Christian Villum, 'The Open Data Census Challenge on Open Data Day 2013', *Open Knowledge International blog*, 5 March 2013, https://blog.okfn.org/2013/03/05/the-open-data-census-challenge-on-open-data-day-2013/.
23 Prime Minister's Office, '2013 Lough Erne G8 Leaders' Communiqué', 18 June 2013, https://www.gov.uk/government/publications/2013-lough-erne-g8-leaders-communique.
24 census.okfn.org/g8.
25 Rufus Pollock, 'G8 countries must work harder to open up essential data', *Open Knowledge International blog*, 14 June 2013, https://blog.okfn.org/2013/06/14/g8-countries-must-work-harder-to-open-up-essential-data/.
26 http://lists-archive.okfn.org/pipermail/open-data-census/2013-July/000082.html.

... the census it very tricky for a country like Germany with a federal system. Some of the datasets simply are not available at the national level as they belong to the federal states. To draw a [realistic] picture for Germany, we would need to do a census 16+1 (for the 16 federal states + 1 for the federal government).[27]

Over the coming years the index explored different ways of responding to the tensions between conventionalising the assessment of open data for a range of data types, and the wide range of practices, policies and advocacy initiatives around government data. One way was to provide more support for common assessment practices. As well as having editors and review processes, 2014 saw the introduction of 'mentors', video tutorials and online drop-in sessions catering to different time zones. Continuing to evaluate government data from around the world according to a common set of metrics enabled the production of rankings, as well as claims such as 'only 11% of the world's published datasets are open according to the open definition' (Figure 5). We might consider the value and practical utility accorded to such rankings and claims in relation to their reactive effects in the context of information policy. As with the examples of indices above, activists and public servants were thus provided with material and 'enumerated entities' to make the case for changes.[28]

Figure 5: Graphic to illustrate results of Open Data Index 2014.

Another way was to enable more flexibility and customisation for different practices for assessing the openness of data at different scales and in different settings. In addition to the coun-

---

27 Submission via Google Form for Open Data Census 2013.
28 Helen Verran, 'Number as an inventive frontier in knowing and working Australia's water resources'. *Anthropological Theory* 10 (2010): 171-178. Helen Verran, 'Enumerated Entities in Public Policy and Governance', in Ernest Davis and Philip J. Davis (eds), *Mathematics, Substance and Surmise,* New York: Springer, 2015, pp. 365-379.

try-level censuses that were the basis for the Open Data Index, there were a proliferation of more local censuses and topical censuses, including through collaborations and alliances with other civil society organisations and projects such as the Sunlight Foundation and Code for America.[29] This enabled the inclusion of datasets which were deemed most relevant for different situations. For example, several groups in Belgium ran a series of workshops, consultations and other activities to solicit input on what should be included in their census to create 'a crowdsourced product that is specifically designed for cities in Belgium'.[30]

The 2015 Global Open Data Index (GODI) saw further efforts to both consolidate the transnational assessment process as well as to broaden it to include other interests and concerns. A list of 'dataset definitions' sought to clarify assumptions around how the openness of government data should be assessed, including the role of states in coordinating the production of data. For example, it was claimed:

> Our assumption the national government has a role as a regulator to create and enforce publishing [of] such data. Therefore, even if the data is not produced by the government, we see it as responsible to ensure the open publication of the data.

The question of which forms of data public institutions do create and should create raised further issues and concerns around different histories and contexts of governance and administration, such as the following comment from a Canadian open data advocate:

> This doesn't work for Canada. There is a clear division of powers in our constitution between the federal government and the provinces. The federal government isn't going to walk into a constitutional battle over e.g. education data just to satisfy this index... Different provinces collect health and education data in different ways. It may not be possible to have one consolidated dataset. Please, just respect countries' differences instead of harmonizing everything to a central government structure like the UK.

UK government officials from Government Digital Service also commented that 'some criteria are an awkward fit in different national contexts', contending that changes in the assessment criteria around election data had 'cost [them] the top spot' and that '[they'd] need to change the laws governing our electoral system to make progress'.[31]

There was also a consultation around which datasets should be included in the 2015 edition of the Global Open Data Index, which encouraged participants to vote on different datasets as well as to propose other suggestions (Figure 6). This was part of a repositioning from 'a

---

29 Rufus Pollock, 'Announcing the Local Open Data Census', *Open Knowledge International blog*, 4 February 2014, https://blog.okfn.org/2014/02/04/announcing-the-local-open-data-census/.
30 Pieter-Jan Pauwels, 'Results of Wiki Survey and final steps', 12 September 2014, http://openbelgium.be/2014/09/results-of-wiki-survey-and-final-steps/.
31 Oliver Buckley, 'Open Data - the race to the top', *Gov.Uk blog*, 15 December 2015, https://data.blog.gov.uk/2015/12/15/open-data-the-race-to-the-top/.

simple measurement tool' to 'civil society audit of the open data revolution' exploring 'which datasets are of high social and democratic value', resulting in the addition of five new datasets: government procurement data, water quality, weather forecasts, land ownership and health performance data.[32] Public input and involvement was also encouraged in a forum, which saw more extended discussions about questions and issues around the index.

Which dataset would you like to see in the next Global Open Data Index?

Land use maps (zoning)

Name and locations of schools

I can't decide
0 votes on 16 ideas

Figure 6: "Crowdsourced survey" to inform choice of datasets included in 2015 Global Open Data Index.

The code for the project was used to create a prototype of a 'Global Goals Data Census', in order to track data relevant to the United Nations Sustainable Development Goals (SDGs), raising the question of the relationship between the transnational coordination of societal progress and the openness of governmental data.[33]

The 2016 edition saw a shift from 'countries' to 'places'. This was said to be because national government is not always the most important unit of analysis (especially with regards to sub-national governments with 'administrative and legislative autonomy'). It also aimed to accommodate 'submissions for places that are not officially recognised as independent countries'.[34] A 'dialogue phase' in the assessment process was also introduced in order to enable 'civil society and government [to] talk to one another'.

More recently there has been more reflection about what the Open Data Index does. Blog posts in 2017 have warned against 'volunteer fatigue',[35] guarded against inappropriate com-

---

32   Mor Rubinstein, 'What should we include in the Global Open Data Index? From reference data to civil society audit', *Open Knowledge International blog*, 18 June 2015, https://blog.okfn.org/2015/06/18/what-should-we-include-in-the-global-open-data-index-from-reference-data-to-civil-society-audit/.
33   Mikel Maron, 'Let's Build the Global Goals Data Census', *Medium*, 5 October 2015, https://medium.com/@mikelmaron/let-s-build-the-global-goals-data-census-c38b0458c9a.
34   https://index.okfn.org/methodology/.
35   Oscar Montiel, 'Our Country Sample and What It Tells Us About Our Contributors', *Open Knowledge International blog*, 3 May 2017, https://blog.okfn.org/2017/05/03/our-country-sample-and-what-it-tells-about-our-contributors/.

parisons between years after changes in assessment methodology,[36] and advocated for a 'shift in focus from a mere measurement tool to a stronger conversational device'.[37]

In summary, the Open Data Census and the Open Data Index aim to intervene around what is considered 'good data' by assessing the extent to which the publication of government data conforms with specific legal and technical norms and conventions, such as open licensing and machine-readability. It can thus be read in relation to the history of ideals and practices of open data, as well as free/open source software.[38] In contrast to other civil society indices which aim to advance their issue work by means of specialised research and policy teams, the Open Data Index has been designed to organise public involvement around the assessment of public data. It might thus be considered in terms of its capacities to enable not only *analysis*, but also *interactivity* using digital technologies - as well as structuring participation in particular ways which are not without tension.[39] Through this discussion of the development and social life of the Open Data Index, we suggest how it may be viewed as a participatory device whose function may vary from 'crowd-sourcing' assessment, to facilitating more substantive deliberation and public involvement around the politics of public data. Such indices may thus be viewed as sites where participation is both configured and contested, and where practices of valuation and enumeration are both conventionalised and brought into question.

References

Bruno, Isabelle, Emmanuel Didier, Tommaso Vitale. 'Statactivism: Forms of Action.

Between Disclosure and Affirmation', *Partecipazione e Conflitto* 7 (2014).

Buckley, Oliver. 'Open Data - the race to the top', *Gov.Uk blog*, 15 December 2015, https://data.blog.gov.uk/2015/12/15/open-data-the-race-to-the-top/.

Dawes, Sharon S., Lyudmila Vidiasova and Olga Parkhimovich. 'Planning and designing open government data programs: An ecosystem approach', *Government Information Quarterly* 33 (2016): 15-27.

Eaves, David. 'How To Evaluate The State Of Open Data', *Techpresident*, 8 May 2012, http://techpresident.com/news/wegov/22161/how-evaluate-state-open-data.

Espeland, Wendy N., and Mitchell L. Stevens. 'Commensuration as a Social Process', *Annual Review of Sociology* 24 (1998): 313-343.

Espeland, Wendy N., and Michael Sauder. 'Rankings and Reactivity: How Public Measures Recreate Social Worlds', *American Journal of Sociology* 113 (2007): 1-40.

---

36 Oscar Montiel, 'Our Country Sample and What It Tells Us About Our Contributors', *Open Knowledge International blog*, 3 May 2017, https://blog.okfn.org/2017/05/03/our-country-sample-and-what-it-tells-about-our-contributors/.
37 Open Knowledge International, 'The Future of the Global Open Data Index: Assessing The Possibilities', *Open Knowledge International blog*, 2 November 2017, https://blog.okfn.org/2017/11/01/the-future-of-the-global-open-data-index-assessing-the-possibilities/.
38 Christopher M. Kelty, *Two Bits: The Cultural Significance of Free Software: The Cultural Significance of Free Software and the Internet*, Durham NC: Duke University Press, 2008. Jonathan Gray, 'Towards a Genealogy of Open Data', *European Consortium for Political Research General Conference*, Glasgow, 3-6 September 2014, http://papers.ssrn.com/sol3/papers.cfm?abstract_id=2605828; Jonathan Gray, 'Three Aspects of Data Worlds', *Krisis: Journal for Contemporary Philosophy* (2018).
39 Noortje Marres, *Digital Sociology: The Reinvention of Social Research*, Cambridge: Polity Press, 2017.

Fish, Adam, Christopher M. Kelty, Luis F.R. Murillo, Lilly Nguyen, and Aaron Panofsky. 'Birds of the Internet'. *Journal of Cultural Economy* 4 (2011): 157-187.

Gray, Jonathan. 'Towards a Genealogy of Open Data', *European Consortium for Political Research General Conference*, Glasgow, 3-6 September 2014, http://papers.ssrn.com/sol3/papers.cfm?abstract_id=2605828.

_____. 'Three Aspects of Data Worlds', *Krisis: Journal for Contemporary Philosophy* (2018).

Guyer, Jane. 'Percentages and perchance: archaic forms in the twenty-first century', *Distinktion, Journal of Social Theory* 15 (2014): 155-173.

Kelty, Christopher M. *Two Bits: The Cultural Significance of Free Software: The Cultural Significance of Free Software and the Internet*, Durham NC: Duke University Press, 2008.

Latour, Bruno. 'Why Has Critique Run out of Steam? From Matters of Fact to Matters of Concern', *Critical Inquiry* 30 (2004): 225-248.

_____. *An Inquiry into Modes of Existence: An Anthropology of the Moderns*, trans C. Porter, Cambridge MA: Harvard University Press, 2013.

Law, John, and Evelyn Ruppert. 'The Social Life of Methods: Devices', *Journal of Cultural Economy* 6 (2013): 229-240.

Le Dantec, Christopher A., and Carl DiSalvo. 'Infrastructuring and the formation of publics in participatory design', *Social Studies of Science* 43 (2013).

Maron, Mikel. 'Let's Build the Global Goals Data Census', *Medium*, 5 October 2015, https://medium.com/@mikelmaron/let-s-build-the-global-goals-data-census-c38b0458c9a.

Marres, Noortje. *Digital Sociology: The Reinvention of Social Research*, Cambridge: Polity Press, 2017.

Milan, Stefania and Lonneke van der Velden. 'The Alternative Epistemologies of Data Activism', *Digital Culture & Society* 2 (2016): 57-74.

Montiel, Oscar. 'Our Country Sample and What It Tells Us About Our Contributors', *Open Knowledge International blog*, 3 May 2017, https://blog.okfn.org/2017/05/03/our-country-sample-and-what-it-tells-about-our-contributors/.

Open Knowledge International. 'Government data still not open enough - new survey on eve of London summit', *Open Knowledge International blog*, 28 October 2013, https://blog.okfn.org/2013/10/28/government-data-still-not-open-enough/.

_____. 'The Future of the Global Open Data Index: Assessing the possibilities', *Open Knowledge International blog*, 2 November 2017, https://blog.okfn.org/2017/11/01/the-future-of-the-global-open-data-index-assessing-the-possibilities/.

Pauwels, Pieter-Jan. 'Results of Wiki Survey and final steps', 12 September 2014, http://openbelgium.be/2014/09/results-of-wiki-survey-and-final-steps/.

Pollock, Rufus. 'The Open Data Census - Tracking the State of Open Data Around the World', *Open Knowledge International blog*, 20 February 2013, https://blog.okfn.org/2013/02/20/open-data-census-tracking-the-state-of-open-data-around-the-world/.

_____. 'G8 countries must work harder to open up essential data', *Open Knowledge International blog*, 14 June 2013, https://blog.okfn.org/2013/06/14/g8-countries-must-work-harder-to-open-up-essential-data/.

_____. 'Announcing the Local Open Data Census', *Open Knowledge International blog*, 4 February 2014, https://blog.okfn.org/2014/02/04/announcing-the-local-open-data-census/.

Power, Michael. *The Audit Society: Rituals of Verification*, Oxford: Oxford University Press, 1999.

Prime Minister's Office. '2013 Lough Erne G8 Leaders' Communiqué', 18 June 2013, https://www.gov.uk/government/publications/2013-lough-erne-g8-leaders-communique.

Rottenburg, Richard, Sally E. Merry, Sung-Joon Park and Johanna Mugler (eds). *The World of Indicators: The Making of Governmental Knowledge through Quantification*, Cambridge: Cambridge University Press, 2015.

Rubinstein, Mor. 'What should we include in the Global Open Data Index? From reference data to civil society audit', *Open Knowledge International blog*, 18 June 2015, https://blog.okfn.org/2015/06/18/what-should-we-include-in-the-global-open-data-index-from-reference-data-to-civil-society-audit/.

Strathern, Marilyn. *Audit Cultures: Anthropological Studies in Accountability, Ethics and the Academy*, London: Routledge, 2000.

Thorsby, Jeffrey, Genie, N.L. Stowers, Kristen Wolslegel and Ellie Tumbuan. 'Understanding the content and features of open data portals in American cities', *Government Information Quarterly* 34 (2017): 53-61.

Tkacz, Nathaniel. *Wikipedia and the Politics of Openness*, Chicago: University Of Chicago Press, 2014.

Transparency International. 'Corruption Perceptions Index', *Transparency International blog*, 21 February 2018, https://www.transparency.org/news/feature/corruption_perceptions_index_2017.

Verran, Helen. 'Number as an inventive frontier in knowing and working Australia's water resources', *Anthropological Theory* 10 (2010): 171-178.

_____. 'Enumerated Entities in Public Policy and Governance', in Ernest Davis and Philip J. Davis (eds), *Mathematics, Substance and Surmise*, New York: Springer, 2015, pp. 365-379.

Villum, Christian. 'The Open Data Census Challenge on Open Data Day 2013', *Open Knowledge International blog*, 5 March 2013, https://blog.okfn.org/2013/03/05/the-open-data-census-challenge-on-open-data-day-2013/.

11: DATA JOURNALISM AND THE ETHICS OF OPEN SOURCE

COLIN PORLEZZA

Introduction

Data journalism has enjoyed an increasing amount of attention and success both in media practice and in journalism research. Unlike traditional journalism, which only recently adopted concepts such as openness and accountability, data journalism seems to be deeply rooted in a culture of open source that comes with increased transparency, shareability and participation. This chapter analyzes the question whether and to what extent data journalists effectively reflect the ethical notions of the open source culture in their everyday work routines and what kind of best practices are in place in order to minimize the ethical challenges they are confronted with while accessing, analyzing and publishing data. The proposed chapter offers therefore a structured insight into whether and how data journalists implement the four normative principles - transparency, participation, tinkering, and iteration - that the concept of open source implies. The chapter also highlights and discusses key ethical standards such as sharing source-codes or granting third parties with complete access to raw datasets.

According to Mayer-Schönberger and Cukier,[1] the growing use of data provokes 'a revolution that will transform how we live, work and think'. The datafication of society - the attempt to transform everything into a specific data format in order to be quantified[2] - is a fundamental process because it supersedes both in scope and style the ways in which reality is seen and constructed. This new data abundance is not only reflected in the reliance on data as a secular belief,[3] but also in the increasingly dominant position of algorithms as cultural artifacts that announce a new social order.[4]

Datafication is therefore an all-encompassing transformation that permeates society as a whole. Journalism is no exception to this trend. In addition, the journalistic field is a particularly interesting object of study to observe datafication processes within society: first, because journalism observes datafication in society and brings the related issues into the public sphere. Second, because journalism increasingly embraces data-driven instruments connected to these processes - data and algorithms - to observe and shed light on the datafication in the wider society. These changes in journalism practice lead to new forms of data journalism

---

1 Victor Mayer-Schönberger and Kenneth Cukier, *Big Data: A Revolution That Will Transform How We Live, Work and Think*. London: Murray, 2013.
2 José Van Dijk, 'Foreword', in Mirko Tobias Schäfer and Karin van Es (eds), *The Datafied Society*, Amsterdam: Amsterdam University Press, 2017, p. 11.
3 José van Dijck, 'Datafication, dataism and dataveillance: Big Data between scientific paradigm and ideology', *Surveillance & Society* 12.2 (2014): 197-208.
4 William Uricchio, 'Data, Culture and the Ambivalence of Algorithms', in Mirko Tobias Schäfer and Karin van Es (eds), *The Datafied Society*, Amsterdam: Amsterdam University Press, 2017, p. 126.

that offer new opportunities such as combing through data from public administrations,[5] or uncovering wrongdoings.[6] Data journalism has therefore enjoyed an increasing amount of attention and success in media practice.

The instruments used to observe datafication processes are often developed and brought into the news media by actors from outside the journalistic field such as programmers, computer scientists or hackers. These actors have not been socialized in newsrooms and have different cultural references that increasingly shape contemporary journalism, entailing not only new roles such as hacker journalists,[7] but also changes in the current journalistic epistemology: unlike traditional journalism, data journalism is rooted in a culture of open source that comes with increased transparency, shareability and participation.

This chapter analyzes therefore the question to what extent data journalists reflect the ethical notions of the open source culture in their everyday work routines. By applying Lewis and Usher's four normative values that are necessary to implement the principles of open source in the journalistic field - transparency, participation, tinkering, and iteration - the chapter studies whether Swiss and Italian data journalists are adhering to the notion of open source and, in addition, what kind of ethical quandaries they are facing.[8]

Data Journalism and Open Source

The growing academic literature has prompted many definitions of data journalism. Nevertheless, I understand data journalism, following Coddington's definition, as a 'hybrid form [of journalism] that encompasses statistical analysis, computer science, visualization and web design, and reporting'.[9] The hybridity of data journalism is given by the combination of different roles and tasks, often carried out by different actors and not only by journalists. This kind of hybridity is also reflected in other scholars' definitions: Splendore for instance emphasizes the combination of storytelling and programming by defining data journalism as 'a form of storytelling, where traditional journalistic working methods are mixed with data analysis, programming, and visualization techniques'.[10] However, even if many definitions of data journalism include similar elements such as reporting, programming, statistics and visualizations, 'an all-encompassing working definition of data journalism is rather difficult to achieve'.[11] This is due to the fact that the field of research is relatively young and, in addi-

---

5   Colin Porlezza, 'Dall'open journalism all'open government? Il ruolo del data journalism nella trasparenza e nella partecipazione', *Problemi dell'Informazione* 1 (2016): 167-194.
6   Eddy Borges-Rey, 'Unravelling data journalism', *Journalism Practice* 10.7 (2017): 833-843.
7   Nikki Usher, *Interactive Journalism: Hackers, Data, and Code*, Champaign: University of Illinois Press, 2016.
8   Seth C. Lewis and Nikki Usher, 'Open source and journalism: Toward new frameworks for imagining news innovation', *Media, Culture & Society* 35.5 (2013): 602-619.
9   Mark Coddington, 'Clarifying Journalism's Quantitative Turn: A Typology for Evaluating Data Journalism, Computational Journalism, and Computer-Assisted Reporting', *Digital Journalism* 3.3 (2014): 334.
10 Sergio Splendore, 'Quantitatively Oriented Forms of Journalism and Their Epistemology'. *Sociology Compass* (2016): online first.
11 Borges-Rey, 'Unravelling data journalism', 834.

tion, scholars from different disciplines such as journalism studies, communication sciences, informatics or economics are studying the phenomenon.

Journalism has radically changed in the last twenty years, particularly with respect to its *openness*. There are different reasons for the disruption of the 'fortress-journalism'.[12] One of the first breaches in the longtime impenetrable walls of the newsrooms was the growing phenomenon of citizen journalism that understands users not only as consumers, but also as active producers of information.[13] This change in perception contributed to the development of a new journalistic paradigm that transcends the idea that all aspects of news work are limited to professional journalists only. Especially the emerging practice of crowdsourcing - an open call for users to participate in certain online activities, for instance in collecting information - was one of the main drivers of participatory forms of journalism.[14]

These changes in journalism, as Lewis pointed out, triggered the emergence of an initial form of 'open journalism' based on contributions, or in the case of catastrophes and emergencies, of an information *network*.[15] However, this kind of open journalism relies more on forms of participation or distributed knowledge in the sense of Singer et al.: 'People inside and outside the newsroom are engaged in communicating not only to, but also with, one another. In doing so, they all are participating in the ongoing processes of creating a news website and building a multifaceted community'.[16] Yet, professional journalism remained resistant to change for a very long time, and participatory journalism - understood as a shared news production process between professionals and amateurs - remained an exception rather than the rule. Williams et al. showed that newsrooms tend to co-opt participatory practices to suit traditional routines and ideals.[17] In other cases, journalists tended to see users simply as 'active recipients' who act only on the grounds of what has been reported.[18]

Even if some newsrooms are still hesitant to include participatory instruments into their news production, or dismissed their collaborative experiments, there is a growing body of evidence that 'journalism's ideological commitment to control, rooted in an institutional instinct toward protecting legitimacy and boundaries, may be giving way to a hybrid logic of adaptability and

---

12 Peter Horrocks, 'The end of fortress journalism', in Charles Miller (ed.), *The future of journalism*, London: BBC College of Journalism, 2009, pp. 6-17.
13 Dan Gillmor, *We the Media: Grassroots Journalism by the People, for the People*, Sebastopol CA: O'Reilly Media, 2004.
14 Tanja Aitamurto, 'Motivation factors in crowdsourcing journalism: social impact, social change, and peer learning', *International Journal of Communication* 9 (2015): 3523-3543.
15 Dharma Dailey and Kate Starbird, 'Journalists as crowdsourcerers: responding to crisis by reporting with a crowd', *Computer Supported Cooperative Work* 23.4 (2014): 445-481.
16 Jane Singer et al, *Participatory Journalism: Guarding Open Gates at Online Newspapers*, Chichester: John Wiley, 2011.
17 Andy Williams, Claire Wardle and Karin Wahl-Jorgensen, '"Have they got news for us?" Audience revolution or business as usual at the BBC?' *Journalism Practice*, 5.1 (2011): 85-99.
18 Alfred Hermida, 'Social journalism: exploring how social media is shaping journalism', in Eugenia Siapera and Andreas Veglis (eds), *The Handbook of Global Online Journalism*, Oxford: Wiley-Blackwell, 2012, pp. 309-328.

openness'.[19] Lewis and Usher even note that journalists increasingly find normative purpose in transparency and participation, a culture that is very similar to the open-source technology culture,[20] which is based on a wider understanding of openness in terms of sharing collected data, being transparent about their use, and being actively interactive with users and other journalists.[21]

This slow change in the adaptation of a culture of openness - to see users as peers rather than as an amorphous and anonymous group of consumers or to understand other journalists as colleagues within a network rather than as competitors - was in part due to the rise of new technologies such as social media and their affordances and culture based on participation. One of the most famous social media journalists, Andy Carvin, once described his own work as 'an open-source newsroom that anyone can come and participate in, or observe the process'.[22] In addition, the slow shift to more open journalism in terms of transparency, sharing and collaboration across different newsrooms or divisions may well be due to the entrance of new actors into the core field of journalism. These actors belong to different professions and have thus been socialized differently with a different professional culture.

This process can be well observed in data journalism. Many quantitatively oriented journalists have a background in informatics, and only subsequently moved, through learning by doing and by being part of a data journalism team, to a more journalistically oriented role. This means that new actors, some of whom have not been influenced and socialized by journalistic culture in the first place, have now entered the institutionalized field of journalism, influencing in turn its practices, routines, professional norms and culture with notions originating from other professions. Russell has shown how hackers and hacktivists, among others, are playing an increasingly important role in shaping contemporary journalism, 'expanding what it means to be involved in the production of news and, in the process, gaining influence over how traditional news stories and genres are constructed and circulated'.[23]

However, the field of data journalism evolved unevenly both across and within different media systems, given that news organizations may not be willing or able to offer the necessary resources in terms of time and money either to sustain a specialized team or to develop a sufficient data literacy among their employed journalists - also due to traditional norms and practices still dominating the newsrooms.[24] This means that the openness of data journalism not only depends on the individual dispositions of journalists, but also on organizational logics and constraints that may severely limit the specific implementation of notions such as

---

19 Seth C. Lewis, 'The tension between professional control and open participation', *Information, Communication & Society* 15.6 (2012): 836-866.
20 Seth C. Lewis and Nikki Usher, 'Open source and journalism: Toward new frameworks for imagining news innovation', p. 851.
21 Usher, *Interactive Journalism: Hackers, Data, and Code*.
22 Jeff Sonderman, 'Andy Carvin explains how Twitter is his "open-source newsroom"', *Poynter*, https://www.poynter.org/news/andy-carvin-explains-how-twitter-his-open-source-newsroom.
23 Adrienne Russell, *Journalism as activism. Recoding media power*, Cambridge: Polity Press, 2016, p. 7.
24 Alfred Hermida and Lynn Young, 'Finding the data unicorn. A hierarchy of hybridity in data and computational journalism', *Digital Journalism* 5.2 (2016): 159-176.

open source. Nevertheless, openness has become a new industry standard as professional journalism practice opens up its boundaries not only to participation in news work, but also in the search for future opportunities to solve journalism's many issues.[25]

One of the main traits of these new actors, mainly technologists, entering the field is a clear orientation towards the concept of open source, particularly if their background is in informatics. The general idea behind the concept of open source is that free sharing, collaborative production and free distribution produce the best results in terms of transparency, use and usability, particularly because users are involved in the production process.[26] According to the Open Source Initiative, open source does not only mean allowing access to the source code. It also means that the distribution of the code must comply with specific criteria such as free re-distribution, allowing modifications and derived works, no discrimination against persons, groups and fields of endeavor, and other aspects.[27] However, the concept of open source goes well beyond questions of licensing. Coleman understands open source as an aspiration towards open programming, grounded on the philosophical belief in social responsibility through freedom and openness.[28]

What makes open source such a captivating concept is its dual significance both as a guideline for the practical development of software programming, and the underlying ethos of a culture of free and open distribution, from which society can benefit. This is why open source is mainly 'characterized by a non-market, non-contractual transfer of knowledge among actors, sharing relevant information with a non-definite set of other actors without any immediate recompense'.[29] In this analysis, open source is thus understood as a dual orientation towards open, transparent and collaborative *production* as well as a belief in the social responsibility and freedom of sharing and openness in the *use* of the produced information.

It is in this sense that Lewis and Usher understand open source both as an 'architectural framework and a cultural context'.[30] This dual implication of open source as both *materiality* (what is actually produced) and *culture* (certain normative values such as the ethos of sharing without any immediate recompense) is particularly relevant when it comes to its implementation in journalism: openness and collaboration are therefore not just to be seen as descriptors of a specific journalistic practice, but as a moral principle in the sense of an 'ethical volunteerism' and a 'desire for open technologies and a philosophical belief in serving the public good through openness'.[31]

---

25 Seth C. Lewis, 'Journalism innovation and participation: an analysis of the Knight News Challenge', *International Journal of Communication* 5 (2011): 1623-1648.
26 See Eric S. Raymond, *The cathedral and the bazaar: Musings on Linux and open source by an accidental revolutionary*. Sebastopol CA: O'Reilly, 2001.
27 For the full definition visit: https://opensource.org/osd.
28 Gabriella Coleman, *Coding Freedom: The Ethics and Aesthetics of Hacking*, Princeton, NJ: Princeton University Press, 2012.
29 Kerstin Balka, Christina Raasch and Cornelius Herstatt, 'Open source enters the world of atoms: a statistical analysis of open design', *First Monday* 14.11 (2009), http://firstmonday.org/ojs/index.php/fm/article/view/2670.
30 Lewis and Usher, 'Open source and journalism: Toward new frameworks for imagining news innovation', p. 606.
31 Seth C. Lewis and Oscar Westlund, 'Big data and journalism. Epistemology, expertise, economics, and

Especially in the field of data journalism, where different actors with diverse backgrounds work together, it is a useful approach in order to gauge how journalists, newsrooms and news organizations are collaborating with 'the clear purpose of contributing to a joint development'.[32] These collaborations that transcend traditional and established boundaries contribute to the evolution of the traditional journalism culture,[33] up to the point where it is possible to consider these new forms of reporting relying on data as a 'trading zone',[34] where the crossing of professional boundaries occurs not only more often, but it gets also increasingly accepted. The increasing collaborative setting of journalism reflects, at the same time, the fact that open journalism as well as data journalism are both the consequence - and the cause - of the enlargement of the journalistic field. Deuze and Witschge pointed out that 'journalism takes place in increasingly networked settings, in formal as well as informal contexts, involving a wide range of actors and actants in various instances of both paid and free labor (...) covering news in real-time across multiplying platforms, often in competition or collaboration with publics'.[35]

This groundbreaking transformation of journalism in terms of openness and collaboration require a broader normative perspective in relation to the concept of open source. Lewis and Usher developed a specific framework of four normative values that are necessary to implement the principles of open source in the journalistic field: transparency, participation, tinkering, and iteration.[36]

Applying an open source approach means first of all to be *transparent* about what one is doing. In the case of journalism it means not only to be transparent about the coding, but also about the production routines of journalism. Data and information (also with regard to the adopted source codes) should be freely shared for others to use. Journalism itself strives for transparency in society and should therefore act accordingly, particularly as digital technologies have enhanced the opportunities of opening up the news production.[37] However, transparency as part of an open source concept pushes journalism even further, as news production becomes both 'liquid' and dynamic: a continuous, transparent and networked process of information, open to participation and that can be held accountable by the users.

Participation means that the production process is relying on a distributed network of different contributors. This is also relevant for ethical frameworks because journalism is shifting

---

ethics', *Digital Journalism* 3.3 (2015): 321-330.
32 Ibid.
33 Matt Carlson and Seth C. Lewis (eds), *Boundaries of Journalism. Professionalism, Practices and Participation*, London: Routledge, 2015.
34 Seth C. Lewis and Nikki Usher, 'Code, Collaboration, and the Future of Journalism', *Digital Journalism* 2.3 (2014): 383-393.
35 Mark Deuze and Tamara Witschge, 'Beyond journalism: Theorizing the transformation of journalism', *Journalism* 19.2 (2017): 165-181.
36 Seth C. Lewis and Nikki Usher, 'Open source and journalism: Toward new frameworks for imagining news innovation', *New Media & Society* 35.5 (2013): 602-619.
37 Angela Phillips, 'Transparency and the new ethics of journalism', *Journalism Practice* 4.3 (2010): 373-382.

from a traditional gatekeeper ethics towards a relational ethics.[38] Participation is an inherent dimension of open source because it relies on the fact that an increased number of collaborators and collective intelligence produce better results. Applied to the field of journalism this means that users have more opportunities to collaborate with professional journalists or can at least to monitor their work. The role of users becomes therefore much more active and interlinked with the newsroom.

The normative value of *tinkering* implies playfulness as well as an inclination towards experimentation. This norm becomes particularly relevant as journalism gets increasingly networked due to new actors entering journalism. The result is a form of hybrid journalism, where different actors such as journalists, hackers or whistleblowing platforms, with different professional roles and cultures (for instance in the case of the 'Panama Papers' or the Offshore Leaks) are working together in the public interest. *Iteration* is a norm closely related to tinkering and implies 'the freedom to fail'.[39] While innovation processes in established news organizations are mostly bound to centralized and top-down processes, iterative methods focus more strongly on the process rather than the actual outcome, leaving the involved actors room for testing. This normative framework is useful to analyze the ethical challenges of data journalists, given that they are working in a collaborative, often experimental and transparency-driven environment.

The Study

In order to answer the research goal, we carried out several problem-centered interviews mostly via Skype with 20 data journalists in Switzerland and Italy between the end of 2015 and the end of 2017.[40] The interviews focused on four main areas: their professional career paths, the production process in relation to collaborations, their normative perspectives about data journalism, and ethical issues. The interviews were recorded and subsequently partially transcribed. The interviewed data journalists are working full-time both for established news organizations and specialized agencies. The sampling method was twofold: initially we carried out a desktop research to identify and collect the names of data journalists currently working in Switzerland and Italy. We then interviewed specific data journalists and asked the interviewees to provide us with the names of other data journalists. This snowball sampling method is suited to analyze well-connected communities like those of data journalists.[41]

The comparison between Switzerland and Italy is not only interesting due to the fact that they belong to different journalistic cultures, but also because data journalism evolved differently in the two countries. In Switzerland, data journalism has gradually entered established news organizations throughout the last couple of years. However, due to the small Swiss media

---

38   Jane Singer, 'Norms and the Network: Journalistic Ethics in a Shared Media Space', in Christopher Meyers (ed.), *Journalism Ethics: A Philosophical Approach*, Oxford: Oxford University Press, 2010, pp. 117-129.
39   Seth C. Lewis and Nikki Usher, 'Open source and journalism: Toward new frameworks for imagining news innovation', p. 608.
40   The interviews in Italy were carried out by my esteemed colleague Sergio Splendore.
41   Howard Becker, *Outsiders: Studies in the Sociology of Deviance*, New York: Macmillan, 1963.

market, data journalism emerged with a considerable delay compared to other countries in Europe. In Italy, data journalism is already a highly professional sub-field, even if the journalistic education is (still) not well developed. Additionally, data journalism's origin lies outside the established field of journalism: in the beginning, data journalists were mainly working for specialized agencies and not for legacy news media.[42]

The Ethics of Transparency

Transparency is a well-established concept in both countries. All interviewed data journalists declare that one of the core tenets of the work of data journalists consists in being absolutely transparent about their practice. However, there are some differences when it comes to the scope of transparency. Not in every case do Swiss data journalists share raw data, and neither do they apply complete transparency when it comes to sharing source codes. Although some newsrooms have a GitHub account, where other data journalists or interested citizens can access the code, it is not published for every story. The main reason for not doing so is twofold: on the one hand data journalists argue that there is only a limited interest for this information. On the other hand, news organizations put some constraints to the transparency norm in terms of sharing raw data and source codes in order to avoid freeriding from competitors. However, data journalists cover an active role when it comes to sharing data and fostering a culture of transparency within the news organization.

In Italy, the transparency norm is universally shared among the community of data journalists: 'I absolutely agree with the idea of open journalism. It would be a paradigmatic change in journalism if the production processes were open and transparent.' (I-J3). This can also be observed in the specific mention of the relevance of an *open source approach*. Moreover, for Italian data journalists transparency is a central issue, which is also reflected in their journalistic role conception that is, compared to their Swiss colleagues, far more activist in support of transparency and the availability of open data: 'We want data to analyze!' (I-J1). The clear disposition towards transparency by granting third parties with complete access to raw datasets might also be traced back to the fact that most data journalists in Italy, unlike their Swiss counterparts, have a background in informatics and were thus socialized in a professional culture that has fewer issues with openness.

At the same time, the fact that most data journalists have a background in informatics can become a matter of concern: data journalists might be forced to handle sensitive data. Most data journalists have never been trained on how to handle such data and how to protect it from hacking or surveillance. The same applies to privacy issues that occur in the case of leaks. The protection of anonymity and of sources cannot always be guaranteed because most data journalists in both countries have never been 'educated' in matters of data protection - even if the situation is slowly changing, also due to the discoveries in the wake of the Snowden revelations:

---

42 Sergio Splendore, 'Closed data! Il giornalismo italiano alla ricerca di dati', *Problemi dell'Informazione* 1 (2016): 195-214.

'The freelance data journalist does not have the requested skills to protect the source. This culture in Italy is still rare, but it would be vital to convince those working in the public administration to have more trust in journalists and to offer more data.' (I-J3).

Open source can thus become a serious concern in journalism as well. Particularly nowadays, where journalism is seen as a 'dynamic set of practices and expectations - a profession in a permanent process of becoming', both organizations and individuals need to develop a normative framework that lives up to the standards of a networked, 'liquid' and flexible journalism.

The Ethics of Participation

Participation implies the collaboration with different actors both within and across the boundaries of news organizations. The findings show that Swiss and Italian data journalists apply different strategies when it comes to the participation of users, but demonstrate similar beliefs for collaborative newswork within the boundaries of news organizations. In Switzerland, data journalists declare that participatory strategies that involve users more actively are not central, except maybe for the generation of new ideas. Collaborative strategies like crowdsourcing are thus the exception. With regard to internal collaborations, many data journalists admitted that they served somehow as 'troubleshooters' for problems related to informatics, visuals and, above all, statistics. Even if this is not the form of collaboration originally intended by the normative framework, it nevertheless allows data journalists to propagate specific normative assumptions like transparency within the organization.

In Italy, data journalists specifically rely on the contributions of users, which are seen as co-constructors of reality. In addition, collaborations that go beyond the boundaries of the news organizations are standard. Compared to the Swiss situation, this is easier to implement because in most cases data journalists in Italy are working for startups or agencies. These organizations are considerably smaller than their legacy counterparts and very often collaborations with external experts are paramount and therefore part of the job. Such informal collaborations occur also within the newsrooms, given that the collaborators of the agencies are not exclusively journalists: often they include hackers, programmers, visualization experts and statisticians as well. Crossing organizational boundaries is a normal procedure, something legacy news media in Switzerland are still struggling with because - even informal - collaborations are often not tolerated.

The Ethics of Tinkering

The biggest differences between Switzerland and Italy can be observed with regard to the norm of tinkering. Given that Swiss data journalism mainly developed within established news organizations, the room for experiments is limited compared to startups or agencies, where experimenting and a drive for innovation is a main motivation. In Italy, informal collaborations particularly for experimental reasons are regarded as absolutely central, not only to further develop products and services, but eventually to stay in business. Such experimental collaborations are thus fostered either through networks like Hacks/Hackers or through events like hackathons. There are still considerable differences with regard to this kind of experimental collaboration through established networks between Switzerland and Italy. Nonetheless, Swiss newsrooms started to organize and to participate in similar events like Hacks/Hackers and hackathons during the last couple of years.[43] Even large news organizations in Switzerland such as Tamedia or the Neue Zürcher Zeitung collaborate with these networks and offer room for meetings and discussions.

The Ethics of Iteration

Iteration, or the freedom to fail, presupposes the possibility to experiment. Even if some news organizations allow and invest in experiments, the expected outcomes may differ. Compared to most of their legacy counterparts, small agencies or journalism startups are considerably better equipped when it comes to experimenting without expecting tangible results in the first place. It is in the DNA of startups that they have to continuously evolve and come up with new and innovative ideas: first to go beyond a culture of resistance, and second to avoid an innovation gap that might occur more rapidly for established news organizations that might even detain a quasi-monopolistic status. Particularly journalism startups with their focus on entrepreneurial thinking are more used to reflections on how to do things differently - a rather difficult task in newsrooms of established news media with their strong focus on daily news production. Italian data journalism startups and agencies are thus at the forefront when it comes to implementing strategies that put innovations into place, changing organizations for the better.

Conclusion

The chapter offered an insight into whether and how data journalists in Italy and Switzerland implement four normative principles related to the ethics of open-source: transparency, participation, tinkering and iteration. Most issues are not actually related to differences in the individual moral compass of data journalists, but to the structures they work within. News organizations in Switzerland tend to organize the work of their journalists in traditional ways, largely blocking the development of networks of 'competitor-colleagues'.[44] While in Italy data journalists working in agencies are free from such constraints, established news organizations still struggle to cope with the new and networked news ecosystem that implies a different approach to the role of news media in society and the so called gatekeeper ethics. These structural conditions put serious constraints to the implementation of an ethical framework based on open source.

The structural constraints can also be observed when it comes to experimentation in terms of tinkering and iteration. Even if Swiss news organizations have considerably improved on experimentation for instance within larger networks such as Hacks/Hackers, there is still a gap in terms of *entrepreneurial thinking,* particularly among data journalists working in larger news organizations. The main issue with an entrepreneurial approach, particularly within traditional

---

43   See for instance the SRG SSR, 'Hackdays' https://www.hackdays.ch/.
44   Mark Deuze and Tamara Witschge, 'Beyond journalism: Theorizing the transformation of journalism', p. 176.

news organizations is the fact that informal collaborations and networks often transcend the boundaries of news organizations - diminishing the organizational and managerial control of news work. Nevertheless, both the more networked approach of Italian agencies as well as the traditional institutional approach can be successful, as news organizations in Italy and Switzerland have won Data Journalism Awards in the past.

However, news organizations cannot be blamed for all the ethical constraints data journalists are struggling with. Some of them are also due to missing individual skills that data journalists have never had the opportunity to learn: data journalists coming from traditional newsrooms are rarely trained in data protection techniques against hacking or surveillance. On the other hand, data journalists with an informatics background might have no problems with openness and participation, but lack knowledge in journalism ethics with regard to handling sensitive information. These educational shortcomings entail ethical issues with regard to data and source protection.

The findings show that the emergence of data journalism within the institutionalized field of journalism - although some organizational backfiring - fosters the normative framework of open source. Taking into account the increasing datafication of journalism - and of society at large - it is likely to remain here to stay. The concept of open source offers to journalism, as it gets more networked, the opportunity to adopt specific values in a news ecosystem that relies more and more on a participatory digital media culture. In any case, open source has to be thought of, as Lewis and Usher affirm, as both an architecture and a culture, that is to say, 'as a structural retooling of news technologies and user interfaces, and as a normative rearticulation of what journalism means in a networked media setting'.[45] In this sense, open source offers the opportunity to produce *good data journalism*.

References

Aitamurto, Tanja. 'Motivation factors in crowdsourcing journalism: social impact, social change, and peer learning', *International Journal of Communication* 9 (2015): 3523-3543.

Balka, Kerstin, Christina Raasch and Cornelius Herstatt. 'Open source enters the world of atoms: a statistical analysis of open design', *First Monday* 14.11 (2009), http://firstmonday.org/ojs/index.php/fm/article/view/2670.

Becker, Howard. *Outsiders: Studies in the Sociology of Deviance*, New York: Macmillan, 1963.

Borges-Rey, Eddy. 'Unravelling data journalism', *Journalism Practice* 10.7 (2017): 833-843.

Carlson, Matt, and Seth C. Lewis. *Boundaries of Journalism. Professionalism, Practices and Participation,* Routledge, 2015.

Coddington, Mark. 'Clarifying Journalism's Quantitative Turn: A Typology for Evaluating Data Journalism, Computational Journalism, and Computer-Assisted Reporting', *Digital Journalism* 3.3 (2014): 331-348.

Coleman, Gabriella. *Coding Freedom: The Ethics and Aesthetics of Hacking*. Princeton NJ: Princeton University Press, 2012.

---

45   Seth C. Lewis and Nikki Usher, 'Code, Collaboration, And The Future Of Journalism'.

Dailey, Dharma and Kate Starbird. 'Journalists as crowdsourcerers: responding to crisis by reporting with a crowd', *Computer Supported Cooperative Work* 23.4 (2014): 445-481.

Deuze, Mark and Tamara Witschge. 'Beyond journalism: Theorizing the transformation of journalism', *Journalism* 19 (2018): 165-181.

Gillmor, Dan. *We the Media: Grassroots Journalism by the People, for the People*, Sebastopol CA: O'Reilly Media, 2004.

Hermida, Alfred. 'Social journalism: exploring how social media is shaping journalism', in Eugenia Siapera & Andreas Veglis (eds), *The Handbook of Global Online Journalism*, Oxford: Wiley-Blackwell, 2012, pp. 309-328.

Hermida, Alfred and Lynn Young, 'Finding the data unicorn. A hierarchy of hybridity in data and computational journalism', *Digital Journalism* 5.2 (2016): 159-176.

Horrocks, Peter. 'The end of fortress journalism', in Charles Miller (ed.), *The future of journalism,* London: BBC College of Journalism, 2009.

Lewis, Seth C., and Nikki Usher. 'Code, Collaboration, and the Future of Journalism', *Digital Journalism* 2.3 (2014): 383-393.

Lewis, Seth C., and Nikki Usher. 'Open source and journalism: Toward new frameworks for imagining news innovation', *Media, Culture & Society* 35.5 (2013): 602-619.

Lewis, Seth C., and Oscar Westlund. 'Big data and journalism. Epistemology, expertise, economics, and ethics', *Digital Journalism* 3.3 (2015): 321-330.

Mauss, Marcel. *The Gift*, London: Routledge, 1954.

Mayer-Schönberger, Victor and Kenneth Cukier. *Big Data: A Revolution That Will Transform How We Live, Work and Think,* London: Murray, 2013.

Phillips, Angela. 'Transparency and the new ethics of journalism', *Journalism Practice* 4.3 (2010): 373-382.

Porlezza, Colin. 'Dall'open journalism all'open government? Il ruolo del data journalism nella trasparenza e nella partecipazione', *Problemi dell'Informazione* 1 (2016): 167-194.

Ramge, Thomas and Victor Mayer-Schönberger. *Das Digital. Markt, Wertschöpfung und Gerechtigkeit im Datenkapitalismus*, Berlin: Ullstein, 2017.

Raymond, Eric S. *The cathedral and the bazaar: Musings on Linux and open source by an accidental revolutionary.* Sebastopol CA: O'Reilly, 2001.

Russell, Adrienne. *Journalism as activism. Recoding media power*, Cambridge: Polity, 2016.

Singer, Jane. 'Norms and the Network: Journalistic Ethics in a Shared Media Space' in Christopher Meyers (ed.), *Journalism Ethics: A Philosophical Approach,* Oxford: Oxford University Press, 2010, pp. 117-129.

Singer, Jane, Alfred Hermida, David Domingo, Ari Heinonen, Steve Paulussen, Thorsten Quandt, Zvi Reich and Marina Vujnovic. *Participatory Journalism: Guarding Open Gates at Online Newspapers*, Chichester: John Wiley, 2011.

Sonderman, Jeff. 'Andy Carvin explains how Twitter is his "open-source newsroom"', *Poynter*, 2012, https://www.poynter.org/news/andy-carvin-explains-how-twitter-his-open-source-newsroom.

Splendore, Sergio. 'Closed data! Il giornalismo italiano alla ricerca di dati', *Problemi dell'Informazione* 1 (2016): 195-214.

_____. 'Quantitatively Oriented Forms of Journalism and Their Epistemology'. *Sociology Compass* (2016): online first.

Turner, Fred. 'Where the counterculture met the new economy: the WELL and the origins of virtual community', *Technology and Culture* 46.3 (2005): 485-512.

Uricchio, William. 'Data, Culture and the Ambivalence of Algorithms', in Mirko Tobias Schäfer and Karin van Es (eds), *The Datafied Society*, Amsterdam: Amsterdam University Press, 2017.

Usher, Nikki. *Interactive Journalism: Hackers, Data, and Code*. Champaign IL: University of Illinois Press, 2016.

Van Dijck, José. 'Datafication, dataism and dataveillance: Big Data between scientific paradigm and ideology', *Surveillance & Society* 12.2 (2014): 197-208.

_____. 'Foreword', in Mirko Tobias Schäfer and Karin van Es (eds) *The Datafied Society*, Amsterdam: Amsterdam University Press, 2017, p. 11.

Williams, Andy, Claire Wardle and Karin Wahl-Jorgensen, '"Have they got news for us?" Audience revolution or business as usual at the BBC?' *Journalism Practice*, 5.1 (2011): 85-99.

12: GOVERNANCE OF COMMUNAL DATA SHARING

CHIH-HSING HO [1] AND TYNG-RUEY CHUANGT [2]

Introduction

The rapid development of the data economy calls for innovative research into its social and ethical impacts. When enormous opportunities emerge along with making use of vast amounts of data, challenges are generated and concerns arise around monopoly and market enclosure. Current legal and regulatory frameworks for data protection fail to address these devastating problems. By focusing on consent and the anonymisation of data, these legal techniques echo the neoliberal methods of governance which promise individual autonomy and choice as an advanced liberal strategy. This article proposes theoretical and computational approaches to the analysis of an alternative data sharing model, which is based on community participation in decision making and self-governance. We consider several examples, such as user data cooperatives and collaborative data projects, to further explore how a community is formed and how the governance of communal data sharing is being established. We will then develop frameworks for the governance of communal data sharing by combining common pool resource management and a socio-legal perspective on the commons.

Today we see many states as well as *private* initiatives to promote a *data*-driven industrial revolution across the globe. Data, said to be like oil a century ago, has been cast as a new type of resource fuelling an emerging, lucrative digital-era industry.[3] However, the wealth derived from this digital revolution is not being evenly distributed. According to a study by the Economist, all five of the most valuable listed companies in the world - Apple, Alphabet (Google's parent company), Amazon, Facebook and Microsoft are tech titans.[4] Digital wealth is being monopolized and concentrated in very few hands. Such dominance has led to such side effects as unfair competition, manipulation, routine intrusion of privacy, and the undermining of democracy.[5] These tech giants provide the infrastructure undergirding much of the data economy, and stand to gain the most from it. Although most of their services appear to be free, what underlies the transactions of the digital economy is an exchange of services for control over data. The challenges posed by capitalist accumulation of data raise the question: is this monopoly inevitable?

---

1 Assistant Research Fellow, Institute of European and American Studies, Academia Sinica, Taipei Taiwan; LLM (Columbia), JSM (Stanford), PhD in Law (LSE), Email: chihho@sinica.edu.tw (corresponding author).
2 Associate Research Fellow, Institute of Information Science, Academia Sinica, Taipei, Taiwan, PhD (NYU), Email: trc@iis.sinica.edu.tw.
3 'The world's most valuable resource is no longer oil, but data', *The Economist*, 6 May 2017.
4 'Tech firms hoard huge cash piles', *The Economist*, 3 June 2017.
5 An example can be illustrated by the Facebook scandal, see: Tam Adams, 'Facebook's week of shame: the Cambridge Analytica fallout', *The Guardian*, 24 March 2018, https://www.theguardian.com/technology/2018/mar/24/facebook-week-of-shame-data-breach-observer-revelations-zuckerberg-silence.

How are we to imagine and create different systems, fairer systems featuring greater participatory control?

This article proposes theoretical and computational approaches to the analysis of an alternative data sharing model, which is based on community participation in decision making and self-governance. When we talk about 'community', we use this term in a non-conventional way. We try not to see community as a fixed group or a predefined collective identity. Rather, it refers to a set of ongoing engagement and practices of group making.[6] In other words, it is this dynamic process of community making - acts of mutual support, negotiation and experimentation, as David Bollier has argued - that are needed to build innovative systems to manage shared resources.[7] Along with these curiosities, we consider several examples, such as user data cooperatives[8] and collaborative data projects,[9] to further explore how a community is formed and how the governance of communal data sharing is being established. We will then develop frameworks for the governance of communal data sharing by combining common pool resource management and a socio-legal perspective on the commons.

Data for All? A Communal Approach

Historically, the governance of shared resources has challenged many great minds. For those who hold the view that competitive market promotes economic efficiency, the privatization of shared resources is one of the best ways to achieve their goal. As promoting efficiency is the core value under this endeavor, *how* the surplus is generated and *who* makes decision about its distribution are not central concerns of capitalists. That said, the social practice of commoning is a political-economic alternative to standard capitalist practice.[10] For commoners, what is more important is the *fair* conditions under which surplus is produced, and that the decision making about the surplus to be distributed involves those who take part in the process of production.[11] Applying the idea of the commons to the data economy, this participatory form of data sharing addresses the well-being of others through a process of democratizing ownership.[12] But the differences between the market and the commons go even beyond participation. Commoners need to communicate with one another to develop the norms, protocols or rules that govern access and the management of shared resources they co-own. In this process of commoning, all parties are stakeholders and are equally affected and bound by the governing rules they discuss, negotiate and then agree upon.

---

6   J.K Gibson-Graham et al, 'Cultivating Community Economies' (2017), https://thenextsystem.org/cultivating-community-economies: 5.
7   David Bollier, 'Commoning As A Transformative Social Paradigm', the Next System Project (2016).
8   For example, see Trebor Scholz and Nathan Schneider (eds), *Ours to hack and to own: The rise of platform cooperativism, a new vision for the future of work and a fairer internet*, New York: OR Books, 2017.
9   For more information on this, see: *2016 Workshop on Collaborative Data Projects,* held at Academia Sinica, Taipei, Taiwan, 8 Dec 2016, http://odw.tw/2016/.
10   Ibid.
11   J.K Gibson-Graham et al, p. 14.
12   David Bollier, 'Reclaiming the commons', *Boston Review* 27.3-4 (2002).

By taking responsibility and claiming entitlement to form and govern the common pool, commoners develop spaces of ethical and social connection. It is such ongoing social relationships that help build distinct communities in which commoners form their own subjectivities.

Current legal and regulatory frameworks for data protection fail to address the devastating problem of market enclosure. By focusing on consent and the anonymisation of data, these legal techniques echo the neoliberal methods of governance which promise individual autonomy and choice as an advanced liberal strategy. The Facebook-Cambridge Analytical scandal is one example of the inadequacy of these mechanisms in which trust was breached when Facebook failed to perform its role as a dutiful data controller by allowing Cambridge Analytical, a third party user, to access user data for very different purposes than that agreed to by data subjects who contributed their data only to access free services provided by Facebook. A communal data sharing model can be an alternative providing a bottom-up initiative to address these challenges.[13] However, how to set up this adequate model remains an issue yet to be solved. On the one hand, an effective system is required to encourage the establishing of incentives for data sharing within the community in a confidential and trustful manner. On the other hand, commoners have to recognise the need to differentiate between the degree of confidentiality within and outside of the communal boundaries. In this paper we will investigate and develop normative principles and computational frameworks to fully address these issues.

For communal data sharing, we refer to a communal approach of data management where members of a community voluntarily pool their data together to create a common pool for mutual benefits.[14] This common pool of data acts as a common resource of collective ownership to be accessed by third party users when properly aggregated and distilled according to its governance framework, which is initiated and agreed by all members of the community. Usually, three main actors are involved in data governance - data subjects, data controllers (and processors), and third party data users. Although data subjects contribute data, it is up to data controllers to decide how data is accessed and processed. In most cases, third party users who plan to access the data pool may hold very different, if not conflicting, interests from the data subjects. In reality, it becomes difficult for data subjects to trace and verify if data controllers have fulfilled their duties and the promises made prior to data collection.

What challenges this conventional model of data governance is that the three actors - data subjects, data controllers, and data users - do not share common views and interests on how they wish the data to be shared and reused. In practice, a common approach is for data controllers to anonymize personal data before the data to be released, and/or adopt restricted access model so that only certain users or queries are allowed to access data warehouses. However, this operation is not without limitations. As data science makes progress, thorough

---

13 Yves-Alexandre de Montjoye, Ce´sar A. Hidalgo, Michel Verleysen and Vincent D. Blondel, 'Unique in the crowd: The privacy bounds of human mobility', *Scientific Reports* 3 (2013): 1376.
14 Chao-Min Chiu, Meng-Hsiang Hsu and Eric T.G. Wang, 'Understanding knowledge sharing in virtual communities: An integration of social capital and social cognitive theories', *Decision Support Systems* 42.3 (December, 2006): 1872-1888.

anonymisation may not be possible when risks of re-identification remain.[15] As for restricting data access on a case-by-case basis, meeting the different expectations and requirements of data subjects and third party users challenges the possibility of stakeholders negotiating and agreeing to their data governing rules.

A Decentralized & Self-Governance Model

A communal approach to data sharing aims to create a decentralized model under which data subjects and data controllers are united rather than separated.[16] In other words, norms and principles for data use can be decided upon data subjects who are members of the community. Also, it is up to them to negotiate how their data shall be collected and used, as well as who can access to this communal data pool. Several notable experiments illustrate this kind of peer-based information production and sharing. Wikipedia,[17] OpenStreetMap,[18] and Social.Coop[19] are examples. They demonstrate that data can be aggregated, shared and managed by the peers themselves for the maximum of communal benefits. In addition, these initiatives also show that data management can be achieved from the bottom-up through grass root efforts.

Take Social.Coop as a case study. It is a social network platform operated through Mastodon,[20] a free and open-source software for microblogging. The operation of Mastodon is done via open protocols as its main purpose is to provide a decentralized alternative to commercial, monopolizing services in communication. Mastodon emphasizes a distributed and federated network of peer communication nodes. Attracted by its ethical design and non-commercial characteristic, Mastodon has been used by many communities to provide a service platform of no data advertising, mining and no walled gardens. Social.Coop follows these similar non-commercial and non-monopoly principles and operates itself as a co-operative microblogging service based on Mastodon. Its co-op operation emphasizes democratic principles of transparency and participation. In practice, it relies on several functional committees composed by members to establish a code of conduct and other policies in order to reach collective decisions for platform governance. All members of the Social.Coop are entitled to co-manage the platform where the community is served, and to take part in creating their own bylaws. The philosophy behind such self-governance model is to foster trust by means that increase data subjects' control over their data management based on their co-ownership.

Under this communal based, self-governance framework, the aggregated data becomes a common-pool resource. Its management is governed by community norms and bylaws set up by the peers who contribute to the data pool. Aggregation, distribution, and all other data management tasks can be facilitated by this open and transparent system. Further, all the

---

15 Latanya Sweeney, 'K-anonymity: A model for protecting privacy', *International Journal of Uncertainty, Fuzziness and Knowledge-Based Systems*, 10.5 (October, 2002): 557-570.
16 Ibid.
17 Wikipedia, https://www.wikipedia.org/.
18 OpenStreetMap, http://www.openstreetmap.org/.
19 Social.Coop, https://social.coop/about.
20 Mastodon, https://mastodon.social/about.

source code of the entire information system of this communal design is open and free for everyone to review and improve upon. Based on these cases of communal data sharing, we will further propose norms, principles and techno designs to help lead to success of the communal data sharing model.

Governing the Data Commons

The Data Commons generates important benefits in terms of building civic trust and shared commitments. The question is how to govern such a commons to make it sustainable. This is perhaps the main challenge we would face while finding ways to protect not only the interests of individual members, but also the integrity of the community, namely the shared resource itself. David Bollier has studied the origins of free software and the Creative Commons licenses. He found that although commoners may assert different notions of social norms and community boundaries, there is one similarity among them, and that is the use of the commons to connect people.[21] For Bollier, a commons serves not only as a shared resource, but appeals to something very deep in humanity. How have commoners organized to build their commons, such as online communities, to improve data management and reclaim their common wealth remains an interesting question worthy of further study.

Garrett Hardin argued in his famous 1968 essay 'The Tragedy of the Commons'[22] that the commons is a failed management regime as when everything is free for the taking, the common resource will be overused. He proposed that the best solution to this tragedy is to allocate private property rights to the resource in question. However, what Hardin observed is not really a commons but an open, or we can say unlimited access, regime. The main difference between the two is that in a commons, commoners share a mutual interest to maintain their shared resources. This common expectation helps form a distinct community, which is lacking in the unlimited access regime in which people do not interact with one another and therefore there is no community consensus being formed. Later, economist Elinor Ostrom offered eight principles based on which she thinks that a commons can be governed in a more sustainable and equitable way.[23] These principles are proposed in order to address issues associated with the tragedy of the commons. Several questions were raised to be considered: what are mechanisms to incentivise sharing? What ways can benefits be fairly distributed? What are the methods to enforce the boundary of a group? What workable procedures are available to form censuses and decisions, among others?

---

21 David Bollier, *Viral Spiral: How the Commoners Built a Digital Republic of Their Own*, New York: The New Press, 2009.
22 Garrett Hardin, 'The Tragedy of the Commons', *Science* 162 (1968): 1243-1248
23 Elinor Ostrom, *Governing the Commons: The Evolution of Institutions for Collective Action*, Cambridge: Cambridge University Press, 1990.

Here are Ostrom's eight principles for the governance of a commons:[24]

1. Define clear group boundaries;
2. Match rules governing use of common goods to local needs and conditions;
3. Ensure that those affected by the rules can participate in modifying the rules;
4. Make sure the rule-making rights of community members are respected by outside authorities;
5. Develop a system, carried out by community members, for monitoring members' behavior;
6. Use graduated sanctions for rule violators;
7. Provide accessible, low-cost means for dispute resolution, and;
8. Build responsibility for governing the common resource in nested tiers from the lowest level up to the entire interconnected system.

After further analysis, it is found that these principles may well apply not only to classic common-pool resources (CPRs), which are made available to all by consumption but access to which are limited by high costs (e.g. fishing grounds and irrigation system), but also to intangible information resources, such as knowledge and data (e.g. software programs).[25] Free software, whose source code is distributed under licenses like the GNU General Public Licenses (GPL),[26] is an example of information commons. A GPL'ed software package can be used and improved upon by anyone, and the enhancements to the package are also free for all to reuse due to the copyleft nature of GPL. The GPL license can be viewed as a way to set up boundaries. GPL'ed software is free for all to use, and such freedom cannot be revoked. However, in general, data is not copyrightable. Although some jurisdictions have sui generis database rights, similar copyleft database licenses have been developed. For example, the Open Database License (ODbL)[27] has been used to set a boundary for OpenStreetMap datasets.

When individuals are willing to pool their data for mutual benefits, similar arrangements can be made to purposely restrict the information flow of the pool. While GPL and ODbL aim to ensure that improvements are free for all to reuse, the pool needs to remain within the community boundary unless other arrangements have been made. Issues such as how to formulate suitable data restriction polices, and how to effectively enforce them, are central to any data sharing community. In addition, due to the sensitivity of personal data, each individual may only want to share partial data to the pool, and/or to remain anonymous when sharing the data.

In addition, there are some proprietary structural designs being developed to improve cooperative legalities in the management of shared resources. A general asset lock is one example. It is often used in the common ownership to set out a number of conditions to prevent residual

---

24 Ibid.
25 Charlotte Hess and Elinor Ostrom (eds), *Understanding Knowledge as a Commons: From Theory to Practice*, Cambridge MA: MIT Press, 2006.
26 GNU General Public License, Version 3, http://www.gnu.org/licenses/gpl-3.0.en.html.
27 ODC Open Database License (ODbL) Summary, http://opendatacommons.org/licenses/odbl/summary/.

assets to be distributed amongst members when the organisation winds up.[28] But it also allows members to vote to change these provisions in the governing document to convert the nature of the organisation from a co-operative into a company. On the contrary, a statutory asset lock includes provisions in the governing document in a prescribed format to incorporate an organisation under specific legislation.[29] It sets out conditions so that assets can only be used for the benefit of the community on dissolution of the organisation or be transferred outside of a community interest company (CIC) when the prescribed requirements are satisfied.[30] These mechanisms of proprietary designs help not only address problems of the tragedy of the commons, but also provide a possible resolution for the sustainability of the commons.

Computational Methods

There are several computational methods that can be used to facilitate communal data sharing while maintaining confidentiality of data subjects. When members share their private data with others in a community, they often wish to ensure that their contributions are confidential, at least to some degree. For example, they may not want their identities to be revealed by other members in the same group. Even if, under certain circumstances, they have to reveal their identities to the group, they may not wish to disclose the same to those who are outside of the group. When members' data leaves the boundaries of the community for third party reuse, the data must be properly de-identified to keep the data subjects anonymous. In some cases, such de-identification efforts are futile, as even de-identified datasets can still reveal characteristics of the entire community that is harmful to every member of the group. For example, an anonymized dataset could reveal that many data subjects come from higher income groups (e.g. by their shopping habits and/or ZIP codes) or are susceptible to a particular disease (e.g. by the characteristics and/or areas of their upbringing).

These examples show that confidentiality is contextual and relative. A person may be more willing to trust others in her or his own community, but not feeling the same for those who are outside of the group. Data use within the group, therefore, shall be treated differently than that used outside of the community. When people form an ad hoc community to share personal information about themselves (e.g. drug abuse), a certain degree of anonymity is warranted; but they may still need ways to identify one another in the group just to be able to communicate with each other properly and in context. As for communication with others outside of the group, however, member anonymity must be maintained. Now, considering a situation where members can leave and join an ad hoc group freely and at any time, maintaining workable group boundaries turns out to be crucial if members are to be adequately protected.

---

28 For example, at the dissolution of the commons, commoners must pass assets on to another common ownership enterprise or choose to retain them within the sector, otherwise donate them to charity if either of these is not possible.

29 Alex Nicholls, https://www.sciencedirect.com/science/article/pii/S0361368209000798#!, 'Institutionalizing Social Entrepreneurship in Regulatory Space: Reporting and Disclosure by Community Interest Companies', *Accounting, Organisations and Society* 35.4 (2010): 394-415.

30 Rory Ridley-Duff, 'Communitarian Perspectives on Social Enterprise', *Corporate Governance: An International Review* (March 2007).

Likewise, there is a need to call for suitable methods for auditing the communal data sharing system. While maintaining confidentiality, members of a community would still want to ensure that their data is, and will always be, incorporated accurately and in full into the communal data pool. In addition, they need ways to validate that other members' contributions are authentic.[31] When the communal data pool is considered to be common resources, the community may want to keep track of contributions from its members and to make sure that members access the resource accordingly. This communal data pool needs to be used wisely by people both within and outside of the group. We shall also emphasize that in many scenarios, auditability needs to be achieved when data are anonymised.

Here we list several computational methods that can be used for trustful group communications. Many of these methods involve parties who would like to cooperate anonymously to produce verifiable outcomes. A typical scenario, for example, is to ask a group of strangers to form a consensus without meeting face-to-face, and that each be able to verify later that a certain consensus has been reached without knowing the opinions offered by others. Below we exemplify three areas of this promising research.

- **Secure multiparty computation** is a subfield of cryptography that aims to provide methods for multiple parties to jointly compute a function over their private values without revealing them.[32] For example, two employees can use a private equality test to see if they are paid the same while not revealing the amount of one's own salary. There are several methods for such a test. Methods for secure multiparty computation have been used for privacy-preserving data mining.

- **Open-audit e-voting** is with regard to developing protocols and systems for online voting in which each voter gains assurance that his or her vote was correctly cast, and any observer can verify that all cast votes were properly counted. Helios[33] is a protocol and a Web-based system for open-audit voting.[34] It is shown that one can set up an election on the Web using Helios, and invite voters to cast a secret ballot, compute a tally, and generate a validity proof for the entire process. In many cases, a group can use secret ballot voting to aggregate sensitive information and to form consensus, such as selecting a leader to the group while not revealing the preference of anyone involved.

- **User-centric online services** let Web users keep their personal data in their own devices and/or on storage servers that act as intermediaries to other online services. The data is likely stored encrypted. When user data is requested by a Web site, for example, while a user is logging into a social media site, encrypted user data is sent to the site on a need-to-know basis and decrypted. Sieve is such a system.[35] Dissent is a general protocol

---

31 Susan J. Eggers and Tor E. Jeremiassen, 'Eliminating False Sharing', *ICPP* (1991).
32 Carsten Baum et al, 'Publicly Auditable Secure Multi-Party Computation', *the 9th International Conference on Security and Cryptography for Networks, Lecture Notes in Computer Science,* vol. 8642, Springer, 2014.
33 Helios, https://heliosvoting.org/.
34 Ben Adida, 'Helios: Web-based Open-Audit Voting', *the 17th USENIX Security Symposium*, 2008.
35 Frank Wang et al, 'Sieve: Cryptographically Enforced Access Control for User Data in Untrusted Clouds',

offering provable anonymity and accountability for group communication.[36] It addresses the need to balance between provably hiding the identities of well-behaved users, while provably revealing the identities of disruptive users.

Confidentiality and auditability requirements are highly contextual. While these computational methods and systems are effective in their respective application domains, they may not meet the communication needs in a communal setting for data sharing. Many of the existing methods assume two kinds of actors: individuals and their adversaries. The assumption often is that every individual acts only for oneself. In a communal setting, there are various data sharing communities, and an individual can belong to many different groups. As each community may have its own data sharing policy (intra-group and inter-group), we anticipate that existing methods may require combination and/or use in layers to effectively address technical problems arising from communal sharing of personal data.

Here, we use a hypothetical example to further illustrate how the above computational methods can be used together to initiate and facilitate group communication concerning sensitive personal information. Suppose that there was an outbreak of disease in a population, but people were not willing to share their personal information. For those suspecting that they were exposed to similar hazards, they may be more willing to communicate with one another. Secure multiple-party computation methods can be developed to allow people to check whether they have a similar travel history - countries visited in last six months, for example, but without revealing where they went exactly. Open-audit e-voting methods will then allow these people to aggregate and share information without revealing their identities ('write in' one's major medical conditions and make tallies, for example). After the vote and tally, and based on the outcome, some people may be more willing to engage in group conversations (though remain private among themselves). In such a case, user-centric online services can be deployed to help host such conversations.

Conclusion

The rapid development of the data economy calls for innovative research into its social and ethical impacts. When enormous opportunities emerge along with making use of vast amounts of data, challenges are generated and concerns arise around monopoly and market enclosure. We need to ensure that the rapidly developing data economy evolves in fair and justifiable ways. In order to make possible this goal, it is crucial that an innovative, bottom-up and de-centralized data governance framework be designed, through which a trustful space arises such that all stakeholders are able to fruitfully engage and take responsibility for their communities.

13th USENIX Symposium on Networked Systems Design and Implementation, Santa Clara, CA, USA, 16-18 March 2016.
36 Ewa Syta et al, 'Security Analysis of Accountable Anonymity in Dissent', *ACM Transactions on Information and System Security* 17.1 (2014).

A communal data sharing model is established based on these principles. By forming a communal data pool, each member of the community is entitled to take her or his entitlement and participates in the collective decision-making on an equal footing. This involves also incorporating collective ownership in data governance frameworks. The central aspect of engagement facilitates communication among members of the community. Such initiative relies not only on an effective information system, but also on the process of commoning through which a collective identity is formed. In contrast to the conventional data protection framework paying primary attention to consent and data anonymisation, the communal data sharing model emphasizes the amount of control that individual subjects have over their data. It also deals with who may have access to data in the communal pool, and with whom such data may be shared. We therefore propose a communal data sharing model to help create fairer platforms for everyone who takes part in this brave new data-driven revolution.

Acknowledgements

This study is supported by Academia Sinica's three-year thematic project 'Socially Accountable Privacy Framework for Secondary Data Usage' under grant number AS-TP-106-M06. The authors would like to thank the editors and two anonymous reviewers for their constructive suggestions and comments.

References

Adams, Tam. 'Facebook's week of shame: the Cambridge Analytica fallout', *The Guardian*, 24 March 2018.

Adida, Ben. 'Helios: Web-based Open-Audit Voting', *USENIX security symposium*, 28 July-1 August 2008, https://www.usenix.org/legacy/event/sec08/tech/full_papers/adida/adida.pdf.

Angiuli, Olivia, Joe Blitzstein and Jim Waldo. 'How to de-identify your data', *Queue* 13 (8, September-October 2015): 20, https://dl.acm.org/citation.cfm?id=2838930.

Baum, Carsten, Ivan Damgård and Claudio Orlandi. 'Publicly Auditable Secure Multi-Party Computation', *International Conference on Security and Cryptography for Networks*, Springer, Cham, 3-5 September 2014, https://eprint.iacr.org/2014/075.pdf.

Bollier, David. 'Commoning as a transformative social paradigm'. *The Next System Project*, 2016, http://www.operationkindness.net/wp-content/uploads/David-Bollier.pdf.

_____. 'Reclaiming the commons', *Boston Review* 27 (3-4, 2002).

_____. *Viral Spiral: How the Commoners Built a Digital Republic of Their Own*, New York: The New Press, 2009, http://barcelonacomuns.pbworks.com/f/Viral+Spiral_How+the+Commoners+Built+a+Digital+Republic+of+Their+Own+%5Bdavid+bollier%5D.pdf.

Chiu, Chao-Min, Meng-Hsiang Hsu and Eric T.G. Wang. 'Understanding knowledge sharing in virtual communities: An integration of social capital and social cognitive theories', *Decision Support Systems* 42.3 (December 2006): 1872-1888.

De Montjoye, Yves-Alexandre, Ce´sar A. Hidalgo, Michel Verleysen and Vincent D. Blondel. 'Unique in the crowd: The privacy bounds of human mobility', *Scientific Reports* 3 (2013): 1376.

Eggers, Susan J. and Tor E. Jeremiassen. 'Page-level Affinity Scheduling for Eliminating False Sharing'. *ICPP* (1995), https://pdfs.semanticscholar.org/34fe/b586363fead853fa7e7d6dc5678d1159a8be.pdf?_ga=2.132910156.372523520.1542619879-1465787887.1542619879.

Garrett Hardin. 'The Tragedy of the Commons', *Science* 162 (1968): 1243-1248.

Gibson-Graham, J.K., Jenny Cameron, Kelly Dombroski, Stephen Healy and Ethan Miller. 'Cultivating Community Economies', 2017, https://thenextsystem.org/cultivating-community-economies.

GNU General Public License, Version 3, http://www.gnu.org/licenses/gpl-3.0.en.html.

Helios, https://heliosvoting.org/.

Hess, Charlotte and Elinor Ostrom (eds). *Understanding Knowledge as a Commons: From Theory to Practice*, Cambridge MA: MIT Press, 2006.

Kosba, Ahmed, Andrew Miller, Elaine Shi and Zikai Wen. 'Hawk: The Blockchain Model of Cryptography and Privacy-Preserving Smart Contracts', *2016 IEEE Symposium on Security and Privacy (SP)*, California, USA 22-26 May 2016, https://ieeexplore.ieee.org/document/7546538.

Lane, Julia, Victoria Stodden, Stefan Bender and Helen Nissenbaum (eds). *Privacy, Big Data, and the Public Good: Frameworks for Engagement*, Cambridge: Cambridge University Press, 2014.

Mastodon, https://mastodon.social/about.

Nicholls, Alex. 'Institutionalizing social entrepreneurship in regulatory space: Reporting and disclosure by community interest companies', *Accounting, Organizations and Society*, 35 (4, 2010): 394-415.

ODC Open Database License (ODbL) Summary, http://opendatacommons.org/licenses/odbl/summary/.

OpenStreetMap, http://www.openstreetmap.org/.

Ostrom, Elinor. *Governing the Commons: The Evolution of Institutions for Collective Action*, Cambridge: Cambridge University Press, 1990.

Ridley Duff, Rory. 'Communitarian perspectives on social enterprise', *Corporate governance: an international review*, 15.2 (2007): 382-392.

Satoshi, Nakamoto. 'Bitcoin: A Peer-to-Peer Electronic Cash System' (2008), https://bitcoin.org/bitcoin.pdf.

Scholz, Trebor and Nathan Schneider (eds). *Ours to hack and to own: The rise of platform cooperativism, a new vision for the future of work and a fairer internet*, New York: OR Books, 2017.

Social.Coop, https://social.coop/about.

Solon, Olivia. 'Facebook says Cambridge Analytica may have gained 37m more users' data', *The Guardian*, 4 April 2018.

Summers, Hannah and Nicola Slawson, 'Investigators complete seven-hour Cambridge Analytica HQ search', *The Guardian*, 24 March 2018.

Sweeney, Latanya. 'K-anonymity: A model for protecting privacy', *International Journal of Uncertainty, Fuzziness and Knowledge-Based Systems* 10.5 (October 2002): 557-570.

Syta, Ewa, et al. 'Security analysis of accountable anonymity in Dissent', *ACM Transactions on Information and System Security (TISSEC)*, 17.1 (2014): 4.

Tene, Omer and Jules Polonetsky. 'Big data for all: Privacy and user control in the age of analytics', *Nw. J. Tech. & Intell. Prop.* 11 (2013): xxvii.

'The world's most valuable resource is no longer oil, but data', *The Economist*, 6 May 2017.

'Tech firms hoard huge cash piles,' *The Economist,* 3 June 2017.

Wang Frank et al. 'Sieve: Cryptographically Enforced Access Control for User Data in Untrusted Clouds', *Proceedings of the 13th USENIX Symposium on Networked Systems Design and Implementation*, Santa Clara, CA, USA, 16-18 March 2016, https://www.usenix.org/sites/default/files/nsdi16_full_proceedings.pdf.

Wicks, Paul et al. 'Sharing health data for better outcomes on PatientsLikeMe', *Journal of medical Internet research,* 12.2 (June 2010), https://www.ncbi.nlm.nih.gov/pmc/articles/PMC2956230/.

Wikipedia, https://www.wikipedia.org/.

Wilkinson, Mark D et al. 'The FAIR Guiding Principles for scientific data management and stewardship', *Scientific Data* 3 (March 2016).

Workshop on Collaborative Data Projects, Academia Sinica, Taipei, Taiwan. 8 Dec 2016, http://odw.tw/2016/.

THEME 4:
GOOD DATA ACTIVISM AND RESEARCH

13: PROVOCATIONS FOR SOCIAL MEDIA RESEARCH: TOWARD GOOD DATA ETHICS

ANDREA ZEFFIRO

Introduction

As academics continue to collect, scrape, integrate and analyse social media data, technical knowledge to acquire, analyse, secure and disseminate data is needed, but so too is a refined understanding of evolving ethical norms and values embedded within data protocols and practices. In fact, the requirement of technical understanding coupled with the contemporary rate of technological evolution itself presents complex ethical conundrums when it comes to the collection, maintenance, and dissemination of social media research data. Institutions and funding agencies champion research using social media data, but few, if any have ethical guidelines for social media research. In part, current policies are too broad for social media research and are therefore left open to interpretation. At the same time, however, codifying ethical considerations means disavowing a situational ethics principle, which recognizes how each social media research context is unique with a distinct set of traits and ethical challenges. This chapter outlines provocations for ethical decision making and provides prompts for researchers to engage with throughout the life-cycle of research.

This chapter sets forth considerations for social media research by identifying provocations for how academic research methods, practices, and norms can foster 'good' social media research data ethics. Over the last year I conducted a pilot study examining institutional research ethics guidelines from Canadian universities in order to assess the current trends, standards and norms for working with social media data in a national research context. My research has shown that institutions from funding bodies, to universities, to research ethics boards share a piecemeal approach to research ethics in the face of changing technologies. The considerations culminating from the pilot study register with international researchers, scholarly communities and institutions that are grappling with the same issues, and add to existing efforts at establishing ethical guidelines for research using social media platforms and data.[1] My contribution to *Good Data* outlines provocations for ethical decision making

---

1   Australian National Data Service, *Data Sharing Considerations for Human Research Ethics Committees*, June 2018, http://www.ands.org.au/guides/data-sharing-considerations-for-hrecs; Ellen Broad, 'Australia, we need to talk about data ethics', *The Ethics Centre*, 25 January 2017, http://www.ethics.org.au/on-ethics/blog/january-2017/australia-data-ethics; dana boyd, 'Where do we find ethics?' *Points*, 5 April 2016, https:// points.datasociety.net/where-do-we-find-ethics-d0b9e8a7f4e6; Karin Clark, Matt Duckham, Marilys Guillemin, Assunta Hunter, Jodie McVernon, Christine O'Keefe, Cathy Pitkin, Steven Prawer, Richard Sinnott, Deborah Warr and Jenny Waycott, *Guidelines for the Ethical Use of Digital Data in Human Research*, The University of Melbourne, 2015, https://www.carltonconnect.com.au/read-ethical-use-of-digital-data-in-human-research/; Huw Davies et al, 'Ethics Guidelines and Collated Resources for Digital Research', British Sociological Association, 2017, https://www.britsoc.co.uk/media/24309/bsa_statement_of_ethical_practice_annexe.pdf; Annette N Markham and Elizabeth

and provides prompts for researchers to engage with when navigating ethical considerations during research design, but also throughout the life-cycle of research. These provocations and prompts do not aim to define a 'one size fits all model' for social media research, but rather intend to generate a dialogue between interdisciplinary researchers to better understand some of the key concerns pertaining to the integration of social media data into a range of scholarly projects, and engage with pressing questions as to how access to and use of social media data is mandated and governed, and how these practices impact scholarly research and the production of knowledge.

'Big Data'

'Big data' remains an elusive term. My understanding of it emerges in part from a digital humanities research context, wherein emerging digital tools and techniques contribute to an expanding array of research methods and sources of evidence. 'Big data' in this sense concerns the application for research of computational tools, techniques and methods used in the extraction, analyses and visualization of data from social media platforms and the Internet. In this respect, 'big data' summons disciplinary domains like data science, data analytics, and data management, curation and stewardship, among others. But I also comprehend the term from a critical media and communication studies perspective, wherein it signals approaches that question and challenge the notion of data as a neutral phenomenon.[2]

Outside of the academic contexts I describe, big data has been cited as an agent in healthcare, entertainment, education, personal wellness, and city planning to name but a few domains.

Buchanan, 'Ethical Considerations in Digital Research contexts', in James D. Wright (ed.), *Encyclopedia for Social & Behavioral Sciences,* Waltham MA: Elsevier, 2015, *pp. 606-613;* Joanna and Claudia Pagliari, 'Mining Social Media Data: How are Research Sponsors and Researchers Addressing the Ethical Challenges?', *Research Ethics* 14.2 (October 2017): 1-39; Katie Shilton, 'Emerging Ethics Norms in Social Media Research', *Big Data Ethics*, 2016, https://bigdata.fpf.org/papers/emerging-ethics-norms-in-social-media-research/; Chris Allen Sula, 'Research Ethics in an Age of Big Data', *Association for Information Science and Technology*, 6 January 2016, https://www.asist.org/publications/bulletin/decemberjanuary-2016/research-ethics-in-an-age-of-big-data/; Katrin Tilenberg, 'Ethics in Digital Research', in Uwe Flick (ed.), *The SAGE Handbook of Qualitative Data Collection*, Thousand Oaks: SAGE, 2018, pp. 466-481; Leanne Townsend and Claire Wallace, '*Social Media Research: A Guide to Ethics*', University of Aberdeen, 2015, https://www.gla.ac.uk/media/media_487729_en.pdf; University of Sheffield, *The Ethics of Internet-based and Social Media Research,* 2016, https://www.sheffield.ac.uk/polopoly_fs/1.644904!/file/Report_Ethics_of_Social_Media_Research_Jul16.pdf.

2   dana boyd and Kate Crawford, 'Critical Questions for Big Data: Provocations for a Cultural, Technological and Scholarly Phenomenon', *Information, Communication & Society* 15.5 (2012): 662-679; Kate Crawford, Kate Miltner and Mary L. Gray, 'Critiquing Big Data: Politics, Ethics, Epistemology', *International Journal of Communication* 8 (2014): 1663-1672; Viginia Eubanks, *Automating Inequality: How High-Tech Tools Profile, Police, and Punish the Poor*, New York: St. Martin's Press, 2018; Andrew Guthrie Ferguson, *The Rise of Big Data Policing: Surveillance, Race, and the Future of Law Enforcement*, New York: NYU Press, 2017; Andrew Iliadis and Federica Russo, 'Critical Data Studies: An Introduction', *Big Data & Society*, December 2016, https://doi.org/10.1177/2053951716674238; Safiya Umoja Noble, *Algorithms of Oppression: How Search Engines Reinforce Racism*, New York: NYU Press, 2018; Miriam Posner and Lauren F. Klein, 'Editor's Introduction: Data as Media', *Feminist Media Histories*, 3.3 (2017): 1-8; Jose van Dijck, 'Datafication, Dataism and Dataveillance: Big Data Between Scientific Paradigm and Ideology', *Surveillance & Society 12*.2 (2014).

The public safety sector, for instance, harnesses self-reported data from social media, publicly available data sets, physical sensors, and surveillance systems to respond quickly to emergency alerts. During Hurricane Harvey, when local 911 systems were failing, residents took to Facebook and Twitter to ask for assistance, and emergency respondents gathered crowd sourced information from social media platforms to refine their situational awareness and respond to requests for help.[3] Thus, big data allegedly stands to improve nearly every facet of our lives.[4] The general optimism for it has rendered it infallible, even in light of 'public' data breaches and leaks,[5] focused inquiries into social media platforms taking liberties with user data,[6] and disclosures of academic studies that have strained the limits of ethical conduct in the use of data.[7] As of late, however, nebulous big data practices have received significant public attention and contempt.

In March 2018, *The Guardian* and *Observer* first reported on a Facebook and Cambridge Analytica data breach in which the political consulting firm was given access to the data of more than 87 million Facebook users.[8] It was later revealed that data had been harvested

---

3   Maya Rhodan, "Please send help.' Hurricane Harvey victims turn to Twitter and Facebook', *Time*, 30 August 2017, http://time.com/4921961/hurricane-harvey-twitter-facebook-social-media/; Deepa Seetharaman and Georgia Wells, 'Hurricane Harvey Victims Turn to Social Media for Assistance', *The Wall Street Journal*, 29 August 2017, https://www.wsj.com/articles/hurricane-harvey-victims-turn-to-social-media-for-assistance-1503999001.
4   Randall E. Bryant, Randy H Katz and Edward D. Lazowska, 'Big-Data Computing: Creating Revolutionary Breakthroughs in Commerce, Science, and Society', *Computing Research Consortium*, 22 December 2008, https://cra.org/ccc/wp-content/uploads/sites/2/2015/05/Big_Data.pdf; Viktor Mayer-Schönberger and Kenneth Cukier, *Big Data: A Revolution that will Transform How we Live, Work, and Think*, Boston, MA: Houghton Mifflin Harcourt, 2013.
5   Alan Rusbridger and Ewen MacAskill, 'Edward Snowden Interview - The Edited Transcript. *The Guardian*, 18 July 2014, https://www.theguardian.com/world/2014/jul/18/-sp-edward-snowden-nsa-whistleblower-interview-transcript.
6   Sam Biddle, 'Stop Using Unroll.me, Right Now. It Sold Your Data to Uber', *The Intercept*, 24 April 2017, https://theintercept.com/2017/04/24/stop-using-unroll-me-right-now-it-sold-your-data-to-uber/; Alex Hearn, 'Google will Stop Scanning Content of Personal Emails', *The Guardian*, 26 June 2017, https://www.theguardian.com/technology/2017/jun/26/google-will-stop-scanning-content-of-personal-emails.
7   Sauvik Das and Adam Kramer, 'Self-censorship on Facebook', *Proceedings of the Seventh International AAAI Conference on Weblogs and Social Media*, 2013, pp. 120-127, https://research.fb.com/publications/self-censorship-on-facebook/; Michelle V. Hauge, Mark D. Stevenson, Kim D. Rossmo and Steven Le Comber, 'Tagging Banksy: Using Geographic Profiling to Investigate a Modern Art Mystery', *Journal of Spatial Science* 61.1 (2016): 185-190; Adam Kramer, Jamie Guillory and Jeffrey Hancock, 'Experimental Evidence of Massive-Scale Emotional Contagion Through Social Networks', *Proceedings National Academy of Science* 111.24 (2014): 8788-8790; Inder M Verma, 'Editorial Expression of Concern and Correction', *Proceedings National Academy of Science* 111.29 (2014): 10779; Yilun Wang and Michal Kosinski, 'Deep Neural Networks are More Accurate than Humans at Detecting Sexual Orientation from Facial Images', *Journal of Personality and Social Psychology* 114.2 (2018): 246-257.
8   Richard Adams, 'Cambridge University asks Facebook for Evidence About Role of Academic', *The Guardian*, 20 March 2018, https://www.theguardian.com/uk-news/2018/mar/20/cambridge-university-asks-facebook-for-evidence-about-role-of-academic-alex-kogan; Carole Cadwalladr and Emma Graham-Harrison, 'Revealed: 50 Million Facebook Profiles Harvested for Cambridge Analytica in Major Data Breach', *The Guardian*, 17 March 2018, https://www.theguardian.com/news/2018/mar/17/cambridge-

through a personality app called *thisisyourdigitallife*. In 2013, Dr. Aleksandr Kogan developed the app separately from his research at Cambridge University, and through his company Global Science Research (GSR), and in collaboration with Cambridge Analytica, hundreds of thousands of Facebook users were paid to take the personality test and agreed to have their data collected for research purposes. The app worked under Facebook's pre-2014 terms of service, which authorised the harvesting of data from not only the 270,000 users who installed it, but from their friends as well. Data mining was largely limited to what was published on public profiles, such as political beliefs, interests, and friends' information. However, a small number of users had their data harvested from timelines, posts, and private messages. Cambridge Analytica was granted access to the data, and without authorization, the firm used it to build psychological profiles of voters in the lead up to the 2016 US Presidential Election and subsequently targeted individuals with personalized political advertisements. Under the pretences of 'research', corporate and political interests sustained the normalization of deceptive data gathering and marketing tactics, and Facebook, Cambridge Analytica and Kogan benefited financially from the exploitation of personal data. Facebook is a market leader in stockpiling personal data, which is at the core of its $40.6 billion annual business.[9] On the heels of the scandal, Facebook's Chief Technology Officer Mike Schroepfer revealed in a post published on the company's news site that most of Facebook's 2.2 billion members have had their personal data scraped by 'malicious actors' at some point.[10] This concession further emphasizes the platform's haphazard procedures for safeguarding user data as well as a wilful lack of disclosure to its participants about the extent to which personal data was collected and shared.[11]

Public outrage in the aftermath of the scandal bolstered concerns scholars have voiced for numerous years in regards to 'big data'.[12] Interdisciplinary scholars invested in critical data

---

    analytica-facebook-influence-us-election; Matthew Weaver, 'Facebook Scandal: I am Being Used as Scapegoat - Academic Who Mined Data', *The Guardian*, 21 March 2018, https://www.theguardian.com/uk-news/2018/mar/21/facebook-row-i-am-being-used-as-scapegoat-says-academic-aleksandr-kogan-cambridge-analytica.

9   Natasha Singer, 'What You Don't Know About How Facebook Uses Your Data', *The New York Times*, 11 April 2018, https://www.nytimes.com/2018/04/11/technology/facebook-privacy-hearings.html.

10   Mike Schroepfer, 'An Update on Our Plans to Restrict Data Access on Facebook', *Facebook Newsroom*, 4 April 2018, https://newsroom.fb.com/news/2018/04/restricting-data-access/.

11   Tim Adams, 'Facebook's Week of Shame: The Cambridge Analytica Fallout', *The Guardian*, 24 March 2018, https://www.theguardian.com/technology/2018/mar/24/facebook-week-of-shame-data-breach-observer-revelations-zuckerberg-silence; Cadwalladr and Graham-Harrison, 'Revealed: 50 Million Facebook Profiles Harvested for Cam bridge Analytica in Major Data Breach'; Keith Collins and Larry Buchanan, 'How Facebook Lets Brands and Politicians Target You', *The New York Times*, 11 April 2018, https://www.nytimes.com/interactive/2018/04/11/technology/facebook-sells-ads-life-details.html; Sheera Frenkel, Matthew Rosenberg and Nicholas Confessore, 'Facebook Data Collected by Quiz App Included Private Messages', *The New York Times*, 10 April 2018, https://www.nytimes.com/2018/04/10/technology/facebook-cambridge-analytica-private-messages.html?action=click&contentCollection=Personal%20Tech&module=RelatedCoverage&region=Marginalia&pgtype=article; Matthew Weaver, 'Facebook Scandal: I am Being Used as Scapegoat - Academic Who Mined Data'.

12   Mark Andrejevic and Kelly Gates, 'Big Data Surveillance: Introduction', *Surveillance & Society* 12.2 (2014): 185-96; Tom Boellstorff, 'Making Big Data, in Theory', *First Monday* 18.10 (2013); Finn

studies consider the historical conditions that have contributed to 'big data', with focused attention on the public and private entities that exert levels of control over the production, analysis and management of data, and the ways in which emerging computational practices, techniques and methods contribute to forms of knowledge production in industry and the academy.[13] In this sense, 'big data' as it is deployed in critical data studies frames urgent concerns about the production of knowledge in an effort to render transparent the ways in which data shape and are shaped by the instruments, practices, and contexts used to generate, collect, process, analyse, and store data. Orit Halpern refers to these assumptions about the value of data as effectuating 'communicative objectivity', which are new forms of observation, rationality and epistemology.[14] For instance, it is common practice for the 'digital traces' or residues of information that are produced, abandoned or captured throughout social media exchanges to stand in for the digital identity of individuals and collectives.[15] The risk in interpreting digital traces as the raw material of human identity,[16] especially in academic

---

Brunton and Helen Nissenbaum, 'Vernacular Resistance to Data Collection and Analysis: A Political Theory of Obfuscation', *First Monday* 16.5 (2011); Finn Brunton and Helen Nissenbaum, *Obfuscation: A User's Guide for Privacy and Protest*, Cambridge MA: MIT Press, 2016; danah boyd and Kate Crawford, 'Critical Questions for Big Data: Provocations for a Cultural, Technological and Scholarly Phenomenon'; Kate Crawford, Kate Miltner and Mary L. Gray, 'Critiquing Big Data: Politics, Ethics, Epistemology'; Lisa Gitelman (ed.), *Raw Data is An Oxymoron*, Cambridge MA: MIT Press, 2013; Rob Kitchin, *The Data Revolution: Big Data, Open Data, Data Infrastructures and Their Consequences*, London: SAGE, 2014; Rob Kitchin, 'Big Data, New Epistemologies and Paradigm Shifts', *Big Data & Society* 1.1 (2014): 1-12; Jacob Metcalf, Emily Keller and danah boyd, *Perspectives on Big Data, Ethics, and Society*, Council for Big Data, Ethics, and Society, 23 May 2016, https://bdes.datasociety.net/council-output/perspectives-on-big-data-ethics-and-society/; Mike Michael and Deborah Lupton, 'Toward a Manifesto for the Public Understanding of Big Data', *Public Understanding of Science* 25.1 (2015): 104-116; Philip Napoli and Robyn Caplan, 'Why Media Companies Insist They're Not Media Companies, Why They're Wrong, and Why it Matters', *First Monday* 22.5 (2017); Gina Neff, Anissa Tanweer, Brittany Fiore-Gartland and Laura Osburn, 'Critique and Contribute: A Practice-Based Framework for Improving Critical Data Studies and Data Science', *Big Data* 5.2 (2017): 85-97; Cathy O'Neil, 'On Being a Data Skeptic', O'Reilly Media, 2013, http://www.oreilly.com/data/free/files/being-a-data-skeptic.pdf; Jose van Dijck, 'Datafication, Dataism and Dataveillance: Big Data Between Scientific Paradigm and Ideology'.

13   Lisa Gitelman (ed.), *Raw Data is An Oxymoron*; Craig Dalton and Jim Thatcher, 'What Does a Critical Data Studies Look Like, and Why Do We Care? Seven Points for a Critical Approach to "Big Data"', *Society & Space Open Site* (2014), http://societyandspace.org/2014/05/12/what-does-a-critical-data-studies-look-like-and-why-do-we-care-craig-dalton-and-jim-thatcher/; Craig Dalton, Linnet Taylor and Jim Thatcher. 'Critical Data Studies: A Dialog on Data and Space', *Big Data & Society* 3.1 (2014): 1-9; Rob Kitchin and Tracey Lauriault, 'Towards Critical Data Studies: Charting and Unpacking Data Assemblages and Their Work', *The Programmable City Working Paper* 2 (2014), http://papers.ssrn.com/sol3/papers.cfm?abstract_id=2474112; Andrew Iliadis and Federica Russo, 'Critical Data Studies: An Introduction'; Gernot Rieder and Judith Simon, 'Datatrust: Or, the Political Quest for Numerical Evidence and the Epistemologies of Big Data', *Big Data & Society*, 3.1 (2016).

14   Orit Halpern, *Beautiful Data: A History of Vision and Reason Since 1945*, Durham: Duke University Press, 2015.

15   Tyler Butler Reigeluth, 'Why Data is Not Enough: Digital Traces as Control of Self and Self-Control', *Surveillance & Society* 12.2 (2014), 249.

16   Mark Andrejevic and Kelly Gates, 'Big Data Surveillance: Introduction'; Tyler Butler Reigeluth, 'Why Data is Not Enough: Digital Traces as Control of Self and Self-Control'; Jose van Dijck, 'Datafication, Dataism and Dataveillance: Big Data Between Scientific Paradigm and Ideology'.

research, is that it displaces the figure of the human subject and fundamentally reshapes practices and processes of knowledge production. Jacob Metcalf and Kate Crawford outline the ways in which 'big data' research challenge research ethics conventions in regard to the 'human subject'.[17] As the authors explain, the figure of the human subject in big data research is reconfigured into a 'data subject', marking a shift from an individual to a wider networked and distributed grouping or classification of people. 'If the familiar human subject is largely invisible or irrelevant to data science', ask Metcalf and Crawford, 'how are we to devise new ethical parameters? Who is the 'data subject' in a large-scale data experiment, and what are they owed?'.[18] Arguably, the 'human subject' has not been deemed inconsequential to data science, but rather digital platforms, networks and data have challenged conventional and static understanding of 'research participant' and in turn, created unprecedented tensions between the researcher and the researched.

Research Ethics

In the decades following World War II, the development of principles of research ethics and the ethical treatment of persons were codified in national and international policies and documents, such as the Nuremberg Code (1948), the Declaration of Helsinki (1964), the Belmont Report (1979), and the UN Declaration of Human Rights (1948). These policies and documents, which were formulated in response to experiments performed on human test subjects illegally and without their knowledge or informed consent, sought to define the ethical and legal terms of research involving human subjects.[19] In broad terms, 'human research ethics' encompass the norms and values that frame ethical considerations, such as 'good' behaviours, protocols and practices for research involving human subjects. In the context of academic research in particular, research ethics policy documents identify ethical issues in the design, coordination and management of research and signal practical and ethical considerations for responding to these issues.[20] In Canadian universities, Research Ethics Boards (REBs) are responsible for reviewing research involving human participants and ensuring the safety and well-being of human participants. However, REBs in and of themselves are not perfect mechanisms to gauge ethical research. The long-standing model of evaluating all research through criteria designed for positivistic, biomedical modes of inquiry is deficient.[21] 'When research design and conduct is guided directly by regulatory bodies'

---

17 Jacob Metcalf and Kate Crawford, 'Where are Human Subjects in Big Data Research? The Emerging Ethics Divide', *Big Data & Society* (June 2016), http://journals.sagepub.com/doi/full/10.1177/2053951716650211.
18 Jacob Metcalf and Kate Crawford, 'Where are Human Subjects in Big Data Research? The Emerging Ethics Divide', *p. 3*.
19 Mary Simmerling, Brian Schwegler, Joan E, Sieber and James Lindgren. 'Introducing a New Paradigm for Ethical Research in the Social, Behavioral, and Biomedical Sciences: Part I', *Northwestern University Law Review* 101.2 (2007): 837-858; Laura Stark, *Behind Closed Doors: IRBs and the Making of Ethical Research*, Chicago: University of Chicago Press, 2011; Paul Weindling, 'The Origins of Informed Consent: The International Scientific Commission on Medical War Crimes and the Nuremberg Code', *Bulletin of the History of Medicine* 75.1 (2001): 37-71.
20 Government of Canada, *Tri-Council Policy Statement: Ethical Conduct for Research Involving Humans*, 2014, http://www.pre.ethics.gc.ca/pdf/eng/tcps2-2014/TCPS_2_FINAL_Web.pdf, p.6.
21 Kirsten Bell, 'Resisting Commensurability: Against Informed Consent as an Anthropological Virtue',

reflects Annette Markham, 'issues of ethics can be obscured; ethics is more like directives than dilemmas or quandaries'.[22] In turn, REBs function at times more like gatekeepers to the advancement of knowledge, rather than as institutional bodies assisting researchers to navigate ethical dilemmas.[23]

In regard to social media research, the norms and values of 'human research ethics' upheld by REBs are strained by the complexity of interactions between individuals, networks and technical systems. For instance, any conventional understanding of 'informed consent' is circumvented by third-party disclaimers in platform policies and renders refusal of participation defunct. In turn, ethical standards are left to interpretation. For some, this may counteract concerns about 'ethics creep' and the continued bureaucratization of research.[24] But at the same time, short of clear guidelines, certain forms of social media research are required to undergo REB review while others are not, which is not to say that all social media research should be exempt from REB review, but rather that such inconsistencies could very well denote exempted research as ethical simply by virtue of exemption. Additionally, a lack of guidance could encourage researchers to abide by a social media platform's terms of service as 'rules' for research, yet these terms do not clarify the conditions for ethical research, but instead govern how a researcher is permitted to access and use the data.

In Canada, the principles to guide the design, conduct and review process of research involving humans are outlined in the *Tri-Council Policy Statement: Ethical Conduct for Research Involving Humans (TCPS 2)*,[25] a joint policy of Canada's three federal research agencies or Tri-Council, which is comprised of the Canadian Institutes of Health Research (CIHR), the Natural Sciences and Engineering Research Council of Canada (NSERC), and the Social Sciences and Humanities Research Council of Canada (SSHRC). Canadian researchers and

---

American Anthropologist 116.3 (2014): 511-522; Robert Dingwall, 'The Ethical Case Against Ethical Regulation in Humanities and Social Science Research', *Twenty-First Century Society 3.1 (2008)*: 1-12; Malcom M. Feeley, 'Legality, social research, and the challenge of institutional review boards', *Law & Society Review 41 (2007)*: 757-776.

22   Annette Markham, 'Ethic as Method, Method as Ethic', *Journal of Information Ethics* 15.2 (2006): 37-54, 39.
23   Kirsten Bell, 'Resisting Commensurability: Against Informed Consent as an Anthropological Virtue'; Kakali Bhattacharya, 'Consenting to the Consent Form: What are the Fixed and Fluid Understandings Between the Researcher and the Researched?', *Qualitative Inquiry* 13.8 (2007): 1095-1115; Robert Dingwall, 'The Ethical Case Against Ethical Regulation in Humanities and Social Science Research'; Malcom M. Feeley, 'Legality, social research, and the challenge of institutional review boards'; Kevin D. Haggerty, 'Ethics Creep: Governing Social Science Research in the Name of Ethics', *Qualitative Sociology* 27.4 (2004): 391-414.
24   Kirsten Bell, 'Resisting Commensurability: Against Informed Consent as an Anthropological Virtue'; Kakali Bhattacharya, 'Consenting to the Consent Form: What are the Fixed and Fluid Understandings Between the Researcher and the Researched?', Robert Dingwall, 'The Ethical Case Against Ethical Regulation in Humanities and Social Science Research'; Malcom M. Feeley, 'Legality, social research, and the challenge of institutional review boards'; Kevin D. Haggerty, 'Ethics Creep: Governing Social Science Research in the Name of Ethics'; Sheeva Sabati, 'Upholding "Colonial Knowing" Through the IRB: Reframing Institutional Research Ethics', *Qualitative Inquiry* (August 2018), DOI: https://doi.org/10.1177/1077800418787214.
25   Government of Canada. *Tri-Council Policy Statement: Ethical Conduct for Research Involving Humans*.

their institutions are required to implement the principles and articles of the TCPS 2 as a condition of federal funding.[26] That said the Policy, which has been informed, in part, by leading international ethics norms and disciplinary and professional codes of conduct, is not merely a contract for funding. Rather, it serves as a benchmark for the ethical conduct of research involving humans. Ultimately, the TCPS 2 assists Canadian researchers and research institutions navigate the contours of ethical research, and it sets forth in unadorned terms a framework for research that emanates from three core principles: Respect for Persons, Concern for Welfare, and Justice.

'Respect for Persons' pertains to a person's ability to exercise autonomy in a research context and encompasses, 'the dual moral obligations' to respect autonomy and safeguard individuals with developing, impaired or diminished autonomy.[27] A crucial apparatus for respecting participants' autonomy is to seek their free, informed and ongoing consent. In this regard, ethical conduct of research reflects a commitment to participation in research as a matter of informed choice that is based on a thorough understanding of the research project, including its potential benefits and risks to participants and others. The second principle, 'Concern for Welfare' relates to a 'person's experience of life in all its aspects', and considers the impact on physical, mental and spiritual health, and physical, economic and social circumstances.[28] Thus, concern for welfare means that researchers and research ethics boards not only protect the welfare of participants by providing them with sufficient information to adequately assess the risks and potential benefits associated with their participation in the research, but they also deliberate on the welfare of participants through the design, review and administration of research and in a manner that safeguards participants from any unnecessary or avoidable risks.[29] Finally, the third principle, 'Justice' refers to a researcher's commitment to treat participants fairly and equitably. Individuals or groups in vulnerable circumstances may need to be provided with focused attention in order to ensure just treatment. As the Policy insinuates, sustaining the principle of justice necessitates a consideration of vulnerability throughout the lifecycle of research.

By all measures, the TCPS 2 dispenses a model and guide for the ethical conduct of research involving humans.[30] Thus, it serves as a template for researchers navigating the contours of established research norms. However, emerging computational tools, methods and sources of evidence such as social media data, strain our understanding of traditional research and ethics norms. A commitment to 'Respect for Persons' as it pertains to upholding participants' autonomy by seeking their free, informed, and ongoing consent is weakened in those instances where consent is derived from vague privacy policies as outlined by social media service providers.[31] For example, prior to public knowledge of Facebook's Cambridge Analytica

---

26 Ibid, p 3.
27 Government of Canada. *Tri-Council Policy Statement: Ethical Conduct for Research Involving Humans*, p 6.
28 Ibid, p. 7
29 Ibid, p.22.
30 Ibid, p.4.
31 Catherine Flick, 'Informed Consent and the Facebook Emotional Manipulation Study', *Research Ethics* 12.1 (2016): 14-28; Jacob Metcalf and Kate Crawford. 'Where are Human Subjects in Big Data

scandal, the company had already spearheaded studies that frayed the contours of ethical research. Most notably, Facebook's dubious research practices became public in 2014 when it was revealed how researchers at Facebook and Cornell University manipulated the news feed of 689,003 subjects by deliberately changing the number of positive and negative posts in their News Feed over a week in January 2012.[32] The study was intended to examine how the changes affected the emotional tone of users' ensuing Facebook posts, in order to assess how emotion spreads through large populations.[33] Some commentators were quick to note how 'permission' was derived from Facebook's Data Use Policy, which outlined how the company used information they received for 'internal operations, including troubleshooting, data analysis, testing, research and service improvement'.[34] However, this version of the data policy, which explicitly references 'testing' and 'research' was updated in May 2012, four months after the study. Moreover, as Flick argues, even if Facebook's terms of service had stipulated at the time of the study that participant data could be used for research, this would not have constituted valid informed consent because the study violated the normative expectations of users, and the terms of service do not allow for a participant to actively waive their expectations in any straightforward manner.[35]

As gleaned from the 'emotional contagion' study, the capacity to uphold a 'Concern for Welfare' is diminished when a research participant is lured into a covert study; they are unable to assess the risks and potential benefits of their involvement and to willingly choose to participate or not. But even in overt research contexts it is increasingly difficult to notify research participants about foreseeable harms, especially when risk is measured by far less discernible outcomes, such as the erosion to information privacy.[36] As made evident from Facebook's Cambridge Analytica scandal, the possible harms extend far beyond immediate risks. The 270,00 users who installed Kogan's app *thisisyourdigitallife* were unaware that data collected would be used for 'research' purposes, or that the app would harvest the data from their friends, or that data mined through Kogan's company would be sold to Cambridge Analytica, who in turn would wield the data for controversial electoral purposes. One might define 'immediate risk' in this scenario as the harvesting of data from each of the friends of the 270,000 users who installed the app. However, if we understand 'risk', as Sheeva Sabati

---

Research? The Emerging Ethics Divide'.
32 Adam Kramer, Jamie Guillory and Jeffrey Hancock, 'Experimental Evidence of Massive-Scale Emotional Contagion Through Social Networks'.
33 Vindu Goel, "As Data Overflows Online, Researchers Grapple with Ethics", *New York Times*, 12 August 2014, http://www.nytimes.com/2014/08/13/technology/the-boon-of-online-data-puts-social-science-in-a-quandary.html?_r=0.
34 Robert Booth, 'Facebook Reveals News Feed Experiment to Control Emotions', *The Guardian*, 30 June 2014, https://www.theguardian.com/technology/2014/jun/29/facebook-users-emotions-news-feeds; Erin Egan, 'Enhancing Transparency in Our Data Use Policy', *Facebook Newsroom*, 11 May 2012, https://newsroom.fb.com/news/2012/05/enhancing-transparency-in-our-data-use-policy/; Robinson Meyer, 'Everything we Know About Facebook's Secret Mood Manipulation Experiment', *The Atlantic*, 28 June 2014, https://www.theatlantic.com/technology/archive/2014/06/everything-we-know-about-facebooks-secret-mood-manipulation-experiment/373648/.
35 Catherine Flick, 'Informed Consent and the Facebook Emotional Manipulation Study'.
36 Jacob Metcalf and Kate Crawford, 'Where are Human Subjects in Big Data Research? The Emerging Ethics Divide'.

explains it, as extending 'into the knowledge that is produced, disseminated, and enacted from the data, rather than merely what is collected',[37] then we have yet to fully grasp the risks or adequately assess the harms in their entirety.

As academics continue to collect, scrape, integrate and analyse social media data, technical knowledge to acquire, analyse, secure and disseminate data is needed, but so too is a refined understanding of evolving ethical norms and values embedded within data protocols and practices. In fact, the requirement of technical understanding coupled with the contemporary rate of technological evolution itself presents complex ethical conundrums when it comes to the collection, maintenance, and dissemination of social media research data. Institutions and funding agencies champion research using social media data, but few, if any have ethical guidelines for social media research. In part, current policies are too broad for social media research and are therefore left open to interpretation. At the same time, however, codifying ethical considerations means disavowing a situational ethics principle, which recognizes how each social media research context is unique with a distinct set of traits and ethical challenges. A standardized research ethics template cannot account for these unique characteristics or ethical considerations that arise on a contextual basis.[38]

This dearth of guidance reflects broader trends in digital data policies and practices. As Sandra Soo-Jin Lee explains, the 'vacuum in policy has placed unrealistic expectations on existing review structures to address the changing social and commercial arrangements that characterize these online platforms'.[39] In turn, researchers are left struggling to understand their ethical obligations when it comes to the collection and management of 'public' data associated with social media. For example, big data collection and analysis of social media may reveal more information about people than what they choose to expose 'publicly'. The interoperability of datasets demands ethical considerations beyond the matter of disclosing risk from a single dataset or individual control of personal data.[40] Datasets that would otherwise be innocuous and adequately anonymized on their own can be used to reveal highly sensitive information when analysed in conjunction with other datasets. Thus, concerns over the privacy of personal data in large datasets depend not only on the safeguards applied to a primary dataset, but also those used in other auxiliary datasets. Likewise, permitting data to be identifiable beyond the context it was intended for and without explicit consent, such as integrating a screen grab or using a quote in scholarly dissemination from a social media user who is not a public figure, can expose the identity and profile of the user. Researchers are responsible for protecting the privacy and anonymity of unknowing participants, such as paraphrasing or narrativizing data reproduced for research output, and they ought to seek informed consent from each individual if data is used in ways that can identify them. This of

---

37 Sheeva Sabati, 'Upholding 'Colonial Knowing' Through the IRB: Reframing Institutional Research Ethics', *Qualitative Inquiry* (August 2018), DOI: https://doi.org/10.1177/1077800418787214, p.6.
38 Matthew L. Williams, Pete Burnap and Luke Sloan, 'Towards an Ethical Framework for Publishing Twitter Data in Social Research: Taking into Account Users' View, Online Context and Algorithmic Estimation', *Sociology* 51.6 (2017): 1149-1168.
39 Sandra Soo-Jin Lee, 'Studying "Friends": The Ethics of Using Social Media as Research Platforms', *The American Journal of Bioethics* 17.3 (2017): 1-2.
40 Jacob Metcalf, Emily Keller, and danah boyd, *Perspectives on Big Data, Ethics, and Society*.

course is further complicated by a platform that may insist on units of data being published only in their original form and attributed to its original poster.[41] In these instances, researchers are tasked with safeguarding participants which may very well defy a platform's definition of publicness.

Research Context

My research has shown that few institutions in Canada have ethics guidelines that apply directly to social media research. Institutional research ethics documents that refer to digital data collection do so in terms of 'internet research' and redirect to the requirements of the TCPS 2. Increasingly more common in Canada are research data management (RDM) plans that outline protocols for data management and stewardship. In June 2016, the three federal research funding agencies - the Canadian Institutes of Health Research (CIHR), the Natural Sciences and Engineering Research Council of Canada (NSERC), and the Social Sciences and Humanities Research Council of Canada (SSHRC) - released a *Statement of Principles on Digital Data Management*,[42] in which it called on researchers, research communities, and institutions to develop data management plans and standards that 'are consistent with ethical, legal and commercial obligations, as well as tri-agency requirements'.[43] It is envisioned by the tri-agencies that these Principles will guide 'the responsible collection, formatting, preservation and sharing of their data throughout the entire lifecycle of a research project and beyond'.[44] The tri-agencies have since developed a draft *Research Data Management Policy*,[45] and invited institutions, associations, organizations and individuals to offer feedback on it. This initiative is a significant development for RDM practices in Canada and internationally. However, data management and stewardship are not interchangeable with research ethics, but rather these practices ought to be integrated with ethical considerations of working with social media data and from the outset of research, that is, prior to data collection.

Again, the TCPS 2 puts forth clear recommendations and requirements that match established research norms for the ethical conduct of research involving humans. Social media research data, as I have tried to argue, challenge these conventions and norms, and researchers are obliged to interpret codes of ethical conduct that were written in the mid-20th century to guide the collection, analysis and representation of data in the 21st century.[46] While institutions continue to refer to the TCPS 2, the contours of what constitutes ethical considerations for research involving social media data remains murky. For example, the Policy stipulates how, 'information contained in publicly accessible material may, however, be subject to copyright

---

41   Leanne Townsend and Claire Wallace, '*Social Media Research: A Guide to Ethics*'.
42   Government of Canada, 'Tri-Agency Statement of Principles on Digital Data Management', 21 December 2016, http://www.science.gc.ca/eic/site/063.nsf/eng/h_83F7624E.html.
43   Ibid.
44   Ibid.
45   Government of Canada, 'DRAFT: Tri-agency Research Data Management Policy for Consultation', 25 May 2018, http://www.science.gc.ca/eic/site/063.nsf/eng/h_97610.html.
46   Matthew L. Williams, Pete Burnap and Luke Sloan, 'Towards an Ethical Framework for Publishing Twitter Data in Social Research: Taking into Account Users' View, Online Context and Algorithmic Estimation', p. 1150.

and/or intellectual property rights protections or dissemination restrictions imposed by the legal entity controlling the information'.[47] Social media platforms are the legal entities that control user generated content and set out and enforce the terms and conditions to data, including how scholars can use and access data for research. But scholarly access to data does not render data practices more transparent. On 11 April 2018, the second day of Mark Zuckerberg's testimony before Congress, the *New York Times* published a piece in which journalist Brian Chen described in detail the process of downloading his Facebook data.[48] Chen learned that approximately 500 advertisers had his contact information, which included his email address, phone number and full name, and he also discovered that Facebook had stored his entire iPhone's address book. As Chen clarified, when he had installed the platform's messaging app, rather than retain relevant information for only those contacts also on Facebook and Messenger, it kept a copy of the names and numbers of all 764 contacts, including his apartment door buzzer, a mechanic and a pizzeria. 'My Facebook data' reflects Chen, 'also revealed how little the social network forgets'.[49] We know very little as to what kind of participant data is collected and stored, how it is stored, for how long, the entities that gain access to the data, and the cost of access. Social media research implicates us into these deceptive practices.

The following section puts forward preliminary thoughts on two provocations for social media research data: negotiated relationships and transparency. These nascent considerations are guided by an expansive body of scholarship on digital ethics[50] that considers the ethical issues in social media research[51] and outlines practical considerations for determining the obligations researchers have towards their participants.[52] These provocations join existing

---

47 Government of Canada, *Tri-Council Policy Statement: Ethical Conduct for Research Involving Humans*, p. 16.
48 Brian X. Chen, 'I Downloaded the Information that Facebook has on Me. Yikes', *The New York Times*, 11 April 2018, https://www.nytimes.com/2018/04/11/technology/personaltech/i-downloaded-the-information-that-facebook-has-on-me-yikes.html.
49 Ibid.
50 Huw Davies et al, 'Ethics Guidelines and Collated Resources for Digital Research'; Charles Ess, *Digital Media Ethics*, Cambridge: Polity Press, 2014; Annette Markham, 'Ethic as Method, Method as Ethic'; Annette Markham and Elizabeth Buchanan, *Ethical Decision-Making and Internet Research 2.0: Recommendations From the AoIR Ethics Working Committee*, 2012, www.aoir.org/reports/ethics2.pdf; Omer Tene and Jules Polonetsky, 'Beyond IRBs: Ethical Guidelines for Data Research', *Washington and Lee Law Review Online*, 72.3 (2016): 457-471, https://scholarlycommons.law.wlu.edu/wlulr-online/vol72/iss3/7/; Michael Zimmer, 'Research Ethics in the Big Data Era: Addressing Conceptual Gaps for Researchers and IRBs', School of Information Studies University of Wisconsin, Milwaukee, 2015, https://bigdata.fpf.org/papers/research-ethics-in-the-big-data-era-addressing-conceptual-gaps-for-researchers-and-irbs/; Andrej Zwitter, 'Big Data Ethics', *Big Data & Society* (July 2014), https://journals.sagepub.com/doi/abs/10.1177/2053951714559253.
51 Axel Bruns, 'Faster than the Speed of Print: Reconciling 'Big Data' Social Media Analysis and Academic Scholarship', *First Monday 18*.10 (2014); Katie Shilton, 'Emerging Ethics Norms in Social Media Research'; Joanna Taylor and Claudia Pagliari, 'Mining Social Media Data: How are Research Sponsors and Researchers Addressing the Ethical Challenges?'; Matthew L. Williams, Pete Burnap and Luke Sloan, 'Towards an Ethical Framework for Publishing Twitter Data in Social Research: Taking into Account Users' View, Online Context and Algorithmic Estimation'.
52 Mary Elizabeth Luka and Mélanie Millette, '(Re)framing Big Data: Activating Situated Knowledges and a Feminist Ethics of Care in Social Media Research', *Social Media + Society*, April 2018, http://journals.

efforts to motivate research communities to consider their ethical obligations in light of the challenges social media research brings to research ethics norms and conventions.

Negotiated Relationships

Navigating the ethical complexities of social media research occurs not in isolation, but in deliberation between three seemingly disparate relations: a researcher and their participants, a researcher and the data platform, and finally, a researcher and their Research Ethics Board (REB). Navigating these can be viewed also as a means through which a researcher refines their sense of accountability.[53] Like negotiation, accountability is multi-directional. It requires rigorous thinking about the ramifications of the choices one makes in the lifecycle of research, rather than assuming that a platform's terms and conditions or a research ethics board will fulfill the task of ensuring that research is conducted ethically.

Researcher and Participants

As touched on previously, social media research displaces the figure of the human subject with data often standing in for the identity of individuals and groups.[54] This distancing of the researcher from research participant makes it easier to approach social media data as non-human research, especially in circumstances when a researcher is working with social media corpora. One may recognize the corpus as produced intentionally or unintentionally by human participants throughout their social media exchanges, while also disavowing the place of the human subject in a traditional sense. As Michael Zimmer notes, 'the perception of a human subject becomes diluted through increased technological mediation'.[55] Researchers ought to consider how social media participants are conditioned into the role of data producers. Social media have been glorified for encouraging and promoting 'sharing', however, this goes only so far when one considers how sharing online is no longer a form of mere exchange but also a requisite for communication and distribution. 'Sharing', as Claire Birchall explains, 'has to be understood today not as a conscious and conscientious act but as a key component of contemporary data subjectivity'.[56] Birchall reframes sharing protocologically, as 'the constitutive logic of the Internet'.[57] Sharing, in other words, is a standard of the system. Activities and practices online that appear to be driven by a free will to share are in effect

---

sagepub.com/doi/full/10.1177/2056305118768297; Jacob Metcalf, Emily Keller, and danah boyd, *Perspectives on Big Data, Ethics, and Society*, Council for Big Data, Ethics, and Society; Chris Allen Sula, 'Research Ethics in an Age of Big Data'; Leanne Townsend and Claire Wallace, '*Social Media Research: A Guide to Ethics*'; University of Sheffield, The Ethics of Internet-based and Social Media Research.

53 danah boyd and Kate Crawford, 'Critical Questions for Big Data: Provocations for a Cultural, Technological and Scholarly Phenomenon'.
54 Tyler Butler Reigeluth, 'Why Data is Not Enough: Digital Traces as Control of Self and Self-Control'; Jacob Metcalf and Kate Crawford, 'Where are Human Subjects in Big Data Research? The Emerging Ethics Divide'.
55 Michael Zimmer, 'Research Ethics in the Big Data Era: Addressing Conceptual Gaps for Researchers and IRBs', p. 6.
56 Clare Birchall, 'Shareveillance: Subjectivity between Open and Closed Data', *Big Data & Society* 3.2 (2016), https://journals.sagepub.com/doi/abs/10.1177/2053951716663965, p.5.
57 Ibid, p. 3.

preconditions to participation and standardized practice. If social media data are generated in large part from individuals who are compelled to 'share' data as a prerequisite for participation, then how might this infringe on a researcher's capacity to uphold 'Respect for Persons' and a 'Concern for Welfare'? Recognition of one's dataset as having been generated by human participants who are likely unaware of how their thoughts, emotions, and observations have been quantified, and in turn, applied by researchers, is imperative in advancing evolving ethical benchmarks.

Researcher and Data Platform

The term 'platform' is synonymous with social media and is often used to refer to those web-based interfaces through which individuals are able interact with other people and share content. For instance, Twitter, Facebook, YouTube and Instagram are some of the more prominent social media platforms in North America. Thus, a social media platform has social characteristics, as I described, but it also has specific technical attributes. Technologically, a platform provides a mark-up language for creating applications, an Application Programming Interface (API) for third-party application integration ,[58] and a back-end administrative console for managing site architecture and functionality. As scholars have argued, a 'platform' is not simply a social or technological tool. Rather, digital intermediaries employ the term as a discursive strategy to frame their services in a particular manner and present themselves as transparent entities in the facilitation of public dialogue and communication, rather than as entities who serve and profit from content providers, advertisers and others.[59]

When researchers seek out social media data from a particular platform, they are in effect entering into a relationship with that platform. First and foremost, a researcher is governed by the terms and conditions set forth by the platform. This is beneficial in instances when agreements articulate how one is permitted to access and use data for research via the platform's standards, but these do not necessarily align with 'ethical research'. Platforms are not simply neutral data portals through which researchers are permitted access to troves of data. Platforms are data gatekeepers that create and specify constraints as to who can access data, in which forms, and under which conditions.[60] As Taina Buchner argues, researchers employing data collection tools like APIs need to know how these tools collect and provide access to the data and functionality contained by platforms, but they also have a responsibility to understand how a seemingly neutral tool like an API is not a conduit for data, but is instead

---

58   An API is an interface that facilitates controlled access to the functionality and data contained by a software service or program, or in this case the Twitter platform. See Taina Bucher, 'Objects of Intense Feeling: The Case of the Twitter API', *Computational Culture* 3 (November, 2013), http://computationalculture.net/objects-of-intense-feeling-the-case-of-the-twitter-api/.
59   Tarleton Gillespie, 'The Politics of "Platforms"', *New Media & Society 12*.3 (2010): 347-364; Jean-Christophe Plantin, Carl Lagoze and Paul N. Edwards, 'Re-Integrating Scholarly Infrastructure: The Ambiguous Role of Data Sharing Platforms', *Big Data & Society* (January 2018), https://doi.org/10.1177/2053951718756683.
60   Jean-Christophe Plantin, Carl Lagoze and Paul N. Edwards. 'Re-Integrating Scholarly Infrastructure: The Ambiguous Role of Data Sharing Platforms'.

is a 'technique for governing the relations they contain'.[61] Following Tarleton Gillespie,[62] platforms and their data tools have 'politics', meaning they can be understood as having 'powerful consequences for the social activities that happen with them, and in the worlds imagined by them'.[63] Thus, rather than asking what these data platforms are, researchers are better served to ask what these platforms do.

A researcher's contractual obligation to a platform ought to be reframed as a partnership with a data gatekeeper, rather than as an agreement with terms and conditions. A researcher wanting to access data will have to do so according to the platform's policies, which may misalign with ethical research. Researchers are therefore left to negotiate what Mark Andrejevic has called the 'big data divide'.[64] There exist unequal ways of accessing and using data that intensify power imbalances. Thus, a 'big data divide' describes the asymmetrical relationship between those who collect, mine, store and analyse data, and those whom data collection targets. Perhaps framing the relationship in this way will render transparent the ways in which social media research data are not neutral, objective, and pre-analytic in nature. Data are a by-product of the politics of platforms. What if research communities conceived of these platforms not simply as sources of research evidence, but as collaborators in the construction of emerging research practices and knowledge production? Would this compel researchers to dig deeper into the politics of platforms as a condition of working with social media data? Perhaps a first step in challenging prescriptive data regimes is for researchers to make concerted efforts to reflect on and make clear in their methodologies the key role platforms play in the co-construction of knowledge.

Researcher and Research Ethics Boards

A researcher's relationship with their Research Ethics Board (REB) ought to be positioned as a continuous dialogue, rather than as an obstacle to research. This is a tall order given how fraught this relationship can be. Indeed, the REB model itself is discordant at times with contemporary research practices and overburdened by risk management and bureaucratic box ticking.[65] In many instances, REBs are also struggling to understand the ethical complexities of social media research, and uncertainty may lead to trepidation. In this respect, social media research may be deemed too risky because it is not well understood. Thus, with few

---

61 Taina Bucher, 'Objects of Intense Feeling: The Case of the Twitter API'.
62 Tarleton Gillespie, 'The Politics of "Platforms"'; Tarleton Gillespie, 'The Stories That Tools Tell', in John Caldwell and Anna Everett (eds), *New Media: Theses on Convergence Media and Digital Reproduction*, New York: Routledge, 2003, pp. 107-123.
63 Tarleton Gillespie, 'The Stories Digital Tools Tell', p. 2.
64 Mark Andrejevic, 'Big Data, Big Questions: The Big Data Divide', *International Journal of Communication* 8 (2014): 1673-1689.
65 Kirsten Bell, 'Resisting Commensurability: Against Informed Consent as an Anthropological Virtue'; Kakali Bhattacharya, 'Consenting to the Consent Form: What are the Fixed and Fluid Understandings Between the Researcher and the Researched?'; Robert Dingwall, 'The Ethical Case Against Ethical Regulation in Humanities and Social Science Research'; Malcom M. Feeley, 'Legality, social research, and the challenge of institutional review boards'; Kevin D. Haggerty, 'Ethics Creep: Governing Social Science Research in the Name of Ethics'; Sheeva Sabati, 'Upholding 'Colonial Knowing' Through the IRB: Reframing Institutional Research Ethics'.

guidelines or protocols for social media research specifically, researchers find themselves seeking expertise and guidance on ethical considerations. In part, I view this productively because it requires that researchers confront the challenges and conundrums of evolving research norms through practical application and beyond the limited scope of regulatory guidelines.[66] Researchers have leeway in interpreting and applying existing ethics protocols to emerging research practices, permitting them to establish new benchmarks for research. At the same time, however, a lack of standardized practices[67] with regards to social media research leads to inconsistent views about how to handle ethical issues,[68] while interpretations of existing protocols for new research contexts may also betray broader ethical conventions, as evidenced by the emotional contagion study and Facebook's Cambridge Analytica scandal.

What is needed are guidelines to allow for social media research to remain flexible but that would foreground ethical considerations to steer research design and methodological considerations, even in those instances when data is deemed 'public'. Ethical considerations for and about social media research must trouble the public/private dichotomy instituted and governed by the terms and conditions established by platforms. In other words, simply because information is stipulated as 'public' does not absolve researchers of ethical concerns because of the presumed 'publicness' of data.[69] For instance, according to the TCPS 2, REB review is 'not required for research that relies exclusively on secondary use of anonymous information', 'so long as the process of data linkage or recording or dissemination of results does not generate identifiable information'.[70] According to this provision, research using social media corpora, which falls within the parameters of 'secondary use of anonymous information', is exempt from REB review. However, if we reconsider how social media data is generated by human participants who are likely unaware of the parameters of secondary data, and how platforms are also data gatekeepers that co-produce knowledge, should we not then reexamine REB exemption? Or, should this fall onto researchers to advocate for ethical considerations, like REB review, that go beyond Tri-Council recommendations and requirements? As explored in this chapter, informed consent is deficient in social media research contexts. As agencies push for 'open data' as a requirement of funding and compel researchers to share research datasets, even if consent is obtained for a particular research study, how is it transferred when a data set is shared? Can it be transferred? In these emerging contexts, how can a researcher possibly guarantee confidentiality? The simple answer is that it cannot be guaranteed. Perhaps in the process of acquiring informed consent for social media research, a 'no guarantee' clause needs to be accentuated. Penn State for instance recommends the following statement be used: 'Your confidentiality will be maintained to the degree permitted

---

66 Annette Markham, 'Afterword: Ethics as Impact-Moving from Error-Avoidance and Concept-Driven Models to a Future-Oriented Approach', *Social Media + Society* (July-September 2018): 1-11.
67 Barry Rooke, 'Four Pillars of Internet Research Ethics with Web 2.0', *Journal of Academic Ethics*, 111.4 (2013): 265-268.
68 Barry Rooke, 'Four Pillars of Internet Research Ethics with Web 2.0'; Katie Shilton, 'Emerging Ethics Norms in Social Media Research'.
69 Jacob Metcalf and Kate Crawford, 'Where are Human Subjects in Big Data Research? The Emerging Ethics Divide'.
70 Government of Canada, *Tri-Council Policy Statement: Ethical Conduct for Research Involving Humans*, p. 14.

by the technology used. Specifically, no guarantees can be made regarding the interception of data sent via the Internet by any third parties'.[71] I would go so far as to endorse a version of a 'no guarantee' clause on all research dissemination.

Transparency

> 'Are you willing to change your business model in the interest of protecting individual privacy?' - *Democratic Representative Anna Eshoo*[72]

> 'Congresswoman, I'm not sure what that means.' - *Mark Zuckerberg*[73]

Privacy in relation to social media data has received significant attention as of late.[74] The Facebook and Cambridge Analytica revelations have attracted scrutiny over the lack of autonomy over one's data and (re)focused debates about privacy with demands for formal governance and regulation. But an emphasis on privacy alone is limiting in our ability to rethink not only our relationship to the data we generate, but also the processes and tools through which we access social media research data. For this reason, I am more invested in the concept of transparency. Transparency discloses the parameters of privacy but also the ways in which social media data operate as a kind of currency, that is, as an accepted source of evidence in academic research, and as a medium of exchange.

Privacy, as it is guaranteed by social media platforms, at least in theory, tends to register as an assurance that data is secure from 'malicious actors', and that it is collected, shared and used in ways we have consented to. And yet, platforms alter their terms of service and renegotiate the conditions of their user agreements to work in their favour,[75] and they grant a multitude of unfamiliar entities access to our data including researchers.[76] In academic research contexts,

---

71 Penn State, 'IRB Guideline X - Guidelines for Computer and Internet-Based Research Involving Human Participants', Office of the Vice President for Research, 2018, https://www.research.psu.edu/irb/policies/guideline10.
72 Bloomberg Government, 'Transcript of Zuckerberg's Appearance Before House Committee', *The Washington Post*, 11 April 2018, https://www.washingtonpost.com/news/the-switch/wp/2018/04/11/transcript-of-zuckerbergs-appearance-before-house-committee/?noredirect=on&utm_term=.71d99a22271d.
73 Ibid.
74 Keith Collins and Larry Buchanan. 'How Facebook Lets Brands and Politicians Target You'; Brian X. Chen, 'I Downloaded the Information that Facebook has on Me. Yikes'; Sheera Frenkel, Matthew Rosenberg and Nicholas Confessore, 'Facebook Data Collected by Quiz App Included Private Messages'; Natasha Singer, 'What You Don't Know About How Facebook Uses Your Data'.
75 Kashmir Hill, 'Facebook Added 'Research' to User Agreement 4 Months After Emotion Manipulation Study', *Forbes*, 30 June 2014, www.forbes.com/sites/kashmirhill/2014/06/30/facebook-only-got-permission-to-do-research-on-users-after-emotion-manipulation-study; Chris Walters, 'Facebook's New Terms of Service: 'We Can Do Anything We Want with Your Content. Forever', *Consumerist*, 15 February 2009, https://consumerist.com/2009/02/15/facebooks-new-terms-of-service-we-can-do-anything-we-want-with-your-content-forever.
76 Brian X. Chen, 'I Downloaded the Information that Facebook has on Me. Yikes'; Keith Collins and Larry Buchanan, 'How Facebook Lets Brands and Politicians Target You'; Alex Hearn, 'How firms you have never interacted with can target your Facebook', *The Guardian*. 21 April 2018, https://www.theguardian.

researchers have an ethical duty of confidentially to participants, which includes upholding a research participant's right to privacy and safeguarding their information. This version of privacy is at odds with the conditions supported by data platforms. Thus, if researchers integrate data from platforms that overstep moral imperatives like privacy, then are researchers also straining the ethical contours of privacy norms and conventions in academic research?

What is 'privacy' in the context of social media research? If we follow Helen Nissenbaum's lead, concerns over privacy are not simply concerns about control over personal information. A 'right to privacy', reflects Nissenbaum, 'is neither a right to secrecy nor a right to control, but a right to the appropriate flow of personal information'.[77] Nissenbaum advocates for a 'contextual integrity approach' to privacy, wherein 'we locate contexts, explicate entrenched informational norms, identify disruptive flows, and evaluate these flows against norms based on general ethical and political principles as well as context specific purposes and values'.[78] In this respect, privacy is tied to the norms governing distinct social contexts, but at the same time, privacy online is not something distinct from privacy offline. Rather, social norms, including informational norms, are inextricably linked with existing structures of social life.[79] If information is flowing beyond the context it was intended for and without regard for a context's particular norms and values, then privacy is not upheld or safeguarded.[80]

Revisiting momentarily the question Democratic Representative Anna Eshoo asked Mark Zuckerberg during his Congressional hearing in April 2018, and reframing it for an academic context, we might find ourselves inquiring, 'are you willing to change your research model in the interest of protecting individual privacy?'. If Eshoo's query to Zuckerberg insinuates that Facebook's business model is at odds with safeguarding privacy, then that same question reformulated for an academic context implies those same business models infringe on the established norms and conventions of privacy in academic research. Zuckerberg's reply, 'I'm not sure what that means', deflects accountability. Researchers are not at liberty to divert privacy concerns. One possible means of respecting privacy in social media research is to approach it contextually, meaning that a researcher's reading of 'expectations of privacy' is a negotiation between a particular platform's terms of privacy, its audience, and aims. And by a nuanced understanding of how privacy expectations vary from platform to platform, group to group, and individual to individual. Despite a researcher's best efforts to uphold expectations of privacy, its limits are tested by virtue of a researcher's negotiated relationship with data platforms. I am putting forward transparency as a conceptual counterpoint to work through the limitations of privacy guarantees.

---

com/technology/2018/apr/21/how-firms-you-have-never-interacted-with-can-target-your-facebook.
77   Helen Nissenbaum, *Privacy in Context: Technology, Policy and the Integrity of Social Life*, Palo Alto: Stanford University Press, 2009, p.127.
78   Helen Nissenbaum, 'A Contextual Approach to Privacy Online', *Daedalus 140.4* (2011): 32-48, https://www.amacad.org/publications/daedalus/11_fall_nissenbaum.pdf, p.38.
79   Helen Nissenbaum, 'A Contextual Approach to Privacy Online'.
80   Helen Nissenbaum, *Privacy in Context: Technology, Policy and the Integrity of Social Life*; Helen Nissenbaum, 'A Contextual Approach to Privacy Online'; Solon Barocas and Helen Nissenbaum, 'Big Data's End Run Around Procedural Privacy Protections', *Communications of the ACM* 57.11 (2014): 31-33.

Transparency in scholarly research is often conflated with 'openness' in the sense of open source, open access and open data, and with the replication of results. To be exact, I am employing transparency here as a marker of intentionality on the part of the researcher, but also in terms of the platform and its policies and practices, which may not be transparent to the researcher. When a researcher deliberately carries out research in a way for others to comprehend the actions, negotiations, and deliberations performed as part of the research process, they are in effect enacting transparency. How then does one sustain transparency as an ethical consideration? At the very least, a researcher considers a process-oriented approach to research, wherein the process itself is just as important as the final output. By this I mean that one's research process is fore grounded, particularly in scholarly output and dissemination. Researchers make clear their methods of data collection and analysis, and reflect on the negotiations between key actors and diverse relations facilitating research and the co-production of knowledge. Transparency in this respect helps to deconstruct processes of knowledge production: how knowledge is produced, who produced it, and for whom. Rather than sustaining 'communicative objectivity',[81] transparency discloses new modes of observation engendered by data tools and sources through which scholarly communities are observing and analysing the world.

Transparency describes how researchers engage in ongoing processes of reflexive practice and revision by foregrounding research intentions, limitations, negotiations, and methods of data collection and analysis. I stand by the term as a provocation, but I also seek to trouble it. As I argued, transparency in social media research is radically important because it is a characteristic lacking from social media platforms. Platforms, as previously discussed, tend to be obtuse technical systems that purport to facilitate social engagement without full disclosure as to how participation is mediated for other individuals and entities that profit from data production. For instance, users of social media are well aware of how in exchange for a 'free' service like Facebook, the company collects their data and uses it to serve them ads both on Facebook and around the web. It is a seemingly simple exchange. But social media platforms like Facebook have proven to be poor stewards of user data, often demanding and doing more with it but without unambiguously disclosing their practices. When Facebook supposedly discovered in 2015 that Aleksandr Kogan provided data to Cambridge Analytica, it took until March 2018, after the publication of stories from *The Guardian*, *Observer* and *The New York Times*, for Facebook to both disclose it and suspend Kogan and Cambridge Analytica from its platform. Arguably, there is a fundamental lack of transparency.[82] But at the same time, Facebook increasingly touts transparency as a catchphrase to signal to users that it is committed to disclosing its practices and that its activities are open to public scrutiny.[83] Facebook recently released ad transparency tools that enable users to see more information than ever before about how advertisers are using the platform.[84] For the average user, these

---

81 Orit Halpern, *Beautiful Data*.
82 Brian Barrett, 'Facebook Owes You More Than This', *Wired*, 19 March 2018, https://www.wired.com/story/facebook-privacy-transparency-cambridge-analytica/.
83 Chris Sonderby, 'Reinforcing Our Commitment to Transparency', *Facebook Newsroom*, 15 May 2018, https://newsroom.fb.com/news/2018/05/transparency-report-h2-2017/.
84 Rob Leathern, 'A New Level of Transparency for Ads and Pages', *Facebook Newsroom*, 28 June 2018, https://newsroom.fb.com/news/2018/06/transparency-for-ads-and-pages/.

tools may reveal the amount of advertising activity carried out on these platforms, but they do not make transparent exactly how ads operate on the platform. Moreover, just because users are given access to more information does not mean it is easy to parse. In turn, Facebook's transparency serves to uphold its core policies and practices without revealing any more about how our data is trafficked.

To reiterate, transparency as an ethical consideration in social media research is radically important, but because it has been co-opted by technology companies, perhaps we need an additional term to address the messiness and complexities of working with social media data. To this end, I propose 'c/overt research'. In their reflection on their experiences in a c/overt research project, Virtová, Stöckelová, and Krásná conceived of the term as a way to interrogate how IRB standards and the 'ethical fiction' of informed consent serve to insulate researchers from having to openly acknowledge uncertainties in field work.[85] Thus, 'c/overt research' troubles the distinctions between overt and covert forms of research and insinuates that all research is covert in some ways, becoming overt only during the research process itself. **

C/overt research as I adopt it fractures the myth that researchers are absolved of ethical concerns by virtue of seeking REB approval and abiding by ethical guidelines or codes of ethic. In following Alexis Shotwell's work on purity politics, we are better served to view the aspiration for ethical purity as simultaneously, inadequate, impossible and politically dangerous.[86] As I have argued, researchers working with social media data enter into a relationship with a platform. Rather than view the REB process as a means through which one is able to neutralize this relationship, we might consider highlighting the ways in which relying on the terms set forth by a social media platform legitimizes their nebulous data practices, and how this renders us complicit in these practices. As Shotwell explains, '[s]ince it is not possible to avoid complicity, we do better to start from an assumption that everyone is implicated in situations we (at least in some way) repudiate'.[87] Complicity, and indeed complexity, is not something we should avoid in research contexts. Understanding not only how researchers are complicit, but REBs and institutions as well, is a 'starting point for action'.[88] In this respect, the ways in which researchers conduct themselves in the c/overt practice of their research is a mode of achieving, rather than applying, 'ethical research'.

Good Data

'Negotiated relationships' and 'transparency' are but two provocations for social media research. These terms outline some of the ethical complexities of working with social media data and the ethical concerns researchers may consider when entangled within contemporary data practices. Yet neither identify a pathway to good data practices. This section formulates questions for researchers to navigate ethical considerations during research design, that is,

---

85 Tereza Virtová, Tereza Stöckelová and Helena Krásná. 'On the Track of C/overt Research: Lessons from Taking Ethnographic Ethics to the Extreme', *Qualitative Inquiry* 24.7 (2018): 453-463.
86 Alexis Shotwell, *Against Purity: Living Ethically in Compromised Times*, Minnesota: University of Minnesota Press, 2016, p.107.
87 Alexis Shotwell, *Against Purity: Living Ethically in Compromised Times*, p.5
88 Ibid.

prior to data collection, but also to spur reflexivity throughout the life-cycle of research. These prompts are meant as an exploratory guide towards establishing definitive good data ethics. '[E]thics, when practiced', write Markham, Tiidenberg and Herman, 'becomes a matter of method'.[89] Good data ethics can engender good data methods and vice versa.

Research Questions: What are some of the questions driving the research? What conceptual and/or theoretical frameworks are shaping these questions? How have other disciplines explored similar questions and to what end?

Research Data: What are my data sources? How will I acquire them? Is REB approval required? If not, will I seek out approval? How will data be managed and by whom? Who will be responsible for anonymizing and encrypting data? How and where will data be stored? Who will have access to the data and in what form?

Research Tools: What computational tools and techniques will be employed for research? Why these and not others? What skills and expertise are required? Who will conduct this portion of the research and how will they be acknowledged? What are other ways of doing the research?

Research Relations: What are some of my negotiated relationships? To whom do I feel accountable towards? With whom do I share this accountability? Where am I in the research and what is my situated perspective?

Research Participants: Who and/or what constitute my research participants? Is REB approval required? If not, will I seek it out anyway? How will participants be made aware of their involvement in the research? If this is not practical, then how will participation be made c/overt? What do I feel is my duty to these participants? How will I safeguard contextual integrity? How will I uphold participant autonomy? What are some possible ways in which I may disappoint research participants?

Research Beneficiaries: For whom is this research for? Who and/or what is the driving force? Why do I care about it? How will it benefit me? How will it be of benefit to others? Who will derive advantage from it?

Research Dissemination: How do I intend to share results of research? In what forms and with whom? How will I uphold contextual integrity when sharing results? Will a 'no guarantee' accompany research dissemination?

---

89 Annette Markham, Katrin Tiidenberg and Andrew Herman, 'Ethics as Methods: Doing ethics in the Era of Big Data Research-Introduction', *Social Media + Society* 4.3 (2018): 1-9, 2.

Conclusion

The provocations and prompts offered here are far from exhaustive, but rather are a preliminary effort at identifying some of the tensions inherent in upholding good data research practices. As I have discussed throughout this chapter, there is a lack of ethical guidelines for social media research. In turn, researchers are often dependent on a mixed bag approach when it comes to ethics. That said, even if codes of ethics for social media were institutionalized, the ethical conundrums addressed throughout this chapter are not simply solved by reference to ethics documents and policies. My hope is that researchers and their institutions approach social media research as iterative and deliberative, rather than cement data ethics protocols or a one-size-fits-all model. Flexibility of this kind will enable research communities to transparently respond to emerging data tools, instruments, practices, contexts and epistemologies and develop further strategies for good data ethics that will empower researchers to respond to the prescriptive data regimes set forth by social media platforms that indubitably impact scholarly research practices and the production of knowledge. Finally, instead of fixating on the deficit of guidance, perhaps we are better served to interpret these challenges as opportunities, and rather than focus on codes of conduct imposed from the outside, we focus on the hidden ethical practices from the inside, that is, through ethical practices as they unfold in social media research contexts.[90] Indeed, in this way, ethics are achieved, not applied.

References

Adams, Richard. 'Cambridge University asks Facebook for Evidence About Role of Academic', *The Guardian*, 20 March 2018, https://www.theguardian.com/uk-news/2018/mar/20/cambridge-university-asks-facebook-for-evidence-about-role-of-academic-alex-kogan.

Adams, Tim. 'Facebook's Week of Shame: The Cambridge Analytica Fallout', *The Guardian*, 24 March 2018, https://www.theguardian.com/technology/2018/mar/24/facebook-week-of-shame-data-breach-observer-revelations-zuckerberg-silence.

Andrejevic, Mark, and Kelly Gates. 'Big Data Surveillance: Introduction', *Surveillance & Society* 12.2 (2014): 185-96, DOI: doi:10.24908/ss.v12i2.5242.

Andrejevic, Mark. 'Big Data, Big Questions: The Big Data Divide', *International Journal of Communication* 8 (2014): 1673-1689.

Australian National Data Service. *Data Sharing Considerations for Human Research Ethics Committees*, June 2018. http://www.ands.org.au/guides/data-sharing-considerations-for-hrecs.

Barocas, Solon, and Helen Nissenbaum. 'Big Data's End Run Around Procedural Privacy Protections', *Communications of the ACM* 57.11 (2014): 31-33.

Barrett, Brian. 'Facebook Owes You More Than This', *Wired*, 19 March 2018, https://www.wired.com/story/facebook-privacy-transparency-cambridge-analytica/.

Bell, Kirsten. 'Resisting Commensurability: Against Informed Consent as an Anthropological Virtue', *American Anthropologist* 116.3 (2014): 511-522.

---

90 Annette Markham, 'Ethic as Method, Method as Ethic', p.39; Annette Markham, 'Afterword: Ethics as Impact-Moving from Error-Avoidance and Concept-Driven Models to a Future-Oriented Approach'.

Bhattacharya, Kakali. 'Consenting to the Consent Form: What are the Fixed and Fluid Understandings Between the Researcher and the Researched?', *Qualitative Inquiry 13*.8 (2007): 1095-1115.

Biddle, Sam. 'Stop Using Unroll.me, Right Now. It Sold Your Data to Uber', *The Intercept*, 24 April 2017, https://theintercept.com/2017/04/24/stop-using-unroll-me-right-now-it-sold-your-data-to-uber/.

Birchall, Clare. 'Shareveillance: Subjectivity between Open and Closed Data', *Big Data & Society* 3.2 (2016).

Bloomberg Government. 'Transcript of Zuckerberg's Appearance Before House Committee', *The Washington Post*, 11 April 2018, https://www.washingtonpost.com/news/the- switch/wp/2018/04/11/transcript-of-zuckerbergs-appearance-before-house- committee/?noredirect=on&utm_term=.71d99a22271d.

Boellstorff, Tom. 'Making Big Data, in Theory', *First Monday* 18.10 (2013).

Booth, Robert. 'Facebook Reveals News Feed Experiment to Control Emotions', *The Guardian*. 30 June 2014, https://www.theguardian.com/technology/2014/jun/29/facebook-users-emotions- newsfeeds.

boyd danah and Kate Crawford. 'Critical Questions for Big Data: Provocations for a Cultural, Technological and Scholarly Phenomenon', *Information, Communication & Society* 15.5 (2012): 662-679.

boyd danah. 'Where do we find ethics?' *Points*, 5 April 2016, https:// points.datasociety.net/where-do-we-find-ethics-d0b9e8a7f4e6.

Broad, Ellen. 'Australia, we need to talk about data ethics', *The Ethics Centre*, 25 January 2017, http://www.ethics.org.au/on-ethics/blog/january-2017/australia-data-ethics.

Bruns, Axel. 'Faster than the Speed of Print: Reconciling 'Big Data' Social Media Analysis and Academic Scholarship', *First Monday 18*.10 (2014).

Brunton, Finn, and Helen Nissenbaum. *Obfuscation: A User's Guide for Privacy and Protest*, Cambridge MA: MIT Press, 2016.

Brunton, Finn, and Helen Nissenbaum. 'Vernacular Resistance to Data Collection and Analysis: A Political Theory of Obfuscation', *First Monday* 16.5 (2011).

Bryant, Randall E., Randy H Katz and Edward D. Lazowska. 'Big-Data Computing: Creating Revolutionary Breakthroughs in Commerce, Science, and Society', *Computing Research Consortium,* 22 December 2008, https://cra.org/ccc/wpcontent/uploads/sites/2/2015/05/Big_Data.pdf.

Bucher, Taina. 'Objects of Intense Feeling: The Case of the Twitter API', *Computational Culture* 3 (November, 2013), http://computationalculture.net/objects-of-intense-feeling-the-case-of-the-twitter-api/.

Cadwalladr, Carole and Emma Graham-Harrison. 'Revealed: 50 Million Facebook Profiles Harvested for Cambridge Analytica in Major Data Breach', *The Guardian*, 17 March 2018, https://www.theguardian.com/news/2018/mar/17/cambridge-analytica-facebook-influence-us-election.

Chen, Brian X. 'I Downloaded the Information that Facebook has on Me. Yikes', *The New York Times*, 11 April 2018, https://www.nytimes.com/2018/04/11/technology/personaltech/i-downloaded-the-information-that-facebook-has-on-me-yikes.html.

Clark, Karin, Matt Duckham, Marilys Guillemin, Assunta Hunter, Jodie McVernon, Christine O'Keefe, Cathy Pitkin, Steven Prawer, Richard Sinnott, Deborah Warr and Jenny Waycott. *Guidelines for the Ethical Use of Digital Data in Human Research*, The University of Melbourne, 2015, https://www.carltonconnect.com.au/read-ethical-use of-digital-data-in-human-research/.

Collins, Keith and Larry Buchanan. 'How Facebook Lets Brands and Politicians Target You', *The New York Times*, 11 April 2018, https://www.nytimes.com/interactive/2018/04/11/technology/facebook-sells-ads-life-details.html.

Crawford, Kate, Kate Miltner and Mary L. Gray. 'Critiquing Big Data: Politics, Ethics, Epistemology', *International Journal of Communication* 8 (2014): 1663-1672.

Dalton, Craig, and Jim Thatcher. 'What Does a Critical Data Studies Look Like, and Why Do We Care? Seven Points for a Critical Approach to "Big Data"', *Society & Space Open Site*, (2014), http://societyandspace.org/2014/05/12/what-does-a-critical-data-studies-look-like-and-why-do-we-care-craig-dalton-and-jim-thatcher/.

Dalton Craig, Linnet Taylor and Jim Thatcher. 'Critical Data Studies: A Dialog on Data and Space', *Big Data & Society* 3.1 (2014): 1-9.

Das, Sauvik and Adam Kramer. 'Self-censorship on Facebook', *Proceedings of the Seventh International AAAI Conference on Weblogs and Social Media*, 2013, pp. 120-127, https://research.fb.com/publications/self-censorship-on-facebook/.

Davies, Huw et al. 'Ethics Guidelines and Collated Resources for Digital Research', British Sociological Association, 2017, https://www.britsoc.co.uk/media/24309/bsa_statement_of_ethical_practice_annexe.pdf.

Dingwall, Robert. 'The Ethical Case Against Ethical Regulation in Humanities and Social Science Research', *Twenty-First Century Society 3.1 (2008)*: 1-12.

Egan, Erin. 'Enhancing Transparency in Our Data Use Policy', *Facebook Newsroom*, 11 May 2012, https://newsroom.fb.com/news/2012/05/enhancing-transparency-in-our-data- use-policy/.

Ess, Charles. *Digital Media Ethics*, Cambridge: Polity Press, 2014.

Eubanks, Virginia. *Automating Inequality: How High-Tech Tools Profile, Police, and Punish the Poor*, New York: St. Martin's Press, 2018.

Feeley, Malcom M. 'Legality, social research, and the challenge of institutional review boards', *Law & Society Review 41 (2007)*: 757-776.

Ferguson, Andrew Guthrie. *The Rise of Big Data Policing: Surveillance, Race, and the Future of Law Enforcement*, New York: NYU Press, 2017.

Flick, Catherine. 'Informed Consent and the Facebook Emotional Manipulation Study', *Research Ethics* 12.1 (2016): 14-28.

Frenkel, Sheera, Matthew Rosenberg and Nicholas Confessore. 'Facebook Data Collected by Quiz App Included Private Messages', *The New York Times*, 10 April 2018. https://www.nytimes.com/2018/04/10/technology/facebook-cambridge-analytica- privatemessages.html?action=click&contentCollection=Personal%20Tech&module= RelatedCoverage&region=Marginalia&pgtype=article.

Gillespie, Tarleton. 'The Stories That Tools Tell', in John Caldwell and Anna Everett (eds), *New Media: Theses on Convergence Media and Digital Reproduction*, New York: Routledge, 2003, pp. 107-123.

_____. 'The Politics of 'Platforms', *New Media & Society, 12*.3 (2010): 347-364.

Gitelman, Lisa (ed.), *Raw Data is An Oxymoron*, Cambridge MA: MIT Press, 2013.

Goel, Vindu. 'As Data Overflows Online, Researchers Grapple with Ethics', *New York Times*, 12 August 2014, http://www.nytimes.com/2014/08/13/technology/the-boon- of-online-data-puts-social-science-in-a-quandary.html?_r=0.

Government of Canada. *Tri-Council Policy Statement: Ethical Conduct for Research Involving Humans*, 2014, http://www.pre.ethics.gc.ca/pdf/eng/tcps2- 2014/TCPS_2_FINAL_Web.pdf.

_____. 'Tri-Agency Statement of Principles on Digital Data Management', 21 December 2016, http://www.science.gc.ca/eic/site/063.nsf/eng/h_83F7624E.html.

_____. 'DRAFT: Tri-agency Research Data Management Policy for Consultation', 25 May 2018, http://www.science.gc.ca/eic/site/063.nsf/eng/h_97610.html.

Halpern, Orit. *Beautiful Data: A History of Vision and Reason Since 1945*, Durham: Duke University Press, 2015.

Haggerty, Kevin D. 'Ethics Creep: Governing Social Science Research in the Name of Ethics', *Qualitative Sociology 27*.4 (2004): 391-414.

Hauge Michelle V., Mark D. Stevenson, Kim D. Rossmo and Steven Le Comber. 'Tagging Banksy: Using Geographic Profiling to Investigate a Modern Art Mystery', *Journal of Spatial Science,* 61.1 (2016): 185-190.

Hearn, Alex. 'Google will Stop Scanning Content of Personal Emails', *The Guardian*, 26 June 2017, https://www.theguardian.com/technology/2017/jun/26/google-will-stop- scanning-content-of-personal-emails.

_____. 'How firms you have never interacted with can target your Facebook', *The Guardian*. 21 April 2018, https://www.theguardian.com/technology/2018/apr/21/how- firms-you-have-never-interacted-with-can-target-your-facebook.

Hill, Kashmir. 'Facebook Added 'Research' to User Agreement 4 Months After Emotion Manipulation Study', *Forbes*, 30 June 2014, www.forbes.com/sites/kashmirhill/2014/06/30/facebook-only-got-permission-to-do- research-on-users-after-emotion-manipulation-study.

Iliadis, Andrew, and Federica Russo. 'Critical Data Studies: An Introduction', *Big Data & Society*, December 2016, https://doi.org/10.1177/2053951716674238.

Kitchin, Rob. *The Data Revolution: Big Data, Open Data, Data Infrastructures and Their Consequences*, London: SAGE, 2014.

_____. 'Big Data, New Epistemologies and Paradigm Shifts', *Big Data & Society* 1.1 (2014): 1-12.

_____, and Tracey Lauriault. 'Towards Critical Data Studies: Charting and Unpacking Data Assemblages and Their Work', *The Programmable City Working Paper 2* (2014), http://papers.ssrn.com/sol3/papers.cfm?abstract_id=2474112.

Kramer, Adam, Jamie Guillory and Jeffrey Hancock. 'Experimental Evidence of Massive- Scale Emotional Contagion Through Social Networks', *Proceedings National Academy of Science,* 111.24 (2014): 8788-8790.

Leathern, Rob. 'A New Level of Transparency for Ads and Pages', *Facebook Newsroom*, 28 June 2018, https://newsroom.fb.com/news/2018/06/transparency-for-ads-and-pages/.

Lee, Sandra Soo-Jin. 'Studying 'Friends': The Ethics of Using Social Media as Research Platforms', *The American Journal of Bioethics* 17.3 (2017): 1-2.

Luka, Mary Elizabeth, and Mélanie Millette. '(Re)framing Big Data: Activating Situated Knowledges and a Feminist Ethics of Care in Social Media Research', *Social Media + Society*, April 2018, http://journals.sagepub.com/doi/full/10.1177/2056305118768297.

Markham, Annette. 'Ethic as Method, Method as Ethic', *Journal of Information Ethics* 15.2 (2006): 37-54.

_____, and Elizabeth Buchanan. *Ethical Decision-Making and Internet Research 2.0: Recommendations From the AoIR Ethics Working Committee*, 2012, http://www.aoir.org/reports/ethics2.pdf](http://www.aoir.org/reports/ethics2.pdf.

_____, and Elizabeth Buchanan. 'Ethical Considerations in Digital Research contexts', in James D. Wright (ed.), *Encyclopedia for Social & Behavioral Sciences,* Waltham MA: Elsevier, 2015, *pp.* 606-613.

_____. 'Afterword: Ethics as Impact-Moving from Error-Avoidance and Concept-Driven Models to a Future-Oriented Approach', *Social Media + Society* (July-September 2018): 1-11.

_____, Katrin Tiidenberg, and Andrew Herman. 'Ethics as Methods: Doing ethics in the Era of Big Data Research-Introduction', *Social Media + Society* (July-September 2018): 1-9, http://journals.sagepub.com/doi/abs/10.1177/2056305118784502.

Mayer-Schönberger, Viktor, and Kenneth Cukier. *Big Data: A Revolution that will Transform How we Live, Work, and Think*, Boston MA: Houghton Mifflin Harcourt, 2013.

Metcalf, Jacob, and Kate Crawford. 'Where are Human Subjects in Big Data Research? The Emerging Ethics Divide', *Big Data & Society*, June 2016, http://journals.sagepub.com/doi/full/10.1177/2053951716650211.

_____, Emily Keller, and danah boyd. *Perspectives on Big Data, Ethics, and Society*. Council for Big Data, Ethics, and Society, 23 May 2016, https://bdes.datasociety.net/council-output/perspectives-on-big-data-ethics-and- society/.

Meyer, Robinson. 'Everything we Know About Facebook's Secret Mood Manipulation Experiment', *The Atlantic*, 28 June 2014, https://www.theatlantic.com/technology/archive/2014/06/everything-we-know-about- facebooks-secret-mood-manipulation-experiment/373648/.

Michael, Mike and Deborah Lupton. 'Toward a Manifesto for the 'Public Understanding of Big Data', *Public Understanding of Science* 25.1 (2015): 104-116.

Napoli, Philip, and Robyn Caplan. 'Why Media Companies Insist They're Not Media Companies, Why They're Wrong, and Why it Matters', *First Monday* 22.5 (2017).

Neff, Gina, Anissa Tanweer, Brittany Fiore-Gartland and Laura Osburn. 'Critique and Contribute: A Practice-Based Framework for Improving Critical Data Studies and Data Science', *Big Data* 5.2 (2017): 85-97.

Nissenbaum, Helen. *Privacy in Context: Technology, Policy and the Integrity of Social Life*, Palo Alto: Stanford University Press, 2009.

_____. 'A Contextual Approach to Privacy Online', *Daedalus, 140*.4 (2011): 32-48.
Noble, Safiya Umoja. *Algorithms of Oppression: How Search Engines Reinforce Racism*, New York: NYU Press, 2018.

O'Neil, Cathy. 'On Being a Data Skeptic', O'Reilly Media, 2013, http://www.oreilly.com/data/free/files/being-a-data-skeptic.pdf.

Penn State. 'IRB Guideline X - Guidelines for Computer and Internet-Based Research Involving Human Participants', Office of the Vice President for Research, 2018, https://www.research.psu.edu/irb/policies/guideline10.

Plantin, Jean-Christophe, Carl Lagoze and Paul N. Edwards. 'Re-Integrating Scholarly Infrastructure: The Ambiguous Role of Data Sharing Platforms', *Big Data & Society* (January 2018), https://doi.org/10.1177/2053951718756683.

Posner, Miriam, and Lauren F. Klein. 'Editor's Introduction: Data as Media', *Feminist Media Histories* 3.3 (2017): 1-8.

Reigeluth, Tyler Butler. 'Why Data is Not Enough: Digital Traces as Control of Self and Self-Control', *Surveillance & Society,* 12.2 (2014).

Rhodan, Maya. '"Please send help." Hurricane Harvey victims turn to Twitter and Facebook', *Time*, 30 August 2017, http://time.com/4921961/hurricane-harvey->twitter-facebook-social-media/.

Rieder, Gernot and Judith Simon. 'Datatrust: Or, the Political Quest for Numerical Evidence and the Epistemologies of Big Data', *Big Data & Society,* 3.1 (June 2016), http://journals.sagepub.com/doi/abs/10.1177/2053951716649398.

Rooke, Barry. 'Four Pillars of Internet Research Ethics with Web 2.0', *Journal of Academic Ethics,* 111.4 (2013): 265-268.

Rusbridger, Alan and Ewen MacAskill. 'Edward Snowden Interview - The Edited Transcript. *The Guardian*, 18 July 2014, https://www.theguardian.com/world/2014/jul/18/-sp-edward-snowden-nsa-whistleblower-interview-transcript.

Sabati, Sheeva. 'Upholding "Colonial Knowing" Through the IRB: Reframing Institutional Research Ethics', *Qualitative Inquiry* (August 2018), DOI: https://doi.org/10.1177/1077800418787214.

Schroepfer, Mike. 'An Update on Our Plans to Restrict Data Access on Facebook', *Facebook Newsroom*, 4 April 2018, https://newsroom.fb.com/news/2018/04/restricting-data- access/

Seetharaman, Deepa, and Georgia Wells. 'Hurricane Harvey Victims Turn to Social Media for Assistance', *The Wall Street Journal*, 29 August 2017, https://www.wsj.com/articles/hurricane-harvey-victims-turn-to-social-media-for- assistance-1503999001.

Shilton, Katie. 'Emerging Ethics Norms in Social Media Research', *Big Data Ethics*, 2016, https://bigdata.fpf.org/papers/emerging-ethics-norms-in-social-media-research/.

Shotwell, Alexis. *Against Purity: Living Ethically in Compromised Times*, Minnesota: University of Minnesota Press, 2016.

Simmerling, Mary, Brian Schwegler, Joan E, Sieber and James Lindgren. 'Introducing a New Paradigm for Ethical Research in the Social, Behavioral, and Biomedical Sciences: Part I', *Northwestern University Law Review* 101.2 (2007): 837-858.

Singer, Natasha. 'What You Don't Know About How Facebook Uses Your Data', *The New York Times*, 11 April 2018, https://www.nytimes.com/2018/04/11/technology/facebook-privacy-hearings.html.

Sonderby, Chris. 'Reinforcing Our Commitment to Transparency', *Facebook Newsroom*, 15 May 2018, https://newsroom.fb.com/news/2018/05/transparency-report-h2-2017/.

Stark, Laura. *Behind Closed Doors: IRBs and the Making of Ethical Research*, Chicago: University of Chicago Press, 2011.

Sula, Chris Allen. 'Research Ethics in an Age of Big Data', *Association for Information Science and Technology*, 6 January 2016, https://www.asist.org/publications/bulletin/decemberjanuary-2016/research-ethics-in- an-age-of-big-data/.

Taylor, Joanna, and Claudia Pagliari. 'Mining Social Media Data: How are Research Sponsors and Researchers Addressing the Ethical Challenges?', *Research Ethics,* 14.2 (October 2017): 1-39.

Tene, Omer, and Jules Polonetsky. 'Beyond IRBs: Ethical Guidelines for Data Research', *Washington and Lee Law Review Online*, 72.3 (2016): 457-471, https://scholarlycommons.law.wlu.edu/wlulr-online/vol72/iss3/7/.

Tilenberg, Katrin. 'Ethics in Digital Research', in Uwe Flick (ed.), *The SAGE Handbook of Qualitative Data Collection*. Thousand Oaks: SAGE, 2018, pp. 466-481.

Townsend, Leanne, and Claire Wallace. '*Social Media Research: A Guide to Ethics*', University of Aberdeen, 2015, https://www.gla.ac.uk/media/media_487729_en.pdf.

University of Sheffield. The Ethics of Internet-based and Social Media Research, 2016, https://www.sheffield.ac.uk/polopoly_fs/1.644904!/file/Report_Ethics_of_Social_Me dia_Research_Jul16.pdf.

Van Dijck, Jose. 'Datafication, Dataism and Dataveillance: Big Data Between Scientific Paradigm and Ideology', *Surveillance & Society 12*.2 (2014), http://ojs.library.queensu.ca/index.php/surveillance-and-society/article/view/datafication.

Verma, Inder M. 'Editorial Expression of Concern and Correction', *Proceedings National Academy of Science* 111.29 (2014): 10779, http://www.pnas.org/content/111/29/10779.1.

Virtová, Tereza, Tereza Stöckelová and Helena Krásná. 'On the Track of C/overt Research: Lessons from Taking Ethnographic Ethics to the Extreme', *Qualitative Inquiry,* 24.7 (2018): 453-463.

Walters, Chris. 'Facebook's New Terms of Service: 'We Can Do Anything We Want with Your Content. Forever', *Consumerist*, 15 February 2009, https://consumerist.com/2009/02/15/facebooks-new-terms-of-service-we-can-do- anything-we-want-with-your-content-forever.

Wang, Yilun, and Michal Kosinski. 'Deep Neural Networks are More Accurate than Humans at Detecting Sexual Orientation from Facial Images', *Journal of Personality and Social Psychology* 114.2 (2018): 246-257.

Weaver, Matthew. 'Facebook Scandal: I am Being Used as Scapegoat - Academic Who Mined Data', *The Guardian*, 21 March 2018, https://www.theguardian.com/uk- news/2018/mar/21/facebook-row-i-am-being-used-as-scapegoat-says-academic- aleksandr-kogan-cambridge-analytica.

Weindling, Paul. 'The Origins of Informed Consent: The International Scientific Commission on Medical War Crimes and the Nuremberg Code', *Bulletin of the History of Medicine* 75.1 (2001): 37-71.

Williams, Matthew L, Pete Burnap and Luke Sloan. 'Towards an Ethical Framework for Publishing Twitter Data in Social Research: Taking into Account Users' Views, Online Context and Algorithmic Estimation', *Sociology* 51.6 (2017): 1149-1168.

Zimmer, Michael. 'Research Ethics in the Big Data Era: Addressing Conceptual Gaps for Researchers and IRBs', School of Information Studies University of Wisconsin, Milwaukee, 2015, https://bigdata.fpf.org/papers/research-ethics-in-the-big-data-era- addressing-conceptual-gaps-for-researchers-and-irbs/.

Zwitter, Andrej. 'Big Data Ethics', *Big Data & Society* (July 2014), https://journals.sagepub.com/doi/abs/10.1177/2053951714559253.

14: DATA FOR THE SOCIAL GOOD: TOWARD A DATA-ACTIVIST RESEARCH AGENDA

BECKY KAZANSKY, GUILLÉN TORRES, LONNEKE VAN DER VELDEN, KERSTI WISSENBACH AND STEFANIA MILAN[1]

Introduction

'Big data' is a hyped buzzword - or rather, it has been for a while, before being supplanted by 'newer' acclaimed concepts such as artificial intelligence. The popularity of the term says something about the widespread fascination with the seemingly infinite possibilities of automated data collection and analysis. This enchantment affects not only the corporate sector, where many technology companies have centered their business model on data mining, and governments, whose intelligence agencies have adopted sophisticated machinery to monitor citizens. Many civic society organizations, too, are increasingly trying to take advantage of the opportunities brought about by datafication, using data to improve society. From crowdsourced maps about gender-based violence ('feminicide') in Latin America, to the analysis of audio-visual footage to map drone attacks in conflict zones, individuals and groups regularly produce, collect, process and repurpose data to fuel research for the social good. Problematizing the mainstream connotations of big data, these examples of 'data activism' take a critical stance towards massive data collection and represent the new frontier of citizens' engagement with information and technological innovation.

In this chapter we survey diverse experiences and methodologies of what we call 'data-activist research' - an approach to research that combines embeddedness in the social world with the research methods typical of academia and the innovative repertoires of data activists. We argue that such approach to knowledge production fosters community building and knowledge sharing, while providing a way to fruitfully interrogate datafication and democratic participation. By exploring what we can learn from data-activist projects and investigating the conditions for collaboration between activist communities and academia, we aim at laying the groundwork for a data-activist research agenda whose dynamics are socially responsible and empowering for all the parties involved.

The chapter is organized as follows. We begin offering a working definition of data-activist research. We explain how the notion has developed within the DATACTIVE research collective at the University of Amsterdam, whose work investigates the politics of datafication and massive data collection from the perspective of civil society. We describe how our commitment to 'engaged research' feeds into our ideas about data-activist research.[2] We build upon interdis-

---

1 * This project has received funding from the European Research Council (ERC) under the European Union's Horizon2020 research and innovation programme (grant agreement No 639379-DATACTIVE, awarded to Stefania Milan as Principal Investigator). See https://data-activism.net.
2 By engaged research we indicate systematic, evidence-based, social science research which is

ciplinary literature on datafication and the valuable insights shared by activists, civil society organizations and engaged researchers at the *Data for the Social Good* workshop (University of Amsterdam, November 2017).[3] We discuss concrete examples of existing research projects and their novel tools and approaches. Since our main goal is to call for more interaction between activists and academics, we conclude with a reflection on the ethics of collaboration, as we deem these two elements to be central questions today. We hope that this discussion will encourage the two communities to appropriate and build upon the powerful approach of data-activist research.

Defining Data-activist Research

The label data-activist research emerges at the intersection of 'traditional' research and the set of critical and/or activist practices that deal or 'act upon' datafication.[4] The roots of data-activist research are to be found in data activism itself, which critically engages with the manifold impact of datafication on social life.[5] Processes of turning aspects of social life into data are of course not new and have always been at the core of the practices of science and knowledge production.[6] Nor are efforts to challenge how social life is turned into data a new thing. For example, where statistics have long been used to steer city and health planning, official numbers and calculations have been challenged by 'statactivists' to produce impactful public policy reform.[7] However, over the last decade, datafication has become a fundamental component of people's lived reality and a major driver of knowledge production. Whether it is through social media use, engaging with the government, buying online goods, or using public transport, people are continuously digitally 'measured', included in databases,[8] and interact with such measurements through the feedback they get via apps and other devices.[9] Furthermore, these data are afterwards used in various types of knowledge production activities that feed political and economic decision-making and governance processes.

---

designed to actively involve and possibly empower disempowered communities and people beyond the academic community. See Stefania Milan, 'Toward an Epistemology of Engaged Research', *International Journal of Communication* 4 (2010), p. 856.

3 DATACTIVE, *Workshop Report: Data for the Social Good*, University of Amsterdam, 2017, https://data-activism.net/wordpress/wp-content/uploads/2018/01/DATACTIVE_DataSocialGood2017_Report.pdf.
4 Sebastian Kubitschko, 'Acting on Media Technologies and Infrastructures: Expanding the Media as Practice Approach', *Media, Culture & Society* 40.4 (2018).
5 Stefania Milan, 'Data Activism as the New Frontier of Media Activism', in Goubin Yang and Viktor Pickard (eds), *Media Activism in the Digital Age*, Oxford: Routledge, 2017.
6 See Viktor Mayer-Schönberger and Kenneth Cukier, *Big Data: A Revolution That Will Transform How We Live, Work, and Think*, Boston: Houghton Mifflin Harcourt, 2013; and Michel Foucault, *The Will to Knowledge: The History of Sexuality*, London: Penguin Books, 1998 (1976).
7 See Isabelle Bruno, Emmanuel Didier and Tommaso Vitale, 'Statactivism: forms of action between disclosure and affirmation', *Partecipazione e conflitto* 7.2 (2014).
8 Kevin D. Haggerty and Richard V. Ericson, 'The Surveillant Assemblage', *The British Journal of Sociology* 51.4 (2000).
9 Kashmir Hill, 'What Happens When You Tell the Internet You're Pregnant', *Jezebel*, https://jezebel.com/what-happens-when-you-tell-the-internet-youre-pregnant-1794398989.

The specific way in which civil society actors have responded to the new possibilities and risks brought about by datafication has informed our research into data activism, an umbrella term which embraces, for instance, socio-technical practices that provide counter-hegemonic responses to the discrimination, social exclusion and privacy infringement that go hand in hand with big data.[10] Data activism 'interrogates the politics of big data',[11] and it does so in a variety of ways: for instance, '[t]he action repertoire of data activists includes examining, manipulating, leveraging, and exploiting data, along with resisting and meddling in their creation and use'.[12] In other words, data activism includes both the use, mobilization or creation of datasets for social causes (providing an alternative to what big data corporations or state agencies do with data), as well as the development and employment of technologies that frustrate massive data collection (providing protection to what big data corporations or state agencies do with data).[13]

Studying the methods and strategies of data activism led us to question our own *research processes, practices and relationships*. This is because data activism signals the emergence of innovative 'epistemic cultures',[14] namely experimental and context-specific ways of producing knowledge about and with data. As Milan and van der Velden suggested, by '[p]ostulating a critical/active engagement with data, its forms, dynamics, and infrastructure, data activists function as producers of counter-expertise and alternative epistemologies, making sense of data as a way of knowing the world and turning it into a point of intervention'.[15] Take for instance the artist Mimi Onuoha, who created a 'Library of Missing Datasets' to strategically draw attention to important issues of social justice which could benefit from more data,[16] or the experience of the activists using drones to counter decades of injustice over oil exploitation in the Amazon rainforest.[17] These cases signal that (data) activism is a powerful location for knowledge production able to fuel political projects, through practices that draw from institutionally entrenched approaches to research while simultaneously subverting, expanding and questioning their components.

---

10 Stefania Milan, 'Data Activism as the New Frontier of Media Activism', p 152.
11 Ibid p. 153.
12 Ibid p. 143.
13 See also Becky Kazansky, 'Privacy, Responsibility, and Human Rights Activism', *The Fibreculture Journal*, 26 (2015); Lonneke van der Velden, 'Leaky Apps and Data Shots: Technologies of Leakage and Insertion in NSA Surveillance', *Surveillance & Society* 13.2 (2015).
14 The notion of 'epistemic culture' is used in science studies and refers to the 'specific strategies that generate, validate, and communicate scientific accomplishments'. See Karin Knorr-Cetina and Werner Reichmann, 'Epistemic Cultures' in *International Encyclopedia of the Social & Behavioral Sciences*, second edition, Oxford: Elsevier, 2015 pp. 873-80. The concept highlights the diversity in scientific practices. Here we use it to discuss the diversity in knowledge making in the context of datafication.
15 Stefania Milan and Lonneke van der Velden, 'The Alternative Epistemologies of Data Activism', *Digital Culture & Society*, 2.2 (2016).
16 Mimi Onuoha, 'The Library of Missing Datasets', http://mimionuoha.com/the-library-of-missing-datasets/.
17 If not us then who?, 'Detecting Disasters'. https://ifnotusthenwho.me/films/using-drone-technology-detect-oil-spills/. See also Stefania Milan and Miren Gutiérrez, 'Technopolitics in the Age of Big Data', in Francisco Sierra Caballero and Tommasso Gravante (eds), *Networks, Movements & Technopolitics in Latin America: Critical Analysis and Current Challenges*, London: Palgrave Macmillan, 2017, pp. 95-109.

It is in collaboration with these novel epistemic cultures that we see possibilities for constructive interaction between activism and academia, and for a joint discussion about what 'data activist research for the social good' could look like. This entails not only a reflection *about* data activism that tries to locate its most innovative and empowering research practices, but also entails paying attention to what engaged and productive role academia could play in the process. In other words, can we do data-activist research ourselves, and if so, how? What could academia learn from these emerging practices and what could it offer back? What are the conditions of possibility for joint research projects? We argue that to provide the best answer to these questions it is necessary to move beyond doing research *about* (data) activism, towards conducting institutional boundary-crossing research that finds common grounds and opportunities for collaboration *with* (data) activists.[18] In the next section we further explore this claim.

Data-activist Research is Engaged Research

Several members of the DATACTIVE research group have known or have been involved for long with the communities they study. They have faced an important question that arises when researching groups one is closely affiliated with: how to develop and deploy a research pathway that is most relevant for the community, making sure that the community itself can contribute to shape both the project's goals and practices? In other words, how can we do research that matters also to those being researched? These concerns are certainly not new in academia, and there are several examples of individuals and groups who approached research *in a different way*. Early attempts at co-producing knowledge while reflecting upon its connection to community empowerment can be found in the 1960s and 1970s. They were influenced by the writings of Brazilian educator Paolo Freire and the *con-ricerca* (co-inquiry) experiments in Italy, for example involving factory workers in analyzing the social impact of capitalism.[19] Since the 1980s, Charlotte Ryan, co-director of the now dormant Movement/Media Research Action Project (MRAP) at Boston College (US), has been experimenting with producing recursive 'two-way, dialogic exchanges that create new, generalizable knowledge' expected to contribute to the 'democratization of theorizing'.[20] Because both theorizing and practice benefit if scholars 'embed themselves in movements, not simply as active citizens but as skilled learners',[21] MRAP members encouraged activists and scholars to establish 'learning communities; based on shared learning practices and work routines. More recently, Lovink and Rossiter have pointed to the importance of working together with actors in the field, since 'collaborative concept production' is needed in order to keep theory up to date.[22] Similarly, the *DataCenter: Research for Justice* organization in Oakland, California, have characterized its Research Justice Model as having three main tenets:

---

18 This argument was made earlier in a series of articles published in the Feature 'Making Communication Matter' of *the International Journal of Communication* (4/2010) edited by Stefania Milan (see http://ijoc.org/index.php/ijoc/issue/view/5).
19 Paulo Freire, *Pedagogy of the Oppressed*, New York: Continuum, 2007 (1968).
20 C. Ryan and K. Jeffreys, 'The Practice of Collaborative Theorizing', unpublished manuscript (2008).
21 Ibid, p. 3.
22 Geert Lovink and Ned Rossiter, *Organization after Social Media*, Colchester: Minor Compositions, 2018, p. 75.

1. It defines research processes as a collective endeavor and a shared knowledge creation process between and academic and community researchers;

2. It creates, maintains, and engages with the knowledge that is produced by community experts, traditional knowledge keepers, as well as cultural leaders in ways that envision research as a ceremonial act of mutual respect and co-sharing; and

3. Only research that is responsive to the social, legal, economic cultural, and political policy needs as identified by community experts should be conducted.[23]

Drawing from these sources of inspiration, DATACTIVE proposes an 'engaged' approach to research that questions the impact that empirical inquiry has over people and communities, and strives to contribute to their causes.[24] Such an approach entails to do research 'with' instead of merely 'about', thus entering into a continuous dialogue with the fields of action and interaction being observed.[25] Nevertheless, an engaged approach to research does not lose sight of the wider context and maintains a sharp attention to the question of power.

In our view, data-activist research should thus emerge as the result of community endeavors whose perspectives and self-definitions can be located in specific and contested discourses about technology, information, activism, marginalization, exclusion and even selfhood, rather than being merely the result of the interaction between disembodied agents in a universal field of knowledge. In what follows we present four case studies that give a sense of what data-activist research might mean in practice.

Data-activist Research in Practice

Forensic Oceanography, *The Syrian Archive*, and the local instances of the *Alaveteli* software are good examples of data-activist research which succeed at performing a series of steps allowing activist-researchers to do 'research that matters'. The three projects managed to remain close to the problems they identified, to then take a step back to develop an abstract understanding and analysis of the reality, only to return to the field to address the community issues that had been identified. As we will see, what these projects demonstrate is that research processes are more productive when they are meaningful to specific communities rather than merely a product of 'disembodied scientific objectivity'.[26]

---

23 Andrew J. Jolivette, *Research Justice: Methodologies for Social Change*, Bristol: Policy Press, 2015.
24 Stefania Milan, 'Toward an Epistemology of Engaged Research.'; Chiara Milan and Stefania Milan, 'Involving Communities as Skilled Learners: The STRAP Framework', in Norbert Wildermuth and Teke Ngomba (eds), *Methodological Reflections on Researching Communication and Social Change*, Cham: Springer, 2016, 9-28.
25 Cf. C. Ryan, V. Salas-Wright, M. Anastario & G. Camara, 'Making Research Matter... Matter to Whom?'.
26 Donna Haraway, 'Situated Knowledges: The Science Question in Feminism and the Privilege of Partial Perspective', *Feminist Studies*, 14.3 (1988): 576.

Forensic Oceanography: In search of a 'disobedient gaze'

Forensic Oceanography is the maritime counterpart of *Forensic Architecture* focusing specifically on migration and bordering. *Forensic Architecture* started in 2011 as an ERC-funded research project at Goldsmiths, University of London (UK), to turn later into a stand-alone research agency focused on the production of evidence of human rights violations. Through the analysis of architecture, the environment, and its media representations, researchers have provided prosecution teams, political organizations and international institutions alike with evidence that can be used in court. The research agency has engaged in a variety of projects spanning from the analysis of deadly drone attacks in Syria, to the disappearance of 43 Mexican students, to the ecocide in Indonesia.[27] The data sources that Forensic Architecture relies upon to fuel its investigation are of varied nature - from satellite images, to publicly available data and media produced by the communities involved in the events under scrutiny.

The 'Left to Die Boat', a project by *Forensic Oceanography,* is a good example of the work of *Forensic Architecture*: it reconstructs the story of a vessel that left Libya with 72 people on-board in the midst of the NATO-led military intervention in the country. The boat ran out of fuel, drifted for two weeks and was finally washed back to the Libyan coast. Most of its passengers died. The survivors stated that they had contact with several ships and helicopters, but no one intervened to help. Using publicly available databases on sea traffic, the researchers traced and visualized the contacts made by the boat, proving that a number of ships, including military vessels, were indeed navigating close by, but chose not to intervene. The evidence allowed advocates to start a number of legal petitions against NATO member states, accused of the crime of non-assistance at sea.[28]

Forensic Oceanography shows how it is possible to use as research input monitoring technologies, including those typically used by police forces, with the goal of bringing about a 'disobedient gaze' - a perspective that challenges the dominant narrative. As Pezzani and Heller explain it, this disobedient gaze performs a reversal of the surveilling action, turning its sight to the act of policing itself.[29] Through this inversion, *Forensic Oceanography* brings to light events and issues that the surveilling system prefers to hide. It also shows how monitoring technologies can be used to hold accountable the very agents who set them in place to exert power. Thus, this project - as well as the rest of *Forensic Architecture*'s work - makes evident how the availability of data can foster the creation of new mechanisms of participation that take advantage of technologies designed for other purposes. In this sense, *Forensic Oceanography* is a great example of the diverse politics of datafication, since the data produced by surveilling technologies can also be processed to provide backing evidence to strengthen the politicization of contemporary social issues.

---

27 For the project about Syria, see: http://www.forensic-architecture.org/case/al-jinah-mosque/; for the case of the missing Mexican Students, see: http://www.forensic-architecture.org/case/ayotzinapa/; for the Indonesia case see: http://www.forensic-architecture.org/case/ecocide-indonesia/.
28 http://www.forensic-architecture.org/case/left-die-boat/.
29 Lorenzo Pezzani and Charles Heller, 'A Disobedient Gaze: Strategic Interventions in the Knowledge(s) of Maritime Borders', *Postcolonial Studies*, 16.3 (September, 2013).

Departing from *Forensic Oceanography*'s work, it could be interesting for data-activist research to think about what other kinds of 'disobedient data politics' are possible,[30] and what their ethical implications are. For example, given that many of the technologies used by *Forensic Oceanography* have been designed with the goal of performing surveillance, it is important to remain attentive to the question of whether there are risks in using them. If data-activist research engages with scraping, data monitoring, etc., how can activist-researchers engage in these activities in a responsible way that does not reproduce the extractive and exploitative rationality of the mainstream discourse and practices? What we learn from this type of projects is that researchers and the communities they work with benefit from 'continuously reflecting upon whether their investigation contributes to a "disobedient gaze", rather than merely a vigilant one.'[31]

The Syrian Archive: Turning Open Source Intelligence Upside-down

The *Syrian Archive* is an Open Source Intelligence (OSINT) effort to document and preserve information about human rights violations committed by all sides of the Syrian conflict.[32] Started in 2014, the project brings together developers and human rights activists focusing on the preservation of media evidence under threat of being deleted or censored from the online platforms where it is uploaded. Its main goals are to secure data, verify its authenticity, and categorize it. The resulting database allows the wider public to reuse the material for various purposes, although evidence gathering concerning human rights violations is the primary rationale.

The *Syrian Archive* aims at implementing ethical principles starting from the design of the technology that powers its activities, the methodologies, and the way its activist-researchers preserve findings. The tools built in the context of the project are open source and most of the code used to process and organize the data is made available in the software repository GitHub. The project also follows a user-centered approach maintaining regular contact with media sources, who have provided so far more than 1 million entries to the archive, all of which have undergone verification and categorization. The project's ultimate goals are to identify reliable sources of data collection, organize the material in a database, establish the trustworthiness of the content, and automatizing data collection and preservation.

The *Syrian Archive*'s methodology makes evident that even working with publicly available data has severe ethical implications. For example, one of the many thorny issues its activist-researchers constantly reflect upon is how to acquire the consent of those depicted in the footage, or how to decide what should be preserved and what should be discarded. To

---

30 On disobedient sensing and listening see Charles Heller, Lorenzo Pezzani, and Maurice Stierl, 'Disobedient Sensing and Border Struggles at the Maritime Frontier of Europe', *Spheres: Journal for Digital Cultures* 4 (June, 2017).
31 Pezzani cited in DATACTIVE, 'Workshop Report', p. 14.
32 https://syrianarchive.org/en/about. Open Source Intelligence is data gathering based on publicly available sources.

guide decisions, the project follows a 'do no harm' approach,[33] taking care to exclude certain sensitive data. 'Do no harm' refers to a set of protocols intended to make sure that humanitarian practitioners do not end up further harming the situation they intend to improve.[34] Additionally, for the *Syrian Archive*, 'open source' does not only refer to the public availability of its materials, but also a specific approach to the transparency of protocols and practices. Keeping the software tools open allows other activists to replicate the work of the organization.

In conclusion, the activities of the *Syrian Archive* stress that, even if one purses an urgent goal through activism - such as collecting data about human rights violations before it disappears or gets censored - it is still of paramount importance to pay attention to the consequences of data gathering, processing and sharing facilitated by digital technology. Furthermore, the project shows how it is possible to build databases with a rationality that does not aim at maximizing control or private benefit, but focuses on its political potential.

Alaveteli: Engaging with communities across borders

Alaveteli identifies a Freedom of Information (FOI) request platform and the community that emerged around it. It is currently implemented in 25 countries across the world.[35] The original platform was launched in 2008 in the UK under the name 'What do They Know'. The open source code of the platform, however, was quickly picked up by other civil society actors (the first in New Zealand), before the e-democracy project *mySociety* made its own iteration available for everyone under the name *Alaveteli*, offering support for groups who were interested in adopting it locally. *Alaveteli* enables citizens to openly request information from government institutions, allowing the whole process to be tracked online and the institutional replies to be available for everyone. In each local deployment, the success or failure of advocating for FOI and engaging civil society through the platform depends on a multitude of factors, such as cultural dynamics, political restrictions, and infrastructural limitations. For example, the backgrounds of the actors who have picked up the code locally are very diverse, ranging from political activists to journalists, from technologists to human rights organizations. The responses to context-related challenges are therefore also varied. While some platform implementations are deeply rooted in an activist ethos, with people spending significant proportion of their volunteer time into platform management and mobilization, other *Alaveteli* communities have been more efficient in pursuing social innovation grants to localize the platform and engage in awareness-raising. The long-term success of the platform usually depends on the ability of the actors involved to establish wider collaborations. For instance, if a group of techies has set up the platform, collaborations with advocacy groups help to create awareness, increase engagement and establish links with potential users such as journalists.

---

33 Mary B. Anderson, *Do No Harm. How Aid Can Support Peace or War*, Boulder CO/London: Lynne Rienner Publishers, 1999.
34 At the same time, this is not an easy approach when a researcher has to deal with unethical actors such as perpetrators of human rights violations.
35 See http://alaveteli.org/. Alaveteli is a good example of Civic tech activism, an emerging instance of organizing collective action that engages in institutionally regulated governance processes through the crafting of direct engagement spaces for civil society and, thus, pushing governing institutions toward more accountability.

Cycling back to our original quest for 'good' collaborations between researchers and the communities on the ground, *Alaveteli* well exemplifies the crucial role of human interaction and relationship-building around technological innovation if this is to become relevant for local communities. The platform's reliance on the local context and its specificities underscores also the importance of making use of the already existing infrastructure - encompassing both technology and human relations - and building on the previous experience of local activists. In sum, data-activist research requires paying attention not only to infrastructure practices, but also to local contexts and human dynamics.

One from the house: Studying collaboration in online communities

The DATACTIVE research group has contributed to the development of a computational research tool called *BigBang*, 'a toolkit for studying communications data from collaborative projects'.[36] Our interest in *BigBang* grew out of the desire to understand how the human rights discourse has evolved within multi-stakeholder discussions about the governance of international data flows. Thus far, this research has targeted a number of community mailing lists within the Internet Corporation for Assigned Names and Numbers (ICANN).[37]

Among other functionalities, *BigBang* allows researchers to scrape large swaths of data from a mailing list database and easily search for keywords. *BigBang* has proven especially useful to the study of ICANN because the large majority of community interactions takes place on mailing lists. As a large community with thousands of contributors across the globe, ICANN produces many data traces. This amount of data can prove cumbersome for manual analysis, hence automating the search for keywords makes the task of investigating the discursive evolution in internet governance processes more manageable. However, the toolkit brings up some concerns because it facilitates research techniques in the realm of 'big data' analysis - a set of techniques which the DATACTIVE project investigates with a critical eye. Partaking in the development and use of this tool presents an interesting opportunity for us to reflect on our research ethics, the 'why' of our research, and our connection with the issues at stake.

Take for example the distinct understandings and expectations of privacy in different community-contexts - a question which is relevant to most data-activist research projects given their reliance on publicly available data. During DATACTIVE's internal discussions we have raised concerns about the expectations of privacy that can be found in different online contexts, and asked how these expectations are affected when the data can be more easily collected and analyzed by third parties - as *BigBang* makes possible. ICANN is a community which conducts much of its work 'in the open' - a fundamental requisite of its multi-stakeholder nature. Because of the open nature of the data the organization produces, DATACTIVE felt it was ethically sound to use it after producing a list of conditions guiding its acceptable use.

---

36 See https://github.com/datactive/bigbang. *BigBang*'s initiator and Lead Developer is computer scientist Sebastian Benthall (UC Berkley & NYU).

37 See Stefania Milan and Niels ten Oever, 'Coding and encoding rights in internet infrastructure', *Internet Policy Review* 6.1 (2017).

These conditions are the result of questioning our goals and intentions: why do we harvest these data? Do we need it to achieve the goals of our research? Who is affected by our data collection and analysis, and how? Who benefits from our research? Among others, we learnt that when it comes to online content the level and the modalities of publicity, including academic publications, need to be determined on a case by case basis and in collaboration with the participant communities themselves.

Inspired by these examples and acknowledging that data activism, in its many forms, emerges from a plurality of social worlds and identities,[38] we deem crucial to reflect upon issues of collaboration. We now turn our attention to this aspect, in order to contribute to sketch the groundwork for a joint research agenda between data activists and academics.

What Collaborations for Data-Activist Research?

Reflecting on the politics of collaboration must be seen as a central methodological task when dealing with the production and use of data to fuel political projects in the interest of society at large. Such reflection has to be guided by the recognition of the existing difference in organizational cultures, modus operandi, goals and values that characterize activists on the one hand, and researchers on the others.[39] Collaborative data-activist research strategies can benefit from researchers and communities developing questions and research practices jointly from the start, remaining open for the exchange of different types of know-how despite the apparent difference in expertise.[40] Such approach aims to go beyond the 'distant reading' of the data points activists produce, moving instead towards a 'critical proximity' that remains close to the issues approached, participating in their development.[41]

The *researching with* that we highlighted as a crucial feature of data-activist research can benefit from the process of building a 'we'; a shared identity resulting from a set of iterative activities, dialogues and reflections connected to fundamental questions such as how do we, as a community, define what the issue at stake is? How do we identify mechanisms to address

---

38   Eliana Herrera Huérfano, Francisco Sierra Caballero and Carlos del Valle Rojas, 'Hacia una Epistemología del Sur. *Decolonialidad* del saber-poder informativa y nueva Comunicología Latinoamericana. Una lectura crítica de la mediación desde las culturas indígenas', *Chasqui. Revista Latinoamericana de Comunicación* 131 (April-June, 2016).
39   Milan, 'Toward an Epistemology of Engaged Research.'; Milan & Milan, 'Involving Communities as Skilled Learners: The STRAP Framework.'.
40   Milan, 'The Ethics of Social Movement Research', in Donatella della Porta (ed.), *Methodological Practices in Social Movement Research*, Oxford: Oxford University Press, 2014. See also Graeme Chesters, 'Social Movements and the Ethics of Knowledge Production', *Social Movement Studies*, 11.2 (2012); Milan & Milan, 'Involving Communities as Skilled Learners: The STRAP Framework'; Donatella Della Porta and Elena Pavan, 'Repertoires of Knowledge Practices: Social Movements in Times of Crisis', *Qualitative Research in Organizations and Management*, 12.4 (2017).
41   See for instance Lorenzo Pezzani and Charles Heller, 'A Disobedient Gaze: Strategic Interventions in the Knowledge(s) of Maritime Borders'; Andreas Birkbak, Morten Krogh Petersen and Torben Elgaard Jensen, 'Critical Proximity as a Methodological Move in Techno-Anthropology', *Techné: Research in Philosophy and Technology*, 19.2 (2015).

it? What core values guide us in the process?[42] From this perspective research is a social process that demands a careful consideration of 'for whom' and 'to what end' it is conducted.[43]

How, then, do we enable collaborative data activist research? This question addresses how the relations between, and the engagement of researchers, activists, and wider civil society look like.[44] Charlotte Ryan has highlighted the importance of working in cycles of dialogue rather than a one-off exchange, continuously assessing the meaningfulness of one's research and the conditions of inequality between researchers and activist/communities.[45] As we have mentioned before, a collaborative, dialogue-based data-activist research methodology that fosters the process of community building and knowledge sharing has to depart from a joint reflection on what knowledge and its production mean, and what building a 'we' entails. However, no process by itself has the ability to erase power asymmetries - imbalances can very well occur within activist communities themselves along lines of race, class, gender, expertise, etc. Therefore, processes of collective research design and analysis need to take into account the power asymmetries prevalent among the actors involved and consciously reduce space for hierarchies. What are, then, the building blocks of an ethics of data-activist research?

The Ethics of Data-Activist Research

Within a data-activist research methodology, ethics should be understood as a process rather than a mere checklist. In conceiving of it as a process we take inspiration from the ethics guidelines by the Association of Internet Researchers (AoIR),[46] and feminist 'ethics of care',[47] which puts a caring relationship with research subjects at centre stage. In what follows, we offer a list of potential starting points in thinking about research ethics.

1. Do no harm

Data-activist research goes beyond the idea of attempting not to negatively impact the communities involved. The guideline is to collectively bring about a difference for such communities,

---

42 See Ryan in DATACTIVE, 'Workshop Report'.
43 The discipline of Social Movement Studies has to some extent engaged with the question of making research relevant for the research subjects. See e.g. David Croteau, William Hoynes and Charlotte Ryan (eds), *Rhyming Hope and History: Activists, Academics, and Social Movement Scholarship*, Minneapolis: University of Minnesota Press, 2005; the Special issue on 'The Ethics of Research on Activism', *Social Movement Studies*, 11.2 (2012); Milan, 'The Ethics of Social Movement Research'.
44 The concept of inclusive participation has been addressed in fields such as Critical Development Studies or communication for social change. See Alfonso Gumucio Dagron and Thomas Tufte (eds), *Communication for Social Change Anthology: Historical and Contemporary Readings*, South Orange NJ: Communication for Social Change Consortium, 2006. It is here that we also find an analytical/methodological account of dialogue: see e.g. Alejandro Barranquero, 'Rediscovering the Latin American Roots of Participatory Communication for Social Change', *Westminster Papers in Communication and Culture* 8.1 (May 2011); and Freire, 'Pedagogy of the Oppressed'.
45 See, for example, Ryan in DATACTIVE, 'Workshop Report'.
46 See AoIR, Ethical Decision-Making and Internet Research: Recommendations from the AoIR Ethics Working Committee (Version 2.0), https://aoir.org/reports/ethics2.pdf.
47 Virginia Held, *Ethics of Care*, New York/London: Oxford University Press, 2005.

aiming for a positive impact as one of the main outcomes of the research.[48] Researchers should ask whose goals the research does or might further serve, as well as what harms might come from having particular experiences or vulnerabilities exposed and made public as research findings.

2. Setting equitable research agendas

If we talk about data-activist research from a perspective centered on collaboration, one key consideration comes to mind: data, where it is meant to be produced and used in the interest of activists or the wider civil society, has to be representative of the needs and interests of those it means to 'support'.[49] However, from a methodological perspective, the reflection around collaboration must go beyond a focus on representation; it builds on the idea that people are in charge of the decision-making processes on which their very realities are constructed.[50] Also in the emerging field of data activism, in which data forms the main currency of engagement in advocacy tactics,[51] forms of collaboration and engagement with civil society in order to identify relevant tactics proves crucial for realizing representative data structures.[52]

3. Re-centering perspectives pushed to the periphery

Researchers should be critical of overly focusing on expert opinions, as these can be used as proxies for the issue or groups being studied, while much of the labor of knowledge production is being done elsewhere.[53] To this end, researchers should strive to look beyond the most prominent names when 'sampling' and selecting research subjects, and adopt a conscious strategy of seeking out expert opinions from underrepresented populations such as women, people of color, affected populations, and other minority groups.

4. Transparency of research objectives (and funding)

Researchers should disclose the aims of their projects and communicate the 'why' of the research to those involved in any research activities - whether an interview, ethnographic participant observation or a joint policy advocacy project. Researchers should be clear that theirs is not a 'view from nowhere', but a situated perspective.[54] Issues of class, race, and locality of the researchers should be reflected upon within the research.

---

48 Anderson, 'Do no harm'; Milan, 'Toward an epistemology of engaged research'.
49 Linnet Taylor and Dennis Broeders, 'In the Name of Development: Power, Profit and the Datafication of the Global South', *Geoforum* 64 (August, 2015).
50 Freire, 'Pedagogy of the Oppressed'.
51 Milan and Velden, 'The Alternative Epistemologies of Data Activism'.
52 Geoffrey Bowker and Susan Leigh Star, *Sorting Things Out: Classification and Its Consequences*, Cambridge MA: MIT Press, 1999.
53 In DATACTIVE, 'Workshop Report'.
54 Haraway, 'Situated Knowledges'.

5. Recognizing research as labor

Researchers should understand that interacting with researchers and 'being researched' is a form of labor.[55] Sitting in for interviews or engaging in other research activities takes time away from urgent work, including gaining an income. Thus, researchers should strive to minimize disruptions caused by their participation in activities.[56] On the other hand, there may be instances in which researchers should also clearly lay out expectations around their own labor of research, for example, by explaining why it might take a certain amount of time for findings to be 'fed back' or published.[57]

6. Contextualizing data and data collection

Researchers should examine the context and potential consequences of studying communities, identities, projects, networks, and dynamics. Some data that is considered public is actually just 'publicly available (sensitive) data.[58] A minimum standard for much of social science research is to obtain the consent of research subjects. Yet in projects using 'big data', this can be difficult. Data-activist researchers should thus put adequate attention to strategizing how they will anonymize any data they use on online communities and consider if it is ethical to collect it in the first place - and they should be up to date with respect to data protection regulations which might prohibit its collection.

7. Responsible data management and sharing

Researchers should strive to create an information management plan prioritizing the privacy and security of research data. The development of a plan should root itself in the particular scenarios of the research life and should consider all phases of a research project.[59] This also includes a plan of how to store and back up research data; how to share data with other researchers; how to transport data while traveling across borders; how to guard data while at field sites; and how to communicate sensitive details within the research team as well as with research subjects.

8. Fair attribution

Researchers should provide correct attribution, anonymizing and pseudonymizing as necessary, or should mention interviewees by name if requested. This is a fundamental step in the recognition of social actors as knowledge producers in their own right, no less than external observers.

---

55 Arne Hintz and Stefania Milan, 'Social science is police science: Researching grassroots activism', *International Journal of Communication* 4 (2010).
56 Ibid.
57 See Ryan in DATACTIVE, 'Workshop Report'.
58 Jacob Metcalf and Kate Crawford. 'Where Are Human Subjects in Big Data Research? The Emerging Ethics Divide', *Big Data & Society* 3.1 (January, 2016).
59 Milan and Milan, 'Involving Communities as Skilled Learners: The STRAP Framework'.

9. Sharing research results

An ethical stance forces researchers to 'share back' with their informants. Are research subjects able to access the work they have contributed to freely, or are publications beyond paywall? Are research subjects able to provide feedback and discuss findings (in terms of time and accessibility of language) before it is published? For example, our hope within the DATACTIVE project is that researching strategies to enhance privacy, digital security, and open source investigations in the midst of human rights and social justice related activities can provide useful information back to civil society actors for their own purposes.

Conclusions and Open Issues

In this chapter we have dealt with a number of methodological and ethical questions that need to be addressed while using and producing data to fuel political projects in the interest of society at large. With the help of four examples, we discussed several aspects from the field of data activism that researchers - particularly those aiming to work with (data) activists - could incorporate in their own work. We have taken a brief look over matters of (disobedient) data research, collaboration and empowerment, and data ethics. These examples have helped us to build a series of recommendations for researchers in light of our own interest in developing joint research projects between data activists and academia. Much work is however needed to expand the range of problems and solutions addressed in a data-activist fashion. Only a broad, collaborative discussion can help us moving this agenda forward: we thus call upon the engaged-researchers and researching-activists across the globe to experiment and share in a long-term exercise of re-thinking what doing 'research that matters' means in the age of datafication.

References

Anderson, Mary B. *Do No Harm. How Aid Can Support Peace or War*, Boulder CO/London, 1999.

Barranquero, Alejandro. 'Rediscovering the Latin American Roots of Participatory Communication for Social Change', *Westminster Papers in Communication and Culture* 8.1 (2011), 154–177.

Birkbak, Andreas, Morten Krogh Petersen, Torben Elgaard Jensen, and Philosophy Documentation Center. 'Critical Proximity as a Methodological Move in Techno Anthropology', *Techné: Research in Philosophy and Technology* 19.2 (2015): 266-90.

Bowker, G, and SL Star. *Sorting Things Out: Classification and Its Consequences*. Cambridge MA: MIT Press, 1999.

Bruno, Isabel, Emmanuel Didier and Tommaso Vitale. 'Statactivism: forms of action between disclosure and affirmation', *Partecipazione e conflitto. The Open Journal of Sociopolitical Studies* 7 (2014), 198-220.

Chesters, Graeme. 'Social Movements and the Ethics of Knowledge Production', *Social Movement Studies* 11.2 (1 April, 2012): 145-60.

Dagron, Alfonso Gumucio, and Thomas Tufte (eds). *Communication for Social Change Anthology: Historical and Contemporary Readings*, South Orange NJ: Communication for Social Change Consortium, 2006.

Dalton, Craig M, Linnet Taylor, and Jim Thatcher. 'Critical Data Studies: A Dialog on Data and Space', *Big Data & Society* 3.1 (2016).

DATACTIVE. 'Workshop Report: Data for the Social Good', Amsterdam: University of Amsterdam, November 2017.

Della Porta, Donatella, and Elena Pavan. 'Repertoires of Knowledge Practices: Social Movements in Times of Crisis', *Qualitative Research in Organizations and Management: An International Journal* 12.4 (2017): 297-314.

Michel Foucault. *The Will to Knowledge: The History of Sexuality:* 1, London: Penguin Books, 1998 [1976].

Freire, Paulo. *Pedagogy of the Oppressed*, New York: Herder and Herder, 1968.

Haggerty, Kevin D., and Richard V. Ericson. 'The Surveillant Assemblage', *The British Journal of Sociology*, 51.4 (2000): 605-22.

Haraway, Donna. 'Situated Knowledges: The Science Question in Feminism and the Privilege of Partial Perspective', *Feminist Studies* 14.3 (1988): 575-99.

Heller, Charles, Lorenzo Pezzani, and Maurice Stierl. 'Disobedient Sensing and Border Struggles at the Maritime Frontier of Europe', *Spheres: Journal for Digital Cultures*, 4 (2017), http://spheres-journal.org/disobedient-sensing-and-border-struggles-at-the-maritime-frontier-of-europe/.

Hill, Kashmir. 'What Happens When You Tell the Internet You're Pregnant', *Jezebel*, https://jezebel.com/what-happens-when-you-tell-the-internet-youre-pregnant-1794398989.

Jolivette, Andrew J. *Research Justice: Methodologies for Social Change*, Bristol: Policy Press, 2015.

Knorr-Cetina, Karin, and Werner Reichmann. 'Epistemic Cultures', in *International Encyclopedia of the Social & Behavioral Sciences* (Second Edition), Oxford: Elsevier, 873-80, http://www.sciencedirect.com/science/article/pii/B9780080970868104544.

Kubitschko, Sebastian. 'Acting on Media Technologies and Infrastructures: Expanding the Media as Practice Approach', *Media, Culture & Society* 40.4 (May 2018): 629-35.

Lovink, Geert and Ned Rossiter. *Organization after Social Media*, Colchester: Minor Compositions, 2018.

Mayer-Schönberger, Viktor, and Kenneth Cukier. *Big Data: A Revolution That Will Transform How We Live, Work, and Think*, Boston: Houghton Mifflin Harcourt, 2013.

Metcalf, Jacob, and Kate Crawford. 'Where Are Human Subjects in Big Data Research? The Emerging Ethics Divide', *Big Data & Society* 3.1 (2016).

Milan, Chiara, and Stefania Milan. 'Involving Communities as Skilled Learners: The STRAP Framework,' in Norbert Wildermuth and Teke Ngomba (eds), *Methodological Reflections on Researching Communication and Social Change*, Cham: Springer, 2016, 9-28.

Milan, Stefania. 'Between Datafication and Encryption: Media Activism in Times of Big Data', Annenberg School of Communication: University of Pennsylvania, 2014.

---------. 'Data Activism as the New Frontier of Media Activism', in Goubin Yang and Viktor Pickard (eds), *Media Activism in the Digital Age*, Oxford: Routledge, 2017.

---------. 'The Ethics of Social Movement Research', in *Methodological Practices in Social Movement Research*, 446-64. Oxford: Oxford University Press, 2014.

---------. 'Toward an Epistemology of Engaged Research', *International Journal of Communication* 4 (2010): 856-58.

Milan, Stefania, and Miren Gutiérrez. 'Technopolitics in the Age of Big Data', in F. Sierra Caballero & T. Gravante (eds.), *Networks, Movements & Technopolitics in Latin America: Critical Analysis and Current Challenges,* London: Palgrave MacMillan, 2017, pp. 95-109.

Milan, Stefania and Niels ten Oever. 'Coding and encoding rights in internet infrastructure', *Internet Policy Review*, 6.1 (2017).

Milan, Stefania, and Lonneke van der Velden. 'The Alternative Epistemologies of Data Activism', *Digital Culture & Society,* 2.2 (2016): 57-74.

Pezzani, Lorenzo, and Charles Heller. 'A Disobedient Gaze: Strategic Interventions in the Knowledge(s) of Maritime Borders', *Postcolonial Studies* 16.3 (September 2013): 289-98.

Ryan, Charlotte, V., Salas-Wright, M. Anastario and G. Camara. 'Making Research Matter... Matter to Whom', *International Journal of Communication* 4 (2010): 845-55.

Ryan, C. and K. Jeffreys. 'The Practice of Collaborative Theorizing', Unpublished manuscript (2008).

Tactical Technology Collective and Becky Kazansky. 'FCJ-195 Privacy, Responsibility, and Human Rights Activism', *The Fibreculture Journal* 26 (2015): 190-208.

Taylor, Linnet, and Dennis Broeders. 'In the Name of Development: Power, Profit and the Datafication of the Global South', *Geoforum* 64 (2015): 229-37.

Velden, Lonneke van der. 'Leaky Apps and Data Shots: Technologies of Leakage and Insertion in NSA Surveillance', *Surveillance & Society* 13.2 (2015): 182-96.

Wildermuth, Norbert, and Teke Ngomba (eds). *Methodological Reflections on Researching Communication and Social Change*, Cham: Springer, 2016.

Wolfinger, Emily. '"But it's Already Public, Right?": The Ethics of Using Online Data', http://datadrivenjournalism.net/news_and_analysis/but_its_already_public_right_the_ ethics_of_using_online_data.

Zimmer, Michael. '"But the Data Is Already Public": On the Ethics of Research in Facebook.', *Ethics and Information Technology* 12.4 (2010): 313-25.

15: GOOD DATA IS CRITICAL DATA: AN APPEAL FOR CRITICAL DIGITAL STUDIES

CHIARA POLETTI AND DANIEL GRAY

Introduction

In social science, approaches that call themselves critical tend to be concerned with advancing some kind of emancipatory political cause, often drawing in some way on Marxian perspectives. In Fairclough's words, such approaches ask, 'how do existing societies provide people with the possibilities and resources for rich and fulfilling lives, how on the other hand do they deny people these possibilities and resources?'. They are critical of prevailing social and material relations, and the ideologies that justify these unequal relations. Critical digital research is a field of study that often focuses on the tip of the spear of ideology and capitalist production in contemporary society. In this chapter we will discuss different critical approaches to this field, and how they relate to ethical standards and good data, arguing that they demand new ideas in terms of what research we do, and how we do it.

Data produced by people in their online interactions and transactions has become a vital tool and commodity in digital capitalism, and is likewise vitally important for many areas of critical digital studies: we cannot analyse online sociality, interaction and labor unless we have data produced by these processes. Digital social data present troubling questions for critical digital researchers: What can be a way to improve knowledge and understanding of digital society while fostering an ethical approach towards digital data? How can we make sure that academics avoid harming subjects? and at the same time, how can we avoid reinforcing structures of domination/exploitation in our data collection, storage and dissemination? In short, what is 'Good Data' when it comes to critical research? In this chapter we want to use a Marxian perspective as well as theoretical ideas developed in critical media studies and digital sociology to discuss the use of digital data, and suggest a methodology based on a critical ethical approach. We will begin by discussing the online context where this data is produced, and providing an overview of ethical and methodological literature related to digital social data, before we focus in particular on the works of Christian Fuchs, Antonio Casilli and Karen Gregory. We have selected these authors because we feel that together they provide a politico-economic interpretation of digital social data. Through this, we will advance the argument that 'Good Data' is data that can be used to highlight and critique the power dynamics connected to the use of digital social data, by stressing the particular economic and technological environment from where they are generated.

Digital social data and platforms

Under contemporary capitalism, digital data is becoming increasingly central in the relationship between companies, workers and consumers, and a new site of growth and profitability following the decline in manufacturing.[1] This is most visible in areas of global informational capitalism, where data is exploited by giant transnational corporations (Google, Apple, Facebook, Amazon, and Microsoft etc). In this context, 'The platform has emerged as a new business model, capable of extracting and controlling immense amounts of data':[2] platforms enroll people in the production process, and provide a variety of services or commodities on a peer-to-peer level. These can be social interactions, as in Facebook or Twitter, or services such as Airbnb, Uber, Deliveroo and so on. Data are at the centre of this 'platform capitalism'.[3] 'Clicks', 'likes', 'tweets', as well as geolocation, traffic information, food preferences, and all other activities and behaviors that leave digital traces (including body data from wearable devices), are routinely gathered and monetized by platforms. User-generated data, either as a by-product of transactions or as metadata produced within platforms online, are very valuable for data brokers, data analytics industries, advertisement companies, artificial intelligence developers, but also public bodies such as intelligence agencies.[4]

Despite their massive value, the public lacks awareness of the importance of their digital data. Platforms emphasize the joy of participation rather than the 'costs' connected to these services, creating an opaque system where the majority of users (with the exception of technologists, activists and academics) are generally unaware of their role in generating value for companies. Only very recently, with the Cambridge Analytica case, a public discussion has started. Cambridge Analytica has demonstrated how the personal data of Facebook users (and similar platforms) are routinely employed without their full awareness by corporations interested not only in commercial but also political targeting and 'surveillance capitalism'.

Methodological and Ethical Problems Raised by Academics About Digital Data

Discussions about opportunities and limitations of digital social data have run for almost a decade. Scholars have been particularly concerned with the possible ways to adapt methodologies to these new data,[5] and the relationship between 'old' methods and new 'natively

---

1   Nick Srnicek, *Platform Capitalism*, Cambridge: Polity Press, 2017.
2   Ibid, p.5.
3   Ibid.
4   Antonio Casilli, Digital Labor Studies Go Global: Toward a Digital Decolonial Turn, *International Journal of Communication* 11 (2017): 3934-3954; Karen Gregory, *The Future of Work*, Public Services International Congress, Geneva, Switzerland (2018) http://congress.world-psi.org/karen-gregory-talks-about-the-negatives-and-positives-of-computer-platform-capitalism/.
5   Mike Savage and Roger Burrows, 'The Coming Crisis of Empirical Sociology', *Sociology,* 41.5 (2007): 885-899, DOI: 10.1177/0038038507080443; danah boyd and Kate Crawford, 'Critical Questions for Big Data: Provocations for a Cultural, Technological, and Scholarly Phenomenon', *Information, Communication, & Society* 15.5 (2012): 662-679; Adam Edwards et al, 'Digital Social Research, Social Media and the Sociological Imagination: surrogacy, re-orientation and augmentation', *International Journal of Social Research Methodology,*16.3 (2013): 245-260; Zeynep Tufekci, 'Big Questions for Social Media Big Data: Representativeness, Validity and Other Methodological Pitfalls', in *ICWSM '14: Proceedings of the 8th International AAAI Conference on Weblogs and Social Media*, 2014; Noortje Marres and Carolin Gerlitz, 'Interface methods: renegotiating relations between digital social research', *The Sociological Review* 64 (2016): 21-46, DOI: 10.1111/1467-954X.12314.

digital' methods.[6] Optimistic and pessimistic views have piled up. A 'computational turn' in social research, initially fuelled by enthusiasm for the opportunities of volume, velocity and variety of 'Big Data'[7] has been especially influential, but also widely criticized. Authors have stressed the shortcomings of user-generated data (e.g. not suitable for statistical sampling), especially when coupled with a strong 'data-driven'/empirical approach.[8] Big Data have been especially troubling because of their ideological implications: the belief that if 'bigger is better', and if we can analyse large data sets, then the type of knowledge produced will be truer, more objective and accurate.[9] In contrast, more critical approaches to data studies have stressed that data are 'never simply neutral, objective, independent, raw representations of the world',[10] but are produced by - and influence - economy, society, and knowledge.[11] This is why stronger normative reflections on the ethics and politics of digital data and the role of researchers are urgently needed.[12]

Debates on the ethics of digital social data have been developing for the past 20 years.[13] Internet research ethics, and particularly their practical application in the context of ethical approval of research projects, are geographically and historically contingent. It is important to acknowledge that what is considered best practice can vary a great deal by time and place. In their overview of the preceding of 20 years of internet research ethics, Elizabeth Buchanan emphasises that early ethical issues and positions, drawing on biomedical conceptions of

---

6   Richard Rogers, *Digital Methods*, Cambridge MA: MIT Press, 2015.
7   Chris Anderson, 'The End of Theory: The Data Deluge Makes the Scientific Method Obsolete', *Wired* 16.7 (2008); David M. Berry, 'The computational turn: Thinking about the digital humanities' *Culture Machine*, 12 (2011) http://www.culturemachine.net/index.php/cm/article/view/440/470; Rob Kitchin, 'Big Data, new epistemologies and paradigm shifts', *Big Data & Society* (April-June 2014): 1-12.
8   Craig Dalton and Jim Thatcher, 'What does a critical data studies look like, and why do we care? Seven points for a critical approach to "big data."' *Society and Space* (2014) http://societyandspace.org/2014/05/12/what-does-a-critical-data-studies-look-like-and-why-do-we-care-craig-dalton-and-jim-thatcher/.
9   danah boyd and Kate Crawford, 'Critical Questions for Big Data: Provocations for a Cultural, Technological, and Scholarly Phenomenon', *Information, Communication, & Society* 15.5 (2012): 662-679; Rob Kitchin, *Big Data, new epistemologies and paradigm shifts;* Cornelius Puschmann and Jean Burgess, 'Big Data, Big Questions, Metaphors of Big Data', *International Journal of Communication*, 8 (2014): 1690-1709, DOI: 1932- 8036/20140005; Merja Mahrt and Michael Scharkow, 'The value of big data in digital media research', *Journal of Broadcasting & Electronic Media*, 57.1 (2013): 20-33, DOI:10.1080/08838151.2012.761700.
10 Rob Kitchin and Tracey P. Lauriault, 'Towards critical data studies: Charting and unpacking data assemblages and their work', in J Eckert, A Shears and J Thatcher (eds), *Geoweb and Big Data*, Lincoln: University of Nebraska Press, 2014; Craig Dalton and Jim Thatcher, 'What does a critical data studies look like, and why do we care? Seven points for a critical approach to "big data."'.
11 Evelyn Ruppert, John Law and Mike Savage, 'Reassembling Social Science Methods: The Challenge of Digital Devices', *Theory, Culture & Society*, 30.4 (2013): 22-46; Karen Gregory, *The Labor of Digital Scholarship*, talk given at the University of Edinburgh (2017), audio and slides available: https://ed.hosted.panopto.com/Panopto/Pages/Viewer.aspx?id=41552549-5650-4cdf-bf62-05999534c270.
12 Rob Kitchin and Tracey P. Lauriault, 'Towards critical data studies: Charting and unpacking data assemblages and their work'.
13 Elizabeth Buchanan, 'Internet Research Ethics Twenty Years Later', in Michael Zimmer and Katharina Kinder-Kurlanda (eds), *Internet Research Ethics for the Social Age*, New York: Peter Lang Publishing, 2017, pp. xxix-xxxiii.

research participants and concerned with fundamental questions, were problematised by the emergence of the social internet, and challenged again by the increasing prominence of Big Data research.[14] The rapid pace of change driving digital technologies has consistently presented new challenges for ethical research standards. For contemporary researchers, Big Data is of particular concern. Conceptualising Big Data as a social phenomenon as well as a collection of technologies, boyd and Crawford define it as interplay of phenomena, combining the technologies of very large data sets, the tools and techniques to analyse them, and the resulting '*Mythology*' of knowledge claims associated with this technology and analysis.[15] In this paper we are concerned with Big Data associated with 'social media interactions',[16] but Big Data itself extends far beyond social media, and into many disciplines and industries besides digital social science. In discussing the ethical implications of Big Data, boyd and Crawford emphasise what are now familiar issues: the ambiguity around public and private spaces, as well as issues around informed consent and potential harm, and the 'highly context-sensitive' nature of online spaces .[17] While they argue that it 'may be unreasonable to ask researchers to obtain consent from every person who posts a tweet',[18] they are also skeptical of approaches that treat publicly available social data as 'fair game' simply because it is public. Overall, they stress that ethically sound research should reflect on issues of accountability, 'both to the field of research and to the research subjects',[19] which involves considering the implications of a given research project.

Similarly, Zimmer[20] uses Nissenbaum's[21] idea of 'Contextual integrity' as a decision heuristic to help researchers to understand and address the ethical dimensions of big data research projects. The theory of contextual integrity ties adequate privacy protection to the preservation of informational norms within in specific contexts, providing a framework for evaluating the flow of personal information between agents to help identify and explain why certain patterns of information flow are acceptable in one context, but viewed as problematic in another.

While our research has occurred in a British context, what counts as ethical internet research can vary extensively by country, and even institution. Based in Denmark, Klastrup states that at the time of their research, Danish universities did not have ethical review boards, nor formal standards for ethical internet research, instead utilising a system of 'collegial mentoring', though even in this case the AoIR guidelines were adhered to by many researchers.[22] In a specifically United States context, the rapid pace of technological change appears to have led to a situation where 'research regulations have not kept up with the methods and stake-

---

14   Ibid.
15   Danah boyd and Kate Crawford. *Critical Questions for Big Data*.
16   Ibid, p.663.
17   Ibid, p.673.
18   Ibid, p.672.
19   Ibid, p.672.
20   Michael Zimmer, 'Addressing Conceptual Gaps in Big Data Research Ethics: an Application of Contextual Integrity'. *Social Media + Society*, 4.2 (2018).
21   Helen Nissenbaum, 'Privacy as contextual integrity', *Washington Law Review* (2004): 79, 119-157.
22   Lisbeth Klastrup, 'Death, Affect and the Ethical Challenges of Outing a Griefsquatter', in Michael Zimmer and Katharina Kinder-Kurlanda (eds), *Internet Research Ethics for the Social Age*, New York: Peter Lang Publishing, 2017, pp. 235-243.

holders', [23] typified by the lack of regulatory response to the infamous Facebook contagion study.[24] And although there were widespread debates around the issue, there is still a lack of broad institutional consensus as to whether such studies are even unethical.[25] Discussing internet research ethics in a non-western context, Honglandarom[26] highlights that internet research in Thailand 'apparently suffers from lack of attention to ethical concerns',[27] due to a lack of clear national or institutional guidelines and awareness, which they argue is broadly the case 'for other Asian countries also'.[28] Some, however, are more similar to our experience of ethical review in a British university in terms of restrictions. In their discussion of the Canadian system, where a national ethical framework is applied by individual institutional ethical review boards, Seko and Lewis [29] emphasise that there exists a 'gap in pragmatic guidelines' in how to best apply ethical judgements concerning internet research.[30] This lack of clear guidelines, combined with the 'Unique ethical issues' presented by the blurred private/public divide,[31] difficulties in maintaining participant anonymity, and difficulties in obtaining informed consent can lead reviews to '*err on the side of caution*'.[32] Clearly there is variation in how researchers across the world experience obtaining ethical approval, likely exacerbated by the aforementioned newness of internet technologies and research methods.

In discussing other dimensions of digital ethics, some authors have stressed that a robust approach should interrogate how subjectivity is constructed in research datasets.[33] However this storing of user data in datasets can complicate the traditional identification of subjects, and methods to protect personal data can still leave participants identifiably, making consent and anonymity almost impossible to attain. Metcalf and Crawford stress how precursor disciplines such as data science computer science, applied mathematics and statistics have not historically conducted human-subject research.[34] As with some of the cases outlined above, in many situations researchers are left to rely on the underlying principles and guidelines

---

23   Elizabeth Buchanan, 'Internet Research Ethics Twenty Years Later', in Michael Zimmer and Katharina Kinder-Kurlanda (eds), *Internet Research Ethics for the Social Age*, New York: Peter Lang Publishing, 2017, p. xxxii.
24   Adam D.I. Kramer et al, 'Experimental evidence of massive-scale emotional contagion through social networks', *Proceedings of the National Academy of Sciences of the United States of America*, 111.24 (2014): 8788.
25   Elizabeth Buchanan, 'Internet Research Ethics Twenty Years Later', p.xxxii.
26   Soraj Hongladarom, 'Internet Research Ethics in a Non-Western Context', in Michael Zimmer and Katharina Kinder-Kurlanda (eds), *Internet Research Ethics for the Social Age,* New York: Peter Lang Publishing, 2017, pp. 151-163.
27   Ibid, p.159.
28   Ibid, p.152.
29   Yukari Seko and Stephen P. Lewis, '"We Tend to Err on the Side of Caution" Ethical Challenges Facing Canadian Research Ethics Boards When Overseeing Internet Research', in Michael Zimmer and Katharina Kinder-Kurlanda (eds), *Internet Research Ethics for the Social Age*, New York: Peter Lang Publishing, 2017, pp. 133-147.
30   Ibid, p.135.
31   Ibid, p.143.
32   Ibid, p.143.
33   Jacob Metcalf & Kate Crawford, 'Where are human subjects in big data research? The emerging ethics divide'. *Big Data & Society*, 3.1 (2016): 1-14, DOI: doi:10.1177/2053951716650211.
34   Ibid.

of general research ethics 'stemming from shared principles of respect, beneficence, and justice',[35] as well as principles of informed consent as 'a general rule'.[36] One prominent set of ethical guidelines are those produced by the Association of Internet Researchers (AoIR). As Ess discusses, in the 2002 first AoIR guidelines 'primary ethical theories and approaches rested on the assumption that human identity is primarily singular and individual'.[37] However, he stresses how our idea of identity has changed towards a more relational and collective conception. Necessarily the idea of subject protection has to change towards a broader and more inclusive conception of the different relationships (familial, social, natural, and so on) that compose identity. In 2012, AoIR guidelines extended the basic ethical tenets (i.e. fundamental rights of human dignity, autonomy, protection, safety, maximization of benefits and minimization of harms for research subjects) to digital research, at the same time stressing the necessity to maintain a processual and flexible approach.[38] In general, it is recognised that a 'one-size-fits-all' approach with regard to ethical decision-making is not viable. Researchers have been developing empirical approaches to data collection and reproduction aimed at reducing harms to subjects in research, for example by reconstructing empirical examples, or making required changes in order to maintain the original meaning and message while ensuring the original content cannot be retrieved through searches.[39]

In our view one of the most important aspects, as it has been stressed by Savage and Burrows, boyd and Crawford as well as Andrejevic and others, is the fundamental role of the specific production system where the data are created and collected. Ten years ago, Mike Savage and Roger Burrows argued that the mechanisms of capitalist organisation of society were challenging the empirical methods in sociology.[40] Thanks to digital technologies, research and social data produced and gathered by private actors outside academia were multiplying. They recognized the necessity for a critical methodological approach, a 'politics of methods', challenging the collection, use and deployment of social data produced by 'knowing capitalism'. Despite this, they did not especially explore the ethical implications that follow from critical methodological innovation and research.[41] However, Savage and Burrows raised the point that academic research is now competing with market research, and it is no longer the dominant party when it comes to providing interpretations of society. boyd and Crawford use the concept of 'ecosystem' to describe the new set of actors connected to the analysis of

---

35 Michael Zimmer, 'Addressing Conceptual Gaps in Big Data Research Ethics: an Application of Contextual Integrity', p.2.
36 Katrine Utaaker Segadal, 'Possibilities and limitations of Internet research: A legal framework', in Hallvard Fossheim and Helene Ingierd (eds), *Internet Research Ethics*, Oslo: Cappelen Damm Akademisk, 2015.
37 Charles Ess, 'New selves, New research ethics?', in Hallvard Fossheim and Helene Ingierd, *Internet Research Ethics*, Oslo: Cappelen Damm Akademisk, 2015, p.48.
38 Ethical Decision-Making and Internet Research: Recommendations from the AoIR Ethics Committee. Approved by the Ethics Working Committee (Version 2.0), 08/2012.
39 Marika Lüders, 'Researching social media: Confidentiality, anonymity and reconstructing online practices', in Hallvard Fossheim and Helene Ingierd. *Internet Research Ethics*. Oslo: Cappelen Damm Akademisk, 2015.
40 Savage and Burrows, *The Coming Crisis of Empirical Sociology*.
41 Ibid, p.896.

digital data and the power relationship that exists between them.[42] Given this, it is increasingly apparent that the technological and economical structure of platforms is the crucial aspect when dealing with digital data in research.

Mark Andrejevic presents a critical account of the economic system where digital data, and Big Data are produced, shared and processed.[43] In particular, Big Data allows the largest amount of information to be available (Andrejevic calls it 'infoglut'), while data mining and automated processing have become the core tenet of economic, marketing and research methods. In this system, traditional concepts such as anonymity and privacy lose their place, as even though subjects names are anonymised, their information is systematically gathered and stored by automated systems that have interest in profiling groups rather than individuals. Moreover, these systems complicate the reliability of data, as the data we use, especially content data, are data that are created in the specific context of platform capitalism. Platforms' algorithms curate and edit contents automatically. Recommendations and automated system of curations have built-in priorities that have nothing to do with content, but rather with the response they can get (in terms of likes, retweets...). This may present the risk that researchers who are using data uncritically risk basing their research on data that is unduly influenced by the economic dynamic where it was created.

Based on this, a challenge for critical researchers is to produce valid, ethical research in an ecosystem of capitalist production, while being under pressure from private industry, and ethical regulations that differ from one country to another. One possible approach to this is through the concept 'accountability', which can be understood as more encompassing than the concept of privacy protection.[44] As we have outlined above, accountability is not only directed towards the research subject, but also towards the research field in a broader sense. Accountability implies reflecting on the consequences of research related to individuals, organizations and the public sphere, and towards potential shifts in the ecosystem regarding the production, collection and analysis of digital data. What can be a way to improve knowledge and understanding of digital society while fostering an ethical approach towards digital data? How can we make sure that academics avoid harming subjects? and at the same time avoid reinforcing structures of domination/exploitation in our data collection/storage and dissemination? In short, what is 'good data' when it comes to critical research? In formulating these questions we are particularly drawing on Staksrud,[45] whose questions for digital social research capture concerns for ethical treatment of participants, as well as a concern for critical and original inquiry. What we find fundamental in ethical assessment of the use of digital data in research is that: Digital social data are generated and circulated within a very specific technological, political, social and above all economic order and, what

---

42 Kari Steen-Johnsen and Bernard Enjolras, 'Social research and Big Data - the tension between opportunities and realities', in Hallvard Fossheim and Helene Ingierd. *Internet Research Ethics*, Oslo: Cappelen Damm Akademisk, 2015.
43 Mark Andrejevic, *Infoglut: how too much information is changing the way we think and know*. New York: Routledge, 2013.
44 danah boyd and Kate Crawford. *Critical Questions for Big Data*.
45 Elisabeth Staksrud, 'Counting Children', in Hallvard Fossheim, and Helene Ingierd. *Internet Research Ethics,* Oslo: Cappelen Damm Akademisk, 2015.

we do as researchers, the type of data we choose and the methods we use, actively shape, change or re-shape this order.[46]

A critical approach to ethics

Here we will draw together the work of Antonio Casilli, Christian Fuchs and Karen Gregory, to suggest a critical approach to ethics that considers the economic and political order at the origin of digital social data. These authors share similar perspectives on good data in digital research, stressing the necessity to ground data ethics in a critique of neoliberal economic system and digital labor. We will build on their work to suggest that good data is data conceived in a way that emphasizes the role of the internet in the extension and reproduction of capitalist relations of production and subjectivity, and is used for positive, progressive political and social change through critical, empirical research. The authors (Fuchs, Casilli, Gregory) challenge the positive idea of digital social data and related ideas of 'participatory culture', by considering economic and political relations, and seeing social media as capitalist relations of production extended into an online space. Researchers have to contrast the positive rhetoric associated with big data and platforms, helping to raise critical awareness of the issues related to digital social data. In this view, good data are the ones that help pointing out the subordination processes enacted through the platform economy, with the explicit aim of obtaining the recognition of fundamental rights for users, the redistribution of the value extracted by users' data and the rebalancing of power relations connected to digital technologies. At the same time researchers can reach outside academia and valorize the initiatives of civil society, unions and other movements also by using the very same platform structure for the purpose of creating a democratic programme, based on the idea of commons, abolition of wage labor and private property.[47]

Data as a product of labor

As we mentioned previously, platforms are elements of global informational capitalism,[48] and serve as an extension of capitalist material processes and tendencies into online spaces and infrastructure.[49] 'Platformization' (i.e. the gradual movement of companies towards a platform organisation) is at the origin of the increased amount of digital social data available to academic research.[50] In this system, social media users are essentially configured as laborers, who in their internet use perform different forms of work. Value in platform capitalism is captured and extracted from users' data.[51] This process is presented as an improvement in the supply of goods and services, either public or private, often instrumentalising concepts such as 'sharing', 'participation', 'collaboration' for commercial purposes. On Facebook the activities that users

---

46   Karen Gregory, 'Marx, Engels and the Critique of Academic Labor', *Workplace: The Journal for Academic Labor*, 28 (2016).
47   Antonio Casilli, 'Lavoro e capitalismo delle piattaforme'. Talk given at the Centro per la Riforma dello Stato, Roma, 7 November 2017.
48   Christian Fuchs. *Internet and Society, Social theory in the information age*, London: Routledge, 2008.
49   Christian Fuchs, *Social Media, A Critical Introduction*. Thousand Oaks: SAGE, 2014.
50   Antonio Casilli, 'Lavoro e capitalismo delle piattaforme'.
51   Ibid.

typically engage in all produce commodities in the form of information, social relationships and social networks. Facebook makes money off of these activities by selling ad space, and through targeted advertising, with users enabling this through the visibility and engagement their interactions generate, and by being the recipients of targeted advertising. These relations extend to other social media platforms: Twitter, YouTube and Google all make their money off of users' labor in similar ways.

Ethical problems from this point of view

As mentioned above, Big Data's nature is quite opaque, and when owned by private companies may be subject to restrictions and suffer from a lack of transparency. Moreover, as stressed by Andrejevic, data do not happen in a vacuum, they are produced within specific technological and economic environment. However, the algorithms that regulate data visibility, extraction and processing are closed for technical and commercial reasons. Digital social data are also at risk of discriminatory practices. Companies have been eroding privacy of users through the massive recovery of information about individuals (e.g. geolocalisation, expenses, health, opinions and behaviours). Cross-referencing users data, companies are able to profile individuals (also non users) into different 'populations' in order to direct advertisement and policies. Implicit in this 'data-veillance' system is the idea of intrusion, both from public as much as private actors (i.e. state surveillance revealed by Edward Snowden in 2013 and more recently Cambridge Analytica), which can lead to forms of discrimination, making it very easy to penalize individuals for their gender, age, ethnic origin, place of residence or socio-economic status. The rhetoric of choice and entrepreneurialism associated to the use of these platforms hides the social cost connected to these data, costs in terms of exploitation, privacy, and the extreme lack of transparency on their usage.[52] People are said to have a choice, and told that they can improve their opportunities through the use of these platforms, however all activities monetized by platforms are denied the 'materiality' as real work, eroding users of their rights, and profoundly enriching transnational companies. Created to parse users into database of population, digital data will never be neutral, as they are with all the concerns connected to the division of population into categories.[53] From this perspective, individual privacy without critique remains part of the neoliberal rhetoric behind digital platforms. Casilli highlights how in this diffuse system of surveillance and extraction of value, privacy can no longer be conceived as an individual, but rather as a collective right. Conceiving privacy as something that an individual can negotiate, contributes to maintain users' weakness in face of the giant corporations.[54]

---

52 Paola Tubaro and Antonio Casilli, 'Enjeux sociaux des Big Data' in Mokrane Bouzeghoub and Rémy Mosseri (eds), *Les Big Data à découvert*, Paris: CNRS Editions, 2017: 292-293.
53 Karen Gregory, *The Labor of Digital Scholarship*; Karen Gregory, *The Future of Work,* Public Services International Congress. Geneva, Switzerland, 2018. http://congress.world-psi.org/karen-gregory-talks-about-the-negatives-and-positives-of-computer-platform-capitalism/.
54 Antonio Casilli, 'Four Theses on Digital Mass Surveillance and the Negotiation Of Privacy', 8th Annual Privacy Law Scholar Congress, June 2015, Berkeley, United States, https://www.law.berkeley.edu/centers/berkeley-center-for-law-technology/upcoming- events/june-2015-the-8th-annual-privacy-law-scholars-conference/.
Antonio Casilli, 'Lavoro e capitalismo delle piattaforme'. Talk given at the Centro per la Riforma dello

Ethical approach in research

For Fuchs, research ethics is dominated by contradictory positions: on one hand 'big data positivism' contends that since social media data is generally public, both in visibility and in the sense that users are not guaranteed privacy by terms and conditions, privacy and ethical concerns can be disregarded. On the other hand, 'research ethics fundamentalism' argues that since user intention and the consequences of reproducing data cannot be guaranteed, informed consent should always be sought Fuchs.[55] Clearly, neither is ideal for critical social research, and while some more recent guidelines have recommended that digital scholars 'neither ignore nor fetishize' ethics in conducting research, there is a need to develop this position.[56]

Challenging dominant rhetoric

Researchers have to contrast the positive rhetoric associated to big data and platforms, helping to raise critical awareness of the issues related to digital social data. In this view, good data are the ones that help pointing out the subordination processes enacted through the platform economy, with the explicit aim of obtaining the recognition of fundamental rights for users, the redistribution of the value extracted by users' data and the rebalancing of power relations connected to digital technologies. At the same time researchers can reach outside academia and valorize the initiatives of civil society, unions and other movements also by using the very same platform structure for the purpose of creating a democratic programme, based on the idea of commons, abolition of wage labor and private property.[57]

Reflexivity

Drawing from Marx and Engel's historical materialist method, Gregory presents a critical definition of the work of digital researchers. Intellectual thought, ideas and concepts produced by academic work are themselves a product of the capitalist mode of production and contribute to reproduce the order.[58] For this reason, researchers should engage in a reflexive critique of methods and data, documenting and making more transparent the challenges presented by data created in a capitalist system of production. Against the common practice of omitting the discussions on complications, researchers have to make their methods more transparent, helping to understand how difficulties and obstacles contributed to shape their research. Such a reflexive approach is necessary to realize how we as academics are reproducing the world that we live in. In particular, digital researchers should help developing new political vocabulary, rethinking concepts and developing new methods and tools of analysis to create new models outside the profit-driven logic of the extractive system and move towards anti-racist

---

Stato, Roma 7 November 2017 https://www.dinamopress.it/news/event/lavoro-e-capitalismo-delle-piattaforme-con-antonio-casilli/.
55   Christian Fuchs, 'From digital positivism and administrative big data analytics towards critical digital and social media research!', *European Journal of Communication* 32.1 (2017): 37-49.
56   Christian Fuchs, *Digital Labour and Karl Marx*. New York: Routledge, 2014.
57   Antonio Casilli, 'Lavoro e capitalismo delle piattaforme'.
58   Karen Gregory, *Marx, Engels and the Critique of Academic Labor*.

justice, political, and economic solidarity.[59]

Fuchs' 'critical moral real[ist]'[60] approach is useful here. This position argues that since beliefs about the social world are themselves part of the social world, it is entirely appropriate for social scientists to make value judgments about them and to work towards resisting them through research. In the case of critical digital research, this means doing research in a way that works towards 'participatory democracy, freedom, justice, fairness and equality',[61] and opposes things that work against those goals. In short, a critical moral realist approach to social media may prioritize the political goal of critique of power over the interests of participants who are reproducing systems of power. Something similar to this position can be found in existing best practice: the Economic and Social Research Council (ESRC) framework for research ethics stipulates that it may be legitimate to expose research participants to risks, 'in cases where the objectives of the research are to reveal and critique fundamental economic, political or cultural disadvantage or exploitation'.[62] Even in this case of a major research council suggesting that the emancipatory objectives of research may justify the exposure of participants to risk, 'Principles of justice' should still guide researchers to minimise personal harm.[63] As such, critical research should not treat its motivations as carte-blanche justification for potentially harmful or risky practice.

What is to be done?

We began this chapter by posing questions around how researchers might develop a concept of good data that is rooted in an explicitly critical approach: one that allows for rigorous critical research that is cognizant of ethical issues, and also of the nature of social media as a form of capitalist production. Here, we will draw on the concepts we have discussed in order to address these questions.

In adopting more traditional, subject-oriented perspectives on ethical problems connected to digital data, researchers risk constructing users and data in a way that uncritically reproduces neoliberal approaches, becoming 'agents' of the same power system, which is problematic for research that seeks to build foundational critique of digital political economy, subjectivity and ideology online. A critical perspective that situates digital social data within the system of production where the data are produced highlights the exploitation and deep inequalities that are embodied in the data. Personal data online are a lucrative commodity and the basis of an extremely opaque and unequal commercial ecosystem, where users/workers are rarely aware of the different interests connected to them. Critical data scholars, such as Fuchs, Casilli and Gregory stress how data are being employed to produce risky social and economic relations: precarisation of work, data-veillance, profiling, algorithmic management of people.[64]

---

59 Karen Gregory, *The Labor of Digital Scholarship*.
60 Christian Fuchs, 'From digital positivism and administrative big data analytics towards critical digital and social media research!'.
61 Ibid.
62 ESRC, *ESRC Framework For Research Ethics*. p.28.
63 Ibid.
64 Rob Kitchin, 'Big Data, new epistemologies and paradigm shifts', *Big Data & Society* (April-June 2014):

When working to formulate ethical approaches for critical digital research, both big data positivism and research ethics fundamentalism are especially troubling for critical researchers, as each represents a reproduction of the internal logics and ideology found in corporate social media within social research. In the case of big data positivism, users' data is seen as something unambiguously open, something that a user has agreed to forfeit control over by agreeing to terms and conditions, with the only controlling party being the platforms who own said data. The consequence of this logic is best seen in the emerging controversy around the data analytics company Cambridge Analytica. In March 2018, the Guardian and the New York Times published a series of articles that allege the misuse of a huge amount of user data taken from Facebook by a political influence/analytics firm called Cambridge Analytica. The story acquired attention because Cambridge Analytica had important relationships with some of Donald Trump's closest collaborators, especially during the 2016 US election campaign. The case has brought to the attention of the large public how data-veillance capitalism operates, confirming the fact that the vast majority of platforms' users are totally unaware of how their data are monetized and used to influence policies. On the one hand, the case indicates that the rhetoric of individual privacy, stressed for long time by platforms (i.e. 'Facebook users have control of their privacy' option) is a cover for the extraction of value from users' and also non-users data (i.e. profiles and shadow profiles). It is also significant that the resulting scrutiny from the press and public is not confined to Cambridge Analytica, but as it develops seems to be expanding to Facebook itself, and how it handles users' data.

The case is useful to stress the necessity of being critical of accepting the meanings associated with digital data. Digital social data acquire their 'goodness' from the moment we use them not only as indicators of social reality, but also as a means to start questioning the image of society they present as a part of the political and economic system from where they derive.

Applying critical perspectives to digital social data means challenging the real significance of big data metrics and analytics as the product of the specific ecosystem at the origin of digital social data. The social implication of metadata fields structure what is described and what is excluded, and the social categories that are created/reinforced or reproduced. For instance, the most used metadata in academic research are those connected to tweets. Twitter's data includes information about users' accounts names, followers, connections (retweets, replies) location, content, devices.[65] But how are these categories really experienced by users as bodied people? Adopting the number of followers (or retweets) as a measure of influence for instance, are we really measuring a social variable or are we rather describing the results of platforms' internal logic of profit?[66] Asking these questions force us to recognize the power struggles behind the data we scrape or download.

1-12; Rob Kitchin and Tracey P. Lauriault, 'Towards critical data studies: Charting and unpacking data assemblages and their work', in J Eckert, A Shears and J Thatcher (eds) *Geoweb and Big Data,* Lincoln: University of Nebraska Press, 2014.

65 Information available at https://developer.twitter.com/en/docs/tweets/data-dictionary/overview/user-object.

66 Frank Pasquale, *Black Box Society: The Secret Algorithms That Control Money and Information,* Cambridge MA/London: Harvard University Press, 2016; Cathy O'Neil, *Weapons of Math Destruction,* New York: Crown Publishers, 2016.

Likewise, research ethics fundamentalist positions are troubling to critical scholarship. As Fuchs argues, approaches to research ethics that fetishize privacy and ethics do so without regard for wider social issues that may be pertinent to the data being studied,[67] for example by serving as protection for users engaging in the reproduction of hateful discourses.[68] We argue that this position serves to reproduce a kind of neoliberal subjectivity in how we construct research participants, by constructing the social media user as someone who has complete sovereign ownership of their data, of all data being private, of all use of data being subject to some kind of individualistic consent, regardless of what is being studied. In a situation where access to socially relevant data is often predicated on amicable relations between researchers and corporate social media platforms, critical researchers should take great care that we do not reproduce the kind of subjectivities and logics of ethics and methodology that grow from the ideologies found in the social media industry.

In discussing the privacy fundamentalism, Fuchs presents the following question a researcher might ask a potential participant: '"Dear Mr. Misogynist/Nazi, I am a social researcher gathering data from Twitter. Can you please give me the informed consent that I quote your violent threat against X?"'.[69] This scenario may seem ridiculous, but in our personal experience is exceedingly accurate in describing the logical consequences of trying to do critical research. For one of us, critical discursive analysis of misogynistic, anti-feminist and sexist language on Twitter has been the primary focus of their research during their postgraduate education, and the above is broadly indicative of the situation they found themself in when fulfilling the conditions of their ethical approval.[70] While the institutional ethical standards applies to that project were not quite as extreme as the positions outlined by Fuchs, they still required that informative consent be obtained from participants who produced more serious and abusive content. While the motivation behind this is an ostensible concern for the potential consequences to participants' welfare of reproducing their data in another context, the effect was that 'the very act of producing hateful discourse is turned into a barrier to the scrutiny of this discourse'.[71] From a critical perspective, this has the perverse consequence of protecting and privileging those users who produce the most extreme discourse, over those who would be the potential or actual targets. Although this is not necessarily representative of the ethical standards applied to all digital social research, it is still an example of how a particular interpretation of ethical standards can act as a barrier to critical scrutiny.

---

67 Christian Fuchs, 'From digital positivism and administrative big data analytics towards critical digital and social media research!'.
68 Libby Bishop and Daniel Gray, 'Ethical Challenges of Publishing and Sharing Social Media Research Data', in K. Woodfield (ed.), *The Ethics of Online Research*, Bingley: Emerald, 2018, pp.157-189.
69 Christian Fuchs, 'From digital positivism and administrative big data analytics towards critical digital and social media research!'.
70 Libby Bishop and Daniel Gray, 'Ethical Challenges of Publishing and Sharing Social Media Research Data'.
71 Christian Fuchs, 'From digital positivism and administrative big data analytics towards critical digital and social media research!'.

Conclusions

In this chapter we discussed the argument for a critical approach to ethics based on digital labor studies, in order to advocate for what we see as truly good data. The focus on the link between digital social data and the economic and technical environment where they are produced labor is fundamental: big data are not 'just' data, they are labor, they are political representation of the world, produced within a specific system of material relations. We advocate for a view of data that grows from this, one that calls critical researchers to reflect on how they are not simply accountable to their participants as individualized,[72] neoliberal subjects, but accountable to the largest set of relationships that compose contemporary concept of identity. As boyd and Crawford and Ess suggest a form of accountability that move beyond the single individual, we argue that the real ethical position of researcher is to be accountable towards the commons, as a specific alternative to the neoliberal capitalist system of production of data. As critical researchers we have a unique opportunity to occupy the emerging field of digital studies, and counter the rhetoric of reproduction of neoliberal approaches to data, methods and subjectivity, such as participation, entrepreneurialism and individualism. Such approaches are already ubiquitous in the social media and data analytics industries, and while the apparent greater concern for the ethical use of user data expressed in academia is undoubtedly an improvement over the bleak cynicism of big data capitalism, these approaches cannot hope to fundamentally challenge industry unless they problematize the basic assumptions of what makes good data. As we have discussed above, such an alternative - one that identifies social media as a form of capitalist production - would require a critical materialist reading of relations of production on social media, as well as fundamental changes in approaches to subjectivity, and a new approach to research ethics that builds on these ideas, with the intention of empowering critical research to target how systems of domination, exploitation and hate are propagated on social media and through the relations of production that underline it. If critical researchers are going to advance a challenge to the ideology, assumptions and relations of production advanced under digital capitalism, they must develop a way of ethically working with user data that is based on achieving these goals. Away from perspectives that treat data as something uncomplicated, or unsuitable for use in critique, and towards good data: data that can be used to affect meaningful change at the edge of modern capitalism.

References

Anderson, Chris. 'The End of Theory: The Data Deluge Makes the Scientific Method Obsolete'. *Wired*, 16.7 (2008).

Andrejevic, Mark. *Infoglut: how too much information is changing the way we think and know*, New York: Routledge, 2013.

Berry, David M. (2011) The computational turn: Thinking about the digital humanities. *Culture Machine* 12, (2011), http://www.culturemachine.net/index.php/cm/article/view/440/470.

Bhaskar, Roy. *A realist theory of science*, London: Verso, 2008.

---

72 danah boyd and Kate Crawford, *Critical Questions for Big Data*.

Bishop, Libby and Daniel Gray, 'Ethical Challenges of Publishing and Sharing Social Media Research Data', in K. Woodfield (ed.), *The Ethics of Online Research*. Bingley: Emerald, 2018, pp. 157-189.

boyd, danah and Kate Crawford. 'Critical Questions for Big Data: Provocations for a Cultural, Technological, and Scholarly Phenomenon', *Information, Communication, & Society* 15.5 (2012): 662-679.

Buchanan, Elizabeth. 'Internet Research Ethics Twenty Years Later', in Michael Zimmer and Katharina Kinder-Kurlanda (eds), *Internet Research Ethics for the Social Age*, New York: Peter Lang Publishing, 2017, pp. xxix-xxxiii.

Casilli, Antonio. 'Lavoro e capitalismo delle piattaforme'. Talk given at the Centro per la Riforma dello Stato, Roma, 7 November 2017, https://www.dinamopress.it/news/event/lavoro-e-capitalismo-delle-piattaforme-con-antonio-casilli/.

_____. 'Digital Labor Studies Go Global: Toward a Digital Decolonial Turn', *International Journal of Communication*, 11 (2017): 3934-3954.

_____. 'Four Theses on Digital Mass Surveillance and the Negotiation Of Privacy'. 8th Annual Privacy Law Scholar Congress, Berkeley, United States. June 2015, https://www.law.berkeley.edu/centers/berkeley-center-for-law-technology/upcoming- events/june-2015-the-8th-annual-privacy-law-scholars-conference/](https://www.law.berkeley.edu/centers/berkeley-center-for-law-technology/upcoming-%20events/june-2015-the-8th-annual-privacy-law-scholars-conference/.

Dalton, Craig and Jim Thatcher, 'What does a critical data studies look like, and why do we care? Seven points for a critical approach to "big data"', *Society and Space*, 2014, http://societyandspace.org/2014/05/12/what-does-a-critical-data-studies-look-like-and-why-do-we-care-craig-dalton-and-jim-thatcher/.

Edwards, Adam et al. 'Digital Social Research, Social Media and the Sociological Imagination: surrogacy, re-orientation and augmentation', *International Journal of Social Research Methodology*, 16.3 (2013): 245-260.

ESRC, *ESRC Framework for Research Ethics*, 2015.

Ethical Decision-Making and Internet Research: Recommendations from the AoIR Ethics Committee Approved by the Ethics Working Committee, 08/2012. Endorsed by the AoIR Executive Committee, 09/2012.

Ess, Charles. 'New selves, New research ethics?', in Hallvard Fossheim and Helene Ingierd, *Internet Research Ethics*, Oslo: Cappelen Damm Akademisk, 2015.

Fairclough, Norman. *Analysing Discourse,* London: Routledge, 2003.

Foucault, Michel and Gilles Deleuze. 'Intellectuals and Power: A Conversation Between Michel Foucault and Gilles Deleuze'. In Donald F Bouchard (ed.), *Language, Counter Memory, Practice: Selected Essays and Interviews*, trans. Donald F. Bouchard and Sherry Simon. Oxford: Basil Blackwell, 1977.

Fuchs, Christian. *Internet and Society, Social theory in the information age.* New York: Routledge, 2008.

_____. *Digital Labour and Karl Marx.* New York: Routledge, 2014.

_____. 'From digital positivism and administrative big data analytics towards critical digital and social media research!', *European Journal of Communication*, 32.1 (2017): 37-49.

_____. *Social Media, A Critical Introduction.* London Sage, 2014.

Gregory, Karen. 'Marx, Engels and the Critique of Academic Labor', *Workplace: The Journal for Academic Labor*, 28 (2016).

_____. 'The Future of Work'. Public Services International Congress. Geneva, Switzerland, 2018. http://congress.world-psi.org/karen-gregory-talks-about-the-negatives-and-positives-of-computer-platform-capitalism/.

_____. 'The Labor of Digital Scholarship'. Talk given at the University of Edinburgh, 2017, https://ed.hosted.panopto.com/Panopto/Pages/Viewer.aspx?id=41552549-5650-4cdf-bf62-05999534c270.

Hongladarom, Soraj. 'Internet Research Ethics in a Non-Western Context', in Michael Zimmer and Katharina Kinder-Kurlanda (eds), *Internet Research Ethics for the Social Age*, New York: Peter Lang Publishing, 2017, pp. 151-163.

Kitchin, Rob and Tracey P. Lauriault, 'Towards critical data studies: Charting and unpacking data assemblages and their work', in J Eckert, A Shears and J Thatcher (eds), *Geoweb and Big Data,* Lincoln: University of Nebraska Press, 2014.

Kitchin, Rob. 'Big Data, new epistemologies and paradigm shifts'. *Big Data & Society,* (April-June 2014): 1-12.

Klastrup, Lisbeth. 'Death, Affect and the Ethical Challenges of Outing a Griefsquatter', in Michael Zimmer and Katharina Kinder-Kurlanda (eds), *Internet Research Ethics for the Social Age*, New York: Peter Lang Publishing, 2017, pp. 235-24.

Kramer, Adam D.I. et al. 'Experimental evidence of massive-scale emotional contagion through social networks', *Proceedings of the National Academy of Sciences of the United States of America*, 111.24 (2014): 8788.

Lüders, Marika. 'Researching social media: Confidentiality, anonymity and reconstructing online practices', in Hallvard Fossheim and Helene Ingierd. *Internet Research Ethics*, Oslo: Cappelen Damm Akademisk, 2015.

Mahrt, Merja and Michael Scharkow, 'The value of big data in digital media research', *Journal of Broadcasting & Electronic Media*, 57.1 (2013): 20-33, DOI: doi:10.1080/08838151.2012.761700.

Marres, Noortjie and Carolin Gerlitz. 'Interface methods: renegotiating relations between digital social research', *The Sociological Review,* 64 (2016): 21-46, DOI: 10.1111/1467-954X.12314.

Metcalf, Jacob, and Kate Crawford. 'Where are human subjects in big data research? The emerging ethics divide', *Big Data & Society*, 3.1 (2016): 1-14, DOI: doi:10.1177/2053951716650211.

Nissenbaum, Helen. Privacy as contextual integrity. *Washington Law Review* (2004): 79, 119-157.

O'Neil, Cathy. *Weapons of Math Destruction*. New York: Crown Publishers, 2016.

Pasquale, Frank. *Black Box Society: The Secret Algorithms That Control Money and Information*, Cambridge: Harvard University Press, 2015.

Puschmann, Cornelius and Jean Burgess. 'Big Data, Big Questions, Metaphors of Big Data', *International Journal of Communication*, 8 (2014): 1690-1709. DOI: 1932- 8036/20140005.

Rogers, Richard. *Digital Methods*. Cambridge MA: MIT Press, 2015.

Ruppert, Evelyn, John Law and Mike Savage, 'Reassembling Social Science Methods: The Challenge of Digital Devices' *Theory, Culture & Society* 30.4 (2013): 22-46.

Savage, Mike and Roger Burrows, 'The Coming Crisis of Empirical Sociology', *Sociology* 41.5 (2007): 885-899, DOI: 10.1177/0038038507080443.

Seko, Yukari and Stephen P. Lewis. '"We Tend to Err on the Side of Caution" Ethical Challenges Facing Canadian Research Ethics Boards When Overseeing Internet Research', in Michael Zimmer and Katharina Kinder-Kurlanda (eds), *Internet Research Ethics for the Social Age*, New York: Peter Lang Publishing, 2017, pp. 133-147.

Srnicek, Nick. *Platform Capitalism*. Cambridge: Polity Press, 2017.

Staksrud, Elisabeth. 'Counting Children', in Hallvard Fossheim, and Helene Ingierd. *Internet Research Ethics*, Oslo: Cappelen Damm Akademisk, 2015.

Steen-Johnsen, Kari and Bernard Enjolras, 'Social research and Big Data - the tension between opportunities and realities', in Hallvard Fossheim and Helene Ingierd, *Internet Research Ethics*, Oslo: Cappelen Damm Akademisk, 2015.

Tubaro, Paola and Antonio Casilli, 'Enjeux sociaux des Big Data' in Mokrane Bouzeghoub and Rémy Mosseri (eds), *Les Big Data à découvert*, Paris: CNRS Editions, 2017: 292-293.

Tufekci, Zeynep. 'Big Questions for Social Media Big Data: Representativeness, Validity and Other Methodological Pitfalls'. *ICWSM '14: Proceedings of the 8th International AAAI Conference on Weblogs and Social Media,* 2014.

Zimmer, Michael. 'Addressing Conceptual Gaps in Big Data Research Ethics: an Application of Contextual Integrity', *Social Media + Society*, 4.2 (2018).

16: THE FIELDNOTES PLUGIN: MAKING NETWORK VISUALIZATION IN GEPHI ACCOUNTABLE

MARANKE WIERINGA, DANIELA VAN GEENEN, KARIN VAN ES AND JELMER VAN NUSS

Introduction

The network visualizations humanities scholars and social scientists employ to communicate research findings are often imbued with a sense of objectivity. The impression is that these visualizations show facts about rather than interpretations of data. Consequently, suggestions have been made as to what kind of questions and contextual information need to accompany data visualizations. However, practical incorporation of answers to these questions in (academic) publications is absent. In this chapter we engage in and depart from tool criticism taking the most common academic network visualization software Gephi as our case in point. Problematically, Gephi saves only the spatialized network graph, whilst the steps taken and parameters of the algorithms used to get to the particular visualization go undocumented.

Tackling the software tool's 'epistemological affordances,' we elaborate on how the 'interpretative acts' of practitioners - knowingly and unknowingly - privilege certain viewpoints and perpetuate particular power relations. We consider how these can be made accountable in a pragmatic way through an application that supports those working with Gephi in taking procedural 'fieldnotes,' which enables scholarly positioning. By facilitating systematic documentation of the visualization and analysis process it allows for traceability of and reflection on the subsequent results. The application, thus, brings us closer to what can be characterized as 'good technologically mediated' practice in data-related research projects and helps us interrogate what being accountable in a scholarly context entails. We place the development of this plugin in an emerging practice of 'account-ability by design'.

Data visualizations are increasingly used for sense-making and communication in scholarly research.[1] Network visualizations, among the most complex data visualizations, are often seen as little more than unintelligible 'hair balls.'[2] Humanities scholars and social scientists nevertheless employ them to make palpable and communicate (abstract) research findings. These visualizations are often imbued with a sense of objectivity and give the impression

---

1   Stephen Few, 'Data Visualization for Human Perception', in Interaction Design Foundation (ed.), *The Encyclopedia of Human-Computer Interaction*, 2nd edition, Aarhus: Interaction Design Foundation, 2014. https://www.interaction-design.org/literature/book/the-encyclopedia-of-human-computer-interaction-2nd-ed/data-visualization-for-human-perception.
2   See e.g. Carlos D. Correa and Kwan-Liu Ma, 'Visualizing Social Networks', in Charu C. Aggarwal (ed.), *Social Network Data Analytics*, New York: Springer, 2011, pp. 307-26; Navid Dianati, 'Unwinding the Hairball Graph: Pruning Algorithms for Weighted Complex Networks', *Physical Review* 93.1 (2016); Hans-Jörg Schulz, and Christophe Hurter, 'Grooming the Hairball - How to Tidy up Network Visualizations', *IEEE Information Visualization Conference,* Atlanta, United States, 2013.

that they show facts about rather than interpretations of data.[3] Several scholars have made suggestions as to what kind of questions and contextual information need to accompany data visualization: most importantly, the decisions involved in making these data visualizations in order to shed more light on these interpretations.[4] In this contribution we focus on the case of Gephi. Gephi is a popular open-source software program for graph and network analysis used in the humanities and social sciences.[5] However, publications using the software rarely inform their readers about the applied settings and steps taken in the making of the network visualization.

We have taken a first step towards 'account-ability by design' in developing a plugin for Gephi, together with the Digital Humanities Lab of Utrecht University. With 'account-ability by design,' an ethnomethodologically inspired term, we refer to the built-in inspectability of tools providing researchers with adequate means to effectively assess these tools. The plugin's development is situated within a larger trend of other projects such as Datasheets for Datasets, Principles for Accountable Algorithms, and the Data Ethics Decision Aid that seek to make transparent and accountable the work that digital tools do.[6] More specifically, the plugin allows users to export the details of the working process including a time-stamped version of the graph file.

In this chapter we discuss how the 'fieldnotes plugin' helps to make Gephi network visualizations accountable. Logging the interaction of the researcher with the software can facilitate and stimulate scholarly positioning and reflection. To begin, we consider 'critical positioning' and its relation to the notions of reflexivity and accountability.[7] We discuss how reflexivity as an inherent quality of the epistemic process encompasses the opportunity to account for decisive (human and non-human) actions performed in the making of network visualizations. Here we take into account Gephi's (lack of) 'epistemological affordances', as Van Geenen terms it,[8] and demonstrate the need for logging explorative and 'interpretive acts' performed by the

---

3   Johanna Drucker, 'Humanities Approaches to Graphical Display', *Digital Humanities Quarterly* 5.1 (2011).
4   See e.g. Adam Kariv, 'Letting Data Speak for Itself', *Medium*, 2017, https://medium.com/@adam.kariv/letting-data-speak-for-itself-80f1625a8ad1.; Helen Kennedy, Rosemary Lucy Hill, Giorgia Aiello, and William Allen, 'The Work That Visualisation Conventions Do', *Information Communication and Society* 19.6 (2016): 715-35; Karin Van Es, Nico Lopez and Thomas Boeschoten, 'Towards a Reflexive Data Analysis' in Mirko Tobias Schäfer and Karin Van Es, *The Datafied Society: Studying Culture through Data*, Amsterdam: Amsterdam University Press, 2017, pp. 171-82.
5   Mathieu Bastian, Sebastien Heymann and Mathieu Jacomy, 'Gephi: An Open Source Software for Exploring and Manipulating Networks' in *Proceedings of the Third International ICWSM Conference*, 2009, http://www.aaai.org/ocs/index.php/ICWSM/09/paper/download/154/1009.
6   Timnit Gebru, Jamie Morgenstern, Briana Vecchione, Jennifer Wortman Vaughan, Hanna Wallach, Hal Daumé III and Kate Crawford, 'Datasheets for Datasets' 2018, http://jamiemorgenstern.com/papers/datasheet.pdf.; Nicholas Diakopoulos, Sorelle Friedler, Marcelo Arenas, Solon Barocas, Michael Hay, Bill Howe, H. V. Jagadish, et al, 'Principles for Accountable Algorithms. Fairness, Accountability, and Transparency in Machine Learning', http://www.fatml.org/resources/principles-for-accountable-algorithms.; Utrecht Data School, 'Data Ethics Decision Aid (DEDA)', Utrecht Data School, 2018, https://dataschool.nl/deda/?lang=en.
7   Donna J Haraway, 'Situated Knowledges: The Science Question in Feminism and the Privilege of Partial Perspective', *Feminist Studies* 14.3 (1988): 586.
8   Daniela van Geenen, 'The Role of Software Tools in Critical Data Studies Practices. Studying the

use of Gephi, something which Johanna Drucker also argued for with regards to visualization in general.[9] This demonstration focuses on the default and adaptable settings of the ForceAtlas 2 layout algorithm using the example of the 'Les Miserables' data sample which comes prepackaged with Gephi.[10] Subsequently, we examine a sample of academic publications to address how media scholars are currently documenting their working processes in and with Gephi. It reveals that, despite having consequences for the analysis or presentation, a number of influential aspects of the working process are not thoroughly documented. Following this, we return to the plugin itself and explore its promises and pitfalls with regard to accountability. The plugin is a pragmatic but partial solution to making network visualization accountable in Gephi. In conclusion, we consider which work still needs to be done around account-ability by design. Although the development of the plugin is aimed at scholars in the humanities, it should be of relevance to scholars engaged with critical data studies more widely.

Critical Positioning and its Prerequisites

Gephi has served as a notable example in several critical explorations that approach digital methods and tools not as mere instruments but as sites of study.[11] Bernhard Rieder and Theo Röhle, in their engagement with such 'sites of study,' call for a scholarly practice that oscillates between practical and critical work on the research material we investigate and the digital tools we employ.[12] Here they build on the notion of 'reflexivity' in both the traditions of the humanities and science and technology studies. According to Michael Lynch, this notion covers two things: Firstly, Lynch discusses the conscious activity of reflecting on the epistemic process, and in this course, the idea of generating 'objective knowledge'.[13] This idea of 'reflexivity' implies a kind of academic superiority put under scrutiny by Lynch. Secondly, he proposes a more general understanding of the term that includes the assumptions of the researchers of which they may not be actively aware. Donna Haraway, in this sense, calls for the 'critical positioning' of practitioners: the critical review of the bias they reflect on the research outcomes through their academic background and the interpretive choices they make during the research process.[14] The following section will explore the importance of

---

Affordances of Gephi as a Sociotechnical System', in *Explorations in Digital Cultures: On the Politics of Datafication, Calculation and Networking.* Lüneburg: Meson press, forthcoming.

9   Drucker, 'Humanities Approaches to Graphical Display'.
10 Mathieu Jacomy, Tommaso Venturini, Sebastien Heymann, and Mathieu Bastian, 'ForceAtlas2, a Continuous Graph Layout Algorithm for Handy Network Visualization Designed for the Gephi Software', *PLoS ONE* 9.6 (2014).
11 Johannes Paßmann, 'Forschungsmedien erforschen. Über Praxis mit der Mapping- Software Gephi', in *Navigationen. Vom Feld zum Labor und zurück* 1 (2013): 113-129; Bernhard Rieder and Theo Röhle. 'Digital Methods: From Challenges to Bildung', in Mirko Tobias Schäfer and Karin van Es (eds), *The Datafied Society: Studying Culture through Data*, Amsterdam: Amsterdam University Press, 2017, pp. 109-24.
12 Bernhard Rieder and Theo Röhle, 'Digital Methods: Five Challenges', in David Berry (ed.), *Understanding Digital Humanities*, Cham: Springer, 2012, pp. 67-84, p. 80.
13 Michael Lynch, 'Against Reflexivity as an Academic Virtue and Source of Privileged Knowledge', *Theory, Culture & Society* 17.3 (2000), 26-54.
14 Haraway, 'Situated Knowledges: The Science Question in Feminism and the Privilege of Partial Perspective', p. 586.

reflexive practice and how Gephi, through its affordances, makes it difficult to track and record how network visualizations are constructed. As such, we state, it constrains critical positioning.

Reflexivity and Accountability

Working with software is a constant interaction between what the program allows, what the user does, and how the program responds to this. In other words, the interplay of human and non-human actors grants different kinds of agencies, or capacities to act, to both.[15] Sometimes these agencies are so intertwined it becomes difficult to locate who is acting upon whom or what.[16] We want to identify two of these agencies, which we believe are crucial in order to identify the (obscured) scholarly intentions at stake: the agency of the researcher, and the agency of the software. Focusing first on the agency of the software, Gephi is programmed in a specific way, thereby enabling particular actions and constraining others; it is 'inscribed' with (human) agency through its programming.[17] Scholars, in turn, can interact with this software in an analysis process in which they make particular (un)conscious choices stimulated by the (automated) methods and tools they use. For us, this dynamic, the interfacing between researcher and program is of interest, as it shapes the 'interpretative acts' researchers perform in their working practice, and thus, meaning-making with Gephi.[18] It is this dynamic which the plugin will help to document.

To better understand how Gephi structures, facilitates, and influences the working process, we propose to look at its affordances: the 'possibilities for action' presented to the user.[19] Questioning the affordances of software tools, understood as their designed and perceivable action possibilities,[20] directs the attention to the actions such tools allow for, or constrain, including their (hidden) politics.[21] An approach of critical affordance analysis is especially suited for Gephi,[22] which is presented as a tool for 'Visual Network Analysis'.[23] As such, Gephi's strength resides in allowing its users interaction with the underlying data and network through its graphical user interface. An investigation of Gephi's interface affordances allows for cutting critically through the interface level and revealing the tool's executable layers and

---

15 Madeleine Akrich and Bruno Latour, 'A Summary of a Convenient Vocabulary for the Semiotics of Human and Nonhuman Assemblies', in Wiebe E. Bijker and John Law (eds), *Shaping Technology / Building Society: Studies in Sociotechnical Change*, Cambridge MA/London: MIT Press, 1992, pp. 259-64.
16 Adrian Mackenzie, *Cutting Code*. New York: Peter Lang, 2006, p. 10.
17 Ibid.
18 Drucker, 'Humanities Approaches to Graphical Display'.
19 Ian Hutchby, 'Technologies, Texts and Affordances', *Sociology* 35.2 (2001): 441-56, 444.
20 Ibid, 447-50, with reference to Donald Norman, *The Design of Everyday Things*. New York: Doubleday, 1990.
21 Matthew Curinga, 'Critical analysis of interactive media with software affordances', *First Monday* 19.9 (2014).
22 Van Geenen, 'The Role of Software Tools in Critical Data Studies Practices', forthcoming.
23 Tommaso Venturini, Mathieu Jacomy and Débora Pereira, 'Visual Network Analysis', Working Paper (2015), https://www.tommasoventurini.it/wp/wp-content/uploads/2014/08/Venturini-Jacomy_Visual-Network-Analysis_WorkingPaper.pdf.

their role in mediating the research material.[24]

Such a reflective attitude is important, for interpretive acts in Gephi are framed by particular 'situated knowledges'.[25] The notion of situated knowledges refers to how researchers are not neutral observers of reality. The epistemic claims they make reflect their social identity and situation. Scientific visualizations are a prominent example of such research outcomes. Haraway scrutinizes the objectified impression visualizations gain in research communication through a separation of information on their making process from the visual outcomes themselves. The notion of situated knowledge stresses the need to make bias in the knowledge production, and therefore, the manner in which this bias resonates in the interpretive practice of scholars, explicit. In other words, situated knowledge implies that one's ideas are rooted in a particular framework: a paradigm, a (socio-economic) background, a discipline, and so forth. All these aspects, which together make up one's situatedness, influence the kinds of interpretative acts one conducts. Moreover, in the case of Gephi, diverse kinds of situated knowledges deriving from particular academic fields are also *implemented by design* and *mobilized by means of the use of the tool*, such as the mathematical branch of graph theory, and the social sciences approach of social network analysis.[26] We focus particularly on the mobilization of situated knowledge in Gephi's usage and the way in which the plugin can enhance reflection on this.

As a tool that produces visual outcomes - in the shape of a network graph - Gephi is a perfect showcase to pose the question of the reflexivity of (algorithmic) knowledge instruments, or what becomes visible in comparison to the parts of the epistemic process that stay invisible. Reflexivity as an inherent quality of the epistemic process implies that we need an opportunity to *account for* all decisive (human and non-human) actions performed in this process. Accountability here is understood as accepting responsibility for one's actions, and thereby being - potentially - liable.[27] It differs from transparency which concerns disclosing information and privileges seeing over understanding.[28] Our concern, however, is not per se on one's liability, but on one's *account-ability*, which refers to, on the one hand, *being open to inspection* (transparency, if you wish), and on the other hand, *being competent in assessing the subject matter*.[29] Thus, the concept encompasses both the subject and object position of the word.[30]

---

24 For an elaborate critical affordance analysis of Gephi see: Daniela van Geenen, *The Role of Software Tools in Critical Data Studies Practices. Studying the Affordances of Gephi as a Sociotechnical System* MA thesis, 2018, https://dspace.library.uu.nl/handle/1874/367489.
25 Haraway, 'Situated Knowledges: The Science Question in Feminism and the Privilege of Partial Perspective', pp. 581-590.
26 Rieder and Röhle, 'Digital Methods: From Challenges to Bildung', pp. 111, 117-9.
27 Helen Nissenbaum, 'Computing and Accountability', *Communications of the ACM* 37.1 (1994): 72-80.
28 Mike Ananny and Kate Crawford, 'Seeing without Knowing: Limitations of the Transparency Ideal and Its Application to Algorithmic Accountability', *New Media and Society* 20.3 (2018): 973-89.
29 Daniel Neyland, 'Bearing Account-Able Witness to the Ethical Algorithmic System', *Science, Technology, & Human Values* 41.1 (2016): 55.
30 Sara Eriksén, 'Designing for Accountability', *Proceedings of the Second Nordic Conference on Human-Computer Interaction* (2002): 179.

The hyphenated term, account-ability, was coined by Harold Garfinkel as an ethnomethodological concept,[31] dealing with the 'observable-and-reportable', with practices of 'looking-and-telling,' and is very applicable to our situation.[32]

Part of being account-able rests with the documentation of one's research process, but also requires insight in how tools are used and why. As such, the account-ability we promote can be seen as a documentation of one's reflexivity: the researchers' ability to provide an account of what they have done. This is a first and necessary step in terms of legitimization of the outcome. Part of the knowledge production is delegated to Gephi. Thus, ideally, the decisions made by the researcher are informed by an understanding of the concepts and techniques mobilized by the software.

It is in the facilitation of further understanding about the analysis process that we situate the plugin: as a first step on the road to what we term 'account-ability by design.' The design process springs forth from an ethnographic, processual, and systematic engagement with the tool. The reflexive practice we envision for scholars working with the tool considers and offers information about the tools we use and the steps we take to analyze our data. In other words, we attempt to make the interpretive practices of scholars open for scrutiny - account-able - as part of their critical positioning. The lack of such documentation, which we expand on later in this paper, is partly due to the structure of the program itself, and resides in the need for and current lack of its 'epistemological affordances'.[33] The term is inspired by Lev Manovich's call for a 'software epistemology', that interrogates what knowledge is and becomes in relation to software.[34] Such a software epistemology should enable a dialogue on action possibilities that stimulate reflection on how software frames and shifts the production and distribution of knowledge, or in other words its epistemological affordances. To put it differently, epistemological affordances are action possibilities the software tool should enable to enhance accountability. The availability of such action possibilities stimulates the reflective attitude of the researcher towards the epistemic process.

The notion of epistemological affordances allows us to think thoroughly about what is 'good technologically mediated' practice in the scholarly context.[35] Peter-Paul Verbeek's conception of the 'good technologically mediated life' poses the questions whether and how it is possible to 'design the morality of things'.[36] Verbeek advocates that we should adopt a 'limit-attitude'.[37] In Michel Foucault's description of the term, this ethos is defined by a critical scholarly attitude *from within* the 'field' in which one is working, constantly questioning the 'limits' of one's

---

31 Harold Garfinkel, *Studies in Ethnomethodology*. Englewood Cliffs: Prentice-Hall, 1967.
32 Eriksén, 'Designing for Accountability', 179.
33 Daniela van Geenen, 'The Role of Software Tools in Critical Data Studies Practices', forthcoming.
34 Lev Manovich, *Software Takes Command,* New York/London: Bloomsbury, 2013, pp. 337-341.
35 Peter-Paul Verbeek, 'Resistance Is Futile: Toward a Non-Modern Democratization of Technology', *Techné: Research in Philosophy and Technology* 17.1 (2013): 91.
36 Ibid; Peter-Paul Verbeek, *Moralizing Technology. Understanding and Designing the Morality of Things.* Chicago/London: University of Chicago Press, 2011.
37 Verbeek, 'Resistance Is Futile: Toward a Non-Modern Democratization of Technology', pp. 81-2.

knowledge, which also involves the tools a scholar is employing.[38] In designing the fieldnotes plugin we strive to contribute to good 'computationally mediated' data research practice, by adopting a limit attitude with regard to a software tool such as Gephi. Below, we discuss how the affordances of Gephi actually (dis)allow documentation of the research practice with Gephi.

Gephi's (lack of) Affordances

We discuss Gephi's action possibilities in terms of default functionalities and other, in social and technical ways, featured specifications.[39] Gephi's software affordances are promoted by the tool's graphical user interface as well as by the core team of developers, for instance, in official tutorials they share on the Gephi platform.[40] In order to have access to the full array of functionalities and explore the tool's affordances the application software requires data input. When a user opens Gephi the welcome pop-up window offers the opportunity to select one of the three exercise data samples the developers prepared for beginning users. For demonstration purposes, we will draw on the smallest of the three exercise samples: 'Les Miserables.gexf" composed of 77 nodes and 154 edges. The dataset is a graph file prepared in Gephi's own Graph Exchange File Format.[41] Users new to Gephi are encouraged to play with the dataset; the set is prominently placed on the welcome screen and in the 'Quick Start Guide', one of the few tutorials that is branded an 'Official Tutorial' by the Gephi core team.[42] The Les Miserables dataset appeals to the imagination of the user: The nodes represent the novel characters and the edges stand for these characters' co-appearances during the plot development of *Les Miserables*. However, in analytical terms the data sample is moderately 'inoperative' in its current form, such as the following demonstration will show.

Upon opening this dataset from the welcome screen, one is presented with the workable Gephi interface. The program offers the user three tabs: The 'Overview' tab (see Figures 1, 3-5) allows for spatializing and analyzing the data. The 'Data Laboratory' tab (Figure 2) houses the dataset and the metrics from preceding analyses (e.g. Modularity Class values, which classify nodes and group them together). Finally, the 'Preview tab' allows for finetuning the static output of the network graph. Looking at the graph in the Overview tab, we noticed that the network graph was prepared by the application of specific settings. Engaging with the software program and its practice set, however, does not clarify which steps have been taken to prepare the graph. The layout algorithm used and its parameters are not made explicit and related documentation is sparse.

---

38   Ibid, in reference to Michel Foucault, 'What is Enlightenment?', in Paul Rabinow (ed.), *Ethics: Subjectivity and Truth*, New York: The New Press, 1997.
39   For this investigation we applied Gephi 0.9.2., the most recent release of the software tool at the time of writing this paper.
40   For the official website see: https://gephi.org/.
41   The 'Les Miserables' exercise sample builds on Donald Knuth's work on 'literate programming'. On his website, Knuth explains that he prepared the data sample as exercise material for "benchmark tests of competing methods." In Gephi the implementation of the sample can be similarly understood in such a benchmarking capacity: as experimental and comparative material for various analytical principles implemented in Gephi. See: Donald E Knuth, *The Stanford GraphBase: A Platform for Combinatorial Computing*, New York: ACM Press, 1993.
42   Gephi.org., 'Learn how to use Gephi.', https://gephi.org/users/.

The 'Quick Start Guide' tutorial is the only resource that provides the user with some clues about the preparation of the data sample. This tutorial recommends the application of an algorithm of the ForceAtlas series, layout algorithms that were specifically developed for Gephi.[43] To demonstrate how influential the choice for a layout algorithm and its particular properties is, we draw upon the Les Miserables data sample and the spatialization algorithm ForceAtlas 2, the successor of ForceAtlas. ForceAtlas 2 spatializes and clusters the graph based on degree, the number of edges a node possesses. The clustering, addressed by the term 'modularity', is facilitated by attraction forces of edges and repulsion forces of (unconnected) nodes.[44] It results in the visual clustering of nodes in which highly connected nodes are grouped together. This phenomenon of grouping together is amplified by the use of a community detection procedure, implemented in Gephi, coupled with node coloring. The 'Modularity Class' community detection algorithm generates metadata (see the fourth column in Figure 2). Starting from a single node, the algorithm 'snowballs' through the entire graph and assesses with which cluster each node has the most connections. Subsequently, it is possible to color and 'partition' these nodes based on the communities inferred by the algorithm (see Figure 1).[45]

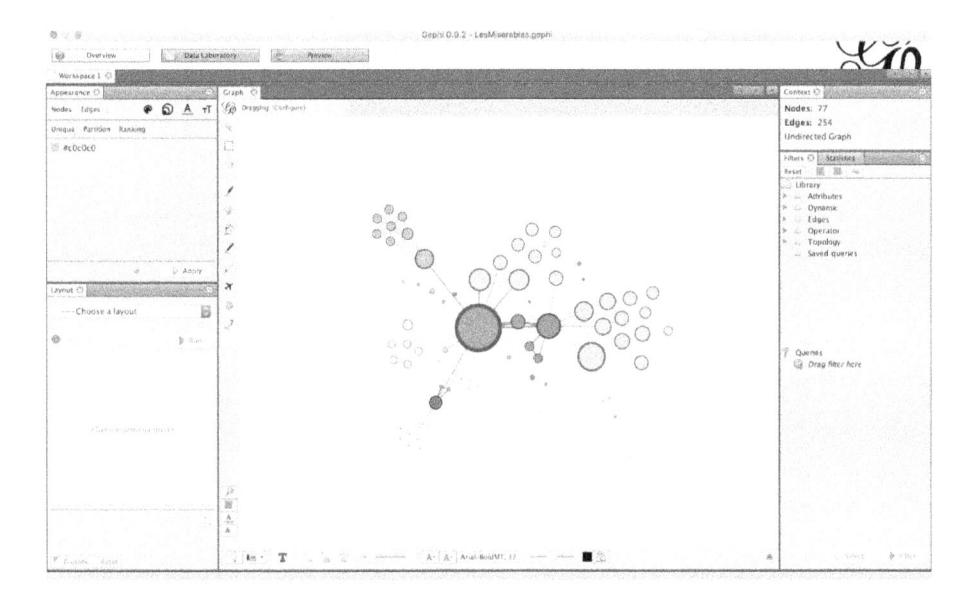

---

43 Jacomy, Venturini, Heymann, and Bastian, 'ForceAtlas2, a Continuous Graph Layout Algorithm for Handy Network Visualization Designed for the Gephi Software'.
44 Ibid, 2-3.
45 See also the steps recommended in the 'Quick Start Guide' tutorial. For academic reference explaining the workings of 'Modularity Class' see: Vincent D Blondel, Jean-Loup Guillaume, Renaud Lambiotte and Etienne Lefebvre, 'Fast Unfolding of Communities in Large Networks', *Journal of Statistical Mechanics: Theory and Experiment,*10 (2008): 1-12.

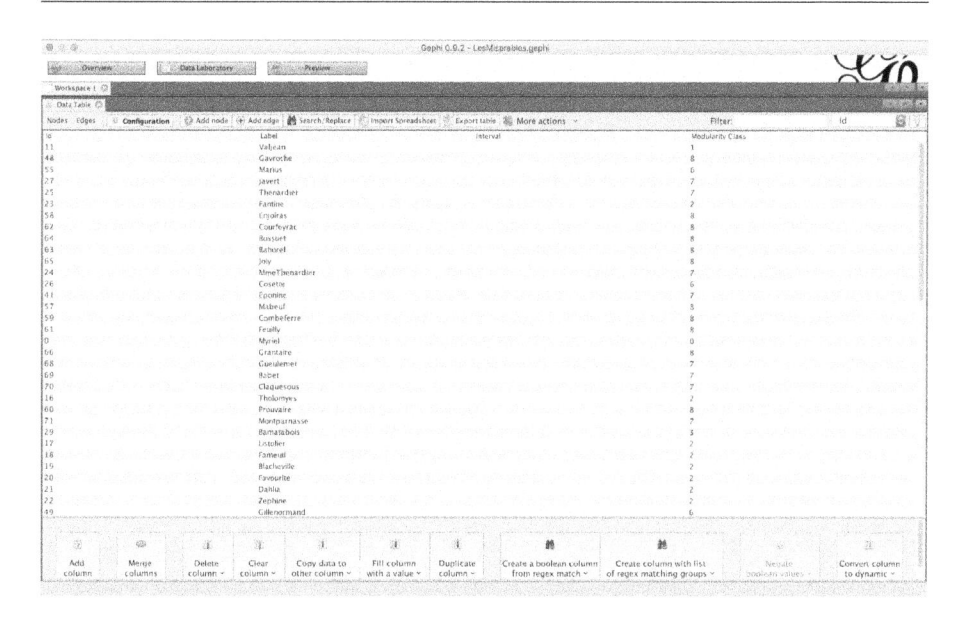

Figures 1 and 2: Gephi's 'Overview' and 'Data Laboratory' tabs after opening the Les Miserables dataset.

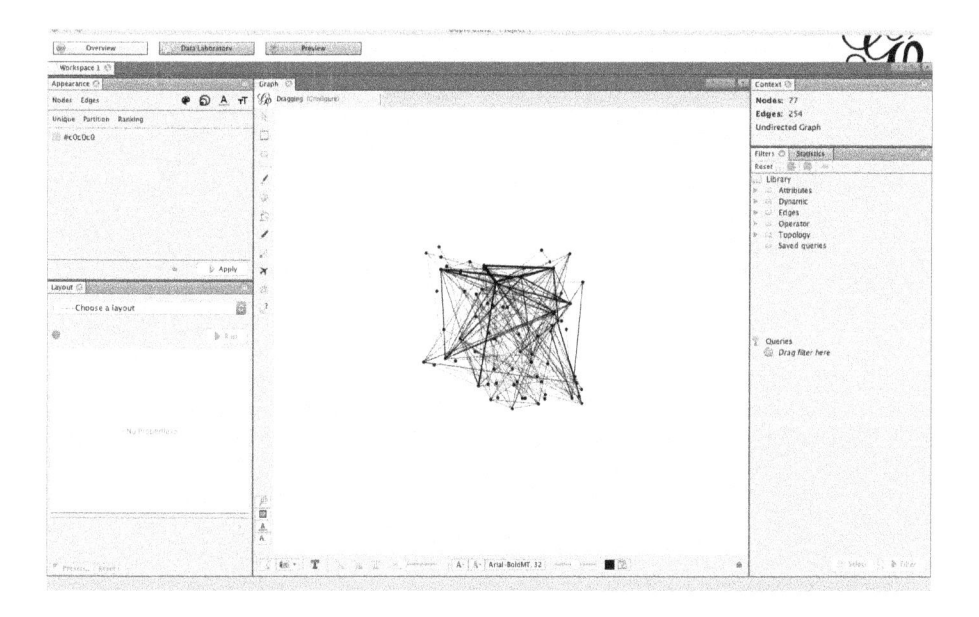

Figure 3: The 'raw' Les Miserables sample.

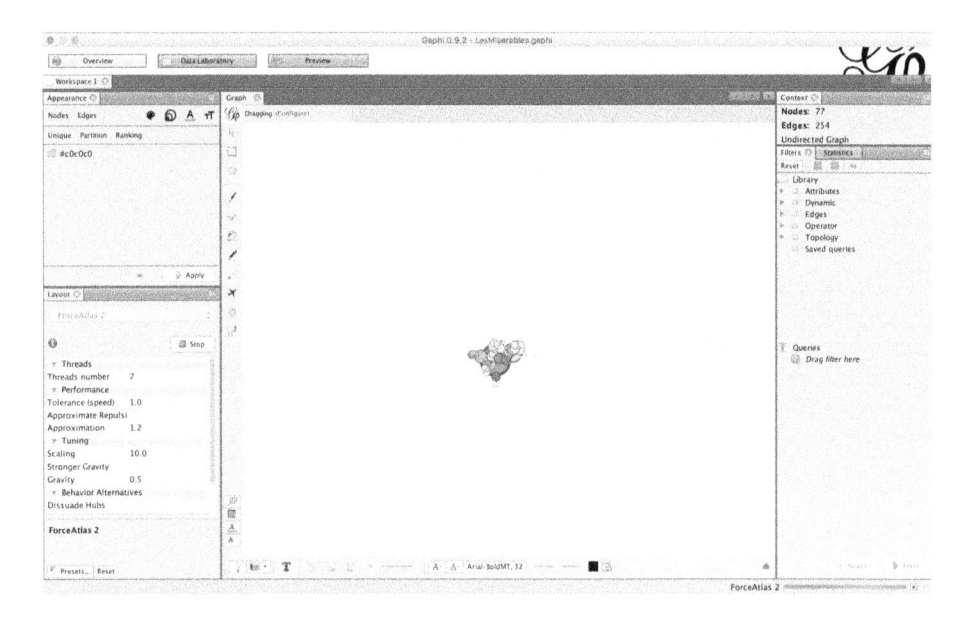

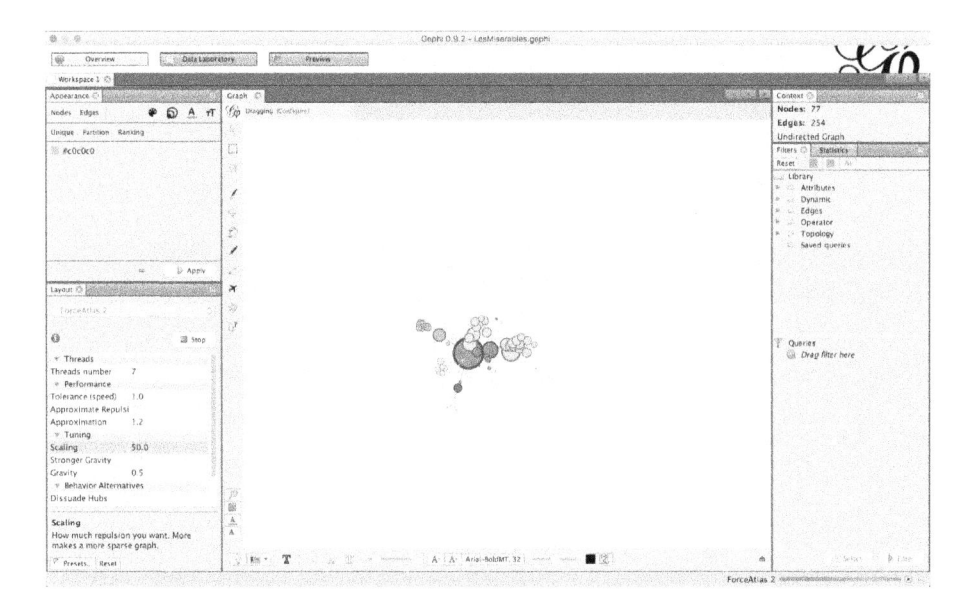

Figures 4 and 5: ForceAtlas 2's default settings applied to the same 'Les Miserables' exercise sample, and after adjusting 'Tuning' and 'Behavior Alternative' settings such as the scaling (from 10 to 50) and the gravity (from 1.0 to 0.5).

In order to stress the importance of recording the applied parameters, the figures above demonstrate how applying a particular layout algorithm and playing with its settings returns network graphs shaped in very specific ways: Figure 3 shows the Les Miserables graph in an unprepared, 'raw' state.[46] In the above figures (4 and 5) we applied ForceAtlas 2 to the prepared graph file and adjusted layout properties under ForceAtlas 2's subheadings of 'Tuning' and 'Behavior Alternatives'. Moreover, selecting "Behavior Alternatives' such as 'Dissuade Hubs' and 'Prevent Overlap' returns a graphical display similar to the starting position (Figure 1). While these adjustments of algorithm property values result in changed node positions in the graph file (GEXF), apart from that this action that changes the algorithm 'behavior' leaves no permanent trail. To be more specific, the work of the software and researcher cannot be traced back. This is exemplified by the lack of otherwise commonplace software features such as 'undo' and 'redo' options.[47]

Gephi's lack of epistemological affordances affect knowledge production. We focused on the default and adaptable settings of the layout algorithm to illustrate their influence on how the data is visualized as graph therein demonstrating the need for recording and accounting for explorative and interpretive activities. The integration of the 'Les Miserables.gexf' dataset reflects the politics of the developer's community: Gephi's sociological focus on community detection and, based on this calculation process, the visual clustering of the network graph.[48] Researchers need to be provided with the opportunity to scrutinize such politics in order to make sense of the interpretative acts performed in, and with, Gephi. We argue that a process of understanding can only be afforded to scholars through a combination of access to the applied parameters and a consultation of the documentation on the software tool.[49] The fieldnotes plugin is a practical solution that offers access to the applied parameters and in doing so can hopefully support Gephi's epistemological affordances. The plugin is needed because, as we demonstrate in the following section, academic publications using Gephi network visualizations only scarcely report the interpretative acts performed by the researcher(s).

Network Visualizations Practices in Scholarly Discourse

About documenting the Gephi work process in academic publications, Axel Bruns writes:

> [T]he various visualization algorithms offered by the well-known, open source network analysis software Gephi, for example, are generally described in some detail in software guides and related literature, but relatively few of the scholarly publications

---

46 The Quick Start Guide tutorial links to such a version of the data sample.
47 See e.g. Van Geenen, 'The Role of Software Tools in Critical Data Studies Practices' for related scholarly discussions, and the discussion feed on the Gephi Wiki that features the call for undo/redo specifications formulated by the Gephi community: https://github.com/gephi/gephi/issues/1175.
48 Most of the default layout algorithms implemented in Gephi are 'force-directed' and cluster the graph based on degree.
49 Documentation could be found, for example, in the academic paper that was published on, and provides insights into, the significance of the applied algorithm settings, see for instance: Jacomy et al, 'ForceAtlas2, a Continuous Graph Layout Algorithm for Handy Network Visualization Designed for the Gephi Software'.

which draw on Gephi to visualize the social networks they study insert any substantive discussion of the benefits or limitations of the particular Gephi network visualization algorithms they have chosen, or of the specific visualization settings which were used to direct the algorithm itself.[50]

We presently seek to validate the observation that there is a lack of documentation empirically, which we find is a cause for concern. In order to gauge if and how scholars are currently discussing their research processes in Gephi, we inventoried a selection of articles which cite the developer's paper 'Gephi: an open source software for exploring and manipulating networks'.[51] Working in a media department ourselves, we decided to sample publications that mention [media].[52] For this selection process, we drew on Google Scholar. In total, 3,251 papers that cite Bastian et al. were found, of which 2,410 also mention [media].[53]

We collected the first 150 academic papers listed by Google Scholar, thereby practicing what Richard Rogers called 'search as research'.[54] Of these 150 papers, we selected the 16 papers stemming from media studies for an exploratory inventory. These papers were assessed on the documentation of the dimensions also logged by the plugin that we will introduce in detail in the next section. We noted on a scale of 0-2 whether the information was not at all (0), to some extent (1), or completely (2) present. Below the inventoried dimensions and their total count are listed.

Dimension	Total count
Amount of nodes	21
Amount of edges	18
Layout algorithm applied	21
Settings algorithm	0
Filters	12

50 Axel Bruns, 'Faster than the Speed of Print: Reconciling 'Big Data' Social Media Analysis and Academic Scholarship', *First Monday* 18.10 (2013).
51 Bastian et al, 'Gephi: An Open Source Software for Exploring and Manipulating Networks'.
52 The block braces are used to denote a query. For an explanation on the nature of query notation, see Richard Rogers, 'Foundations of Digital Methods', in Mirko Tobias Schäfer and Karin Van Es (eds), *The Datafied Society: Studying Culture through Data*, Amsterdam: Amsterdam University Press, 2017, pp. 75-94, p. 83.
53 Bastian, et al, 'Gephi: An Open Source Software for Exploring and Manipulating Networks'.
54 In order to minimize effects of personalization, we logged out of Google and used a clean installation of a normally unused browser, of which all cookies were deleted as an additional precaution. Books/book chapters, duplicates, and non-English work were excluded due to practical constraints. Rogers, 'Foundations of Digital Methods', p. 76.

Appearance N/E (explaining the ranking/partition elements in graph)	24
Color nodes	15
Color edges	5
Size nodes	16
Edge thickness/shape	8
Statistics used	17
Data lab manipulations	1
Preview settings	1

Table 1. Amount of times papers documented aspect of research project. N is 16, the greatest potential score is 32, lowest is 0.

Our sample suggests that media studies papers drawing on Gephi frequently document the layout algorithm that was used and details on the partitioning of the graph. However, none of the papers in our sample reflected on the settings of those (layout) algorithms (e.g. whether scaling was set to 10 or 50). As demonstrated earlier, such settings should be described because of the influence they have on the presentation of the graph. Furthermore, the settings of the applied metrics such as the 'resolution' set for Modularity Class influence the outcome of the calculation process (e.g. more or less smaller communities) and, therefore, the (visual) clustering of the graph and identification of communities based on this clustering. The inventoried dimensions were classified according to three different degrees of attention to documentation: rich documentation, some documentation, and limited documentation. This categorization serves to show the disproportional attention particular aspects of the process receive, as per below.

Rich documentation (>20)	Some documentation (10-20)	Limited documentation (<10)
Amount of nodes	Amount of edges	Settings algorithm
Layout algorithm applied	Filters	Color edges
Appearance N/E (explaining the ranking/partition elements in graph)	Color nodes	Edge thickness/shape

	Size nodes	Data lab manipulations
	Statistics used	Preview settings

Table 2. Spectrum of documentation.

We discovered that a number of influential aspects of the working process are not documented (in detail), despite their fundamental consequences for the analysis or presentation. This includes documentation about the statistics and filters used, the settings of the algorithm applied, data lab manipulations, and the preview settings. These settings should be logged and open for scrutiny as part of an effort for scholarly positioning. Bruns has rightly raised concerns about 'spatial limitations' in the publication of (big) data research that limit detailed documentation of tools, methods, and datasets.[55] As such we propose that at a bare minimum the most relevant settings for the particular network visualization, as established by the researchers working on the project, be included in a legend. It should also be accompanied by either the settings file itself or contact details to retrieve the said file.

The Fieldnotes Plugin

Alluding to a long-standing tradition in field work and the related practice of taking thorough fieldnotes, we decided to baptize the practical contribution to making network visualization in Gephi accountable the 'fieldnotes plugin'.[56] In doing so, we also emphasize the need for more (ongoing) ethnographic work in the domain of digital methods and software tools, their use and development. The plugin is designed to be installed like any other plugin available for Gephi.[57] It can automatically log the following:

- Amount of nodes/edges;
- Algorithms used;
- Filters;
- Statistics;
- Preview settings;
- Time-stamped graph file (including information from Data Laboratory) in gexf format.

The log of the working process can be exported as a settings file (see for example the figure below). In this file, the particular parameters of each step are logged - not only the steps taken. For instance, if one uses a particular filter, besides the type of filter all properties associated with that filter are saved. The settings are exported as a .txt file and can therefore be opened

---

55 Bruns, 'Faster than the Speed of Print'.
56 See e.g. James Clifford and Georg E. Marcus (eds), *Writing Culture: The Poetics and Politics of Ethnography*, Berkeley: University of California Press, 1986; Roger Sanjek (ed.), *Fieldnotes: The Makings of Anthropology*, Ithaca: Cornell University Press, 1990.
57 The project can be found on GitHub: https://github.com/UUDigitalHumanitieslab/gephi-plugins/tree/fieldnotes.

in a wide variety of text editors (e.g. Figure 6).

A limitation, which is important to note, is that we have not yet managed to extract the property values of the layout algorithm, which are influential settings. The back-end of Gephi did not allow for such implementation during the development time allotted, but it is foremost on our priority list for future development. Nevertheless, even with the limited functionality in logging this particular aspect, it still greatly speeds up the logging which would otherwise be done manually.

```
## General settings
isDirectedGraph: true
edgeCount: 1785
nodeCount: 2069

## Filter settings
# filter 0: Edge Type
type: 0
# filter 1: Edge Weight
range: 1.0 - 4.0

## Layout settings
# layout: ForceAtlas 2
scalingRatio: Not extracted
strongGravityMode: Not extracted
gravity: Not extracted
distributedAttraction: Not extracted
linLogMode: Not extracted
adjustSizes: Not extracted
edgeWeightInfluence: Not extracted
jitterTolerance: Not extracted
barnesHutOptimization: Not extracted
barnesHutTheta: Not extracted
threads: Not extracted

## Statistics settings
statisticsModel: org.gephi.statistics.StatisticsModelImpl@5a337198

## Preview settings
edge.show: true
node.border.width: 1.0
node.border.color: java.awt.Color[r=0,g=0,b=0]
node.opacity: 100.0
node.per.node.opacity: false
node.label.show: false
edge.label.show: false
edge.thickness: 1.0
edge.rescale-weight: false
edge.rescale-weight.min: 0.1
edge.rescale-weight.max: 1.0
edge.color: java.awt.Color[r=0,g=0,b=0]
edge.opacity: 100.0
```

Figure 6. Example of settings.txt file

Aside from the settings file, the plugin also automatically saves the graph file (GEXF) with a timestamp that matches the settings file's timestamp. Together these files serve as a complete snapshot of the graph. Additionally, the automatic saving functions as an extra failsafe for Gephi's omission of an undo button and is a hack to cope with the need to continuously save all steps during the working process.[58]

What the Gephi Plugin Does and Does not Solve

The Gephi plugin is intended to make it easier to document the working process, yet it by no means covers all the problems (humanities) scholars face when working with Gephi. We will briefly highlight a couple of problems that will persist, and some others for which we believe the plugin to be a pragmatic solution to.

Several scholars have highlighted the need for a better understanding of the tools we use,

---

58   See e.g. a related discussion on the Gephi Wiki: https://github.com/gephi/gephi/issues/1175.

and therefore, the algorithms we work with.[59] While we acknowledge the importance of such intimate tool understanding - for instance, in the case of statistical measures such as PageRank or algorithms like ForceAtlas 2 - our plugin does not facilitate better understanding of the algorithms themselves. The plugin limits itself to offering information on what parameters were used to influence their workings. Thus, it does not help to open the black box of the applied - in this case mathematical and social - principles themselves, but rather helps to give insight into the 'black box of data research,' by gathering the variables and procedures applied.

By tackling this black box of data research, we hope to stimulate communication between scholars both within research teams and in external communication. Documenting the variables used allows, for instance, for accessing and assessing particular research projects. By logging these, it also makes it easier for scholars to communicate and reflect on key parameters in their publications. As we have shown, much can be gained in this area. Nevertheless, the plugin does not immediately lead to a more reflective engagement with the Gephi working process. As the plugin logs properties automatically, it is still up to the researcher to reflect on the process; our contribution merely facilitates practices of critical positioning.

The plugin is not a fix for all issues arising around inspectability of data research projects. While it helps to make settings known, one still needs the dataset in order to be able to actually assess the research. Furthermore, one needs to know how that dataset has been created, under what circumstances, whether it is the original master version, or whether it has been filtered, in which way, and what motivated these choices.[60] *Seeing* a network graph, then, does not equal *understanding* the data sample and its (partially automatic) creation.[61] Some information on the Les Miserables data sample's preparation, for example, can be found in the Quick Start Guide, but extensive documentation is missing. In other words, the plugin is merely a way station on the road to critical positioning and account-ability by design.

Additionally, the exact way of arriving at particular settings is not always documented. Node size, for instance, can be set through partition or through manual settings. The approach used to get to different node sizes is not logged, only the size change. As discussed, due to the technical makeup of the program, we were not able to program the plugin in such a way that it logs everything we wanted to as of yet. For instance, the pop-up windows used in the case of statistics or splining, and the layout properties during the algorithm's runtime, were impossible to log in the scope allotted for the development of the plugin. It is something we hope to add in future versions.

In sum, we need to distinguish between tackling the black-box of creating network visualizations and that of the tool. Automatically logging the settings used in making the visualization

---

59   See e.g. Paßmann, 'Forschungsmedien erforschen. Über Praxis mit der Mapping- Software Gephi'; Bernhard Rieder and Theo Röhle, 'Digital Methods: Five Challenges'; Rieder and Röhle, 'Digital methods: from challenges to Bildung.'.
60   Gebru et al, 'Datasheets for Datasets'.
61   Ananny and Crawford, 'Seeing without Knowing: Limitations of the Transparency Ideal and Its Application to Algorithmic Accountability'.

with the Gephi plugin, does the former, but not the latter. Rieder and Röhle rightfully point out that 'tools such as Gephi have made network analysis accessible to broad audiences that happily produce network diagrams without having acquired robust understanding of the concepts and techniques the software mobilizes'.[62] It is true then that the plugin does not make everyone domain experts, but merely makes it possible for domain experts and other researchers to *better communicate about the process*,[63] and in that, critically position themselves and their research activities. For us, this is what is at stake in account-ability by design. Automating logging processes can assist the researchers in their reflexive process, but the required reflection on the epistemic process remains a human activity.

Conclusion

In this chapter we introduced the fieldnotes plugin for Gephi, which allows the taking of procedural 'fieldnotes.' By facilitating systematic documentation of the visualization and analysis process, it allows for traceability of and reflection on the subsequent results. By mapping the interaction between the software tool and the researcher, we facilitate a reflexive approach to one's research practice. We situate the development of the plugin in what we call the road to 'account-ability by design.' Recently there have been a number of pragmatic contributions which similarly allow for 'methodological reflexivity' and account-ability, which share a similar vision on what is good computationally mediated scholarly practice.[64]

For us being account-able rests in part with the documentation of one's research process, but it also requires insight in how tools are used and why. The need for the documentation was demonstrated with an exploration of the application of (different properties of) the ForceAtlas 2 algorithm and modularity clustering in the case of the Les Miserables data sample. We have also shown that documentation in scholarly papers drawing on Gephi is in many instances quite poor or nonexistent.

We see the Gephi plugin as a pragmatic solution which only partially aids in account-ability. The plugin enables tracking the interaction between researcher and program but does not address other crucial matters (e.g. why particular choices were made or providing more insight in the workings of an algorithm). The application brings us closer to good computationally mediated practice in data-related research projects and helps us interrogate what being accountable means in a scholarly context. Yet, it needs to be seen as just one step towards the end goal of 'account-ability by design'. The plugin maps the analysis process, which facilitates better documentation in scholarly communication.

The development of the plugin fits in the tradition of research documentation. In the case of network visualization, we argue that many different forms of process documenting can still be explored. Due to practical constraints, we abandoned the idea of accompanying the plugin

---

62 Rieder and Röhle, 'Digital methods: from challenges to Bildung'.
63 In the same line as Gebru et al, 'Datasheets for Datasets'.
64 Rieder and Röhle, 'Digital methods: from challenges to Bildung'; see e.g. Datasheets for Datasets, *Principles for Accountable Algorithms*.

with a list of questions to the researcher to kickstart methodological reflexivity. We consider the development of such (an) accompanying document(s) as a fertile strand of further research. One of such promising strands is, for instance, recording the graph simulation, or more dynamic forms of communication, which demonstrate how the analysis process unfolds over time and based on which choices. With regards to further development of Gephi, we argue in particular for the implementation of the legend module. This was already pitched by Heymann in 2012 and announced on the roadmap for the Gephi 1.0 version that is yet to come.[65]

Acknowledgements

We would like to extend our thanks to the Digital Humanities Lab of Utrecht University, as without their help the plugin could not have been realized. Especially, we want to express our gratitude to José de Kruif and Alex Hebing. Additionally, we would like to thank our research assistant Marjolein Krijgsman who inventoried the academic papers under our guidance.

References

Akrich, Madeleine and Bruno Latour. 'A Summary of a Convenient Vocabulary for the Semiotics of Human and Nonhuman Assemblies', in Wiebe E. Bijker and John Law (eds), *Shaping Technology / Building Society: Studies in Sociotechnical Change*, Cambridge MA/London: MIT Press, 1992, pp. 259-64.

Ananny, Mike and Kate Crawford. 'Seeing without Knowing: Limitations of the Transparency Ideal and Its Application to Algorithmic Accountability'. *New Media and Society,* 20.3 (2018): 973-89.

Bastian, Mathieu, Sebastien Heymann and Mathieu Jacomy. 'Gephi: An Open Source Software for Exploring and Manipulating Networks', *Proceedings of the Third International ICWSM Conference*, 2009. http://www.aaai.org/ocs/index.php/ICWSM/09/paper/download/154/1009.

Blondel, Vincent D., Jean-Loup Guillaume, Renaud Lambiotte and Etienne Lefebvre. 'Fast Unfolding of Communities in Large Networks', *Journal of Statistical Mechanics: Theory and Experiment,* 10 (2008): 1-12.

Bruns, Axel. 'Faster than the Speed of Print: Reconciling 'Big Data' Social Media Analysis and Academic Scholarship', *First Monday* 18.10 (2013).

Clifford, James and Georg E. Marcus (eds), *Writing Culture: The Poetics and Politics of Ethnography*, Berkeley: University of California Press, 1986.

Correa, Carlos D and Kwan-Liu Ma. 'Visualizing Social Networks', in Charu C. Aggarwal (ed.), *Social Network Data Analytics*, New York: Springer, 2011, pp. 307-26.

Curinga, Matthew. 'Critical analysis of interactive media with software affordances', *First Monday* 19.9 (2014).

Diakopoulos, Nicholas, Sorelle Friedler, Marcelo Arenas, Solon Barocas, Michael Hay, Bill Howe, H. V. Jagadish, et al. 'Principles for Accountable Algorithms. Fairness, Accountability, and Transparency in Machine Learning', http://www.fatml.org/resources/principles-for-accountable-algorithms.

---

65   Heymann, Sebastien. "GSoC: Legend Module." *Gephi Blog*, 2012. https://gephi.wordpress.com/2012/09/24/gsoc-legend-module/comment-page-1/; Heymann, Sebastien. "Roadmap." *Wiki*, 2015. https://github.com/gephi/gephi/wiki/Roadmap.

Dianati, Navid. 'Unwinding the Hairball Graph: Pruning Algorithms for Weighted Complex Networks', *Physical Review,* 93.1 (2016).

Drucker, Johanna. 'Humanities Approaches to Graphical Display', *Digital Humanities Quarterly* 5.1 (2011).

Eriksén, Sara. 'Designing for Accountability', *Proceedings of the Second Nordic Conference on Human-Computer Interaction*, 2002: 177-186.

Es, Karin van, Nico Lopez and Thomas Boeschoten. 'Towards a Reflexive Data Analysis', in Mirko Tobias Schäfer and Karin Van Es (eds), *The Datafied Society: Studying Culture through Data*, Amsterdam: Amsterdam University Press, 2017, pp. 171-182.

Few, Stephen. 'Data Visualization for Human Perception', in Interaction Design Foundation (ed.), *The Encyclopedia of Human-Computer Interaction*, 2nd edition, Aarhus: Interaction Design Foundation, 2014. https://www.interaction-design.org/literature/book/the-encyclopedia-of-human-computer-interaction-2nd-ed/data-visualization-for-human-perception.

Foucault, Michel. 'What is Enlightenment?', in Paul Rabinow (ed.), *Ethics: Subjectivity and Truth*, New York: The New Press, 1997.

Garfinkel, Harold. *Studies in Ethnomethodology*, Englewood Cliffs: Prentice-Hall, 1967.

Gebru, Timnit, Jamie Morgenstern, Briana Vecchione, Jennifer Wortman Vaughan, Hanna Wallach, Hal Daumé III and Kate Crawford, 'Datasheets for Datasets', 2018. http://jamiemorgenstern.com/papers/datasheet.pdf.

Geenen, Daniela van. 'The Role of Software Tools in Critical Data Studies Practices. Studying the Affordances of Gephi as a Sociotechnical System', MA thesis, 2018. https://dspace.library.uu.nl/handle/1874/367489.

Geenen, Daniela van. 'The Role of Software Tools in Critical Data Studies Practices. Studying the Affordances of Gephi as a Sociotechnical System.' in *Explorations in Digital Cultures: On the Politics of Datafication, Calculation and Networking,* Lüneburg: Meson Press, forthcoming.

Gephi.org. 'Learn how to use Gephi', https://gephi.org/users/.

Gibson, J.J. *The Ecological Approach to Visual Perception*, Boston: Houghton Mifflin, 1979.

Haraway, Donna J. 'Situated Knowledges: The Science Question in Feminism and the Privilege of Partial Perspective', *Feminist Studies* 14.3 (1988): 575-99.

Heymann, Sebastien. 'GSoC: Legend Module', *Gephi Blog*, 2012, https://gephi.wordpress.com/2012/09/24/gsoc-legend-module/comment-page-1/.

Heymann, Sebastien. 'Roadmap', 2015. https://github.com/gephi/gephi/wiki/Roadmap.

Hutchby, Ian. 'Technologies, Texts and Affordances', *Sociology* 35.2 (2001): 441-56.

Jacomy, Mathieu, Tommaso Venturini, Sebastien Heymann and Mathieu Bastian. 'ForceAtlas2, a Continuous Graph Layout Algorithm for Handy Network Visualization Designed for the Gephi Software', *PLoS ONE* 9.6 (2014): 1-12.

Kariv, Adam. 'Letting Data Speak for Itself', *Medium*, 2017, https://medium.com/@adam.kariv/letting-data-speak-for-itself-80f1625a8ad1.

Kennedy, Helen, Rosemary Lucy Hill, Giorgia Aiello, and William Allen. 'The Work That Visualisation Conventions Do', *Information Communication and Society* 19.6 (2016): 715-35.

Knuth, Donald E. *The Stanford GraphBase: A Platform for Combinatorial Computing*, New York: ACM Press, 1993.

Lynch, Michael. 'Against Reflexivity as an Academic Virtue and Source of Privileged Knowledge', *Theory, Culture & Society* 17.3 (2000), 26-54.

Mackenzie, Adrian. *Cutting Code,* New York: Peter Lang, 2006.

Markham, Annette, and Simon Lindgren, 'From Object to Flow: Network Sensibility, Symbolic Interactionism, and Social Media', *Studies in Symbolic Interaction*, 2013.

Manovich, Lev. *Software Takes Command,* New York, London: Bloomsbury, 2013.

Neyland, Daniel. 'Bearing Account-Able Witness to the Ethical Algorithmic System', *Science, Technology, & Human Values* 41.1 (2016): 50-76.

Nissenbaum, Helen. 'Computing and Accountability', *Communications of the ACM* 37.1 (1994): 72-80.

Norman, Donald. *The Design of Everyday Things*, New York: Doubleday, 1990.

Page, Lawrence, Sergey Brin, Rajeev Motwani and Terry Winograd. 'The PageRank Citation Ranking: Bringing Order to the Web', *World Wide Web Internet And Web Information Systems* 54.1999-66 (1998): 1-17.

Paßmann, Johannes. 'Forschungsmedien erforschen. Über Praxis mit der Mapping- Software Gephi', in *Navigationen. Vom Feld zum Labor und zurück* 1 (2013): 113-129.

Rieder, Bernhard, and Theo Röhle. 'Digital Methods: Five Challenges', in David Berry (ed.), *Understanding Digital Humanities*, Cham: Springer, 2012, pp. 67-84.

Rieder, Bernhard, and Theo Röhle. 'Digital Methods: From Challenges to Bildung' in Mirko Tobias Schäfer and Karin Van Es (eds), *The Datafied Society: Studying Culture through Data*, Amsterdam: Amsterdam University Press, 2017, pp. 109-24.

Rogers, Richard. 'Foundations of Digital Methods', in Mirko Tobias Schäfer and Karin Van Es (eds), *The Datafied Society: Studying Culture through Data*, Amsterdam: Amsterdam University Press, 2017, pp. 75-94.

Sanjek, Roger (ed.). *Fieldnotes: The Makings of Anthropology*, Ithaca: Cornell University Press, 1990.

Schulz, Hans-Jörg and Christophe Hurter. 'Grooming the Hairball - How to Tidy up Network Visualizations', *IEEE Information Visualization Conference*, Atlanta, United States, 2013.

Utrecht Data School. 'Data Ethics Decision Aid (DEDA)', *Utrecht Data School*, 2018, https://dataschool.nl/deda/?lang=en.

Venturini, Tommaso, Mathieu Jacomy and Débora Pereira. 'Visual Network Analysis', Working Paper (2015), https://www.tommasoventurini.it/wp/wp-content/uploads/2014/08/Venturini-Jacomy_Visual-Network-Analysis_WorkingPaper.pdf.

Verbeek, Peter-Paul. *Moralizing Technology. Understanding and Designing the Morality of Things.* Chicago/London: University of Chicago Press, 2011.

____. 'Resistance Is Futile: Toward a Non-Modern Democratization of Technology', *Techné: Research in Philosophy and Technology* 17.1 (2013): 72-92.

THEME 5:
GOOD DATA AND SMART CITIES AND HOMES

17: ALGORITHMIC MAPMAKING IN 'SMART CITIES': DATA PROTECTION IMPACT ASSESSMENTS AS A MEANS OF PROTECTION FOR GROUPS

GERARD JAN RITSEMA VAN ECK

Introduction

Maps are powerful communication tools, and mapmaking used to be a privileged affair. In recent times, this has changed as 'smart cities' have been outfitted with video, audio, and other kinds of 'Internet of Things' sensing devices. The data-streams they generate can be combined with volunteered data to create a vast multitude of interactive maps on which individuals are constantly (re)grouped based on abnormality, deviation, and desirability. Many have argued that under these circumstances personal data protection rights should extend to groups.

However, group rights are an awkward fit for the current European Data Protection Framework, which is heavily focused on individuals. One possible opening for better protection is offered by Data Protection Impact Assessments (DPIAs), which are mandatory to carry out when the 'systematic monitoring of a publicly accessible area on a large scale'[1] necessary for mapmaking takes place. They form an opportunity to recognize the risks of e.g. discrimination at an early stage. Furthermore, by including representatives of local (disadvantaged) groups, the strong performative qualities of maps can offer occasions for groups of citizens in smart cities to proactively shape the environments in which they live.

There are serious limitations. Although DPIAs are mandatory, the inclusion of affected data subjects and their representatives is not. This undermines many of the possible advantages. Finally, the high costs associated with the process might mean many companies engage with it only superficially and temporarily. Establishing effective data protection for groups negatively impacted by mapmaking software through DPIAs thus seems nigh on impossible in lieu of substantial legislative change.

In late 2017, Strava revealed its 'global heatmap' which shows popular running and cycling routes around the world. Although first reported as a 'striking visualization of over one billion activities',[2] the tone of the reporting quickly changed when it was discovered that secret (mili-

---

1 Regulation (EU) 2016/679 of the European Parliament and of the Council of 27 April 2016 on the protection of natural persons with regard to the processing of personal data and on the free movement of such data, and repealing Directive 95/46/EC (General Data Protection Regulation (GDPR)) [2016] OJ L119/1, point (c) of art 35(3).
2 'Strava: A Global Heatmap of Athletic Activity', *The Guardian*, 2 November 2017, https://www.theguardian.com/lifeandstyle/the-running-blog/gallery/2017/nov/02/strava-a-global-heatmap-of-athletic-activity.

tary) locations could also be located using the heatmap.[3] The Stratumseind, a popular nightlife area in the Dutch city of Eindhoven received similarly negative press when it transformed into a 'Living Lab' 'where massive amounts of data about people's activities will be used [...] to study which factors contribute to violence and discomfort.'[4] This data is overlaid on a map of the area, and the police can quickly intervene when and where suspicious patterns emerge. One reporter dubbed it 'Having a beer with Big Brother'.[5]

Clearly, the usage of large amounts of data to draw maps raises concerns. The practice, however, seems to be booming rather than decreasing. 'Smart' and dumb cities alike are increasingly being outfitted with video, audio, and various other 'Internet of Things' (IoT) sensing devices in order to gather ever more data,[6] and an even more potent, and often cheaper, stream of data can be crowdsourced or scraped from (the smartphones of) city dwellers. Once generated, the data needs to go somewhere, and often they end up in maps.

This chapter will consider these developments by combining insights from critical geography and data protection law, particularly the General Data Protection Regulation (GDPR) that recently came into force in the European Union. Specifically, the chapter will begin by investigating the relationship between data and maps, and why they are such salient artifacts. In the next section, the issue of maps is problematized and the lack of legal protections for affected groups is discussed. Then, Data Protection Impact Assessments (DPIAs), a tool that has received renewed interest as a result of the introduction of the GDPR, are introduced as a possible solution in the absence of strong legislation. But are they really a panacea that can provide meaningful safeguards, or an expensive Band-Aid that will be avoided, ignored, and brushed aside?

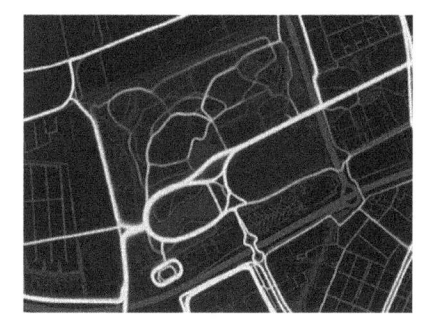

Figure 1. Screenshot taken by the author on https://labs.strava.com/heatmaps on 2 February 2018.

---

3   Alex Hern, 'Fitness Tracking App Strava Gives Away Location of Secret US Army Bases', *The Guardian*, 28 January 2018, https://www.theguardian.com/world/2018/jan/28/fitness-tracking-app-gives-away-location-of-secret-us-army-bases.
4   'Eindhoven Living Lab', European Network of Living Labs, http://www.openlivinglabs.eu/livinglab/eindhoven-living-lab.
5   Author's translation. Peter de Graaf, 'Een Biertje Met Big Brother Erbij', *De Volkskrant*, 23 November 2015.
6   Privacy International, 'Smart Cities: Utopian Vision, Dystopian Reality', 31 October 2017, https://privacyinternational.org/node/638.

Shown is the Stadspark in Groningen, the Netherlands. The clearly visible small semi-circle in the bottom is a 400-meter running track whereas the larger oval above it goes around a pond and measures almost exactly one kilometer; it therefore constitutes a popular running route.

How Maps Are Made

Drawing a map is a powerful act. Who draws a map, decides what is shown on it: physical features of the landscape, roads, settlements, or claims to certain territories by various (imagined) groups.[7] Maps provide a representation of a certain geographical area that, even if not fully objective, at least is claimed to represent the truth.[8] Map drawing has historically been a privileged affair that is only undertaken by those with the means and motivation to do so, including 'scientists, planners, urbanists, technocratic subdividers and social engineers'.[9] However, over the past two decades, the global north has seen a dizzying multiplication of geotagged databases visually overlaid on maps, each of which comprises a new map in itself.[10] Such 'Geographic Information Systems', or simply GIS as they are referred to in the technocratic jargon, are often not carefully constructed by single authors but are based on aggregations of data from a multiplicity of sources, each of which might have been collected differently.[11]

Outfitting an environment with enough IoT sensors to collect the critical mass of geotagged data needed to feed a GIS can be prohibitively expensive for all but the most well-funded smart cities. A cheap and therefore popular alternative, or addition, is crowdsourcing. Roughly, organizations that crowdsource the collection of georeferenced data in order to make maps have three options. One option is that data is collected purposefully by participants that have knowledge of (and perhaps an interest in) how it will be processed further. This is the approach taken by, for example, OpenStreetMap, which is 'built by a community of mappers that contribute and maintain data about roads, trails, cafés, railway stations, and much more'.[12] Another option is to scrape together the various geotagged data trails that smartphone

---

7   For an interesting example of how the national map of Indonesia/the former Dutch East Indies was used in this way, see Benedict R. Anderson, *Imagined Communities: Reflections on the Origin and Spread of Nationalism*, 2nd edition, London/New York: Verso, 2006, from p. 175. For a contrasting example of the same phenomenon, see Jeremy W. Crampton, 'Bordering on Bosnia', *GeoJournal* 39.4 (1996): 353-61.
8   Camilo Arturo Leslie, 'Territoriality, Map-Mindedness, and the Politics of Place', *Theory and Society* 45.2 (April 2016): especially 172-73, DOI: 10.1007/s11186-016-9268-9.
9   Henri Lefebvre, *The Production of Space*, trans. Donald Nicholson-Smith, Malden MA: Blackwell, 1991 (1974), p. 38.
10 Note that from hereon, the term 'map' in this article will be used to describe any visual representation of geographic or georeferenced data that claims to describe some spatial territory, i.e. maps in paper atlases as well as interactive Geographic Information Systems such as Waze.
11 For some examples of differing input arrangements in this context, see Oskar Josef Gstrein and Gerard Jan Ritsema van Eck, 'Mobile Devices as Stigmatizing Security Sensors: The GDPR and a Future of Crowdsourced "Broken Windows"', *International Data Privacy Law* 8.1 (2018): 70-74, DOI: 10.1093/idpl/ipx024.
12 OpenStreetMap Foundation, 'About', https://www.openstreetmap.org/about.

users leave behind,[13] as is done by the Living Lab in Eindhoven and various others.[14] The third option is to combine these two strategies. This model is successfully employed by the navigation app Waze, which takes into account the current traffic situation to calculate the fastest routes. To be able to do so, it scrapes data on the speed and location of its users and combines this with data on for instance road closures that users are encouraged to add using a gamified system of badges and achievements. Furthermore, in various cities such as Rio de Janeiro, New York City, and Ghent, Waze receives data on upcoming road closures from local governments through its Connected Citizens Programme - in exchange, the local governments gain access to information on accidents and other traffic disruptions.[15] As Gekker and Hind point out, this makes it 'not necessarily easy to make a clean split between those who "produce" the map, those who "edit" the map and those who "consume" the map'.[16]

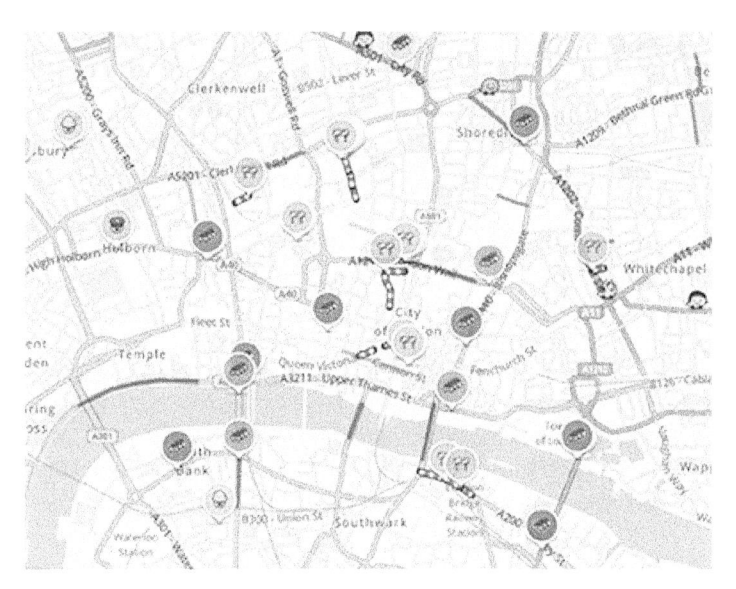

Figure 2. Screenshot taken by the author on https://www.waze.com/livemap on 5 February 2018. Shown is part of the center of London, England. The three data sources are clearly visible: the coloration of the streets is based on scraped movement data, the balloons are based on user submitted reports, and the map data comes from Google Maps.

Once collected, the manner in which crowdsourced georeferenced data is presented further blurs the lines between producers, editors, and consumers. Georeferenced datasets are

---

13 Gavin J. D. Smith, 'Surveillance, Data and Embodiment: On the Work of Being Watched', *Body & Society* 22.2 (2016): 108, doi: 10.1177/1357034X15623622.
14 See e.g. Federico Botta, Helen Susannah Moat and Tobias Preis, 'Quantifying Crowd Size with Mobile Phone and Twitter Data', *Royal Society Open Science* 2.5 (May 2015), DOI: 10.1098/rsos.150162.
15 'Connected Citizen's Programme', Waze, https://www.waze.com/ccp.
16 Alex Gekker and Sam Hind, '"Outsmarting Traffic, Together": Driving as Social Navigation', in Clancy Wilmott et al (eds.) *Playful Mapping in the Digital Age*. Theory on Demand #21, Amsterdam: Institute of Network Cultures, 2016, p. 83.

visualized as cartographic imagery in interactive environments overlaid on Google Maps or similar services like OpenStreetMaps or Bing Maps,[17] engaging the user in acts of active sense making.[18] This makes *prima facie* sense, as the public is accustomed to engaging with large data sets visually.[19]

Interestingly, something else is also gained when crowdsourced georeferenced data is offered as a map. This mode of presentation immediately embeds the data within what Leslie calls 'the "system of maps," the full panoply of mutually-reinforcing, mutually referential map images that subjects are exposed to [...], a system ultimately grounded in a generalized awareness of cartography's scientism'.[20] Thus, by becoming maps, crowdsourced georeferenced data sets also gain the performative power that comes with the claim to truth-correspondence of maps. Put differently: Because people tend to take maps at face value, any data overlaid is also taken at face value, whether it purports to show a crime hotspot or a traffic jam.

Maps and (Missing) Group Rights

The role of many modern algorithms is to render 'big data' actionable on the basis of hyper-complex probalistics.[21] They do this by categorizing people into groups: for example, those who should be shown a certain advertisement, those who should not be let into an airplane without an extra security check, or those who should receive special police attention because they know a victim of a recent shooting.[22]

In public spaces, the push to make cities smart by outfitting them with a multitude of sensors also increases the influence of grouping algorithms.[23] Take, for example, those who are unwittingly part of a suspicious pattern in the Stratumseind Living Lab in Eindhoven. Once identified, the location of the pattern is shown on a map, which, as outlined above, forms an effective communication method for the end-result of such algorithms: it embeds the abstract

---

17   Which itself also provides a seamless transition between multiple 'views' of the same area, such as 'map,' 'terrain,' 'traffic,' and 'satellite.'
18   Jeremy W. Crampton, 'Maps as Social Constructions: Power, Communication, and Visualization', *Progress in Human Geography* 25.2 (2001).
19   Helen Kennedy et al, 'Engaging with (Big) Data Visualizations: Factors That Affect Engagement and Resulting New Definitions of Effectiveness', *First Monday* 21.11 (3 November 2016), DOI: 10.5210/fm.v21i11.6389.
20   Leslie, 'Territoriality, Map-Mindedness, and the Politics of Place', 172.
21   Louise Amoore, 'Data Derivatives: On the Emergence of a Security Risk Calculus for Our Times', *Theory, Culture & Society* 28.6 (November 2011): pp. 24-43, DOI: 10.1177/0263276411417430.
22   Ali Winston, 'Palantir Has Secretly Been Using New Orleans to Test Its Predictive Policing Technology', *The Verge*, 27 February 2018, https://www.theverge.com/2018/2/27/17054740/palantir-predictive-policing-tool-new-orleans-nopd; David Lyon (ed.), *Surveillance as Social Sorting: Privacy, Risk, and Digital Discrimination*, London; New York: Routledge, 2003.
23   Lilian Edwards, 'Privacy, Security and Data Protection in Smart Cities: A Critical EU Law Perspective', *European Data Protection Law Review* 2.1 (2016) DOI: 10.21552/EDPL/2016/1/6.

(and perhaps highly contestable)[24] output of the algorithm in the 'panoply of maps'.[25] Private security personnel can then be deployed to re-establish order. The Strava example mentioned before shows that an environment does not need to be highly saturated with IoT sensors for such groupings to have an effect: only a few smartphones in the Syrian Desert were enough to give away the locations of various secret military bases.

The most problematic side product of map-making algorithms can be geographical biases. Although they do not directly affect individuals, they can deeply impact local communities[26] through, for instance, increased police surveillance.[27] This can, inter alia, be caused by a skew in the collection of crowdsourced geographic data, in which marginalized communities tend to be underrepresented,[28] or conversely, their overrepresentation in historical data.[29] After the collection phase, bias can also creep in during analysis. At this stage though, it may be harder to detect any biases[30] because the inner workings of many algorithms can be difficult to understand for non-experts and, in the case of self-learning algorithms, for the developers of the algorithm itself.[31] Such biases can easily turn into disparate impacts and discrimination when the output of an algorithm is taken at face value. This is especially salient for mapmaking algorithms because, as was discussed above, representing abstract outputs on maps increases their performativity.

The enigmatical nature of refined data processing means that even if strong anti-discrimination legislation exists, it might not provide much protection.[32] This follows from the simple fact that,

---

24 See e.g. Matthew L. Williams, Pete Burnap, and Luke Sloan, 'Crime Sensing with Big Data: The Affordances and Limitations of Using Open Source Communications to Estimate Crime Patterns', *British Journal of Criminology*, 31 March 2016, doi: 10.1093/bjc/azw031, who found that the same Twitter data can reveal juxtaposed phenomena in areas with either high or low levels of crime.
25 Leslie, 'Territoriality, Map-Mindedness, and the Politics of Place', 172.
26 Alessandro Mantelero, 'Personal Data for Decisional Purposes in the Age of Analytics: From an Individual to a Collective Dimension of Data Protection', *Computer Law & Security Review* 32.2 (April 2016): 240, doi: 10.1016/j.clsr.2016.01.014.
27 Elizabeth E. Joh, 'The New Surveillance Discretion: Automated Suspicion, Big Data, and Policing', *Harvard Law & Policy Review* 10.1 (2016): 31-32; Note in this context that Andrew D. Selbst recently proposed an impact assessment framework specifically for predictive policing solutions, see 'Disparate Impact in Big Data Policing', *Georgia Law Review* 52.1 (2018).
28 Burak Pak, Alvin Chua, and Andrew Vande Moere, 'FixMyStreet Brussels: Socio-Demographic Inequality in Crowdsourced Civic Participation', *Journal of Urban Technology*, 10 April 2017, DOI: 10.1080/10630732.2016.1270047; Monica M. Brannon, 'Datafied and Divided: Techno-Dimensions of Inequality in American Cities', *City & Community* 16.1 (March 2017): 20-24, DOI: 10.1111/cico.12220.
29 Selbst, 'Disparate Impact in Big Data Policing', 133; Elizabeth E. Joh, 'Policing by Numbers: Big Data and the Fourth Amendment', *Washington Law Review* 89.1 (2014): 58; Delbert S. Elliot, 'Lies, Damn Lies and Arrest Statistics' Center for the Study and Prevention of Violence, 1995.
30 Brent Mittelstadt, 'From Individual to Group Privacy in Big Data Analytics', *Philosophy & Technology* 30.4 (December 2017): 479 and 490, doi: 10.1007/s13347-017-0253-7.
31 Joh, 'The New Surveillance Discretion', 21; Frank Pasquale, *The Black Box Society: The Secret Algorithms That Control Money and Information*, Cambridge: Harvard University Press, 2015.
32 Mantelero, 'Personal Data for Decisional Purposes in the Age of Analytics', 248; Bryce Goodman, 'Discrimination, Data Sanitisation and Auditing in the European Union's General Data Protection Regulation', *European Data Protection Law Review* 2.4 (2016): 502, DOI: 10.21552/EDPL/2016/4/8 on the GDPR, and specifically art 9 juncto art 22(4).

in order to bring a claim, for instance in a class action setting, claimants need to be aware that they belong to a group that has been negatively impacted. In the context of algorithmic grouping, where groups are constantly being made, re-made, and deleted on the basis of hypercomplex probalistics, this awareness is usually lacking.[33]

Furthermore, relying on the current EU data protection framework often falls short. Consider for instance the idea of consent, a cornerstone in individual data protection law.[34] It seems questionable whether the (often heavily intoxicated) visitors to the Stratumseind gave informed consent to use their personal data for research purposes. And what about their rights to receive access to the data kept on them, in order to see if it is correct,[35] or whether so-called 'special categories' of data such as their ethnicity or sexual orientation - easily guessed by observing e.g. the entrance to an LGBT nightclub - have been processed?[36] Both questions are, from a legal perspective, moot because the Living Lab and Strava anonymize all data before analysis. The latter even gives users an opt-out to making their anonymized data available.[37] The individual focus of the human rights framework means that the analysis of anonymous data that by definition cannot be traced back to any individual can never infringe any data protection rights. However, it is clear that groups can suffer the consequences of the processing of data that does not identify anyone in the group, for instance when a map clearly indicates where extra police presence might be needed or where antagonists can strike secret military bases.

Many have argued that under these circumstances it no longer makes sense to only defend the personal data protection rights of individuals.[38] Rather, we should be protecting group rights, which are rights 'possessed by a group qua group rather than by its members severally',[39] and more specifically, the data protection rights of groups created by classification algorithms.

However, group rights are an awkward fit for the current European Data Protection Framework, which is heavily focused on individuals.[40] Combined with the recent adoption of the GDPR

---

33 Mittelstadt, 'From Individual to Group Privacy in Big Data Analytics', 487-88; Alessandro Mantelero, 'AI and Big Data: A Blueprint for a Human Rights, Social and Ethical Impact Assessment', *Computer Law & Security Review* 34.4 (August 2018): 764, doi: 10.1016/j.clsr.2018.05.017.
34 GDPR, point (a) of art 6(1).
35 ibid, art 15.
36 ibid, art 9.
37 Drew Robb, 'The Global Heatmap, Now 6x Hotter', *Medium*, 1 November 2017, https://medium.com/strava-engineering/the-global-heatmap-now-6x-hotter-23fc01d301de.
38 See e.g. Mantelero, 'Personal Data for Decisional Purposes in the Age of Analytics', 241; Mittelstadt, 'From Individual to Group Privacy in Big Data Analytics'; Linnet Taylor, Luciano Floridi, and Bart van der Sloot, (eds.), *Group Privacy: New Challenges of Data Technologies*, Philosophical Studies Series #126. Berlin: Springer, 2017, p. 2.
39 Peter Jones, 'Group Rights', *Stanford Encyclopedia of Philosophy*, 29 March 2016, http://plato.stanford.edu/archives/sum2016/entries/rights-group/.
40 Bart van der Sloot, 'Do Groups Have a Right to Protect Their Group Interest in Privacy and Should They? Peeling the Onion of Rights and Interests Protected under Article 8 ECHR', in Linnet Taylor, Luciano Floridi, and Bart van der Sloot (eds), *Group Privacy: New Challenges of Data Technologies*,

and the associated legislative fatigue, which prevents any major innovations in data protection rights in the foreseeable future, it seems unlikely that group data protection rights will become a staple of data protection law in Europe anytime soon.[41] This section has accentuated why this might be problematic. Therefore, the next section will introduce DPIAs, which might provide a workable solution that can be implemented without completely overhauling the legislative framework.

Making Group Rights Real Through DPIAs?

DPIAs have been around for several decades,[42] but the GDPR has renewed interest in them. The GDPR became directly applicable in the member states of the European Union (EU) on 25 May 2018.[43] It aims to create 'first-rate data protection rules providing for the world's highest standard of protection.'[44] Some of the central tools the GDPR employs in order to ensure this high standard are preventative measures, such as storage limitations,[45] codes of conduct,[46] certification,[47] data protection by design and by default,[48] and rules on the security of personal data.[49] This approach aimed at reducing risks seems fitting for personal data protection, as it can be difficult to predict harms,[50] and it might be even more complicated to reverse them.

Philosophical Studies Series 126. Berlin: Springer, 2017, pp. 197-224, DOI: 10.1007/978-3-319-46608-8_9; Lilian Edwards and Michael Veale, 'Enslaving the Algorithm: From a "Right to an Explanation" to a "Right to Better Decisions"?', *IEEE Security & Privacy* 16.3 (May 2018): 47, DOI: 10.1109/MSP.2018.2701152. Note that the existence of group (or collective) rights in general has long been a topic of debate within legal and political philosophy scholarship. There is not sufficient room within the current chapter to provide an overview that would do justice to this debate, but the interested reader may, for both pro and contra perspectives, refer to inter alia Peter Jones, 'Human Rights, Group Rights, and Peoples' Rights', *Human Rights Quarterly* 21.2 (1999): 80-107; Miodrag A. Jovanović, *Collective Rights: A Legal Theory,* Cambridge ; New York: Cambridge University Press, 2012; Tamir Yeal, 'Against Collective Rights', in Christian Joppke and Steven Lukes (eds), *Multicultural Questions*, Oxford: Oxford University Press, 1999, pp. 150-80; David Miller, 'Group Rights, Human Rights and Citizenship', *European Journal of Philosophy* 10.2 (August 2002), DOI: 10.1111/1468-0378.00155; Neus Torbisco Casals (ed.), *Group Rights as Human Rights: A Liberal Approach to Multiculturalism*, Law and Philosophy Library #75. Dordrecht: Springer, 2006, DOI: 10.1007/1-4020-4209-4.

41 Taylor, Floridi, and van der Sloot, *Group Privacy*, p. 233.
42 Although they already existed in a primordial form in the 1970s, their development really took flight after the mid-1990s. Roger Clarke, 'Privacy Impact Assessment: Its Origins and Development', *Computer Law & Security Review* 25.2 (January 2009), DOI: 10.1016/j.clsr.2009.02.002.
43 GDPR, art 99(2).
44 European Commission, 'Joint Statement on the Final Adoption of the New EU Rules for Personal Data Protection', 14 April 2016, http://europa.eu/rapid/press-release_STATEMENT-16-1403_en.htm.
45 GDPR, point (e) of art 5(1).
46 ibid, art 40.
47 ibid, art 42.
48 ibid, art 25.
49 ibid, art 32.
50 Arvind Narayanan, Joanna Huey and Edward W. Felten, 'A Precautionary Approach to Big Data Privacy', in Serge Gutwirth, Ronald Leenes, and Paul De Hert (eds), *Data Protection on the Move: Current Developments in ICT and Privacy/Data Protection,* Issues in Privacy and Data Protection #24. Dordrecht: Springer Netherlands, 2016, p. 358, DOI: 10.1007/978-94-017-7376-8_13.

DPIAs are a central instrument in this toolbox, and required if the processing of personal data is 'likely to result in a high risk to the rights and freedoms of natural persons.'[51] In cases where it is unclear whether high risks will materialize, the Article 29 Working Party recommends that a DPIA be carried out nonetheless in order to minimize risks and ensure compliance.[52] 'A DPIA is a process designed to describe the processing, assess its necessity and proportionality and help manage the risks to the rights and freedoms of natural persons resulting from the processing of personal data'.[53] This process can take many forms depending on, inter alia, the type of personal data processing being assessed.[54] But its minimum requirements are a description of the processing; an assessment of the proportionality and necessity of the processing (i.e. can the same aim be achieved with less personal data processing); measures to minimize risks to data subjects; and an active involvement of those data subjects.[55]

Crowdsourced maps are usually of publicly accessible areas such as streets, neighborhoods and parks, if only because it would be hard to find a crowd in an area that is *not* publicly accessible.[56] In particular, the GDPR requires DPIAs if 'systematic monitoring of a publicly accessible area on a large scale' takes place.[57] The Article 29 Working Party points out that such data collection can be especially problematic because data subjects might not be aware of the data processing. Furthermore, they might not be able to prevent their data from being collected without avoiding the public area in question, rendering the public place less public and any form of consent meaningless.[58] Therefore, safeguards to gauge and minimize risks are certainly needed, and it seems it will be nigh on impossible to avoid doing a DPIA when gathering crowdsourced data for making maps.

As DPIAs are thus a necessary step in the development of crowdsourced maps, they might form a promising avenue to address the problems identified in the previous section. As we have seen however, trying to deal with group data protection rights within the EU data protection framework achieves unsatisfactory results. So why should Data Protection Impact Assessments be better suited to deal with mapmaking algorithms that analyze crowdsourced data if they are a part of that same framework? In the next two sub-sections, only those aspects that are pertinent to this specific question will be dealt with. Many others have already written extensively on DPIAs and proposed various models and frameworks.[59] The object here is not

---

51   GDPR, art 35(1).
52   Article 29 Data Protection Working Party, 'Guidelines on Data Protection Impact Assessment (DPIA) and Determining Whether Processing Is "Likely to Result in a High Risk" for the Purposes of Regulation 2016/679 (WP 248 Rev.01)', 4 October 2017, 8, ec.europa.eu/newsroom/document.cfm?doc_id=47711.
53   ibid., 31. Note that the Article 29 Working Party has been renamed the European Data Protection Board (EDPB) when the GDPR came into force. GDPR, art 68-76.
54   Article 29 Data Protection Working Party, 'Guidelines on DPIA', annex 1.
55   ibid, annex 2.
56   Although not completely impossible if one for instance invites a crowd of people to their private castle or estate.
57   GDPR, point (c) of art 35(3).
58   Article 29 Data Protection Working Party, 'Guidelines on DPIA', 9.
59   See, among many others, e.g. the interactive software released by the French Data Protection Authority, the Commission Nationale de l'Informatique et des Libertés, 'The Open Source PIA Software

to duplicate their work or add yet another model, but to suggest how, within existing models, a small extension could yield significant results.

Opportunities

Counter-intuitively, the embeddedness of DPIAs provides an opportunity to enhance the protection of group data protection rights *within* the current legal framework. Many other proposals exist to include various ethical, social, and human rights considerations in a plethora of impact assessment tools.[60] These can serve as important inspirations and templates in the context of crowdsourced map-making initiatives. However, they form an additional financial and administrative burden that data controllers are called upon to voluntarily shoulder. By adding group rights to an already existing requirement, these costs could be significantly decreased.

The most straightforward way in which group data protection rights for crowdsourced map-making initiatives can be safeguarded is the same way in which personal data protection rights are safeguarded: by 'assessing [risks] and determining the measures to address them'.[61] Many already established personal data protection principles can be applied to address any identified risks for groups. Consider, for example, how the data minimization principle could also be applied to anonymous data. In the Strava example mentioned above this simple procedure could have prevented the company great reputational loss, not to mention the unknown costs to military operations.

This example also shows how important the proactive nature of DPIAs is in making group rights real. DPIAs should be engaged in 'as early as is practicable'[62] in order to prevent risks from materializing. As was discussed in the section 'Maps and (Missing) Group Rights', it

---

Helps to Carry out Data Protection Impact Assessment', CNIL, 31 May 2018, https://www.cnil.fr/en/open-source-pia-software-helps-carry-out-data-protection-impact-assesment; Commission Nationale de l'Informatique et des Libertés, 'Privacy Impact Assessment (PIA) Templates', 2018, https://www.cnil.fr/sites/default/files/atoms/files/cnil-pia-2-en-templates.pdf; Information Commissioner's office, 'Sample DPIA Template', 2018, https://ico.org.uk/media/for-organisations/documents/2258857/dpia-template-v1.docx; The 'Guidelines on DPIA' by the Article 29 Working Party could be read in this light; Mantelero, 'AI and Big Data'; See also various contributions to the edited volume by David Wright and Paul de Hert (eds), *Privacy Impact Assessment*, Law, Governance and Technology Series #6. Dordrecht: Springer, 2012.

60 See e.g. Nora Götzmann et al, 'Human Rights Impact Assessment Guidance and Toolbox (Road-Testing Version)' The Danish Institute for Human Rights, 2016, https://www.humanrights.dk/sites/humanrights.dk/files/media/dokumenter/business/hria_toolbox/hria_guidance_and_toolbox_final_may22016.pdf_223795_1_1.pdf; David Wright and Michael Friedewald, 'Integrating Privacy and Ethical Impact Assessments', *Science and Public Policy* 40.6 (1 December 2013), DOI: 10.1093/scipol/sct083; David Wright and Emilio Mordini, 'Privacy and Ethical Impact Assessment', in David Wright and Paul De Hert (eds), *Privacy Impact Assessment,* Dordrecht: Springer Netherlands, 2012, pp. 397-418, DOI: 10.1007/978-94-007-2543-0_19; Barbara Skorupinski and Konrad Ott, 'Technology Assessment and Ethics: Determining a Relationship in Theory and Practice', *Poiesis & Praxis* 1.2 (1 August 2002), DOI: 10.1007/s102020100010.
61 Article 29 Data Protection Working Party, 'Guidelines on DPIA', 4.
62 ibid, 14.

can be difficult to reliably reconstruct what has happened once an algorithm has grouped individuals. Therefore, it is preferable to set limits and objectives beforehand,[63] by for instance auditing algorithms for disparate impacts using simulated data.[64]

Besides these more general opportunities for the inclusion of group data protection rights within DPIAs, the GDPR contains a clause with specific relevance for crowdsourced map-making initiatives: 'where appropriate, the controller shall seek the views of data subjects or their representatives on the intended processing'.[65] At its most basic, this clause allows data controllers to seek these views and perhaps include them in the final report of the DPIA, but then for all intents and purposes discount them. However, if properly engaged with, it also allows for data subjects to co-produce the environments in which they live.[66]

This opportunity is created by the considerable performative power of maps, as discussed in the section 'How Maps are Made'. By affording local groups access to the development process, they gain ownership[67] over the production of the map and thus their surroundings. For instance, they can have a voice in what maps will and will not show, in which way, and to whom.[68] This ability to contribute to the meaning of places makes DPIAs for crowdsourced maps especially well-suited for empowering residents;[69] it allows them to change their environment from a place that they happen to live in and that others map, to a place that is mapped and co-produced by them.[70]

Such a co-production can be modelled after consent, one of the pillars of personal data protection law. Consent should always be given beforehand,[71] and by the affected data subject itself. Consent is only valid if, inter alia, it meets the connected requirements that it is informed, granular, and specific.[72] By integrating these requirements into DPIAs, groups are given a way

---

63 Mittelstadt, 'From Individual to Group Privacy in Big Data Analytics', 489.
64 Goodman, 'Discrimination, Data Sanitisation and Auditing in the GDPR', 503.
65 GDPR, art 35(9).
66 Henri Lefebvre, 'Right to the City', in Eleonore Kofman and Elizabeth Lebas (eds), *Writings on Cities*, Cambridge MA: Blackwell, 1996, p. 79.
67 To be understood in the manner that e.g. Michiel de Lange and Martijn de Waal use for the term; 'Owning the City: New Media and Citizen Engagement in Urban Design', *First Monday* 18.11 (27 November 2013), DOI: 10.5210/fm.v18i11.4954.
68 Adam Greenfield and Mark Shepard, *Urban Computing and Its Discontents*, Architecture and Situated Technologies Pamphlets #1. New York: The Architectural League of New York, 2007, p. 44.
69 For a parallel argument, see Simon Walker, *The Future of Human Rights Impact Assessments of Trade Agreements*, School of Human Rights Research Series #35. Antwerp: Intersentia, 2009, p. 41, https://dspace.library.uu.nl/bitstream/handle/1874/36620/walker.pdf.
70 Lefebvre, 'Right to the City', p. 79; For a similar argument from the disciplines of human geography and urban studies, see Paolo Cardullo and Rob Kitchin, 'Being a "Citizen" in the Smart City: Up and down the Scaffold of Smart Citizen Participation in Dublin, Ireland', *GeoJournal* (12 January 2018), DOI: 10.1007/s10708-018-9845-8; and the seminal work by Sherry R. Arnstein, 'A Ladder Of Citizen Participation', *Journal of the American Institute of Planners* 35.4 (July 1969), DOI: 10.1080/01944366908977225.
71 Although consent can also be withdrawn at any time (GDPR, art 7(3)); this can be difficult in this context as will be discussed below.
72 Article 29 Data Protection Working Party, 'Guidelines on Consent under Regulation 2016/679', 29

to meaningfully co-produce the crowdsourced maps and the GIS software - and thus their living environments - at a stage when some of the processing operations are still unknown.[73]

The inclusion of as many views as possible is essential for this process. However, as it seems quite impractical to have all (potential) data subjects fully engaged in any and all DPIAs for crowdsourced mapmaking initiatives that might affect them, the selection of data subjects and their representatives is crucial. These should come from at least two categories: on the one hand representatives of local communities and local disadvantaged groups, and on the other hand, representatives from digital rights associations with a broader basis in society.

Delegates from local[74] communities should be included to directly speak for those affected and in turn, affect the mapmaking process and the places they inhabit. Also, they alone can meaningfully and actively co-produce their environment on behalf of its inhabitants. The inclusion of representatives from disadvantaged groups can help in trying to avoid bias and discrimination. As was pointed out above, georeferenced data gathering tends to underrepresent already disadvantaged groups,[75] and if data is collected on these groups, it usually further stigmatizes them.[76] The inclusion of these groups should draw the attention of mapmakers to their specific concerns at an early stage.[77]

The benefit of including digital rights associations is that they can represent groups of which the existence is not yet known and can contribute expert knowledge.[78] As was pointed out in the section 'Maps and (Missing) Group Rights' it can be impossible to predict, or even reconstruct after the fact, which groups the algorithms constantly (re)generate. This would mean that any unforeseen groups are automatically excluded from the DPIA. In order to prevent this, digital rights associations may represent them. Note that it would seem appropriate for representatives of such associations to be cautious beyond this specific remit.

The selection of representatives is a difficult task,[79] but the GDPR gives a hint at who might be welcome at the table regardless. Article 80 outlines how individual data subjects can mandate a 'not-for-profit body, organisation or association which [...] has statutory objectives which are in the public interest, and is active in the field of the protection of data subjects' rights and freedoms with regard to the protection of their personal data'[80] to represent them when lodging

---

November 2017, pp. 11-15, http://ec.europa.eu/newsroom/document.cfm?doc_id=48849.
73   Article 29 Data Protection Working Party, 'Guidelines on DPIA', 14.
74   The exact scale of 'local' is not defined here, as it will depend on the mapmaking effort in question. When making a global map, 'local' might thus very well include the world population.
75   Pak, Chua and Moere, 'FixMyStreet Brussels'.
76   Brannon, 'Datafied and Divided'.
77   Wright and Mordini, 'Privacy and Ethical Impact Assessment', p. 402.
78   Mantelero, 'Personal Data for Decisional Purposes in the Age of Analytics', 252; Alessandro Mantelero, 'From Group Privacy to Collective Privacy: Towards a New Dimension of Privacy and Data Protection in the Big Data Era', in Linnet Taylor, Luciano Floridi, and Bart van der Sloot (eds) *Group Privacy: New Challenges of Data Technologies*, Philosophical Studies Series 126. Berlin: Springer, 2017, p. 153, DOI: 10.1007/978-3-319-46608-8_8.
79   See also the next sub-section.
80   GDPR, art 80(1).

a complaint with a DPA,[81] or when seeking a judicial remedy against a DPA, data controller, or processer.[82] This list could be expanded - either informally by data controllers currently executing a DPIA, or eventually by the European legislator - to include the representation of data subjects during DPIAs in the sense of Article 35(9) of the GDPR.

Limitations

Although the EU legislator pays lip service to the ethical and social issues that result from large scale data processing and have an impact beyond the individual, these are included neither in Article 35 of the GDPR which describes Data Protection Impact Assessments, nor in the various DPIA models provided by the Data Protection Authorities (DPA) of the Member States.[83] As a result, despite the many opportunities listed above, a number of important limitations to DPIAs as a tool for enhancing group data protection rights in the context of crowdsourced mapmaking needs to be considered.

A fundamental limitation to the possibility of using DPIAs as embedded in the GDPR is formed by the voluntary nature of the inclusion of groups and their representatives in the process. Article 35(9) is qualified as follows: '*Where appropriate*, the controller shall seek the views of data subjects or their representatives on the intended processing [...]' (emphasis added). It remains unclear, at least for the moment, where this would and would not be appropriate; a situation that the Article 29 Working Party failed to remedy in its opinion on DPIAs.[84] It seems improbable that companies will interpret this provision widely and be eager to engage in the time-consuming, costly, and potentially politically laden process[85] if it can easily be avoided. As seen above, however, it would be exactly this inclusion that engenders many opportunities.

If we assume that companies do engage in DPIAs and include affected data subjects and representatives of local (disadvantaged) groups, many limitations still remain. First of all, when we compare the data protection rights of groups that can be protected through DPIAs to the rights that individuals have over their personal data, it seems that it is chiefly the prohibition on the processing of special categories of data that can be somewhat enhanced through engaging in DPIAs. Left by the wayside are many other principles, such as for example accuracy, accountability, confidentiality, or a lawful basis for processing such as informed and freely given consent.[86] For now, these data protection principles seem out of reach for groups.

---

81 ibid, art 77.
82 ibid, art 78 and 79.
83 Mantelero, 'AI and Big Data', 756; GDPR, recital 75. See also footnote 61.
84 Raphaël Gellert, 'The Article 29 Working Party's Provisional Guidelines on Data Protection Impact Assessment', *European Data Protection Law Review* 3.2 (2017): 215, DOI: 10.21552/edpl/2017/2/11; Atanas Yordanov, 'Nature and Ideal Steps of the Data Protection Impact Assessment Under the General Data Protection Regulation', *European Data Protection Law Review* 3.4 (2017): 493, doi: 10.21552/edpl/2017/4/10; Dariusz Kloza et al, 'Data Protection Impact Assessments in the European Union: Complementing the New Legal Framework towards a More Robust Protection of Individuals' d.pia.lab, 2017, 3, https://cris.vub.be/files/32009890/dpialab_pb2017_1_final.pdf.
85 Mantelero, 'AI and Big Data', 755.
86 See GDPR, art 5 for a more comprehensive set of data processing principles.

The selection of groups to be represented would also present a data controller eager to conduct a DPIA with major difficulties. As was discussed in the section 'How Maps are Made' it is impossible to pinpoint exactly who produces, edits, or consumes a contemporary map; we could add to this confusion those who are impacted by a map. Even if it would be possible to neatly separate these roles and find suitable representatives for each affected group, the composition of all the groups that will (or might) be formed by an algorithm cannot always be known beforehand. Furthermore, many distinct local communities are not neatly divided in classical neighborhoods,[87] and the involvement of neighborhood associations, which may be easy to access for data controllers, might not lead to accurate representation. Finally, assuming that a somewhat complete overview of groups to be represented has been established, it is extremely difficult to decide who can speak on behalf of each group.[88] As the success of a DPIA hinges on the accurate composition of the groups and involvement of their representatives, careful consideration for each separate DPIA is warranted.[89]

Finally, even if companies do engage in the process initially and include as many views as possible, for a DPIA to be truly successful it should be a circular process that is regularly repeated. This is even more important if self-learning algorithms are employed as their outcomes can show unexpected changes over time. This can include changes in the groups targeted, thus necessitating a constant updating of the composition of representatives. The costs necessary to continually assess the possible negative impacts of crowdsourced mapmaking software that has already been written and released might not, in the view of profit maximizing companies, be justified by the possible results.

Conclusion

The question asked at the beginning of the chapter was whether DPIAs could form a panacea or a Band-Aid when protecting group data protection rights in crowdsourced mapmaking initiatives. It laid out the strong performative power of maps and how crowdsourced data is used to make them. Then, it introduced how this practice interacts with the current personal data protection framework in the European Union, leaving undesirable gaps in the safeguarding of group rights. Finally, it introduced Data Protection Impact Assessments and discussed how they could help in alleviating these problems without overhauling the current legislative framework in the EU.

When taking stock of both the opportunities and limitations that DPIAs offer for group data protection rights in crowdsourced mapmaking initiatives it seems that they could easily be circumvented, their effect would be limited at best, that the proper representation of groups is nigh impossible, and that their long-term impact is uncertain in the face of self-learning

---

87 Alan Harding and Talja Blokland-Potters, *Urban Theory: A Critical Introduction to Power, Cities and Urbanism in the 21st Century* Los Angeles: SAGE, 2014, p. 179.
88 Mantelero, 'Personal Data for Decisional Purposes in the Age of Analytics', 254; Mantelero, 'From Group Privacy to Collective Privacy', p. 150.
89 The permanent ad-hoc committees proposed by Mantelero might provide some solace for specific data controllers, although it remains unclear who would be responsible for solving the underlying problem: 'AI and Big Data', 771.

algorithms. Still, companies interested in retaining consumer trust - and gaining a competitive advantage when dealing with responsible customers and partners - would be well-advised to make the investment. This goes doubly so for governmental bodies and institutions: DPIAs form an opportunity to use group rights to put the performative power of maps in the hands of those being mapped. Despite the many gaps and pitfalls, DPIAs for mapmaking initiatives that utilize crowdsourced georeferenced data should be performed, and they should include as many views as possible; Public space should belong to the public, not to companies writing mapping software.

It is up to the EU legislator - and in the meantime: the European Data Protection Board, formerly known as the Article 29 Working Party, whose importance 'for the EU data protection cannot be overstated'[90] - to ensure that group data protection rights can be properly incorporated within the European Data Protection framework. This is the only way to ensure that the uncomfortable Band-Aid proposed in this chapter becomes unnecessary and can be ripped off.

Acknowledgments

An early version of this paper was presented to my colleagues at the department of Transboundary Legal Studies in Groningen. I thank them for the frank comments, which helped to sharpen the argument. I thank Prof. Jeanne Mifsud Bonnici for her many comments on various early drafts. Thanks are due to Lauren Elrick for her careful language check. Finally, I would like to thank the participants of the Surveillance Studies Network 8th Biennial Conference at Aarhus University, Denmark, who provided valuable feedback and inspiration.

References

Amoore, Louise. 'Data Derivatives: On the Emergence of a Security Risk Calculus for Our Times', *Theory, Culture & Society* 28.6 (November 2011): 24-43, DOI: 10.1177/0263276411417430.

Anderson, Benedict R. *Imagined Communities: Reflections on the Origin and Spread of Nationalism*, 2nd ed. London; New York: Verso, 2006.

Arnstein, Sherry R. 'A Ladder of Citizen Participation', *Journal of the American Institute of Planners* 35.4 (July 1969): 216-24, DOI: 10.1080/01944366908977225.

Article 29 Data Protection Working Party. 'Guidelines on Consent under Regulation 2016/679', 29 November 2017, http://ec.europa.eu/newsroom/document.cfm?doc_id=48849.

---------. 'Guidelines on Data Protection Impact Assessment (DPIA) and Determining Whether Processing Is "Likely to Result in a High Risk" for the Purposes of Regulation 2016/679 (WP 248 Rev.01)', 4 October 2017. ec.europa.eu/newsroom/document.cfm?doc_id=47711.

Botta, Federico, Helen Susannah Moat and Tobias Preis. 'Quantifying Crowd Size with Mobile Phone and Twitter Data', *Royal Society Open Science* 2.5 (May 2015). DOI: 10.1098/rsos.150162.

---

[90] Paul de Hert and Vagelis Papakonstantinou, 'The New General Data Protection Regulation: Still a Sound System for the Protection of Individuals?', *Computer Law & Security Review* 32.2 (April 2016): 193, DOI: 10.1016/j.clsr.2016.02.006.

Brannon, Monica M. 'Datafied and Divided: Techno-Dimensions of Inequality in American Cities', *City & Community* 16.1 (March 2017): 20-24. DOI: 10.1111/cico.12220.

Cardullo, Paolo, and Rob Kitchin. 'Being a "Citizen" in the Smart City: Up and down the Scaffold of Smart Citizen Participation in Dublin, Ireland', *GeoJournal* (12 January 2018). DOI: 10.1007/s10708-018-9845-8.

Casals, Neus Torbisco (ed.). *Group Rights as Human Rights: A Liberal Approach to Multiculturalism*, Law and Philosophy Library #75. Dordrecht: Springer, 2006.

Clarke, Roger. 'Privacy Impact Assessment: Its Origins and Development', *Computer Law & Security Review* 25.2 (January 2009): 123-35, DOI: 10.1016/j.clsr.2009.02.002.

Commission Nationale de l'Informatique et des Libertés. 'Privacy Impact Assessment (PIA) Templates', 2018, https://www.cnil.fr/sites/default/files/atoms/files/cnil-pia-2-en-templates.pdf.

---------. 'The Open Source PIA Software Helps to Carry out Data Protection Impact Assessment', CNIL, 31 May 2018, https://www.cnil.fr/en/open-source-pia-software-helps-carry-out-data-protection-impact-assesment.

'Connected Citizen's Programme', Waze, https://www.waze.com/ccp.

Crampton, Jeremy W. 'Bordering on Bosnia', *GeoJournal* 39.4 (1996): 353-61.

---------. 'Maps as Social Constructions: Power, Communication, and Visualization', *Progress in Human Geography* 25.2 (2001): 235-52.

De Lange, Michiel, and Martijn De Waal. 'Owning the City: New Media and Citizen Engagement in Urban Design', *First Monday* 18.11 (27 November 2013), DOI: 10.5210/fm.v18i11.4954.

Edwards, Lilian. 'Privacy, Security and Data Protection in Smart Cities: A Critical EU Law Perspective', *European Data Protection Law Review* 2.1 (2016): 28-58, DOI: 10.21552/EDPL/2016/1/6.

Edwards, Lilian, and Michael Veale. 'Enslaving the Algorithm: From a "Right to an Explanation" to a "Right to Better Decisions"?', *IEEE Security & Privacy* 16.3 (May 2018): 46-54, DOI: 10.1109/MSP.2018.2701152.

'Eindhoven Living Lab', European Network of Living Labs, http://www.openlivinglabs.eu/livinglab/eindhoven-living-lab.

Elliot, Delbert S. 'Lies, Damn Lies and Arrest Statistics'. Center for the Study and Prevention of Violence, 1995.

European Commission. 'Joint Statement on the Final Adoption of the New EU Rules for Personal Data Protection', 14 April 2016, http://europa.eu/rapid/press-release_STATEMENT-16-1403_en.htm.

Gekker, Alex, and Sam Hind. '"Outsmarting Traffic, Together": Driving as Social Navigation', in Clancy Wilmott, Chris Perkins, Sybille Lammes, Sam Hind, Alex Gekker, Emma Fraser, and Daniel Evans (eds.) *Playful Mapping in the Digital Age*, Theory on Demand #21. Amsterdam: Institute of Network Cultures, 2016, pp. 78-92.

Gellert, Raphaël. 'The Article 29 Working Party's Provisional Guidelines on Data Protection Impact Assessment', *European Data Protection Law Review* 3.2 (2017): 212-17, DOI: 10.21552/edpl/2017/2/11.

Goodman, Bryce. 'Discrimination, Data Sanitisation and Auditing in the European Union's General Data Protection Regulation', *European Data Protection Law Review* 2.4 (2016): 493-506, DOI: 10.21552/EDPL/2016/4/8.

Götzmann, Nora, Tulika Bansal, Elin Wrzoncki, Cathrine Poulsen-Hansen, Jacqueline Tedaldi, and Roya Høvsgaard. 'Human Rights Impact Assessment Guidance and Toolbox (Road-Testing Version)'. The Danish Institute for Human Rights, 2016, https://www.humanrights.dk/sites/humanrights.dk/files/media/dokumenter/business/hria_toolbox/hria_guidance_and_toolbox_final_may22016.pdf_223795_1_1.pdf.

Graaf, Peter de. 'Een Biertje Met Big Brother Erbij', *De Volkskrant*, 23 November 2015.

Greenfield, Adam, and Mark Shepard. *Urban Computing and Its Discontents*, Architecture and Situated Technologies Pamphlets #1. New York, NY: The Architectural League of New York, 2007.

Gstrein, Oskar Josef, and Gerard Jan Ritsema van Eck. 'Mobile Devices as Stigmatizing Security Sensors: The GDPR and a Future of Crowdsourced "Broken Windows"', *International Data Privacy Law* 8.1 (2018): 69-85, DOI: 10.1093/idpl/ipx024.

Harding, Alan, and Talja Blokland-Potters. *Urban Theory: A Critical Introduction to Power, Cities and Urbanism in the 21st Century*, Los Angeles: SAGE, 2014.

Hern, Alex. 'Fitness Tracking App Strava Gives Away Location of Secret US Army Bases', *The Guardian*, 28 January 2018, https://www.theguardian.com/world/2018/jan/28/fitness-tracking-app-gives-away-location-of-secret-us-army-bases.

Hert, Paul de, and Vagelis Papakonstantinou. 'The New General Data Protection Regulation: Still a Sound System for the Protection of Individuals?', *Computer Law & Security Review* 32.2 (April 2016): 179-94, DOI: 10.1016/j.clsr.2016.02.006.

Information Commissioner's office. 'Sample DPIA Template', 2018, https://ico.org.uk/media/for-organisations/documents/2258857/dpia-template-v1.docx.

Joh, Elizabeth E. 'Policing by Numbers: Big Data and the Fourth Amendment', *Washington Law Review* 89.1 (2014): 35-68.

---------. 'The New Surveillance Discretion: Automated Suspicion, Big Data, and Policing', *Harvard Law & Policy Review* 10.1 (2016): 15-42.

Jones, Peter. 'Group Rights', Stanford Encyclopedia of Philosophy, 29 March 2016, http://plato.stanford.edu/archives/sum2016/entries/rights-group/.

---------. 'Human Rights, Group Rights, and Peoples' Rights', *Human Rights Quarterly* 21.2 (1999): 80--107.

Jovanović, Miodrag A. *Collective Rights: A Legal Theory*, Cambridge: New York: Cambridge University Press, 2012.

Kennedy, Helen, Rosemary Lucy Hill, William Allen and Andy Kirk. 'Engaging with (Big) Data Visualizations: Factors That Affect Engagement and Resulting New Definitions of Effectiveness', *First Monday* 21.11 (3 November 2016), DOI: 10.5210/fm.v21i11.6389.

Kloza, Dariusz, Niels van Dijk, Raphaël Gellert, István Böröcz, Alessia Tanas, Eugenio Mantovani and Paul Quinn. 'Data Protection Impact Assessments in the European Union: Complementing the New Legal Framework towards a More Robust Protection of Individuals'. d.pia.lab, 2017, https://cris.vub.be/files/32009890/dpialab_pb2017_1_final.pdf.

Lefebvre, Henri. 'Right to the City', in Eleonore Kofman and Elizabeth Lebas (eds.), *Writings on Cities*, Cambridge MA: Blackwell, 1996 (1968), pp 61-181.

---------. *The Production of Space*, trans Donald Nicholson-Smith, Malden MA: Blackwell, 1991 (1974).

Leslie, Camilo Arturo. 'Territoriality, Map-Mindedness, and the Politics of Place', *Theory and Society* 45.2 (April 2016): 169-201, DOI: 10.1007/s11186-016-9268-9.

Lyon, David (ed.). *Surveillance as Social Sorting: Privacy, Risk, and Digital Discrimination*. London/New York: Routledge, 2003.

Mantelero, Alessandro. 'AI and Big Data: A Blueprint for a Human Rights, Social and Ethical Impact Assessment', *Computer Law & Security Review* 34.4 (August 2018): 754-72, DOI: 10.1016/j.clsr.2018.05.017.

---------. 'From Group Privacy to Collective Privacy: Towards a New Dimension of Privacy and Data Protection in the Big Data Era', in Linnet Taylor, Luciano Floridi and Bart van der Sloot *(eds.), Group Privacy: New Challenges of Data Technologies*, Philosophical Studies Series #126. Berlin: Springer, 2017, pp. 139--58, DOI: https://doi.org/10.1007/978-3-319-46608-8_8.

---------. 'Personal Data for Decisional Purposes in the Age of Analytics: From an Individual to a Collective Dimension of Data Protection', *Computer Law & Security Review* 32.2 (April 2016): 238-55, DOI: 10.1016/j.clsr.2016.01.014.

Miller, David. 'Group Rights, Human Rights and Citizenship', *European Journal of Philosophy* 10.2 (August 2002): 178-95, DOI: 10.1111/1468-0378.00155.

Mittelstadt, Brent. 'From Individual to Group Privacy in Big Data Analytics', *Philosophy & Technology* 30.4 (December 2017): 475-94, DOI: 10.1007/s13347-017-0253-7.

Narayanan, Arvind, Joanna Huey and Edward W. Felten, 'A Precautionary Approach to Big Data Privacy', in Serge Gutwirth, Ronald Leenes, and Paul De Hert (eds), *Data Protection on the Move*, Issues in Privacy and Data Protection #24, Dordrecht: Springer Netherlands, 2016, pp. 357-85, DOI: 10.1007/978-94-017-7376-8_13.

OpenStreetMap Foundation. 'About', https://www.openstreetmap.org/about.

Pak, Burak, Alvin Chua, and Andrew Vande Moere. 'FixMyStreet Brussels: Socio-Demographic Inequality in Crowdsourced Civic Participation', *Journal of Urban Technology* (10 April 2017), 1-23, DOI: 10.1080/10630732.2016.1270047.

Pasquale, Frank. *The Black Box Society: The Secret Algorithms That Control Money and Information*. Cambridge: Harvard University Press, 2015.

Privacy International. 'Smart Cities: Utopian Vision, Dystopian Reality', 31 October 2017, https://privacyinternational.org/node/638.

Robb, Drew. 'The Global Heatmap, Now 6x Hotter', *Medium*, 1 November 2017, https://medium.com/strava-engineering/the-global-heatmap-now-6x-hotter-23fc01d301de.

Selbst, Andrew D. 'Disparate Impact in Big Data Policing', *Georgia Law Review* 52.1 (2018): 109-95.

Skorupinski, Barbara, and Konrad Ott. 'Technology Assessment and Ethics: Determining a Relationship in Theory and Practice', *Poiesis & Praxis* 1.2 (1 August 2002): 95-122, DOI: 10.1007/s102020100010.

Sloot, Bart van der. 'Do Groups Have a Right to Protect Their Group Interest in Privacy and Should They? Peeling the Onion of Rights and Interests Protected under Article 8 ECHR', in Linnet Taylor, Luciano Floridi, and Bart van der Sloot (eds), *Group Privacy: New Challenges of Data Technologies*. Philosophical Studies Series #126. Berlin: Springer, 2017, pp. 197-224, DOI: 10.1007/978-3-319-46608-8_9.

Smith, Gavin J. D. 'Surveillance, Data and Embodiment: On the Work of Being Watched', *Body & Society* 22.2 (2016): 108-39, DOI: 10.1177/1357034X15623622.

'Strava: A Global Heatmap of Athletic Activity', *The Guardian*, 2 November 2017, https://www.theguardian.com/lifeandstyle/the-running-blog/gallery/2017/nov/02/strava-a-global-heatmap-of-athletic-activity.

Taylor, Linnet, Luciano Floridi, and Bart van der Sloot (eds). *Group Privacy: New Challenges of Data Technologies*, Philosophical Studies Series 126, Berlin: Springer, 2017.

Walker, Simon. *The Future of Human Rights Impact Assessments of Trade Agreements*, School of Human Rights Research Series #35. Antwerp: Intersentia, 2009, https://dspace.library.uu.nl/bitstream/handle/1874/36620/walker.pdf.

Williams, Matthew L., Pete Burnap, and Luke Sloan. 'Crime Sensing with Big Data: The Affordances and Limitations of Using Open Source Communications to Estimate Crime Patterns', *British Journal of Criminology* (31 March 2016): 320-340, DOI: 10.1093/bjc/azw031.

Winston, Ali. 'Palantir Has Secretly Been Using New Orleans to Test Its Predictive Policing Technology', *The Verge*, 27 February 2018, https://www.theverge.com/2018/2/27/17054740/palantir-predictive-policing-tool-new-orleans-nopd.

Wright, David, and Michael Friedewald. 'Integrating Privacy and Ethical Impact Assessments', *Science and Public Policy* 40.6 (1 December 2013): 755-66, DOI: 10.1093/scipol/sct083.

Wright, David, and Paul de Hert (eds). *Privacy Impact Assessment*, Law, Governance and Technology Series 6. Dordrecht: Springer, 2012.

Wright, David, and Emilio Mordini. 'Privacy and Ethical Impact Assessment', in David Wright and Paul De Hert (eds), *Privacy Impact Assessment*, Dordrecht: Springer Netherlands, 2012, pp. 397-418, DOI: 10.1007/978-94-007-2543-0_19.

Yeal, Tamir. 'Against Collective Rights', in Christian Joppke and Steven Lukes (eds), *Multicultural Questions*, Oxford: Oxford University Press, 1999, pp. 150-80.

Yordanov, Atanas. 'Nature and Ideal Steps of the Data Protection Impact Assessment under the General Data Protection Regulation', *European Data Protection Law Review* 3.4 (2017): 486-95, DOI: 10.21552/edpl/2017/4/10.

18: TRULY SMART CITIES. BUEN CONOCER, DIGITAL ACTIVISM AND URBAN AGROECOLOGY IN COLOMBIA

JUAN-CARLOS VALENCIA AND PAULA RESTREPO

This chapter comes out of two research projects carried out in Colombia, South America. One of them, finished in 2017, was called *City of Data*. It was an exploration of government-led, centralized Smart City projects being implemented in the cities of Bogotá and Medellín. The other one, still ongoing, is called *Communication Practices in the Medellín's Gardeners Network: Knowledge, Territory and Social Fabric.* It is an exploration of knowledge construction, and virtual and real territorialization through grass-roots gardening initiatives in Cali and Medellín. Both research projects had to do with approaches to public data: some 'centralized', government-led in the form of Smart City projects and others, more in the form of citizen-led initiatives. We analysed project documents, conducted semi-structured interviews with dozens of officials and citizen group leaders, and carried out participatory research with a citizen collective in the city of Medellín. Our main goal was to analyze government-led and grass-roots-led initiatives producing and managing data to empower citizens in Medellín and Bogotá. Our theoretical perspective comes from Critical Data Studies, Surveillance Studies, Decoloniality and Relational Ontologies. We found very closed and centralized data production practices in the government-led, smart city initiatives studied, but discovered what could be described as promising 'good data' citizen-led approaches in Medellín's Gardeners Network (RHM). We also found some issues and challenges arising from the particular, non-western, highly unequal context of these citizen-led initiatives.

A Brief Review of Smart City Literature

Smart City projects are being implemented around the world, from Amsterdam to New Delhi, from Los Angeles to Rio de Janeiro. The definition of what a Smart City is differs from place to place, from project to project and between theoretical perspectives. The concept has evolved from a sector-based, corporate or government focused approach to a more comprehensive view that pays more attention to governance and stakeholders' involvement at the core of strategies.[1] According to some proponents and to optimistic academic perspectives, Smart City projects promise to improve the quality of life of urban populations and, at the same time, to make better use of both tangible and intangible resources and public infrastructures.[2] Networked infrastructures would improve economic and political efficiency and enable social, cultural and urban development,[3] but this would only happen when Smart City projects take

---

1 Victoria Fernandez-Anez, José Miguel Fernández-Güell, and Rudolf Giffinger, 'Smart City implementation and discourses: An integrated conceptual model. The case of Vienna', *Cities*, 78 (August 2018):4.
2 Paolo Neirotti et al, 'Current trends in Smart City Initiatives: Some Stylised Facts', *Cities* 38 (June 2014): 27.
3 Andrea Caragliu, Chiara Del Bo and Peter Nijkamp, 'Smart cities in Europe', *Journal of urban technology* 18.2 (2011): 69.

all the stakeholders' opinions into account and seek a compromise between their views and the implementation of the strategies. This literature still believes in Smart City approaches that are government-facilitated but purposefully citizen-centric or even citizen-led. There is a growing emphasis on collaborative economies and innovation.[4] It remains to be seen whether these later approaches fulfil their goals thoroughly and if there are socially successful, really democratic and participative Smart City projects being implemented around the world.

But from the perspective of Critical Data Studies and Surveillance Studies scholars, to whom we feel closer, these projects are based on an illusion of technocratic efficiency and a highly suspicious discourse of digital democratization that hides the economic interests of technology corporations and the designs of neoliberal governments around the world. Daniel McQuillan explains that the Smart City 'is inscribed by an endless stream of heterogeneous data points that pour from our networked daily experiences'.[5] It marks a shift in government intervention in social space from discrete forms of 'intermittent and/or specific information-gathering to continuous processes of management based on total and unremitting surveillance'.[6]

Data is produced by citizens even when they are not specifically creating content: their use of public transport cards and public hot-spots, the traffic they generate while driving, the amount of taxes they pay, their consumption of power, water and other utilities, the crimes they report to the police, their location coordinates;[7] all these activities are being translated into data flows that are correlated with other sources of information to manufacture metadata that could be understood as data commons and should be available to all,[8] but that in fact are the domain of government agencies and corporations.

Top-down Smart City Projects in the Global South

In the Global South, Smart City projects are promoted by resorting to the decades-old myth of Development:[9] traditional societies must embrace new technology and science to finally modernize and join the ranks of developed nations. This myth, denounced by Decolonial scholars and activists such as Esteva and Escobar, dictates that it is necessary:

> [...] to take knowledge to an uneducated society under the assumption that the life of citizens is impoverished by the lack of scientific and technological know-how. It is also based on the idea that science and technology are naturally beneficial and are not related to political and economic interests.[10]

---

4   Boyd Cohen, Esteve Almirall and Henry Chesbrough, 'The City as a Lab. Open Innovation Meets the Collaborative Economy', *California Management Review* 59.1 (1 November 2016): 5.
5   Daniel McQuillan, 'Counter Mapping the Smart City', *Livingmaps Review* 2 (2017): 1-7.
6   Nick Couldry and Alison Powell, 'Big Data from the Bottom up', *Big Data & Society* 1.2 (July 2014): 1.
7   Nick Couldry and Alison Powell, 'Big Data from the Bottom up', 3.
8   Dana Cuff, Mark Hansen and Jerry Kang, 'Urban Sensing: Out of the Woods', *Communications of the ACM* 51.3 (2008): 29.
9   Gustavo Esteva, 'Development', in Wolfgang Sachs (ed.), *The Development Dictionary: A Guide to Knowledge as Power*, London: Zed Books, 1992, pp. 1-23.
10 Manuel Franco-Avellaneda and Tania Pérez-Bustos, 'Tensiones y Convergencias en Torno a la

But both in the Global North and the South, data collection enables what McQuillan describes as a colonial mapping that extends to our feelings, our physiology and even our faces. For analysts like Kitchin and Lauriault,[11] the data captured, processed and constructed by technologies are never neutral; they are immersed in ideologies and worldviews, and get their meaning in concrete socio-historic contexts, where data serves particular goals. What is considered relevant and significant, and constructed as useful data, ignores the perspectives, goals and concerns of different social actors.

Critical analysts are also concerned about the biopolitical implications of Smart City projects: the increased surveillance, the privatization and exploitation of the commons, the neoliberal necropolitics that data-supported governance could allow, the consolidation of what Lash has called 'Algorithmic power'.[12] Smart City projects serve 'the purposes of power, and as the sensors of the smart city see more deeply in to our lives, they colonize the new spaces that they find'.[13] We agree with Colding and Barthel when they propose that Smart City literature and research should include analysis around social sustainability issues for city dwellers, reflect more about whom the Smart City is for, address issues of cultural diversity, resilience and cyber security, and think about the impact of Smart City projects on human-nature relations.[14]

The implementation of Smart City projects differs greatly from place to place, their scopes are diverse, and the uses given to the data and metadata collected are not monolithic and sometimes not even coherent or thorough.[15] This happens both in the Global North where projects and applications fail, are based on racial prejudices,[16] and targeted by special interests, as in the Global South,[17] so diverse and culturally rich, but so uneven, chaotic and plagued by corruption.

Our research of Smart City projects in Bogotá and Medellín analyzed the work of city government agencies and hybrid private and public institutions like Empresa de Telecomunicaciones de Bogotá, the National Police, *Medellin Ciudad Inteligente* and *Ruta N*.[18] It was

---

Apropiación Social de la Ciencia y la Tecnología en Colombia', in Tania Pérez-Bustos y Mayali Tafur Sequera (eds), *Deslocalizando la Apropiación Social de la Ciencia y la Tecnología: Aportes Desde Prácticas Diversas,* Bogotá: Maloka-Colciencias, 2010, p. 13.

11 Rob Kitchin and Tracey Lauriault, 'Towards Critical Data Studies: Charting and Unpacking Data Assemblages and Their Work', in Joe Eckert, Andrew Shears and Jim Thatcher (eds), *Geoweb and Big Data*, Lincoln: University of Nebraska Press, 2014.
12 Scott Lash, 'Power after hegemony: Cultural studies in mutation', *Theory, Culture & Society* 24.3 (May 2007): 55-78.
13 Daniel McQuillan, 'Counter Mapping the Smart City', *Livingmaps Review,* 2 (2017): 1-7.
14 Johan Colding and Stephan Barthel, 'An urban ecology critique on the "Smart City" model', *Journal of Cleaner Production* 164 (October 2017): 95-101.
15 Nick Couldry and Alison Powell, 'Big Data from the Bottom up', *Big Data & Society* 1.2 (July 2014): 1.
16 Simone Browne, 'Digital Epidermalization: Race, Identity and Biometrics', *Critical Sociology* 36.1 (February 2010): 131-150.
17 Claudio Altenhain, 'Tropicalizing Surveillance: How Big Data Policing "Migrated" from New York to São Paulo', *Big Data from the South: From media to mediations, from datafication to data activism, IAMCR Preconference Paper*, Cartagena, Colombia, 15 July 2017, http://cartagena2017.iamcr.org/big-data/.
18 Dario Amar, *Estudios de casos internacionales de ciudades inteligentes,* Documento para discusión No. IDB-DP-443, Banco Interamericano de Desarrollo, 2016.

difficult for us to establish a relationship of trust with governmental or public-private institutions. For example, the Medellín Metro never agreed to give us information, *Ruta N* stopped responding our requests for additional interviews when we refused to organize a meeting of grassroots organizations to have a *Ruta N*-lead conversation about data and collaborative work, and *Medellín Ciudad Inteligente* was dismantled and reorganized soon after our first and only visit. With Medellín's Gardeners Network we established a relationship that allowed us to get closer to what they were doing, and to also understand the complexity and some of the internal conflicts in the organization. For these reasons, this chapter takes a panoramic look at government and public-private led Smart City projects, but delves much more into a citizen-led initiative, the RHM case.

In the case of government-led Smart City projects our interviews with officials, members of citizen collectives and individuals allowed us to discover a complex situation: conflicts and rivalry between government agencies and institutions result in the misuse of data or in its transformation into abstract figures and charts, confusedly mentioned to legitimize policies and political propaganda. New administrations discard previous and ongoing efforts, dismantle research and policy units and force projects to start from scratch. Sophisticated data that contradicts special interests is ignored or discarded. The capacity to collect and process vast amounts of data overwhelms the capacity of existing political institutions and agents to analyze it and use it. Smart City projects may buy and use complex sensor systems and software but people, working in stressful and contradictory conditions, run them. The Smart City projects that we selected and studied in Colombia seem to be developed in a vertical, fragmented and discontinuous way. They are not citizen-led at all and it is dubious that they could be described as purposefully citizen-centric. At least in the case of a Latin American city like Medellín, the projects are full of contradictions, lack transparency and in some cases become pockets of corruption that benefit corporations and an industry of mercenary international advisers. This does not mean that big data are not used by some government agencies to try to control populations for questionable purposes. We just want to point out that the control grid is not completely sealed.

The government and public-private-led Smart City projects that we selected as case studies largely considered citizens as disempowered, uneducated, disorganized individuals whose capacities and knowledge could be fostered and canalized by the institutions. Some officials considered citizens as a potential threat in case they were given access to public data. They insisted that data could be released to the public only when solid organizations and initiatives emerge, but not before. We understood that they feared that adopting open data policies or even just releasing limited sets of data would give ammunition to their political foes and make government initiatives, agencies and policies vulnerable to partisan, intolerable scrutiny. This was the case, for example, of the Medellín Metro system. It is a public company. We and other researchers and citizen collectives have been requesting access to simple data such as station congestion, peak traffic hours and power consumption with no significant response.

Ruta N Corporation considered that citizens could be convened to help co-create solutions to urgent urban problems. Their officials distrust top-down smart city projects that did not connect somehow to the local population and did not take into account their cultural context. They celebrated the fact that at the time of our field work, more than 15,000 citizens of Medellín had become involved in co-creating solutions to city problems, together with *Ruta N*, interacting with officials through social networks and in special events. But nevertheless, it was the agency that played the role of identifying the key problems, recruited citizens to create solutions and recognized them as such.

Another agency called *Medellin Ciudad Inteligente* (Medellín Smart City) has gone through different reorganizations, depending on the local government in turn. When we contacted them in 2015, the agency had become a sort of local news outlet: a group of more than sixty web designers and journalists collecting and publishing information about Medellín and its citizens. They were training people in the city's neighborhoods in basic internet tools, digital photography and writing, to get them to produce local content. A year later, this goal was abandoned and most staff were sacked. Currently, this is the name of the public internet network of the city, but it is not possible to find an agency with such a name.

Social Movements, *Buen Conocer*, Good Data and Postcolonial Computing

But are citizens so unknowledgeable about data technologies? Are they unaware of its potentials? Do they lack the organization and ideas to develop alternative, more democratic uses of data? Aren't they producing any form of *Good Data*?

Most critical approaches to Smart City projects leave little room for agency on the part of citizens. This is why we agree with Couldry and Powell when they argue that 'emerging cultures of data collection deserve to be examined in a way that foregrounds the agency and reflexivity of individual actors as well as the variable ways in which power and participation are constructed and enacted'.[19] As mentioned, our research also focused on citizen strategies for building alternative economies of information. We tried to underscore human agency in relation to data and technology.[20] We did find pockets of resistance to datafication but more interestingly, we came across some urban collectives fighting for the release of public, high quality, socially relevant data. These citizen organizations create communities of resistance and action that demand open data and transparency from public administrators. They also strive to achieve different forms of technological appropriation, the creation of citizen technologies, the production of *Good Data* and the constitution of networks that materialize new forms of communality and become spaces of collective intellect. They demand that government proposals be 'based more on bottom-up approaches in which cities provide access to data and allow citizens to make their own decisions'.[21]

Their efforts are creating more diverse Smart City projects from the bottom up and could be

---

19 Nick Couldry and Alison Powell, 'Big Data from the Bottom up'.
20 Stefania Milan and Lonneke van der Velden, 'The Alternative Epistemologies of Data Activism', *Digital Culture & Society*, 2.2 (2016): 57-74.
21 Paolo Neirotti et al, 'Current trends in Smart City Initiatives: Some Stylised Facts', *Cities* 38 (June, 2014): 8.

understood as what some theorists in Latin America are describing as *Buen Conocer*, 'an interesting process of creative collaboration, 'significant collective intelligence' that mixes knowledges, avant-garde challenges and contextualized solutions to everyday realities'.[22] Some Global South digital activists are engaging in what academics have called Postcolonial Computing:[23] a way of creating software that is critically aware of its context of production and its power relations, not as something to ignore or solve technocratically but as a reality that must be taken into account. They propose a shift from expert designed software and privatized, capital-enhancing data that fundamentally follow the prescriptions of corporations and the Eurocentric worldviews of IT specialists[24] to community designed software and open data that benefits all, humans and non-humans. Truly Smart Cities would operate from the bottom up, taking into consideration the well-being of all, humans and non-humans. They work based on the Marxist idea that general social knowledge has become a direct force of production. Truly Smart Cities could only emerge from citizen-led, communitarian efforts, an expression of the general intellect arising from social practice, of the real life process.

Red de Huerteros Medellín

We will focus now on the work of an independent network of urban agriculture, the Medellín's Gardeners Network (Red de Huerteros Medellín or RHM for its initials in Spanish). First we will offer a brief description of Medellín, the context where this citizen-led initiative operates.

Medellín is the second largest city in Colombia. It has been an important industrial hub since the early 20th Century. Textile, chemical and plastics factories were established in the area. The population rose from 358,189 inhabitants in 1951 to more than 2.5 million in 2017, a sevenfold increase. The industrial sector has taken a hit due to competition from Asia, but factories still operate in the city, many of them with poor waste and pollutant management practices. Cars and motorcycles overflow the streets and this, together with large migration from the countryside and a construction boom, has resulted in a serious environmental crisis. Air pollution has triggered alarms frequently since 2017. Furthermore, Medellín, like so many cities around the world, has been experiencing an increased symbolic and material privatization of space. The dangerous levels of air pollution, the persistent violence and real estate speculation generate visible and invisible borders and deepening socioeconomic gaps. But the city has also become a pocket of environmental resistance, where various citizen collectives are pushing for alternative ways to manage urban space, denounce and monitor air pollution and criticize the felling of trees.

---

22 David Vila-Viñas & Xabier Barandiaran (eds), *Buen conocer. Modelos sostenibles y políticas públicas para una economía social del conocimiento común y abierto en Ecuador*, Quito: FLOK Society, 2015, p.8.
23 Lilli Irani, Janet Vertesi, Paul Dourish, Kavita Philip & Rebecca Grinter, 'Postcolonial computing: A lens on design and development', *Proceedings of the 28th International Conference on Human Factors in Computing Systems,* Atlanta, Georgia, USA, 10-15 April 2010, https://www.cc.gatech.edu/~beki/c50.pdf.
24 Iván Székely, 'What do IT Professionals Think about Surveillance?´, in Christian Fuchs, Kees Boersma, Anders Albrechtslund and Marisol Sandoval (eds), *Internet and Surveillance. The Challenges of Web 2.0 and Social Media*, London: Routledge, 2011.

The RHM is a citizen collective that emerged around 2013 at the initiative of residents of central-western Medellín. They started orchards in their terraces and front yards, and later in abandoned buildings, sidewalks and parks. The members of the RHM come from different backgrounds, professions, genders and economic conditions, but share the goal of making Medellín greener. With the passing of time, the network grew and spread. Interest in different forms of urban agriculture, strategies to manage organic waste, concern with the quality of food, the survival of bees and other insects, the defense of traditional, non-genetically-modified seeds, the control of air pollution and urban soil contamination by heavy metals and the strengthening of communities became topics of discussion and action. Some members consider that despite the examples of Cuba[25] and Argentina,[26] urban agriculture cannot fully supply the demand of such a big and polluted city as Medellín. But they want to do something, they want to learn, meet and take action.

The Network has been growing gradually, adding various parts of the city and connecting with people around the world. It has turned its original urban planting and gardening activities into spaces of social articulation, construction of commonality and knowledge dialogues.[27] They use different communication means to organize their activities, to foster social links in a city with so many scars dating from the years of drug cartel wars and the many conflicts of Colombia. The Network organizers do not know exactly how many people compose it, but current membership in the RHM Facebook group tops 6800 people. Like any network, the RHM is composed of nodes and relationships between them. Some of these nodes work to keep the network well connected, while others are dedicated to maintaining their individual and group projects. In this way, the RHM is not a homogeneous structure. However, there is a node that calls itself the base group, and that has more or less homogeneous intentions, articulated in a Manifesto called 'Sowing Sovereign and Solidarity Worlds'.[28] Some of the nodes are aware and subscribe to the ideas of the Manifesto, others do not know it, do not understand many of its ideas or do not fully subscribe to them. When we refer to the network of 'huerteros', we refer then to the base group and the activities that it develops in articulation with other nodes and grassroots organizations.

Territory, Data and Relational Ontologies

One of the sections of the Manifesto refers to open data and free knowledge, and states: 'We promote the use of open data, software and free knowledge without barriers as a way to transform culture, to grow as a society and to rescue the community values of collective sharing and doing'. This section is articulated with others related to the Earth as a living organism,

---

25 Sinan Koont, *Sustainable urban agriculture in Cuba*, Heidelberg: Springer, 2011.
26 Eduardo Spiaggi, 'Urban Agriculture and Local Sustainable Development in Rosario, Argentina: Integration of Economic, Social, Technical and Environmental Variables', in Luc Mougeot (ed.), *Agropolis. The Social, Political and Environmental Dimensions of Urban Agriculture,* London: Routledge, 2010.
27 http://tupale.co/e50.
28 Red de Huerteros Medellìn, *Manifiesto red de huerteros* Medellìn (March 2017), https://ia601601. us.archive.org/17/items/ManifiestoRedDeHuerterosDeMedelln/Manifiesto_Red%20de%20 huerteros%20de%20Medell%C3%ADn%20.pdf.

food autonomy, food as a political act, agroecology as practice and as social movement, free seeds, food diversity, territorial connection through the activity in the gardens, creativity, community learning, collaborative work for the common good, rural-urban solidarity, conscious consumption practices, re-use of organic waste and bicycles as a form of transport.

The members of the Network reject the understanding of territory as just a commodity. Urban planning views the city as a place for the realization of Capital through real estate projects and other actions aimed at stimulating economic growth and development, regardless of their consequences. The RHM is involved in an ontological struggle that takes place in the urban space.

Proponents of an ontological turn in the Social Sciences have been largely focused on exploring alterity in Indigenous and to a lesser extent Afro-descendant communities, but following Marisol de la Cadena,[29] we consider that we can analyze the dynamics of some non-Indigenous and non-Afro-descendant urban actors as ontologies. De la Cadena puts on the table the dispute between those who seek to preserve 'the networks of emplacement that enable local life' in their dynamics of action (or enaction as Escobar, following Varela, explains),[30] and those who destroy them while converting territory into immaterial assets that support financial speculation[31].

For the RHM the urban territory is a *network of emplacement*.[32] The Network views the city as a melting pot where it should be possible to rearticulate the social fabric and where human and non-human actors could coexist. Furthermore, the city cannot be understood in isolation from the surrounding countryside that supports it. For these reasons, the RHM is constantly developing initiatives that connect people, non-humans and spaces with the goal of protecting the environment and the life that inhabits it.

Resistance to economic and political power arises from micro-territories inhabited by active, empowered communities. While knitting a micro-territorial network,[33] the RHM is trying to redistribute power and to replace a hegemonic mercantilist vision with a different set of relations between the environment, urban nature and people. The activities that allow these micro-territories to intersect and overlap also occur in virtual spaces; but virtual interventions in social or personal spaces are necessarily guided by the real contacts occurring in material, defended territories. These contacts catalyze the virtual interactions.[34]

---

29 Marisol de la Cadena, 'Naturaleza Disociadora', *Boletín de Antropología* 31.52 (July-December 2016): 256.
30 Arturo Escobar, 'Territorios de diferencia: ontología política de los "derechos al territorio"', in Sheila Gruner et al (eds) *Des/dibujando el País/aje. Aportes Para la Paz con los Pueblos Afrodescendientes e Indígenas*, Medellín: Ediciones Poder Negro, 2016.
31 Saskia Sassen, *Expulsions: Brutality and Complexity in the Global Economy*, Boston: Harvard University Press, 2014.
32 Marisol de la Cadena, 'Naturaleza Disociadora'.
33 Rogério Haesbaert, 'Del mito de la desterritorialización a la multiterritorialidad', *Cultura y representaciones sociales* 8.15 (2013): 9-42.
34 Rogério Haesbaert, 'Del mito de la desterritorialización a la multiterritorialidad', 29.

The RHM has been slowly redefining space through a combination of various activities: bike tours of the network's gardens, communitarian activations of gardens, workshops and organic waste management. But to direct and support their *guerrilla gardening*,[35] territorial appropriation and social fabric enhancing activities, the RHM has been increasingly collecting, producing and using what could be called *Good Data*. The Network considers citizen-produced, not for profit data as a key element in the dispute over the urban territory of Medellín. Data such as the location coordinates of gardens, their dimensions and crops, the people taking care of them, their waste management initiatives, the productivity and the local suppliers of agroecological products that reinforce the ideas of the RHM are being stored in open source, free software systems. A few members of the Network with computer programming knowledge manage these applications. They are currently using tools such as OpenStreetMap,[36] Mapillary, OsmAnd and OSM Tracker. They designed a platform called Tupale, totally open and free, that has become the computer base for the work of the Network.

The RHM resists data manipulations that create a world in which humans are opposite or outside nature and are in permanent search for its domination. In this sense we can speak of an articulation between territorial networks, data and worlds (ontologies) defended, appropriated and lived.

Besides its commitment to food sovereignty, the redesign of cities, agroecological food production and reduction of the carbon footprint, the RHM is also turning orchards into multifunctional spaces of social articulation, construction of communality and knowledge dialogues.[37] Some members of the Network create applications designed with free software to store information about their activities, agroecological techniques and databases of the gardens that they are establishing in public and private spaces, through social mapping tools such as OpenStreetMap.[38]

The Network members have grown increasingly conscious of corporate and government data mining and undemocratic, technocratic Smart City initiatives and have switched most of their communications to highly encrypted platforms like Telegram. Yet, the RHM is very active in Facebook as this platform is widely used in Colombia and it allows new nodes, gardens and people to connect with the Network. Google applications are also used but the long-term goal is to have all the Network activities based on open source, free platforms, not only to store information but to create *Good* metadata and visualizations to communicate the RHM activities and objectives.

However, sometimes, the open data and the other ideas of the RHM's Manifesto collide or result in contradictions. Since there are few members of the RHM who possess the knowledge to follow the rules of free software and open data, the registration of activities by other means

---

35 Glenda Amayo Caldwell & Marcus Foth, 'DIY media architecture: Open and participatory approaches to community engagement', in Peter Dalsgaard & Ava Fatah gen Schieck (eds.), *Proceedings of the 2014 Media Architecture Biennale*, Aarhus: ACM Denmark, pp. 1-10.
36 https://www.openstreetmap.org.
37 https://tupale.co/e50.
38 https://www.openstreetmap.org.

such as forms or Google email account end up being the most expeditious and effective way to advance the work. The difficulty of using messaging programs that are more respectful of open data such as Telegram, has ended up causing the communications of the base group to be re-channeled via WhatsApp at the suggestion of the majority. This generates frictions between different members of the group. We identified three factions that are frequently disputing: those closest to the discourse and the technical knowledge of open data constantly try to convince the others of the dangers of proprietary and of the benefits of migrating to computer tools that respect privacy; the less informed often do not understand the discussion and do not participate in it; a third faction which is quite informed about the principles of open data but pragmatically wishes the work to continue and thinks that sometimes open data principles have to be sacrificed to obtain results.

Although the goal is the free circulation of knowledge and a strong articulation of do-it-yourself, maker cultures, the reality is complex. The defense of open data, the fear of corporate and government data mining and the design of free and open platforms all demand specialized knowledge. The hacker and maker culture ethics assume that a large number of people are autonomous and knowledgeable, that they never use and do not trust private platforms despite the fact that they are tried and tested and very user-friendly. However, the level of expertise required to produce, update and maintain free software applications and visualization tools is high. Data activists in the Global South develop apps in contexts of extreme inequality and job insecurity. They are volunteers working in their scarce spare time, and their activism collides with the normal work they do, the one that allows them to make a living. Sharing their knowledge with other activists and training more of them is very difficult. These conditions close the door to greater participation of other volunteers and the public. Therefore, technology remains a domain of experts and maintains an air of complexity and inaccessibility. This is why the creation of apps and the production of *Good Data* at the RHM are still in the hands of few people.

The Network is currently exploring the development of sensors and applications that could be categorized as forms of participatory sensing,[39] citizen data collected by citizens and used by them in a decentralized way for democratic purposes. They are counterposing commonality to markets and self-governance to distributed assimilation.[40] Besides promoting food self-reliance and commonality in urban spaces, the Network is contributing to the creation of data countercultures that challenge the mainstream readings of reality produced by Smart City projects.

Final Thoughts

The *Good Data* produced by the RHM is transforming the vision of the city for its members. Paraphrasing Milan and van der Velden,[41] data activism supports the new visibility of alter-

---

39 Dana Cuff, Mark Hansen and Jerry Kang, 'Urban Sensing: Out of the Woods', 28.
40 Daniel McQuillan, 'Counter Mapping the Smart City'.
41 Stefania Milan and Lonneke van der Velden, 'The Alternative Epistemologies of Data Activism', *Digital Culture & Society*, 2 (2016): 57-74.

native epistemic cultures and ontologies present in Latin America, making sense of data as a way of knowing the world and turning it into a point of intervention, from the bottom up. The cartographies being created, shared and commented contribute to *enact* a world that clearly differs from that lived by entities such as *Medellín Ciudad Inteligente* or *Ruta N*. In this other world, humans are not outside nature, they are not striving to dominate it. This is why we speak of an articulation between territorial networks, data and worlds (ontologies) defended, appropriated and lived: of truly Smart Cities.

This discussion and our enthusiasm for the results of our research do not mean that we are not finding contradictions and challenges. Not every member of RHM is aware of the risks of datafication, of the privatization of seeds by corporations, the colonization of space by real estate developers and the monopolization of knowledge by governments. In this kind of urban social movements, there are different discourses in different layers and nodes. The Network's purpose and actions are understood differently by its members.

We also conclude that hacker philosophy and ethics must be read with a healthy dose of skepticism in order to develop more realistic approaches to citizen technologies that produce and use *Good Data*. Social movements attempting to follow maker culture ethic manifestos to the letter could find themselves in dead ends or find that their efforts at incorporating technology to their efforts become paralyzed.

Our ongoing participatory research with the RHM aims to help the Network collect *Good Data* from gardens and gardeners in Medellin, make most of it available to everyone in the Tupale platform and allow the Network to make strategic decisions to achieve its goals and turn Medellín into what the RHM's manifesto has described as a *gardening territory*. We planned this research together with members of the RHM for more than two years. We are trying to meet the requests and concerns of the Network organizers and we have become organizers and gardeners ourselves as well. We as researchers and the Network are trying to understand how communication flows among the members. We have come to realize that communication occupies a central place in the dynamics of social movements. At the same time, we are trying to understand what information and knowledge is required in the long term by the RHM, in order to construct a research program that allows organizers to make decisions, plans and to respond the permanent demands of academics, journalists and filmmakers, curious about the Network.

References

Altenhain, Claudio. 'Tropicalizing Surveillance: How Big Data Policing "Migrated" from New York to São Paulo', *Big Data from the South: From media to mediations, from datafication to data activism, IAMCR Preconference Paper*, Cartagena, Colombia, 15 July 2017, http://cartagena2017.iamcr.org/big-data/.

Amar, Dario. *Estudios de casos internacionales de ciudades inteligentes,* Documento para discusión No. IDB-DP-443, Banco Interamericano de Desarrollo, 2016.

Amayo Caldwell, Glenda and Marcus Foth. 'DIY media architecture: Open and participatory approaches to community engagement', in Peter Dalsgaard & Ava Fatah gen Schieck (eds.) *Proceedings of the 2014 Media Architecture Biennale*, Aarhus: ACM Denmark, pp. 1-10.

Browne, Simone. 'Digital Epidermalization: Race, Identity and Biometrics', *Critical Sociology* 36.1 (February 2010): 131-150.

Caragliu, Andrea, Chiara Del Bo and Peter Nijkamp, 'Smart cities in Europe', *Journal of Urban Technology* 18.2 (August 2011): 65-82.

Cohen, Boyd, Esteve Almirall and Henry Chesbrough. 'The City as a Lab. Open Innovation Meets the Collaborative Economy', *California Management Review* 59.1 (November 2016): 5-13.

Colding, Johan and Stephan Barthel. 'An urban ecology critique on the "Smart City" model', *Journal of Cleaner Production* 164 (October 2017): 95-101.

Cuff, Dana, Mark Hansen and Jerry Kang. 'Urban Sensing: Out of the Woods', *Communications of the ACM* 51.3 (2008), pp. 24-33.

De la Cadena, Marisol. 'Naturaleza Disociadora', *Boletín de Antropología* 31.52 (July-December 2016): 253-263.

Escobar, Arturo. 'Territorios de diferencia: ontología política de los "derechos al territorio"', in Sheila Gruner et al (eds), *Des/dibujando el País/aje. Aportes Para la Paz con los Pueblos Afrodescendientes e Indígenas*, Medellín: Ediciones Poder Negro, 2016, pp. 91-108.

Esteva, Gustavo. 'Development', in Wolfgang Sachs (ed.), *The Development Dictionary: A Guide to Knowledge as Power*, London: Zed Books, 1992, pp. 1-23.

Fernandez-Anez, Victoria, José Miguel Fernández-Güell and Rudolf Giffinger. 'Smart City implementation and discourses: An integrated conceptual model. The case of Vienna', *Cities* 78 (August 2018): 4-16.

Franco-Avellaneda, Manuel and Tania Pérez-Bustos. 'Tensiones y Convergencias en Torno a la Apropiación Social de la Ciencia y la Tecnología en Colombia', in Tania Pérez-Bustos and Mayali Tafur Sequera (eds), *Deslocalizando la Apropiación Social de la Ciencia y la Tecnología: Aportes Desde Prácticas Diversas,* Bogotá: Maloka-Colciencias, 2010, pp. 30-61.

Haesbaert, Rogério. 'Del mito de la desterritorialización a la multiterritorialidad', *Cultura y representaciones sociales* 8.15 (2013): 9-42.

Irani, Lilli, Janet Vertesi, Paul Dourish, Kavita Philip and Rebecca Grinter. 'Postcolonial computing: A lens on design and development', *Proceedings of the 28th International Conference on Human Factors in Computing Systems*, Atlanta, Georgia, USA, 10-15 April 2010, https://www.cc.gatech.edu/~beki/c50.pdf.

Kitchin, Rob and Tracey Lauriault. 'Towards Critical Data Studies: Charting and Unpacking Data Assemblages and Their Work', in Joe Eckert, Andrew Shears and Jim Thatcher (eds), *Geoweb and Big Data*, Lincoln: University of Nebraska Press, 2014.

Koont, Sinan. *Sustainable urban agriculture in Cuba*, Heidelberg: Springer, 2011.

Lash, Scott. 'Power after hegemony: Cultural studies in mutation', *Theory, Culture & Society* 24.3 (May 2007): 55-78.

McQuillan, Daniel. 'Counter Mapping the Smart City', *Livingmaps Review* 2 (2017): 1-7.

Milan, Stefania and van der Velden, Lonneke. 'The Alternative Epistemologies of Data Activism', *Digital Culture & Society* 2.2 (10 October 2016).

Neirotti, Paolo, et al. 'Current trends in Smart City Initiatives: Some Stylised Facts', *Cities* 38 (June, 2014): 25-36.

Red de Huerteros Medellìn, *Manifiesto red de huerteros Medellín. Sembrando mundos soberanos y solidarios* (3 March 2017), https://ia601601.us.archive.org/17/items/ManifiestoRedDeHuerterosDeMedelln/Manifiesto_Red%20de%20huerteros%20de%20Medell%C3%ADn%20.pdf.

Sassen, Saskia. *Expulsions: Brutality and Complexity in the Global Economy*, Boston: Harvard University Press, 2014.

Spiaggi, Eduardo. 'Urban Agriculture and Local Sustainable Development in Rosario, Argentina: Integration of Economic, Social, Technical and Environmental Variables', in Luc Mougeot (ed.), *Agropolis. The Social, Political and Environmental Dimensions of Urban Agriculture*, London: Earthscan and the International Development Research Centre, 2005, pp. 187-202.

Székely, Iván. 'What do IT Professionals Think about Surveillance?´, in Christian Fuchs, Kees Boersma, Anders Albrechtslund and Marisol Sandoval (eds), *Internet and Surveillance. The Challenges of Web 2.0 and Social Media*, London: Routledge, 2011, pp. 198-219.

Vila-Viñas, David and Barandiaran, Xabier (eds). *Buen conocer. Modelos sostenibles y políticas públicas para una economía social del conocimiento común y abierto en Ecuador*, Quito: FLOK Society, 2015.

19: Intelligent Warning Systems: 'Technological Nudges' to Enhance User Control of IoT Data Collection, Storage and Use

RACHELLE BOSUA, KARIN CLARK, MEGAN RICHARDSON AND JEB WEBB

Abstract

The modern digital world of networking and connectivity enabled by the Internet of Things (IoT) has the paradoxical result of introducing a new era of 'smart computing' while reducing the intelligent control that individuals can exercise over their personal data. In this digital realm of big data and predictive analytics, we argue that users should be able to exert greater control over the collection, storage and use of their personal data. Our focus groups with IoT designers and users indicate that they are worried about the handling of their data, with users voicing concerns including surveillance and insecure storage of their data in the Cloud. Overall users wish for greater involvement in the management of their data. In response, we propose a high-level design prototype of an *Intelligent Warning Application* ('IWA') titled 'DataMind', empowering users to better control their IoT data collection, storage and use through: i) registering devices they wish to control; ii) setting and controlling required risk levels of their personal data flows; and iii) reacting on app warnings in the form of 'technological nudges' that report risky data flows. We present three illustrating scenarios of the latter together with corrective user actions, and conclude with a discussion of further steps of the design of this app.

Introduction

As we move into an era of big data, the mass collection, aggregation and processing of personal data through multiple connected devices signal many concerns. In particular, the uncontrolled collection, storage and use of individuals' data enabled by the Internet of Things (IoT) is unsettling in a world of more connectivity, networking and collaboration. The research question that can be asked is: *how can users better control the management of their personal data in an increasingly connected and digitised world?* While this is a key question, we acknowledge that new technologies and their accompanying data collection practices provide multiple new services and promises to significantly ease and enrich our lives in many different ways. For example, the flick of a single switch can instantaneously set a variety of devices into operation and customise information fed back to users based on unique predetermined individual needs. However, the mass collection of personal data, unknown methods of storage of this data (e.g. in the cloud), and the analyses, aggregation and processing of big data sets using modern data mining techniques, are growing concerns. In short, there is a serious question about how intelligent IoT users are really allowed to be in the new world of 'smart computing' - especially when it comes to their personal information. Specific concerns at the global level relate to privacy, data protection and cybersecurity.[1] In this chapter we respond to

---

1   See, for instance, Sachin Babar, Parikshit Mahalle, Antonietta Stango, Neeli Prasad and Ramjee Prasad 'Proposed Security Model and Threat Taxonomy for the Internet of Things (IoT)' in *International Conference on Network Security and Applications*, Berlin/Heidelberg: Springer, 2010: 420-429; Denis

our initial research question by introducing a new generation of protective systems designed to enable users to better control data flows associated with their personal data.

The chapter consists of four substantive sections. The first describes more background to the problem, followed by our research methodology and findings of our IoT project. The third section outlines the conceptual architectural model and a wireframe mock-up of our IWA prototype design, followed by a description of three scenarios that illustrate instances of nudging based on a user's profile built from knowledge garnered about the user's data privacy needs and inappropriate data flow patterns. A short discussion precedes the conclusion that elaborates on next stages of the study with some limitations and recommendations for further research.

Background Description of the Problem

The new world of computing is one of smarter living involving mass collection of IoT data from multiple devices, sensors and 'gadgets' we use in person as part of our daily lives. While it is already clear that mass IoT data collection and processing will bring significant positive change to our lives, the open internet-based infrastructure on which the IoT is based also raises some concerns. Firstly, 'interaction' comprises data collection, storage and sharing between multiple machines, devices and embedded sensors excluding any human intervention, immediate reception, or control of any personal data.[2] Secondly, entities, organisations or individuals other than those whose data is collected may take control of the data collected and shared through IoT devices. Finally, without their knowledge or consent, users are more vulnerable to surveillance, as personal data from multiple sources can be combined and processed intelligently to infer new insights about user actions, interactions and patterns of behaviour.[3] In addition, current legal frameworks in many jurisdictions, such as those in Australia, are often dated and immature in responding effectively to the diverse ongoing problems that may arise as a result of IoT processing of individuals' personal data.[4] In contrast, the new European General Data Protection Regulation (GDPR) which came into effect on 25 May

---

Kozlov, Jari Veijalainen and Yasir Ali, 'Security and Privacy Threats in IoT Architectures' in *Proceedings of the 7th International Conference on Body Area Networks*, ICST (Institute for Computer Sciences, Social-Informatics and Telecommunications Engineering), 2012: 256-262; Rolf H Weber, 'Internet of Things - New Security and Privacy Challenge', *Computer Law & Security Review 26* (2010): 23-30; Megan Richardson, Rachelle Bosua, Karin Clark, and Jeb Webb with Atif Ahmad and Sean Maynard, 'Privacy and the Internet of Things', *Media, Law & Arts Review* 21 (2016): 336-351; and Megan Richardson, Rachelle Bosua, Karin Clark, and Jeb Webb with Atif Ahmad and Sean Maynard, 'Towards Responsive Regulation of the Internet of Things: Australian Perspectives' *Internet Policy Review: Journal on Internet Regulation* 6 (2017). Note that, unless otherwise specified, in this essay we use the generic label 'data privacy' to cover privacy and data protection.

2 Weber, Internet of Things - New Security and Privacy Challenge'.
3 Ibrahim AT Hashem, Ibrar Yaqoob, Nor Badrul Anuar, Salimeh Mokhtar, Abdullah Gani and Samee Ullah Khan, 'The Rise of 'Big Data' on Cloud Computing: Review and Open Research Issues Information Systems', *Information Systems* 47 (2014): 98-115.
4 See Rolf H Weber, 'Internet of Things - Need for a New Legal Environment?' *Computer Law & Security Review* 25 (2009): 522-527; Richardson, Bosua, Clark and Webb, 'Privacy and the Internet of Things'; Richardson, Bosua, Clark and Webb, 'Towards Responsive Regulation of the Internet of Things'.

2018,[5] represents the biggest overhaul of modern data protection regulation in more than 20 years. Designed to give EU citizens more control over their personal data, GDPR aims to simplify and reshape ways in which EU organizations approach data collection and protection. It values data subjects' wishes signifying their agreement to processing of their personal data.[6] Hence, the GDPR is a timely response to a key problem associated with big data collection and processing using Information and Communications Technologies (ICTs).

Of course, another way to regulate for data protection is through more intelligent design of technologies themselves - and this is something that the GDPR also encourages.[7] A difficulty is that modern ICTs and applications (or 'apps') i) currently tend to present complex processes simplistically through heuristic interfaces that hide most of this complexity from the user, and ii) rely on the fact that users have been conditioned to accept personal disempowerment while using the internet. The former condition extends beyond using graphical user interfaces, saving users the effort of dealing with programming code. Actual audiences, relationships between entities, and information flows (to include who is doing what with data) are all effectively hidden from the average user of internet-connected services. The latter is self-evident insofar as users are routinely presented with situations engineered by other parties: i.e. programs that work in certain ways, allowing some forms of interaction while disallowing others. In other words, while people can engage in navigational and interactive behaviour in the online environment, they often do so with limited insight or control over the implications of their online behaviours. Furthermore, providers of services enabled by ICTs may have vested interests in data collection that lead them to actively obscure these interests or details of how data is used within their business models. Conditioning users to accept situations that serve these interests can also clearly be beneficial to the provider.

These problems are heightened in the case of the IoT. Personal IoT data collection is often unencrypted and uncontrolled e.g. automatically collected by sensors worn by users, embedded or concealed in the environment. In addition, IoT users are unaware of the following:

i. how and to what extent users' data is used or combined with other data sets;
ii. who acts as 'responsible owners' of collected data;
iii. when are users' data made available to external parties, or;
iv. how users' data is ultimately managed over time and by whom.

On the other side, the desire of consumers to exert control over their data has experienced a major shift over the last two decades. While a minority concern in the 1980s, individual fears about the potential abuse of personal (consumer) information have become a major concern by the 2000s.[8] Consumer concerns became focused on the ways in which users personal information is collected and used, with one study indicating that almost 88% of

---

5   See General Data Protection Regulation (GDPR) (Regulation (EU) 2016/679), in effect 25 May 2018.
6   Article 4(11) GDPR.
7   Art. 25 GDPR (Data protection by design and by default).
8   Batya Friedman, Peyina Lin and Jessica K Miller, *Informed Consent by Design in Security and Usability 2001*, (2005): 503-530.

US internet users expressed wishes to have an 'opt-in' privacy policy (in 2001) whereby internet companies need to first obtain users' permission to share their personal information with others.[9] This desire is becoming more pressing with the increased emittance of data as a by-product of user engagement with technological devices and services. The progressive 'giving-out' of individual data has both practical and political implications for ways in which people are seen and treated by the private sector and the state. In view of these concerns, the notion of minimal informed consent has evolved through political, legal, economic, social and technological realms.

Informed consent has been introduced as a mechanism to gain more user trust by articulating business practices for collecting and using personal information and giving users autonomous choice in terms of data collection and use. An Information Systems model of informed consent has been introduced in 2000,[10] constituting values associated with 'being informed' (including disclosure and comprehension) and 'giving consent' (i.e. voluntariness, competence and agreement). This model has since inception been incorporated in 'Value-Sensitive Design' frameworks touted by many authors as an integral part of large-scale real-world software systems.[11] Value sensitive designs appreciate and take account of human values in a principled and comprehensive way throughout the technological artefact design process.[12]

While the Information Systems model of informed consent is an attribute of many modern apps and technology artefacts, its ethical underpinnings related to informed consent are considered inadequate, outdated and limited in today's modern technology world.[13] More specifically, there are concerns that data collection, storage and use practices are not communicated 'in a manner that enables [users] to make an informed decision as to whether or not they want to divulge personal information' in the circumstances.[14] This problem is exacerbated in the interconnected world of the IoT. Prior studies indicate that users often unknowingly and even mindlessly 'consent' to data collection and use practices of online apps in exchange for services - and in fact this may well be encouraged by the apps themselves. Anecdotes from our empirical research confirm this aspect and also indicate that the inclusion of value-sensitive design frameworks in internet applications as a form of gaining informed

---

9   Ibid.
10 David Friedman, 'Privacy and Technology,' *Social Philosophy and Policy* 17 (2000): 186-212.
11 See, for instance, Batya Friedman and Peter H Kahn Jr., 'Human Values, Ethics, and Design', in Andrew Sears and Julie Jacko (eds), *The Human-Computer Interaction Handbook, Boca Raton:* CRC Press, 2003, pp. 1177-1201; Batya Friedman and Helen Nissenbaum, 'Bias in Computer Systems', *ACM Transactions on Information Systems (TOIS)* 14 (1996): 330-347; and Jennifer Hagman, Ann Hendrickson and Amanda Whitty, 'What's in a Barcode? Informed Consent and Machine Scannable Driver Licenses', *CHI'03 Extended Abstracts on Human Factors in Computing Systems*, ACM (2003): 912-913.
12 Friedman and Nissenbaum, 'Bias in Computer Systems'.
13 Scott D Rhodes, DA Bowie and Kenneth C Hergenrather, ‚Collecting Behavioural Data using the World Wide Web: Considerations for Researchers', *Journal of Epidemiology and Community Health* 57 (2003): 68-73.
14 Irene Pollach, 'A Typology of Communicative Strategies in Online Privacy Policies', *Journal of Business Ethics* 62 (2005): 221, 231.

consent is often ignored or bypassed.[15] Considering these and the increasing vulnerability of online personal data, the increasing collection and use of users' personal information require users to be more cognisant of IoT data collection and use, allowing users to control these activities in a more systematic way.

In response to our initial research question, the above challenges and limited-to-no practical control currently exercised by or on behalf of the users or data subjects concerned, and based on our empirical findings, we propose a conceptual architectural model and mock-up prototype design for an intelligent warning app (IWA) titled 'DataMind'. This app gives users more personalised control over the collection, storage and use of their individually collected IoT and social media. It deploys the idea of 'nudges' to alert users of changes in their known data collection and usage patterns allowing them to make decisions how they will respond and take further preventative steps[16] - in the same way that technological nudges employed in other contexts serve as 'soft reminders' that prompt users to take courses of action consistent with self-interest. For example, reinforcement for smokers trying to quit, or more recently, as part of the Facebook web interface, nudging users to more carefully consider the content and audience of their online disclosures.[17]

We believe that the IWA could be a useful example of the familiar 'privacy-by-design'/'data-protection-by-design' principle which has now been given legislative support with a special statutory provision encouraging such technologies in the GDPR.[18]

Research methodology and findings

Research Methodology

Our IoT research project funded by the University of Melbourne's Networked Society Institute was conducted from October 2015 to April 2017 and involved research teams from both

---

15 Richardson, Bosua, Clark and Webb, 'Privacy and the Internet of Things'; Richardson, Bosua, Clark and Webb, 'Towards Responsive Regulation of the Internet of Things'.
16 We appreciate that nudges can themselves sometimes be coercive: see Karen Yeung 'Nudge as Fudge', *Modern Law Review* 75 (2012): 122-148; Karen Yeung '"Hypernudge": Big Data as a Mode of Regulation by Design' *Information Communication & Society* 20 (2017): 118-136; Robert Baldwin 'From Regulation to Behaviour Change: Giving Nudge the Third Degree', *Modern Law Review* 77 (2014): 831-857. However, our design aims to minimise this problem by allowing users to effectively build their own preferences into the process of nudging.
17 Yang Wang, Pedro G Leon, Alessandro Acquisti, Lorrie Cranor, Alain I Forget and Norman Sadeh, 'A Field Trial of Privacy Nudges for Facebook', *CHI*, 26 April-1 May 2014, Toronto, Canada. The notion of 'reminders' is not new and originated as computer-based 'reminder systems' in the 1990s, specifically in the context of ambulatory preventative care systems. In the medical domain reminder systems serve as invaluable prompts to alert medical staff to necessary interventions associated with treatment practices to enhance patient safety: Jennifer Meddings, Mary AM Rogers, Michelle Macy and Sanjay Saint, 'Systems Review and Meta-Analysis: Reminder Systems to Reduce Catheter Associated Urinary Tract Infections and Urinary Catheter Use in Hospitalized Patients, *Clinical Infectious Diseases* 55 (2010): 550-560.
18 See Art. 25 GDPR (Data protection by design and by default).

the Melbourne Law School (Clark and Richardson) and the University's Computing and Information Systems Department (Bosua and Webb). We were specifically interested in regulatory aspects related to data privacy in a world of more connectivity and the IoT. In view of this our project commenced with an intensive requirements elicitation phase to get a deeper understanding of IoT data collection, use practices problems and concerns. Our overall aim was to gain specific knowledge of these concerns from two groups - IoT users and software engineers involved in the development of IoT software. We were specifically interested in privacy, data protection and security and wanted to hear views of both sets of stakeholders to verify whether and to what extent problems and concerns could be tackled.

Following ethics approval, our first study comprised 24 interviews with 14 IoT users and 10 experienced IoT designers/software engineers in October 2015 to April 2016. Individual one-hour face-to-face interviews were conducted in Melbourne with IoT users and software engineers in the 28 to 55-year age group. One of the authors (Webb) conducted the interviews and transcribed the audio-recorded interview data, followed by data analysis to identify key functional requirements. The other three authors participated in the data analysis to ensure triangulation and agreement of the key themes that emerged from the data. We reported on this study in two published papers,[19] where we argued (based on comments from users and designer findings) that laws ideally should go further in providing responsive regulation of IoT data practices, encouraging the inclusion of minimal standards of transparency and control integrated into the design of IoT.

Our second data collection stage involving 2 focus groups with 4 and 7 (total 11) users and 6 IoT designers/software engineers followed in April 2017. Four participants in our first stage participated in the stage 2 focus groups, while the other focus group participants were new - selected on the basis of their knowledge of or interest in privacy, data protection and/or security related to data practices of the IoT. With a deeper understanding of users' concerns about IoT data collection practices we used our initial study's findings to design a set of discussion questions. The second data collection stage aimed to confirm the veracity of the first stage's findings before moving on to obtain a more refined understanding of user requirements for data privacy and data security of IoT devices and comparing these with options that designers' thought were feasible. Both focus groups were conducted on the same day (one in the morning and the other in the afternoon), each lasting one and a half hours. All four authors were present with two authors (Bosua and Webb) leading the focus group discussions and the other two acting as observers. The focus group discussions were audio-recorded and used to confirm the key themes in the form of functional requirements to inform our architecture and initial app design.

Findings

As in the case of Stage 1, a large majority of participants who are users, said that they would like to have more transparency and control over their information as one commented about

---

19 Richardson, Bosua, Clark and Webb, 'Privacy and the Internet of Things'; Richardson, Bosua, Clark and Webb, 'Towards Responsive Regulation of the Internet of Things'.

his personal data: *'once you have given [your] data out you are out of control and there is no way that you know where it is'*,[20] with another confirming: *'as an end user I want to know what my information is being used for, who is using it, for what - I want that sort of control of my information - I want to be able to say I want that information deleted'*,[21] and *'I just want to have my own control [over my privacy]'*.[22] Another participant stated *'from the perspective of a user you don't actually know what data is collected by these devices concerning you and your habits.... cheaper, faster and smarter often means unregulated'*.[23] Interestingly designer/engineers (who were also, of course, often users) often agreed with this summation with some emphasising the laissez-fare attitude of developers who monetise on data collection: *'..it all comes down to money, this profit to be made'*.[24] Particular examples were given of the treatment of sensitive data including health data (*'a lot of the stuff shared now is far more revealing than you could ever imagine and people are large unaware of it'*),[25] surveillance practices especially using geolocation data,[23] (*'if people knew the ramifications of the [geolocation] option on my phone and the consequences of that, they would drop it like a rock'*), the use of photographs or images going online,[26] (*'the one thing I find most disturbing is online baby monitors [images]'*), and data transferred overseas,[27] (*'the best form [of privacy] is do not plug it into the Internet'*). But participants also agreed there might be individual and cultural variations in terms of what information was considered particularly sensitive and how it should be treated.[28]

At the same time, participants generally questioned the value of the standard term consent regimes that IoT systems typically employ. In the words of one: *'who reads these terms and conditions, it's about 10 pages of really fine print - everyone just wants the facilities and it's only when there is a security incident then you go like I do have to read this'*. [29] Others said in terms of consent *'Australia is a bit cowboy land and in other countries it's not. In Germany consent is very explicit and its legally binding*,[24] and *'some have hidden uses that you as a user do not understand'* and essentially they are '*"click, click, click" regimes'* that allowed *'little scope for negotiation or individual variance'*.[30] As one of the participants summarised the situation, the current '*regime*' is a result of *'...the design of the [typical modern] user interface and having been trained as a user - that is the user experience -* '*...to click-click and don't worry about the rest of it*' the result is that '*there is no actual conscious thought in the [software design] process*'.[31]

---

20 Designer/software engineer #1.
21 Designer/software engineer #2.
22 Designer/software engineer #3.
23 Designer/software engineer #1.
24 Designer/software engineer #3.
25 Designer/software engineer #4.
26 User #1.
27 User #2.
28 Designer/Software engineer #1.
29 User #3.
30 Designer/Software engineer #5.
31 Designer/Software engineer #5.

As to legal standards, another participant expressed concern that these terms and conditions [of use] are subject to change without any notice,[32] while another participant indicated another issue with consent forms - '...*the difference is that US law is very different to Australian law with respect to fair and reasonable use - so you have this problem with terms and conditions which may be enforceable under a different law*'.[33] Another participant expressed his concern about the storage of the data, stating there is also this danger of terms and conditions and where data is stored: '*having all the data in the cloud, I do not know where it is.* [34]

The questions of data ownership once collected also came up especially when data is in the cloud, ('*Amazon provides fantastic services and things and if we record group meetings and basically use their IoT and there is a private discussion, who owns it [the data]?*').[35]

Instead, some participants expressed a preference for more targeted '*warnings*' or '*notifications*'[36] that would '*allow them choices*' as to how to respond, ('*...you want to give out some level of access or granting access*'). The idea once raised quickly became the subject of more discussion. One software engineer indicated that '*I talk about notification, about different actions you take within the software system. If a software engineer designs notifications keeping in mind "what are the side effects [of data collection] of whichever action I have taken within the software", it will help give users awareness about the implications of what you [the data collector] are doing*'.[37] One theme that came up a few times is user naivety with one participant mentioning that the privacy problem is '*a social issue*' stating that '*there is not such thing as absolute security... we need to do better as developers in educating users in what the downside of these technologies are - so it's not enough to wait until there is a security incident before mitigating*'[38] and '*have the user know what s/he wants to give out*' educating users to '*be aware that they [external organisations] are using your data... you kind of guarantee that people are using your data, I give them my data so if something gets wrong, you the user is responsible*'.[39]

These findings were from a small sample, but they were insightful and a crucial part of the key considerations which informed our Intelligent Warning app architecture and prototype design as discussed in the next section.

Conceptual Architecture and Prototype Design of the IWA *The Conceptual Architecture*

Figure 1 proposes a conceptual model illustrating the client-server model comprising the IWA architecture. This distributed model presents the key app building blocks indicating

---

32 User #3.
33 Designer/Software engineer #6.
34 Designer/Software engineer #1.
35 Designer/Software engineer #1.
36 Designer/Software engineer #6.
37 User #3.
38 Designer/Software engineer #5.
39 Designer/Software engineer #6.

the division of tasks between the client (service requests from the user) and servers i.e. the application server, the database server with the data files and cloud storage and the Artificial Intelligence (AI) analytics engine. The application layer coordinates the app through the processing and analysis of user demands and logical decision-making related to the movement of data between the other remaining server layers. The AI analytics engine draws on logged historical user data, privacy settings customised by users through the app, IoT and Application Programming Interface (API) data stored in the Cloud to identify and learn more about a user's behaviour and data usage patterns. These patterns can be inferred over time through the user's customised privacy settings in combination with his/her historical data logs and interaction based on data flows to and from various APIs e.g. Google, IoT sensors/devices and social media APIs and external servers. Any deviations from the initial privacy settings will be alerted back to the user through the client in the form of one or more 'nudges' requesting corrective action. This could call for increasing specific API privacy settings or corrective user interventions (e.g. disconnecting from a specific Wi-Fi network).

Initially users set up their preferred data protection levels based on individual preferences, for example, control settings for i) GPS location; ii) processing of images and iii) data movement/transfer of data overseas. An initial period of use may lead to modification of the privacy settings stored in the app. The app engine will monitor data flows to and from various APIs in an inter-connected network with the consent and cooperation of the IoT service provider who may treat this as a way of offering an externalised system of privacy-by-design to users and complying with any relevant legal obligations in the jurisdiction (or jurisdictions). Figure 1 also presents the three data flow scenarios A, B and C that are described in the next section.

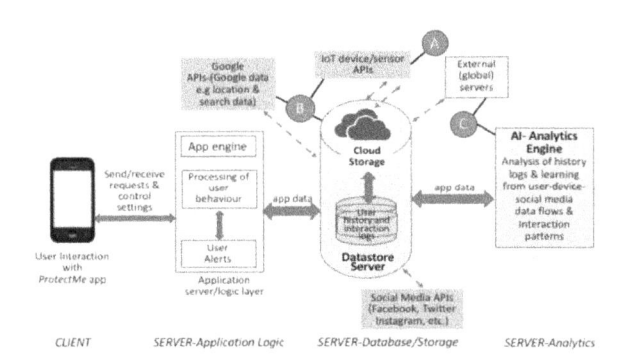

Figure 1: Conceptual Architectural Model of the Intelligent Warning app (IWA).

Three Scenarios Illustrating Instances of Nudging

The next three scenarios describe how the IWA 'nudges' users to update their 'DataMind' app's privacy settings or intervene through corrective actions. The scenarios relate to some particular dataflow concerns raised during our consultations and make provision for specific informed consent to be provided or requested for adapting a user's pre-set controls for IoT data collection, storage, processing and use.

i) **Dataflow A** as set up by Abigail: The IWA will sense or track Abigail's fitness-monitoring IoT device, which is connected to her phone, access her location data through the mobile phone's geolocation technology and integrate this geolocation data with fitness i.e. health IoT data to target localised advertising about health and fitness services. Based on controls set up through control settings of the app by Abigail, this activity will either inform or alert Abigail for possible actions that include closing the port through which the geolocation data flows.

ii) **Dataflow B** as set up by Beatrice: The IWA will assess whether Beatrice's images or videos collected by her security camera which is linked to her smart phone (or her smart phone turned into a security camera) are encrypted prior to storing these on one or more server(s). The checking of encryption is not limited to images and videos but can also be applied to any other type of data being sent via one or more channels from an IoT device to a server. Beatrice will be aware through nudging that the collected data is not encrypted, as this data is sent out of a specific environmental boundary. Once again, Beatrice can decide to take preventative actions to stop the flow of her unencrypted data, for instance disconnecting the device or putting the device behind a 'firewall'.

iii) **Dataflow C** as set up by Chester: In this scenario, the IWA makes Chester aware of voluminous data flowing through one or more channels (e.g. connected to Chester's Wi-Fi network) to a third-party server overseas. Once again, the IWA will sense or track uncontrolled data movement. Hence the IWA should 'learn' of destinations of data and by knowing this and being aware of the setting of user controls the app will nudge Chester of any uncontrolled movement of data through specific communication channels. Chester might then formally act on this by consenting or reporting inadequate behaviour to an appropriate regulatory entity.

Wireframe mock-up prototype design

Figure 2 presents a wireframe diagram with a few initial mock-up screens of the IWA prototype design giving an idea of the IWA app's look and feel from a usability perspective. The aim is to design an interactive user-friendly app that is fairly intuitive in terms of use and functionality.

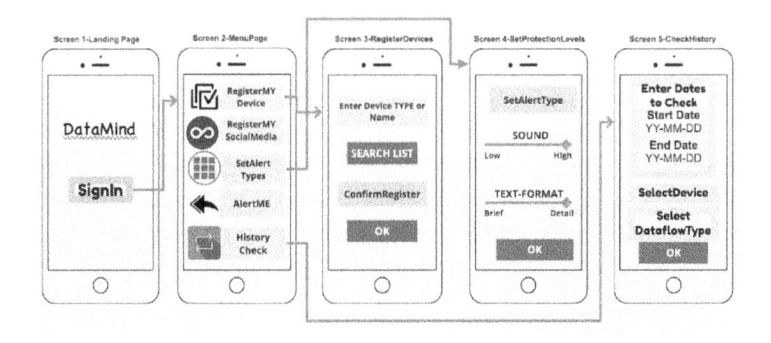

Figure 2: Excerpt of wireframe mock-up of the IWA prototype.

The initial landing page requires a secure user login taking the user to a second Menu Page screen which allows the user to provide his/her own control settings (for dataflows A, B and C mentioned above) based on the APIs in use (e.g. of social media applications) and IoT device apps. A third screen (Screen 3-RegisterDevices), allows the user to register specific IoT devices he/she wishes to control based on the device name or type using a search list (e.g. the fitness monitor for dataflow A and security camera for dataflow B). A similar screen (not yet shown here), will allow the user to register the social media applications in use he/she wishes to 'watch' or be 'nudged' about through linking to each application's API (e.g. Facebook, Twitter or Instagram). Screen 4 shows that users can also set their preferred alert types in the form of prompting sounds and/or 'nudges' in the form of textual warnings guiding the user for corrective action. The last screen (Screen 5) visualises how users can check a history of specific data flow interactions and/or violations for a specific period of time.

Discussion

Our recommended prototype design architecture is considered an initial attempt to address and illustrate the gaps in individually controlled data/information collection, processing and use through the IoT. While we only considered three different types of data flows that could compromise an individual's data through IoT devices, there are other more complex scenarios that involve the flow of collected data. We therefore consider the illustrated conceptual architecture in Figure 1 and the small prototype excerpt in Figure 2 as first steps towards developing a fully functional version of our proposed IWA. We acknowledge that the rich aspects of our initial prototype design cannot be presented in this limited space.

We envision that the IWA will create a greater user awareness of unauthorised data collection practices, while also helping users make more informed and conscious decisions about the different levels of privacy they require for their personal data. In addition, users will learn over time which devices, APIs and specific IoT devices and gadgets can be trusted from a privacy-by-design perspective. We envisage that the type of support to be provided by the IWA, would educate users to be more cautious with respect to sharing their personal data in a more digitised and connected world.

We aim to follow an agile systems development approach to build and test the current prototype version of the IWA in order to gauge feedback about the look and feel of the app. Following this we will continue with the design and building of a more comprehensive version to test the next stages of the IWA app's design. More specifically, the finer details of the IWA's application, and interaction between the AI analytics engine utilizing machine learning and data logs representing user activity, need to be developed. For this, a comprehensive set of algorithms drawing on artificial intelligence pattern matching techniques will be designed as the AI Engine's core functionality.

Conclusion

Our research confirms that users are concerned about data management practices in a new era of IoT computing. In particular, it highlights the need for users to have more control over the personal data and emphasises the need to incorporate Value Sensitive Design principles in a new generation of control software. Our study introduces the importance of 'nudges' as a way to alert users of violations in the management of their digital personal data and proposes an architectural view of an IWA app that draws on customised user control levels, nudging users to more intelligently control the use of their personal data collected and processed through the IoT. We consider our design and dataflow scenarios a first in incorporating the notion of 'nudges' with privacy by design into an intelligent warning app.

We acknowledge that this research is work in progress and in its early conceptual design and prototyping stages. As a result, the app development can only proceed once a fully functional prototype version of the IWA has been tested with a variety of users. We plan to further the app development following an Agile development approach. Another limitation is that the actual form of nudging as a means for users to control the flow of their data, is at this stage, unspecified. We hope that user-specific requirements in this regard can be elicited through in-depth testing of our prototype and also through further interviews and discussions with focus group members to identify the more nuanced aspects of the IWA's deeper design aspects.

References

Babar, Sachin, Parikshit Mahalle, Antonietta Stango, Neeli Prasad and Ramjee Prasad. 'Proposed Security Model and Threat Taxonomy for the Internet of Things (IoT)' in *International Conference on Network Security and Applications*, Berlin/Heidelberg: Springer, 2010: 420-429.

Baldwin, Robert. 'From Regulation to Behaviour Change: Giving Nudge the Third Degree', *Modern Law Review* 77 (2014): 831.

Friedman, Batya, Peyina Lin and Jessica K Miller. 'Informed Consent by Design' in *Security and Usability 2001*, (2005): 503.

Friedman, Batya, and Peter H Kahn Jr. 'Human Values, Ethics, and Design', in Andrew Sears and Julie Jacko (eds), *The Human-Computer Interaction Handbook, Boca Raton:* CRC Press, 2003, pp. 1177-1201.

Friedman, Batya and Helen Nissenbaum. 'Bias in Computer Systems' *ACM Transactions on Information Systems (TOIS)* 14 (1996): 330.

Friedman, David. 'Privacy and Technology,' *Social Philosophy and Policy* 17 (2000): 186.

General Data Protection Regulation (GDPR) (Regulation (EU) 2016/679, enforcement date: 25 May 2018.

Hagman, Jennifer, Ann Hendrickson and Amanda Whitty. 'What's in a Barcode? Informed Consent and Machine Scannable Driver Licenses', in *CHI'03 Extended Abstracts on Human Factors in Computing Systems*, ACM (2003): 912.

Hashem, Ibrahim, A.T., Ibrar Yaqoob, Nor Badrul Anuar, Salimeh Mokhtar, Abdullah Gani and Samee Ullah Khan. 'The Rise of 'Big Data' on Cloud Computing: Review and Open Research Issues Information Systems', *Information Systems* 47 (2014): 98-115.

Kozlov, Denis, Jari Veijalainen, and Yasir Ali. 'Security and Privacy Threats in IoT Architectures' in *Proceedings of the 7th International Conference on Body Area Networks*, ICST (Institute for Computer Sciences, Social-Informatics and Telecommunications Engineering) (2012): 256-262.

Meddings, Jennifer, Mary AM Rogers, Michelle Macy and Sanjay Saint. 'Systems Review and Meta-Analysis: Reminder Systems to Reduce Catheter Associated Urinary Tract Infections and Urinary Catheter Use in Hospitalized Patients', *Clinical Infectious Diseases* 55 (2010): 550.

Pollach, Irene. 'A Typology of Communicative Strategies in Online Privacy Policies', *Journal of Business Ethics* 62 (2005): 221.

Rhodes, Scott D., DA Bowie and Kenneth C Hergenrather. ,Collecting Behavioural Data using the World Wide Web: Considerations for Researchers', *Journal of Epidemiology and Community Health* 57 (2003): 68.

Richardson, Megan, Rachelle Bosua, Karin Clark, and Jeb Webb with Atif Ahmad and Sean Maynard, 'Privacy and the Internet of Things', *Media, Law & Arts Review* 21 (2016): 336.

Richardson, Megan, Rachelle Bosua, Karin Clark, and Jeb Webb with Atif Ahmad and Sean Maynard, 'Towards Responsive Regulation of the Internet of Things: Australian Perspectives' *Internet Policy Review: Journal on Internet Regulation* 6 (2017).

Wang, Yang, Pedro G Leon, Alessandro Acquisti, Lorrie Cranor, Alain I Forget and Norman Sadeh, 'A Field Trial of Privacy Nudges for Facebook' *CHI*, Toronto Canada, 26 April-1 May 2014.

Weber, Rolf H., 'Internet of Things - Need for a New Legal Environment?', *Computer Law & Security Review* 25 (2009): 522.

_____. 'Internet of Things - New Security and Privacy Challenge', *Computer Law & Security Review* 26 (2010): 23.

Yeung, Karen. 'Nudge as Fudge', *Modern Law Review* 75 (2012): 122.

_____. '"Hypernudge": Big Data as a Mode of Regulation by Design', *Information Communication & Society* 20 (2017): 118.

20: *DOMESTICATING DATA*: SOCIO-LEGAL PERSPECTIVES ON SMART HOMES AND GOOD DATA DESIGN

MARTIN FLINTHAM, MURRAY GOULDEN, DOMINIC PRICE AND LACHLAN URQUHART

Introduction

In this chapter, we focus on the so-called 'smart home' as an archetypal group space into which the Internet of Things is spreading. As most homes are shared spaces we focus on what 'good data' might look like in a space that is essentially defined by the interpersonal relations between their occupants; how good is it really, and how do we avoid it becoming 'bad data'? We engage with this problem in two ways. First, we consider the grey area that is interpersonal data from a legal perspective, by considering transparency and accountability of smart home data, ownership and responsibilities. Second, through short narrative design fictions we speculate on how the smart home might provoke unconsidered, problematic or unexpected data practices both good and bad. We draw on these to conclude with reflections on and implications for the specific but complex challenges that designers and occupants of the modern smart home face in trying to engage in good data practices.

In 2012, a New York Times story on the most banal of subjects - store card data - went viral. An American man, it was claimed, had discovered that his daughter was pregnant after a retail store began targeting the family with pregnancy-related products. The retail store had inferred the pregnancy through purchase patterns in the family's store card data. The algorithms knew before the girl's family did.

This story has commonly been read as a lesson in the power of Big Data to reveal our most intimate secrets. We see it as something different: a warning of a future in which the Internet of Things (IoT) creates torrents of *group data* that overwhelm the efforts of group members to manage the personal information that other members have access to. We call this group data *interpersonal data*,[1] because it is drawn from, and carries consequences for, the relationships between intimate groups like the family above. Public discussions around the ethics of data have, to date, overwhelmingly focused upon what institutions - state or corporate - know about individuals. We do not deny the importance of this framing, but wish to complement it with a focus on what happens when data capture is no longer restricted to individuals' devices, but instead embedded in our social environments and involves multiple actors. What does 'good data' look like in this space defined by interpersonal relations, how good is it really, and how do we avoid it becoming 'bad data' through inappropriate design, or legal consequence?

---

[1] Murray Goulden, Peter Tolmie, Richard Mortier, Tom Lodge, Anna-Kaisa Pietilainen and Renata Teixeira, 'Living with Interpersonal Data: Observability and Accountability in the Age of Pervasive ICT', *New Media & Society* 20.4 (2018): 1580-99.

In addressing this question, we focus on the 'smart home', as the archetypal group space into which the IoT is extending. After introducing the technologies which are currently being designed for this space, we turn our attention to how law regulates data in this space (or not). This focus reflects the importance of law in shaping the future design of technologies, through concepts like privacy by design. But just as importantly, it provides an example of the challenges that external frameworks have when engaging with domestic spaces. Our analysis is limited to European Union (EU) law, on the basis that, as the most proactive regulator in this space, the EU is highlighting the challenges that lie ahead for technology designers, and society more broadly.

We argue the 'goodness' of data in the home is strictly contextual. The socially complex nature of the domestic space means that, even with best intentions, good applications can result in bad outcomes if they do not attend to what users actually want and do in practice. For example, the Samaritans Radar[2] app garnered significant criticism by collecting, sharing and drawing attention to Tweets labelled as indicative of distress despite aiming to do good by preventing suicide. When designing for the home, there is clearly a need to engage with the setting, and actors therein. From the legal perspective, whilst the EU's General Data Protection Regulation (GDPR) may provide high level requirements and norms, these need to be appropriately and carefully situated so as not to become problematic themselves. As Nissenbaum has long argued, privacy can be seen as the contextual integrity of information, where harms occur if that information moves outside what individuals expect, to unanticipated channels of sharing.[3] Accordingly, within the home, to understand if applications will result in good or bad data they need to be designed with an appreciation of the expectations and uses *specific to* the practice(s) implicated by the data.

Viewed through the prism of interpersonal data, the specific forms of sociality in this space take on greater importance for design. Single-occupier homes are becoming more common, yet are still in the minority. Most homes are shared spaces, indeed even single-occupier homes may regularly host guests that otherwise live elsewhere. Most commonly, this sharing is between family members, though this itself is a concept which defies easy categorisation for technical systems. The once widespread notion of the family as a nuclear unit, clearly structured according to its social functions, and distinct from wider kin and community,[4] has little support today amongst those that study it. Instead, drawing on empirical study, family is seen as diverse, fluid and dynamic.[5] Defining what family *is* has accordingly become far less deterministic, based not on any applied template, but rather on *doings*[6] - in other words, the shared practices of members who identify as family. The notion of family and the experience

---

2   Jamie Orme, 'Samaritans pulls 'suicide watch' Radar app over privacy concerns', *The Guardian*, 7 November 2014, https://www.theguardian.com/society/2014/nov/07/samaritans-radar-app-suicide-watch-privacy-twitter-users.
3   Helen Nissenbaum, 'Privacy As Contextual Integrity', *Washington Law Review* (2004): 79.
4   Talcott Parsons, 'The American Family', in Talcott Parsons and Robert Freed Bales, *Family, socialization and interaction process*, New York: Free Press, 1955.
5   Deborah Chambers, *A Sociology of Family Life*, Cambridge: Polity Press, 2012; David Cheal, *Sociology of Family Life*, Cham: Springer, 2002.
6   David Morgan, *Family Connections: An Introduction to Family Studies*, Cambridge: Polity Press, 1996.

of it are then co-producing. Families may fit the nuclear template, but they may also be made up of cohabiting couples, those 'living apart but together', they may be gay or lesbian. Agency in families is unevenly distributed, often along lines of generation and gender, but the specifics of the distribution are situated in the particular instance in question. In some cases, this distribution is so uneven it becomes coercive, and members subject to violence at the hands of other family members.[7] In their totality, these characteristics are deeply challenging for technological systems that rely on the application of machine-readable formal structures for their operations.

To explore what the outcomes of these technical and legal developments might mean for the home, we engage in *design fiction*. Design is commonly concerned with solving problems. Design fiction uses the same design practices but for asking questions instead. Through several short narratives, our design fiction seeks to show how the smart home might provoke unconsidered, problematic or unexpected data practices within the smart home. We draw on these to conclude with reflections on the specific but complex challenges that designers and participants of this new world face in trying to design good data practice, or at least in avoiding the bad.

The Smart Home

The smart home marks a coordinated industry programme to bring IoT technologies, and the associated service platforms to which they connect, into the home. Smart devices span heating, security, entertainment, lighting and appliances, but the vanguard has proved to be the smart speaker. In 2017 it was predicted that smart speakers will be installed in over 60 million homes by the end of 2018,[8] by summer 2018 it was predicted they would be in 100 million homes.[9] Currently these devices' adoption is geographically limited to the most lucrative and accessible markets - Amazon's Alexa for example was, as of 2017, only available in English, German and Japanese (Google's offering covered an additional four languages). Their availability can be expected to expand greatly in the next five years however - whilst Apple lags in smart home offerings, it's voice assistant already covers 21 languages. In regard to data, the application of pervasive computing to such shared environments presents a qualitatively different set of challenges from designing discrete computing technologies for individual users, as the industry has done in the four decades since the computer was reconfigured as *personal*. In the existing era of personal devices, the challenge has been one of protecting personal data from 'bad actors' - third parties who would exploit that data for their own gain. The standard defence has been to secure such data behind a user account, gated by biometric data or a password, leaving the data only accessible to the user and the service provider.

---

7   Julia Wardhaugh, 'The Unaccommodated Woman: Home, Homelessness and Identity', *The Sociological Review* 47 (2001): 91-109.
8   Associated Press, 'Smart Speaker Sales More Than Triple in 2017', *Billboard*, 28 December 2017, https://www.billboard.com/articles/business/8085524/smart-speaker-sales-tripled-25-million-year-2017.
9   Bret Kinsella, 'Smart Speakers to Reach 100 Million Installed Base Worldwide in 2018, Google to Catch Amazon by 2022', *Voicebot AI Blog*, 10 July 2018, https://voicebot.ai/2018/07/10/smart-speakers-to-reach-100-million-installed-base-worldwide-in-2018-google-to-catch-amazon-by-2022/.

In recent years this challenge has become increasingly fraught. First, a procession of large-scale hacks weakened the notion that user data was secure from third parties. The consequences of these hacks ranged from the inconvenience of required password changes, to credit card fraud, to - at least in the case of the Ashley Madison hack[10] - at least two suicides. More recently, the focus has turned away from third party interventions, to the intentions of the service providers themselves. At the time of writing the likes of Facebook and Google are facing intense pressure from the public, media and regulators over their own gathering and use of personal data.

In the coming era of the IoT the challenges posed by personal data collection remain, but are joined by those of interpersonal data. Data collected from, and actuated by, pervasive computing in the environments around us implicates not only the individual user of a device, but the multiple users of the space. In smart homes, as our focus is here, these multiple users have existing relationships, as families; flatmates; host-guests; owner-pets. Here the elegance of the secured user account solution breaks down. This approach is predicated upon the uncontroversial identification of data subject, which is to say the data collected from a device logged into a specific user account is assumed to belong to that user, and hence accessible to them alone.

In practice, within intimate settings this is already more complex than is acknowledged. The introduction of 'incognito' or 'private' browsing windows[11] is in part a reflection of the recognition that in settings like homes, devices are often shared, and that some users may wish to hide parts of their browsing history from subsequent users. Such a solution is problematic in that it requires the user remember to select the option every time they wish to avoid the risk of 'social surveillance'.[12] In the context of IoT it becomes even more problematic, because data collection is no longer so obviously tied to specific practices (e.g. browsing on a shared laptop), but is embedded in the world around us, potentially tracking us through every waking, and sleeping, moment. Temporarily 'opting-out' of tracking becomes unviable.

The specific danger here is not some distant bad actor accessing personal data, but rather its exposure to those closest to us. Our intimates may know more of our secrets than anyone else, but what we hide from them is that which is most potentially consequential. When people are asked about breaches of their privacy, it is not abstract third parties that concern them the most, but those they know best.[13] This appears borne out by the suicides which followed the

---

10 The Ashley Madison hack in 2015 saw the leaking of millions of users' details from the infidelity website (tagline: 'Life is short. Have an affair'). In the aftermath, as well as suicides, there are reports of much larger numbers of users experiencing distress as they feared their loved ones would find out. Tom Lammont, 'Life after the Ashley Madison affair', *The Observer*, 28 February 2016, https://www.theguardian.com/technology/2016/feb/28/what-happened-after-ashley-madison-was-hacked.
11 'Incognito' or 'private' browsing windows do not store browsing history and related cookies locally, preventing subsequent users from tracking activities.
12 Alice Marwick, 'The Public Domain: Surveillance in Everyday Life', *Surveillance & Society* 9 (2012).
13 A.E. Marwick and danah boyd, 'Networked privacy: How teenagers negotiate context in social media', *New Media & Society* 16.7 (2014): 1051-1067; Peter Tolmie & Andy Crabtree, 'The practical politics of sharing personal data', *Personal Ubiquitous Computing* 22 (2018): 293, DOI: https://doi.org/10.1007/

Ashley Madison hack, which revealed infidelity, or attempted infidelity, to users' loved ones. It is the potential breach of the trust held between these closest ties, and the consequences of such breaches, that makes such data exposure so troublesome.

The IoT raises questions of how such interpersonal data should be secured, but also how it should be used, for the use of data often entails exposure of it in some form. The content recommendation systems of video-on-demand services like Amazon Video, for example, reveal in their suggestions the type of content previously consumed. If, for example, a user had a preference for erotic content, this will be apparent on subsequent visits to the site by other members of the household.

Amazon is also the creator of Echo, which, along with Google's Home, has become front runner in the smart home market. Echo and Home have established their respective parent companies as the default platform providers in the smart home. Increasingly, other companies are integrating their devices into one or both platforms. As such, Amazon and Google find themselves at the sharp end of the question of how best to manage interpersonal data. Their response has been *Amazon Household* and *Google Families*. These are a set of interlinked user accounts with prescribed relationships - specific adult, teen and child arrangements - through which the smart home and its data are to be managed. In doing so, they create what we refer to as 'platform families' - domestic kinship groups which are constituted within proprietary digital systems.

At root, these interlinked accounts comprise of taxonomies defining relationships between different users, devices, and services. Amazon separates Household into three roles: Adults (18-), Teens (13-17), Children (-12). *Google Families* also consist of three roles, but these are Parents, Family Members, and Family Manager. *Household* allows for ten members - two Adults, four Teens, four Children; *Families* allows for six. Children/Family Member accounts allow for only limited agency, and Adults/Parents can set limits on what media and services they can access, and when. Amazon's Teen accounts do not have these constraints, and can make purchases through Amazon using the family payment option, but orders must be reviewed by an Adult before they can be executed. Google's Family Manager role, alongside parental controls, also has executive functions including '*Decide who is in the family group*', and '*Delete the family group*'. Then there are the restrictions, for example *Families'* members must all reside in the same country, and can only be a member of one family at a time. *Household* defines Adults as over 18, except in Japan where they are over 20, because this is the age at which Japanese people can hold a credit card. These taxonomies, including the relationships they encode, and the limitations placed around them, are the result of a set of culturally, commercially and legally informed choices by designers - about what family looks like - and as such are inherently ethical acts.[14]

Whilst seeking to manage the challenges of interpersonal data, the deployment of tools such as *Families* and *Household* do much more. By intervening in both the information available

---

s00779-017-1071-8.
14   Geoffrey C. Bowker & Susan Leigh Star, *'Sorting Things Out'*, Cambridge MA: MIT Press, 2000.

between members, and the agency and accountability members hold over smart devices in the home, and by extension other users of those devices, they mark a radical intervention into domestic life, seeking to digitise domestic interpersonal relations. In doing so, they demonstrate how IoT technologies carry novel implications for interpersonal relations, and the data generated around them. This is the context in which data will be evaluated as 'good', or otherwise.

Legal Perspectives on Interpersonal Data & Smart Homes

Domestic IoT technologies, and the platform families they establish, intervene in a space that, historically, law has been reticent to enter. Data protection law provide rights for individuals over their own data but deal less effectively with group or collective rights.[15] Furthermore, human rights law has long recognised a right to private and family life, and any limitations on privacy need to be proportionate, necessary and legally justified, showing the value placed on keeping the home free from external privacy intrusions.[16] Similarly, EU data protection laws exempt data processing carried out by individuals during purely household or personal activities,[17] meaning they are not classified as 'data controllers' with the responsibilities that come with it. However, the growth of smart homes as ad-hoc collections of smart devices is complicating this, with case law that narrows this exemption and bringing data protection law into the home, and reframing family dynamics by potentially forcing members into managing their legal obligations internally.[18]

In this section, we consider a number of questions that are raised when we apply current data protection law to smart home environments. However, like with technology, law can be a blunt instrument as it needs to be contextualised. Given the focus on regulation through technology design in the GDPR, the way legal requirements are built into technology need to account for the context of use and needs of users better, particularly in the home. At one more technical level, actually embedding legal principles into technology is complex due to the importance of interpretation and law being language based, requiring translation and assumptions about meaning of terms: something that is technically difficult to account for. At another, targeting the designers and developers of IoT to support their understanding and engagement with legal requirements has its own problems around comprehension and accessibility of language.[19] However, even if these challenges could be addressed, the variety of deployment settings for these technologies mean challenges will arise that were not foreseen during the design stage. Regulation through design may have good intentions to address

---

15 Linnet Taylor, Luciano Floridi and Bart van der Sloot, *Group Privacy: New Challenges of Data Technologies*, Philosophical Studies Series #126. Berlin: Springer, 2017, pp. 197-224, DOI: 10.1007/978-3-319-46608-8_9.
16 Article 8, European Convention on Human Rights; United Nations Declaration on Human Rights; African Charter on Human and Peoples' Rights.
17 Article 2(2)(c), General Data Protection Regulation 2016.
18 EU European Court of Justice - Case C212/23; *Lindqvist*, 2003; EU European Court of Justice - C101/01; Rynes, 2014.
19 Ewa Luger, Lachlan Urquhart, Tom Rodden, Mike Golembewski, 'Playing the Legal Card', *Proceedings of ACM SIGCHI 2015*: 457-466.

the lag between legal regulation and technological innovation, but it needs to attend to the way these systems are used in practice too. In homes, this could mean making a system too transparent where inferences about daily life are made trackable and visible to co-habitants, leading to social surveillance. Or perhaps setting up accounts where permissions over data processing prevent control by some household members, despite data being co-constructed and interpersonal. As the law normally does not go into this space, the appropriate responses remain to be seen, but it is important to consider in more detail some of the challenges below, in order to open up the problem space.

Who owns interpersonal data, what are their rights, and who is responsible for fulfilling them?

Even if members seek to exercise legal rights over interpersonal data, because such data does not relate to just one individual, understanding to what extent new individual data rights in Europe for GDPR apply is problematic. Rights to data portability[20] or to be forgotten[21] are already technically complex to exercise, but when data relates not just to one person, but to many, it adds another layer of difficulty. With the right to data portability, for example, it applies to raw data, but not any statistical inferences or analysis made, perhaps to provide personalisation. Thus if someone leaves the family home, they may not have a right to the personalisation of the home's devices, such as the smart thermostat's heating profile which is tailored to their activities.

A related challenge is determining who the rights may be exercised against. Smart home technologies create opacity around data flows, coupled with a complex ecosystem of stakeholders seeking access to the data. This is legally challenging, as accountability is often lacking.[22] There are difficulties establishing who is legally responsible, and who users need to contact to exercise their rights. As mentioned above, by bringing IoT devices into the home, there is increasing volume of domestic personal data processing ongoing, which threatens the household exemption. This may give rise to a new class of 'domestic personal data controllers' (DPDC) who might need to respond to right to be forgotten claims for smart fridge consumption by family friends or to create consent notices for babysitters captured on their Nest cams.

There is a tension in how they might reconcile their social obligations, as members of the household, with legalistic requirements of responding to rights requests. As gatekeepers to the home, DPDCs are also mediating data flows internally and externally. Given the current business model, data on Nest Cam or a fridge does not stay within the confines of the home, it travels to the cloud. This is particularly problematic for interpersonal data, as unlike within individual personal data that is wholly within the realm of GDPR, the law is not as clear on

---

20   Article 20, General Data Protection Regulation 2016.
21   Article 17, General Data Protection Regulation 2016.
22   Lachlan Urquhart, Tom Lodge and Andy Crabtree, 'Demonstrably Doing Accountability in the Internet of Things', *International Journal of Law and Technology* (forthcoming, 2018); Lachlan Urquhart and Tom Rodden, 'New directions in information technology law: learning from human - computer interaction', *International Review of Law, Computers & Technology*, 31:2 (2017): 150-169, DOI: 10.1080/13600869.2017.1298501.

protection of co-constructed data or even group privacy as a whole.

This poses issues for the family unit in smart homes, especially over time. Navigating what rights individuals have and against whom becomes a complex exercise. Can children apply for subject access requests for data processing to their parents? Can family visitors demand a right to be forgotten when they leave the home? These challenges are exacerbated when family dynamics are tested by disruption (break-ups, divorce, domestic violence etc.). How do DPDCs manage these issues if they are proximate to data subjects? They may find themselves having to balance legal responsibilities against the normative expectations attached to their roles within the family unit, potentially having to choose between risking censure from either the law or their loved ones.

Who can access the data?

Often with IoT, to be more legally compliant, trustworthy and responsible, the proposed solution is to increase transparency and accountability around data flows to end users.[23] The smart home is no exception, however, how accountability is managed needs to account for the domestic order. Disclosure of information within relationships may cause harm, especially during times of disruption. Information collection is fractured and distributed across smart home devices. How and if this information is presented to different family members can impact relationships and even lead to privacy harms, as in the example we began this chapter with. Given many IoT services are mediated by contracts and accounts, family members beyond the lead account holder may have limited rights. If privacy harms occur to spouses, partners or children through information sharing, they may have no recourse as they are not account holders.

Design Fictions - Domestic Data, Good and Bad

Design fiction is the practice of exploring possible futures by creating speculative and provocative fictional narratives. Here we use design fiction to create scenarios around data in the home which integrate legal, sociological and IT perspectives, and these help us both to understand what it will be like to live with future technologies, but also to think more carefully about that future.[24]

Bad Data

Fiction 1: For that Special Someone

Susan and Bill Anderson live with their children Josh and Angela. They have recently signed up for the FutureHome Smart Ecosystem™. This package interconnects practically all electronic devices in the home, from appliances like the TV and the oven down to electric

---

23 Articles 5(2), 12, 15, General Data Protection Regulation 2016.
24 Paul Coulton, Joseph Lindley and Rachel Cooper, *The Little Book of Design Fiction for the Internet of Things,* 2018, https://www.petrashub.org/the-little-book-of-design-fiction-for-the-internet-of-things/.

toothbrushes. It also includes home security devices like internal and external cameras. In order to save money on the installation, the family sign up for the AdConnect package. This package is billed as a '*data-driven brand loyalty discount package*': by sharing their data and delegating some control of the smart home to third parties, significant savings can be made on the package price.

AdConnect™ utilises interpersonal advertising, algorithmically combining user preference data with data on family relationship and events. When, on the eve of Bill's birthday, the family is targeted with ads promoting vouchers for a seedy motel on the edge of town, the kids see mum get really mad and shout at dad a lot. As the AdConnect™ package stipulates a minimum spend for all family occasions, dad still gets a present, but Angela notices he doesn't look that happy about the PieceOfMind™ location tracker that mum says he will have on him the whole time from now on.

Fiction 2: Watching Me Watching You

John and Mary are an estranged couple with three kids. Several months ago, John moved out of the family home where Mary and the children still live. The house was bought new three years ago with a full complement of smart devices. It still has 25 years on the mortgage. John, Mary and the children are all registered to a Kinship™ group account on the platform that controls the smart house. It was John that set up the group account originally, and his remains the admin account. As such he has executive control over the both home devices, and user privileges.

One evening in his rented flat John notices the *Ironman* film he was planning to watch has already been viewed. Mary would normally never choose to watch action films. John starts monitoring the devices in the house, noting when Mary turns the lights off at night, uses the shower, has the oven turned on long enough that John figures she must be cooking for someone else. He remembers the doorbell has a video camera feed, and starts watching it on his laptop when he gets in from work. The next Sunday when he picks up the kids from Mary he asks her why the electric toothbrush was used twice the night before. Mary tells him to leave. The next day she speaks to her lawyer, but she says as John is still paying half the mortgage he has a case for continuing to control the Kinship™ account. Instead she has an idea. On Wednesday morning, John receives a letter. Inside is a Subject Access Request - as Data Controller, he has 72 hours to catalogue all data he is holding on Susan. Failure to comply with the request in the inventory format could result in a fine of €20m or 4% of his global annual turnover, whichever is the greater. John calls his lawyer.

Fiction 3: Equality in the Eyes of the IoT

A legal case comes before the Supreme Court, concerning the abuse of smart home data during a family breakup. The Court creates new case law in its finding that the admin account holder is indeed a data controller, and thus under the terms of the GDPR is liable for sizeable fines. Furthermore, the co-defendant, Kinship™ LLC, is also found guilty of selling software that was judged to be non-compliant.

Even as Kinship™ lawyers prepare an appeal, the company stock price tanks, as does those of its competitors. Within days, software updates to smart homes are being issued which attempt to head off further legal action. Families across the continent wake to find that all members of the family have been granted equal status by the digital systems running the home. The continuing operation of all smart devices in the home now requires the consent of all family members. The manufacturers believe that this requirement gives their systems the utmost compatibility with legal requirements.

For the Anderson family parents, life suddenly becomes more a lot more complicated. Angela and Josh quickly realise their new found powers. Josh manages to get them off school for a whole morning, just by refusing to accept the Terms and Conditions of the front door's smart lock. Angela discovers the Restricted section of mum's video library, and learns a great deal from it. She does worry about getting caught by one of her parents coming home early, but the risk is lowered by the fact that she can now access dad's PieceOfMind tracker, and see where he is at all times. All in all, the kids are very pleased with their newfound privileges.

Good Data

Fiction 4: Smart Home Truths

Sam and Leslie have just moved in together. Leslie loves new tech, and has already outfitted the house with the latest IoT gadgets and smart control system. In order to fully use the integrated system each occupant needs to be registered as a user in the system although basic functionality, such as changing TV channels and switching on and off lights, is still available to an unregistered user. Leslie fails to register Sam as a user, always seeming to not get around to doing it. A year later, the system still only recognises Sam as a 'guest', not a partner.

Sam can't seem to get on with the smart home. Leslie has to choose the music to play as only official family members have access to the house's media library. Other things keep happening. Sometimes the smart shower switches to cold when Sam is using it and refuses to alter temperature, or the washing machine somehow uses the wrong profile and ruins Sam's delicate clothing. Leslie tells Sam that it's all in their head, and that they are fantasizing that they're being persecuted by the smart home.

When Leslie's out at work, Sam's old friend Alex stops by for a long overdue cup of tea, and a tearful Sam confesses that they feel they're losing the plot. Alex thinks something sounds very wrong and convinces Sam to request a SafePersonalDataAudit from the smart home company. She does so by using utility bills and government records to evidence her membership of the home. The audit exhaustively logs every action Leslie has taken on the system, revealing a campaign of control and coercion, effectively weaponizing the smart home against Sam. Sam packs a bag. The doorbell camera glares balefully as Sam and Alex depart.

Fiction 5: Machine Learning Magic

Susan and Bill Anderson are having marital problems. Having come to suspect Bill of having an affair, Susan has grown distant. Their sex life is almost non-existent, and Susan has turned to online pornography as a means of finding satisfaction. Bill has noticed his wife's distance but finds himself unable to initiate a conversation about it, fearful about where it might lead. Each carries on going through the motions, unable or unwilling to address the dark cloud hanging over them.

Part of the Anderson's installed FutureHome Smart Ecosystem™ is an inbuilt recommender system - Synygy™. Unlike traditional systems designed around individual users (inevitably resulting in parents being pestered with recommendations for their kids' favourite cartoons), Synygy is designed to not only recognise multiple users, but to use machine learning to identify from their individual preferences, content that would appeal to any subset of them, if and when they sit down to watch together.

Bill and Susan often spend some time after the children have gone to bed in the living room, watching television - it's a way of being together without actually having to talk. At first, some of Synygy's suggestions make Susan uncomfortable, because they clearly drawn on some of her viewing habits which she wishes to keep private. However, Synygy promotes the inclusion of 'wildcard' content into its suggestions, and is explicit to users that is it doing so - without identifying which recommendations specifically. Susan knows full well that its suggestion of *Visit from the Plumber Vol.III* isn't a wildcard, but it is easy enough to confirm Bill's belief that it is. They share a rare joke about how stupid this recommender systems are.

Drawing on their full viewing profiles, their demographics, and fine-grained data on daily routines as captured by Smart Ecosystem, and combining it with its full user base datasets, Synygy begins to suggest both romantic films and films that reflect the Anderson's current domestic turbulence. The shared experiences that follow generate some uncomfortable moments on the Anderson sofa, but over the weeks Bill and Susan begin to talk, properly, for the first time in months.

What Makes Good Domestic Data, Good?

The rise of the Internet of Things marks the latest chapter in Weiser's ubiquitous computing vision of the 'disappearing computer'.[25] Formerly innocuous devices such as toothbrushes, thermostats, televisions, speakers and even dolls[26] are now imbued with so-called 'smart' functionality, ostensibly harnessing the power of the digital but more specifically the 'good' that can be leveraged from reasoning about data at scale to enhance previously mundane

---

25 Mark Weiser, 'The computer for the 21st century', *SIGMOBILE Mobile Computing and Communications*, 3.3 (July 1999), 3-11, DOI: http://dx.doi.org/10.1145/329124.329126.
26 Wolf Richter, 'Our Dental Insurance Sent us "Free" Internet-Connected Toothbrushes. And this is What Happened Next', *Wolf Street*, 14 April 2018, https://wolfstreet.com/2018/04/14/our-dental-insurance-sent-us-free-internet-connected-toothbrushes-and-this-is-what-happened-next/.

household activities and to enable new experiences. Furthermore, while previously operating as a collection of disparate artefacts, the voice interfaces of Google Home and Amazon Echo seek to make sense of, unify and integrate this ecosystem of devices into an ad-hoc infrastructure for the modern smart home. The end-game of this trajectory is currently uncertain. In the above we have used design fiction to explore possible future interactions between social, legal and technical systems in this place; three we have labelled as 'bad data'; two 'good'. However, even within these short scenarios the picture is more complicated. We argue that the data itself in these fictions is agnostic, and is only meaningful when considered in a broader socio-legal-technical context. Our goal with the Fictions was not to present answers, but to open up questions.

Our data fictions are deliberately playful, but all are plausible. Fiction 1 demonstrates how the most ostensibly mundane of data implicitly has the potential to be momentous because, when it comes to data about the situated arrangements of tight-knit groups, *meaning is in the eye of the beholder*. What may appear in one domestic context unremarkable may in another be revelatory, and vice versa.[27] This Fiction also highlights how data itself does not have to be exposed to be consequential, instead here it is the output of algorithmically-processed data which is read as being revealing of moral impropriety. This scenario points at the commercial imperatives that are often at play here, which can drive the generation of potentially revealing interpersonal data. Interest in such possibilities has already been shown - Facebook announced, in 2017, that it was going to begin to enable the targeting of advertising at family groups.[28] There are potentially considerable conflicts between the commercial interests of industry, and those of smart home occupants, and a real danger that careless, or simply short-termist approaches to developing the smart home ultimately result in the kind of toxicity which has now surrounded Facebook, in the form of fake news and the Cambridge Analytica scandal, during 2017-18. We must hope that the technology industry learns from its current travails, if only for its own long-term self-interest.

Fiction 2 focuses on how kinship groups' membership and roles are dynamic, both changing gradually with the unfolding of time, but also occasionally in great lurches. This has profound implications for the intimate data which accumulates around such relationships, and how control over it is maintained.[29] Similarly to Fiction 1, it shows how data from the most quotidian of objects - like toothbrushes and ovens - can be imbued with critical meaning by users interpreting data through the prism of past experience and current belief. The current design of platform families does not suggest due care is being exercised here - Amazon Household, for example, allows either Parent to remove their partner account from the family, but the agency to do so is reserved solely for those who click first - once out, the ejected is powerless to return.

---

27 Murray Goulden et al, 'Living with Interpersonal Data: Observability and Accountability in the Age of Pervasive ICT'.
28 Marty Swant, 'Facebook Will Soon Let Brands Target Ads at Entire Families or Specific People Within Households', *Adweek*, 27 June 2017, https://www.adweek.com/digital/facebook-will-soon-let-brands-target-ads-at-entire-families-or-specific-people-within-households/.
29 Jimmie Manning and Danielle M. Stern, 'Heteronormative Bodies, Queer Futures: Toward a Theory of Interpersonal Panopticism', *Information, Communication & Society* 21.2 (1 February 2018): 208-23, DOI: https://doi.org/10.1080/1369118X.2016.1271901.

At the heart of Fiction 3 is the current uncertainty regarding how regulatory frameworks, with their household exemptions, will apply to a technology platform that renders the boundaries between home and world outside so porous as to be almost meaningless. The absurd outcome of the court case points to a very good reason why the law may be reticent to intervene in the home, namely its bluntness as an instrument in comparison to the nuances of situated domestic practices, a challenge that faces technology designers too, albeit arguably to a lesser degree. The scenario also flags the capacity of these systems, through remote updates, to change form and function literally overnight, and how consequential such changes might be[30] when the technologies involved are fully embedded in domestic life.

Fiction 4 has similarities to 2, describing an abusive partner denying their victim control over many aspects of their shared physical-digital lives, purely by exploiting administrative privileges. One way in which it differs is in how accountability is established between members. In Fiction 2 Mary *can* ultimately use the law to turn the tables on John's intrusions, but only in a way in which it was not intended. In Fiction 4 by contrast Sam is able to access the devices' logs via a mechanism designed for such purposes, by presenting evidence of her occupancy of the home. Users are both empowered and marginalised by data, to both positive and negative affect.

Fiction 5 demonstrates how situated such evaluations of good or bad must be. In contrast to 1, where Bill is made accountable by data for his infidelity, the systems here allow those implicated by the exposure of personal data a means of deflecting their accountability. Unlike the advertising system which incriminates Bill, Synygy explicitly includes wildcard suggestions, which in this instance act as 'noise' which Susan can appropriate to hide what she wants to keep hidden. Accountability is itself nuanced - whilst we label as good Susan's avoidance of it, we apply the same label to Leslie's exposure in Fiction 4. This particular distinction hinges on the actions in question, one set - Susan's - which we judged to be personal, the other - Leslie's - we judged to require disclosure. Our justification relies on the impact of Leslie's actions on Sam, but nevertheless these are normative judgements that we make, and must be reflexive of, just as designers should be.

These Fictions raise difficult moral questions, which the terminology of 'good' data invokes. The reader might see it as justifiable that Susan's pornography tastes are hidden, but have little sympathy when similar systems reveal Bill's infidelity. In an intimate space such as the home, inevitably smart technologies impinge on normative judgments of behaviour. As Bowker and Star remind us,[31] the decisions of the designs of these systems are always ethical in nature. There is no single standardised solution for designing smart domestic technologies, but an awareness of what is at stake, and when individual's right to privacy may conflict with another's right to know, is necessary. In portraying Synygy's recommendations altering Susan

---

30   The inspiration for this element of the scenario comes from the news in 2017 that a remotely-issued firmware update bricked several hundred Lockstate customers' door locks. Iain Thomson, 'Firmware update blunder bricks hundreds of home 'smart' locks', *The Register*, 11 September 2017, 'https://www.theregister.co.uk/2017/08/11/lockstate_bricks_smart_locks_with_dumb_firmware_upgrade/.
31   Geoffrey C. Bowker and Susan Leigh Star, *Sorting Things Out*, Cambridge MA: MIT Press 2000.

and Bill's relationship, Fiction 5 also poses a question of political philosophy. How should we think about such systems using use algorithmic processing to change our behaviour? Synygy is not directed by a human designer to rescue their marriage, but here the algorithms' goal of getting them to watch content has that effect. Does the fact that the outcome could be considered positive make this unambiguously good data? Is the fact that it is unintentional rather than by design important - would the alternative be creepily paternalistic? Does our response change if the algorithm has negative impacts on users - as many systems have been shown to?[32]

Conclusion

With little regulatory oversight, the technology industry has propelled societies towards a ubiquitous, 'smart' future, one that was barely conceivable at the turn of the millennium. However, the wholesale application of these technologies in disciplinary isolation may lead to unforeseen social impacts, both good and bad, or more likely impossibly difficult to characterise so simply, but potentially risking very real harms. The IoT-enabled home industry is built upon but also hopelessly addicted to data, and the distributed nature of ambient data collection means there that we are quickly becoming surrounded by digital ears. There are many concerns to be raised about how the companies which own those ears are monetising what they hear, whether that be Amazon selling transcripts of our conversations with Alexa,[33] or Roomba selling the floor plans of our homes[34]. Here though our focus has been on the dangers of interpersonal data. We would argue that data is agnostic, that it is neither good nor bad - but rather that the Internet of Things enables vastly powerful tools that can reason about data created by 'the user' but also complicated by, as we have seen, data about others. Activities in the home are inextricably linked with the activities of other family members, and this is a point we believe is largely overlooked by the current crop of smart devices. Whether considering the commercial interests of the technology company seeking a foothold into the domestic space through data analysis at scale, or the privacy of the teenage daughter's purchases via the shared Amazon account, these data driven technologies must respect interpersonal relationships, and the distribution of agency amongst them, both socially and legally. They must also, in doing so, recognise the moral choices they are making in involving themselves in these spaces, and redefining their possibilities.

Information privacy law traditionally stops at the front-door of the home. It is not clear whether data protection law provides redress for the actual harms faced by the occupants of the modern smart home, or whether it is too far removed from the practical challenges faced by users - however in the interim compliance mechanisms like privacy by design[35] are bringing it

---

32 Virginia Eubanks, *Automating Inequality: How High-Tech Tools Profile, Police, and Punish the Poor*, New York NY: Macmillan USA, 2018.
33 Rob LeFebvre, 'Amazon may give developers your private Alexa transcripts', *Engadget Blog*, 7 July 2017, https://www.engadget.com/2017/07/12/amazon-developers-private-alexa-transcripts/.
34 Natalie O'Neill, 'Roomba maker wants to sell your home's floor plan', *NYPost*, 25 July 2017, https://nypost.com/2017/07/25/roomba-maker-wants-to-sell-your-homes-floor-plan/.
35 Article 25, General Data Protection Regulation 2016.

in by the backdoor. If technology embeds regulatory norms,[36] these can structure relationships in the home. Even if done with the best of intentions, these are external interventions into complex, intimate spaces, and the consequences of them are difficult to anticipate. The extent to which they are negotiable or legible to end users, and compliant with the situated norms of any particular household, will affect their impact. A good example is requirements for parents to consent on behalf of under-16s to access services like social media or online shopping.[37] Depending on family dynamics, such a requirement may impact autonomy and agency of young people in negative ways, and neglect developmental differences of different users.

Our conclusion, then, is to suggest that for the Internet of Things and the smart home to be considered as 'good' - or rather, harmless - in their use of data, they must be grounded in an interdisciplinary conversation about the tensions at the intersection of human-computer interaction, or increasingly human-data interaction,[38] the social life of the home and the law. There are significant implications for the designers of technologies of the future smart home:

- The next generation of smart devices should, potentially actively and disruptively, deliver data protection norms into the home, perhaps by considering what a meaningful and recognisable digital front-door should look like.

- They must involve their users in a legitimate conversation about the value of their data - not just engaging in privacy by design, but affording *informed and visible* transactions around data that can be integrated into the socially negotiated work of the home.

- Where interpersonal data is concerned, its visibility, and the potential accountabilities that flow from that for those implicated by it, requires careful thought on the part of designers. Predicting all outcomes is impossible, but certain data, in certain systems, may require the maintenance of *personal* privacy, even where that undermines the possibilities presented by merging user data. In other situations, the deliberate, and explicit, insertion of noise into the data may offer a solution which mediates between individual and group interests.

- Technology blunders into ordering the home in different ways. We need to better understand the implications of using technology design to bring structural and legal norms into the 'sacred space' of the home. The smart home should be made configurable, not seek to configure, the family schema to reflect the complex, fluid and inherently non-standard domestic environment.

Finally, we consider how some of the challenges we have raised can and are beginning to be addressed through research and design.

---

36 Lawrence Lessig, *Code v2*, http://codev2.cc/download+remix/Lessig-Codev2.pdf.
37 Article 8, General Data Protection Regulation 2016.
38 Richard Mortier, Hamed Haddadi, Tristan Henderson, Derek McAuley and Jon Crowcroft, 'Human-Data Interaction: The Human Face of the Data-Driven Society' (1 October 2014), https://ssrn.com/abstract=2508051.

Human-Computer Interaction (HCI), and its focus on user centric design, can address some of these regulatory challenges by surfacing social practices and how users orientate around a technology. Furthermore, the growing interest in embedding socially desirable values and norms into technology is one approach to addressing the risks of bad data. However, in practice, as phenomenologists such as Don Ihde have argued for a long time, how a technology is designed and how it is used differ considerably.[39]

Technologies designed for one purpose can be repurposed for another. So whilst a smart camera entry system can be designed to spot intruders, it can also be used to track movements of a spouse, to question on why they are arriving so late. A smart thermostat can be used to help users manage energy more efficiently, but it can also be used by social workers to argue a house was too cold, showing evidence of neglect of children. A smart fridge can be used to manage consumption of food to address waste, but it can also be a trigger for those with eating disorders by questioning their consumption practices.

Many of these technologies assume social harmony within the home, in the same way socio-technical research in the early years of Computer-Supported Cooperative Work (CSCW) research often assumed harmony between worker and employer when new systems were deployed. As more critical school lines of thought emerged, particularly in Scandinavia, this assumption was challenged and a more conflict driven model of the setting for technology deployment was given attention. For the smart home, the complexity needs attention. The power relationships and domestic hierarchies cannot be neglected in design.

Relatedly, there is a risk in this design space of the assumption that social problems can be fixed by technology. Without considering the context of deployment, ostensibly good data applications can fall into bad data. Accordingly, the fallacy of a binary good/bad is not productive when designing for the home, and arguably for any data driven technology that humans interact with. It neglects the subtleties, and how people use and domesticate technologies into their everyday lives.

Furthermore, with its focus on individual rights, for example in data protection, the law can also neglect these subtleties. Data in homes is often co-constructed, yet protection is constrained to individualised notions of one user, one device. This is not the case, and whilst the home is posing challenges for technology design, equally the law will need to face up to the limitations of not attending to the social context of use too. Privacy by design is a good idea in the abstract, but if the protections, or understanding of what is needed do not tally with the reality, then these safeguards are likely to miss the mark.

If designers cannot give these questions the attention they require, or resolve them in a way that does not place all implicated members interests over primarily commercial interests, the ethical choice is to not pursue the smart home at all.

---

39 Don Ihde, *Technology and the Lifeworld: From Garden to Earth*, Bloomington IN: Indiana University Press, 1990.

References

African Charter on Human and Peoples' Rights.

Article 8, European Convention on Human Right.

Articles 2(2)(c), 5(2), 8,12, 15, 17, 20, and 25, General Data Protection Regulation 2016.

Associated Press, 'Smart Speaker Sales More Than Triple in 2017', *Billboard*, 28 December 2017, https://www.billboard.com/articles/business/8085524/smart-speaker-sales- tripled-25-million-year-2017.

Bowker, Geoffrey C. and Susan Leigh Star. *Sorting Things Out*, Cambridge MA: MIT Press, 2000.

Chambers, Deborah. *A Sociology of Family Life*, Cambridge: Polity Press, 2012.

Cheal, David. *Sociology of Family Life*, Cham: Springer, 2002.

Coulton, Paul, Joseph Lindley and Rachel Cooper. *The Little Book of Design Fiction for the Internet of Things*, 2018, https://www.petrashub.org/the-little-book-of-design-fiction-for-the-internet-of-things/.

EU European Court of Justice - Case C212/23; *Lindqvist*, 2003.

EU European Court of Justice - C101/01; *Rynes*, 2014.

Goulden, Murray, Peter Tolmie, Richard Mortier, Tom Lodge, Anna-Kaisa Pietilainen and Renata Teixeira. 'Living with Interpersonal Data: Observability and Accountability in the Age of Pervasive ICT', *New Media & Society* 20.4 (2018): 1580-99.

Ihde, Don. *Technology and the Lifeworld: From Garden to Earth*, Bloomington IN: Indiana University Press, 1990.

Kinsella, Bret. 'Smart Speakers to Reach 100 Million Installed Base Worldwide in 2018, Google to Catch Amazon by 2022', *Voicebot AI Blog*, 10 July 2018, https://voicebot.ai/2018/07/10/smart-speakers-to-reach-100-million-installed-base- worldwide-in-2018-google-to-catch-amazon-by-2022/.

Lammont, Tom. 'Life after the Ashley Madison affair', *The Observer*, 28 February 2016, https://www.theguardian.com/technology/2016/feb/28/what-happened-after-ashley- madison-was-hacked.

LeFebvre, Rob. 'Amazon may give developers your private Alexa transcripts', *Engadget Blog*, 7 July 2017, https://www.engadget.com/2017/07/12/amazon-developers- private-alexa-transcripts/.

Lessig, Lawrence. *Code v2*, http://codev2.cc/download+remix/Lessig-Codev2.pdf.

Luger, Ewa, Lachlan Urquhart, Tom Rodden, and Mike Golembewski. 'Playing the Legal Card', *Proceedings of ACM SIGCHI 2015*: 457-466.

Manning, Jimmie and Danielle M. Stern. 'Heteronormative Bodies, Queer Futures: Toward a Theory of Interpersonal Panopticism', *Information, Communication & Society* 21.2 (1 February 2018): 208-23, DOI: https://doi.org/10.1080/1369118X.2016.1271901.

Marwick, Alice. 'The Public Domain: Surveillance in Everyday Life', *Surveillance & Society* 9 (2012).

Marwick, A.E. and danah boyd, 'Networked privacy: How teenagers negotiate context in social media', *New Media & Society* 16.7 (2014): 1051-1067, DOI: https://doi.org/10.1177/1461444814543995.

Morgan, David. *Family Connections: An Introduction to Family Studies*, Cambridge: Polity Press 1996.

Mortier, Richard, Hamed Haddadi, Tristan Henderson, Derek McAuley and Jon Crowcroft. 'Human-Data Interaction: The Human Face of the Data-Driven Society', (1 October 2014), https://ssrn.com/abstract=2508051.

Nissenbaum, Helen. 'Privacy As Contextual Integrity', *Washington Law Review* (2004): 79.

O'Neill, Natalie. 'Roomba maker wants to sell your home's floor plan', *NYPost*, 25 July 2017, https://nypost.com/2017/07/25/roomba-maker-wants-to-sell-your-homes-floor- plan/.

Orme, Jamie. 'Samaritans pulls 'suicide watch' Radar app over privacy concerns', *The Guardian*, 7 November 2014, https://www.theguardian.com/society/2014/nov/07/samaritans-radar-app-suicide-watch-privacy-twitter-users.

Parsons, Talcott. 'The American Family', in Talcott Parsons and Robert Freed Bales, *Family, socialization and interaction process*, New York: Free Press, 1955.

Richter, Wolf 'Our Dental Insurance Sent us "Free" Internet-Connected Toothbrushes. And this is What Happened Next', *Wolf Street*, 14 April 2018, https://wolfstreet.com/2018/04/14/our-dental-insurance-sent-us-free-internet- connected-toothbrushes-and-this-is-what-happened-next/.

Swant, Marty. 'Facebook Will Soon Let Brands Target Ads at Entire Families or Specific People Within Households', *Adweek*, 27 June 2017, https://www.adweek.com/digital/facebook-will-soon-let-brands-target-ads-at-entire- families-or-specific-people-within-households/.

Taylor, Linnet, Luciano Floridi, Bart van der Sloot, *Group Privacy: New Challenges of Data Technologies*, Philosophical Studies Series #126. Berlin: Springer, 2017, pp. 197-224, DOI: 10.1007/978-3-319-46608-8_9.

Thomson, Iain. 'Firmware update blunder bricks hundreds of home 'smart' locks, *The Register*, 11 September 2017, https://www.theregister.co.uk/2017/08/11/lockstate_bricks_smart_locks_with_dumb_firmware_upgrade/.

Tolmie, Peter and Andy Crabtree, 'The practical politics of sharing personal data', *Personal Ubiquitous Computing* 22 (2018): 293, DOI: https://doi.org/10.1007/s00779-017-1071-8.

United Nations Declaration on Human Rights.

Urquhart, Lachlan, Tom Lodge and Andy Crabtree. 'Demonstrably Doing Accountability in the Internet of Things', *International Journal of Law and Technology* (forthcoming, 2018).

Urquhart, Lachlan and Tom Rodden, 'New directions in information technology law: learning from human - computer interaction', *International Review of Law, Computers & Technology* 31.2 (2017):150-169, DOI: 10.1080/13600869.2017.1298501.

Wardhaugh, Julia. 'The Unaccommodated Woman: Home, Homelessness and Identity', *The Sociological Review* 47 (2001): 91-109.

Weiser, Mark. 'The computer for the 21st century', *SIGMOBILE Mobile Computing and Communications* 3.3 (July 1999): 3-11. DOI: http://dx.doi.org/10.1145/329124.329126.

BIOGRAPHIES

Bruce Baer Arnold is an Assistant Professor at Canberra Law School (University of Canberra). Dr Arnold's doctoral dissertation explored the nature of legal identity, including the information state, autonomy and population-scale data-mining. He has served on OECD health informatics and data protection working parties, alongside Vice-Chairmanship of the Australian Privacy Foundation, the Australia's preeminent civil society body concerned with data protection. His work on new technology law and privacy has appeared in leading journals and collections. He is a contributor to Australia's authoritative privacy/confidentiality practitioner resource. Dr Arnold's current research focus is on regulatory incapacity regarding medical products and data.

Wendy Elizabeth Bonython is an Adjunct Associate Professor at Canberra Law School (University of Canberra). Dr Bonython has graduate qualifications in molecular genetics and law, with a background in health research, public administration and policy development. She serves on government and professional committees, in addition to providing invited expert testimony to a range of legislative and law reform inquiries. Dr Bonython's work has appeared in leading Australian and overseas law journals, including studies of the interaction between tort law and practitioner regulation, tort theory and law's understanding of property in bodies and intangibles. Her research encompasses professional and public understandings of risk, harm and innovation.

Rachelle Bosua is Assistant Professor in the Business Process Management & IS Dept of the Management Science and Technology Faculty at the Open University of The Netherlands. She is also an Honorary Senior Fellow in the Department of Computing and Information Systems (CIS) at the University of Melbourne. She is co-author of the book *Knowledge Management in organizations: a critical introduction* (Oxford University Press 2018). Her research focuses on data and information privacy that relates to human behavior and the use of information and communication technologies.

Ellen Broad is Head of Technical Delivery, Consumer Data Standards at CSIRO's Data61. Previous roles include Head of Policy for the Open Data Institute (ODI), an international non-profit founded by Sir Tim Berners-Lee and Sir Nigel Shadbolt, and adviser to senior UK government minister Elisabeth Truss on data, both in the UK. She has also held roles as Manager of Digital Policy and Projects for the International Federation of Library Associations and Institutions (Netherlands) and Executive Officer for the Australian Digital Alliance. Ellen has written and spoken about AI, open data and data sharing issues in the New Scientist, the Guardian and a range of technology publications, and is the author of *MADE BY HUMANS: The AI Condition* published by Melbourne University Publishing (MUP) in August 2018.

Anna Bruce is a Senior Lecturer in the School of Photovoltaic and Renewable Energy Engineering at UNSW and Research Coordinator (Engineering) at the Centre for Energy and Environmental Markets. Her research focuses on energy transitions, including renewable and distributed energy system and energy market modelling. Current research projects include Energy Data for Smart Decision Making through the Australian Government's Smart Cities and

Suburbs Program, and Integrated Smart Home Energy Management Technologies through the CRC-P program. She participates as an Australian expert in the IEA's Photovoltaic Power Systems and Demand Side Management technology collaboration programs.

Stephanie Carroll Rainie (Ahtna Athabascan), MPH, DrPH, is Assistant Professor, Public Health Policy and Management at the Community, Environment and Policy Department, Mel and Enid Zuckerman College of Public Health; Assistant Research Professor, Udall Center for Studies in Public Policy (UC); Associate Director and Manager - Tribal Health Program for the Native Nations Institute (http://nni.arizona.edu/) in the UC; and Assistant Director for the Center for Indigenous Environmental Health Research(http://ciehr.arizona.edu/), MEZCOPH at the University of Arizona (UA). Stephanie's research explores the links between governance, health care, the environment, and community wellness. Stephanie is the co-founder of the United States Indigenous Data Sovereignty Network and the International Indigenous Data Sovereignty Interest Group at the Research Data Alliance.

Donna Cormack (Kati Mamoe, Kai Tahu) is a Senior Lecturer and researcher with joint positions at Te Kupenga Hauora Maori, University of Auckland and Te Ropu Rangahau Hauora a Eru Pomare, Univeristy of Otago. Donna has had a long-standing interest in data issues, particularly as they relate to measuring and monitoring Maori health and ethnic health inequities. She is a member of the Te Mana Raraunga Maori Data Sovereignty Network.

Karin Clark is a Senior Fellow (Melbourne Law Masters) at the University of Melbourne. Previously, she was Special Counsel with the Melbourne office of the Allens law firm and practised in the firm's Communications, Media and Technology Practice Group specialising in advising on compliance with privacy laws.

Tyng-Ruey Chuang is an Associate Research Fellow at the Institute of Information Science, Academia Sinica (Taipei, Taiwan) with a joint appointment at both the Research Center for Information Technology Innovation and the Research Center for Humanities and Social Sciences. He was trained as a computer scientist (PhD, NYU 1993) and has been working with ecologists, historians and legal scholars to make better use of research data. He serves on the Executive Committee of CODATA (The Committee on Data for Science and Technology) at the International Science Council. He is also a member of CODATA's International Data Policy Committee.

Angela Daly is a critical socio-legal scholar of the regulation of new technologies. She is currently based in the Chinese University of Hong Kong Faculty of Law and holds adjunct positions at Queensland University of Technology Faculty of Law (Australia) and the Tilburg Institute of Law, Technology and Society (Netherlands). She is the author of *Private Power, Online Information Flows and EU Law: Mind the Gap* (Hart 2016) and *Socio-Legal Aspects of the 3D Printing Revolution* (Palgrave Macmillan 2016).

S Kate Devitt is a philosopher and cognitive scientist working as a social and ethical robotics researcher for the Australian Defence Science and Technology Group. She is an Adjunct Fellow in the Co-Innovation Group, School of Information Technology and Electrical Engineering,

University of Queensland. Her research includes: the ethics of data, barriers to the adoption of technologies, the trustworthiness of autonomous systems and philosophically designed tools for evidence-based, collective decision making.

Martin Flintham is an Assistant Professor of Computer Science at the University of Nottingham, where he is a member of the Mixed Reality Lab and Horizon Digital Economy Research Institute. His research focus on deploying and studying interactive experiences and disruptive technology probes, including domains such as the Internet of Things, ubiquitous computing, mixed reality and games. He has led successful 'in the wild' collaborations with the creative industries, leading to several highly-cited publications at ACM CHI, and winning the Prix Ars Electronica and two BAFTA nominations.

Murray Goulden is an Assistant Professor of Sociology at the University of Nottingham, and current holder of a Nottingham Research Fellowship. Through the Fellowship he is exploring the sociological implications of Internet of Things technologies for domestic life. His most recent work addresses the political economy of the 'smart home', and the implications of IoT-generated 'interpersonal data' for intimate social groups. He has worked extensively on research applying novel digital technologies to real world settings, with a focus on networking, digital data, and smart energy, their role in reconfiguring associated social practices, and the implications for policy making and design.

Timothy Graham is Postdoctoral Fellow in Sociology and Computer Science at the Australian National University. His research combines computational methods with social theory to describe, explain, and predict the dynamics of social systems. He is currently a Chief Investigator of an ARC Discovery Project that utilises large-scale hyperlink network analysis and web experiments to comparatively assess the government web presence of 10 high-tech countries. He develops open source software tools for the analysis of socially-generated data, and has published in journals such as Information, Communication & Society, Information Polity, Big Data & Society, and Critical Social Policy.

Daniel Gray (@DanielGray00) is a PhD researcher based at Cardiff University, United Kingdom. His undergraduate and postgraduate studies have focused on critical discursive approaches to social media. At the time of writing this takes the form of an analysis of neoliberal and misogynistic discourse on Twitter, blending big data and computational methods with critical, qualitative research. His research interests are focused on Marxist and radical approaches to digital sociology, particularly political, ethical and methodological issues on social media. More generally, his interests also include the intersections of radical left politics and Christianity, and teaching in university.

Jonathan Gray is Lecturer in Critical Infrastructure Studies at the Department of Digital Humanities, King's College London, where he is currently writing a book on data worlds. He is also Cofounder of the Public Data Lab; and Research Associate at the Digital Methods Initiative (University of Amsterdam) and the médialab (Sciences Po, Paris). More about his work can be found at jonathangray.org and he tweets at @jwyg.

Miren Gutiérrez (@gutierrezmiren) holds a PhD in Communication Studies. She is the Director of the postgraduate program 'Analysis, Research and Data Communication' and lectures on Communication at the University of Deusto and is a guest lecturer at the University of Navarra. She is also an Associate Researcher at the Overseas Development Institute (ODI) in London and DATACTIVE at the University of Amsterdam. Her interest is data activism or how people and organizations use data infrastructure, in combination with other technologies, for social change, equality and environmental conservation. She is also the author of the book *Data activism and social change (*Palgrave Macmillan 2018).

Chih-hsing Ho is Assistant Research Fellow at Academia Sinica, Taiwan. Her research focuses on the nexus of law and medicine in general, with particular attention to the governance of genomics and newly emerging technologies, such as big data, biobanks and artificial intelligence (AI). She is currently a Co-PI in law for a health cloud project in Taiwan and is responsible for designing an adequate regulatory framework for the secondary use of health data and data linkage. She holds a PhD in law from the London School of Economics (LSE), a LLM from Columbia Law School, and a JSM from Stanford University.

Becky Kazansky is a PhD candidate with the DATACTIVE project at the University of Amsterdam. She has a joint affiliation with the Media Studies and Political Science departments, additionally serving on the ethics committee of the Informatics Institute. Her research focuses on resistance to surveillance amidst datafication, looking specifically at practices that try to predict and preempt surveillance. Alongside her academic research, she has worked for a decade with different human rights and social justice organisations on technology issues.

Declan Kuch is a Research Fellow in the School of Humanities and Languages at UNSW. His research is motivated by problems of reconciling public values, technoscience and democracy in an era characterized by profound environmental constraints. His research spans climate change, energy policy and the social dimensions of the life sciences, and his primary role is as a co-leader of the Social Dimensions stream of the ARC Centre of Excellence in Convergent Bio-Nano Science and Technology. He is the author of *The Rise and Fall of Carbon Emissions Trading* (Palgrave Climate Energy and Environment Series 2015).

Tahu Kukutai (Ngati Tipa, Ngati Kinohaku, Te Aupouri) is Professor of Demography at the National Institute of Demographic and Economic Analysis, University of Waikato. Tahu specialises in Maori and Indigenous demographic research and has written extensively on issues of Maori population change, Maori identity and official statistics. Tahu is a founding member of the Maori Data Sovereignty Network Te Mana Raraunga and co-editor (with John Taylor) *of Indigenous Data Sovereignty: Toward an Agenda* (ANU Press 2016). She was previously a journalist.

Danny Lämmerhirt is researcher and research coordinator at Open Knowledge International. His work focuses on the sociology of quantification, metrics and policy, data ethnography, and the data commons. Among other activities, he leads the methodology around the Global Open Data Index and co-chairs the measurement and accountability working group at the Open Data Charter. Working at the intersection between practice and theory, he explores the 'social life of metrics' and how metrics intervene and reshape organisational cultures and vice versa. He shares his work on Twitter @danlammerhirt.

Vanessa Lee (Yupungathi and Meriam people, Cape York and the Torres Strait), is a social epidemiologist and senior academic within the discipline of Behavioural and Social Sciences in the Faculty of Health Sciences at University of Sydney. Vanessa's overarching focus addresses the social issues of the burden of disease to break the cycle of inequality that potentially lead to suicide in First Nations communities, and to strengthen the health and wellness of Aboriginal and Torres Strait Islander cultural identity, particularly for women. She is a founding member of the Indigenous Data Sovereignty group in Australia - Maiam nayri Wingara.

Raymond Lovett (Wongaibon/Ngiyampaa) is an Associate Professor and leader of the Aboriginal and Torres Strait Islander health program at the National Centre for Epidemiology and Population Health, Research School of Population Health, the Australian National University. Ray is a social epidemiologist with extensive experience in health services research, public health policy development and health program evaluation. He is a founding member of the Indigenous Data Sovereignty group in Australia (Maiam nayri Wingara) and is a member of the International Indigenous Data Sovereignty Interest group at the Research Data Alliance.

Iain MacGill is an Associate Professor in the School of Electrical Engineering and Telecommunications at the University of New South Wales, and Joint Director (Engineering) for the University's Centre for Energy and Environmental Markets (CEEM). Iain's teaching and research interests include electricity industry restructuring and the Australian National Electricity Market, sustainable energy generation technologies, renewable and distributed energy integration, energy efficiency and demand-side participation, and broader energy and climate policy opportunities and challenges.

Daniel McNamara is a PhD candidate in the Research School of Computer Science at the Australian National University. He is affiliated with the Machine Learning Research Group at CSIRO Data61. Daniel's research interests include fair machine learning and representation learning. He was a visiting student researcher during 2016-17 at the Carnegie Mellon University Machine Learning Department, supported by a Fulbright Postgraduate Scholarship. His work experience includes roles as a campaign data specialist at the Australian Labor Party, as a management consultant at the Nous Group, and as an intern at Microsoft and Google.

Monique Mann is the Vice Chancellor's Research Fellow in Technology and Regulation at the Faculty of Law, Queensland University of Technology. Dr Mann is advancing a program of socio-legal research on the intersecting topics of algorithmic justice, police technology, surveillance, and transnational online policing.

Luke Marshall is a PhD student in the School of Photovoltaics and Renewable Energy Engineering and Centre for Energy and Environmental Markets in the University of New South Wales. His research centres on the intersection between energy market rules, and the integration of solar resources into the electricity grid. He loves to code (including projects such as http://energyopensource.org/) and also to surf.

Nikita Melashchenko is a PhD Candidate at Victoria University of Wellington. He focuses on intellectual property and regulatory theory in application to the knowledge economy. His dissertation examines data localization policies under the WTO law. Nikita is a Fulbright alumnus and earned degrees from Vanderbilt University (LLM) and SPbU (LLB & LLM). Before joining the academy he practiced in the field of law and technology.

Stefania Milan (stefaniamilan.net) is Associate Professor of New Media at the University of Amsterdam. Her work explores the intersection of digital technology, governance and activism, with emphasis on critical data practices and autonomous infrastructure. Stefania is the Principal Investigator of the DATACTIVE project, funded with a Starting Grant of the European Research Council (639379) and exploring the evolution of citizenship and participation vis-à-vis datafication and surveillance (data-activism.net), and of the spin-off ALEX project (ERC Proof of Concept 825974). She is the author of *Social Movements and Their Technologies: Wiring Social Change* (Palgrave Macmillan 2013/2016) and co-author of *Media/Society* (Sage 2011).

Cheng Soon Ong is a principal research scientist at the Machine Learning Research Group, Data61, CSIRO(http://data61.csiro.au/). He is also an Adjunct Associate Professor at the Australian National University. His PhD in Computer Science was completed at the Australian National University in 2005. He was a postdoc at the Max Planck Institute of Biological Cybernetics and the Fredrich Miescher Laboratory in Tübingen, Germany. From 2008 to 2011, he was a lecturer in the Department of Computer Science at ETH Zurich, and in 2012 and 2013 he worked in the Diagnostic Genomics Team at NICTA in Melbourne. Since 2014, Cheng Soon is researching ways to enable scientific discovery by extending statistical machine learning methods with the Machine Learning Research Group in Data61, CSIRO in Canberra. Prior to his PhD, he researched and built search engine and Bahasa Malaysia technologies at Mimos Berhad, Malaysia. He obtained his B.E. (Information Systems) and B.Sc. (Computer Science) from the University of Sydney, Australia.

Sefa Ozalp is a research assistant and a PhD student at the Social Data Science Lab, Cardiff University. His main research interests are computational sociology and computational criminology, particularly focusing on dissemination of multiple typologies of cyberhate and xenophobia on social media platforms. He is also interested in regulation of digital platforms and abuse of personal (meta)data by oppressive regimes, focusing particularly on Turkey.

Rob Passey is a Senior Research Associate at the Centre for Energy and Environmental Markets (CEEM), and Postdoctoral Fellow at the School of Photovoltaic and Renewable Energy Engineering (SPREE), both at UNSW Sydney. He is also a Senior Consultant with ITP Renewables, and Policy Analyst and Treasurer at the Australian PV Institute. He focuses on policy research and analysis, particularly renewable energy, distributed energy resources, energy efficiency and carbon pricing. He has published widely on market-like policies to reduce greenhouse emissions, the uptake of low emission technologies and energy efficiency, as well as distributed generation and its integration into electricity networks, including smart grids.

Chiara Poletti (@ccpollon) is an ESRC funded PhD researcher in the School of Social Sciences at Cardiff University. Her research interests cover digital rights, digital labour, cybersecurity, digital methodologies and ethics of research on big data. In the last years, she has been working on Internet governance, social media platforms and big data. Her PhD project focuses on the discursive and socio-economic aspects of social media platforms' content regulation. Previously, she studied the public discourse on social media platforms in the aftermath of terrorist attacks. She is one of the co-founders and chair of the Digital Stuff Post Graduate research group in Cardiff University (https://digitalstuffcardiff.com).

Colin Porlezza is Senior Lecturer in Journalism with the Department of Journalism at City, University of London. He is also a Visiting Professor at the Institute of Media and Journalism at the Università della Svizzera italiana. His research focuses on data journalism, media accountability and transparency, as well as innovation in digital journalism. His research so far has resulted in more than 30 peer-reviewed publications. He is a Board Member of the Swiss Association of Communication and Media Research (SACM) and a founding member of the European Journalism Observatory. He has featured on the the Swiss Public Service Broadcaster SRG SSR, Poynter, the Neue Zürcher Zeitung and other news outlets.

Dominic Price is a researcher at the Horizon Digital Economy Research Institute at the University of Nottingham. His research focuses on the software engineering aspect of Human-Computer Interaction and the development of platforms that bridge the gap between system level computing and human interfaces. He has most recently been involved in work in the areas of crowd-sourcing and social-networking.

Paula Restrepo is an Associate Professor at the Department of Social Communication, Faculty of Communication, Universidad de Antioquia, Medellín, Colombia. She has a degree in Anthropology and a Masters in Philosophy from Universidad de Antioquia, and a PhD in Philosophy from the Basque Country University. She is a member of the Research Group 'Grupo de investigación Comunicación Periodismo y Sociedad' at Facultad de Comunicaciones, Universidad de Antioquia UdeA, Calle 70 No. 52-21, Medellín, Colombia. This chapter is a product of the Project "Prácticas comunicativas de la agricultura urbana en Medellín" (cod. 2016-12689) approved by Convocatoria Programática 2016, from the Universidad de Antioquia.

Megan Richardson is a Professor of Law, Co-Director of the Centre for Media and Communications Law, and Director of the Intellectual Property Research Institute of Australia at the University of Melbourne. Recent books include *The Right to Privacy: Origins and Influence of a Nineteenth-Century Idea* (Cambridge University Press 2017), and she is currently writing an *Advanced Introduction to Privacy Law* (Edward Elgar, forthcoming 2020).

Gerard Jan Ritsema van Eck is a PhD researcher at the Security, Technology, and e-Privacy (STeP) research group at the University of Groningen. His research focuses on participatory surveillance and privacy issues in public spaces. In particular, he is interested in how new and rapidly evolving technologies, such as smartphones and predictive analytics, enable states and large corporations to enrol citizens as data gatherers. His work combines insights from sociology and surveillance studies with work on European (Union) data protection law to generate new insights on the changing nature of urban public spaces.

Mike Roberts is a Research Associate at the Centre for Energy and Environmental Markets (CEEM) and in the School of Photovoltaic and Renewable Energy Engineering (SPREE) at UNSW Sydney. His research interests include technical and policy aspects of integration of distributed renewable generation, storage and demand management, co-operative approaches to energy planning, including embedded networks, micro grids and community renewable energy, and solar potential assessment. Mike's doctoral thesis explored opportunities for photovoltaics and storage in multi-occupancy residential buildings.

Adam Steer is a serial multi-disciplinarian, whose career has ranged from neurophysiology laboratories to web site management to professional bicycle repair to Antarctic logistics, sea ice field research and most recently working on massive high resolution geospatial data management. The intersection of technology and human evolution is a key driver in Adam's outlook on science and data and life - looking at when we cast human problems as engineering problems, and how we can become better humans in order to build a better future. He runs the consultancy Spatialised (http://spatialised.net).

Naomi Stringer is undertaking a PhD in the School of Photovoltaics and Renewable Energy Engineering and Centre for Energy and Environmental Markets in the University of New South Wales. Her research is driven by a fascination with the opportunities and challenges afforded by distributed energy resources (namely rooftop PV and home battery systems) and research interests include the technical, social and regulatory aspects of distributed energy integration. Her current work examines the behaviour of rooftop solar PV systems during major electricity system disturbances. Undertaken in collaboration with the Australian Energy Market Operator and solar monitoring company, Solar Analytics, her work is heavily data driven.

Guillén Torres joined DATACTIVE as a PhD candidate to develop a project on how data mediates the interaction between organised citizens and the state. His main areas of interest are transparency, resistance and the anthropology of the state. He also serves as an advisor to the Mexican NGO ControlYourGovernment. He has a background in Urban Studies and Sociology and is a recidivist Actor-Network Theory enthusiast.

Claire Trenham has research and data experience spanning a range of physical sciences, including radio astronomy, ocean waves, and climate models, as well as substantial experience more broadly managing large scale 'nationally significant' research data collections at the Australian National Computational Infrastructure. Claire currently works for CSIRO's Climate Science Centre in the Sea level rise, waves and coastal extremes team alongside the regional climate team. Claire is heavily involved in climate modelling, data processing, data preparation and software to enhance science capabilities, as well as supervising student volunteers in historical data digitisation. Claire has a passion for making maths and science fun, relevant and accessible.

Lachlan Urquhart is a Lecturer in Technology Law at the University of Edinburgh. He is also a visiting researcher at the Horizon Digital Economy Research Institute, where he was a Research Fellow in Information Technology Law from 2016-2018. He is a multidisciplinary researcher, having degrees in both law and computer science, with an LL.B, (Hons) from University of Edinburgh, an LL.M in IT & Telecoms Law (Distinction) from University of Strathclyde and & a Ph.D in Human Computer Interaction from University of Nottingham. He works at the boundaries of information technology law (mainly privacy & information security), HCI, and computer ethics. His research mainly considers the technical, legal, social, and ethical implications of living with ambient interactive computing.

Juan Carlos Valencia is an Associate Professor of Communication at Universidad Javeriana in Bogotá, Colombia. He holds a degree in Electronics Engineering and a Masters in Communication from Universidad Javeriana, and a PhD from the Department of Music, Media and Cultural Studies at Macquarie University (Australia). He is a member of the Research Group 'Comunicación, medios y cultura' at Universidad Javeriana.

Karin van Es is an Assistant Professor at Utrecht University and coordinator of the Datafied Society research platform. Her current research interests revolve around tool criticism and public values in the digital age. Karin is author of the book *The Future of Live* (Polity Press 2016), co-editor of the volume *The Datafied Society* (AUP 2017) and the issue 'Big Data Histories' (2018) for TMG-Journal for Media History. She has published in outlets such as Television & New Media, Media, Culture & Society, M/C Journal and First Monday. Her publications cover critical data studies, social media, and the concept liveness.

Daniela van Geenen is a Lecturer and researcher in data journalistic practice and data visualization at the University of Applied Sciences Utrecht and an affiliated researcher at the Datafied Society research platform. Her work tackles the question of the scholarly conduct that the work with digital methods demands, challenged by the need to design accountable software tools. She wrote her MA thesis on tool criticism investigating the case of Gephi. Daniela published on the role of social and technical actors on social media platforms, and their meaning for social and political practices such as public debate and cultural consumption.

Jelmer van Nuss is a developer at the Digital Humanities Lab at Utrecht University and a computing science master's student at Utrecht University. He specializes in artificial intelligence with a particular interest in data science. His work at the Digital Humanities Lab consists of supporting humanities researchers by providing software and tools for their research.

Lonneke van der Velden is a postdoctoral researcher with DATACTIVE and a Senior Lecturer at the Department of Media Studies at the University of Amsterdam. Her work deals with surveillance and data activism, with a special focus on Open Source Intelligence. She is part of the editorial board of Krisis: Journal for contemporary philosophy in the Netherlands and is on the Board of Directors of the Dutch digital rights organisation Bits of Freedom.

Jennifer Walker (Haudenosaunee), PhD, is a Canada Research Chair in Indigenous Health and Assistant Professor, School of Rural and Northern Health, Laurentian University. She is the Indigenous Lead at the Institute for Clinical Evaluative Sciences in Ontario, Canada. Jennifer works to support and advance the governance and use of population health data by Indigenous nations to address community health and wellbeing. Her program of research integrates Indigenous perspectives on multi-morbidity and culturally safe care for Indigenous older adults. Jennifer is a member of the Indigenous Data Sovereignty Interest group at the Research Data Alliance.

Jeb Webb is a research fellow at Australia's Oceania Cyber Security Centre, which works in partnership with the University of Oxford's Global Cyber Security Capacity Centre to conduct maturity reviews for countries in the Oceania region. He received a Bachelor of Arts in Political Science from the University of California at Berkeley, a Master of Arts in Intelligence Studies from American Military University, and a PhD from the University of Melbourne's School of Engineering (Department of Computing and Information Systems).

Maranke Wieringa is a PhD candidate at Utrecht University and has a background in Cultural Studies and Media Studies, with a specialization in software and data. Her dissertation investigates algorithmic accountability in Dutch municipalities, and, following from this insight, Maranke develops a toolkit to empower municipal data professionals to give testimony of the (decisions around the) algorithm. At Utrecht University, Maranke is part of the Datafied Society research platform, and teaches various courses on (scholarly) data analysis. Her academic interests lie at the intersection of software and data (e.g. tool criticism, algorithm studies).

Kersti Wissenbach (kerstiwissenbach.com) is a researcher and senior consultant working on the crossroads of communication, governance, responsible data, and civic tech. She is specialised in participatory methods and has worked with activist groups, NGOs, and government institutions in over 15 countries. Since 2011 Kersti runs her own consulting firm providing strategy and policy advice and facilitating co-creation processes. Kersti lectures in the Communication for Development Master of Malmö University. She is a researcher with the DATACTIVE project where she merges social movement and communication for social change scholarship for her study of power dynamics within transnational civic tech activism.

Sharon Young has recently submitted her PhD thesis to the University of New South Wales, investigating the influence of tariffs on the impacts of decentralised energy resources on the Australian electricity industry and is currently working with the Centre for Energy and Environmental Markets (CEEM).

Andrea Zeffiro is an Assistant Professor in the Department of Communication Studies and Multimedia, and Academic Director for the Lewis & Ruth Sherman Centre for Digital Scholarship at McMaster University.